THE HERITAGE OF SUFISM

VOLUME I

THE HERITAGE OF SUFISM

VOLUME I

Classical Persian Sufism from its Origins to Rumi (700–1300)

EDITED BY LEONARD LEWISOHN

ONEWORLD
OXFORD

THE HERITAGE OF SUFISM
VOLUME I

Oneworld Publications
(Sales and Editorial)
185 Banbury Road
Oxford OX2 7AR
England
http://www.oneworld-publications.com

Oneworld Publications
(US Marketing Office)
160 N. Washington St.
4th floor, Boston
MA 02114
USA

Previously published by Khaniqahi Nimatullahi Publications 1993

A CIP record for this title is available
from the British Library

Reproduction of the illustrations in this volume has been made possible by a generous grant from the British Institute of Persian Studies.

ISBN 1-85168-188-4

Cover design by Design Deluxe
Printed and bound in England by Clays Ltd, St Ives plc

Contents

IV. METAPHYSICS & HERMENEUTICS

V. LITERATURE & POETRY

VI. DIVINE LOVE, SAINTHOOD, SPIRITUAL DISCIPLINES & STATIONS

VII. SPIRITUAL CHIVALRY & MALĀMATĪ SPIRITUALITY

Illustrations

Contributors

JAVAD NURBAKHSH, Professor Emeritus and Former Head of the Department of Psychiatry, University of Tehran; Master of the Nimatullahi Sufi Order

SEYYED HOSSEIN NASR, University Professor of Islamic Studies, The George Washington University, Washington, D.C.

BRUCE B. LAWRENCE, Professor of Islamic Studies and the History of Religions, Duke University, Durham, North Carolina

AHMAD MAHDAVI DAMGHANI, Professor of Arabic Literature, Harvard University, Cambridge, Massachusetts

ANNEMARIE SCHIMMEL, Professor Emeritus of Indo-Muslim Culture, Harvard University, Cambridge, Massachusetts

HERBERT MASON, University Professor of History and Religion, Boston University, Boston, Massachusetts

TERRY GRAHAM, Editor, Persian Translation Series, Khaniqahi Nimatullahi Publications, London, England

HAMID DABASHI, Assistant Professor of Persian Literature, Department of Middle Eastern Languages and Cultures, Columbia University, New York, N.Y.

AHMET T. KARAMUSTAFA, Assistant Professor of Islamic Thought, Department of Asian and Near Eastern Languages and Literatures, Washington University, St. Louis, Missouri

GERHARD BÖWERING, Professor of the History of Islamic Religion, Yale University, New Haven, Connecticut

NICHOLAS HEER, Professor Emeritus of Arabic, Former Head of the Department of Near Eastern Languages and Civilization, University of Washington, Seattle

MEHDI AMINRAZAVI, Assistant Professor, Department of Classics, Philosophy and Religion, Mary Washington College, Fredericksburg, Virginia

LEONARD LEWISOHN, Research Associate, Institute of Ismaili Studies, London, England

WILLIAM C. CHITTICK, Professor of Religious Studies, State University of New York, Stony Brook, New York

J.T.P. DE BRUIJN, Professor of Persian and Iranian Cultural History, Leiden University, Leiden, The Netherlands

A.G. RAVAN FARHADI, Associate Professor, Department of Near Eastern Studies, University of California, Berkeley, California

MUHAMMAD ESTE'LAMI, Professor of Persian Language, Institute of Islamic Studies, McGill University, Montreal, Canada

JOHN COOPER, E.G. Browne Lecturer in Persian Studies, University of Cambridge, England

CARL ERNST, Professor of Religious Studies, University of North Carolina, Chapel Hill, North Carolina

IAN RICHARD NETTON, Professor of Arabic Studies and Head of the Department of Arabic and Islamic Studies, University of Leeds, England

BERND RADTKE, Lecturer in Arabic and Persian, University of Utrecht, The Netherlands; Associate Professor of Arabic Language and Culture, University of Bergen, Norway

MUHAMMAD ISA WALEY, Curator of Persian and Turkish, British Library, London, England

MUHAMMAD JA'FAR MAHJUB, Professor of Persian Literature, University of California, Berkeley, California

SARA SVIRI, Lecturer in Medieval Hebrew and Jewish Studies, University College, London, England

System of Transliteration

CONSONANTS

ء	ʾ	ظ	ẓ
ب	b	ع	ʿ
پ	p	غ	gh
ت	t	ف	f
ث	th	ق	q
ج	j	ك	k
چ	ch	گ	g
ح	ḥ	ل	l
خ	kh	م	m
د	d	ن	n
ذ	dh	ه	h
ر	r	و	w
ز	z	ی	y
ژ	zh	ة	-a (-*at* in construct state)
س	s		
ش	sh		
ص	ṣ		
ض	ḍ		
ط	ṭ		

VOWELS

Long:	آ	ā
	اُو	ū
	اِی	ī
Doubled:	ـِيّ	iyy
	ـُوّ	uww
Diphthongs:	اَو	aw
	اَی	ay
Short:	ـَ	a
	ـُ	u
	ـِ	i

Preface to the First Edition

Every sort of praise marches on
behind the Light of God.
The praise of forms and persons
is all just gilt and fiction.

Jalāl al-Dīn Rūmī[1]

The aim of the present volume is to trace the rise and development of Persian Sufi spirituality and literature in Islam, focusing upon the first six Muslim centuries (seventh to thirteenth Christian centuries). The essays have been contributed by some of the foremost scholars in the field of Islamic studies and Persian mysticism and cover a wide range of subjects, from literature and poetry to metaphysics and Koranic exegesis—from Sufi institutions and schools to the mysticism of love, the concept of sainthood, contemplation, chivalry, and the origins of the Malāmatī movement. Many great figures among the Sufis of this period have never before been examined within the context of the early development of Sufism, but simply discussed by individual scholars in separate monographs or essays,

1. R.A. Nicholson (ed., trans. and comm.), *The Mathnawí of Jalálu'ddín Rúmí* (London and Leiden 1925-40; repr. London 1982), vol. 2, Bk. III: 2125. "Individuals are praised for qualities which are thought to be their own; but really these qualities are Divine Attributes reflected in them: hence all praise is due, and of necessity is rendered, to God," wrote R.A. Nicholson in his commentary *(ibid.,* vol. 8, p. 60) upon the above verse from the *Mathnawī.*

so that the influences exerted by their personalities upon later Muslim society have been neglected. Extensive discussion is devoted in this collection to the rise of the two Sufi 'Schools' of Baghdad and Khurāsān, and to the role played by key personalities among the mystics such as Abū Ḥāmid Ghazālī, 'Ayn al-Quḍāt Hamadānī, Abū Sa'īd ibn Abī'l-Khayr, the two Suhrawardīs—Abū'l-Najīb and Shihāb al-Dīn Yaḥyā (Shaykh al-Ishrāq)—as well as Ḥallāj, Anṣārī, Rūzbihān Baqlī, and of course, Rūmī, in the development of Islamic culture during the Classical period. In their totality, the twenty-four studies in this book cover many of the significant achievements of the Muslim intellectual and cultural tradition in history, mysticism, philosophy and poetry—achievements which in themselves demonstrate the high calibre attained by Islamic societies in early times.

The inspiration and devotion of many people animate the spiritual and material form of the present work. First and foremost, we would like to thank Dr. Javad Nurbakhsh, Master of the Nimatullahi Sufi Order, for lending his inspiration to the conference on which this collection was based, and for consenting to its inclusion among other KNP publications.

The editor especially wishes to thank all the scholars and specialists who have contributed to this collection. This endeavor is indebted to every one of them, without whom nothing would have been possible. Most of the contributors featured herein first pursued their discussions at a conference organized by the Nimatullahi Research Centre on "Persian Sufism From its Origins to Rumi," held at The George Washington University from 11th to 13th May, 1992. Initial drafts of most of the essays featured in this book were written as contributions to that conference. In this regard, we are greatly indebted to The George Washington University for furnishing the venue for this conference and, in particular, to Prof. Seyyed Hossein Nasr for his prolonged exertions in helping to convene it. Our gratitude likewise extends to Lu A. Kleppinger, Director of the George Washington University Conferences and Institutes' Center, and A. Renee Battle, Conference Coordinator, for their efficiency and enthusiasm in facilitating the realization of the conference.

Special thanks are also due to all those who helped with the conference organization—most particularly to Phillip Edmundson, Assistant Professor of English in the Department of English as a

Foreign Language at The George Washington University. I would also like to thank Dr. Ayman El-Mohandes for his considerable assistance during the conference, and Carol Baldwin for her dedication and professional expertise at conference organization, all of which were indispensable to its convening, and hence, in compilation of this book. We are beholden to Maestro Muḥammad Reza Lotfi, who directed the Nimatullahi Sufi Music Ensemble in a concert of Classical Persian Music on May 11, 1992 at the Lisner Auditorium on the campus of The George Washington University. We would like to thank Mr. Lotfi along with all the other performing artists in the Nimatullahi Music Ensemble for the donation of their time and talent towards making the conference a success. I would like to acknowledge warmly the contribution of Robert Bly to the conference in providing an inspired evening of poetry on May 12, 1992, in which he read his translations of the poetry of Rūmī and Ḥāfiẓ accompanied by Hasan Nahid on ney and Mr. Lotfi on tar.

The editor is greatly indebted to Elizabeth Leach and Janet Jones for their outstanding devotion in typing much of the original manuscript of the book. I am grateful to Mehmet Yalcin of the Harvard Divinity School for generously donating some of his rare photographs as illustrations to this work. I must also thank Heather Sacco, Terry Graham and Wendy Moulang for their care and diligence in proofreading the final manuscript. I would like to acknowledge my profound gratitude to Dr. Muhammad Isa Waley for his continued encouragement, criticism and advice throughout the editing of the present volume. Two more principle debts I must lastly acknowledge: to my wife Jane for formatting and designing the book and to the readers whose pain and need were the raison d'être of this volume.

Leonard Lewisohn
London, November 1993

Preface to this Edition

During the six years since the first publication of *Classical Persian Sufism: from its Origins to Rumi* in 1993, a wealth of monographs have appeared in English reaffirming the key spiritual, literary and cultural role played by Sufism during the period under consideration in this volume (700–1300). Many of these works have been penned by contributors to this volume, treating in detail some of the same historical themes and figures found covered in these pages, and often enlarging on themes originally introduced herein. Prominent among these works are Michael Sells' *Early Islamic Mysticism: Sufi, Qur'an, Mi'raj, Poetic and Theological Writings* (New York 1996), Bernd Radtke and John O'Kane's *The Concept of Sainthood in Early Islamic Mysticism* (London 1996), Ravan-Farhadi's *'Abdullah Ansari of Heart: An Early Sufi Master* (London 1996), Carl Ernst's *The Shambhala Guide to Sufism* (London 1997) as well as his *Ruzbihan Baqli: Mysticism and the Rhetoric of Sainthood in Persian Sufism* (London 1996). An important edited collection devoted to the theme of *Recurrent Patterns in Iranian Religions: From Mazdaism to Sufism* (Paris 1992) should also be cited in this context.

In addition to the foregoing studies, English translations of a number of key early Persian Sufi works have also appeared in the last decade. Mention should be made of the following: Muhtar Holland's rendition of 'Abd al-Qādir Jilāni's *Sufficient Provision for Seekers of the Path of Truth* in five volumes (Florida 1995–97), two different translations of Qushayrī's celebrated *Risāla* on Sufism (by B.R. Von Schlegell, Berkeley 1990; by Rabia Harris, Chicago 1997), not to mention John O'Kane's superb translation of Ibn Munawwar's *Asrār al-Tawhīd* (as *The Secrets of God's Mystical Oneness*, Costa Mesa 1992) which appeared simultaneously with the first edition of this volume.

Despite the abundance of scholarly works which have emerged since this book's first publication, I am happy to say that there is scarcely anything in the present work which today requires modification. Furthermore, it retains a breadth of perspective which be said to underlie the more specialized monographs and studies which have appeared more recently.

The first two volumes of *The Heritage of Sufism* were originally published in London by Khaniqah-I Nimatullahi Publications (KNP) in a reduced print run. Because of the rapid sales of the first two books in this series, as the third volume (devoted to the late classical period of Persianate Sufism) was in preparation, it was thought appropriate to issue all three together as a three-volume set. Realization of this project, entitled *The Heritage of Sufism*, spanning an entire millennium (750–1750) of Persianate Sufism, owes much to the goodwill and kind heart of Mr Novin Doostdar, director of Oneworld Publications, and his efficient staff. I am delighted to congratulate the present publishers on their initiative in fostering the temporal continuation of the spiritual life of the Persian Sufis in such an inspiring literary vestiture.

Leonard Lewisohn
London, March 21 (*Nawrūz*), 1999

Foreword

The Key Features of Sufism in the Early Islamic Period

Dr. Javad Nurbakhsh

A thorough-going examination of the particular characteristics of early Sufism would be a lengthy and time-consuming enterprise—far beyond the scope of a foreword. In what follows I propose to provide a general outline of the development of certain salient concepts in the history of early Sufism, touching on its high points in this period, points that for the most part have been lost today. From its very inception the school of Sufism in Islam was characterized by a stress on certain fundamental spiritual issues. These provide a key to its esoteric doctrines as they unraveled over the course of later centuries, and may be subsumed as follows:

1. THE PRACTICAL AND VISIONARY APPROACH TO THE 'UNITY OF BEING'

Masters of this early period concentrated on the visionary and practical, versus the purely speculative or theoretical, understanding of the notion of the 'Unity of Being'.[1]

Visionary 'Unity of Being' implies heart-insight, a faculty of vision known only to 'possessors-of-heart', those Sufis who distance themselves from the realm of the ego and the temporal personality by means of divine love, and contemplate God through God's vi-

1. For further discussion of the significance of the 'Unity of Being' in Sufism, see Dr. Javad Nurbakhsh, "Two Approaches to the Principle of the Unity of Being" in L. Lewisohn (ed.), *The Heritage of Sufism II*, pp. xv–xviii.

sion.

Theoretical 'Unity of Being', on the other hand, is a philosophy concocted by the ratiocinative reason *('aql),* and as such, belongs to the realm of the ego. Belief in this philosophy is devoid of all spiritual benefit—in fact, it only serves to send a person socially and morally astray, since one may easily misuse this philosophy to justify indulgence in various vices or offensive behavior by claiming that "since all is Unity, anything goes." Thus, reasonable adherence to this philosophy is suspect, because it actually may lead to moral decay, lowering an individual from the sublime station of humanity.

Jalāl al-Dīn Rūmī (d. 672/1273) illustrates this danger in his story of the thief who enters an orchard and steals some apricots. The owner happens to come by at that moment and seizes him. "Are you not afraid of God?" he asks the thief. "Why should I be afraid?" replies the man. "This tree belongs to God, the apricots belong to God and I am God's servant. God's servant is but eating God's property." At this, the owner orders his servants to fetch a rope and tie the man to the tree. "Here is my answer," explains the owner as he begins to beat the thief. In response, the thief exclaims, "Are you not afraid of God?" Smiling, the owner replies, "Why should I be afraid? This is God's stick, the rope belongs to God and you are God's servant. Thus, I am only beating God's servant with God's stick."

In contrast to the theoretical approach to the Unity of Being, the visionary approach is founded on love and practised solely by those free of self-interest. This school fosters and emphasizes service to society, tolerance of and kindness to one's fellow human beings, and produces such exemplars of human excellence as Abū Sa'īd ibn Abī'l-Khayr (d. 440/1049), Abū'l-Ḥasan Kharaqānī (d. 426/1034), Bāyazīd Basṭāmī (d. 260/874), Manṣūr Ḥallāj (d. 309/992) and Rūzbihān Baqlī (d. 606/1210).

Whereas theoretical Unity of Being is a matter of talk and conjecture, visionary Unity of Being involves a practical spiritual path in which the Sufi sees all things as one, for his eyes are focused in but one direction. The former is a doctrine taught and learned by the mind; the latter a practice based on direct experience and realization. The former is taught from the classroom's lecture podium; the latter is gnosis gleaned in the school of revelation and vision. The former increases one's intellectual awareness; the latter frees one from consciousness of self and brings one to life in God. So when Ḥallāj cried out, "I am the Truth!" he was a flute being played by God's breath. When Bāyazīd exclaimed, "Glory be to me!", it was God speaking through him.

2. DIVINE LOVE

As its basic assumption, Sufism teaches that Reality cannot be known by logical or rational methods. God must be approached through love, and only through divine grace and favour may intimacy with Him be attained. From the perspective of the Sufis, as long as 'you' remain 'yourself', you cannot know God: the greatest veil between you and Reality being 'yourself'. Only the fire of divine love can burn away this egocentricity. Moreover, such divine love appears spontaneously; it cannot be learned through study.

Divine love may arise in the Sufi in one of two ways: 1) through divine attraction *(jadhba)* and 2) through wayfaring and methodical progression on the Path *(sayr wa sulūk).* By 'attraction', God's love arises within the Sufi directly, without intermediary, so that the Sufi forgets everything but God. By the second route, that of wayfaring and methodical progression on the Path, the Sufi becomes devotedly in love with the spiritual master, who then transforms this love into divine love. To present another simile, the Sufi sets out in search of a spiritual master, holding in hand the lantern of the Search for Truth; then the master kindles the flame of his lamp with the breath of his own holy spirit, causing the Sufi to burn with divine love. Ḥāfiẓ (d. 791/1389) alludes to this in the following verse:

In this intense heat which scorches our insane heart
The straw of one hundred dry intellects
would burn up in an instant.

In this context, when Bāyazīd was asked the significance of Sufism, he replied, "It is as if someone had stumbled on a buried treasure in a corner of his heart, and in that treasure trove had uncovered a valuable jewel called 'love'. Only one who has found this treasure is a Sufi." In the same vein, Khwāja 'Abdullāh Anṣārī (d. 481/1089) remarked, "Most people say 'One', yet remain attached to a hundred thousand. When Sufis say 'One', however, they flee from their very identities."[2] Or, in Abū'l-Ḥusayn Nūrī's (d. 295/907) words:

> Sufis are the wisest of all people. Most people look to God's bounty, while Sufis look to Him alone, seeking His intimacy. Others are content with His gifts; the Sufis are content only with Him. This is not a task which they accomplished of their own freewill; rather they saw something, their eyes were drawn to it, and everything fell away from them, all their powers reverting to Him. All people pursued and contented themselves with the Qualities, in place of the divine One Qualified; the Sufis sought the Essence and beheld naught but It. The entire world denied the Sufis, the world's wisest men most vehement in their denial of them—for the ignorant man is impotent and cannot reject anything; it is the 'wise' who reject.[3]

Thus for the Sufi masters, the consequence of divine love is that they become focused in one direction, concentrating on God alone. The following story is an excellent illustration of this attitude:

> Sultan Maḥmūd of Ghazna visited the town of Kharaqān to pay his respects to the Sufi master Abū'l-Ḥasan Kharaqānī. He pitched his tent nearby and sent an emissary ahead to announce that the King had arrived after traveling a great distance to visit him, requesting that Kharaqānī leave his *Khānaqāh* and meet him in his tent. If Kharaqānī refused, the emissary was instructed to quote the following verse, "O ye who believe! Obey God, and obey the messenger and those of you who are in authority."[4] The emissary conveyed his message. When Kharaqānī tried to politely excuse himself, the emissary recited the Koranic verse as instructed.
>
> The master replied, "Tell Maḥmūd that I still am so immersed in 'Obey God', that I am embarrassed to admit that I have not yet realized 'Obey the messenger', let alone, 'those of you who are in authority'."[5]

Rābi'a's (d. ca. 180-5/788-92) account of how once she beheld the Prophet in a dream carries essentially the same message:

---

2. *Ṭabāqāt al-ṣufiyya,* ed. by Muḥammad Sarwar Mawlāyī (Tehran: Sahāmī 'ām 1362 A.Hsh./1983), p. 94.
3. *Ibid.,* p. 72. (On Nūrī, see the essay by Annemarie Schimmel in this volume.–ED.)
4. Koran IV: 59.
5. 'Aṭṭār, *Tadhkirat al-awliyā',* edited by Muḥammad Este'lami (Tehran: Zawwār 1365 A.Hsh., 3rd ed.), p. 668.

> He asked me if I loved him. "Who doesn't love you," I told him, "but my heart is so totally transported with God's love that no place for love or hate of another remains."

Another version of this anecdote is given by the Arab author, Zabīdī (d. 602/1205) in the *Itḥāf al-sādah al-muttaqīn*, who renders it in the following fashion:

> Rābi'a was asked, "How much do you cherish the Prophet of God?"
>
> "Excessively... I love him indeed," Rābi'a avowed, "but the Love of the Creator inhibits me from love of His creatures."[6]

3. THE CALL TO WORSHIP OF GOD

Masters of the Path call their disciples to God, not to themselves. Their aim is to liberate disciples both from self-worship and the worship of other individuals, and guide them toward worship of God alone, rather than attracting others to themselves for egotistic purposes or through the display of miracles and powers in order to eke out a living for themselves.

In this context, 'Aṭṭār recounts the story of a man who went to Imam Ja'far al-Ṣādiq (d. 148/765), challenging him to "Show me God."

> "Have you not heard what God said unto Moses, replied Ja'far al-Ṣādiq, that 'You shall not see Me'?" [Koran VII: 146]
>
> "Oh yeah, I've heard it," said the man, "but now we live in the community of Muḥammad, where one man was known to exclaim, 'My heart has seen my Lord' and another cried out, 'I do not worship a Lord I cannot see.'"
>
> "Bind his limbs and throw him into the Tigris," ordered Ja'far al-Ṣādiq. He then commanded the water to carry him under. He sank and rose to the surface again.
>
> "O son of the Prophet of God! Help! Help!" cried the man.
>
> Ja'far al-Ṣādiq commanded the water to drag him under again. The man then rose to the surface again, repeating his desperate plea for help. Again the master commanded the water to drag him under. Several times this was repeated. At last the man totally despaired of receiving assistance from any created being, and having

6. See Dr. Javad Nurbakhsh, *Sufi Women*, 2nd ed., trans. L. Lewisohn (London: KNP 1990), p. 47. For yet another version of this tale see 'Aṭṭār, *op. cit.*, p. 80.

abandoned hope in human succour he resorted to God, crying, "O Lord! Help! Help!"

"Now draw him forth from the Tigris," commanded Ja'far al-Ṣādiq.

They pulled him forth and left him on the shore to rest and recover. When he had recovered his wits, they asked him if he had, when drowning, seen God.

"As long as I relied on aught but God," he related, "I remained veiled. But once I finally took refuge in Him, in my heart an orifice opened. Therein I gazed and saw the object of my quest. 'Whenever you are rendered impotent, then supplicate'."

So Ja'far al-Ṣādiq commented, "Until you cried out 'al-Ṣādiq!' ['the Truthful'] you were but a liar *(kādhib).*"[7]

This idea of total detachment from all but God is similarly emphasized by 'Aṭṭār in the following story concerning Dhū'l-Nūn al-Miṣrī (d. 246/860):

Dhū'l-Nūn relates as follows.

I was wandering in the mountains when I observed a party of afflicted folk gathered together.

"What befell you?" I asked.

"There is a devotee living in a cell here," they answered. "Once every year he comes out and breathes on these people and they are all healed. Then he returns to his cell, and does not emerge again until the following year."

I waited patiently until he came out. I beheld a man pale of cheek, wasted and with sunken eyes. The awe of him caused the mountain to tremble. He looked on the multitude with compassion. Then he raised his eyes to heaven, and breathed several times over the afflicted ones. All were healed.

As he was about to retire to his cell, I seized his skirt.

"For the love of God," I cried. "You have healed their outward sickness; pray heal my inward sickness!"

Dhū'l-Nūn," he said, gazing at me, "take your hand from me. The Friend is watching from the zenith of might and majesty. If He sees you clutching at another than Him, He will abandon you to that person, and that person to you, and you will perish at each other's hands."

So saying, he withdrew into his cell.[8]

---

7. 'Aṭṭār, *Tadhkirat al-awliyā'*, p. 16.
8. *Ibid.*, p. 140. Adapted from A.J. Arberry's *Muslim Saints and Mystics: Episodes from the Tadhkirat al-Auliya'* (London: RKP 1966), pp. 93-4.

Again, expounding this same theme of the worship of God above and beyond any created intermediary, 'Aṭṭār recounts the story of the son of a nobleman who one day stopped in at the assembly of Abū Sa'īd ibn Abī'l-Khayr. Upon hearing the master speak, he was so smitten with remorse that he repented of his misguided life and pledged everything he owned to the master, who subjected him to several years of degrading labor. With the passing of time the man had become an object of contempt to the local folk. The master then instructed his own disciples to ignore him as well. Finally, he expelled the man entirely from his assembly of disciples and forbade him to return to his *Khānaqāh.*

Severed completely from any expectation of society, the disciple took refuge in a mosque, where he flung himself to the earth and cried, "O Lord! You see and you know that no one accepts me. I have no pain but pain for you, and no refuge but in you." Weeping copiously for a period, suddenly he was vouchsafed the state and given the fortune which he had sought so long.

Back in the *Khānaqāh,* Abū Sa'īd told his disciples to go with him to find the man he had expelled. They set out and soon found him, still weeping. When the disciple saw the master, he asked him why he had been subjected to such humiliations. Abū Sa'īd replied, "Before, you had despaired of all created beings, that is true: but one veil yet remained between you and God—that veil was me. Now we have removed this too. Arise and rejoice."[9]

Certain Sufi masters in fact were so rigorous in their emphasis on the call to the worship of God to exclusion of intermediaries, that they insisted that after death their graves remain concealed, thus preventing people from visiting their tombs and hence becoming distracted from God! Hence, we hear from 'Aṭṭār that "Dāwūd Ṭā'ī instructed his disciples, 'Bury me behind a wall, so that no one will pass before my face.' This they did, and so it remains unto today."[10]

9. *Tadhkirat al-awliyā',* p. 807.
10. *Ibid.,* p. 207.

4. ENGAGEMENT IN A PROFESSION, SHUNNING SLOTH AND UNEMPLOYMENT

The great mystics and masters of the Sufi Path endorsed the necessity of having employment, and themselves engaged in various trades, encouraging their disciples to emulate in deed their industrious example. For example, Sarī Saqaṭī (d. 255/871) was a wholesale merchant in the bazaar, Abū'l-Qāsim Junayd (d. 295/910) ran a glass-cutter's shop and Qushayrī (d. 465/1072) relates of Abū'l-Ḥusayn Nūrī:

> Every morning he would set out from his house for his shop, and pick up a few loaves of bread on the way. These he gave away as alms, then went on to the mosque where he performed his prayers until the hour of noon prayers. He would then go and open his shop while still fasting. His fellow merchants supposed he had eaten at home, while his household assumed he ate in the bazaar. For twenty years during his initial years on the Path, he maintained this practice.[11]

Ibn Khafīf tells us that "In my day most masters had a profession whereby they earned their living. I myself learned spinning through which trade I managed to support myself."[12]

5. SERVICE TO PEOPLE AND LOVE FOR HUMANITY

The classical Sufi masters essentially strove to foster an attitude of mutual fellowship and service to humanity and to promote the development of positive human qualities among their brethren, and through their own example set themselves to uphold this ideal. Thus Anṣārī recounts:

> When Abū 'Abdullāh Sālimī was asked what the friends of God are known for, he replied, "Subtlety of expression, pleasant dispositions, cheerful countenances, generosity of nature, tolerance, forgiveness of those who beg their pardon, and kindness—

11. Qushayrī, *Tarjuma-yi Risāla-yi Qushayriyya,* Persian trans. Abū 'Alī Ḥasan ibn Aḥmad al-'Uthmānī, ed. B.Z. Furūzānfar (Tehran 1321 A.Hsh./1942), p. 55.
12. Abū'l-Ḥasan Daylamī, *Sīrat-i Shaykh-i kabīr Abū 'Abdullāh Ibn Khafīf Shīrāzī,* translated into Persian by Rukn al-Dīn Yaḥyā ibn Junayd Shīrāzī, edited by Annemarie Schimmel (Tehran: Intishārāt-i Bānk 1363 A.Hsh./1984), p. 24.

regardless of others' virtue or iniquity—towards all beings."[13]

This sentiment of altruistic love is likewise reflected in Abū'l-Ḥasan Kharaqānī's remark:

> If only I could die for all mankind so that they would not have to endure death! If only I could atone for all mankind's sins, so that on the Day of Judgement they would not be called to reckoning. If only I could endure the torments of the life hereafter instead of people, that they be saved from the Inferno.[14]

The words of Sarī Saqaṭī strike the same note:

> "I would that all the sorrow and grief which burdens the hearts of others descend upon my heart, that they be delivered from grief."[15]

Sarī also recounted,

> It was the feast-day. I saw Ma'rūf Karkhī collecting date-stones. I asked him the purpose of his occupation.
>
> "I saw a child crying," he said. "I asked him why he was crying. The boy said: 'I am an orphan, deprived of mother and father. Today, on the feast-day, other children are given new clothes. Not me. Other children get marbles to play with, but not me'.
>
> "So I am collecting these date-stones to sell," said Ma'rūf, "to buy him marbles to play with, that he weep no more."[16]

In the same vein, Ibn Munawwar tells us that one day Abū Sa'īd ibn Abī'l-Khayr reflected to himself,

> I had realized both knowledge *('ilm),* spiritual practice *('amal),* and meditation *(murāqaba).* I needed to experience being deprived of these things. When I pondered how to achieve such a thing, I realized that the inner reality of this could be found in nothing else except service to the Sufis. So I waited on the Sufis, making it my personal task to clean out their chambers and scrub their lavatories. After doing this assiduously for a time, I became accustomed to it and realized its inner significance. Then I took up begging, becoming a professional mendicant in order to fill the Sufis' coffers. There came a day, however, that alms were not

---

13. Anṣārī, *Ṭabaqāt al-ṣūfiyya,* p. 312.
14. 'Aṭṭār, *Tadhkirat al-awliyā',* p. 678.
15. *Ibid.,* p. 331.
16. *Ibid.,* p. 326.

forthcoming. So I sold my turban, then my shoes and finally, the embroidered lining on my robe for the Sufis. My father chanced to see me bareheaded in my threadbare robe:

"Son!" he said, distressed, "What do you call this?"

I replied, "They call it 'look at it but don't ask about it'."[17]

It is said that, when asked how many ways there are from creation to God, Abū Sa'īd replied, "According to one account, there are a thousand ways, according to another, there are as many as there are particles in existence, but the shortest, the best, and the easiest way to God is to bring comfort to someone else."[18]

It is in the same context that Rūmī writes:

For God's pleasure should you do your service;
What care have you whether you bear peoples'
praise or censure? [19]

Or, in Sa'dī's words:

Service to people is the whole of worship:
The worship of God is not done
by rosary beads, robes of piety or prayer carpets.

Sahl al-Tustarī related,

"I was once traveling with Ibrāhīm ibn Adham, when I fell ill. Whatever he owned he sold in order to cover my expenses. I asked him a favor. He even sold his own donkey to fulfil it. When I recovered, I asked what had become of his donkey. He said he had sold it.

"What then will I ride on?" I asked.

"O brother," he replied, "mount up on my shoulders."

So he carried me on his back for three leagues.[20]

Likewise, 'Aṭṭār recounts how three men once prayed together in a ruined mosque. When they fell asleep, Ibrāhīm ibn Adham stood by the door until the morning. In the morning the devotees

---

17. *Asrār al-tawḥīd fī maqāmat al-Shaykh Abū Sa'īd,* ed. Dhabīḥullāh Ṣafā (Tehran: Sipihr 1354 A.Hsh./1975, 3rd ed.), p. 34.
18. *Ibid.,* p. 302.
19. *Mathnawī-yi ma'nawī,* ed. R.A. Nicholson, Gibb Memorial [New] Series n.s. 4(London: Luzac 1925-40), Bk. VI: 845.
20. Qushayrī, *Tarjuma-yi Risāla-yi Qushayrī,* p. 26.

asked him why he had done this. "It was bitterly cold weather," he explained, "with a freezing wind. So I made myself into a door, that you would suffer less, and the hardship be my portion."[21]

6. NOT TAKING OFFENCE AT MALTREATMENT

We'll keep the faith, endure blame and rejoice,
For on this path it's infidelity to take offence.

Ḥāfiẓ

For the Sufis, not taking offence has two aspects:

First of all, being offended is an attribute of self-existence and egocentricity, whereas the Sufi is 'non-existent' and ego-less. Thus one who becomes piqued and takes offence is still a 'somebody', conscious of his separate self-identity as distinct from God—a person who associates others with God, rather than a Unitarian.

Second, the Sufi is one who has submitted to God and is content with God's will. Whatever affliction befalls him, or whatever harassment he receives, he considers it sent by God. As the poet says:

Since grief and dolor have come from the Friend,
I delight in this pain; this suffering
is the cause of my awakening.

Not taking offence at maltreatment is the touchstone, the criterion which distinguishes the Sufi from the non-mystic: thus the more profound one's equanimity when receiving rough treatment, the more selfless, the more 'Sufi' one actually is. The following tales concerning some of the early classical Sufi masters: Ibn Khafīf, Abū'l-Ḥasan Būsanjī, Abū 'Uthmān Ḥīrī[22] and Bāyazīd Bisṭāmī provide ample illustration of this principle:

A traveller once visited Shaykh Ibn Khafīf, robed in a black dervish cassock and with a black turban on his head. The Shaykh, noting his strange attire, was inwardly overcome by zealous indignation. Having performed two *rak'at*s of prayer, the visitor

21. 'Aṭṭār, *Tadhkirat al-awliyā'*, p. 114.
22. On Ḥīrī, see Sara Sviri's essay in this volume. –Ed.

conveyed his salutations to the Shaykh.

"Brother, what means your black vesture?" demanded the Shaykh.

"These clothes attest to the death of my gods," said the guest (he meant his 'lower soul' *[nafs]* and desire). "Have you not heard the verse: 'Have you ever considered what kind of person it is who makes a deity of his own desires?' [Koran XXV: 43]"

"Throw this man out!" cried the Shaykh. Ibn Khafīf's disciples dragged the man outside in disgrace.

"Now bring him back inside," the master commanded. Forty times he was similarly expelled from and summoned into the assembly. At last the master rose and kissed the brow of his black-robed guest and offered his apologies, saying,

"Indeed, it befits you to wear black, for you withstood forty rounds of disgraceful treatment without becoming once discomposed."[23]

* * *

Ibn Khafīf received a traveller suffering from diarrhoea. The Shaykh remained sleepless, at the guest's bedside the entire night, emptying his bedpan. He didn't catch a wink of sleep that night. At dawn the sick guest cried out, "God damn you! Where are you?"

The master leapt up, fearful of the man's condition, and approached him with his bedpan.

Later in the morning his disciples approached him. "What sort of guest is this," they protested, "who uses such abusive language? We have had enough of his obscenity! Our patience is exhausted!"

Ibn Khafīf said, "Oh – all I heard him say was, 'God bless you'."[24]

* * *

Once Abū'l-Ḥasan Būshanjī was travelling in full Sufi regalia. A Turk passed by and punched him. The crowd accosted the Turk and demanded an explanation for his disrespectful behavior.

"Are you not aware who it is you struck? That is Abū'l-Ḥasan Būshanjī, the master of this age?" they said.

Smitten with remorse, the Turk returned and begged the Shaykh's apologies. Abū'l-Ḥasan dismissed him, "Begone my friend! Forget this matter! I do not regard you as the Agent of this act anyway. The place where it was coming from is never involved in error."[25]

---

23. 'Aṭṭār, *Tadhkirat al-awliyā'*, p. 576.
24. *Ibid.*, p. 577.
25. *Ibid.*, p. 522.

* * *

"For forty years," said Abū 'Uthmān Ḥīrī, "whatever state God has kept me in I have not resented and to whatever state He has transferred me I have not been angry."

The following story bears out this assertion. A man who disbelieved in Abū 'Uthmān sent him an invitation. Abū 'Uthmān accepted, and got as far as the door of his house. The man then shouted at him.

"Glutton, go home! There is nothing here for you."

Abū 'Uthmān went home. He had gone only a little way when the man called out to him.

"Shaykh, come here!"

Abū 'Uthmān returned.

"You are very eager to eat," the man taunted him. "There is still less. Be off with you!"

The Shaykh departed. The man summoned him again, and he went back.

"Eat stones, or go home!"

Abū 'Uthmān went off once more. Thirty times the man summoned him and drove him away. Thirty times the Shaykh came and went, without showing the least discomposure. Then the man fell at his feet in tears and repented, becoming his disciple.

"What a man you are!" he exclaimed. "Thirty times I drove you off in shame, and you showed not the slightest discomposure."

"That is easy." Abū 'Uthmān replied. "Dogs do the same. When you drive them away they go, and when you call them they come, without showing any discomposure. Something at which dogs equal us cannot really be counted anything important. Men's work is something else."[26]

* * *

"Bāyazīd often wandered about amongst the tombs. One night he was returning from the cemetery when a young nobleman approached playing a lute. "God save us," Bāyazīd exclaimed. The youth lifted the lute and dashed it against Bāyazīd's head, breaking both his head and the lute.

Bāyazīd returned to his convent and waited till morning. Then he summoned one of his companions. He wrapped the sum of the price of the lute in a cloth, added a piece of sweetmeat, and sent these to the youth.

---

26. *Ibid.*, p. 477. Adapted with minor changes from Arberry's translation, *Memoirs of the Saints,* pp. 234-35.

"Tell the young gentleman," he said to his companion, "that Bāyazīd asks his pardon. Say to him, 'Last night you struck me with that lute and it broke. Accept this money in compensation, and buy another. The sweetmeat is to remove from your heart the sorrow over the lute's being broken.'"

When the young nobleman realized what he had done, he came to Bāyazīd and apologized. He fell at the Shaykh's feet and repented."[27]

Ibn Khafīf recounts the following anecdote about Abū 'Alī Rudbarī's (d. 323/934) remarkable forbearance under harassment:

One day a reception to entertain all the Sufi Shaykhs in Mecca was held, wherein all of them were present. Among them was a dervish from Khurāsān unknown to Abū 'Alī. When the dinner-cloth was laid out, Abū 'Alī arose, and as was the custom of the Sufis, took a pitcher of water and passed among the guests, serving each of the eminent masters, joking and exchanging pleasantries with all of them. Just as he behaved with cheer and conviviality with the masters, so he approached the stranger, when, to the astonishment of the gathered guests, the dervish snatched the pitcher from him and smashed it over his head, breaking his head and drawing blood. The disciples of Abū 'Alī rose to strike the dervish.

Abū Alī said, "Allah! Allah! Do not hurt him. Do not ruffle his temper."

At this, the dervish was disconcerted and abashed at his own behavior.

Seeing the dervish had been put to shame, Abū Alī said, "O brother! Forget it! I was feeling quite feverish and wished to draw off a little blood to relieve this bad fever until you struck me. Now, without recourse to bloodletting or getting myself a cupping-glass, I have gotten rid of the fever altogether, for a good amount of blood has been let out already!"

So saying, he continued his light-hearted repartee with the dervish, putting him in a good humor, until the dervish had forgotten his sense of shame and had regained his former cheer and joviality.[28]

Bāyazīd's forbearance in face of affliction is the subject of Sa'dī's famous verses in the *Būstān:*

---

27. *Ibid.,* p. 171. Adopted with minor changes from Arberry's translation, *Memoirs of the Saints,* p. 117.
28. Abū'l-Ḥasan Daylamī, *Sīrat-i Shaykh…Ibn Khafīf Shīrāzī,* p. 63.

A bowl of ashes is poured over the head of Bāyazīd Bisṭāmī as he emerges from the baths. From the *Būstān* of Sa‘dī; Mughal period, ca. 1039/1629. British Library, MS. Add. 27262, folio 67v.

I've heard that once, before dawn, on a feast-day,
From a bathhouse there emerged Bāyazīd;
All unaware, a pan of ashes
Was poured from a mansion down onto his head,
At which he said, turban and hair dishevelled,
And rubbing his palms in gratitude upon his face:
'My soul! I'm fit for the Fire –
Shall I, then, look askance at ashes?'[29]

7. SPIRITUAL CHIVALRY

Spiritual chivalry[30] has a very special significance for the Sufis. They understand it to mean the performance of altruistic service to others while remaining free of any self-consciousness with respect to the value of that service. Many Sufi masters have spoken about such chivalry.

Abū Ḥafṣ Ḥaddād has said, "Chivalry means being fair to others, while not expecting fairness in return."[31]

Junayd remarked, "Chivalry occurs without any awareness of the act of being chivalrous. One who performs such an act never says, 'I did this'."[32]

When Kharaqānī was asked about chivalry, he replied, "Were God to bestow a thousand bounties upon your brother and only one upon you, you would nevertheless give that one bounty to your brother as well."[33]

8. RELIGIOUS TOLERANCE

The classical Sufi masters extended their respect to the followers of all other religions, rejecting sectarian infighting, fanaticism, bigotry and the persecution of others in the name of religion.

In this respect, Kharaqāni reflected, "I do not reckon anyone to

---

29. Translation by G.M. Wickens: *Morals Pointed and Tales Adorned: The* Būstān *of Sa'dī* (Leiden: E.J. Brill 1974), p. 123.
30. See the essay by M.J. Mahjub in this volume.–ED.
31. 'Aṭṭār, *Tadhkirat al-awliyā'*, p. 394.
32. *Ibid.*
33. *Aḥwāl wa aqwāl-i Shaykh Abū'l-Ḥasan Kharaqānī wa muntakhab-i Nūr al-'ulūm*, ed. Mujtabā Mīnuwī, (Tehran: Ṭahūrī 1359 A.Hsh./1980), p. 92.

be spiritually realized if he still permits his heart to discriminate in thought between so-called 'gospel truth' *(ḥaqq)* and 'credal error' *(bāṭil).*" Maghribī (d. 810/1408) later expressed this idea in verse:

An eye which sees the Truth
For lies has no sight at all:
For all 'untruth' that is conceived
Or what is perceived as lies, mendacity
Lies in the eyes, themselves deceived,
The viewpoint of men without veracity.[34]

The following story also illustrates the attitude of religious tolerance maintained by the classical Persian Sufis:

Once a group of Sufis set out to visit Abū'l-Ḥasan Kharaqānī. Among them was a Christian posing as a Sufi. When they reached Kharaqān, Abū'l-Ḥasan rose and insisted on serving them individually with his own hands. He was especially kind and considerate towards the Christian. One day he suggested that his guests go the public baths. While his other guests were delighted at this idea, the Christian became apprehensive: What would he do with his cincture?[35] While he was preoccupied with this thought, Abū'l-Ḥasan summoned him aside and whispered in his ear, "While you bathe, you may leave your cincture with us: my servants can be trusted to keep your secret, I assure you."

When he returned from the bath, the master pulled him aside in confidence and quietly gave him back his cincture.

* * *

'Abdullāh ibn Ṭāhir Azdī said, "I had a dispute with a Jew in the bazaar and in the heat of our debate, called him a dog.

"At that moment Ḥusayn ibn Manṣūr [Ḥallāj] passed by and overhearing me, looked at me in rage and said, 'Stop *your own dog* from barking!' He passed on in fury.

"When I had freed myself from this disputation, I sought out Ḥallāj. He turned away and refused to face me when he saw me. I begged his forgiveness until I regained his goodwill."[36]

---

34. *Dīwān-i Muḥammad Shīrīn Maghribī,* edited by Leonard Lewisohn (Tehran: McGill Institute of Islamic Studies 1993), ghazal 35. Trans. L. Lewisohn.
35. A belt worn by religious minorities in Islamic countries; in this case, hidden under the Christian's outer garments.

9. INDEPENDENCE, CHARITY AND DETACHMENT FROM THE WORLD

Among the distinctive qualities exhibited by Sufi masters, especially those of the early period, one should also include: independence *(istighnā),* charity *(īthār)* and detachment from worldly interests and concerns. Selflessly committed to the service of others, these Sufi masters possessed nothing and generously gave away to other Sufis and to the poor whatever came to them, showing no concern for the possession of financial means, estates or landed properties.

Even if a Sufi lacked adequate means, he would not hesitate to sacrifice robe and turban to relieve another's material hardship. From the depths of personal material deprivation they thus realized the meaning of spiritual 'needlessness'—indicating the spiritual station of 'independence' by their severance of all ties with temporal being and their utter unworldliness and lack of selfishness.

The classical masters detached their hearts from everything but the Absolute Truth and, just as dispassionate detachment *(tajrīd)* characterized their outward relations to society, so in their inner life they were completely unaffected by illusions of phenomenal being. Standing on the threshold of Absolute Being they knocked on the door of Non-Existence, beholding Being in non-being.

10. KINDNESS TO ANIMALS

Beholding all beings as creatures of God, the classical Sufi Shaykhs likewise extended their affection and compassion to animals. 'Aṭṭār relates that

> Ma'rūf Karkhī had an uncle who was mayor of the city. One day, he was passing by some wasteland when he observed Ma'rūf sitting there eating bread. Before him was a dog, and Ma'rūf was putting one morsel in his own mouth and then one in the dog's.
>
> "Are you not ashamed to eat with a dog?" cried his uncle.
>
> "It is out of shame that I am giving bread to him," replied Ma'rūf.[37]

---

36. Mujtabā Mīnuwī, *Āzādī wa āzād-fikrī,* p. 124.
37. 'Aṭṭār, *Tadhkirat al-awliyā',* p. 326. Arberry, trans., *Muslim Saints and Mystics,* p. 164.

In the following story related by ʻAṭṭār the special relationship of Manṣūr Ḥallāj to dogs[38] is represented:

> One day, Shaykh ʻAbdullāh Turughbādī, of the city of Ṭūs, had spread his tablecloth and was breaking bread with his disciples, when Manṣūr Ḥallāj arrived from the city of Qashmir, dressed in a black *qabā'*, and holding two black dogs on a leash. The Shaykh said to his disciples: "A young man arrayed in this way is going to come; get up all of you, and go out to him, for he does great things."
>
> And they went out to this man and brought him back with them. The Shaykh, as soon as he saw him, yielded his place to him; [Ḥallāj] took it, brought his dogs to the table close to him... The Shaykh looked at him. He ate bread, and gave some to his dogs, which shocked the disciples. Only when he was leaving did the Shaykh get up to say good-bye to him.
>
> Upon the Shaykh's return, his disciples said to him: "Why do you let such a man who eats with his dogs sit in your place, a passerby whose presence here renders our entire meal impure?" "These dogs, responded the Shaykh, were his self *(nafs);* they stayed outside him, and walked behind him, while our dogs remain inside ourselves, and we follow behind them... This is the difference between the one who follows his dogs and the one whom his dogs follow. His dogs are outside, and you can see them; yours are hidden. His state is a thousand times superior to yours. He desires to be in the creative will of God, whether there be a dog there or not, he wants to direct his act toward God."[39]

* * *

On the way back from Mecca, relates ʻAṭṭār,

> Bāyazīd stopped off in Hamadān, where he bought some saffron seeds. He put these into the pockets of his cassock and brought them back to Bisṭām. On his return, he emptied out his pockets, and found therein an ant. "I have displaced the poor creature from his native habitat," he reflected. So he rose and returned to Hamadān with the ant and deposited it in the same place he had bought the seeds.

---

38. For a detailed exposition of this theme, see Javad Nurbakhsh, *Dogs From a Sufi Point of View,* (London: KNP 1989).
39. ʻAṭṭār, *Tadhkirat al-awliyā',* p. 556. The following version of this famous story is taken from Herbert Mason's translation of Massignon's version of ʻAṭṭār (based on that of Nicholson and Pavet de Courteille); see *The Passion of al-Ḥallāj: Mystic and Martyr of Islam* (Princeton University Press 1982), I, p. 182.—ED.

> None shall attain such a degree in 'the realm of compassion to created beings' until he has realized to its farthest extent the station of giving 'reverence to God's command'.[40]

11. ACCENTUATION OF THE INTERIOR DIMENSION OF THE *SHARI'Ā* OVER THE EXTERIOR

Through both oral discourse and poetic and prose composition the classical Sufi masters attempted—whether by direct statement or symbolic allusion—to enlighten their audiences concerning the transformal *Reality* of the *Sharī'a.* Their sayings and writings must be viewed as a kind of passage from the outer kernel of formal liturgics found in the Islamic religious Law, to the inner core of truth-worship therein. Although the vast number of sayings dedicated to this theme of 'transcending the fetishes of religious formalism' can hardly be covered in this brief discussion, the selections provided below suffice to illustrate the profundity of their views:

Pilgrimage *(ḥajj)*

Regarding the rite of Pilgrimage in Islam (the visit made, at least once in a lifetime, by Muslims to the Ka'ba in Mecca), the classical masters attempted to direct attention away from idolatrous concentration on the 'House of the Lord' – the Ka'ba in Mecca – to the 'Lord of the House'. In this respect, Muḥammad ibn Faḍl Balkhī remarked, "It amazes me that these people take the trouble to traverse deserts to reach God's House and see the relics of His Prophet, yet do not attempt to suppress their own passions and sensual desires *(nafs wa ḥawā)* so as to reach the heart and contemplate God's Signs therein."[41]

Abū Sa'īd ibn Abī'l-Khayr used to direct all his disciples who wished to make the Pilgrimage to visit the grave of his master, Abu Faḍl, instead, telling them to circumambulate his tombstone until their goal was attained."[42]

---

40. 'Aṭṭār, *Tadhkirat al-awliyā',* p. 164.
41. *Tarjama-yi Risāla-yi Qushayriyya,* p. 57
42. *Asrār al-tawḥīd,* p. 61.

Once Kharaqānī asked a man where he was going and the man replied, "To the Ḥijāz on pilgrimage."

"Why?" Kharaqānī asked.

"I go there to seek God."

The master retorted, "Where then is the God of Khurāsan, that you must journey to the Ḥijāz?"[43]

Once Shiblī was seen running with a burning brand in hand. Asked his destination, he replied, "To the Ka'ba, to set it afire, so people, instead of worshipping the House of God, make the *God of the House* the focus of their devotion.[44]

It is reported that, while performing the pilgrimage to Mecca, Rābi'a remarked, "Here is the House (Ka'ba) which is idolized upon the earth, whereas God neither enters it nor leaves it."[45]

Abū'l-Ḥasan Kharaqānī said, "I abstained from all but God. Then, when I summoned my self, heard God reply instead. I realized that I had transcended created being. So I cried out, 'O God, here I am! O God, at Your service!'[46] I made my ablutions, donned the pilgrim's garments and performed the rites of pilgrimage by circumambulating God's Unity. The Ka'ba then circumambulated me, hymning my praises, while the angels extolled and lauded me."[47]

Kharaqānī also said, "Some people circumambulate the Ka'ba, some the Sacred Mosque in the heavens, and some the Divine Throne, but the companions of chivalry *(jawānmardān)* circumambulate God's Unity."[48]

Once Kharaqānī even remarked to Abū Sa'īd ibn Abī'l-Khayr, "May they keep you from going to Mecca, for you are too precious to go there. May they bring the Ka'ba to you, to circumambulate you!"[49]

This interiorized vision of pilgrimage animated and inspired much later Persian Sufi poetry. Thus the poet Kamāl Khujandī (d.

---

43. *Aḥwāl wa aqwāl Kharaqānī,* p. 81.
44. 'Aṭṭār, *Tadhkirat al-awliyā',* p. 617.
45. Dr. Javad Nurbakhsh, *Sufi Women,* p. 58.
46. An invocation uttered by pilgrims to Mecca.
47. *Aḥwāl wa aqwāl Kharaqānī,* p. 50.
48. *Ibid.,* p. 65.
49. *Ibid.,* p. 19.

Abū'l-Ḥasan Kharaqānī holding a snake in each hand while riding a panther. From the *Kulliyyāt* of Sa'dī. Shiraz, Safavid period, 974/1566. Add. 24944 folio 9a. (Courtesy of the British Library).

803/1400) wrote:

> *The 'Arafāt of lovers is at the head of the Beloved's lane;*
> *It would be shameful for me to leave this door*
> *to circle the Ka'ba.*[50]

Heaven and Hell

Abū'l-Ḥasan Kharaqāni said, "I'm not telling you that heaven and hell do not exist, but I do say neither heaven or hell have any place around me, for they are both created things and in my sphere and place, no place exists for any temporal created being."[51]

Abū Sa'īd ibn Abī'l-Khayr said, "Wherever the delusion of your ego appears, that is hell. Wherever you are not, that is heaven."[52]

The Koran

Kharaqāni said, "I have seen people who devote themselves to exegesis and interpretation of the Koran; the companions of chivalry devote themselves to self-exegesis."[53]

Asceticism *(zuhd)*

Aḥmad Ḥarb sent Bāyazid a prayer rug with the message: "Spread this under your feet when you pray at night." Bāyazid sent it back to him.

"Send me a pillow stuffed with the asceticism of both this world and the next, that I may place it under my head and sleep soundly," he demanded.[54]

Supplication *(dū'ā)*

"Pray for me," someone entreated Mimshād Dīnawarī.

"Go, seek the quarter of God, that you be independent of

---

50. *Dīwān-i Kamāl al-Dīn Mas'ūd Khujandī* , ed. K. Shīdfar (Moscow 1975), Ghazal 440, p. 464.
51. *Ibid.*, p. 47.
52. *Asrār al-tawḥīd,* p. 299.
53. *Aḥwāl wa aqwāl-i Kharaqānī,* p. 91.
54. *Aḥwāl wa aqwāl-i Kharaqānī,* p. 127.

Mimshād's supplication," replied the Shaykh.

"Where is God's quarter?" queried the man.

"Wherever 'you' are naught," he replied.[55]

***

'Abdullāh Anṣārī declared, "The creed *(madhhab)* of the Sufis does not permit supplication, for they believe in eternal pre-ordainment, that is to say: all that was will be."[56]

The Mosque

"Are there Men of God to be found in mosques?" Abū Sa'īd ibn Abī'l-Khayr was asked. "Yes," he replied, "but they can also be found in taverns *(kharābāt).*"[57]

The Direction of Prayer *(qibla)*

Kharaqānī said, "The *qibla,* for the companions of chivalry, is God, for 'Wherever you turn, there is the face of God'." [Koran II 109].[58]

Ritual Prayer *(namāz)*

When Abū Sa'īd ibn Abī'l-Khayr was asked where one should put one's hands when performing one's daily prayers, he replied, "Place your hands upon your heart and set your heart upon God, may He be glorified."[59]

He also said, "Ritual prayer and fasting are the work of devotees *('ābidān);* removing blemishes and defects from the heart is the work of Men [i.e. realized human beings]."

---

55. 'Aṭṭār, *Tadhkirat al-awliyā',* p. 610.
56. *Ṭabaqāt al-ṣūfiyya,* p. 323.
57. *Asrār al-tawḥīd,* p. 297.
58. *Aḥwāl wa aqwāl-i Kharaqānī,* p. 75.
59. *Asrār al-tawḥīd,* p. 299.

Enjoining Righteousness; Dissuading from Evil *(amr bi'l-ma'rūf wa nahy az munkar)*

When Bāyazīd was asked about 'enjoining righteousness' and 'dissuasion from evil', he replied, "Inhabit a realm wherein these two are not to be found, for both of these pertain to the realm of created being. On the plane of divine Unity, neither enjoining righteousness nor dissuading from evil exist."[60]

Divine Chastisement *('adhāb)*

In order to expound the Sufi vision of God's wrath and chastisement, I will conclude my remarks with the following quatrain:

O God! You said You would subject me to torment.
I wonder how will You undertake this?
Wherever You are there can be no torment
And where is the place where You are not?

***

In conclusion, on behalf of Khaniqahi Nimatullahi Publications, I would like to thank all the contributors to this volume for gracing it with the results of their valuable research, thus keeping alight the flame of divine love and humane spirituality in the Fire Temple of Persian Sufism.

Translated from Persian by
L. Lewisohn

60. *Tadhkirat al-awliyā'*, p. 199.

The Mausoleum of Bāyazīd Bisṭāmī. Photo by Asad Behroozan

I

The Rise and Development of Persian Sufism

Seyyed Hossein Nasr

Although the focus of this volume of essays is on the history of Persian Sufism up until the late thirteenth century, the 'Age of Rūmī' (d. 672/1273), let me begin with a poem by the greatest of all Sufi poets who is, for that matter, the greatest of all poets in the Persian language: the spiritual friend of Rūmī, Ḥāfiẓ:

The fortune for which none need worry for its decline,
Listen, do not belabor yourself—that is the fortune of the Sufis.
From one shore to the other stand the armies of oppression,
Yet from pre-eternity to post-eternity
lies the opportunity of the Sufis.

Although we have from pre-eternity to post-eternity, the constraints of the present essay provide me only a short space to accomplish a very difficult task. This task was set upon me during a visit with my friend Dr. Javad Nurbakhsh in the *Khānaqāh* of the Nimatullāhī Sufi Order, of which he is the present master, in 1991 in London, England. At that time it was put upon my shoulders to devise the format and structure of this volume and also to try to summarize the whole scope of its contents in an introduction. Dr. Nurbakhsh chose the easy part of dealing with matters of the heart, and cast the more difficult philosophical issues on my shoulders.

The contributors to this volume have dealt with issues both spiritual and intellectual, combining both the theoretical and practical aspects of Sufism. My attempt here will be to summarize the rise and development of Persian Sufism and provide a taste of the vast riches of the history and literature of this period. I think it is very important to state that this volume was devised from the very beginning not as merely a dry academic book, but as one which would deal with Sufism from within.

One matter of extreme importance as far as the Sufi tradition itself is concerned should first be mentioned here. That is, the rise of Persian Sufism did not come about in any way except through the blessings given to the Persian people through the revelation of the Koran and by grace of the inner being of the Prophet Muḥammad. Persian Sufism may be compared to a vast tree with roots and branches extending all the way from Albania to Malaysia, and casting its shadow upon all the lands in between. However, the ground from which this tree grew was the soil of Persia. While it is one of the greatest glories of Persian culture and civilization to have been able to produce this tree from the land of its own people, and for the heart and soul of Iranian nation to have nurtured this tree—its seed came from heaven, from the divine descent of the Koranic revelation. No serious Sufi would ever say anything else, for to reduce Sufism to the genius of a people is to make it something purely human. And if it is purely human it cannot enable us to transcend the human.

If we were to expound upon all the great glories—cultural, philosophical and of course, most of all, spiritual—of Sufism in its Persianate milieu we must recollect the origins of Sufism. It is not accidental that all the Persian Sufi Orders—like all the other Sufi Orders, Arab, Turkish and otherwise—trace the origin of their *silsila,* or initiatic chain, to the Prophet, and (in the case of Persia) in addition, to the half-mythical figure of 'Salmān the Persian'(Salmān-i Fārsī), the famous Persian companion of the Prophet. The latter personage is the link which relates not only Persian Islam but especially Persian Sufism to the Prophet and his household.

From the early centuries practically all the important developments in Sufism's early history are geographically related to greater Persia. Although the precise territory in which these developments occurred is not confined to the borders of the present-day Iran, but includes more precisely the land of Mesopotamia, from the third/ninth century onwards, many if not most of the great figures of

Sufism were of Persian stock. This phenomenon is discussed in some detail by Prof. Mahdavi-Damghani below (pp. 33-57).

By the third/ninth century one finds the co-temporaneous development of two parallel and contending schools of Sufism, which have come to be known today as the schools of Khurāsān and Baghdad.[1] However, this was not really a 'contention' between the Arab and Persian expressions of Sufism, for—aside from Ḥasan al-Baṣra (d. 110/728) and Rābi'a al-'Adawiyya (d. ca 180-85/796-801), the great woman saint from Baṣra—most of the important figures of Baghdadian Sufism were in fact of Persian origin. These included Abū'l-Qāsim al-Junayd (d. 298/910), Abū'l-Ḥusayn al-Nūrī (d. 295/908), and Abū Bakr al-Shiblī (d. 334/945). Of course, Manṣūr Hallāj, the most famous of the Baghdadian Sufis in the west, was born in the province of Fars in southern Persia. Rather, the 'contention' between these two schools, if it exists at all, runs on intellectual and spiritual rather than ethnic lines: the school of Khurāsān being more associated with so-called *sukr* or intoxication, and the school of Baghdad being associated with *ṣaḥw* or sobriety.

At this juncture it may be useful to briefly summarize all the various literary manifestations and spiritual motifs which characterized early Persian Sufism. Without pretending to be exhaustive, there are respectively some dozen important aspects in the early development of Sufism within the cradle of Islamic civilization which I shall attempt to enumerate. These are as follows: the literature of ecstatic sayings, ethics, Sufi manuals of practice, Sufi Koranic commentary, doctrinal Sufism, teachings of divine love, Sufi historical writings, institutionalized Sufism (the 'Orders'), spiritual chivalry, the Persian Sufi prose and poetic tradition, the fine arts (both the visual arts and music), philosophy and theology *(kalām)*.

ECSTATIC SAYINGS IN EARLY PERSIAN SUFISM

From the third/ninth century to the seventh/thirteenth century, an incredible development in Persian Sufism was visible in practically every field of thought. One of the most interesting occurrences dur-

1. See the essays by Terry Graham, Herbert Mason and Sara Sviri in this volume. – ED.

ing this period is the development of the type of literature known as 'ecstatic sayings' or 'theophanic locutions' *(shaṭḥ).*[2] Javad Nurbakhsh in his foreword points outs that the Sufi is like a flute through which God plays his own tune; it is by means of such inspired sayings, one could say, that the divine Being in a particular mystic holds forth, for from a purely human point of view such utterances are incomprehensible. One may recall in this context the ecstatic cry uttered by Bāyazīd Bisṭāmī (d. 875) of "*Subḥānī*—Praise be to Me, how great is my Glory!" and the famous theopathic maxim of Ḥallāj: *Anā al-Ḥaqq*—"I am the Truth," a statement which has been quoted through the centuries of the history of Sufism.

The *shaṭḥ*-genre reached its peak during this period in the great *Commentary on the Paradoxes of the Sufis (Sharḥ-i shaṭḥiyyāt)* by Rūzbihān Baqlī of Shirāz (d. 606/1210) who was known as the *Sulṭān al-shaṭḥāṭīn*—or King of those who utter such ecstatic sayings. This genre represents a large part of the spiritual legacy of early Persian Sufism. Although one may study Sufism a whole lifetime and examine numerous long-winded treatises and commentaries, one always returns in the end to such short pithy sayings which seem to contain almost all that there is to say on the subject of the mystical quest. Almost like the basic formula of Islam: 'There is no god but God'—*Lā ilāha illā'Llāh* itself, but on a lower level of inspiration, these ecstatic sayings contain in a synthetic fashion the whole truth and inspiration of Sufism. In studying such sayings, one comes to realize how they contain the entire ethos of Sufism in a nutshel: just as the small plant contains every single element of the growth of the later tree, these early locutions and sayings contain all the most profound doctrines and expressions of Sufism found in the more extended commentaries and didactic and poetical works of the later centuries.

2. Carl Ernst, who has contributed an essay to the present collection, has written the only existing book in the English language on this subject: *Words of Ecstasy in Sufism* (Albany: SUNY Press 1985).

ETHICS

This same period also saw the compilation of the first Sufi texts; it was the age of the great masterpieces of early Sufi ethical thought, such as the *Qūt al-qulūb—The Food for Hearts* by Abū Ṭālib al-Makkī (d. 380/990) and perhaps the most famous of all such treatises, the *Risāla al-Qushayriyya* by Abū'l-Qāsim al-Qushayrī (d. 465/1072) of Khurāsān and later, the *Iḥyā' 'ulūm al-dīn – The Revivification of the Sciences of Religion* of Abū Ḥāmid al-Ghazālī (d. 505/1111). From its very beginnings, the whole field of ethics *(akhlāq)* in Islam was dominated by the Sufis. In fact, in both the Sunni and the Shi'ite sects of Islam, the major ethical works composed over the centuries were all indebted to the inspiration of the Sufis. Throughout all the various sectarian divisions of the Islamic world, it is really the breath of the Sufism which brought life to and gave sustenance to ethics. Many people are not aware that the ethical works that they are reading come in fact from Sufi sources, even if, outwardly, they have nothing to do with Sufism.

MANUALS OF PRACTICE

During this period, Sufi ethical teachings are combined with practical manuals on *sayr* and *sulūk:* that is, on both the inner spiritual voyage and the outer conduct of the Sufis. Thus, from the very beginning, these ethical works exhibit a synthesis of the practical and applied dimensions of the spiritual quest. Such treatises on *sayr* and *sulūk* are likewise concerned with *adab*, that is to say, spiritual courtesy: how one must comport oneself before others—so important in the practice of Sufism. The various stages and states of human soul, the mystical states *(aḥwāl)* and spiritual stations *(maqāmāt)*—of which the celebrated Khwāja 'Abdallāh Anṣārī of Herat (d. 481/1089) was perhaps the greatest exponent in the early history of Islam—are also given extensive coverage in these early tracts.

KORANIC COMMENTARIES

This period also witnessed the efflorescence of the esoteric commentaries on the Koran by the Persian Sufis. From the traditional Islamic point of view these commentaries are said to derive their inspiration from the example of 'Alī ibn Abī Ṭālib (d. 41/661), the first Imam of the Shi'ites and the fourth caliph of the Sunnis. According to both Sunni and Shi'ite traditions, 'Alī wrote an esoteric commentary on the Koran which some Western orientalists mistook for another version of the Koran. They tried to destroy the definitive nature of the Sacred Text, claiming that it was an alternative Koran and that the Shi'ites (followers of 'Alī) did not accept the text of the Koran as it then existed. What seems apparent from this early polemic is that such historical references were actually to an *esoteric commentary* on the Koran attributed to 'Alī which has unfortunately been lost to us today.

However, we do have some pages of the esoteric commentary on the Koran by Imām Ja'far al-Ṣādiq (d. 45/765), 'Alī's descendent. The esoteric commentaries of the Koran by the Persian Sufis were first composed on the basis of the latter text, beginning with the commentary by Sahl al-Tustarī (d. 283/896). This was followed later on by perhaps the most ambitious esoteric commentary of this period, the *Kashf al-asrār—The Revelation of Mysteries* of Rashīd al-Dīn Maybudī (d. 520/1126), Anṣārī's disciple and commentator, and eventually by the remarkable mystical Koranic commentaries by Abū Ḥamīd Ghazālī. Ghazālī certainly must be considered one of the greatest Koranic commentators in delineating the methods and limits of esoteric commentary.[3] This is exemplified in his famous *Mishkat al-anwār—Niche of Lights,* a commentary on the Light Verse of the Koran and a *ḥadīth* of the Prophet concerning the veils of light and darkness.

DOCTRINAL SUFISM

The same era also saw the seeds of doctrinal Sufism sown on Persian soil. Although this type of Sufism was mainly associated in subsequent centuries with the teachings of Muḥyī al-Dīn ibn 'Arabī (d. 638/1240), the actual founders of doctrinal Sufism were two late sixth/twelfth-century Sufi philosophers, Abū Ḥamīd Ghazālī and 'Ayn al-Quḍāt Hamadānī (executed 526/1132 at the age of 33). If the latter had lived longer, he might have been the greatest expound-

3. On which, see the essay by Nicholos Heer in the present volume.—ED.

er of Sufi metaphysics. Despite his premature demise, however, he did write two major works which are really among the foundations of theoretical Sufism.

DIVINE LOVE

This period also brings to an apogee the type of Sufi expression which has to do with love. Here we are not solely concerned with the expression of ordinary human love, but with an entire philosophy of being expressed in the language of human emotion. Thus we find, for instance, that the great founder of the Philosophy of Illumination *(ishrāq),* Shihāb al-Dīn Yaḥyā Suhrawardī (d. 587/1191) associates his doctrine of light with love, while the Peripatetic philosophers associated love with God as the principle of existence. This wide spectrum of early Sufi reflections on love is given extensive coverage by Carl Ernst's essay in this volume.

The most prominent figure among exponents of the path of love during this period was Aḥmad Ghazālī (d. 520/1126), the brother of Abū Ḥamīd Ghazālī, and author of the *Sawāniḥ al-'ushshāq—The Incidents of the Lovers,* one of the most important tracts on love theory in early Persian Sufism. With the *Sawāniḥ* begins an extremely rich spiritual tradition, leading to that elusively subtle treatise by Rūzbihān, the *Abhār al-'āshiqīn—The Lover's Jasmine,* and on down to Fakhr al-Dīn 'Irāqī (d. 688/1289)—all of those early troubadours of love whom Henry Corbin rightly calls the *fideli d'amore* of Persia (comparing them to the *fideli d'amore* of late thirteenth-century Italy).

SUFI HISTORIES

Sufis during this period were also very much interested in their own history and genealogy—a fascination which devolved upon the crucial question of the preservation of spiritual authenticity. As 'Aṭṭār remarked, perfume is what smells sweet, but not necessarily what the druggist labels as fragrance: the sense of this saying being that an authentic Sufi Order would never produce anything not genuine, and likewise, a non-authentic Sufi Order can never produce anything which is authentic.

In accord with this interest in spiritual genealogy, in the third/

ninth century the first histories of Sufism made their appearance. Although most of the authors were Persian, this interest eventually culminated in the Arabic-language *Ḥilyat al-awliyā' – The Ornament of the Saints,* that vast compendium of early Sufi history by Abū Nu'aym al-Iṣfahānī (d. 428/1037). The majority of such works, at least up until the fifth/eleventh century, were written in Arabic.

SUFI ORDERS

The first Sufi Orders made their appearance in the late fourth/tenth and early fifth/eleventh century. One of the earliest of these was the Rifā'īyya Sufi Order founded by Aḥmad ibn 'Alī al-Rifā'ī (d. 578/1182), an Arab, not a Persian, from southern Iraq. His Order is one of the oldest which survives to this day. Another early Order, and the certainly most expansive throughout the Islamic world to this day, was founded by Shaykh 'Abd al-Qādir Jīlānī (d. 528/1134). His last name is Jīlānī, of course, because he was from the province of Gilan in northeastern Iran. 'Abd al-Qādir is surely the most famous of all the citizens of that province, although many Persians are unaware of this. It is interesting that when one travels to lands as far away as the Philippines today, despite the existence of many other famous Gilanis, the only name people know from Gilan is Shaykh 'Abd al-Qādir Jīlānī. Today the Order is known after his first name, as the Qādiriyya.

Another early Sufi Order was the Suhrawardiyya, which traced its lineage back to Ḍiyā' al-Dīn Abū'l-Najīb al-Suhrawardī (d. 503/1168), a disciple of Aḥmad Ghazālī, whose *Ādāb al-murīdīn – The Etiquette of Disciples* (the first manual of Sufi discipline ever to be written, in Arabic), is the subject of I.R. Netton's essay in this volume (see below, pp. 457-82). The Suhrawardiyya Order itself was founded by his nephew, Shihāb al-Dīn Abū Ḥafṣ al-Suhrawardī (d. 632/1234). The Suhrawardī family was part of a group of remarkable Sufis who flourished in sixth/twelfth-century Persia and Iraq, but who were originally from this otherwise totally obscure town of Suhraward in Central Persia, a town which has produced so many great figures in the history of Sufism and Islamic philosophy.

SPIRITUAL CHIVALRY

As Dr. Nurbakhsh pointed out in his Foreword, this period also witnessed the development of what is called *jawānmardī* in Persian and *futuwwat* in Arabic, a word which is best translated as 'spiritual chivalry'. Until the last two or three decades this important phenomenon had been insufficiently studied. Since then, thanks to the efforts of Henry Corbin, Ja'far Maḥjūb and others, some of the more fundamental texts have been published.[4]

Chivalry deals at once with knightly chivalry (similar to the chivalric orders of warrior knights, such as the Templars of mediæval Western Europe) as well as with the economic life of the Islamic community as it developed in the late Abbasid period (just before the time of Rūmī when *futuwwat* became a basic socio-economic element of early mediæval Anatolia and Persia). Here, what meets the eye is the influence of Sufism on the social fabric, that is to say, on the most external aspect of economic and social life. The social bonds created through the institutions of *futuwwat* and the guilds of artisans affiliated to these chivalric orders exercised a profound influence over the whole of Persian society at this time. This was not solely due to economic causes, but represented the wedding of economic activity with ethics on the one hand and with beauty and art on the other.[5]

Spiritual chivalry became closely integrated into Sufism in the 3rd/9th and fourth/tenth centuries. Reading the earliest texts on *futuwwat*, such as the *Risāla al-futuwwa* by Sulamī (d. 412/1021), one realizes that it is impossible to engage seriously in the mystical disciplines of Sufism without simultaneously putting into practice the ethical virtues of chivalry. Thus the phenomenon of the organization of the Orders of chivalry and the guilds or artisans affiliated with these Orders is an inseparable and integral element of the religious experience of early Persian Sufism.

---

4. Dr. Maḥjūb's essay in this volume is devoted to the early development of Sufi chivalry in its Persian milieu.
5. For a more detailed study of this phenomenon, see S.H. Nasr, "Spiritual Chivalry" in S.H. Nasr (ed.), *Islamic Spirituality II: Manifestations* (New York: Crossroad 1991), pp. 304-315.

PERSIAN SUFI POETRY AND PROSE

Another aspect of Sufism which merits our consideration is the development of classical Sufi literature in the Persian language during this period. This is an important phenomenon, not only from the spiritual point of view but also from the cultural and political standpoint, since, deprived of the rich productions of the Persian sages and poets, Islam would never have spread into the subcontinent of India nor into Central or Southeast Asia to the extent that it did. However, the rise of Persian Sufi literature is a whole subject in itself, which would require a separate monograph, so I will limit myself here to a few general remarks:

Persian Sufi poetry contains perhaps the richest mystical poetry in the world (in the Islamic world, for example, it is richer than Arabic Sufi poetry, although Arabic non-mystical poetry is extremely rich and in many ways richer than early Persian court poetry). All of the early Sufi poets in the Arabic language, except for Rābi'a al-'Adawiyya, were of Persian origin; the great Sufi poetry written by the Arabs in Arabic only occurs at a much later date. If one considers the works of the great Arab Sufi poets (that is, the verse of Ibn Fāriḍ, Ibn 'Arabī, and others), it was all composed *after* the early period of Sufism under consideration here.

Persian Sufism from its inception was inextricably linked with poetry. The reason for this it that the Persian language and Persian Sufism met at a time when the Persian language had not yet become crystallized. Its vocabulary, as well as its prosody and metrics along with its use of technical and poetic language, was still unformed, and thus much more malleable.

The Persian language was born in the third/ninth century in Khurāsān and Transoxiana and was based on Middle Persian and Dari but enriched by an Arabic vocabulary of a strong religious orientation, deeply influenced by the Koran. During this formative period the influence of Sufism was very strong and so, in a sense, it was much easier for Sufism to leave its imprints upon Persian literary culture and language than upon Arabic which had also a highly developed prosody and poetic tradition.

From the early simple quatrains of Bābā Ṭāhir in the local language of Hamadān to the quatrains attributed to Abū Sa'īd Abī'l-

Khayr (d. 440/1049—although as several European scholars, such as Fritz Meier, have shown they probably belong to a period earlier than his, in fact[6]), a remarkable flowering of early Persian Sufi poetry took place. This was followed by the more elaborate works of the Persian poetical renaissance of the sixth/twelfth and seventh/thirteenth centuries, which featured, first of all, the vast mystical *mathnawī*s of Sanā'ī, who in turn set the background for the Sufi epics of 'Aṭṭār and the ecstatic ghazals and didactic *Mathnawī* of Rūmī.

Persian Sufi poetry is perhaps the most conspicuous and influential production of Persian culture to date, and no other expression of Persian culture has had such a world-wide influence as the poetry of that period. One proof of this is that in the last two years over ten volumes of the poetry of Rūmī have been translated into English. (Although these are not all first-class scholarly or literary translations, the fact that they have been translated into English at all proves that despite the passage of over seven centuries, the poetry of that period is very much a living force).

This period also witnessed the rise of Persian Sufi prose literature. Although the salient prose works of this epoch are not as well-known outside of Persia as their poetical counterparts, their impact was hardly less significant in the Islamic world. Here we may mention the *Munājāt—Invocations* of Khwāja 'Abdallāh Anṣārī (d. 481/1089) the *Kīmīyā-yi sa'ādat—Alchemy of Happiness* of Abū Ḥamīd Ghazālī, and of course the *Rawḥ al-arwāḥ—The Refreshment of Spirits* by Aḥmad Sam'ānī (d. 534/1140), to which W.C. Chittick has consecrated a special study in this volume. From a purely literary point of view such works are the peak of Persian prose in that period; there are no comparable works in the fields of either history, philosophy or theology nor of other types of literature which matches the beauty of language found in the Persian Sufi prose of that period.

6. See Terry Graham's essay in the present volume.

MUSIC AND THE FINE ARTS

Turning now to an important ancillary aspect of Persian Sufi poetry, as far as its influence was felt upon other modes of cultural expression during this period, we come to the field of the arts. Gradually, although begrudgingly, the Western world is beginning to realize that Islamic art is not just an odd collection of *objets de art* or quaint relics created by some people who call themselves Muslims, but that it is essentially the spiritual fruit of the Islamic revelation.

Of all the forms of art created in the vast Islamic civilization, Persian art is certainly the most diverse and extensive, possessing its own distinct ethos, world-view and particular symbolic meaning, one which is inextricably connected with Sufism. The majority of the great practitioners of this art were Sufis and in fact, the entire theoretical world-view that made this art possible actually emanated from Sufi metaphysical and philosophical teachings. On a more external plane, the rise and adaptation of certain art forms by Sufis made possible their continued survival. This is especially true in regard to the art of music.

Since every type of art usually required a patron, scholars often debate who was the patron of a particular art. We know that monumental architecture survived on royal patronage which favored the construction of major mosques and palaces, and that the patrons of carpet-making were, of course, the consumers of carpets, all the way from the vizier down to the merchant.

But who, precisely, were the patrons of music—whose patronage made possible the survival of a tradition which remains one of the greatest and profoundest expressions of music found anywhere in the world and which has survived to the present day? (As far as Persian culture is concerned, although court music is quite important, it was really secondary to the music performed by the Sufis). The answer is that it was the organized network of the Persian Sufi *khānaqāhs* which spanned the entire Islamic world during the latter part of this period, that provided the only viable physical substructure and spiritual framework within which classical Persian music could develop, enabling it to survive and preventing it from succumbing to the attacks of certain of the exoteric *'ulamā'*.

It is interesting to note that although classical Persian music had its admirers in the court up until the Safavid period, nevertheless its greatest performers were always the Sufis.[7] Perusing the annals of Persian music in the later Qajar period, when it underwent a great revival, one constantly finds echoes of the influence of the Sufis—as anyone who knows the history of Persian music will acknowledge. Recalling the names of such famous Qajar-period musicians as ʻAbdallāh Khān or Darwīsh Khān, for instance—one finds that they were almost all people who were either practising Sufis or related to Sufism in one form or another. There is also the long story of the relationship between Sufism and the visual arts, which however, is beyond the scope of the present introduction.[8]

PHILOSOPHY, THEOLOGY *(KALĀM)* AND SUFISM

Dr. Nurbakhsh in his foreword provided ample warning about the dangers of philosophy of a purely ratiocinative bent, that is, philosophy divorced from the source of the Truth. The role of Sufism in Islamic philosophy was basically to counterbalance the dangers of this exercise of pure reason by emphasizing the virtues of the gnosis of the heart.

Sufism's effect upon Islamic philosophy[9] was basically twofold: first of all, it served to preserve for every generation the possibility of an *experience* about which the philosopher philosophizes. By this we mean that the philosopher always philosophizes about an *experience* that he has undergone—his intellectual data or analysis are but by-products of this unique *philosophical experience*. One of the reasons why Western philosophy suddenly veered off from Islamic philosophy and went in a completely different direction—towards rationalism—is because in the sixteenth century, in Paris, Descartes was unable to gain access to the kind of *philosophical*

7. See S.H. Nasr, "The Influence of Sufism on Traditional Persian Music," in S.H. Nasr, *Islamic Art and Spirituality* (Suffolk, U.K.: Golgonooza Press 1987), pp. 163-176.
8. Cf. S.H. Nasr, "The Relationship between Islamic Art and Spirituality," in S.H. Nasr, *Islamic Art and Spirituality*, pp. 3-14.
9. For an extended discussion, see S.H. Nasr, "The Relationship between Sufism and Philosophy in Persian Culture," trans. H. Dabashi," *Hamdard Islamicus,* vol. 6, no. 4 (1983), pp. 33-47.

experience which his near-contemporary Mīr Dāmad (d. 1041/1631) realized in Iṣfahān, in Iran. It was this *philosophical experience* which makes possible access to the Ultimate Reality. The ever-living possibility of this *experience* of the Ultimate Reality provided Islamic philosophy, especially that of the later period, with the experiential foundation which complemented intellection.

Secondly, it was the spiritual method and meditative disciplines of Sufism which continually resurrected the power of the contemplative intellect (rather than reason) in Islamic thought. The Sufi method, which is exercised not through ratiocination but by a faculty which knows the Truth immediately by illumination, does not function properly unless all of the veils of forgetfulness and passion are removed from it. The achievement of Sufism was to unite the philosophical experience of the philosophers with the inner experience of the mystics and enable the intellect to function without the impediment of the carnal soul.

In this fashion a gradual wedding of Islamic philosophy with Sufism occurred. Although in the early period under analysis here there were only two Islamic philosophers who were interested in Sufism—the first being al-Fārābī, who practiced Sufism himself, and the second being Avicenna who moved on its outskirts despite a constant interest in it—in subsequent centuries this dance between the two worlds united into one single movement.

After the eighth/fourteenth century, we find that almost all Islamic philosophers, from Quṭb al-Dīn Shīrāzī (d. 710/1311) onwards were either practising Sufis themselves, or at least, very interested in the world view which *taṣawwuf* presented. This process finally culminated in the synthesis of the doctrinal teaching of Sufism or 'gnosis' *('irfān)* and philosophy in the thought of Mullā Ṣ adrā (d. 1050/1641). As John Cooper demonstrates in his essay in this volume (see below, pp. 409-33) Mullā Ṣadrā was deeply influenced by poetical teachings of Persian Sufism in the person of Rūmī.

If, as a general rule, it can be stated that the Sufis usually avoided the study of scholastic theology *(Kalām),* there were great exceptions to this rule as well, the most important of whom was Abū Ḥamīd Ghazālī, the greatest of all the Sunni theologians, whose theology is still taught throughout the Islamic world. Ghazālī, however, was also a dedicated Sufi. Thus, the rupture in the Islamic intellectual world between Ash'arīte theology *(Kalām)* and Sufism is not really so profound as some scholars maintain. There were, in fact, many thinkers besides Ghazālī and 'Ayn al-Quḍāt Hamadānī who were profoundly versed in both Sufism and theology at the same time. However, a real obstacle in the way of the synthesis of these two fields of thought did exist in the case of most theologians. This is illustrated by a story from the biography of Fakhr al-Dīn Rāzī of Herat (d. 600/1203), one of the most famous of Ash'arīte theologians and perhaps the most learned of the theologians of Islam. Rāzī had composed poetry in both Arabic and Persian, and was also deeply versed in geometry, medicine, history, and astronomy, having written treatises in all of these fields.

One day he went to see a Sufi master and expressed his interest in following the *Ṭarīqat.* This master agreed to initiate him on the condition that he grant him his unquestioning obedience as a disciple. Rāzī readily assented.

"Are you willing to give up all of your wealth?" the Sufi master asked.

Although he was an extremely wealthy man, Fakhr al-Dīn consented.

"Are you willing to give up your fame?" asked the master.

Although a man of great renown, he readily acquiesced to this condition as well.

"Are you willing to give up your power and influence?" the Sufi master queried.

"Yes." said Rāzī.

"Are you willing to give up your knowledge?" the Sufi master asked at last.

At this request Fakhr al-Dīn Rāzī balked, saying, "Of course, I cannot do that."

"Then you are unsuitable to become a Sufi," said the master.

Unfortunately, that was the end of Fakhr al-Dīn Rāzī's Sufi novitiate.

The story is very telling, I think, insofar as it exemplifies the eternal debate which is carried on in all the world's civilizations in one form or another, between that immediate form of knowledge—based on inner peace, tranquillity, union and illumination—and purely theological knowledge, typical of the academic milieu of the seminary school in which scholars such as Fakhr al-Dīn Rāzī were educated, especially in the discipline of *Kalām.*

THE CROSS-CULTURAL INFLUENCE OF PERSIAN SUFISM

One of the dominant characteristics of early Persian Sufism was an all-embracing universalism, which, like an tree, cast the shade of its influence not only upon the country of Persia but far beyond the borders of the Persian world. When we say 'Persian world' our reference is to the entire Persian-speaking world, not merely to the geographical boundaries of the present country of Iran. And it was this 'Greater Persia' which was one of the main homelands of early Sufism. Early Persia embraced a vast area, far broader than present-day Iran, stretching north to south: from present-day Central Asia to the Persian Gulf, and east to west: from Kashghar in present-day China to Ctesiphon in modern-day Iraq. This area was the main homeland of the Persian tradition and culture in the early centuries of Islamic history.

Strange to say, the effect of this 'Persianate civilization' was hardly felt in the Arab world of letters—aside from the fact that the literary works of many erudite Persians, such as Ghazālī, were written in Arabic and thus became known throughout the Arab world. Its deepest effect was on the other literatures and cultures which came into being during the Islamic period. The question of the Islamization of the Turks and the Turkic people, especially the Seljuk Turkmens who migrated from Central Asia to Transoxiana in the fifth/eleventh century, so often debated by scholars, is less explicable in terms of certain Turkish garrisons who converted to Islam under the Abbasid Caliphs in Baghdad, than in terms of the spread of Sufism. This influence of Sufism extended from present-day Pakistan up through Central Asia and into the Turkic part of the northern lands of Persia, that is to say, Khurāsān and upper Transoxiana, which today comprise the newly independent countries of Turkmenistan, Uzbekistan, Tajikistan, Kyrgyzstan, and part of southern central Kazakhistan.

Persian Sufi literature played a very important role in this process: the literary models of Persian Sufism formed the basis of

Turkish Sufi literature, from the early to the classical poetry of the Ottoman Empire. The reason why the Ottomans used Persian so much (and why, for example, Sultan Mehmet, the first Turkish conqueror of Constantinople, wrote in Persian) was not because they were in love with the Sassanian kings of ancient Iran, Jamshīd and Bahrām, but because of their devotion to Persian Sufism. In fact, to this day, Sufism still exercises a vast influence in the Turkish world—although not in the name of Persia *per se,* but in the name of Jalāl al-Dīn Rūmī. Since people sense an innate need to transcend the ethnocentric pettiness created by modern nationalism, in this respect Jalāl al-Dīn Rūmī assists them, figuring as a patron saint of the Turks and the Persians at the same time. Thus, during this early period, Persian Sufi literature played a profound role in the spiritual life of the emerging Ottoman civilization.

Little space is left to consider the effect of Persian Sufism upon the vast world of Islamic Southeast Asia and India, although Bruce Laurence has contributed an essay to the present volume (below, pp. 19-33) touching on Sufism in India. Persian language and culture played a formidable role in mediæval India and only after the rise of Shah Walīullāh of Dehli in the eighteenth century did Urdu emerge as a language of literary expression in Islamic culture. We may also recall that it was Shah Khalīlullāh, the son of Shāh Ni'matullāh (d. 834/1431), who ordered his children to go to India, and who of course spoke in Persian, and thus introduced the Ni'matullāhī Order into the Deccan. However, the world of Indian Islam and Indian Sufism is itself a separate concern, and would demand another volume of its own.

Finally, a few brief remarks about Sufism in the Arab world are in order. As mentioned above, Arabic Sufi literature never enjoyed intimate contact with the cultural milieu of Persian Sufism. In fact, Arabic Sufism became acquainted with this milieu primarily as a result of the Ottoman invasion of the Arabic world. It was actually the Ottomans who, inspired by their own love of the poetry and philosophy of Persian Sufism, conveyed the Persian mystical tradition to the Arab world. For example, the *Mathnawī* of Jalāl al-Dīn Rūmī was translated only once into Arabic during the entire mediæval period, and that was shortly after his death. Then, as the Mawlawiyya Order's influence grew through the expansion of the Ottoman influence in Egypt, the Arabs became acquainted with his great masterpiece. The same is true of 'Aṭṭār and the other great Persian Sufi poets; at first, they were not easily accessible in Arabic, until, at last, under the aegis of Ottoman influence, their writings were gradually made available in the Arab world.

CONCLUSION

By way of conclusion, I would just like to offer the following reflections on the contemporary interest in Sufism in the West. This interest is not merely a passing fad, but does have a timeless dimension. Interest in the reality of Sufism or the reality of all that comes from the Spirit, is something genuine, for Sufism emanates from the Reality beyond time, and being timeless, it necessarily manifests itself at various times and climes in different forms. We happen to be living in a time when the needs of human beings in the West have turned them towards the study of Sufism—for the second time in two hundred years: the first being in the early nineteenth century, in a somewhat shallow and superficial manner, and the second, today, in the late twentieth century, with, one hopes, greater depth.

Outside of greater Persia there is also an increasing interest in Persian culture and Sufism in the community of Iranian and Afghan exiles: this being a vivid commentary on their own spiritual condition. At its root this interest reflects the profound nostalgia of the soul for its own home, for when the earthly home is lost the celestial home is all that remains. Sufism is the Way of taking us back to our celestial home. This Way is a vivid reality not only for Persians or Afghans in physical exile from their homelands—but for all people who feel a sense of spiritual exile. All human beings having intimations of their spiritual being are already in exile in this world. "Islam began as a stranger and it will end up as a stranger," said the Prophet of Islam, and concluded, "and happy are those who are strangers." This is a spiritual maxim which reflects the condition of all those who feel themselves in exile in this world. Sufism is not only a call to those Persians or Afghans who feel themselves in exile from their native lands, but for all men and women who are beckoned by the call of the Spirit.

II

An Indo-Persian Perspective on the Significance of Early Persian Sufi Masters

Bruce B. Lawrence

Marc Bloch once observed that religious history has been muddled by the confusion between origins and beginnings.[1] Bloch's project was to recuperate emphasis on beginnings and downplay the significance of origins. With respect to Sufism, neither beginnings nor origins can be ignored. Yet they also can not be conflicted. One might suggest that beginning moments, together with their actors and stories, provide a frame narrative for the uninformed inquirer, while ordinary markings offer the sources of motivation for the involved and engaged.

Unfortunately, too much of EuroAmerican scholarship on Sufism, from R.C. Zaehner to Julian Baldick,[2] has focused on beginnings. Influences and borrowings are accounted for, and Sufis labeled by whom they resemble, that is, antecedent others, whether Muslim or non-Muslim. In studies of Sufi biographical texts that stress beginnings two approaches predominate. Both embrace, even as they perpetuate, an outdated style of intellectual history, its goal to press Sufi narratives into the service of a narrowly positivist agenda. One approach takes historical date in general and Sufi biographies in particular as test cases for rules of methods. The real

---

1. Marc Bloch, *The Historian's Craft,* translated by Peter Putnam (New York 1953), pp.32-35.
2. R.C. Zaehner, *Hindu and Muslim Mysticism* (New York 1969) and Julian Baldick, *Mystical Islam* (New York 1989).

purpose of scholarship, their proponents argue, is to winnow the few pellets of truth lying beneath all the accumulated dross of legend and superstition concocted by over zealous biographers. Both Baldick and P.M. Currie[3] epitomize this approach. The other approach is to excavate and then array massive chunks of obscure information about little known saints, on the assumption that once their story has been told 'in their own words', the message of their quest for Truth will be self-evident. In scholarship on Indian Sufism this approach is best represented by S.A.A. Rizvi.[4]

What is ignored in both approaches is what La Capra, glossing Weber and Collingwood, has stressed as the crucial analytical precept for historians, to wit, that "a fact is a pertinent fact only with respect to a frame of reference involving questions that we pose to the past." Moreover, La Capra goes on to note, "It is the ability to pose the 'right' questions that distinguishes productive scholarship."[5]

With reference to the origins of Persian Sufism, the right questions are not easily posed. They occupy a penumbral zone between this time and former times. They require attention to origins in order to understand beginnings. For Marc Bloch was only half-right: even though logically beginnings do have to be accounted for apart from origins, in practice the two invariably commingle. To trace the multiple histories of Persian Sufism, each historian must engage in a struggle with both. The exclusive quest for beginnings is wrong-headed because it presumes that beginnings matter and origins do not. The former are deemed to be clear and 'factual', the latter muddled and 'legendary'. Yet to isolate origins from beginnings is equally futile; it makes of origins a timeless myth marked by human names yet unshaped either by human initiatives or by unforeseen social circumstances. Persian Sufism demands something more; it demands attention to both its historical beginnings and its transhistorical origins.

---

3. . P.M. Currie, *The Shrine and Cult of Mu'īn al-Dīn Chishtī of Ajmer* (New Delhi 1989).
4. . S.A.A. Rizvi, *A History of Sufism in India,* 2 vols. (New Delhi 1978, 1983).
5. Dominick LaCapra, *Rethinking Intellectual History: Texts, Contexts, Language* (Ithaca 1983), p. 31.

To chart a path of interpretive value through the minefields of extant scholarship on Persian Sufism, one must ask questions that combine origins with beginnings. Two perspectives loom large: the perspective of a discrete biographical author and the perspective of a modern researcher. The latter can be omitted only at the cost of obfuscating basic presuppositions. I am a modern researcher, and so are all of us. We combine our endeavors in this setting as modern researchers who have chosen to investigate pre-modern writings from a non-Western part of the globe. A chasm of time and space separates us from our subjects, they from us. Our subjects' world view, in common with all pre-modern world views, eschewed both the Galilean mode of reasoning and the Cartesian conception of knowledge. In their stead our subjects privileged "textual exegesis, cosmic analogies and above all appeals to authority, both genealogical and literary, scriptural and juridical."[6]

We presume to study pre-modern Persian Sufis, knowing that their world view is not ours, no matter how great our affection for their writings or our immersion in the quest that motivated them. Our perspective is at once individual and collective. While each of us may demur from aspects of the place and time in which we live, we cannot fully escape its dominant mood. We are shaped by what Bourdieu calls the *habitus,* the taken-for-granted outlook of late twentieth century global capitalism. From that perspective we are all marked as post-Galilean, post-Cartesian and, horror of horrors, even post-modern. We investigate the past as a social datum filtered through our own present. We approach it with handles that are provisional labels in the service of our own enquiry. We enjoy no secure frames of reference; we possess no incontestable or incontrovertible facts. Even the title "Classical Persian Sufism" is a term of convenience. "Classical Persian Sufism?" From the perspective of those discussed there is no 'Persian Sufism' separable from *taṣawwuf* as a universal impulse pervading all of *Dār al-Islām,* the global Muslim community. *Taṣawwuf* is limited neither to one kind of language, however refined and subtle, nor to one body of

6. Adapted from Steven Lukes, "Relativism in its Place" in Martin Hollis and Steven Lukes, eds. *Rationality and Relativism* (MIT Press 1982) p. 297.

literature, however varied and satisfying. It is we who are limited in how we approach *taṣawwuf*. We are limited by our modernity, even as we are privileged by it. We are also limited by our focus on the Persian language, Persian actors, and Persian texts, despite the evident organizational benefit and the hoped for explanatory yield of that stricture.

Having excused ourselves from premature self-congratulation, we can still try to ask the 'right' questions. In our case, the prior question is to ask how Sufi authors themselves viewed their task. Instead of culling from their writings grist for a historical grindstone, we can ask: how did Sufi biographers in the pre-modern period recall the formation of those institutional structures, brotherhoods dedicated to preserving the Divine Trust, that had marked their lives?

That question opens up a view of the Muslim past as interpreted and reinterpreted through spiritual exemplars. But it is not a uniform, homogeneous past which offers a cornucopia of equivalent figures. While all were Muslim, not all excelled on the Path. Some did not even pursue the Path. The biographers had to make choices in how they presumed to recall and re-present certain figures from the Muslim past to their readers. Were the exemplars whom they cited and about whom they wrote only saints of bygone eras or were they also noble persons esteemed by all Muslims? Wadad al-Qadi, after surveying the entire range of Islamic biographical dictionaries written in Arabic, noted:

> [The pioneer of Sufi biography] al-Sulamī (d.412/1021) arranged the biographies in *Ṭabaqāt al-ṣūfiyya* chronologically, beginning with the earliest Sufi (al-Fuḍayl b. 'Iyāḍ) and ending with contemporary Sufis (the last one is Abū 'Abdullāh al-Dinawarī) ...And the same principles are noted in some of following dictionaries, such as al-Qushayrī's (d.465/1072) *al-Risāla al-Qushayriyya.* [But at the same time another format is initiated by] Abū Nu'aym Iṣfahānī (d. 430/1038) in his *Ḥilyat al-awliyā'*. There almost all the great figures of Islam who have been known for their outstanding piety or great learning are considered *awliyā'*– just like the Sufis. Thus the biographies of the Companion 'Umar b. al-Khaṭṭāb stands side by side in the book with that of the Follower al-Ḥasan al-Baṣrī, the jurist al-Shāfi'ī, and the Sufi al-Junayd. The underlying assumption of the author is further strengthened by

> lengthy citations from the words/works of all those people, giving credibility to the criterion used.[7]

The same double option—to limit oneself to Sufi exemplars or to include all pious Muslim 'heroes'—is present in the Persian and Indo-Persian *tadhkira* tradition. (There is, of course, a third option, to write biographies limited to an individual saint or a single spiritual brotherhood retrospectively linked to an eponymous ancestor, but we are not concerned with that genre here, since it reveals little about the transition from Arabic to Persian to Indo-Persian in Sufi biographical writing.) For instance, 'Abdullāh Anṣārī first expanded Sulamī's *Ṭabaqāt* to include Persian-speaking saints. Four centuries later Jāmī in his massive *Nafaḥāt al-uns* (completed in 883/1477), further enlarged Anṣārī's *Ṭabaqāt* while also embellishing its Persian style. What resulted was the classic Persian *tadhkira* of Sufi and Sufi-affiliated saintly figures. Jāmī begins with a minor figure, Hāshim al-Ṣūfī, and, five hundred and sixty-six entries later, concludes with another minor figure of the generation preceding his own, Mīr Sayyid Qāsim Tabrīzī (d. 837/1433). He adds notices on thirteen Persian Sufi poets as well as thirty-four notices on woman saints.

The 'chaste' tradition of Sulamī/Anṣārī/Jāmī is continued in Indo-Persian. Its premier pre-Mughal exponent is the Suhrawardī adept, Shaykh Jamālī (d. 971/1536): in *Siyar al-'ārifīn* he offers a wealth of information about thirteen major Chishtī and Suhrawardī saints of the Delhi Sultanate. In the Mughal period Jamālī is followed by the Qādirī loyalist, Shaykh 'Abd al-Ḥaqq Muḥaddith Dihlawī: his *Akhbār al-akhyār,* though limited to entries on saints, depicts over two hundred and sixty Sufi exemplars from the Chishtiyya, Suhrawardiyya, Firdawsiyya, Shaṭṭāriyya, Qalandariyya and also, of course, the Qādiriyya Order. A short appendix includes fourteen pious women, all of Indian extraction. 'Abd al-Ḥaqq's work is a saint's biographical dictionary intended for the edification of all those who either pursue the Path or admire those who

7. Wadad al-Qadi, "The Islamic Book in the Form of the Biographical Dictionaries: Inner Structure and Cultural Significance," paper given at a Conference on the Islamic Book, Washington, D.C., Summer 1989.

do. It was often emulated in later generations.[8]

But the other option for writing *tadhkiras* is also broached: though seldom evident in Persian, it attracts some major biographers in the high period of Indo-Persian culture, particularly during the reign of the Great Mughals. That option is to write not only about saints and select poets but rather about all the formative personalities who have helped to forge a distinct galaxy of Persian spiritual luminaries with their individual repertoires of attributes, skills and paradoxical utterances as saints.[9] Among the most famous *tadhkira* deploying this approach is Dārā Shikūh's *Safinat al-awliyā',* completed in 1640 when the Mughal prince was but twenty-five years old. Though it has been hailed as "a standard work of reference" on the Sufi brotherhoods extant in seventeenth-century Mughal India,[10] it in fact offers but fragmentary biographical resumes of some four hundred saints, both Indian and non-Indian. Preceding these accounts are other biographies of Muslim notables, beginning with the Prophet Muḥammad, the first four Caliphs, the eleven Imāms ('Alī's biography being given as 'Caliph'), and the four eponymous founders of Sunni legal schools. The significance of these non-Indian, non-Sufi entries is made evident in the concluding section on "wise, virtuous, perfected and united" women. It begins with the Prophet's wives, then depicts his daughters before turning to women saints. In effect, claims Dārā Shikūh, the legitimacy of the Path he pursues is affirmed by the most esteemed and lauded exemplars from the foundational period of Islam. He tries to map his own beginnings as a Qādirī adept through an appeal to the origins of Islam as an historical movement. Fascinated with the miraculous, he nonetheless takes account of temporal markings. "For example," explains Perwaiz Hayat, "he did not accept the age of Salman or the Prophet Muḥammad as cited in the traditional accounts. He narrates different sources, but accepts that account which for him seems to

8. For fuller details on *Akhbār al-akhyār,* see my article in *Encyclopaedia Iranica* I.7, pp. 711-712.

9. I have explored these paradoxes in "The Chishtīya of Sultanate India: A Case Study of Biographical Complexities in South Asian Islam" in Michael A. Williams, ed. *Charisma and Sacred Biography* (Chico 1982), pp. 47-67.

10. C.A. Storey. *Persian Literature: A Bio-Bibliographical Survey* 1/2, (London 1953-1972), p. 993.

be nearer to historical fact. He was also interested in providing as complete an account of the *awliyā'* as possible: he tries his best to furnish birthdates, deathdates and the places of the tombs of every *walī.*" [11]

Yet Dārā Shikūh's apparent concern for historical accuracy, like his list of Muslim 'heroes' from the seventh and eighth centuries, is a mask for his overriding goal: not only to affirm 'Abd al-Qādir as the foremost Sufi exemplar and the Qādiriyya as the paramount Sufi brotherhood, but to underpin his own authority *vis-à-vis* rival claims to Qādirī spirituality. As noted above, his was not the first Indo-Persian biographical dictionary written by a Qādirī. He was preceded by the formidable scholar of *ḥadīth*, himself a Qādirī adept, Shaykh 'Abd al-Ḥaqq Muḥaddith Dihlawī (d. 1052/1642). 'Abd al-Ḥaqq's *Akhbār al-akhyār*, completed in 1028/1618, had already gained considerable fame by 1640, and Dārā Shikūh models many of his own entries on Indian saints after the longer, fuller entries of *Akhbār al-akhyār.* Yet in presenting the Qādiriyya, he bypasses the lineage traced by 'Abd al-Ḥaqq, acknowledging only that line of Qādirī affiliation traceable through 'Abd al-Qādir al-Thānī to 'Abdullāh Bhitī to Miyān Mīr (d. 1046/1635) and then to his own preceptor, Mullā Shāh (d. 1070/1660).

The significance of the Islamic past for Dārā Shikūh is functional: its retelling helps to affirm his status as a Qādirī adept. Giants of Persian Sufism like 'Alā' al-Dawla Simnānī and Jalāl al-Dīn Rūmī, while mentioned, are accorded half a page devoted mostly to biographical, travel and literary data. Their inclusion affirms Dārā Shikūh's awareness of the long tradition in which he stands, but their sole purpose is to provide a backdrop for the stage onto which he parades as central actor the Qādiriyya, especially his own immediate spiritual mentors.

Dārā Shikūh's *Safīnat al-awliyā'* contrasts with another biographical dictionary from Mughal India. While much has been written about *Safīnat al-awliyā'*, mention is seldom made of the Chishtī master, Shaykh 'Abd al-Raḥmān (d. 1094/1683) or his *tadhkira,* the

11. Perwaiz Hayat, "The Concept of Wilaya in the Early Works of Dara Shukoh (1024/1615-1069/1659)," M.A. Thesis submitted to McGill University, May 1987, p. 63.

Dārā Shikūh in Conversation with a Muslim Sage. Attributed to La'l Chand, ca. 1650. B.M. 1941-10-10-04. (Courtesy of the British Museum).

Mir'āt al-asrār, which appears in several published catalogues. Although it has never generated a fraction of the interest directed to *Safinat al-awliyā',* the two works merit comparison, if only because their authors were near contemporaries and also because they employed the same inclusive method of *tadhkira* writing. In the *Mir'āt al-asrār,* after noting the twelve family clusters into which Sufi brotherhoods may be parceled, Shaykh 'Abd al-Raḥmān reviews no less than twenty-three generations of spiritual exemplars. He brackets the Prophet Muḥammad and his three immediate successors as the first generation, followed by 'Alī and the other eleven Imāms in the second generation in which the first Chishtī master is said to have lived and died in Syria (ca. 328/940). Appearing in the same generation with him were his contemporaries Shiblī (d. 334/945) and Ḥallāj (d. 309/922). By the time of the fourteenth generation when Quṭb al-Dīn Mawdūd (d. 537/1132) became the successor at Chisht he counted among his contemporaries both Abū Ḥāmid and Aḥmad Ghazzālī (d. 505/111 and 520/1126) as well as 'Ayn al-Quḍāt Hamadānī (martyred 526/1132). Successive generations boasted still more illustrious names. For instance, by the sixteenth generation when 'Uthmān Ḥarūnī (d. 607/1210) became the Chishtī standard bearer, he welcomed as fellow Sufi Shaykhs 'Abd al-Qādir Jilānī (d. 561/1166) and Abū Madyan Maghribī (d. 595/1198.

Most intriguing, however, are the last six generations depicted in the *Mir'āt al-asrār.* The initial two depict well-known non-Indian Sufis alongside scarcely known Indian exemplars. These generations are decisive for the beginnings of Sufism in the Asian subcontinent. They mark the historical period when the Chishtī Order was first introduced to India and began to establish itself as the sole brotherhood linked exclusively with South Asia. Their roll call includes:

1) Under Mu'īn al-Dīn Chishtī (d. 633/1236) in the seventeenth generation:
Najm al-Dīn Kubrā (d. 618/1221),
Shihāb al-Dīn Abū Ḥafṣ Suhrawardī (d. 632/1234),
Muhyī al-Dīn Ibn 'Arabī (d. 638/1240),
Ruzbihān Baqlī (d. 606/1210),
Bahā' al-Dīn Walad (d. ca 628/1231),

Sa'd al-Dīn Ḥamūya (d. 650/1253),
Sayf al-Dīn Bākharzī (d. 659/1261),
and Farīd al-Dīn 'Aṭṭār (d. 618/1221).

2) Under Quṭb al-Dīn Bakhtiyār Kākī (d. 633/1235) in the eighteenth generation:
Jalāl al-Dīn Rūmī (d. 672/1273),
Ṣadr al-Dīn Qūnyawī (d. 673/1274),
Awḥad al-Dīn Kirmānī (d. 635/1238),
Muṣliḥ al-Dīn Sa'dī (d. between 691/1292 – 695/1296),
and Sulṭān Walad (d. 712/1312).

The arbitrariness of these two clusters is evident, not only from the near identical death-dates of the two Chishtī masters but also from the wide disparity in the death-dates of the Persian masters: while Najm al-Dīn Kubrā expired in 618/1221, Sayf al-Dīn Bākharzī, one of his disciples, did not expire till 659/1261. Moreover, both Rūmī and Qunyāwī survived till the 670's/1270's, while Sa'dī's death-date is usually given as 691/1292. Such temporal disparities, however, do not detract from 'Abd al-Raḥmān's primary purpose: to retell the saga of Persian/Indo-Persian Sufism as a single dramatic endeavor shaped by the Unseen for the benefit of humankind.

Yet from the time of Farīd al-Dīn Ganj-i Shakar (Quṭb al-Dīn's successor, d. 664/1265) to the end of *Mir'āt al-asrār,* the Indo-Persian actors begin to overshadow their Persian predecessors. After the eighteenth generation, scarcely any non-Indian saints are mentioned, the few notable exceptions being 'Alā' al-Dawla Simnānī (d. 736/1336), Bahā' al-Dīn Naqshband (d. 791/1389) and 'Abdullāh Yāfi'ī (d. 1768/1367) in the twenty-first generation, and Muḥammad Parsā (d. 822/1421) and Shāh Ni'matullāh (d. 834/1431) in the twenty-second generation. The reason is not hard to discover: Shaykh 'Abd al-Raḥmān is not only a Chishtī master, he is also the incumbent of a shrine in Awadh, well to the east of Delhi in modern-day Uttar Pradesh. He traces his own spiritual lineage back through the Ṣābiriyya rather than the Niẓāmiyya sub-branch of the Chishtiyya. That lineage is beset with chronological difficulties that cloud its initial years. Its eponymous founder was one Shaykh 'Alā' al-Dīn 'Alī ibn Aḥmad Ṣābir who died in Kalyar, a town in northern

Uttar Pradish in 691/1291. He is said to have been identical with the Shaykh 'Alī Ṣābir who is briefly mentioned in *Siyar al-awliyā'* as a disciple of Shaykh Farīd al-Dīn Ganj-i Shakar. No less an authority than Shaykh 'Abd al-Ḥaqq , however, questions the conflation of the two names and persons. Even if it is accepted, there seems to be more than a generation between 'Alī Ṣābir's successor, Shams al-Dīn Turk Pānīpatī (d. 718/1318) and his successor, Jalāl al-Dīn Pānīpatī (d. 765f/1364). Further comprising the historical markings of the lineage is the fact that Aḥmad 'Abd al-Ḥaqq (d. 837/1434), who succeeds Jalāl al-Dīn and is the biological as well as the spiritual ancestor of 'Abd al-Raḥmān, was not born till ca. 751/1350.

'Abd al-Raḥmān, rather than linger on these hiatuses and discrepancies, paints a colorful canvas of spirituality that includes all the major figures of the Niẓāmiyya sub-branch of the Chishtiyya as part of his own mystical legacy. Unlike Dārā Shikūh's brief reminders, these are full, vivid accounts of both Persian and non-Persian saints of earlier eras. The organization by successive *ṭabaqāt* or generations, despite the chronological discrepancies, draws attention to the pre-eminent Sufi authority (the 'axis' or *quṭb*) of each age. From the perspective of 'Abd al-Raḥmān's lineage, the *quṭb* of each age, since the appearance of Shaykh 'Alī Ṣābir, had to be, and has been, a Ṣābirī Chishtī master. Yet his is not a partisan view which argues for Ṣābiris over Niẓāmīs, Chishtīs over other Sufis, Sufis over other Muslims or Muslims over Hindus. Instead he shows a wide acquaintance with classical Persian Sufism and an appreciation for the luster that its exemplars bring each to his own generation and to his own place. While each generation is marked by a *quṭb*, he is situated among, not apart from, other Sufi masters: though he stands at their head, they add to his preeminence. By this ingenious artifice the author of *Mir'āt al-asrār* accomplishes a double purpose: 1) he makes clear how vital was the connection to a Persian Sufi tradition for all Ṣābiri Chishtīs while 2) at the same time conferring the highest spiritual rank on a handful of obscure saints, most of whom lived and toiled and died in Northeastern India.

The reputation of 'Abd al-Raḥmān does not rest on the *Mir'āt al-asrār* alone. He was a curious figure who existed on the margins of several worlds. A member of the Indo-Tūrānī elite, he lived in Agra for awhile but chose to settle far east of Agra in the region of Lucknow. Though a member of the Chishtī Order, he was affiliated with the lesser Ṣābiriyya branch, not the dominant Niẓāmiyya branch. A skilled Persian prosodist, he nonetheless shows scant interest in Arabic, except for the usual familiar quotations. His real 'second' language is Sanskrit, from which he does translations into Persian.[12] In a sense he seems to be as much the legatee of the emperor Akbar (1566-1605) as was Akbar's great-grandson, Dārā Shikūh. It was Akbar who in 1582 made Persian the official government language of the Mughal empire. It was also Akbar who authorized and subsidized translations from Sanskrit into Persian. 'Abd al-Raḥmān, like Akbar and also like Dārā Shikūh, wanted to make Persian the bridge language between a nomothetic Islamic world shaped by distant scriptural sources and juridical norms and an Indian domain privileging local resources of myth, miracle, and magic. Many of 'Abd al-Raḥmān's 'heroes', such as the two Simnānīs, 'Alā' al-Dawla and Ashraf Jahāngīr, Mu'in al-Dīn Chishtī, Gīsū-Darāz, Muḥammad b. Ja'far and Shāh Madār, accent the visionary and the miraculous. They are also peripatetic, traveling, or claiming to have traveled, to many parts of the Islamic world. 'Abd al-Raḥmān's world-view cannot be strait-jacketed into one or another vision of Sufi metaphysics. It is more a kaleidoscope than a coherent system of thought. Praxis reigns over theory, anecdotes and poetry over metaphysical treatises.

In reviewing the progression of biographical writing among Indian Sufis, we rediscover the Persian legacy of all subcontinent Muslims. While the first efforts at biographical writing were launched in Arabic, they were continued and embellished in Persian. The models provided in Khurāsān and Isfahan proved useful in Hindustan, first during the Delhi Sultanate and then during the subsequent period of Mughal ascendancy. This literary production was restricted to elites, even when, as in the case of 'Abd al-Raḥmān, a biographer branched out from the *ashrāf* classes to include practices

12. This point is amplified and documented in Roderic Vassie, "Persian Interpretations of the Bhagavadgita in the Mughal Period, with special reference to the Sufi version of 'Abd al-Raḥmān Chishtī," Ph.D thesis submitted to SOAS (University of London 1988).

and beliefs common to *ajlāf*, or non-elite Muslims.

The resulting picture is much more complicated than a simple diffusionist theory would allow. To understand the origins of Mughal Sufism, one must look again at the figures who are most often linked to its beginnings. Sixteenth and seventeenth century Indo-Persian Sufi adepts saw themselves as parts of a chain that extended back to the earliest period of Islamic history but had its strongest links during the eleventh, twelfth and thirteenth centuries when Persian Sufism crystallized its distinctive world view. Yet even those authors, like Dārā Shikūh and 'Abd al-Raḥmān Chishtī, who seem to share so much as Indo-Persian Sufi polymaths, have a radically different perception of their common past.

How does one account for such differences? At least, in part, one accounts for them by acknowledging that despite the spirit of tolerance that prevailed among Sufis there was a rivalry for spiritual excellence. It is not clear that Dārā Shikūh was irenic in his view of fellow Indo-Persian elites who claimed a different lineage to Shaykh 'Abd al-Qādir Jīlānī. His search for a metaphysical unity between Hindu and Muslim world views may not have extended to finding a common ground for accepting all Sufis as spiritual equals. 'Abd al-Raḥmān, on the other hand, did feel that his quest was marked by a visionary union with all past saints, of his own and parallel lineages. In the long entry on Farīd al-Dīn, for instance, he quotes from the Shaṭṭārī exemplar, Muḥammad Ghawth (d. 969/1562), who wrote about a dream in which he found himself in one of the highest celestial realms. There he came face-to-face with Farīd al-Dīn Ganj-i Shakar. Farīd al-Dīn explained that he shared that station with three other saints: Bāyazīd, Junayd, and Dhū'l-Nūn![13] By such visionary accounts 'Abd al-Raḥmān seeks to confirm his own vision that pre-Indian and Indian exemplars merge in their common striving to become heirs to the blessing of the Prophet Muḥammad.

While the genre of *tadhkiras* offered saints such as 'Abd al-Raḥmān a literary vehicle to demonstrate their imagination as well as their saintliness, his *tadhkira* underscores the extent to which Indo-Persian Sufism was dependent on its perception of its origins

13. . 'Abd al-Raḥman, *Mir'āt al-asrār,* British Museum copy, f. 302.

in struggling to account for its beginnings. The tradition of Persian Sufism flourished in the subcontinent because it could be simultaneously cosmopolitan and local. There was no single story of ancestry but many stories with a varying array of ancestors. The appropriation of saintly forebears, far from being uniform or incremental, depended on the narrator and his narrative strategies. The legacy of Indo-Persian Sufism was continually being reshaped as both an extension and a replacement of Persian antecedents. And not only in each period, in each region and in each Order. It was also reshaped to suit the temporal-spatial needs of particular adepts. In 'Abd al-Raḥmān Chishtī we witness how a learned member of the Indo-Turani elite privileged the legacy of Persian Sufism at the same time as he transformed that legacy into a local narrative. His paramount need was, in Carl Ernst's words, "to create a local sacred geography for Indian Islam."[14] By being local, his message was not divorced from extra-Indian territorial referents but it did reconfigure them to exalt the tastes and affirm the spiritual authority of his own Indian masters. 'Abd al-Raḥmān's, far from being a solitary quest, illumines how durative yet malleable is the legacy of Persian Sufism – beyond its formative period and also beyond the geographical limits of Iran.

14. Carl Ernst, "Sufism in the Deccan: the Khuldabad-Burhanpur Axis." Paper delivered at a conference on 'Regional Varieties of Premodern Islam in India', University of Heidelberg, 17-22 July 1989.

Persian Contributions to Sufi Literature in Arabic

Ahmad Mahdavi Damghani

In Islamic culture the word *adab* is employed in basically two senses. The first denotes 'intellectual education and cultivation' leading to the creation of a certain virtuous quality *(malaka)* within an individual, inhibiting one from indulgence in vices and improprieties and bringing one ultimately, both in act and deed, in public and private, to the highest reaches of learning and accomplishment. This type of *adab* has also been referred to in diverse terms as respectively: tradition *(sunna),* asceticism *(zuhd),* ethics *(akhlāq),* discipline of the soul *(adab-i nafs)* and so on. Roughly speaking, one of the best and most concise ways of defining this aspect of *adab* is what was axiomatically referred to as the essence of human morality and proper behavior by the Persians during the pre-Islamic period, *viz.* 'good thoughts, good words, and good deeds' *(pindār-i nīk, guftār-i nīk, kirdār-i nīk).* One endowed with such *adab* is thus known as a 'person of refinement, courtesy, and culture' (Arabic: *mu'addab,* Persian: *bā-adab).* Religious creeds, philosophical doctrines and mystical teachings both east and west have also endeavoured to develop and perfect this type of culture or *adab.*

The second significance of the word is simply 'learning' *(adab-i dars)* or 'literary lore', 'humanistic or literary studies' *('ilm-i adab),* a person 'cultured' in this sense being described as a 'man (or woman) of letters' *(adīb):* from whence was derived both the adjective 'literary' *(adabī)* and the collective noun 'literature' *(adabiyyāt).*

Now, it should be emphasized that the Sufis in general, and Persian Sufis in particular, played a very important role in the development and expansion of both these types of *adab* in the Islamic world. So to simplify our discussion of the Persian Sufi contribution to the development of Arab Sufi *adab,* we may consider the first type of *adab* (*ādāb-i nafs:* tradition, asceticism, ethics, discipline of the soul)—as roughly equivalent to what is known as 'practical Sufism' *(taṣawwuf-i 'amalī),* and the second type of *adab* (learning, literary lore, or literary studies) as corresponding to what is known as 'Sufi literature' and 'speculative Sufism' *(taṣawwuf-i naẓarī).*

Here, we should note that the Persian Sufis were among the first to set hand to pen and make substantial contributions to the development of Arabic literature *(adab-i 'arab)* in respect to both of these branches mentioned above. Insofar as the 'discipline of the soul' *(adab-i nafs)* was first cited above and the oldest Sufi compositions generally concerned the exposition of this branch of ethical *adab* and practical Sufism, in what follows we will first examine the contributions made by Persian Sufis and ascetics to this field.

If we consider the Persians among the companions of the Prophet of Islam—such as Salmān Fārsī (d. 36/656),[1] or those who belonged to the second generation of pious Muslims: the so-called 'followers' or *tābi'ūn,* such as Ḥabīb 'Ajamī (d. 156/772)—as the first Sufis, and this is indeed, the actual fact of the matter, a great deal of their noteworthy and pithy sayings are to be found in the extant literature of ethics, *adab* and biography. These sayings represent not only some of the finest examples of literary eloquence and style of their period, but also are key texts and primary sources in the science of the 'discipline of the soul' *(ādāb-i nafs).* However, since the actual composition of books and treatises did not occur until the end of the second/eighth century, no literary works from these early Sufis remain.

During this early period of the literary development of Islamic thought the first treatise to be composed on the 'discipline of the soul' was *Al-Zuhd wa'l-raqā'iq* by 'Abdullāh ibn Mubārak Marwazī (118/736 –181/797) of Khurāsān, a work divided into sixteen fascicles of one hundred and two chapters.[2] 'Abdullāh ibn

1. For further information on the veneration maintained by the Sufis for Salmān Fārsī, cf. Ibn 'Arabī, *Futūḥāt al-makkiyya,* chapter 29, "On the Wisdom of Salmān Fārsī."

Mubārak expounds and comments on traditions *(ḥadīth)* and works which served as guidelines for ascetics who observed strict discipline in following the Sufi path, explaining the various doctrines of 'practical Sufism'. His book is not only the first text written on 'practical Sufism', but can also be considered as the earliest history of Sufism, since it contains descriptions of the *exempla* and *dicta* of eight of the most famous saints of early Islam, the chief founders of Islamic Sufism. These are mentioned as: Rabī' ibn al-Khaytham, Uways al-Qaranī, Harim ibn Ḥayyān, 'Āmir ibn 'Abd Qays, Abū Muslim Khawlānī, Masrūq ibn al-Ajda', Ḥasan al-Baṣrī, and Aswad ibn Yazīd.

This famous Persian's book had a profound impact, prompting many Islamic religious leaders and ascetics of the Sufi persuasion, as well as some of the foremost traditionists of the period, to adopt it as a model for their own thoughts and practice. In fact, through their imitation of this work a new chapter in Islamic theology was opened up: thus, only four years after Ibn Mubārak's death, these scholars had each written their own books emulating his style, with titles such as *Al-Zuhd* or *Al-Raqā'iq*. It also prompted many of the eminent traditionists of the period to add separate chapters to their own collections of *ḥadīth* under the title of 'asceticism' *(zuhd)*. Hence, one finds a separate chapter allocated to the subject of asceticism in the *Saḥīḥ al-Bukhārī,* the *Saḥīḥ al-Tirmidhī,* the *Sunan al-Nasā'ī,* and the *Sunan Ibn Māja*—all of which were composed during this period. The importance of Ibn Mubārak's book can also be deduced from the words of the great Ḥanbalite jurisprudent of the sixth/twelfth century, Ibn Taymiyya, who wrote, "One of the highest ranking books written on this subject is *Al-Zuhd wa'l-raqā'iq* by 'Abdullāh ibn Mubārak."[3]

By the same century, more than twenty books by the name of *Al-Zuhd* or *Al-Raqā'iq*—even including a work called *Al-Zuhd* by Aḥmad ibn Ḥanbal, the founder of one of the four main legal schools in Islam—had been written in imitation of Ibn Mubārak's work. Muḥammad ibn Isḥaq Nadīm, author of *Al-fihrist,* a text which has

---

2. This work has been published in many editions.
3. 'Abdullāh Ibn Mubārak Marwazī Khurāsānī, *Al-Zuhd wa'l-raqā'iq,* p. 14.

been a staple reference source for scholars of the Islamic sciences for over a thousand years, indicates that Bishr ibn Ḥārith Ḥāfī (d. 227/842), the renowned Sufi from Merv in Khurāsān had also composed a book entitled *Al-Zuhd,* a work which considerably antedated Ibn Ḥanbal's work on the same subject.

Featured in the fifth section of the fifth chapter ("Notices of the Devotees, Ascetics and Sufis") of this same *Al-Fihrist* is also mention of compositions by such Persian Sufis as Yaḥyā ibn Mu'ādh Rāzī (from Ray, near modern-day Tehran, d. 258/871) and Sahl ibn 'Abdullāh Tustarī (d. 273/887, from Shushtar in southwestern Iran), both contemporaries of Bishr Ḥāfī. Another Persian Sufi from Nīshāpūr—to whom 'Aṭṭār was to give the sobriquet, the "Master of Khurāsān"—Aḥmad ibn Ḥarb (d. 234/848), also composed a book entitled *Al-Zuhd.*

Therefore, the first person to write a book on the 'discipline of the soul', *(adab-i nafs)* and 'practical Sufism' *(taṣawwuf-i 'amalī)* was this same 'Abdullāh ibn Mubārak of Khurāsān. Following in his footsteps the great Ḥārith ibn Asad Muḥāsibī of Baghdad (d. 243/857) compiled his *Kitāb al-Ri'āya li-ḥuqūq Allāh* as well as other long and short treatises such as *Risāla al-qaṣd, Risāla al-a'mal al-qalb wa al-jawāriḥ, Risāla al-makāsib* and the *Risāla al-'aql.*[4]

Muḥāsibī was one of the foremost intellectual luminaries of his age, at once mystic, scholar, theologian, and philosopher. Although his works should certainly be accounted amongst the earliest Arabic texts on Sufism, and include explanations and exposition of much Sufi technical terminology, such as self-examination *(muḥāsaba),* contemplation *(murāqaba),* fear *(khawf),* hope *(rajā'),* patience *(ṣabr),* contentment *(riḍā')* and loving-kindness *(maḥabba)*—nonetheless, probably owing to the recent vogue enjoyed by such mystical terms and themes, he provides only very brief definitions of them. He does, however, frequently quote many of the older Persian Sufis, such as Ibn Mubārak, Ibrāhīm ibn Adḥam (d. 161/778), Fuḍayl ibn 'Iyāḍ (d. 187/803), Bishr Ḥāfī (d. 227/842), Muḥammad ibn Yūsuf Iṣfahānī, Shaqīq Balkhī (d. 194/810) and others, using

---

4. It should be mentioned that the late Louis Massignon speculated that, prior to Ḥārith Muḥāsibī, Aḥmad ibn 'Āsim Anṭākī Shāmi had composed a book covering these same themes.

their words to illustrate his ideas.

After Muḥāsibī and Aḥmad ibn Āṣim, many of the Sufis of Baghdad and Khurāsān, such as the 'Leader of the Sufis' Abū'l-Qāsim Junayd of Baghdad (d. 298/910, born in Nahāvand in Western Persia), Yaḥyā ibn Mu'ādh of Ray, Saḥl Tustārī and Muḥammad ibn Faḍl Balkhī also composed treatises on Sufism. Among such masters, Muḥammad ibn 'Alī al-Ḥakīm Tirmidhī (d. c. 295/908),[5] the author of several comprehensive books[6] on mystical gnosis and *adab-i nafs* should be mentioned. Tirmidhī was also an eminent scholastic theologian *(mutakallim)*, having composed treatises and books on such themes of 'divine Unity' *(tawḥīd)*, the 'divine Essence and Attributes' *(dhāt, ṣifāt)*, as well as on 'Friendship with God' *(walāya)*.

Nonetheless, because the scope of all these works was very limited, being devoted to the exposition of specific issues in Sufi gnostic thought, or else composed in the form of 'epistles' explaining particular matters which concerned only the author and his correspondent, none of them managed to give a thoroughgoing account of all the theoretical and practical principles of Sufism, and analyse in detail the various belief-systems and spiritual practices of the mystics. Hence, it was not until the fourth/tenth century when two eminent Persian Sufis, Abū Naṣr Sarrāj of Ṭūs (d. 378/988) and Abū Bakr Muḥammad Kalābadhī[7] of Bukhārā (d. 380/990), contemporaries of one other, wrote their respective classic manuals of Sufi doctrine: *Al-Luma'* and *Al-Ta'arruf li-madhhab ahl al-taṣawwuf*, that the principles of theoretical and practical Sufism became clearly delineated. It came to be said of Kalābadhī's work, that 'If it had not been for *Al-ta'arruf*, none would have known *taṣawwuf*'.

Prior to the appearance of these two books, the dominant attitude of the Sufis towards themselves might have been summed up in two maxims: "Sufism is neither science nor tradition but rather, ethics

---

5. See the essays by B. Radtke and S. Sviri in the present volume. –ED.

6. Among which may be cited his *Sharḥ al-ṣalāt, Khatm al-awliyā'* (or *Khatm al-wilāya)*, and the *Kitāb al-uṣūl.*

7. The name "Kalābadhī" is, incidentally, an Arabicization of the Persian place-name: "Gulābadī."

(akhlāq)" (Abū'l-Ḥusayn Khurāsānī),[8] and "The Sufi cannot be qualified with descriptive attributes and customs" (Ibn Abī Sa'dān Baghdādī).[9] However, with the publication of these two books, Sufism was formally presented to Islamic society as a science and tradition inclusive of both discursive literary expressions *(qāl)* and direct spiritual experience *(ḥāl),* possessed of a specific formal methodology suited to particular individuals' private and social needs, while being beyond the capacity of certain others. It was also introduced as a spiritual path *(ṭarīqat)* which in every state and circumstance professed perfect adherence to Koranic principles and the Prophetic tradition or Sunna.

It was in these two books that for the first time Sufi beliefs concerning the Essence and Attributes of God was discussed in detail and in the same style as that employed by the scholastic theologians in their discussions. Kalābādhī, precisely in the fashion of an erudite theologian, first introduces and then establishes the veracity of his theories concerning the subject-matter of scholastic theology *('ilm al-kalām),* before proceeding to discuss the states and stations of Sufism, expounding and putting the principles of the Sufis' spiritual and ethical progression *(sayr wa sulūk)* on a scholastic basis. Abū Naṣr Sarrāj, on the other hand, in the *Al-Luma',* devotes more space to discussion of the mystical states *(aḥwāl)* and etiquette *(ādāb),* and is much less concerned with matters of a purely scholastic nature.

Many contemporary scholars of Islamic mysticism, Muslim and non-Muslim, Iranian and non-Iranian alike, while admitting that prior to the composition of these two books the Sufis did not possess a book which comprised the entire spectrum of their basic beliefs, intellectual tenets and spiritual disciplines, are nonetheless partisan to the notion that early Sufism consisted of two 'schools'. These were known as the schools of Baghdad and Khurāsān.[10] The former school propagated its doctrines by means of the pulpit and public religious assembly, and the latter made known its principles through the composition of books and treatises on Sufism. Due mainly to the

8. Sulamī, *Ṭabaqāt al-ṣūfiyya,* p. 167
9. *Ibid.,* p. 422.
10. See the essays by Herbert Mason and Terry Graham in the present volume. -ED.

latter school's literary orientation, from the time of Kalābādhī and Sarrāj onwards, all the famous Sufis with literary aspirations did in fact belong to this 'School of Khurāsān', and it was these same Persian scholars who composed their fascinating treatises and comprehensive manuals on the principles and practices of Sufism, thus contributing to the richness of Arabic literature.

It may be pointed out, however, that there were several studies of lesser importance written in Arabic by *non-Persian* Sufis during the same period. These include the *Qūt al-qulūb* by Abū Ṭālib Makkī (d. 386/996), which enjoyed a considerable reputation among the Sufis, and the *Al-Mawāqif* and *Al-Mukhātabāt* of Muḥammad ibn 'Abdī al-Jabbār Niffarī (d. 354/965).[11] Niffarī's two books consist of imaginal recitals and visions written as a series of divinely infused prayers or inspired orations, divided respectively into seventy-seven sections of separate 'stopping places' *(mawqif)* and fifty-six different 'addresses' *(mukhāṭaba).* The actual texts of these 'stopping places', each of which has a different subtitle, consist of esoteric allusions and subtle mysterious aphorisms inspired by the author's own powers of reflection and discursive reason. Niffarī's writing seems to be colored both by neo-Platonic *(ishrāqī)* ideas and Islamic philosophical speculation, in which the relation between the creature and Creator, and material to spiritual being appears as the central concept. His books are, in my opinion, absolutely devoid of practical benefit or instructive value for novices on the Sufi Path, but rather resemble certain apocryphal Jewish and Christian works modeled on the Torah and the New Testament, such as the Lamentations of the Prophet Jeremiah and the Revelations of St. John and similar literary compositions.

From this period down to the beginning of the seventh/thirteenth century, when the pole star of Sufism, Ibn 'Arabī, appeared, few works by Arab Sufis of any importance are left to us, and even if in certain anthologies and biographical studies mention of books by Arab Sufis is made, nothing of their texts beside their title has remained to posterity. However, it is during these last two and a half

11. See *The Mawāqif and Mukhātabat of Muḥammad Ibn Abdī 'l-Jabbār al-Niffarī with other fragments,* edited with translation by A.J. Arberry (London: Luzac & Co., 1978).

centuries—from the fifth/eleventh to the seventh/thirteenth century—that many of the major Persian Sufis made their appearance. In this regard, one should mention Sayyid Sharīf Abū Manṣūr Mu'ammar Aḥmad Iṣfahānī (d. 418/1027), author of the *Ādāb al-mutaṣawwafa,* Abū 'Abdu'l-Raḥmān Sulamī of Nīshāpūr (d. 412/1021), author of the famous biographical history of the Sufis, *Ṭabaqāt al-ṣūfiyya* and an important exegesis of the Koran, the *Ḥaqā'iq al-tafsīr,* Abū'l-Qāsim Qushayrī of Nīshāpūr (d. 465/1072), author of the *Risāla,* 'Alī Hujwīrī (d. 463/1071), author of the *Kashf al-maḥjūb,* Khwāja 'Abdullāh Anṣārī of Herat (d. 481/1089), author of the first Persian translation of Sulamī's *Ṭabaqāt* and the *Manāzil al-sā'irīn,*[12] Abū Ḥāmid Muḥammad Ghazālī (d. 505/1111), author of the famous *Iḥyā' 'ulūm al-dīn* as well as many other important treatises,[13] Abū Ḥafṣ 'Umar Suhrawardī (d. 632/1234), author of the *'Awārif al-ma'ārif,* Najm al-Dīn Kubrā of Khīva (d. 618/1221), author of the *Fawā'iḥ al-jamāl,* Sayf al-Dīn Bākharzī (d. 658/1260), author of the *Waqā'i' al-khalwa,* and Sa'd al-Dīn Ḥammūya (d. 650/1253), author of the *Al-Miṣbāḥ fī'l-taṣawwuf.*

Some of these texts, such as the *Risāla* of Qushayrī, the *Manāzil al-sā'irīn* of Anṣārī and the *'Awārif al-ma'ārif* of Suhrawardī, from the time of their composition until the present day—that is to say, in regard to the first two texts for a period of over a thousand years, and in respect to the last-mentioned book, over eight hundred and fifty years—were, and still are, considered to be key works and classical sources of reference for the study of both practical and speculative Sufism, such that no Sufi scholar or student of Sufism who engages in research on the principles of Sufism can afford to ignore their importance. Since such books, and dozens of others like them, have been the primary sources relied upon by scholars of Sufism for centuries and are vital documents for illuminating the intellectual, doctrinal and practical methodology of Muslim Sufis throughout the world, and because the greater number of their authors are of Khurāsānī origin, hence, the ascription 'Khurāsānīan' was given to this school.

---

12. See the essay by Ravān Farhādī in the present volume.–ED.
13. On Ghazālī, see the essay by Nicholas Heer in the present volume.–ED.

Although Makkī's *Qūt al-qulūb* may be counted as a prime text for the teachings of practical Sufism, his work is of limited usefulness with respect to its speculative dimension, as it provides but a brief description of some of the mystical states *(aḥwāl)* and spiritual stations *(maqāmāt)* in Sufism. Moreover, some of the great Islamic jurisprudents and traditionists have expressed doubts about the accuracy of much of the traditions *(ḥadīth)* cited therein.[14] Still it is noteworthy that the book, which has been since published in two different editions, (although, unfortunately, neither of these printings provides proper indices), features more quotations from the sayings of eminent Khurāsānī Sufis than from mystics from any other geographical region.

A closer examination of these references is quite rewarding. Makkī was a disciple of Sahl ibn 'Abdullāh Tustarī and constantly addresses his master with epithets such as "our good Master Sahl" or "our Shaykh Abū Muḥammad." Whichever the title, Makkī cites him some 93 times. He also refers to Bishr Ḥāfī: 40 times; to Ibrāhīm ibn Adham: 25 times; to Fuḍayl ibn 'Iyāḍ: 22 times; to Ibn Mubārak: 15 times; to Yaḥyā b. Mu'ādh Rāzī (d. 258/871): 14 times; to Ibrāhīm ibn Khawāṣṣ (d. 291/904): 13 times; to Bāyazīd Bisṭāmī (d. 261/875): 12 times; and less than 10 times to the likes of Shaqīq Balkhī (d. 194/810), Salmān Fārsī, Ḥabīb 'Ajamī, Ḥātim Aṣamm Balkhī (d. 237/852), Abū Ḥafṣ Ḥaddād of Nīshāpūr (d. 265/878), Abū Sahl Pū-shangī, Abū Turāb Nakhshabī (d. 245/859), and Muḥammad b. Yusūf Iṣfahānī, citing their pithy sayings and eloquent poetry.

The Revivification of the Sciences of Religion (Iḥyā 'ulūm al-dīn) by Abū Ḥāmid Ghazālī (d. 505/1111) of Ṭūs in Khurāsān is not only one of the brightest blossoms in the bouquet of Khurāsānian Sufi literature, but one of the most brillant flowers in the entire garden of Islamic literature in general. Scholars and students of Islamic studies throughout the world would unanimously agree, I think, that if one were to select twenty representative works whose contribution marked an occasion of supreme importance in the development

---

14. See, for instance, the comments given by Khaṭīb Baghdādī, *Tārīkh-i Baghdād,* vol. 2, s.v. "Muḥammad b. 'Alī b. 'Atiyya b. Ḥārith Makkī."

of Islamic culture, the *Iḥyā' 'ulūm al-dīn* would certainly be numbered amongst them.

Another aspect of Islamic studies to which the Sufis of Khurāsān were the foremost contributors was Symbolism, which in the mystics' own lexicon was known as 'the science of mystical allusions' *('ilm-i ishārāt),* since it dealt with the hidden correspondences between sensible and intelligible phenomena (the spiritual truths, *ḥaqā'iq).* In this branch of studies the Persian Sufis of Khurāsān led the way and made significant contributions.

Most everyone is familiar with the station of Muḥyī al-Dīn ibn al-'Arabī (d. 638/1240) of Andalusia in Spain, known as the *Shaykh al-akbar,* the 'Supreme Shaykh', and his impact on Sufism. It is also well known that his *Meccan Revelations (Futūḥāt al-Makkiyya)* is not only a vast and comprehensive encyclopedia of both practical and speculative Sufism, but also one of the most brilliant manifestations of enlightened human reason in history. Expounded and explained in the space of its five hundred and sixty chapters lies the entire spectrum of Sufi lore and wisdom with all of its complex intricacy.

It is hardly necessary to mention that we owe to Ibn 'Arabī the full intellectual divulgence and development of the doctrine of the 'Unity of Being' *(waḥdat-i wujūd),* an idea which, prior to him, had been discussed in subtle mystical allusions by Sufis who cloaked it in arcane expressions and an obscure symbolic terminology. The Supreme Shaykh was the first to expose this doctrine to daylight of explicitness, bathing it in the penetrating glare of his thought, expressing its truth with fearless frankness. Where Bāyazīd of Bisṭām (d. 261/875) lounging in a nook of his lodge in Khurāsān, had cried "Naught but God lies beneath this cloak of mine" and where Ḥallāj of Bayḍā (near Shiraz in Fars, d. 309/922)—who, in Ḥāfiẓ's (d. 791/1389) words, "learned to speak so sweetly upon the gibbet's steps")—expressed his secret that "I am the very One I love and the One I love is I; We are two spirits who dwell in one body," Ibn 'Arabī, using logic and demonstration, gave it all the colourful contours of his personal philosophical system.

It is interesting to note, however, that where Ibn 'Arabī concerned himself with analyzing, in his own unique and prolix manner, the details of the concept of the cycle and the 'seal' (that is, the 'end') of the prophets and the friends of God,[15] the substantial portion of his discussion is both derived from and indebted in its inspiration to a series of questions addressed to the same matter by Muḥammad ibn 'Alī Ḥakīm Tirmidhī, who flourished some three hundred and fifty years before Ibn 'Arabī. In a work entitled *The Seal (or 'End') of the Saints (Khatm al-awliyā'),* a study of great depth and detail on the matter of 'Friendship with God' *(walāya),* Ḥakīm Tirmidhī posed some one hundred and fifty-seven questions on this topic, and Ibn 'Arabī proceeded to reply to these queries, sometimes briefly and sometimes in detail, in both the *Futūḥāt al-Makkiyya* as well as in a treatise devoted to answering Tirmidhī's questions, entitled *Al-jawāb al-mustaqīm 'ammā sa'al 'anhu al-Tirmidhī al-Ḥakīm.* Tirmidhī also wrote extensively on the role of 'reason' *('aql),* the soul *(nafs),* the spirit *(rūḥ)* and the heart *(qalb)* in mystical psychology. In later centuries Tirmidhī's ideas became the subject of much discussion and speculation on the part of Sufis, legalists and Koranic experts. Prominent Sufis such as Abū Ḥāmid Ghazālī and jurisprudents such as Ibn Qayyim al-Jawziyya (d. 597/1200) in his treatise *al-Rūḥ,* and Koranic exegetes such as the Spaniard Qurṭubī in his *Tafsīr al-kabīr* (known as *al-Bahr al-muḥīṭ)* came to refer to his theories as sources of authority.

Ibn 'Arabī was also deeply versed in all of the traditional esoteric sciences of his day: familiar with both the imaginative subtleties of the science of numerology and letter symbolism, as well as the science of the 'heart's divine infusions' *(wāridāt-i qalbiyya).* He was acquainted with all types of the mediæval occult sciences, and also expressed his opinion on every single issue relating to the paradoxical ecstatic sayings *(shaṭḥiyyāt, mawājīd)* of his Sufi forbears such as Bāyazīd Bisṭāmī, 'Ayn al-Quḍāt Hamadānī (executed 526/1132) and Najm al-Dīn Kubrā (d. 618/1221).

The final work which should be mentioned in this context is the *'Awārif al-ma'ārif* of Shihāb al-Dīn Abū Ḥafṣ 'Umar Suhrawardī of Zanjan (d. 632/1234), a book which put the finishing touches upon practical and speculative classical Sufism. It is more comprehensive in scope and broader in detail than Qushayrī's *Risāla,* functioning as

15. *walāyat, nabuwwat, khatamiyyat-i nabuwwat wa walāyat.*

a summa of all the principles and *ādāb* of the mainstream Islamic mystical tradition up to the seventh/thirteenth century, remaining today one of the foremost manuals and textbooks of Sufism.

If the above remarks have succeeded in demonstrating and elucidating the genuinely creative role played by the Persian Sufis in the development of mystical gnosis in Islam and Ibn 'Arabī's extensive and detailed commentary upon this tradition, then their purpose has been achieved.[16]

PERSIAN SUFIS AND ARABIC LITERARY STUDIES

The contribution of Persian Sufis to Arabic literature *(adab-i 'arab)* was not just limited to the ethics of practical Sufism (the mystical equivalent of *adab-i nafs).* In the genre of literary studies *(adab-i dars)* and in the creation of literary works in the Arabic language, both in poetry and prose, Persian Sufis also made noteworthy contributions.

From the middle of the second/eighth century to the end of the fifth/eleventh century, that is, for about three hundred and fifty years, constitutes the period when the literary works of Arabs reached their maximum efflorescence. Literary studies on the prose and poetry of the pre- and post-Islamic period, being based on good critical methods and sound scholarly philological principles, reached its zenith during this period. In some respects, this period can be considered as the Golden Age of Arab literature. The greatest works of literature, the most famous anthologies of pre- and post-Islamic poetry and the most complete works in all fields of Arabic literature were all compiled in this period, works which were and still are perennial sources of authority and reference for its study.

16. For further study one may refer to the texts of (as well as Uthmān Yahyā's introduction to) Tirmidhī's *Khatm al-awliyā'* and Najm al-Dīn Kubrā's *Fawā'iḥ al-jamāl,* accompanied by Professor Fritz Meier's masterly introduction.

Mystics Discoursing in a Garden. From Nawā'ī's *Ṣadd-i Iskandar*. Bodleian MS. Elliot 339, folio 95b. (Courtesy of the Bodleian Library, Oxford).

One could cite Ibn Khaldūn's (d. 808/1406) statement[17] in this context, that his masters and teachers mentioned four books as the fundamental source-textbooks of the principles of Arabic *adab*-studies, these being: *al-Kāmil* by Al-Mubarrad,[18] *Al-Bayān wa'l-tabyīn* of Al-Jāḥiẓ (d. 255/869), the *Al-Amālī* by Al-Qālī (d. 356/967), and the *Adab al-kātib* by Ibn Qutayba (d. 276/889-90). Scholars in humanistic studies *(adab)* added two other books to Ibn Khaldūn's list, namely, the *'Uyūn al-akhbār* of the same Ibn Qutayba and the *Al-'Iqd al-farīd* by Ibn 'Abd al-Rabbihī. Of these six books, three are exclusively concerned with lexicography and the principles of *adab*-studies, and the other three, namely: the *Al-Bayān wa'l-tabyīn*, the *'Uyūn al-akhbār*, and the *Al-'Iqd al-farīd* are comprehensive anthologies and detailed literary miscellanies incorporating mention of the literary works as well as the *dicta* and *exempla* of the creators of Islamic and Arabic culture, covering an immense variety of subjects. Each of these three books also features a chapter "On Asceticism" (entitled *Al-Zuhd)*, devoted to exposition of the words and deeds of the prominent Sufis from the time of the Prophet down to the third/ninth century. Of course, from the literary context of their humanistic discourse it is evident that the authors of these works provide citation of sayings only by those Sufi masters whose *dicta* represent the height of literary eloquence as well.

Al-Jāḥiẓ, the supreme master of Arabic *adab*-studies, in his *Al-Bayān wa'l-tabyīn* mentions Salmān Fārsī (d. 36/656) some eighteen times, quoting extensively from other well-known Persian Sufis and ascetics such as 'Abdullāh ibn Mubārak (d. 181/797), Abū Isḥāq Ibrāhīm ibn Adham of Balkh (d. c. 165/782), Fuḍayl 'Iyāḍ (d. 187/803), Shaqīq Balkhī (d. 194/810), Abū Naṣr Bishr ib al-Ḥārith Ḥāfī of Merv (d. 227/841) and Abū 'Abd al-Raḥmān Ḥātim Aṣamm of Balkh (d. 237/852) as well. Ibn Qutayba and the Spaniard Ibn 'Abd Rabbihī (d. 328/940), both of whom flourished after al-Jāḥiẓ and so were naturally more familiar with the literary works and sayings of the Sufis, mention these masters respectively some thirty-three and thirty times in their above-cited works. They also discuss

17. See his *Muqaddima,* trans. F. Rosenthal (New York: Pantheon Bks. 1958), pp. 340-1.
18. Edited by Zakī Mubārak (Cairo: al-Ḥalabī Press 1355/1936)

the *dicta* of other famous Sufi Shaykhs such as Aḥmad ibn Ḥarb of Nīshāpūr (d. 234/849) and Ibrāhīm Khawāṣṣ (d. 291/904). All such quotations by these scholars of Arabic *adab,* needless to say, represent the highest level of literary expression and eloquence.

This admiration for the sayings of the Sufi mystics on the part of such scholars of Arabic *adab*-studies appears to be unmitigated despite the fact that it was said of the likes of certain Sufis, such as Bishr Ḥāfī, for instance, "that he did not know Arabic properly, nor could he properly vocalize its consonants and sometimes committed solecisms *(laḥn).*"[19] Yet, at the same time, it was said of this celebrated saint that, "If the rational faculty *('aql)* with which Bishr Ḥāfī was endowed were subdivided among the inhabitants of Baghdad, all of them would be counted among the foremost thinkers of the world."[20] It is instructive to compare Ḥāfī's personality with that of his forebear and teacher Ibrāhīm ibn Adham of Balkh, who, although known for his eloquent speech and mastery of rhetoric, remarked, "Although we have adorned our speech and have committed no errors in literary expression, yet our deeds have been soiled with error. Better had we corrected and beautified our deeds, rather than merely ornamented our words."[21]

Such in brief was the scope and contribution of the early Persian Sufis to the texts which formed the primary sources and basis of Arabic *adab*-studies in prose. The poetry and deeds of the pious Sufis of both the early and later generations are also fully featured in many of the texts in other branches of Arab *adab,* including grammar *(naḥw),* history *(tārīkh),* the various classes of learned and other illustrious men *(ṭabaqāt),* and moral philosophy *(akhlāq).* Some forty to fifty books might be cited in this context, all full of the eloquent Arabic poetry and the sayings of the Sufis hailing from all the diverse provinces and climes of Persia—from Transoxiana (a region inclusive of Khurāsān and Khwarazm), down to Māzandarān and Gīlān, south to Iṣfahān and Khūzistān and west to Kirmānshāh. However, mention of these texts, all of which are extant and well-

19. Muḥammad ibn Aḥmad Dhahabī, *Siyar a'lām al-nubalā'* (Beirut 1981-85), vol. 10, p. 472.
20. *Ibid.,* p. 475.
21. *Qūt al-qulūb,* vol. 1, p. 337.

known, exceeds the breadth of the present study.

Perhaps one reason why the early non-Persian Sufis left so little written evidence for posterity was their conscious avoidance of the normal academic circles of dictation and instruction. As they themselves often remarked, such association is not always uncontaminated by the vices of conceit and sanctimonious self-display. Furthermore, there was always the tendency to 'conceal the *arcanum* from commoners'—"the lips of those learned in the secret lore of God are sewn and sealed shut," in Rumi's words—so that even when the mystics felt obliged to note something down, it was usually kept carefully hidden. Bishr Ḥāfī's behavior when he willed that all of his literary compositions be buried alongside him, clearly reflects this attitude. Those in charge of executing his will, it is related, entombed some eighteen large tomes of his writings with his corpse. Nevertheless, there is no doubt that a large body of work still remained from such great masters, insofar as in still-surviving Sufi texts one finds ample evidence of their substantial literary contributions.

In his *Ṭabaqāt al-ṣūfiyya* (Classes of the Sufis), Sulamī cites Ja'far Khuldī's claim to have possessed "one hundred and thirty-odd collections of Sufi books."[22] When asked if among these tomes, he owned any of Ḥakīm Tirmidhī's works, he replied, "No, I do not count him among the Sufis." (Apparently, in Khuldī's eyes, Tirmidhī appeared more as a philosopher-sage and scholastic theologian than a Sufi).[23] Among such rare books and treatises should be counted the works of Abū Sa'īd ibn al-A'rābī, one of the pre-eminent Sufi sages of the third/ninth century, and the author of the first biographical study of illustrious Sufis, entitled *Ṭabaqāt al-nussāk.* It is interesting that Abū Naṣr Sarrāj incorporated a large section of A'rābī's treatise *Al-wajd* verbatim into his famous *Kitāb al-Luma'*.

It should be also emphasized that most of the books composed by these early Persian Sufis, today counted among the foremost classics of Sufism, exhibit the highest standards of literary eloquence in Arabic, whether they were written in a simple and austere style or in

22. *Ṭabaqāt al-sūfiyya,* edited by N. Sharība (Cairo 1953), p. 434.
23. See S. Sviri's essay on Tirmidhī in this volume for a detailed discussion of this statement. –ED.

ornate rhymed prose, as regards both their literary style, composition of words and arrangement of ideas. If definitive proof were required to attest to these authors' mastery of the many branches of Arabic *adab* (philology, lexicography, rhetoric, etc.) one need only note the fact that for centuries their books have been (and most likely will so remain) the subject of scholarly exegesis, debate and exposition and that their works have yet to be superseded by others of superior quality. Originally composed in Arabic by Persian-speaking Sufis, these texts became over the intervening centuries the subject of dozens of glosses and commentaries penned by Arabic-speaking Sufis and eminent literary savants versed in the diverse sciences of Arabic *adab.* One could cite in this context the innumerable commentaries written upon Kalābadhī's *Kitāb al-ta'arruf,* Qushayrī's *Risāla,* and Anṣārī's *Manāzil al-sā'irīn.* A further example is Sayyid al-Murtaḍā Zabīdī's (d. 1205/1790)—a renowned lexicographer and Sufi, who, as author of the *Tāj al-'arūs,* a vast encyclopediac dictionary, was unsurpassed in this field by scholars of preceding or succeeding generations—monumental six-thousand page commentary on Ghazālī's *Iḥyā',* entitled *Itḥāf al-sādah al-muttaqīn bi-sharḥ asrār Iḥyā' 'ulūm al-dīn.*

PERSIAN SUFIS' USE OF RHYMED PROSE

Extracts in extant texts from the sayings and expressions of early Persian Sufis, particularly those of Yaḥyā ibn Mu'ādh Rāzī and Sahl ibn 'Abdullāh Tustarī, provide evidence of their extensive use of 'rhymed prose' *(nathr-i musajja').*[24] Among those books and treatises which are today counted among the most treasured classics of Sufism can be found many fine examples of rhymed prose of sublime eloquence and style, some of which might even be characterized as typifying a kind of separate mystical genre complementing the traditional 'academic artistic sermon' *(maqāmāt).* One might recall here the Arabic treatises and letters of Junayd[25] which feature a prose style that is so artistically well-fashioned and ornate, both in terms of his use of verbal embellishments and rhetorical devices,

24. Cf. Ibn Mulaqqin's *Ṭabaqāt al-awliyā',* ed. Nūr al-Dīn Sharība, (Egypt 1973), p. 321 ff.

that it is virtually indistinguishable from that of such masters of the Arabic literary arts as Abū Bakr Khwārazmī (d. 383/992), Badī‘ al-Zamān Hamadānī (d. 398/1007) and al-Ṣabī (d. 384/994). For example, in his first and second letters addressed to various mystics,[26] in his long epistle addressed to Abū ‘Abdullāh ‘Amr ibn ‘Uthmān Makkī (d. 291/904),[27] in his treatise on *Fanā’*[28] and in his discussion of "Rules of Conduct for One who is Dependent upon God,"[29] Junayd appears as one of the most brilliant and accomplished prose stylists of his day. Reading the account given of Junayd after his death by Ja‘far Khuldī, it is also apparent that Junayd still observed the literary strictures demanded of rhymed prose in Arabic well into his Afterlife. When Khuldī saw Junayd in a dream following his demise and asked him how God had treated him, Junayd, responding in phrases steeped in the melodic consonance and assonance characteristic of eloquently rhymed Arabic prose, replied, "All those symbolic allusions were swept to the wind, those intricately fashioned phrases vanished, those sciences and the care taken to observe the required forms of tradition all perished; all that availed me were a few prostrations at dawntide."

Persian Sufis in the succeeding centuries made ample use of rhymed Arabic prose as well. Particularly typical in this regard are the writings of ‘Abdullāh Anṣārī of Herat (d. 481/1089). His *Manāzil al-sā’irīn,* for instance, is replete with rhyming alliteration and Arabic sentences couched in the eloquent and melodic style characteristic of the finest rhymed prose; this literary form also ornamented and pervaded his best Persian writing as well.[30]

---

25. See Ali Hassan Abdel-Kader, *The Life, Personality and Writings of al-Junayd: A Study of a Third/Ninth Century Mystic with an Edition and Translation of his Writings*, (London: Luzac & Co.; E.J.W. Gibb Memorial Series 1976).
26. See *ibid.*, pp. 122-23 (English translation); pp. 1-2 (Arabic text).
27. See *ibid.*, pp. 127-47 (English translation); pp. 2-27 (Arabic text).
28. See *ibid.*, pp. 152-59 (English translation); pp. 31-40 (Arabic text).
29. See *ibid.*, pp. 178-83 (English translation); pp. 58-62 (Arabic text).
30. I should particularly like to draw attention to the lovely short rhyming sentences found in chapters 3, 4, 38, 62-66, 69, 71, 79 and 82 of the *Manāzil.*

PERSIAN SUFIS AND ARABIC POETRY

Despite the fact that the Persian-speaking Sufis have indeed composed much excellent, eloquent and stylistically fine Arabic poetry and their verses adorn many a book of Arabic literature, history and genealogy, I can and hardly would wish to claim that any Persian has ever been introduced as a 'poet' in the history of Arabic literature. Nonetheless there was much good poetry produced by the earliest Persian Sufis: the verse of Ibrāhīm ibn Adham and 'Abdullāh ibn Mubārak is particularly noteworthy in this regard.

From the third/ninth century onwards, as the Sufis gained an increasingly popular and noticeable place for themselves in Islamic civilization, one finds much fine Arabic verse, most of it composed by the mystics themselves, featured in their prose works. A prime example of this tendency appears in the *Kitāb Al-Luma'* of Abū Naṣr Sarrāj who devotes an entire chapter to the poetry composed by Sufis concerning mystical states, spiritual stations and symbolic terminology. In this 'poetic chapter' we find some one hundred Arabic verses written by the likes of Junayd, Abū 'Alī Rūdbārī (d. 323/934), Yaḥyā ibn Mu'ādh Rāzī (d. 258/871), Sahl ibn 'Abdullāh Tustarī and Bishr Ḥāfī.

In addition to the books mentioned in our foregoing discussion of the Arabic-language Persian Sufi prose texts, there is also much excellent Arabic poetry to be found in Persian books composed by Persian Sufis. Such fundamental Persian Sufi texts as Maybudī's *Kashf al-asrār,* Anṣārī's *Ṭabaqāt al-ṣufiyya,* Ibn Munawwar's *Asrār al-tawḥīd,* Junayd Shīrāzī's *Shadd al-izzār,* 'Izz al-Dīn Maḥmūd Kāshānī's *Miṣbāḥ al-hidāya* and Jāmī's *Nafaḥāt al-uns,* as well as the usual Arabic works on biography, history, travel and genealogy feature much Arabic poetry by Persian Sufis. Arabic poetry composed by Persian Sufis from the earliest Islamic period to the time of the author would most often be cited. For instance, Dhahabī in the *Siyar a'lām al-nubalā',* while relating the biography of 'Abdullāh ibn Mubārak, cites some eighty-three lines of his poetry, and Ibn 'Asākir (d. 571/1176) in the *Tārīkh Dimashq,* in his lengthy account of the life of Ibrāhīm ibn Adham, quotes many of the latter's verses. Likewise Ibn Qayyim Ḥanbalī in his *Rawẓat al-muḥibbīn* provides extensive excerpts from Arabic verse composed by Persian

Sufis.

Two Persian Sufis—Manṣūr Ḥallāj and Abū Bakr Shiblī (d. 334/945), the latter from Samarqand by origin but born in Baghdad — did manage to gain considerable acclaim as poets in Arabic. The existence of a full and complete *Dīwān* by Ḥallāj is confirmed in many primary sources, and is mentioned in the fifth/eleventh century by Abū 'Abdu'l-Raḥmān Sulamī. Thus Sulamī's student, Abū'l-Qāsim Qushayrī in his *Risāla* wrote, "My father-in-law, Abū 'Alī Daqqāq [d. 412/1021] ordered me to go to Sulamī's house and to look for a small tome bound in red leather which was the *Dīwān* of Ḥallāj, and to borrow it from Sulamī and bring it to him." Sulamī consented to lend the book to Qushayrī on the condition that he return it immediately because, he related, he was using it for research purposes and needed to cite some of Ḥallāj's verses in a book he was writing.[31]

Of course it should be pointed out that there is a great stylistic difference between the poetry of Shiblī, a native of Baghdad in Iraq, and the verse of Ḥallāj, born in southwestern Persia. Shiblī's poetry is endowed with greater grace and fluency than that of Ḥallāj, who, it would seem, was more interested in the delicacies of divine contemplation than the intricacies of Arabic prosody and metrics. It should also be pointed out that as far as the published poetical works of these two poets goes, the edition of Ḥallāj's *Dīwān* published in Paris by Louis Massignon[32] and the edition of the *Dīwān* of Shiblī published by Kāmil Muṣṭafā Shaybī[33] are neither complete nor definitive texts, since they do not include all the poems by both poets, nor can all the verses cited in these two editions be ascribed to either Ḥallāj or Shiblī with any certainty. Thus the redaction and edition of the *Dīwān*s of these two eminent Sufi poets remains as desiderata for scholars of future generations. There is also a substantial amount of Arabic poetry ascribed to Abū'l-Ḥusayn Baghawī of Khurāsān, known as "Nūrī"[34] in the classical Sufi texts, which, if collected and edited, would constitute a separate *Dīwān* in itself.

---

31. Ibn Mulaqqin, *Ṭabaqāt al-awliyā'*, p. 315.
32. "*Dīwān Ḥusayn ibn Manṣūr al-Ḥallāj.* Essai de reconstitution by Louis Massignon." *Journal asistique,* January-July 1931.
33. Published, Cairo 1967.
34. On whom, see Prof. Schimmel's essay in this book. –ED.

Amongst the most important Persian Sufis who wrote poetry in Arabic in the later centuries, the names of Qushayrī, 'Ayn al-Quḍāt Hamadānī (d. 526/1132) and Shihāb al-Dīn Suhrawardī (author of the *'Awārif)* should be mentioned. Traces of many highly fashioned individual verses by Qushayrī are to be found in his exegesis of the Koran entitled the *Laṭā'if al-ishārāt,* Ibn Mulaqqin's *Ṭabaqāt* and Arab literary histories.

THE QUATRAIN *(RUBĀ'Ī)* IN ARABIC POETRY

Disregarding, if we may, the debate as to the origins of the *rubā'ī* metre (whether it be considered as originating in pre-Islamic Persian poetry or derived from Greek influence[35]), one of the most dramatic indications of Persian influence on Arabic poetry is the appearance and popularity of this metre in Arabic verse. Although prior to the appearance of the greatest of the Arab mystical poets,'Umar ibn Fāriḍ of Egypt (d. 633/1235), the *rubā'ī* metre was not employed by Arab poets, Andalusian Arab poets in Spain, inspired by their own native poetic metres, had used a similar quatrain-like popular lyrical form: the strophic *muwashshaḥ* and *zajal,* as well as the 'double couplet' *(dūbaytī,* a verse-form derived from Persian poetry, long before him.

Ibn Fāriḍ's innovative use of the *rubā'ī* metre in Arabic poetry was no doubt indebted to and inspired by Eastern Sufism and Persian Sufis who had pioneered the use of this metre in their musical concerts *(samā')* long before him, not to mention the itinerant Persian mystics who, in his day could be found throughout Asia Minor, North Africa and Arabia. We know, for instance, that *samā'* was a common phenomenon among the Sufis of Khurāsān in

35. In the chapter on Poetics in his *Manṭiq shifā',* Ibn Sīnā (Avicenna) mentions the possibility that the *rubā'ī* may be of Greek origin. Shams al-Dīn Muḥammad ibn Qays Rāzī, however, in his *Al-Mu'ajjam fī mu'āyīri ash'ār al-'ajam* (ed. M. Qazwīnī and Mudarris Raḍawī, Tehran: n.d., p. 114) asserts it to be of Persian origin, and invented by Rūdakī (p. 113), considering it to be derived from the *Hazaj* metre (p. 115). After describing how the Arab poets adopted this metre from the Persians, Rāzī notes, "at the present time, the most creative and original Arab poets tend to employ this metre, and the composition of *rubā'iyyāt* in Arabic is common throughout all Arabic-speaking lands." (p. 115)

particular and Persian Sufis in general from the fourth/tenth century onwards. The most common poetical forms employed by cantors in these assemblies in order to evoke the required ecstatic ambience were the ghazal, 'ballad' or *tarāna,* the *rubā'ī* and the *dubaytī.*

Sulamī's testimony in this regard is quite revealing. Narrating the biography of Abī'l-'Abbās ibn Masrūq Ṭūsī, he notes,

> When asked to deliver his opinion concerning listening to quatrains *(samā'-i rubā'iyyāt),* he declared, "Listening to [the singing of] of quatrains is only permissible for those whose inner and outer beings are of an upright nature, whose hearts are strong and whose knowledge is completely mature. Others should not engage in it."[36]

Thus it seems a foregone conclusion that Ibn Fāriḍ's delightful Arabic quatrains were deeply indebted in their inspiration to the cultivation of the *ghazal,* the *tarāna,* the *dubaytī,* and the *rubā'ī* genres by Persian Sufis such as Anṣārī, Abū Sa'īd ibn Abī'l-Khayr, Bābā Ṭāhir and 'Ayn al-Quḍāt Hamadānī. By the seventh/thirteenth century, following Ibn Fāriḍ's lead, the *rubā'ī* entered the mainstream Arabic literature as one of its most popular and widespread poetical forms.

PERSIAN SUFI KORANIC EXEGESIS

Another important aspect of the Persian contribution to Arabic *belles-lettres* which should not be passed over in silence—since the Persians were the inventors and originators of the genre itself—is commentary on the Koran. Many of the commentaries by these Persians are peerless models of artistic excellence and literary eloquence. It would appear that the poetic sensibility of the Iranian national character naturally caused the Persians to excel in uncovering esoteric subtleties of obscure passages in the Koran, being guided in the science of hermeneutics by allowing their spiritual intuition to reign supreme.

36. Sulamī, *Ṭabaqāt al-ṣūfiyya,* p. 239.

The Persian commentaries seem each to have been indebted to the other in inspiration. The many beautiful passages devoted to Sufi themes in Anṣārī's/Maybudī's multi-volume Koranic exegesis, the *Kashf al-asrār,* which are to be found in the third 'Persian-language' section following each chapter, are mostly adapted from and inspired by Qushayri's *Laṭā'if al-ishārāt*, composed some twenty years before Anṣārī's death. Qushayrī was also deeply influenced in his commentary by the *Ḥaqā'iq al-tafsīr* ('Realities of Koran Exegesis') composed by his teacher, Abū 'Abd al-Raḥmān Sulamī.[37] Sulamī's *tafsīr,* which unfortunately remains unpublished and in manuscript form, constitutes an important contribution to the genre, notwithstanding the objections raised by certain legalists to it.

There are two important points to be stressed concerning the Persian Sufis' contribution to Arabic Koranic exegesis. First, to my knowledge, the Persian Sufis initiated the literary genre of Sufi Koranic interpretation. Second, they produced more commentaries than writers of Arab background. In fact, as far as I know, between the third/ninth and sixth/twelfth centuries, there are no extant commentaries on the Koran composed by Arab Sufis at all. The earliest mystical *tafsīr* is the renowned commentary on the verse "In the Name of the Most Compassionate and Merciful" of the Opening Surah of the Koran by Sahl ibn 'Abdullāh Tustarī (d. 283/896). In order of their importance down to the seventh/thirteenth century, the chief commentaries and their authors may be listed as follows:

1) A partially extant commentary by Ḥakīm Tirmidhī, the surviving portions of which are featured in his *Nawādir al-uṣūl* and *Al-masā'il al-maknūna.*

2) A commentary by Abū Bakr ibn Mūsā Farghānī (d. 231/846)

3) The *Ḥaqā'iq al-tafsīr* by Sulamī.

4) Qushayrī's *Laṭā'if al-ishārāt*, published in three large volumes in Egypt some thirty years ago.

5) The *Ḥaqā'iq al-ishārāt* by 'Ayn al-Quḍāt Hamadānī.

6) The *Laṭā'if al-bayān fī tafsīr al-Qur'ān,* and the *'Arā'is al-*

37. For a detailed study of the extant MSS. of this work, see Gerhard Böwering, "The Qur'ān Commentary of al-Sulamī" in (eds.) W.B. Hallaq & D. Little, *Islamic Studies Presented to Charles J. Adams* (Leiden: Brill 1991), pp. 40-56.–Trans..

bayān fī ḥaqā'iq al-Qur'ān[38] of Rūzbihān Baqlī of Shiraz (d. 606/1210)

CONCLUSION

The last Arabic-language text composed by a Persian Sufi incumbent upon us to mention here is the 'Ornament of the Saints' or *Ḥilyat al-awliyā'*[39] by the high-ranking traditionist and eminent Sufi saint Ḥāfiẓ Abū Nu'aym Iṣfahānī (d. 430/1038). This work is the lengthiest and most complete biographical history of Sufism *(ṭabaqāt al-ṣūfiyya)* written up to its period and is indeed one of the greatest cultural and literary legacies bequeathed by Persian Sufism to Islamic civilization. Its published text, which amounts to more than four thousand pages, includes seven hundred and twenty-three entries, and provides, not only the *dicta* and *exempla* of eminent Sufis up to his own time along with relevant historical, biographical and anecdotal information *(akhbār)* given for each entry, but also a great many Prophetic traditions whose narrative chains *(isnāds)* are as carefully recorded as those featured in the *ḥadīth* collections. These traditions alone were vast enough to have formed the subject of an independent book written by a scholar under the title of *Al-Bughyat fī tartīb aḥādīth al-Ḥilyat,* which has been a constant source of reference since its compilation for the majority of specialists in Prophetic traditions, Koran exegetes, and high-ranking Sufis interested in the *Ḥilyat.*

Although Abū Nu'aym's literary style is fluent and graceful, he demonstrates his skill in and mastery of Arabic rhyming prose by a deliberate use of ornamentation at the beginning of each entry—the same style to be used centuries later in Persian by 'Aṭṭār of Nīshāpūr (d. 618/1221) in the 'Memoirs of the Saints' *(Tadhkirat al-awliyā').* Boldly, but nonetheless with complete confidence, one may state that the *Ḥilyat al-awliyā'* is the supreme gift and work which Persian Sufism has given to Islamic culture in general and Arabic culture in particular.

In conclusion, although it is correct to state that our discussion

38. Published in two volumes, Calcutta 1883.
39. Abū Nu'aym Iṣfahānī, *Ḥilyat al-awliyā',* 10 vols., (Cairo 1932-38)

above has focused with some exclusivity on eminent names among the *Persian-speaking* Sufi mystics who hailed from that dear land and cherished clime which goes by the name of 'Persia'—we should not forget that these beloved brethren and spiritual equals, whether Arab, Turk, Spaniard or Indian, are first and foremost brethren in spirit, rather than simply members of nations which go by the name of Egypt, Turkey, Spain or India.

The Sufis are of too liberal a nature to be concerned with ethnic origin or place of birth. While in bodily form they may hail from Merv, Ṭūs, Baghdad, Turkestan or Farghana, in spirit and heart they are all pearls from the grace-giving ocean of Islam. All bask in the light of the Prophet's divine inspiration. Their gnosis is all a grace gained by attendance to the College of the wise counsel of the Koran and the Sunna. Their external difference of ethos, color, race and tongue never taints their inner spiritual unity:

Souls of wolves and dogs are set in castes apart,
but the souls of men: the lions of God are One.

Having recalled this couplet by Rumi, one of the supreme masters of Sufism, it is only fitting to give our discourse a proper denouement with his words as well:

"To speak one tongue and idiom,"
They say, "means consanguinity and kin;"
and "a man's chains are among barbarians."
Yet many Turk and Hindu talk one tongue
and often two Turks are foreign to one another!

Besides these words, signs and mute innuendos
the heart calls up a battalion of interpreters:
So a kindred spirit's speech itself is something else:
It is better to speak one heart-language
than to talk with a common outward tongue.[40]

Translated by L. Lewisohn and M. Bayat

40. R.A. Nicholson (ed.,)*The Mathnawí of Jalálu'ddín Rúmí* (London & Leiden 1925-40; repr. London 1982), Bk. I, lines 1205-8. The Persian text of this article was originally published under the title "Sahm-i īrāniyān dar adab-i ṣūfiyāna-i 'arab: az nathr wa naẓm" in *Iran Nameh,* vol. 11, no. 1 (1993), pp. 17-32.

Dervishes Dancing during Preparation of a Meal. From Sa‘dī’s *Būstān.* Shiraz, *circa* 1580-90. Ms. Laud Or. 241 F.1b. (Courtesy of the Bodleian Library).

III

Abū'l-Ḥusayn al-Nūrī: *"Qibla of the Lights"*

Annemarie Schimmel

Among the great Sufis of Baghdad, many of whom hailed from Persia, Abū'l-Ḥusayn al-Nūrī occupies a special place. Known to most readers mainly by his slightly controversial attitude toward Abū'l-Qāsim al-Junayd (d. 298/910), Nūrī was one of the most attractive figures in Baghdad in the second half of the ninth century. His full name was Aḥmad ibn Muḥammad al-Baghawī, and his background was Khurāsānian. Born about 226/840 (for he still met Dhu'l-Nūn who passed away in 245/859) he belongs to the 'second mystical class' *(ṭabaqa)* among the Sufis. Most of his life was spent in Baghdad, although he also lived for some time it seems, in Raqqa where he, according to 'Anṣārī,[1] did not talk to anyone for a whole year. "That one attracted by Unity...that *qibla* of the lights," as 'Aṭṭār calls him in the *Tadhkirat al-awliyā'*, died in Baghdad in 295/907.

The most extensive information about him is given in Sarrāj's *Kitāb al-Luma' fī'l-taṣawwuf* and in Kalābādhī's *Kitāb al-Ta'arruf;* both of these sources quote many sentences and verses ascribed to him. In the case of some of his lovely short poems, however, the question of authorship is not always clear; verses attributed to Ḥallāj in other sources appear in these books as Nūrī's products, and the poem quoted by Sarrāj[2] is usually ascribed to Jamīl. The brief

1. 'Abdullāh Anṣārī, *Ṭabaqāt al-ṣūfiyya,* edited by A.H. Ḥabībī (Kabul: n.d), p. 158.

biographies in Sulamī's *Ṭabaqāt al-ṣūfiyya* and Abū Nu'aym's *Ḥilyat al-awliyā'* agree almost verbatim as do the Persian notes in 'Abdullāh 'Anṣārī's *Ṭabaqāt* and Jāmī's *Nafaḥāt al-uns,* based on the book of his compatriot 'Ansārī. 'Aṭṭār's biography—of medium length—elaborates romantically on otherwise briefly mentioned details, and Rūzbihān Baqlī devotes five chapters to Nūrī (§§95-100) in his *Sharḥ-i shaṭḥiyyāt*.

It is claimed that he acquired his surname because "he radiated light when talking;" and as Jāmī recounted in the *Nafaḥāt al-uns* he himself stated: "I looked into the light until I became myself that light."[3] A disciple of Junayd's uncle Sarī al-Saqaṭi, from whom he transmitted *ḥadith,* Nūrī underwent hard self-mortification: "Sufism is to leave all pleasures of the lower soul *(nafs),"* he reportedly remarked, and emphasized the true *faqīr*'s reliance upon God alone. "The true *faqīr* does not think of secondary causes but rests all the time in trust of God *(tawakkul),"* and "The Sufi knows God through God; he eats, drinks sleeps, and loves through Him."

Nūrī was very critical of the deterioration of Sufism, and his complaint foreshadows similar words of Hujwīrī: "The patched frocks used to be covers for pearls, and they have turned today into dunghills over corpses."[4]

Nūrī is praised in the biographies for his *īthār,* that is, preferring others to oneself. "Poverty is to keep quiet when nothing is available, and *īthār,* preferring others when something is found," that is, the true *faqīr* will always give from his meager possessions or food to others. For him, this was a religious duty, for "Sufism consists not of forms and sciences but of *akhlāq,* good qualities," he said, probably alluding to the old Sufi adage *tahkallaqū bi-akhlāq Allah,* "Qualify yourselves with God's qualities," that is, substitute for each each of your lowly qualities a praiseworthy one.

Nūrī's emphasis upon *īthār* is illustrated by his attitude during the trial of the Sufis in 264/877. When the Hanbalite Ghulām Khalīl

---

2. Abū Naṣr as-Sarrāj, *Kitāb al-Luma' fī'l-taṣawwuf,* ed. R.A. Nicholson (London-Leiden 1914), p. 305.
3. *Nafaḥāt al-uns,* ed. M. Tawhīdīpūr (Tehran 1957), p. 79.
4. 'Abū'l-Qāsim al-Qushayrī, *Al-Risāla fī 'ilm al-taṣawwuf* (Cairo 1330 A.H./ 1912), p. 50.

denounced the Sufis' teachings of pure divine love to the authorities, Nūrī offered his life for his Sufi brethren. The Qāḍī, amazed at such generosity, exclaimed: "If these are *zanādiqa,* heretics, then there is no *muwaḥḥid,* true monotheist, on the face of the earth." And the Caliph, impressed by Nūrī's words and actions, acquitted the Sufis.

His self-negating love for others, which is reflected in his prayer to be put into Hell to save others, may have grown from his deep emotional warmth. For Nūrī considered intellect to be "incapable,"*'ājiz,* contrary to the sober and prudent Junayd whom he accused of having receded into his *'ilm*—his religious knowledge—during the inquisition, *miḥna*—a term usually applied to the Mu'tazilite persecution of the traditionist scholars, but probably used here for the trial under Ghulām Khalīl during which Junayd preferred to stay away from the Sufis.

Strange miracles are ascribed to him, although he seems to have been critical of miracles: when the banks of the Tigris joined together to enable him to cross he swore that he would cross only in a boat,[5] yet most famous is the story that he daringly addressed God to bring out a fish of a certain weight from the Tigris—and he caught the fish, a miracle that induced Junayd to remark: "It would have been better if a snake had surfaced to bite him."[6] This story is perhaps exaggerated in order to stress the contrast between Nūrī and the Baghdadian leader of whom one of this colleagues said: "If intellect had the shape of a man, it would be Junayd."

Given his—may we say 'anti-intellectual'—attitude, it seems perfectly natural that Nūrī loved *samā',* thus his remark, "The Sufi is one who listens to *samā'.*" Again, his encounter with Junayd in this connection is well known: when he tried to induce this colleague of his to participate in the whirling Junayd only replied with the Koranic verse: "You see the mountains and think them firm, but inside they are like passing clouds." (Koran XVII 90)

That is, the true 'listener' is moved only inside his heart, but does not show any traces of his 'ecstasy'. For Nūrī, on the other hand, ecstasy and music were part of his mystical life, and not in vain does

---

5. Sarrāj, *Kitāb al-Luma',* p. 325.
6. *Ibid.,* p. 327.

Rūzbihān Baqlī ask in his threnody on the Sufis: "Where is the singing, *tarannum,* of Nūrī?"[7] It fits this picture that Nūrī's death was caused by his running in full ecstasy into a freshly cut reedbed; he died from the wounds in his feet and legs.

His complete surrender to the divine beloved, which was probably the basis of his extraordinary ecstatic states, seems to have prompted 'Anṣārī's remark that "he was more worshipping, *a'badu,* than Junayd" —although at times he followed the sobering advice of his colleague. Emotional as he was, Nūrī was seen once weeping bitterly along with a sad old man—who was none else but Iblis—bemoaning his fate.

As Nūrī claimed to be a lover, *'āshiq,* the Ḥanbalites declared him a heretic as the word *'ishq* was not permissible to express the relation between man and God in the Arabic language; but for Nūrī the term *maḥabba* (from the root that occurs in the Koran, V: 59) denoted a higher stage than *'ishq,* for the *'āshiq,* he thought, is kept away, while "Love, *maḥabba,* is to rend the veils and unveil the secrets."[8] Later Sufis would reverse the order.

Dangerous seemed his remark, "Deadly poison," when he heard the *mu'adhdhin*'s call to prayer, while he answered a dog's barking with *Labbayka,* "At Thy service"[9]—with this seemingly impious exclamation he intended to blame a person who performed religious duties for money but understood from the dog's mouth how every creature praises God. His paradoxical statements and actions were certainly not appreciated by many of his colleagues—he threw a considerable amount of money, which he had just received, into the Tigris instead of using it, as his friends advised him, for pious purposes; but he found even the thought of owning money (for a certain time) too distracting. And as he had no desire left, even lions surrounded him obediently.

Kalābādhī mentions that Nūrī wrote about mystical sciences with *ishārāt,* 'symbolic expressions.'[10] But only about two decades ago

---

7. *Sharḥ, §377.*
8. *Ibid.* §100.
9. *Ibid.* §96.
10. *Kitāb at-ta'arruf fī madhhab ahl al-taṣawwuf,* ed. A.J. Arberry (Cairo 1934), p. 13.

P. Nwiya discovered Nūrī's *Maqāmāt al-qulūb,* a treatise which contains fascinating descriptions of the human heart, that house of God, which is inhabited by King 'Certitude' who is aided by two viziers, 'Fear' and 'Hope.'[11] Such an allegorical interpretation of Koranic terms appears also in his comparison of the heart to a castle with seven ramparts—here he seems to prefigure St. Teresa's *Interior Castle,* and, Luce Lopez-Baralt has (convincingly, it seems to me) shown, his influence upon the great Spanish Carmelites, Santa Teresa de Avila and San Juan de la Cruz.[12] A very interesting development in the history of Sufism is that the impact of Nūrī's thought was felt down into later times, especially throughout North Africa.[13]

Nūrī's language, called by 'Aṭṭār *laṭīf ẓarīf,* 'fine and elegant' is highly poetical and Sulamī asserts that "there was no better representative of the Sufi-path nor anyone with more refined expressions."[14] Particularly beautiful is his image of the heart as a garden which is either fertilized or destroyed by the divine rain: the rain of grace or the rain of wrath. It is a garden in which laud and gratitude are the odoriferous herbs—images which certainly are echoed in the garden imagery which was to become such an important aspect of Persian mystical and profane poetry alike.

For a modern historian of religion, however, one aspect of Nūrī's thought is in particular attractive. That is how he describes, based on Koranic terms, the way from the external phenomena of religion to its innermost core. Those who have worked with Friedrich Heiler's immense survey of phenomenology of religion: *Wesen und Erscheinungsformen der Religion* (Stuttgart 1961), know the German scholar's attempt to lead his readers through four concentric rings of

---

11. Abū'l-Ḥasan Nūrī, *Textes mystiques inédits,* introduction and notes by Paul Nywia, vol. 44, no. 9 (Beirut: Mélanges de l'Université Saint-Joseph 1968), and also Nywia's *Exégèse coranique et langage mystique* (Beirut: Dar al-Mashreq 1970), esp. pp. 220ff.
12. See *Huellas de'Islam en la literatura española* (Ch. 4) (Madrid 1985), English translation, Leiden: Brill 1992; and "De Nūrī de Bagdad a Santa Teresa de Jesús: el símbolo de los siete castillos o moradas concéntricas del alma," in *Vuelta,* no. 80 (July 1983), pp. 18-22.
13. Prof. Vincent Cornell, Duke University, drew my attention to this fact, which I believe has been inadequately surveyed until now.
14. *Ṭabaqāt as-ṣūfiyya,* ed. Sharība (Cairo 1953), p. 156.

phenomena and external manifestations of religion into the heart of the heart, the most sacred, unknowable and fathomless Essence. More than a millennium earlier, the Baghdadian Sufi had developed the following stages of understanding:

> *Ṣadr,* breast, is connected with *islām,* according to Surah IXL: 22;
> *Qalb,* heart, is connected with *īmān,* based on Surah IL: 7;
> *Fu'ād,* inner heart, is the seat of *ma'rifa,* intuitive knowledge, as Surah L: 11 indicates, and
> *Lubb,* the innermost kernel of the heart is connected with *tawḥīd,* the essential declaration that God is One, as Nūrī understands from Surah III: 190.

This sequence perfectly corresponds to Heiler's schema in which the outward manifestations of religions are seen first, their interiorization and their use as symbolic figures come next, while the intuitive knowledge shows itself in the different reactions of human to the Divine revelation. But the last step, absolute *tawḥīd,* is something that is realized only in the darkest cell of the heart where one may find the Divine, the one who cannot be grasped by the hands of intellect but only by faith and love.

It shows Nūrī's ingenuity that he was able to develop this detailed description of the path inward by relying completely upon the Koranic words. We understand his biographers who called him *ṣāḥib al-wafā,* a truly faithful man, and *amīr al-qulūb,* 'Prince of Hearts.' And it speaks for the deep understanding of Junayd that he, for all the frictions that may have happened between him and Nūrī, deplored his death with the words: "Half of Sufism is gone."

Ḥallāj and the Baghdad School of Sufism

Herbert Mason

I.

In general terms, Baghdad in the late third/ninth, early fourth/tenth century was an exciting and dangerous place to be: for mystics no less than for politicians and poets, bankers and other speculators, judges and scribes, traditionalists and philosophers.

Though the present brief review[1] focuses on the mystics of the Baghdad school and on Ḥusayn ibn Manṣūr *"al-Ḥallāj"* (d. 309/922) in particular, one finds with each reexamination of the period and the place, an extraordinary convergence of forces and disparate professions pushing these mystics and mysticism itself to a tragic moment in the glare of the world's stage.

The glare was unwanted by the Baghdad school, as guided by its leader Junayd (d. 298/910), who was aware of the potential dangers to the path of mysticism and to mystics in general caused by spiritual imprudence and political exposure. His keen sense of human defects

1. Sources for this paper include the following: *Diwan al-Ḥallāj,* ed. L. Massignon, (Paris 1929); ed. K.M. Shaybī, (Baghdad 1974); L. Massignon (ed.), *Akhbār al-Hallāj, texte ancien relatif à la prédication et au supplice du mystique musulman al-Ḥosayn b. Manṣour al-Ḥallāj,* (1936; 3rd ed., Paris 1957); 'Alī b. Uthmān al-Hujwīrī, *Kashf al-maḥjūb: The Oldest Persian Treatise on Sufism,* trans. R.A. Nicholson, (reprint London 1976). *Muslim Saints and Mystics: Episodes from the Tadhkirat al-Auliya' by Farid al-Din 'Attar,* tr. A.J. Arberry, (University of Chicago Press 1966)). Quotations from Hujwīrī are taken from the named or otherwise identified brief biographical notices in *Kashf.*

Manṣūr Ḥallāj being led to the gallows. From a manuscript of the *Majālis al-ʿushshāq,* dated 959/1552. MS. Ouseley Add. 24, 34b; (Courtesy of the Bodleian Library, Oxford).

and instabilities leading to jealousies and possessiveness of pupils by masters, and to antagonisms toward and within the circle of mystics, led him to concentrate on renunciation of the world *(zuhd)* and patience *(ṣabr)* in the time-honored ascetical spirit of Ḥasan Baṣrī (d. 110/728), and on trust in God *(tawakkul)* in the manner of one of his spiritual guides Muḥāsibī (d. 243/857), and, as he approached prudently the question of mystic love *(maḥabba),* on the yearning for intimacy with God of Rābi'a al-Adawiyya (d. 185/801) and those centered after her in Iran and in the Baghdad of Junayd's own time.[2]

The mystics of Baghdad concentrated and diverged on the question of sobriety *(ṣaḥw)* versus intoxication *(sukr)* in mystical love, and the sober and cautious Junayd became, at least in subsequent legend, a warner if not benign opponent of the imprudent Ḥallāj, who believed that "love as long as it is hidden is in danger," and "better for love when gossip forces it by lies to spread like fire, for it is useless hiding under stone."[3] Ḥallāj was to become the protagonist (and in subsequent legend the tragic emblem) of intoxicated love, who brought mysticism into history's dangerous, and, for him, self-destructive public glare.

Of course, the drama of Ḥallāj, including the allegations of heresy, the trials and atrocious execution, the book burnings, public demonstration, and riots that followed in Baghdad and other cities in response to his martyrdom, can only be understood in the larger context of early fourth/tenth century social, economic, and political realities—a context too large and complex to discuss in the present review. But one might easily conclude that such a figure as Ḥallāj was impelled onto the public stage not only by his particular fusion and witness of mystic love and passion for social justice, but also by his precursors' and followers' collective quest and equally controversial if subtler arguments for intimate union with God. Surely the "Tragedy of Ḥallāj" *(ma'sāt al-Ḥallāj),* to use the modern Egyptian poet-playwright Ṣabbūr's phrase, was in any case, not mere chance or accident, nor did it spring from nothing.

---

2. See Carl Ernst's essay in this volume.—ED.
3. *Dīwān al-Ḥallāj,* ed. L. Massignon, M24; ed. Shaybī, p. 34.

Junayd was considered wise in urging sobriety and teaching acceptance of the inexpressibility of divine mystery, of guarding one's gift from God in secret, of keeping out of harm's way, of common sense. Such a stance was surely no less sincere in its devotion or profound in its adoration of God through love than was the way of those who spoke as if directly with God (by ecstatic utterances or *shaṭḥ)* in public and declaimed against political corruption, social and sectarian divisiveness, economic inequities, and betrayal of the community by the state, and thereby put at risk the security and place of both themselves and their more cautious brothers on the path.

II.

Before turning to Ḥallāj himself, I would like to mention briefly a few of the mystics of the Baghdad school, of both the sobriety and the intoxication persuasion; that is, both those respected figures who, according to Ḥujwīrī, insisted that the verification of spiritual experience required sanity, the ability to see things as they really are, who argued that intoxication, by causing loss of one's normal state was evil; and those by contrast eccentric figures[4] who risked in the ecstasy of love the loss of their human nature by immersion *(istighrāq)* in (and by ascription of all their acts and words to) God.

One of the principal master figures, the teacher of most of the Shaykhs of Iraq, according to Hujwīrī, and who was also the maternal uncle of Junayd, was Sarī al-Saqaṭī (d. 253/867), "the huckster" in the bazaar shop sense, one of the first to teach the doctrine of the mystical states and stages *(aḥwāl* and *maqāmāt).* He is quoted in his notice by Hujwīrī as saying "there is no punishment in Hell more painful and difficult to endure than (the pain) of being veiled (from God)." To Sarī love was the vision of Him in the heart *(qalb);* and like his fellow Iraqi, the aforementioned Muḥāsibī (and subsequently Junayd and other Sufis), he believed in the knowledge of the secrets of the hearts' motions *(al-'ilm bi-ḥarākat al-qulūb).*

To the intoxicated Ḥallāj and his friend and disciple Ibn 'Atā',

4. As footnote to the eccentric, one might recall the words of that strange and elusive mystic from Egypt Dhu'l-Nūn (d. 245/859): "Ordinary men repent of their sins, the elect of their heedfulness."

however, the 'science of hearts' *('ilm al-qulūb)* was a form of communion with God himself achieved by mediation of the friends of God. In this regard one also discovers in Hujwīrī's work, among the Shaykhs of sobriety in or linked with the Baghdad school the presence of a highly active inner spiritual community whose members are similarly in touch with one another, sending messages back and forth, knowing each others' secret thoughts and even dreams (concerning Muḥammad, for instance, and God). That inner community was a rare nurturing, almost epiphanous, moment in that place, whose guides were deeply acquainted with the inward experiences of their disciples. In this sense and spirit, the so-called 'Letters' exchanged between Ḥallāj and Ibn 'Aṭā' were understandable as "letters (written as if) to myself." And indeed Ibn 'Aṭā's adage that, "the way to union with God is through fraternal love" is perhaps a familiar truth to that spiritual community established soundly before him by the Shaykhs of sobriety.

Junayd himself, following Sarī, put emphasis on direct experience as opposed to mere expression, and, according to Hujwīrī, he had an experience with an old man—none other than Iblis—and believed the saints of pure contemplation who had acheived the degree of being "witnesses" *(siddiqīn=mushāhadāt)* were given mysterious powers to resist Iblis, who was of course the subject of Ḥallāj's remarkable tract, the *Ṭawāsīn.*

Another figure deserving of more than brief mention possible here was Abū'l-Ḥusayn al-Nūrī (d. 295/907),[5] a companion of Junayd and disciple of Sarī, whose followers, the so-called Nūrīs, Hujwīrī calls "approved *(maqbūl)* but controversial" among the Sufi sects. To Nūrī, "union with God is separation from all else, and separation from all else is union with Him."[6] Nūrī's position was also close to that of Junayd, echoed by Abū Muḥammad Ruwaym ibn Aḥmad (d. 303/915) among his ascetical disciples, who emphasized the same denudation of self and detachment from the world and the flesh *(tajrīd),* and intense, uncompromising devotion to God.

Another of the mystics close to Nūrī was Sumnūn ibn Ḥamza (d.

5. See Annemarie Schimmel's essay in this volume. –Ed.
6. *Kashf al-maḥjūb,* p. 131.

after 287/900), known as 'the lover' *(al-muḥibb),* who aroused, along with Nūrī the wrath of a leading antagonist to the Baghdad school of Sufis, Ghulām al-Khalīl (d. 275/888). Al-Khalīl's pretended piety and ready accusation of heresy raised against certain openly intoxicate Sufis, along with calls for their execution, was brought as high as to Caliphal attention, and this helped create the atmosphere of persecution conducive to Ḥallāj's own later trials. Sumnūn believed that love, being an attribute of the Beloved, was ultimately inexpressible.[7]

And, of course, there are those figures linked directly to the life of Ḥallāj, such as 'Amr ibn 'Uthmān al-Makkī (d. 297/909), a disciple of Junayd, who also affirmed the inexpressibility of divine mystery; and Sahl al-Tustarī (d. 283/896), the austere concentrator on human fallibility and pious defender of the religious Law as Truth and Truth as Law against those Sufis tending to separate them.

The list of members or distant associates of the Baghdad school is very large indeed. It includes Abū Sa'īd Aḥmad al-Kharrāz (d. 286/899) whose *Kitāb al-ṣidq* mentions the Truth (*al-Ḥaqq)* in what was to become a Ḥallājian manner; Abū Isḥāq Ibrāhīm ibn al-Khawāṣṣ (d. 292/904) who "saw" Khiḍr, the archetypal mythic guide of the Sufis; Abū Ḥamza al-Baghdādī al-Bazzāz (d. after 341/952), a friend of Nūrī who remained close to him through his persecution by Ghulām al-Khalīl; Abū Bakr al-Wāsiṭī (d. 331/942), whose 'decentering' of self led him to regard his recollection of God *(dhikr)* as his only self, amongst many more of this School…

All by their expressions and beliefs, their emphasis on love and their individual introspections and extensions of the stages leading to union with God, helped to 'create' in themselves or, at least, imagine the figure of the divinely embraced lover that was to be realized in life by Ḥallāj. Each of them, in varying degrees, conceived the idea of the martyr of love, even as they recoiled from it in the profundity of their own meditation; but in most cases they drew back from the real consequence that he could not escape.

---

7. *Ibid.,* p. 138.

III.

Now we turn to Ḥallāj, who was given the longest of Hujwīrī's notices (no. 53), with whom "Shaykhs," we are told, "are at variance," but as for ourselves, "we leave him to the judgement of God."[8]

The mention of Sahl Tustarī, "whom [Ḥallāj] left without asking permission, in order to attach himself to 'Amr al-Makkī," whom he also later "left without asking permission," to go to Junayd, "who wouldn't receive him" (hence, Ḥallāj was "banned by all the Shaykhs," due to his conduct, not to his principles), reflects for us the conventional protocol among the Shaykhs along with their proprietary expectations and attitude (in some minds) toward the impulsiveness of Ḥallāj's character. It also underscores Ḥallāj's individualism, so to speak, and points to his actual rejection of any long term association with established Sufism. Other opinions held by close associates of Ḥallāj, as quoted in Hujwīrī's work, include the following:

To Abū 'Abdullah Muḥammad ibn Khafīf, (d. 372/982), known for his self-denudation *(tajrīd)*, Ḥallāj "is a divinely learned man *('ālim-i rabbānī).*" To Abū Bakr ibn Jaḥdar al-Shiblī (d. 334/945), known for his feigned madness and a disciple of Junayd, "Ḥallāj and I are of one belief, but my madness saved me, while his intelligence destroyed him."[9] Hujwīrī himself says, "He is dear to my heart, but his path isn't soundly established on any principle…" etc. He tells us that Ḥallāj wrote fifty works —in Baghdad, in Khurāsān, in Fars, and in Khūzistān. (From other sources we know he also traveled twice to India and once to China. His sobriquet *Ḥallāj al-asrār* ('carder of consciences' or 'reader of hearts') was given him in Ahwāz, (c. 280/893). "He wore the garb of piety, consisting in prayer and praise of God and continual fasts and fine sayings on the subject of Unification. If his actions were magic, all this could not possibly have proceeded from him. Consequently, they must have been miracles, and miracles are vouchsafed only to a true saint. Some orthodox theologians reject him on the ground that that his sayings are pantheistic but the offence lies solely in the expression,

---

8. *Ibid.*, p. 150
9. *Ibid.*, p. 151.

not in the meaning."[10]

Hujwīrī's notice is typically anecdotal, but much of Ḥallāj's thought is included in the last section of *Kashf* dealing with the uncovering of the eleven veils. We touch here briefly on just a few of these uncoverings for comparative views among the Shaykhs:

1.*Tawḥīd* (unification):

According to Junayd, "Unification is the separation of the Eternal (God) from that which originates in time." According to Ḥallāj, however, the first step is the annihilation of separation *(tafrīd),* so that in unity *(waḥdaniyyat)* one affirms nothing other than God. Any other thought than of God is a veil and an imperfection; one is veiled by one's thoughts, not by God. Hence the path is concentration of thought on God alone—to the point of knowing only God, and nothing of oneself.

2. *Imān* (faith)

To Junayd and his circle faith was a matter of verbal expression combined with verification. Faith's root *(aṣl)* finds its verification in the heart. Faith's derivative or branch *(far')* is observance of the command *(amr)* of God. Since faith is equivalent to knowledge, works by themselves are not the key to salvation. We know God by His attributes: Beauty *(jamāl),* Majesty *(jalāl)* and Perfection *(kamāl),* as well as by love, longing and awe, which are states recommended for lifting the veil of human attributes. Thus, faith when fully realized, is equivalent to gnosis *(ma'rifa)*, which is equivalent to love *(maḥabba),* and worship/obedience *('ibādat)* is the sign of love.

To Ḥallāj, the divine attribute which alludes to Unification is *al-Ḥaqq* (the Truth, the Real) which embraces all of the above. But union with God, who is 'the Source' *('ayn al-jam')* and the goal of the mystic lover, is not pure speculation or mere ecstasy, but a permanent and transforming action sanctifying one, realizable only by direct experience. In union, all separation is annihilated, for in Ḥallāj's controversial expression: *Anā'l-Ḥaqq (al-Ḥaqq* is the only true 'I').

---

10. *Ibid.,* p. 152.

3) *Ṣalāt* (ritual prayer; Persian *namāz)*

It is related of Ḥallāj that "he performed 400 *rak'a*s each day and night, a model of self-annihilation *(fana')*," and of Junayd: "even when old he kept up his litanies of youth, a model of *ṣalāt.*"

4.*Maḥabba* (love)

According to Shiblī: "Love obliterates from the heart all but the Beloved." Thus, the first step to union is restlessness of desire for the Beloved, or excessive love *('ishq).* In this context we may recall from Ḥallāj's *Diwān* the expression that, "The realization of God is given to one who craves it in anguish."[11] For Sahl Tustarī however, love was equivalent to obedience.

4. *Ḥajj* (pilgrimage)

Hujwīrī cites two kinds of *Ḥajj*: in absence from God and in the presence of God, remarking that in his view, which followed that of Junayd, "anyone who is present with God in his own house is in the same position as if he were present with God in Mecca," and that "*Ḥajj* is self-mortification for the sake of contemplation as a means to knowledge of God."[12] Here we should recall the legal device for justifying the execution of Ḥallāj, the three-time pilgrim to Mecca: he was accused of advocating the overthrow of the religious Law by preaching that the *Ḥajj* can be fulfilled by sincere prayer performed in one's own home.

IV.

The account of Ḥallāj's death—detailed in its full gruesomeness by 'Aṭṭār[13], indicates more than a legal execution, rather a vengeful murder, indeed a sadistic slaughter, urged and orchestrated by the

---

11. *Dīwān al-Ḥallāj,* ed. L. Massignon, M17.
12. *Kashf al-maḥjūb,* p. 329.
13. *Tadhkirat,* pp. 268-271. For a detailed reconstruction of the events leading up to and including his trials and execution, see Louis Massignon, *The Passion of al-Ḥallāj,* trans. H. Mason (4 vols., Princeton University Press 1983), I, chaps. 5-7. Included is the intrigue generated by Ḥāmid and his supporters to increase their power in court against the pro-Persian Samanid faction which, in league with the Caliph's mother Shaghab, was strongly supportive of Ḥallāj.

brutal vizier Ḥāmid, a figure whose dominance in the Baghdad political arena of 309/922 reflects the corruption and decadence of the Abbasid caliphate of al-Muqtadir and his sycophants.

From fear of a riot, the Caliph (in reality, it was Ḥāmid prodding him) shouted, "Kill him, or beat him with sticks until he retracts."

They beat him with sticks three hundred times. At each blow a clear voice was heard saying, "Do not be afraid, son of Manṣūr!"

Then they took him out to be crucified.

Weighed down with thirteen chains, Ḥallāj strutted proudly waving his hands in the air like a beggar.

"Why do you stand so proudly?" they asked him.

"Because I am on my way to the slaughterhouse," he answered.[14]

The description that follows includes details of his apparel (loincloth and a mantle over his shoulders), his prayer towards Mecca, his communing with God, his ascent onto the gibbet, and his acceptance of death as a sign of the crowd's "belief in one God to uphold the strictness of the Law."

He was then stoned by the crowd. The executioners cut off his hands, then his feet, then they plucked out his eyes; he was stoned again, then they cut off his ears and nose. He uttered his forgiveness of them as they were preparing to cut out his tongue. An old woman shouted "What right has this little woolcarder *(al-Ḥallāj)* to speak of God?" Thereafter, he uttered "It is enough for the lover to (diminish himself) before the uniqueness of the One." Then his tongue was cut out, and, finally, he was beheaded at the time of the evening prayer.

The next day his limbs were burned and his ashes thrown into the Tigris.

V.

The following excerpts from my play, *The Death of al-Ḥallāj,*[15] represent a distillation of his thought in the form of a dramatic recreation of his last days in prison prior to his execution. They are based primarily on his *Diwān,* the *Ṭawāsīn* and the *Akhbār al-Ḥallāj.*

---

14. *Tadhkirat,* p. 268.
15. Published, Notre Dame University Press 1979. By permission of the publisher.

Ibn 'Aṭā'

Then what *is* the meaning of your teaching,
Of your imprisonment, of your life?

Ḥallāj

I have the feeling I shall spend my days
Of confinement being asked the meaning
Of the meaning of the meaning until
My soul and meanings are exhausted by
Analyses. I'm sorry, I did not mean
To hurt you, dear friend. Your face betrays
My selfishness. The meaning is, we are two parrots.
One is imprisoned here so the other may be free
To sing His words. We must be substitutes for each.
It is His desire.
(A pause between them. They muse apart.)

Ibn 'Aṭā'

(after a long silence)
Who is He?

Ḥallāj

He is His lettered sign to us. H-u-W-a.
His essence is separate from His letters.

Ibn 'Aṭā'

How can we enter Him if He is separate?

Ḥallāj

By removing ourself as vowels from His signs
And letting Him be vowels in us. He then enters
The signs with His transforming union. And then
Utters Himself clearly in the only true eloquence.
His Oneness is His wisdom.

Ibn 'Aṭā'

Are you also a grammarian?

Ḥallāj

I am only His parrot in a cage.

Ibn 'Aṭā'

Is the world then a prison? Are you saying that?

Ḥallāj

The world is not something other
Than ourselves and Him.
If I may depart from character,
I think you are really asking
If religion can be action
For improving it. I know that you
Are anxious for more action.

Ibn 'Aṭā'

But you yourself took action
When you marched with the Zanj
Against the war,
When you spoke out for the blacks,
When you preached against the Caliph's
And his bankers' speculating on
Their hidden stores of gold and wheat.

Ḥallāj

But that is not religion in itself.
We must not think that speaking out
Can be a substitute for meditation of Allah.
A breed of empty heroes will emerge,
For all it takes is momentary courage
And the crowd does all the rest. No,

It is harder to contemplate our God
Than to utter a few words on His behalf.
But sometimes we are called to be a mouthpiece
For the inarticulate, maybe to lose our lives.
But even dying on the gibbet is nothing
More than one rung on the ladder,
Not the last... The last is His alone
Where He embraces us. For then we know
Our heart and mind are one like His
Without this separation anymore. I am not a Theologian, as you can see; only a prisoner
Pulled to the Center... the theologian, that is
Who separates the heart and mind, like Satan,
Who was so conditioned in his love he couldn't bear
God's giving unity to man. He always tried
To make God's unity seem inaccessible.
I am worried about those who concentrate
Too much on fine distinctions, as in the case of faith,
Instead of witnessing His nearness.
But I understand, for we are all closer
To Satan's love than to our God's.[16]

***

(After a long silence Ḥallāj speaks:)
We are here, we, Your witnesses.
We ask for refuge in the splendor of Your Glory
That You may show at last what You intended
To fashion and achieve,
O You Who are God in heaven and earth.

It is You Who shine forth when you desire
Just as You shone before the angels and Satan
In the most beautiful form of the unspoiled Adam,
The form in which Your voice resides
Present in knowledge and in speech.

16. *The Death of Ḥallāj,* pp. 24-28.

You have given me, Your present witness,
Your self, Your own desire…
How is it that You Who gave me Your Self
When they had stripped and mocked me for my self,
Who used me to proclaim Your self,
To utter the words which gave me life,
Have let me be taken, imprisoned, judged,
Now to be executed, hung on the cross,
Burned, my ashes to be thrown to the winds
Of the desert, the waves of the Tigris…
Am I of no use once Your words are spoken…?
Should I have not revealed Your gift of Your Self
As my enemies say who love the vanity
Of possessing You alone? Do you abandon me
Or can the smallest particle of my ashes
Burned in this way to Your glory
Assure me of another form in Your love
Than this old temple they are tearing down?[17]

***

Shaghab

In my boredom I have imagined pain
As something beautiful, sorrow as heart-
Filling music. I even dreamed
I saw you crucified, your arms were wings
And you took flight in soaring ecstasy
To God, you flew with other creatures
In your folds. Suffering seemed bliss.

---

17. *Ibid.*, pp. 63-74.

Ḥallāj

I differ with your dream on that.

Shaghab

No, suffering cannot be given you
Except to veil your flight.

Ḥallāj

That is the precious singing bird you cage
But will release in time…

Shaghab

I am a very poor disciple, but I think
I see behind your veils and disguises,
Your talk about your love of pleasure, your
Words that bring you close to men, for I
Am able to distinguish those
Who are captive to our world from those
Who are merely clothed in it. You have no
Attachments, you live an asceticism
Of the heart. For you your final suffering
Will bring you joy, but it will bring us
Pain of loss. That is why I woke up
Crying in my dream. I understand
You though I am a caliph's mother.
You hold the secret truth we can't embrace.
And you must appear in this or that
Disguise, for you are the first of our faith
Who desires to die out of sheer love.
You are very frightening to some and
Even to me. I know the way it will end.

Ḥallāj

You understand our God is a consuming fire.
The rose opens to the light, the Narcissus
Leans to shade. We are more mixtures than we
Like to think. But at some point His light
Penetrates our eyes, destroying our shades
And our distortions, leaving us floating blind
Spots we forget when our vision is clarified in His.
If we are roses we are drawn to light.
We do not think about the end. There is none.

Shaghab

May I ask you something very personal?

Ḥallāj

I have nothing personal that is my own.

Shaghab

I have a very small idea of love:
That it requires two at once, and it lives
On two occurrences: intimacy and laughter.
We must enjoy the presence of the one we love
And find amusement in the world we share.
Have you known that with others or with God
Alone?

Ḥallāj

(*He smiles.)* With both, not God alone.
(She smiles and reaches out to touch his hands.
They break together in releasing laughter.)

***

H. Mason *Ḥallāj and the Baghdad School of Sufism* 81

Ḥallāj

I cry to You, not only for myself
But for those souls who yearn for You,
Whose witness, I myself, goes now to You,
The witness of Eternity.[18]

18. *Ibid.*, p. 75.

Abū Sa'īd ibn Abī'l-Khayr conversing with a young man. From the *Majālis al-'ushshāq,* dated 959/1552. MS. Ouseley. Add. 24, f. 36v. (Courtesy of the Bodleian Library, Oxford).

Abū Sa'īd ibn Abī'l-Khayr and the School of Khurāsān

Terry Graham

PROLOGUE

"There is nothing under this robe but God."
"Introduce me as 'Nobody son of nobody'."

The man who uttered these two apparently contradictory statements was himself a classic paradox. A champion of asceticism in his early years, Abū Sa'īd ibn Abī'l-Khayr became criticized by many for his seemingly indulgent lifestyle in his later life as a spiritual master. A Sufi who stood above politics, he commanded the respect, if not discipleship, of the men of political power. He was also the seminal figure in the process of development of Sufism from the spontaneous gathering of seekers around a master in his home to the formation of a widespread Sufi Order. Yet his influence lies notably in the contrasting domains of the formulation of a disciplinary rule for conduct in the *khānaqāh* as an institutionalized center of Sufi life and of the introduction of *samā'*, the audition of music and poetry and the participation in dance, as part and parcel of the Sufi collective devotional ritual of *dhikr,* or Divine invocation.

The present study attempts to analyse this master's seminal influence on the shaping of Sufism at a critical point in its development. Four aspects of the cultural evolution of Persian Sufism during the early eleventh century will hold our attention, these being:

1) *Literary:* The principal language of Sufism in the eastern lands of Islam was changing from Arabic to Persian;

2) *Political:* Islam was experiencing erosive factional strife and social upheaval from within, on the eve of massive destruction inflicted from without;

3) *Institutional and Pedagogical:* the relationship between master and disciple and the process of spiritual training were becoming systematized, with the institution of the *Khānaqāh* becoming concretized on the eve of the formation of official Sufi Orders; and

4) *Social-Ethical:* Sufism was becoming integrated with ethical doctrines and anti-legalistic ideas deriving from movements based on spiritual chivalry and 'blame-incurring' behavior.

These principal themes will be used as foci around which to assess Abū Sa'īd's particular contribution to this developmental process, in respect to:

1) His application of the spoken word, particularly in the line of spiritual instruction and most notably through the quatrain with its economy of statement;

2) His work in systematizing of the institution of the *Khānaqāh* and the establishment of the use of poetry, music and dance, namely, *samā',* or 'spiritual audition,' in regular congregational Sufi practice; and,

3) His teaching of sincerity and spiritual chivalry *(jawānmardī)* or "selflessness in intention and conduct," as the basis of devotion in Sufism, these principles being founded on contemporary Khurāsānian currents known as *qalandariyya/'ayyāriyya,* 'the way of those who are free-spirited'—and the *malāmatiyya*, 'the way of those who incur blame.'

I. YOUTH AND EDUCATION: JURISPRUDENCE AND SHĀFI'ISM

Abū Sa'īd Faḍlullāh ibn Abī'l-Khayr Aḥmad Mayhanī was born on the first of the month of Muḥarram, the very first day of the Islamic year of 357 A.H., corresponding to 7 December 967 A.D., at Mayhana, a town in the Plain of Khāwarān in the northeastern Iranian region of Khurāsān, fifty miles northwest of the town of

Sarakhs. He died there, as well, on 4 Sha'bān 440 A.H. (12 January 1049 A.D.). While Sarakhs is on the Iranian side of the border of the former Soviet Union today, Mayhana is in the erstwhile Soviet Republic of Turkmenistan.

More is known of the details of Abū Sa'īd's life than those of virtually any other master of his era because of the unique presence of two biographies. The first is the *Ḥālāt u sukhanān-i Shaykh Abū Sa'īd Abī'l-Khayr Mayhanī,* composed by a great-great-grandson, Kamāl al-Dīn Muḥammad b. Jamāl al-Dīn Abū Rawḥ Luṭfullāh b. Abī Sa'īd Sa'd b. Abī Sa'īd As'ad b. Abī Ṭāhir Sa'īd b. Abī Sa'īd Faḍlullāh (d. 541/1147).[1] The other biography is the *Asrār al-tawḥīd fī maqāmāt Shaykh Abī Sa'īd,* written by Luṭfullāh's cousin, Muḥammad b. Nūr-al-Dīn Munawwar b. Abi Sa'īd As'ad b. Abī Ṭāhir Sa'īd b. Abī Sa'īd Faḍlullāh, known as Ibn Munawwar, whose date of death is unknown but who is estimated to have completed the biography sometime between 553/1158 and 588/1192.[2]

Like his equally illustrious fellow Khurāsānian Bāyazid Bisṭāmī (d. 251/875) before him and the renowned founder of the Qādiriyya Order, 'Abd al-Qādir Gīlānī (d. 561/1166) after him, Abū Sa'īd was launched on the Sufi path by his mother, who, in this case, put pressure on his father to take him to Sufi gatherings,[3] where he proved to have spiritual acumen well beyond that of his father.[4] The latter subsequently introduced his son to his first spiritual guide, Abū'l-Qāsim Bishr Yāsīn (d. 380/990), who set an example for his pupil by teaching through verse. In fact, it has been suggested that many

1. Jamāl al-Dīn Luṭfullāh ibn Abī Sa'īd Sa'd, *Ḥālāt u sukhanān-i Shaykh Abū Sa'īd Abī'l-Khayr,* ed. V.A. Zhukovskii (St. Petersburg 1899); ed. Īraj Afshār (Tehran 1963).
2. Muḥammad Ibn Munawwar, *Asrār at-tawḥīd fī maqāmāt Shaykh Abū Sa'īd*, ed. V. A. Zhukovskii, (St. Petersburg 1899), re-edited A. Bahmanyār (Tehran 1978); ed. Dhabīḥullāh Ṣafā, (Tehran 1953; repr. Tehran 1969 and 1975); Arabic tr. E. A. Qandil (Cairo 1966); French transl. M. Achena, *Les étapes mystiques du shaikh Abū Sa'īd* (Paris 1974); and M.R. Shafī'ī-Kadkanī (Tehran 1987), 2 vol., incl. study and notes. Unless otherwise indicated, all references to the *Asrār at-tawḥīd* are to the edition of Ṣafā.
3. Ibn Munawwar, *op. cit.,* p. 4.
4. The *Asrār al-tawḥīd,* p. 5, tells an anecdote which indicates the superior understanding of Abū Sa'īd to that of his father from the lad's earliest experience of Sufism.

of the quatrains attributed to Abū Sa'īd may have actually been uttered by this master.

Abū Sa'īd's education was in two spheres: professional and spiritual. Professionally, he studied law as interpreted by the Sunni Shāfi'ī school of jurisprudence *(fiqh)* in the city of Merv (in modern-day Turkmenistan), where the two leading authorities of the region held classes. His first teacher, Abū 'Abdullāh Muḥammad b. Aḥmad Khiḍrī (d. between 373/983 and 390/1000), was fourth in a pedagogical chain leading from Imām Shāfi'ī (d. 204/820), founder of the school.

Khiḍrī was a pupil of Abū 'Abdullāh al-Muzanī al-Baṣrī, author of the *Mukhtaṣar*, the basic text of the Shāfi'ite school, to which jurists of this *madhhab* continue to refer today. Khiḍrī was also the pupil of Abū'l-'Abbās b. Surayj Shīrāzī (d. 306/918-919), the leading *Qāḍī* of Shīrāz, the principal Shāfi'ite center in western Iran until the Safavid period. It was in Ibn Surayj's generation that Shāfi'ism was introduced to Nīshāpūr, a generation before Abū Sa'īd's arrival in that city. It was brought by two jurists, one a native of Merv, Muḥammad b. Naṣr Mervazī whereby Nīshāpūr "came to shelter a large and vigorous Shāfi'ite community."[5] Khiẓrī was also the Shāfi'īte juridical teacher of the eminent Khurāsānian Sufi master Abū 'Alī Daqqāq (d. 405/1015 or 412/1021), fellow disciple of Abū 'Abd al-Raḥmān Sulamī (d. 412/1021) with Abū Sa'īd, and master and father-in-law of Abū'l-Qāsim Qushayrī (d. 465/1072), fellow Shāfi'ite in jurisprudence and Ash'arite in theology with Abū Sā'id.

Despite the fact that so much is known of Abū Sa'īd's life, no exact dates can be determined, apart from those of his birth and death. In terms of time-frame, all that is known of Abū Sa'īd's stay in Merv is that his first teacher, Khiḍrī, died after Abū Sa'īd had studied five years in his circle, whereupon the pupil went on to study under another important figure in the spread of Shāfi'ism in Khurāsān and Transoxiana, Abū Bakr 'Abdullāh b. Aḥmad Qaffāl Mervazī (d. 417/1026), who also dwelled in Merv.[6] Abū Sa'īd was well on his

5. Wilferd Madelung, *Religious Trends in Early Islamic Iran,* Columbia Lectures on Iranian Studies 4 (Albany: SUNY 1988), p. 26.

way to a career as a Shāfi'īte scholar and 'scholar of Prophetic Traditions *(muḥaddith)'*.

A fellow student of his under Qaffāl was Abū Muhammad Juwaynī, the scholar who was to become father of the leading Shāfi'ite jurist and Ash'arite theologian of his generation in Nīshāpūr, the center of Shāfi'ite thought for the Persian-speaking world: Abū'l-Ma'ālī 'Abd al-Malik Juwaynī (d. 468/1075), known as 'Imām al-Ḥaramayn' (spiritual chief of the two sanctuaries [Mecca and Medina])." 'Abd al-Malik was ultimately to be associated with Abū Sa'īd in both the professional and spiritual realms: as a recipient of accreditation *(ijāza)* from him in the field of the transmission of Prophetic Traditions *(ḥadīth)* and as a disciple on the spiritual Path.[7] Furthermore, as the most important teacher of the famous Abū Ḥāmid Muḥammad Ghazālī (d. 505/1111), the younger Juwaynī served as a direct conveyor of Abū Sa'īd's teaching to the most celebrated theologian in the history of Islam.[8] Abū Sa'īd's association with Qaffāl also prefigured his imminent parallel spiritual development, in that his teacher was also a Sufi.[9]

In fact, with respect to the two schools of jurisprudence *(farīqān),* which dominated Sunni Iran at this time, the Shāfi'ītes were known as the *ahl-i ḥadīth* (Traditionists), while the Ḥanafites were called the *aṣḥāb-i ra'y* (Rationalists). According to Madelung, "Persian Sufism was in this period closely associated with Shāfi'ism and Ash'arism,"[10] the theology of which emphasized faith over reason as the vehicle for understanding. In contrast, rationalist Mu'tazilism tended to attract the Ḥanafites of Khurāsān and Transoxania.

---

6. *Ibid.* Madelung *(ibid.,* p. 26) speaks of "the renowned Shāfi'ite scholar Abū Bakr Muḥammad b. 'Ali al-Qaffāl (d. 365/976)," whose death would have been too soon for Abū Sa'īd to have studied with him; however, the coincidence of both *kunya* ('Abū Bakr') and sobriquet (Qaffāl= 'Locksmith') suggests the possibility of a confusion of records on the participation of cousins in the same field, as was the case with the two biographers of Abū Sa'īd.

7. Ibn Munawwar, *op. cit.,* (Shafī'ī-Kadkanī's ed.), p. xxxi.

8. Montgomery Watt, *Muslim Intellectual: A Study of al-Ghazālī* (Edinburgh 1963) pp. 23-24.

9. Sayyid Muḥammad Damadī, *Abū Sa'īd-nāma: Zindagī-nāma-yi Abū Sa'īd Abī'l-Khayr,* (Tehran 1973), p. 12.

10. Madelung, *op. cit.,* p. 46.

Abū Sa'īd's biographer Ibn Munawwar

> went so far as to assert that all Sufi masters since the time of al-Shāfi'ī had been Shāfi'ites and that even those who originally adhered to another school adopted Shāfi'ite doctrine after God elected them for His friendship. The reason for this was, he explained, that the Sufis were deeply concerned with a meticulous and rigorous practice of the obligatory rites and devotions of Islam and even supererogatory acts in order to mortify their desires, and this attitude was most in harmony with the rigorism of Shāfi'ite law. Although Ibn Munawwar insisted that the Sufis would not discriminate between al-Shāfi'ī and Abū Ḥanīfa, both eminently pious imams, he clearly implied that Ḥanafism, the rationalist school associated with the Mu'tazila who denied the miracles of Sufi saints, was unsuited for Sufis.[11]

After another five years, Abū Sa'īd completed his study with Qaffāl and went south to Sarakhs, nearer his hometown of Mayhana, and joined the circle of Abū 'Alī Ẓāhir Sarakhsī (d. 389/999), with whom he concentrated on Koranic, juridical and theological studies. During this time, Abū Sa'īd focused on the science of establishing legal precedent through citation of Prophetic Traditions, his future profession. As Shafī'ī-Kadkanī points out, the story recounted by Ibn Munawwar[12] that Abū Sa'īd buried his books and never returned to them once he had embarked on the Sufi path is clearly apocryphal (unless meant in a purely symbolic sense); for, later on, in the Shāfi'ite center of Nīshāpūr, he served to accredit a number of prominent *muḥaddithūn,* including the celebrated Juwaynī, and appears in a number of official Shāfi'ite sources as a transmitter of Traditions, such as Sam'ānī's *al-Ansāb* and *al-Taḥbīr fi'l-Mu'jam al-kabīr,*[13] as well as being a distinguished teacher at the prestigious Niẓāmiyya College in Nīshāpūr[14] whose founder, the vizier Niẓām

---

11. *Ibid.*
12. Ibn Munawwar, *op. cit.,* pp. 250-51.
13. Cf. al-Sam'āni, *al-Ansab,* Facsimile ed. D. S. Margoliouth, (Leiden 1912), and *al-Taḥbīr fi'l-mu'jam al-kabīr,* ed. Munīra Najī Sālim, (Baghdad 1395/1975). N. Māyil-Harawī, in his edition of 'Umar ibn Muḥammad ibn Aḥmad Shirakān's Persian translation of Abū'l-Najīb Suhrawardī's *Adāb al-murīdīn* (Tehran 1984; p. 347, no. 59) points out that Suhrawardī, following the Shāfi'ite school, would have quoted Prophetic Traditions from chains of authority which included Abū Sa'īd.
14. Ibn Munawwar, *op. cit.,* (Shafī'ī-Kadkanī's ed.), p. xxxi.

al-Mulk (d. 1092) was a Shāfi'ite and patron of the adherents of this *madhhab.*[15] Indeed, if Ibn Munawwar is to be believed, the intertwining of Sufism and Shāfi'ism in the world of Abū Sa'īd was given a further twist by the possibility that the powerful vizier (fl. 1063-1092) was even a disciple of Abū Sa'īd.[16]

II. *PĪRS* AND *KHIRQAS*: ABŪ SA'ĪD'S SPIRITUAL AFFILIATIONS

It was in the course of his study with Abū 'Alī Ẓāhir in Sarakhs (possibly in the year 387/997)[17] that Abū Sa'īd began his return to the fold of Sufism, prefigured in his early years, by encountering the *'āqil-i majnūn* (saintly fool) Luqmān Sarakhsī. Sitting on an ash-heap, Luqmān was stitching a patch on his cloak. Abū Sa'īd waited while he finished his stiticing, when his shadow fell across it, whereupon this *'āqil-i majnūn* stated, "With this patch, I have stitched you to my cloak." Then he rose and took Abū Sa'īd by the hand, leading him to Abū'l-Faḍl's *Khānaqāh.* Stopping before the door, Luqmān called out to the master. When Abū-Faḍl appeared, Luqmān passed Abū Sa'īd's hand into the master's, thus completing the transition.[18]

In this manner, Luqmān served as the spiritual connection drawing Abū Sa'īd back to the path by presenting him to this master, Abū'l-Faḍl Muḥammad b. Ḥasan Sarakhsī (d. 414/1023).[19] Reflecting back on this discovery of his master, when later asked how he had embarked on the mode of life which he was living, Abū Sa'īd replied,[20] "With a glance *(naẓar)* from Pīr Abū'l-Faḍl (which had fallen upon him one day by a stream even before he had met Luqmān).... From that day to the very present, everything I have I owe

15. Concerning Niẓām al-Mulk's patronage of the Shafi'ītes, see Madelung, *op.cit.*, pp. 33-34.
16. For reference to Niẓām al-Mulk being a disciple of Abū Sa'īd, *cf.* Ibn Munawwar, *op.cit.*, pp. 193-96.
17. Gerhard Böwering, s.v. "Abū Sa'īd Faẓl-Allah b. Abī'l-Khayr," *Encyclopædia Iranica,* II, p. 377.
18. Ibn Munawwar, *op. cit.,* p. 24.
19. *Ibid.*, p. 25.
20. *Ibid.*

to him."

Abū Sa'īd now entered into the fifteen-year period of extreme asceticism for which he became famous in the annals of Sufism, dividing his time between isolation *(khalwat)* in his home in Mayhana, guidance in his master's *khānaqāh* in Sarakhs fifty miles away, and wandering in the wilderness of the Plain of Khāwarān. In the course of his training, Abū'l-Faḍl sent him once to the city of Nīshāpūr to receive the *khirqa-yi irshād* (cloak of guidance) from the master Abū 'Abd al-Raḥmān Sulamī (d. 412/1021).[21] This meeting must have taken place just before this master's death, for Abū Sa'īd had only another two years to continue with Abū'l-Faḍl before the latter died. When he returned to Abū'l-Faḍl, the latter told him that his work was finished, sending him back to Mayhana to begin guiding disciples.

However, although Abū Sa'īd was now authorized to initiate disciples, he was destined to go much further in his spiritual development, so that he observed assiduously all the strictures of the religious law *(Sharī'a),* as well as carrying on the starkest ascetic practice and mortification, even suspending himself upside down in a well, until, as he later put it to his son Abū Ṭāhir:

> Blood ran from my eyes, and I lost consciousness of myself. Then things changed, and it became clear that the indescribable rigors which I had undergone and the attainments therefrom were through God's grace, though I had imagined that they had been from myself. . . It had all been imagination.
>
> Now, if you were to say, "I will not undertake this approach," that would be imagination. I mean to say that your not undertaking it would be imagination. Only when you have gone through this process will you have passed beyond imagination. Only by observing the religious law can this imagination be eliminated. Imagination is in religion, where according to the religious law, non-observance is unbelief, whereas observance and consciousness thereof is duality, whereby you and God are distinct . . . You must disappear from in between [God and the act of worship].[22]

---

21. *Ibid.*, p. 6; Fritz Meier, *Abū Sa'īd-i Abū'l-Ḫayr: Wirklichkeit und Legende* (Tehran/Paris/Leiden 1976), p. 45.
22. Ibn Munawwar, *op. cit.*, p. 38.

Abū Sa'īd went on to say that eventually he became annihilated *(fanā')* from consciousness of self, as a light pierced the darkness of his separate existence and the distinction between him and God-as-Agent vanished and "everything was Divinity, vision and grace."[23] The effect of this state he described in these verses:

> Hama jamāl-i tu bīnam, chū dīda bāz kunam;
> Hama tanam dil gardad ki bā tū rāz kunam.
> Harām dāram bā digarān sukhan guftan;
> Kujā ḥadīth-i tu āmad, sukhan dirāz kunam.[24]
>
> *I see all as Your beauty, when I open my eyes;*
> *All my body becomes heart, communing with You.*
> *I regard it forbidden to speak with others;*
> *When talk turns to you, I discourse at length.*

Having attained this state, Abū Sa'īd suddenly found himself an object of profound veneration, with disciples flocking to his door. Awed by his ascetic example, even his dissolute neighbors were moved to mend their ways, giving up drinking and taking to the path of piety. Popular veneration of the master came to exceed all reasonable limits, for, as Abū Sa'īd recollected,

> If someone picked up a melon rind which I happened to have dropped, he could sell it for twenty dinars; and one day, as I chanced to be riding a mule who deposited its droppings, people rushed over to rub them into their scalps and faces.
>
> God showed me that this situation was none of my doing. A voice called out from the mosque, quoting the Koranic verse: "Has your Lord not sufficed you?" [Koran XLI: 53] A light illumined my breast and more veils lifted. Everyone who had respected me came to reject me, to the point where they went to the Qāḍī [the religious judge], accusing me of irreligion. They swore that whatever ground this man trod was cursed and nothing would grow thereon. Things reached the point where one day when I was sitting in a mosque, women came out on the roof and threw filth down on my head. The voice within me came saying, "As long as this madman is in our mosque, we cannot pray!" Then I recited these verses:

---

23. *Ibid.*
24. *Ibid.*, p. 39.

Tā shīr būdam, shikār-i man būd palang;
Pirūz būdam ba har-chi kardam āhang.
Tā ʻishq-i turā ba-bar dar āwardam tang,
Az bīsha burūn kard ma-rā rūbah-i lang.

When I was a lion, panther was my prey;
I caught everything which I hunted.
When I came to embrace tightly love for You,
A lame fox drove me from my den.[25]

The result of all this was that a state of contraction befell Abū Saʻīd. He sought guidance from the Koran, which responded with the verse: "We try you with ill and good in affliction, and to Us you return" [Koran XXI 35]. Abū Saʻīd replied, "Everything we undergo on Your path is trial, be it good or ill." Then he told his listeners, "Thereafter I was no longer in between. Everything became His grace." He then recited this couplet:

Imrūz ba har ḥālī Baghdād Bukhārā-st;
Kujā Mīr-i Khurāsān ast pīrūzī ānjā'st.

Whatever today brings, Baghdad in Bukhārā—
Wherever Khurāsān's Prince is, Triumph is there.[26]

This clever couplet—whether it be Abū Saʻīd's own or an eulogistic fragment from Rudakī or another court poet adapted to a spiritual context—allows the listener to draw his own conclusion as to who is the "Prince of Khurāsān." Where a courtier would have envisioned him as the reigning Sāmānid Amir or Ghaznavid Sultan, the average Muslim or Sufi would see him as God or the Prophet. In this modest—or as the Sufis would say, "spiritually sly" *(rindāna)* way—Abū Saʻīd described his attainment of the state of possessing "nothing under this robe but God." Because he was sober, that is, non-ecstatic, at the time, he would not express this state in antinomian terms, but in literal, factual terms, which had to be put indirectly, so as not to be misconstrued as pompous or arrogant.

The certification which Abū Saʻīd received from Sulamī was to all intents and purposes that which the *pīr-i ṣuḥbat* (training master) confers when the disciple has completed his training. It appears that

---

25. *Ibid.*
26. *Ibid.*, pp. 39-40.

Abū'l-Faḍl did not want to break the connection with Abū Sa'īd, even when the latter was ready to undertake spiritual guidance on his own. Indeed, Abū Sa'īd made a practice of visiting Abū'l-Faḍl's tomb after his death, as he had consulted his *khānaqāh* while he was alive. In reference to these visits to the tomb, Abū Sa'īd explicitly stated that they were for the purpose of release from contraction *(qabḍ).*[27]

After Abū'l-Faḍl's death, Abū Sa'īd sought out the master Abū'l-'Abbās Aḥmad b. Muḥammad Qaṣṣāb in the Khurāsānian town of Āmul, near Nasā in present-day Turkmenistan. Qaṣṣāb acknowledged Abū Sa'īd's status when he indicated his readiness to assume mastership. According to the *Asrār al-tawḥīd,* the congregants for the collective morning prayer held by Qaṣṣāb

> ...saw Shaykh Bū'l-'Abbās wearing Shaykh Bū Sa'īd's robe and vice versa. They were all astonished, wondering what this signified. Shaykh Bū'l-'Abbās said, "Indeed, last night there were intimations as to what this youth of Mayhana is to receive. May he be blessed!" Thereupon he turned to our Master and said, "Return to Mayhana and wait for a few days, when this sign will be placed upon the door of your house." As our Master tells it, "By his indication I came home, graced with a hundred thousand revelations and investitures; disciples gathered round, and work began." Scarcely had our Master returned to Mayhana than Bū'l-'Abbās back in Āmul died.[28]

So it seemed if he had stayed alive solely to complete the work of Abū'l-Faḍl, who had brought Abū Sa'īd to perfection, while the task of granting him the authority to give spiritual guidance to others lay with Sulamī and Qaṣṣāb.

According to 'Aṭṭār, Qaṣṣāb told Abū Sa'īd, "Mystical intimations *(ishārāt)* and devotion *('ibādat)* are your destiny,"[29] thus indicating in reverse the two phases of Abū Sa'īd's life. On receiving the *khirqa-yi tabarruk* (cloak of blessing) from this master,[30] Abū Sa'īd

---

27. Concerning Abū Sa'īd's visitation of Abū'l-Faḍl's tomb for release from contraction, cf. Ibn Munawwar, *op. cit.*, p. 10.
28. Concerning the incident of the master Qaṣṣāb wearing his disciple Abū Sa'īd's robe, see *ibid.*, p. 8.
29. 'Aṭṭār, *Tadhkirat al-awliyā'*, edited by M. Este'lami (Tehran 1981), p. 641.
30. Ibn Munawwar, *op. cit.*, p. 54.

passed the threshold between his time of ascetic rigor and the era of his life's work of not only guiding disciples through grace and intimations, but subtly influencing even those outsiders who were guiding the course of policy in that age, the era of Seljuk rule, from Niẓām al-Mulk and the Seljuk sultan who had preceded his time of power, Ṭughrïl Beg (reg. 429/1037–455/1063), to the leaders of the warring factions of Nīshāpūr: the Shāfi'ites and Ḥanafites amongst the Sunnis, the Karrāmites, and the Shi'ites.

Abū Sa'īd never traveled out of his home region, the main journeys having been to Merv for his studies, to Āmul to serve Qaṣṣāb, and to Nīshāpūr, where he followed his profession of teaching Shāfi'ite *ḥadith* and established his *Khānaqāh* to guide disciples and receive those who sought solace and inspiration from him. His decision not to undertake the pilgrimage to Mecca is connected with his one other noteworthy journey, to the town of Kharaqān, where the famous master Abū'l-Ḥasan Kharaqānī (d. 426/1034) told him that he would himself be the Ka'ba around which the devoted would circumambulate.[31] When he died in 440/1049, he was buried in Mayhana where his tomb came to serve as a site of pilgrimage (to be destroyed by the Ghuzz Turks in 1074 and rebuilt in the 14th century by the Īkhānid ruler Ghāzān Khān, himself a devoted visitant).

III. SPIRITUALITY IN VERSE: ABŪ SA'ĪD'S USE OF POETRY

Few Sufi masters have been as widely quoted as Abū Sa'īd, who set a standard of instruction not only through pungent aphoristic statements, but through verse as well. This represents the first of the three important areas in which he influenced the course of development of Sufism. Since no work—not even the collection of poetry ascribed to him—can be reliably attributed to Abū Sa'īd, Shafī'ī-Kadkanī callS him the Socrates of Sufi doctrine, being cited and quoted all over as the seminal authority, yet leaving no text to which he might have applied his pen.[32]

31. Concerning Kharaqānī telling Abū Sa'īd that he would be the Ka'ba around which others would circumambulate, *cf.* Ibn Munawwar, *op. cit.*, p. 149; Hujwīrī, *Kashf al-maḥjūb*, ed. V.A. Zhukovskii (Reprinted, Leningrad 1926), p. 204.

The judgment that Abū Sa'īd did not create most of the poetry ascribed to him goes back to a remark quoted in the earliest biography, the *Ḥālāt wa sukhanān:* "I have never composed a poem myself. What you hear from my tongue comes from able men *(mardān-i saturg),* the most part from Abū'l-Qāsim Bishr."[33] This statement seems as much a reflection of his modesty and chivalrous altruism *(ithār, jawānmardī:* 'self-effacement and putting of others' interests before one's own') and identification with this early master who instilled the presence of the God in him, than any representation of literal truth. In fact, the later biographer, Ibn Munawwar, in the same context in the *Asrār al-tawḥīd* omits this quotation; the author apparently considered it specious, or at best, misleading, and deemed it better to replace it with a profounder observation: "There are some who think that these [verses] which fall from the Master's tongue are composed by him, but this is not so, for he is so drowned in God that he has no capacity to speak on his own."[34]

This quotation would seem to indicate his complete selflessness in attributing the source of his poetry (as, indeed, all his actions, in accordance with the Sufi conception of annihilation of self) to God. To take the implication to its logical conclusion, what Ibn Munawwar implies is nothing less than that Abū Sa'īd's poetry was to the speaker thereof as the verses of the Koran were to the Prophet.

Nonetheless, Ibn Munawwar does go on to point out two bits of verse which were not divinely inspired but actually composed by Abū Sa'īd the man. The first is a couplet penned by Abū Sa'īd on the back of a note from a dervish known, for his humility, by the nickname of 'Bu Ḥamza al-Turāb' ('Earthy' Abū Ḥamza). The note, jotted on a scrap of paper, was an expression of his submission to the master, declaring that he was earth under the feet of Abū Sa'īd, who replied:

---

32. Ibn Munawwar (ed. Shafī'ī-Kadkanī), p. xlvi.

33. Cited by Y.E. Bertel's, *Taṣawwuf wa adabiyyāt-i taṣawwuf,* Persian translation by Sīrūs Īzadī, (Tehran 1977), p. 61, fn 40. To Bertel's *(ibid.)* this quotation demonstrates that "Abū Sa'īd cannot be considered as the author of the most ancient poetry of Sufism."

34. Ibn Munawwar, *op. cit.*, p. 218.

Gar khāk shudī, khāk-i tu-rā khāk shudam;
Chūn khāk-i tu-rā khāk shudam, pāk shudam.

If you've become earth, I've become earth for your earth;
When I became earth for your earth, I've become purged.[35]

Abū Sa'īd's humility before such a simple dervish may also be viewed as characteristic of a spiritual attitude stemming from the *jawānmardī* tradition of spiritual chivalry (on which, see below, pp. 131-3). The second bit of poetry which Ibn Munawwar attributes to the person of Abū Sa'īd is following quatrain:

Jānā ba zamīn-i Khāwarān khārī nīst
K'ash bā man u rūzagār-i man kārī nīst;
Bā luṭf u nawāzish-i jamāl-i tu marā
Dar dādan-i ṣad hizār jān 'āri nīst.

There is no thorn, O Soul, in the land of the Khāwarān
That has not dug into me and my affairs;
While I have the grace and caress of Your beauty
I am not ashamed to offer up a hundred thousand lives.

Ibn Munawwar concludes that whatever else besides these lines Abū Sa'īd produced in poetry was learned from "the [Sufi] masters *(pīrān).*"[36] This seems to be a nod to the view expressed in the *Ḥālāt,* contradicting the foregoing claim of Divine inspiration quoted by Ibn Munawwar. However, Sa'īd Nafīsī cites several other passages in the *Asrār* which indicate Abū Sa'īd's use of poetry in his teaching, contending that these prove the master himself to be the author of this verse. He also provides the testimony of later Sufi authorities, such as 'Aṭṭār, Hujwīrī, 'Ayn al-Quḍāt Hamadānī, Shāh Ni'matullāh, and Khwāja Aḥrār, all of whom quote and/or comment on poems which they specifically ascribe to him.[37]

35. Bertel's, *op. cit.,* pp. 59-60, quoting Ibn Abī Sa'īd Sa'd, *ibid.,* p. 75; Ibn Munawwar, *op. cit.,* p. 218.
36. *Ibid.*
37. Sa'īd Nafīsī, *Sukhanān-i manẓūm-i Abū Sa'īd Abī'l-Khayr* (Tehran: Sanā'ī, n.d.), pp. 35-63.

Abū Sa'īd apparently spoke poetry spontaneously, both in ecstasy and by way of conscious instruction, and such verses were certainly noted down by disciples, even as Rūmī's *Diwān* was recorded, or Anṣārī's *Ṣad maydān.*[38] An example of this is the quatrain which Abū Sa'īd spoke to the nurse of Īshī Nīlī, a pious woman of a noble family of Nīshāpūr, when she had been despatched to hear Abū Sa'īd speak at his gathering. Commissioned to report what she heard, she confessed to Abū Sa'īd that she could not remember what he had said, to be able to communicate it to her mistress. Abū Sa'īd then told her this quatrain to sum up the content of his message, in such a way that it would appeal to her state:

Man dāngī-yi sīm[39] dāshtam ḥabba'ī kam;
Du kūza-yi may kharīda-am, pāra'i kam.
Bar barbaṭ-i man na zīr mānd'ast u na bam;
Tā kay gū'ī qalandarī u gham u gham?

I had a sliver sixthpence—well, a fraction less;
I bought two jugs of wine—well, a little less.
Neither tenor nor bass remains upon my lute:
How long will you claim to be a 'qalandar' *and still complain?*[40]

Spiritually speaking, the point of the poem was to take the lady to a higher state, detaching her further from consciousness of 'self'. When she heard the poem, as relayed by the nurse, she fell ill and was ultimately healed (according to the biographer, by the grace of the Master). Hence, such quatrains were used not for their literal content, but for the inner meaning they might convey to whatever recipient for whom they were intended. For literary historians, however, the more mundane issues of authorship still present a problem: thus, Sa'īd Nafīsī includes this quatrain among the five hundred or so that he believes to have been composed by Abū Sa'īd,[41] while Meier is adamant that it pre-dates the Master's time.[42]

---

38. Cf. A.G. Ravān Farhādī's essay in this volume. —ED.
39. In some MSS the line reads *dangī ū nīm* (a measure and a half), which is more obscure in meaning. Bertel's *(op. cit,* p. 59) quotes this version which Ṣafā's edition of Ibn Munawwar *(op. cit.,* p. 82) cites as well; Shafī'ī-Kadkanī's edition (p. 83), however, has *dangī-yi ū nīm.*
40. Ibn Munawwar, *op. cit.*, p. 82.
41. Nafīsī, *op. cit.*, p. 58, quatrain no. 397.

Another instance of the use of poetry to teach on different levels of consciousness is that of Qāḍī Ṣā'id, a jurist who was initially a stern critic of Abū Sa'īd. He was, in fact, the local leader of the adherents to the Ḥanafī school of Sunni jurisprudence. In the course of taking the sanctimonious cleric down a peg or two, the Master said that one could not be impressed by the Qāḍī's claims, because true knowledge and spiritual authority lay with the *'ayyāriyya*, men of true spiritual detachment. He gave the example of Ḥusayn ibn Manṣūr Ḥallāj (d. 309/922), in whose "time there was no one with equal knowledge, east or west." Ḥallāj was not interested in impressing others or gaining their respect, remarked Abū Sa'īd, concluding, "One should be humble before the *ayyār*s, not before hollow men." Then he told the cantor *(qawwāl)* to sing the following quatrain:

Dar maydān ā bā sipar tarkash bāsh;
Sar-i hīch ba-khwūd makish; ba mā sarkash bāsh.
Gū khwāh zamāna āb khwāh ātash bāsh;
Tū shād ba-zī u dar miyāna khwash bāsh.

Enter the arena, armed with shield and quiver;
Ascribe nothing to yourself; abandon all with us.
Let time bring what it will, hell or high water
Live joyfully, delighting in whatever comes your way.[43]

These words of sturdy advice came after a long period of exposure to the Sufism of Abū Sa'īd on the part of Qāḍī Ṣā'id, preparing him to sit in a session of spiritual audition (*samā'*) of which the preamble was the singing of this quatrain. The disciples who had gathered for *samā'* fell into an ecstatic state, which affected the Qāḍī and his companions as well, their hearts having become predisposed to its spiritual influence. The following day Qāḍī Ṣā'id and his followers came to greet the master and offer their repentance. The Qāḍī was positively effusive in his new-found enthusiasm, being moved to praise the "beauty of the moon of Nīshāpūr." At this point Abū Sa'īd called on his cantor to sing another quatrain, which was clearly composed extempore, for it served to answer the Qāḍī's declaration,

42. Meier, *op. cit.*, p. 496.
43. Ibn Munawwar, *op. cit.*, p. 81.

indicating through the master's *firāsat* (heart-discernment)[44] his awareness that the former's inward state was akin to his own, thus dispelling any alienation which Qāḍī Sā'id might have felt towards him.

> Guftī ki manam mah-i Nayshābūr-sarā;
> Ay mah-i Nayshābūr, Nayshābūr tu-rā
> Ān-i tu tu-rā w'ān-i mā nīz tu-rā;
> Ba mā banagū'ī kī khuṣūmat zi chirā.
>
> *You said that "I am the moon of Nīshāpūr town."*
> *O Moon of Nīshāpūr, Nīshāpūr all is yours.*
> *What is yours is yours, and what is ours is also yours;*
> *But won't you tell us: whence this hostility?*[45]

Ibn Munawwar then tells us: "When this verse had been uttered by the Master, the Qāḍī fell at the Master's feet, weeping and begging forgiveness. All his company abandoned their bias, contention and prejudice and arose with gladdened hearts. Thenceforth, no one in Nīshāpūr had the temerity to speak ill of the Sufis."[46]

Given his father's Sufi inclinations, Abū Sa'īd was actively engaged from his earliest years in the mystical tradition. After school he would go to serve and take training from the master Abū'l-Qāsim Bishr Yāsīn to whom he had been introduced by his father. Besides laying the groundwork Abū Sa'īd's later enthusiasm for the Sufi path, Bishr set an example for this pupil in instruction of spiritual subtleties throught the medium of symbolic poetry. This productive use of of poetry was to become a hallmark of Abū Sa'īd's social intercoursewith disciples and visiting outsiders alike. Bertel's noted that in the Sufi gatherings of Abū Sa'īd's day

> most of the people who attended were working folk and city-dwellers of small means. Thus, poems and songs needed to be selected which would have meaning for them and be in accord with their taste and conventions... In his instructive talks Abū Sa'īd

44. Abū Sa'īd's prominence as a possessor of *firāsat* is attested in Māyil Harāwī's introduction to Abū'l-Najīb Suhrawardī's *Adāb al-murīdīn* (p. 20) where the latter states that after years of austerities like those undergone by Abū Sa'īd, he came to possess a *firāsat* "comparable to that of Abū Sa'īd."
45. *Ibid.*, p. 82.
46. *Ibid.*, pp. 82-3.

> Abī'l-Khayr made extensive use of quatrains, a poetic form which had a popular origin and in this period had yet to enter the circles of the elect. Moreover, what is particularly interesting is that Abū Sa'īd did not himself create these quatrains, but used ready-made ones, most of which may be said to have had a popular origin.[47]

Besides the spiritual direction which Bishr gave Abū Sa'īd, he also put him squarely in the Khurāsānian tradition of using poetry in the New Persian *(darī)* court language, the *lingua franca* of the regions of the northeast in the pre-Islamic Sāsānian empire and the Iranic regions of Transoxiana beyond, namely, Soghdiana, Khwārazm and Farghāna, where Persian literature first arose and where it was confined until the end of the fourth/tenth century,[48] the period of Abū Sa'īd. The more exalted forms of the popular poetry in Khurāsān were cultivated by the *dihqāns,* the class of petty aristocratic village farmers which had survived from the pre-Islamic era in the region, which was culturally less affected by the impositions of religious orthodoxy, whether Mazdean (Zoroastrian), with its medium of the Pahlavi language, or Islam, with its medium of Arabic.[49]

Most of the themes of Sufi poetry were already found in the *darī* verse of the local courts, notably those of the Sāmānid rulers (whose reign: 261/875–395/1005 in Khurāsān and Transoxiana ended halfway through Abū Sa'īd's life); these themes in turn enjoyed wide circulation among 'the people of the streets and the marketplace' *(kūcha u bāzār*—as the Persians say), that is, in the folk traditions of the region. Such themes included the celebration of wine and intoxication,[50] philosophical discourse,[51] moral and ethical counsel *(andarz),*[52] a sense of transience of the things of this world,[53] all from the pre-Islamic Persian tradition, and celebration of the beauty of the beloved and mourning of the beloved's absence, adapted from

---

47. Bertel's, *op. cit.,* p. 54.
48. G. Lazard, "The Rise of the New Persian Language," in *The Cambridge History of Iran,* Vol. 4: *From the Arab Invasion to the Seljuqs,* ed. Richard N. Frye, (Cambridge 1975), p. 608.
49. G. Lazard, "Pahlavi, Pârsi, Dari: Les Langues de l'Iran d'apres Ibn al-Muqaffa'," in C. E. Bosworth (ed.), *Iran and Islam,* (Edinburgh,1971), *passim.*
50. G. Lazard, in *The Cambridge History of Iran,* p. 621.
51. *Ibid.*, p. 618.
52. *Ibid.*, p. 615.
53. *Ibid.*

the pre-Islamic Arabic poetic tradition *(Jāhiliyya).*[54]

Bertel's compares the use of Arabic poetry inherited from the Sufis of Iraq to the growing use of Persian in Abū Sa'īd's time, saying that the former was "brilliant but cold," while the latter was "much closer to the expressions of the people at large," being the medium of song *(tarāna)* and communicating "warmth, sincerity and familiarity."[55] An important property of the "song-like quality" of such Sufi poetry was its "intoxicating effect. ...conducive to stimulating ecstasy."[56] "Without question," Bertel's concludes, "the formal literary structure and development of poetic metaphor of the sufi *ghazal* had fully developed by the fifth [eleventh] century [Abū Sa'īd's era]."[57]

The type of poetry which Abū Sa'īd learned from Bishr as a medium of disciplinary instruction and communication of mystical states was the popular and quintessentially Persian *rubā'ī* (quatrain) and *dū-baytī* (double couplet).[58] An example of Abū Sa'īd's use of this popular quatrain form comes in the account of his encounter with a young slave-girl, who was plucking a zither *(duray)* at the slave-market in Nīshāpūr and singing this poem:

> Imrūz dar in shahr chu man yārī nay,
> Awarda ba bazār o kharīdārī nay.
> Ān kas ki kharīdār ba durāyam nay,
> W'ān kas ki ba durāy kharīdāram nay.

> *Today there's no beloved in this city like me,*
> *Brought to sell in the market and finding no buyer.*
> *Whoever would buy me cares naught for my zither,*
> *Yet one who cares for it will not be my buyer.*[59]

---

54. *Ibid.,* p. 621.
55. Bertel's, *op. cit.,* p. 76
56. *Ibid.*
57. *Ibid.*
58. L. P. Elwell-Sutton, "The Ruba'ī in Early Persian Literature,"*The Cambridge History of Iran,* vol. 4, p. 633.
59. Bertel's, *op. cit.*, p. 59-60, citing Ibn Abī Sa'īd Sā'd, *op. cit.*, p. 75.

Bertel's comments:

> There is no question that this quatrain represents an improvised form that Iranians and Tajiksto this very day use to express their sentiments. Moreover, there is no difference between the conventional (literary) quatrain and this *tarāna* (popular song), the quatrain employed by Abū Sa'īd in his instructional talks also being of the popular variety.[60]

Although Elwell-Sutton maintains that the quatrain as a form was not "long enough for the sustained ecstasy of mystical inspiration," such that "even mystics like Abū Sa'īd b. Abī'l-Khayr and Khwāja 'Abdullāh Anṣārī, whose poetic output was confined almost exclusively to the *rubā'ī,* used it rather to emphasize and illustrate points already elaborated in prose sermons and prayers," the fact is that much of the verse employed by Abū Sa'īd and Bishr served as a haiku-like encapsulation of a mystical state. An example of this is the quatrain (cited below, p. 103) which Bishr taught Abū Sa'īd as a form of meditation, or the following:

> Hayhāt ki bāz būyi may mīshinawam:
> Āwāzahā'ī u hū-u-hay mīshinawam.
> Az gūsh-i dilam sirr-i ilāhī har dam
> Ḥaqq mīgūyad valī zi nay mīshinawam.[61]
>
> *O, glory! I scent the aroma of wine again!*
> *I hear the songs and the Sufis' 'Hū!' and 'Ḥayy!'*
> *Each moment God speaks through my heart's ear;*
> *Divine mysteries, but I hear them from the reedpipe.*

Many of Abū Sa'īd's poems tread a middle path between this type of poem inspired by a mystical state and the more aphoristic type of *rubā'ī,* such as the following:

> Mā kushta-yi 'ishqīm u jahān maslakh-i mā'st;
> Mā bīkhwur u khwābīm u jahān maṭbakh-i mā'st.
> Mā-rā nabuwad hawā-yi firdāws az ānk
> Ṣad martaba bālātar az ān dūzakh-i mā'st.[62]

---

60. *Ibid.*
61. Nafīsī, *op. cit.*, p. 66, quatrain no. 455.
62. Elwell-Sutton, *op. cit.*, p. 645.

Through love we're slain, the world's our slaughter-house;
We've no food nor sleep, the world's our cookhouse.
We've no desire for paradise, because
Our hell's a hundred times loftier than that.

This quatrain is among those which Elwell-Sutton cites as typical of the genre ascribed to Abū Sa'īd and for which he implies that he would like to accept his authorship, saying:

> Even if the *rubā'īyāt* are not by Abū Sa'īd himself, they were learnt by him from his teachers, and have certainly been attached to his name from a very early date. Nafīsī notes that of the 726 complete *rubā'īyāt* in his edition, 172 are also attributed to other poets, notably 'Umar Khayyām (55)... This still leaves well over five hundred for whom no other author has ever been suggested. This is not conclusive evidence of Abū Sa'īd's authorship, but it at least leaves it open. What can certainly be stated without qualification is that the *rubā'īyāt* attributed to Abū Sa'īd constitute the first major corpus of Sufi quatrains, and indeed one of the earliest collections of Persian Sufi verse in any form.[63]

Although the quatrain is a purely Persian form, brought from popular to literary use in Khurāsān in Abū Sa'īd's era as part of the renascence and reshaping of Persian literature in that time and region,[64] Sa'īd Nafīsī indicates that there is every evidence that Abū Sa'īd was the one to utilize it in a specifically Sufi context, saying:

> It is evident that he [Abū Sa'īd] was the first person amongst the Persian Sufi masters to express his views and doctrines in Persian [albeit occasionally Arabic] poetry, whereby he must be considered the forerunner of Sanā'ī, 'Aṭṭār, and [Rūmī]; and there is even reason to believe that he has preceded [Khayyām] in the composition of the quatrain in the Persian language.[65]

---

63. *Ibid.*
64. Lazard, *op. cit.*, p. 612.
65. Nafīsī, *op. cit.*, p. 6. There is no difficulty, of course, in distinguishing Khayyām's pen from Abū Sa'īd's, for the former's world-weary cynicism and hedonistic negativism run completely counter to the positive embracing of trials indicated, for example, in the last quatrain quoted above. Where Khayyām's world is all he had in hand before plunging into the abyss, Abū Sa'īd's world is merely the proving ground, the prelude, a stage to be sloughed off when one is ready, for the richness of the Real realm to be attained, that of Divine Unity.

Besides Abū Sa'īd's ecstatic quatrains 'inspired by mystical states', there are two other principal varieties also cast in this positive Sufi mould, these being: 1) purely didactic/instructive and 2) devotional verse.

1. Instructive verse has an ancient Iranian tradition behind it, deriving in spirit from the Sāsānian 'tract on ethical counsel' *(andarz-nāma),* which was continued in the Islamic era in treatises such as the *Qabūs-nāma*, a royal book of advice on social conduct and political policy from Khurāsān's eastern neighbor of Ṭabaristān (modern-day Mazāndarān) composed during Abū Sa'īd's lifetime.[66] "Counsel-giving verse can be traced back to the third/ninth century in the earliest preserved fragments of Persian poetry. . . From then onward it flourished without a break."[67] Such didactic counsel—in Abū Sa'īd's case, wherein Sufism is the moral, media and message—is expressed in his own passionate poetic style in this single verse:

Ay bīkhabar az sūkhta u sūkhtanī,
'Ishq āmadanī buwad, na āmūkhtanī![68]

O you who are unaware of those who are burnt up,
or of being burned—
Love is something that comes of its own; it cannot be taught.

The following quatrain is also another example of mystical *andarz:*

Az hastī-yi khwīsh tā pashīmān nashawī,
Sar ḥalqa-yi 'ārifān u mastān nashawī.
Tā dar naẓar-i khalq nagardī kāfir,
Dar madhhab-i 'āshiqān musalmān nashawī.[69]

If you do not come to repent your existence,
You'll never approach the circle of gnostics and drunkards.
Unless in others' eyes you become an infidel,
In the creed of lovers, you'll never be Muslim.

2. A quatrain written in the devotional mode, as a poem of communion with the Beloved, reflects Abū Sa'īd's experience of his fif-

---

66. G. Ḥ Yūsufī, s.v. "Andarz-Nāma,"*Encyclopædia Iranica,* II, pp. 23-4.
67. Dh. Ṣafā, s.v. "Andarz:In New Persian,"*Ibid.,* II, p. 16.
68. Ibn Munawwar, *op. cit.*, p. 54.
69. Nafīsī, *op. cit.*, p. 101, quatrain no. 688.

teen years of the harshest asceticism and the spiritual goal for which it was undergone:

> Sar tā sar-i dāsht-i Khāwarān sangī nīst
> K'az khūn-i dil u dīda bar ān rangī nīst.
> Dar hīch zamīn u hīch farsangī nīst
> K'az dast-i ghamat nishasta diltangī nīst [70]
>
> *Over all the plain of Khāwarān there is no stone*
> *Unstained by blood of heart and eye.*
> *There is not a furlong or a patch of ground*
> *Where yearning's not imbedded out of grief for You.*

The very lines which Bishr commended to Abū Sa'īd as a sort of *dhikr* in Persian, (indicating the closeness of spirit of master and disciple in the process of poetic creation, this poem being based on the Prophetic Tradition: "I cannot number the praise due to You") also appear in the quatrain form in a devotional mode to express communion with God:

> Bī-tū, jānā, qarār natwānam kard;
> iḥsān-i tu-rā shumār natwānam kard.
> Gar bar tan-i man zafān shawad har mū'ī,
> Yak shukr-i tu az hizār natwānam kard.[71]
>
> *Without You, O Soul, I cannot rest;*
> *Your goodness towards me I can never reckon.*
> *Though every hair on my body turned into a tongue,*
> *I could not render a thousandth part of the thanks due you.*

Following Bishr's inspiration, Abū Sa'īd set about integrating poetry into both his speeches and the litanies of his gatherings. Bertel's attributes this process, which in later centuries infiltrated and characterized Persianate Sufi gatherings from the Nile to the Oxus, to the inspiration of the example set by Abū Sa'īd, saying:

> Apparently the convention of organizing meetings with poetry was initiated by Abū Sa'īd in Khurāsān, whence it spread throughout Iran. On the one hand, masters sought in particular to encapsulate the most difficult material of their doctrine in verse, to make

---

70. Riḍā Qulīkhān Hidāyat, *Majma' al-fuṣaḥā'* (Tehran 1336 A.Hsh./1957), I, p. 143.
71. Ibn Munawwar, *op. cit.*, p. 19.

> comprehension of it easier for their listeners, and at the same time to assist in the inculcation of concepts, aided by the accompaniment of improvised melodies. On the other hand, the singing of poems by specialized cantors *(qawwāl)* facilitated the attainment of ecstatic mystical states *(ḥāl)* which is the principal aim of congregational *dhikr* (invocation).[72]

This brings us to the second of the three main foci of this study: Abū Sa'īd's contribution to the organization of the *Khānaqāh* and the nature of its activities, notably the *majlis* ('meeting' or 'gathering') of *dhikr* and *samā'* (spiritual audition). However, in order to provide a historical backdrop for our discussion of the *Khānaqāh* institution in early Khurāsān, a study of some of the socio-religious currents and the political climate is in order here, which we take up in the following section .

IV. BETWEEN KHURĀSĀN AND BAGHDAD: ABŪ SA'ĪD'S SUFISM IN ITS SOCIO-RELIGIOUS CONTEXT

Due to his support—indeed, promotion—of ecstatic expression as part and parcel of Sufi practice, Abū Sa'īd met with vigorous opposition on the part of those Sufis who were essentially concerned with religious convention and the most sober subordination of Sufism to the strictures of the *Sharī'a,* among the most prominent of whom were Abū'l-Qāsim Qushayrī, with whom he shared the same spiritual lineage leading back to Abū Naṣr Sarrāj Ṭūsī (d. 378/988), author of the influential *Kitāb al-Luma' fi'l-taṣawwuf* and master of both Abū Sa'īd's master, Abū'l-Faḍl Muḥammad b. Ḥasan Sarakhsī, and Qushayrī's own master, the prolific chronicler of Sufi theory and practice, Abū 'Abd al-Raḥmān Sulamī.

It is, indeed, because of his advocacy of ecstatic expression that this pre-eminent possessor of a "joyful heart" and "representative of expansion," in Meier's felicitous terms,[73] is brought forward as one of the prime proofs of the 'intoxicated' nature of the Sufism of the so-called School of Khurāsān in contrast to the purported 'sobriety'

---

72. Bertel's, *op. cit.*, pp. 58-60.
73. Meier, *op. cit.,* p. 134, 192.

of the School of Baghdad. This view, however, is problematic, because it fails to take into account the earlier tradition of Khurāsān, initiated by Ibrāhim ibn Adham (d. ca. 161/778), not to speak of the intoxicated expressions of such 'Baghdadis' as Nūrī,[74] Shiblī and Ḥallāj.[75]

While the distinction between these two 'trends'—perhaps a more appropriate denomination than 'schools'—goes back to a member of the generation succeeding Abū Sa'īd's, 'Ali ibn 'Uthmān Jullābī Ḥujwīrī (d. 463/1071), in his pioneering Persian text, the *Kashf al-maḥjūb,*[76] it is our contention that the matter of "intoxication versus sobriety" or 'ecstasy *vis-a-vis* ascetic rigor' or 'expansion as opposed to contraction' is not a fair criterion for classifying broad Sufi movements, since the two conditions are mutually dependent in any individual mystic, and while certain Sufis may appear to be dominated by one or the other in their expressions, there are perhaps as many exceptions to Hujwīrī's rule as there are substantiations. For example, while Abū'l-Qāsim Junayd (d. 298/910), the most celebrated advocate of 'sobriety' over 'intoxication' as the higher state,[77] is cited as the Baghdadian par excellence, his most famous disciples are set to embarrass his stately position utterly: those prototypical ecstatics whom Ruzbihān celebrates poetically in his *Sharḥ-i shaṭḥiyyāt,* rhetorically asking, "Where is Shiblī's moaning cry?. . . Where is Nūrī's haunting song?. . . Where is the

74. Although Nūrī, of course, came of a Khurāsānian background (cf. A. Schimmel's study in this volume)

75. In fact, Schimmel makes a point of the ascetic nature of the early Sufism in Khurāsān, beginning with Ibrahīm ibn Adham (d. 161/778): "The ascetics of Marv and [Khurāsānian] Tālaqān' became almost proverbial. Among them we may mention Shaqiq Balkhi (d. 809) along with the former highway robber Fuzail b. Iyad. There is also Abū Turab Nakhshabi, the master of *tawakkul*, who paid his complete trust in God with his life. Wandering alone and without provisions in the desert, he was devoured by lions (849). These men and their disciples practised perfect poverty and trust in God, following the injunctions of the religious law even more strictly than the rank and file of the Muslims. Due to their absolute submission to God, they implanted some of the basic tenets of Sufism into the hearts of the following generations." Annemarie Schimmel, "The Ornament of the Saints," *Iranian Studies,* vol. 7 (1974), p. 92.

76. Concerning the various ramifications of the schools of Khurāsān and Baghdad, cf. Ḥujwīrī, *op. cit.*, p. 154.

77. Concerning Junayd on sobriety, *cf. ibid.*

spurting blood of Ḥusayn Manṣūr [Ḥallāj] in 'I am the Truth'"*[Anā'l-ḥaqq]?*"[78]—to cite but a few of these 'sober' Baghdadians!

Thus, while granting the usefulness of a position which makes a fruitful distinction between the trends of Baghdad and Khurāsān, as Trimingham productively does,[79] perhaps one might take a different cue from Trimingham, concerning the move towards what he calls "a distinctively Persian Sufism"[80] in the twelfth century, the transitional period being Abū Sa'īd's eleventh century. The ground for differentiation between the two trends would thus be changed: namely, from a distinction resting on spiritual-temperamental criteria (intoxication vs. sobriety, etc.) to one couched in socio-cultural terms. The Khurāsānian trend was more 'Persian' in the sense that it came to be expressed more and more in the Persian language, although it could also be reasonably argued that the Baghdadians were, culturally speaking, just as Persianate as the Khurāsānians. After all, the 'Abbasid caliphate had been established on Sāsānian royal lines, reinforced by native Khurāsānian Persian vizirs, from the Barmakids of Balkh in the early days, to Khwāja Niẓām al-Mulk in Seljuk times. The majority of the influential Sufis of Baghdad, a city with a Persian name, were also Persians, notably the likes of Junayd, whose family hailed from Nahavand, and Ḥallāj, a native of Fars.[81] What distinguishes the Khurāsānian Sufis from their Baghdadi brethren is neither their purported 'intoxication' versus the latter's 'sobriety', but the different *nature* of their mutual Persianate character. Socio-politically, Baghdad represented a continuation of the authoritarian tradition of Ctesiphon, seat of the Sāsānian Shahs with an etiquette *(adab)* based on courtly behavior, hierarchy, command and obedience, whereas Khurāsān was a region which had constituted the marches of the Sāsānian empire, and after the coming of Islam, had served as the seedbed for revolt against both

---

78. Ruzbihān Baqlī Shīrāzī, *Sharḥ-i shaṭḥiyyāt,* ed. Henry Corbin, (Tehran 1981), pp. 214-15.
79. J.S.Trimingham, *The Sufi Orders in Islam,* (Oxford 1971), pp. 51-52.
80. *Ibid.*, p. 53.
81. Not to speak of those later founders of the important Sufi Orders, 'Abd al-Qādir Jīlānī (d. 561/1166) and Abū Najīb Suhrawardī (d. 563/1168) with his nephew Shihāb al-Dīn Abū Ḥafṣ 'Umar Suhrawardī (d. 632/1234).

Arabic influence and Sāsānian-style despotism, that is, whatever was imposed from the capital in distant Mesopotamia. Here another Persianate tradition held sway, one of a more popular nature, that of an etiquette based on a noble artisanry, known as *jawānmardī* (rendered in Arabic as *futuwwat),* the code of guilds in the cities and of highwaymen in the wilderness (the *'ayyārs),* in a land where farmers tended to be yeomen rather than serfs and where an independent-spirited communitarianism could harbor religious sectarian communities like the Karrāmiyya in Abū Sa'īd's day, along with groups rallying to Ḥallāj or Nāṣir-i Khusraw Qubādiyān (d. 481/1088), the well-known Persian poet and Ismā'īlī activist.

Frye contrasts the character of the two regions in taking into account both their pre-Islamic and their Islamic socio-cultural situations. Compared to the caste-bound rigidity and priestly domination of Sāsānian Mesopotamia, in the Iranian northeast "the society. . . was much more a mercantile, trading one," where the "development of an egalitarian Islamic society...was more propitious," providing for "the well-known 'Iranian Renaissance'...which flourished under the Samanids,"[82] the Perso-Khurāsānian dynasty which ruled the region from 261/875 to 395/1005, half-way through Abū Sa'īd's lifespan.

Although the ruling dynasty changed in the course of Abū Sa'īd's lifetime, there was little change in the socio-cultural situation of Khurāsān or disruption of the life of its major cities and towns. The Persian-speaking bureaucracies and governmental institutions which had developed under the Sāmānid rulers were maintained by their Ghaznavid successors (351/962–431/1040), who, though Turks, continued the Sāmānid policy of patronizing Persian cultural institutions, where it "was perhaps natural that those who became masters of a part of the former Sāsānian empire should look back to the pre-Islamic past and that the victories of the minor dynasties should be seen by some as a preparation for a reconstruction of the glorious past of the Persian empire.[83] As Lambton points out, "in eastern Persia the traditions of Sunni Islam were strong,"[84]

82. R.N. Frye, "The Sāmānids," in *The Cambridge History of Iran,* IV, p. 147.
83. Lambton, *Continuity and Change in Medieval Persia* (London: I.B. Tauris 1988), p. 2.

allowing the more democratic and egalitarian quality of the new religion to meld with the anti-authoritarian tendencies of the society of the region, hand-in-hand with "the development of Persian as a literary language under the Ghaznavids."[85]

Comments by Hermann Landolt about Persian Sufism in general are particularly relevant in the context of defining the unique character of Khurāsānian Sufism. "The Iranian genius," notes Prof. Landolt,

> has often known how to interpret in a mystical way those among the poetic works that detached analysis would see in a very different light, an art which derives from an ancient Sufi practice developed in the *samā'*. One has only to remember the exemplary figure of Abū Sa'īd Abī'l-Khayr… to see that the distinctively Persian Sufism is animated essentially in its practice as well as in its theory by something which must be called the poetic spirit, a spiritual liberty whose corollary is the absence of all rigorous legalism.[86]

This "poetic spirit" in the sense of the employment of verse in the place of, or at least in addition to, conventional religious texts, is, as we have seen, a Khurāsānian innovation, born of the relative freedom of the marches and the greater sense of the Persian language and its lyrical possibilities. Thus, Abū Sa'īd played a key role in one of the defining features of Khurāsānian Sufism, namely, the application of poetry, and generally speaking, poetry of the vernacular, to spiritual instruction.

A second area distinguishing the Sufism of Khurāsān was the blended tradition of *'ayyārī, malāmatī* and *jawānmardī* (see below, part VI); Abū Sa'īd played a crucial role in bringing these uniquely Khurāsānian—if not to say native Persian—traditions together and integrating them into the fabric of Sufism. An anecdote symbolizing the initial divergence of traditions between the Baghdad and Khurāsān schools in this area[87] and their eventual merging concerns

---

84. *Ibid.*
85. *Ibid.*, p. 3. Also cf. Bertel's, *op. cit.*, p. 49.
86. "Two Types of Mystical Thought in Muslim Iran," in *The Muslim World,* vol. 68 (1979), pp. 191-92.
87. See also Sara Sviri's discussion of this anecdote below, pp. 605ff. –ED.

a reputed encounter between Junayd and Abū Ḥafṣ al-Ḥaddād (d. ca. 265/874 - 270/879), a master of Nīshāpūr considered by the preeminent authority, Sulamī, in his *Risāla al-malāmatiyya* to be one of the pioneers of the *malāmatī* trend.

According to the *Kashf al-maḥjūb,* Junayd and al-Ḥaddād had an exchange over the meaning of *jawānmardī/futuwwat,* carried on purportedly in Arabic. Although it is said that Abū Ḥafṣ had no knowledge of Arabic, he dispensed with an interpreter and launched into fluent Arabic for the duration of the discussion; this he was able to do because of his powers of spiritual perspicacity. The fact that the given subject was introduced immediately upon Abū Ḥafṣ presentation to Junayd in his accustomed corner of Baghdad's Shūnīyziyya Mosque indicates the novelty of the concept in the Baghdad mystical milieu, not to speak of Abū Ḥafṣ undoubted reputation as a model adherent of this trend. In fact, the model practitioner in the proper spirit deferred to his interlocutor, Junayd, to offer the first definition.

Junayd stated that in his view *futuwwat* "means not being conscious of one's possession of this trait and not ascribing one's actions to oneself." "What the master has said is fine," responded Abū Ḥafṣ, who then proceeded to present his view, namely, that *jawānmardī* "means being just while not noticing one's justice." At this Junayd excitedly applauded the superiority of Abū Ḥafṣ's definition and called on his disciples and companions to rise and pay tribute to the latter's *jawānmardī.*[88]

A third feature of the school of Khurāsān was the institution of the *Khānaqāh,* its code of conduct and the special character of its community of residents and lay associates (on which, see below, pp. 116ff.) In this area Abū Sa'īd also made a seminal contribution. Malamud, in her study of Abū Najīb Suhrawardī's *Ādāb al-murīdīn,* acknowledges Abū Sa'īd's ten basic rules for *Khānaqāh* life as the precedent for a codification of guidelines for the community associated with such a center, wherein Suhrawardī's book represents the first fully developed text to spell out the code of conduct for such an institution.[89] Hence, the idea of a formalized center for Sufi activity,

---

88. Hujwiri, *op.cit.*, pp.154-55.

representing a community of disciples and lay associates focused on a master, yet conscious of itself as an interactive social body, springs from Khurāsān, nurtured in that more open, egalitarian and diversified society.

The open socio-cultural atmosphere of Nīshāpūr also permitted a ferment of contention to take place among different Islamic schools, such that,

> the Karrāmis played a certain role in Nīshāpūr still in the late eleventh century so that even some internal feud arose between them and the united Ḥanbalite-Shāfi'ite faction of the city, though on other occasions the Ḥanbalis and Shāfi'īs of Nīshāpūr worked against each other.[90]

The Sufi community was not unaffected by such contentions. When the Niẓām al-Mulk came to wield his awesome power as vizier during the reigns of the Seljuk rulers, Ālp-Arslan (455/1063–465/1072) and Malikshāh (467/1072–485/1092), he supported both the Sufis in general and the Shāfi'ite-Ash'arite camp in particular. If his biographer Ibn Munawwar is to be believed, the mighty vizier—possibly the most powerful man in the Islamic world at the time—was very likely a disciple, and certainly a devoted adherent, of Abū Sa'īd, and therefore open to his spiritual and most intimate counsel. In the *Asrār al-tawḥīd* three encounters are recounted between the Master and the Minister beginning from the time of his youth in Nīshāpūr.[91] Before 'his man' came to power, however, the Shāfi'ite-Ash'arite cause was suffering at the hands of the Ḥanafī-favoring Ṭughrïl Beg—who, nevertheless, with all the respect which he had for Abū Sa'īd, left the Sufis, who were strictly Sufis, alone.[92]

---

89. Margaret Malamud., "Sufism in the Twelfth-century Baghdad: The *Ādāb al-murīdīn* of Abū Najīb al-Suhrawardī," unpublished article presented at the 1991 MESA conference, p. 6.
90. Schimmel, *art. cit.*, p. 92.
91. Ibn Munawwar, *op. cit.*, pp. 66-67, 98-99, and 193-196. The most significant encounter involves a ceremonial tying on of a belt, a very Persian custom reminiscent of both the Zoroastrian coming-of-age ritual *(kustī-bastan)* and the *futuwwat* investiture *(kamar-bastan)*. In after-years, at the height of his power, he reflected on this clearly initiatory act on the part of Abū Sa'īd with respect to his person, saying, "Whatever I have gained is through the charisma of Shaykh Bū Sa'īd."

This is not to say that all the Sufis of the region were of the Shāfi'ite-Ash'arite persuasion. Abū Bakr Muḥammad Kalābādhī (d. 380/990), from a village near Bukhara, the Sāmānids' Transoxianan capital, and the author of the most widely read Sufi text of the day, the *Kitab al-ta'arruf li-madhhab ahl al-taṣawwuf,* was a Ḥanafite jurist, and Anṣārī, the celebrated *"Pīr* of Herat," was also persecuted by the very government which had protected Ghazālī as well as Qushayrī "for his strict Ḥanbalīte persuasion."[93]

All of this politico-ideological activity was, of course, very foreign to Abū Sa'īd, who, outside the parameters of pure Sufism, was a supporter of no political cause. Indeed, he eventually abandoned the contentious capital for the peace of his hometown, Mayhana, where he settled down in what he called his *mashhad*[94] ('place of martyrdom', or, where he, according to the Prophetic injunction cited as a byword by the Sufis, "died before he died").[95] In fact, this very title, which he gave to his Mayhana home and *Khānaqāh,* reflects the view of one of his quatrains:

Ghāzī ba-rah-i shahādat andar tak u pū'st,
Ghāfil ki shahīd-i 'ishq fāḍiltar az ū'st.
Dar rūz-i qiyāmat īn ba-dān kay mānad?
K'īn kushta-yi dushman ast u ān kushta-yi dūst.[96]

The holy warrior goes out in search of martyrdom,
Unaware that love's martyr to love is the nobler one.
How could one be as the other on Resurrection Day?
One's been slain by the foe, the other by the Friend.

---

92. "Abū'l-Qāsim al-Qushairī, who was a victim of the persecution of the Ash'arīs, wrote a treatise...defending al-Ash'arī from the heresies with which he had been charged...Alp Arslan, under the influence of Niẓām al-Mulk, who belonged to the Shāfi'i faction of Nīshāpūr, ended the persecution of the Ash'arīs, and gave permission to them to build a second congregational mosque in Nīshāpūr." Lambton, *op. cit.,* p. 238.
93. Schimmel, *op. cit.*, p. 100.
94. Concerning the name *'Mashhad-i muqaddis', cf.* Ibn Munawwar, *op. cit.*, p. 27 et al.
95. Prophetic Tradition quoted in Javad Nurbakhsh, *Traditions of the Prophet,* (New York 1981),I, pp. 66-67.
96. Ḥidāyat, *op. cit.*, p. 143; Nafīsī, *op. cit.* p. 16, quatrain no. 106.

Interestingly enough, the Seljuk ruler, Ṭughrïl Beg (429/1037—455/1063, Ālp-Ārslān's predecessor and founder of the ruling line in Iran), was a zealous proponent of the Ḥanafite school and was, thus, the persecutor of Qushayrī, not on the grounds of the latter's Sufism, but for Qushayrī's committed partisanship of the Shāfi'īte school in Nīshāpūr. Yet, he held such a profound faith in non-sectarian Sufism that he sought out Abū Sa'īd for spiritual guidance on the eve of an important military engagement, the very master of whom Qushayrī so disapproved for theoretically flouting the Shāfi'ite religious legalities which he was so concerned to defend!

As Ibn Munawwar recounts the incident in the *Asrār al-tawḥīd*, the Seljuk brothers, Ṭughrïl and Chaghrï Beg, on the road to the conquest of southern Iran, having advanced southward from Bukhara, had arrived in the Plain of Khāwarān, where they pitched camp in the vicinity of Abīward and Mayhana. People thronged to them, wishing them well in their campaign in Khurāsān because of their despair at the neglectful and corrupt policies of the Ghaznavid Sultan Mas'ūd. The latter sent his challenge to the Seljuks in what was to be the key encounter in their conquest of the region. This was accepted with due alacrity by the brothers, who commended the affair to God in their response.

> Our master was aware of this matter through heart-discernment *(firāsat).* Then Chaghrï and Ṭughrïl, the two brothers together, made a visitation to do homage to our Master, making their greetings and kissing his hand. They remained standing, while the Master, as was his custom, sat with head lowered for a time. When at last he raised his head, he told Chaghrï, "We have bestowed the domain of Iraq upon you." Thereupon they did obeisance and took their leave."[97]

The Seljuk leaders' faith in Abū Sa'īd proved well-founded, for they won the day on the field of Dandānqān in that year of 431/1040, defeating Mas'ūd and bringing to an end the rule of the Ghaznavid dynasty in Khurāsān![98] The Seljuks seem to have kept a special place in their hearts for the master, for some time later, well after

97. Ibn Munawwar, *op. cit.*, p. 170.
98. Lambton, *op. cit.*, p. 5.

they had gained power, another brother, Ibrāhim Ināl, came to pay his respects in Nīshāpūr, a city which was by now the Seljuks' administrative center for Khurāsān. The prince came to visit the Master at his *Khānaqāh* in the neighborhood of 'Adni-kūyān' (the Eden Quarter),[99] where the following episode took place:

> Upon seeing our Master in the lane on the way, he dismounted and bowed his head reverently before the Master, who told him, "Bow lower!" and he did so; but the Master kept on commanding him to bow lower, until the prince's head was almost touching the ground, whereupon the Master said, "That's far enough! *Bismillāh!* Now mount up!" The prince did as he was bidden. Then the Master sent him off and proceeded to the *Khānaqāh.* A Sufi who had just come up asked why the Master had treated Ibrāhīm Ināl thus. Our master turned to the Sufi and told him, "O Sufi, you do not realize that when someone greets me, he is saluting God. My form is merely the focus for man to approach God. I am nothing in between. So, when one pays one's respects, the humbler one is, the closer God permits one to come. Thus, I was simply directing Ibrāhīm Ināl to venerate God all the more, not myself." The Master then explained that, by the same token, God had established the Ka'ba as the focus for every Muslim, for man to prostrate before Him, where the Ka'ba is nothing in between. The Sufi fell down prostrate, aware that whatever the masters do is beyond the consciousness of the average person, and that one should not question whatever they do, either outwardly or inwardly, for such things can be only Divine.[100]

Even after Abū Sa'īd's death, the veneration of the Seljuk princes for his memory continued. Sultan Sanjar (d. 551/1157), the last of the Seljuk rulers of Khurāsān, "and his army are said to have been disciples *(murīd)* of Shaykh Mahdī Marwazī, the *khādim* or keeper

99. The Zhukovskii and Bahmanyar editions of the *Asrār al-tawḥīd* have 'Adnī-Kūbān, which Meier renders as 'Adni-walker in German—meaning "the 'Adnī-fullers (Lane), where *'Adni* is interpreted as referring to a type of felt which is produced by beating, that is, the fuller's trade. Although when the Persian root *kūb* (beat) is used for the trade, it is normally accompanied by a definitive term, such as namad (felt), whereby this should read *'Adnī-namad-kūbān,*suggesting that *'adnī*would be the name of the local fullers' guild. We prefer the version in Shafī'ī-Kadkanī's definitive edition: 'Adnī-kūyān," where *'Adnī* is an adjective referring to *'Adan* (Eden) and *kūy* means 'lane' and *kūyān* 'quarter', from which the lane could take its name. Hence, our reading: Eden Quarter.
100. Ibn Munawwar, *op. cit.*, p. 247-48.

or the shrine [of Abū Sa'īd]. After escaping from the Ghuzz [Turks] Sanjar is alleged to have referred to Mayhana as "a blessed place" and to have given seed corn to the shrine and the surrounding district to restore its prosperity.[101]

However, it is clear that if Abū Sa'īd was popular with the Seljuk rulers, it was not through any worldly connection. Quite apparently, as indicated by the foregoing anecdotes, respect for this master came from those who had the insight to see beyond what was often a deliberate smokescreen of unconventional behavior. I think such conduct must be viewed in the cultural context of two Sufi trends which were becoming increasingly prominent on the Khurāsānian scene: One was the *malāmatiyya* ("incurrers of blame") movement, who, as Schimmel defines it, "deliberately tried to draw the contempt of the world upon themselves by committing unseemly, even unlawful actions, but they preserved perfect purity of heart and loved God without second thought."[102] The other was the *qalandariyya,* examples of which were the *'ayyārs*, who displayed a bounteous generosity of spirit and compassion toward others through a leonine brashness, a devil-may-care boldness. In a master like Abū Sa'īd, these two trends seemed united in one personality whereby an inner core of profound spirituality and grace was given a rugged outward surface facing the world.[103]

V. ABŪ SA'ĪD'S ROLE IN THE DEVELOPMENT OF THE PERSIAN *SAMĀ'* CONCERT & *KHĀNAQĀH* INSTITUTION

Having outlined the historical background, socio-religious currents and the political climate prevalent in Abū Sa'īd's Khurāsān during the eleventh century, we may now turn our attention to more specifically Sufi themes, namely, the *pedagogical* and *institutional* mentioned in our prologue above and the uses of musical audition *(samā')* in Persian mysticism. Abū Sa'īd established the first formal rule for conduct in the *khānaqāh* and hence, played a vital role in

101. Lambton, *op. cit.*, p. 240.
102. *Mystical Dimensions of Islam,* p. 86.
103. See below, section VI.

establishing this Sufi center as not merely a meeting house or a hospice for travelers, but as the focal point for spiritual practice—a practice which he himself further enriched by incorporating the *samā'*, or audition of music and poetry accompanied by ecstatic dancing, into formal Sufi observance, which up to that time had been mostly limited to the chanting of litanies, or *dhikr-i jalī* (vocal remembrance or invocation). On the basis of the classical biographies of Abū Sa'īd, Bertel's estimates that his *Khānaqāh* in Nīshāpūr housed forty regular residents and a virtually constant population of some eighty guests at any given time.[104]

> The Master always recited poetry from the pulpit, bringing numbers of people through poetry into *samā'* and inducing mystical states. His enemies criticized this custom... saying, "He does not interpret the Koran, nor does he cite Traditions of the Prophet *(ḥadīth)*. All he does is recite poetry."[105]

Despite the criticisms, these recitations of poetry, Bertel's points out, had a beneficial effect on people, as the story of the pious Ishī indicated. Furthermore, they were not incidental but fully planned occasions, as a reference cited by Bertel's makes clear.[106]

Qushayrī states that "the audition *(samā')* of poems sung with a fine voice is in principle permissible *(mubāh)* when the auditor does not possess illicit *(ḥarām)* belief and does not undertake *samā'* of anything which is condemned by the religious law *(Sharī'a)* nor give rein to his passions nor be concerned with entertainment. Furthermore, there is no contravention in the audition of poetry, for poetry was sung for the Prophet, who did not discourage the singing thereof."[107] Qushayrī goes on to emphasize that the auditor must be motivated by "desire entirely for devotional practice, fully conscious of what God" has disposed to be forbidden, for the *samā'* to have the proper effect, such that "pure infusions *(wāridāt)* may

104. Bertel's, *op. cit.*, p. 58.
105. *Ibid.*, p. 59.
106. *Ibid.*, p. 62. He goes on to quote a passage from Sa'dī's *Majālis* confirming Abū Sa'īd's precedent had become established Sufi practice by the seventh/thirteenth century. *Ibid.*, pp. 62-65.
107. Qushayrī, *Tarjama-yi Risāla-yi Qushayriyya,* ed. B. Furūzānfar (Tehran 1982), pp. 591-92.

appear in the heart."[108] Further along in the same chapter, Qushayrī states that "Imām Shāfi'ī did not consider it illicit *(ḥarām),* though considering it reprehensible *(makrūh)* for ordinary people, as in the case of someone making a profession of it, maintaining it for the purpose of entertainment, his testimony is invalid, forbidden."[109] It is interesting to contrast Qushayrī's carefully legalistic conditions for audition with Abū Sa'īd's specifications for *samā'*, which are defined in overtly spiritual terms:

> Audition on the part of friends is right for them if they listen with the finest of faces. God declared, "So, give good tidings to My worshippers who listen to the Word and follow it in the best way." [Koran XXXIX: 18] Everyone is affected by his surroundings. One may be listening to the world, another to his passions. One may be listening in terms of love, another in terms of union and separation. These are all unhealthy and erroneous. Audition is correct when it is heard from God.[110]

In his account of one of the master's meetings, Ibn Munawwar quotes Abū Sa'īd instructing the disciples and listeners on the subject of adherence to self versus adherence to God, saying, "As the masters have taught, whatever has to do with material being has nothing to do with God and vice versa." Then the biographer tells how whenever Abū Sa'īd read the Koran, he would skip the grim sections describing the torments of Hell and retribution; instead, he would concentrate on the gracious and merciful passages. When a dervish objected that such selectivity was a travesty of Koran-reading, the master answered with a segment of an ode:

> Sāqī, tu bidih bāda u, muṭrib, tu bizan rūd,
> Tā may khwuram imrūz, ki waqt-i ṭarab-i mā'st.
> May hast u diram hast u but-i lāla-rukhān hast;
> Gham nīst, w'agar hast, naṣīb-i dil-i 'adā'st.
>
> *O Sāqī pour the wine! Minstrel, strike the chord!*
> *Let me drink wine today, for now's my moment of rapture!*
> *There is wine; there's money; there are tulip-faced idols;*
> *There's no grief, and if there is, it's the lot of our foes' heart.*

---

108. *Ibid.*, p. 592.
109. *Ibid.*, p. 594.
110. Ibn Munawwar, *op. cit.*, p. 277.

Using this poem as his text, Abū Sa'īd explained his approach to reading the Koran, saying, "What has to do with us is all good tidings and mercy, while what has to do with the others is torment. What are we to do in the face of their caviling?" "With this," writes the biographer, "something came to the dervish's heart."[111] Thus, the point is not the outward expression except insofar as it embodies a communication which touches the heart, rather than the intellect.

The emphasis that Abū Sa'īd placed on expansion *(basṭ)* over contraction *(qabḍ)* as the state in which one's heart could best be opened to the Divine underlay the master's view of *samā'* as an integral part of Sufi practice. Where Qushayrī in his *Risāla* (completed in 437/1045, four years before Abū Sa'īd's death) is at pains to define the legal ramifications of *samā',* in order to ascertain the limits of its permissibility, Abū Sa'īd is concerned only with its role in bolstering the state of the auditor *(mustammī')* to further his progress on the spiritual path *(ṭarīqat)* and bring him ever closer to the Beloved. Thus, Meier remarks that it is perfectly evident that Abū Sa'īd treated the *samā'* "as a means towards higher experience and as a form of worship," in addition to its having a certain cathartic and restorative function.[112]

Ibn Munawwar tells of the following encounter involving Abū Sa'īd's response to criticism of his approach to *samā':*

> While the Master was in Nīshāpūr, Shaykh Bū 'Abdullāh Bākū [the famous Bābā Kūhī Shīrāzī] was (master of) Shaykh Abū 'Abd al-Raḥmān Sulamī's *Khānaqāh* after the latter's decease. Whenever this Bū 'Abdullāh asked the Master something, he would make it a leading question... Once he put a query in this way to the master: "I see several things from you which I never saw from my masters: One is that you seat elders with youths and that you see the actions of beginners in the same light as those of veterans... and another thing is that you permit youths to dance in the course of *samā'*... My masters never did such things."
>
> The Master asked, "Is there anything else?"
>
> "No," the Shaykh replied.
>
> The Master explained, "On the matter of beginners and veterans, there is no such thing as a beginner from my point of

111. Ibn Munawwar, *op. cit.*, pp. 216
112. Meier, *op. cit.*, p. 229.

view. Whoever embarks on the Path *(ṭarīqat)*, however youthful he may be, his elders ought to consider that possibly he will receive in a single day what they have not received in seventy years."

As for the dancing of youths in the course of *samā'*, the souls of young people are not free of desire; indeed, they they may even be dominated by their passions, which rule all their limbs. If they clap their hands, they shed the desire in their hands. If they kick their feet, the passion in their feet becomes lessened. When, in doing this, they become conscious of their imperfection, they are made aware of their cardinal defects. Taking all of these into account, they seek refuge in God for their sinfulness. The fire of these passions being shed in *samā'* is far better than its dissipation in something else.

Shaykh Bū 'Abdullāh [convinced] declared, "If I had never seen the master, I would never have seen a Sufi."[113]

At one point Abū Sa'īd turned the tables on those who would criticize him for reciting poetry as his text for instruction rather than Scripture, the conventional resource of the preacher. Once a group of important figures of Nīshāpūr came to visit the master, including Qushayrī and the Shāfi'ī jurist Abū Muḥammad Juwaynī, when in the course of discussion Abū Sa'īd recited this line of poetry:

Yak dam zadan az ḥāl-i tu ghāfil nayam, ay dūst!
Ṣāḥib khabarān dāram ānjā ki tau hastī.

O friend! At every breath I know your state—
I have informants wherever you may be.

Saying this, he looked around the assemblage of dignitaries and asked if any of them could cite the Koranic verse to which these words referred. However much they puzzled over it, they could not come up with the answer and were forced to refer back to him. "So it's up to me to tell you?" queried the master, and they said, "Yes." Then he quoted the verse, "Or do they reckon that We do not hear their secret thoughts *(lānasma'u sirrahum)* and their secret confidences *(najwahum)?* Indeed, Our emissaries, present with them, take note." [Koran XLIII: 80][114] In this way he not only reversed the

113. Ibn Munawwar, *op. cit.*, pp. 222-24.
114. Ibn Munawwar, *op. cit.*, pp. 282-83.

formula of the conventionalists but also made allusion for those who had the understanding of the fact that his "hearing" *(samā'*, the key verb in the verse being *lānasma'u* "We cannot hear"), was on a plane entitling him to determine the nature of a disciple's "audition" *(samā')*.

The final word on *samā'* is Abū Sa'īd's dictum that "For *samā'* the heart must be alive and the passions *(nafs)* dead."[115] Meier notes[116] that Qushayrī in his *Risāla* does quote this statement but, consistent with his apparent omission of the mention of Abū Sa'īd, leaves the ascription anonymous. (Of course, Qushayrī characteristically qualified the statement in legalistic terms, saying, "For *samā'* to be licit *(ḥalāl)* the passions *(nafs)* must be dead and the heart alive.")[117]

His evident ability to present the virtues of the complete Persian *samā'* tradition with its repertoire of mystical *ghazals* and quatrains, rather than the mere seated chanting of Koranic verses and litanies which had been the custom among Sufis before Abū Sa'īd's time,[118] points to Abū Sa'īd's key role in the gaining of acceptance of this activity as a formal part of Sufi gatherings by the Sufis of a strictly theological orientation, such as Qushayrī and Ghazālī.

* * *

If Abū Sa'īd began a revolution in Sufi practice, he also made an important contribution to the founding of the very institution in which the practice took place: the *Khānaqāh*. 'Abd al-Ghāfir ibn Ismā'īl al-Fārisī (d. 529/1134), writing in Arabic in the *Kitāb al-*

---

115. Ibn Munawwar, *op. cit.*, p. 318.
116. Meier, *op. cit.*, p. 216
117. Qushayri, *op. cit.*, p. 602.
118. As Ismā'īl Ḥākimī *(Samā' dar taṣawwuf-i Islām* [Tehran 1989], p. 81), puts it: "With the appearance of Abū Sa'īd and the spread of his fame in spite of the jurists and the legalists, *samā'* gatherings of Sufis little by little gained currency. In these gatherings what most appealed to the Sufis were love poems of a delicate nature, interpreted by them in an exoteric manner such that they would not be subject to anathema and condemnation by those opposed. The skill which Abū Sa'īd and his associates exercised in this activity caused the Sufis gradually to be able to recite love poems in their gatherings, inducing ecstasy and spiritual awareness *(ḥāl)*. Imām Ghazālī, moreover, considered interpretations of this sort permissible, allowing *samā'* to be practised in certain cases under certain conditions."

Siyāq li-ta'rīkh Nayshābūr, called Abū Sa'īd "the first person to establish customs for residence and rules of conduct *(adab)* within the *Khanaqah,* describing the spiritual path *(ṭarīqat),* and the necessary procedures *(qiyām wa qu'ūd)* as they have come down to us from that time to the present day."[119] Kiyānī calls Abū Sa'īd's center in Nīshāpūr "the first official *Khānaqāh,"*[120] noting that Abū Sa'īd felt the need to "formalize the program for communal and institutional living" of his disciples. Kiyānī believes that Abū Sa'īd's *Khānaqāh* must have been more extensive than others, thus necessitating a statement of principles for its direction and the behavior and duties of its members.[121] Meier qualifies 'Abd al-Ghāfir's statement above by stressing that Abū Sa'īd could not have actually founded the *Khānaqāh* as an institution, as there is abundant evidence that the institution was already thriving before his time—as, indeed, Abū Sa'īd's own childhood experience with his father indicates. However, Meier would agree that to the view of "Abū Sa'īd as the founder of the first ground-rules for the regulation of the conduct of the residents in Sufi convents."[122] The historian Qazwīnī cites Abū Sa'īd as the founder of the *Khānāqah* as a Sufi institution with provision for the needs of both residents and visitors and the spreading of a generous meal *(sufra)* twice a day, to which all were invited.[123] Abū Sa'īd's *Khānaqāh* in Nīshāpūr became renowned as a very new sort of institution. As Shafī'ī-Kadkanī explains, "Abū Sa'īd and his *Khānaqāh* more often received ordinary people, poor folk and laborers, urban and rural... bestowing attention and favor upon not only such persons, but even the most ostracized outcasts of society, such as a wretched young drunkard in one instance."[124]

---

119. Cited by Muḥammad Dāmādī, *Abū Sa'īd-nāma* (Tehran 1988), p. 65.
120. Muḥsin Kiyānī, *Tārīkh-i khānaqāh dar Īrān* (Tehran: Ṭahūrī 1369 A.Hsh./ 1991), p. 187.
121. *Ibid.*, p. 188.
122. Meier, *op. cit.*, p. 309.
123. Zakariyyā Qazwīnī, *Athār al-bilād wa akhbār al-'ibād* (Beirut 1380 A.H./ 1960), p. 361.
124. Ibn Munawwar, *op. cit.*, (ed. Shafī'ī-Kadkanī), I, p. 231.

What is most important is that in the establishment of the *Khānāqah,* Abū Sa'īd brought together three trends: 1) that of the local border posts or watchtowers *(ribāṭ)* founded on the frontline of the ongoing war between the Persian Muslims and the marauding Turks in the second/eighth and third/ninth centuries, as centers in which the first Sufis and ascetics congregated;[125] 2) the *Khānaqāh* by name (viewed by some scholars as having been founded by the Karrāmiyya, the severest expression of the mystico-ascetic trend in Khurārānian Islam), as a hospice in which the inhabitants resided, took their meals and meditated and 3) the Khurāsānian trend of spiritual chivalry *(jawānmardī),* itself predating Islam, while being enriched by Islam's encouragement of egalitarian communitarianism, giving hospitality to strangers, and helping those in need.

Abū Sa'īd was certainly the first person to formally codify a set of regulations for the running of the *Khānaqāh,* and two of the ten rules he set forth were directly concerned with awakening chivalrous impulses in disciples. Thus Rule 8 instructs the Sufi residents of the *Khānaqāh:* "Let them welcome the poor and needy and all who join their company, and let them bear patiently the trouble of waiting upon them," and Rule 9 reads: "Let them not eat anything, save in participation with one another."[126]

The latter prescription is consistent with the character of the prophet Abraham, called 'Abū Fityān' (Father of the Knights) and 'Abū Ḍayf' (Father of Hospitality). who, according to *jawānmardī* tradition, would never partake of food unless he could share it with a guest. According to Qazwīnī, amongst Abū Sa'īd's contributions was the example he set: that "in his *Khānaqāh* he engaged in feeding the poor and needy and homeless dervishes,"[127] The *Fuṣūṣ al-ādāb* by Yaḥyā Bākharzī[128] gives the most detailed account of Abū Sa'īd's prescriptions for the treatment of Sufi visitors to the *Khānaqāh,* among which is respect for the stranger's privacy:

125. See Kiyānī, *Tārīkh-i khānaqāh dar Irān,* p. 156.
126. Cited by Nicholson, *Studies in Islamic Mysticism,* (Cambridge 1980 rprt.), p. 46.
127. Qazwīnī, *op. cit.,* pp. 241-42, which states further that Abū Sa'īd "established the path of Sufism, building a *Khānaqāh* and providing a full meal *(khwān)* twice a day. All Sufi etiquette *(adab)* derives from him."

> The residents must not ask the visitor where he comes from and where he is going, but let this become known in due course... The residents should yield their places of prayer to newcomers, and speak to them cheerfully and positively, eat with them with a smiling face, and not ask them about conditions of the world and people of the world, and what they are about, but they may ask about the conditions of the Masters, Shaykhs and brethren of purity.[129]

According to the *Ḥālāt u sukhanān*, the earlier biography of Abū Sa'īd, "one of the Master's virtuous traits was not to eat until a visitor would share his bowl with him; and every newly arrived Sufi would be honored by being invited by him to share his bowl on the first night."[130] When Abū Sa'īd prepared to leave Nīshāpūr to return to his hometown Mayhana, he left these instructions: "The *khānaqāh* should be kept open, swept and clean, with a light always lit *(chirāgh rawshan* [a term that has come down through history to indicate that a *Khānāqah* is in active operation]) and all facilities for hygiene *(ṭahārat)* in force and always fully provisioned. Whoever comes should bring his own victuals (if he is able)."[131]

His instructions came to be called the *Rusūm-i Bū Sa'īdī* (the Bū Sa'īdian traditions), for the first time a stated, formalized set of rules that could be passed down from generation to generation. In the thirteenth century, the Kubrawī Shaykh Majd al-Dīn Baghdādī translated Abū Sa'īd's Ten-Point Rule into Arabic, thus insuring its communication to the Western Islamdom.

Simnānī reports one innovation of Abū Sa'īd with a *jawānmardī* reference, which was that of joining separate bowls and servings for each individual at a meal, rather than having everyone dig into one central container. When it was protested that in the Prophet's time, all ate from the same bowl, and as the Prophet had said, people should eat meals with *īthār* (giving priority to others) as the Koran

---

128. For a closer treatment of Shaykh Sayf al-Dīn Bākharzī's own *Khānaqāh* organization, see Muhammad Isa Waley, "A Kubrāwī Manual of Sufism: The *Fuṣūṣ al-ādāb* of Yaḥyā Bākharzī" in L. Lewisohn (ed.) *The Heritage of Sufism II,* pp. 289–310.

129. Abū'l-Mafākhir Bākharzī, *Awrād al-aḥbāb wa Fuṣūṣ al-ādāb: jild-i duwwam: Fuṣūṣ al-ādāb,* ed. Īrāj Afshār (Tehran 1345 A.Hsh./1966), p. 177.

130. Dāmādī *op. cit.*, p. 53.

131. Shafī'ī-Kadkanī, *op. cit.*, introduction, p. cxxxiv.

indicates in the verse, "And they gave priority over themselves..."[132] Abū Sa'īd responded that in the Prophet's day, the greater blessing was due to the greater number of those yielding to their brethren, whereas now people eat by plundering, with the sensual appetites *(nafs)* feeding itself to the point of devouring the bowl's portion as well, ever more voraciously. The Prophet branded this kind of eating unlawful *(ḥarām)* and we dervishes restrain ourselves from unlawful eating by separating each individual's portion."[133]

What Abū Sa'īd institutionalized as part and parcel of the purpose of the functioning of the *Khānaqāh* was 'service to others', the effect of which came to be seen in the expansion of the *Khānāqah* under the patronage of the Seljuks, associated dynasties like the Ayyūbids in Egypt and the Seljuks' successors, the Īl-Khānids, particularly in the Arabic-speaking world, where the prevailing Sufi centers had previously been the *Ribāṭ* and the *Zāwiyya,* both focused on Sufi training in a monastic way, emphasizing retreat *(khalwa),* and divorcing the Sufi from the society around him—even from his family,[134] whereas the Persian *Khānāqah* included these functions in its complex of buildings, but emphasized social interaction through hospitality and service to others. So when Trimingham explains that, "the popularity of the Persian-type hospices in particular is associated with the Seljuk period, as can be seen from any list of the dates when these were founded,"[135]—it should be emphasized that these Seljuk-era patrons were, of course, none other than the likes of Ṭughrīl Beg and Niẓām al-Mulk, those devotees of Abū Sa'īd, sensitive to his spiritual instruction, acting on his example and passing the word, *Khānaqāh,* on with the institution, to enter the Arabic language.

Nicholson is quite positive about Abū Sa'īd's contribution to the institution in Sufism as a whole, calling it "the first Mohammedan example of a *regula ad monachos,*" and saying, "although he

---

132. Amīr Iqbāl Sīstānī, *Chihil majlis* (of 'Alā' al-Dawla Simnānī), ed. 'Abd al-Rafī' Ḥaqīqat (Tehran 1358 A.Hsh./1979), p. 18.
133. *Ibid.*
134. J.S. Trimingham. *op. cit.* p. 17.
135. *Ibid.,* p. 24.

founded no Order, the convent over which he presided supplied a model in outline of the fraternities that were established during the 12th century."[136] Here Nicholson points, of course, to the seminal nature of Abū Sa'īd's ten rules, which appear in the *Asrār al-tawḥīd*[137] and are quoted in full in English by Nicholson himself,[138] Trimingham,[139] and Schimmel;[140] and, in German, by Meier.

Although the term *Khānaqāh* seems to have come from the Karrāmiyya who had established the institution throughout their area of influence, principally Khurāsān (as Madelung explains, deriving his information primarily from al-Maqdisī)[141]—where the nature of the Karrāmite institution was that of a center for both devotional practice and residence, the the Karramiyya's quietism, not believing in work to support themselves, ran counter to the view of Sufis that they should not only support themselves but serve others. Hence, the Sufi institution would necessarily have to be very different in spirit. This brings us to the third focal point of this essay: Abū Sa'īd's sincerity and chivalry.

VI. ABŪ SA'ĪD'S INFLUENCE ON SUFI CHIVALRY AND *MALĀMATĪ* SPIRITUALITY

Judging from the evidence provided by the sources, notably the *Asrār al-tawḥīd,* the *Khānaqāh* up to the time of Abū Sa'īd's maturity was fundamentally a place of spiritual practice, where, as in the case of the master's father, Sufis gathered for collective observance, or, as in the case of Abū Sa'īd's masters—Faḍlullāh Ḥasan, Sulamī, and Qaṣṣāb—a center was provided for disciples to join a master and be trained by him. A clear contribution made by Abū Sa'īd in this context, however, is that in laying down his ground-rules, he provided for that all-important principle of Sufism: *khidmat,* service to others, to be incorporated in the very fabric of the concept of the *Khānaqāh*—a feature which derives from yet another source: the

136. *Studies in Islamic Mysticism,* p. 76.
137. Ibn Munawwar, *op. cit.*, p. 330-32.
138. *Studies in Islamic Mysticism,* p. 46.
139. Trimingham, *op. cit.,* p. 167.
140. *Mystical Dimensions of Islam,* p. 243.
141. Madelung, *op.cit.,* p. 45.

langar of the *qalandars.*[142]

According to Hanaway, "from the fifth/eleventh century onward, some of the *Futuwwa* groups began to adopt an ideology which brought them into contact with mystic circles then seeking corporate forms." Further along, he points out that *'ayyārs* (free-spirited free-booters), identified in the positive sense of *jawānmards* are shown in epics of the centuries after Abū Sa'īd "as members of a corporate, initiatory organization apparently similar to organizations of crafts-men, and Sufi orders in the Iranian world."[143] This close identifica-tion of *'ayyārī* and *jawānmardī,* as well as that of *qalandarī* and *malāmatī,* with Sufism is very much a product of the post-Bū-Sa'īdian age, for Abū Sa'īd was one of the first distinguished mas-ters to make a point of embracing people of all walks of life within the purview of his hospitality and grace, whether or not they were initiates or Sufis. With all these trends being brought together in the fabric of Sufism through a giant figure like Abū Sa'īd, it would be well to say something briefly about the background of these lines in Khurāsān. 'Abd al-Ḥusayn Zarrīnkūb adduces that, from the point of chivalry at least, true Sufism consists in following the 'path of blame':

> Sincerity in one's actions—upon which the *malāmatiyya* based their spiritual path—became a kind of movement aimed at the purification of Sufism from being in thrall to the cultural mores and outer formalities which prevailed among the common ranks of the mystics, tradesmen and the lower classes. Since the spiriutal path *(ṭarīqa)* of the *fityān* was also based, to a certain degree, on sincerity in one's actions and abstinence from the hypocritical dis-play of religious piety—the *ṭarīqa* of the *malāmatiyya* gradually fused with the tradition of chivalry.[144]

The era of the *malāmatiyya* in the Sufism of Nīshāpūr was com-ing to a close in Abū Sa'īd's time. He himself, as Shafī'ī-Kadkanī indicates, was already transforming this mode of approach through his intoxication, a legacy of the tradition of Bāyazīd, (whom,

---

142. 'Abd al-Ḥusayn Zarrīnkūb, *Justujū-yi dar taṣawwuf-i Īrān* (Tehran: Amīr Kabīr 1978), p. 363.
143. *Encyclopædia Iranica,* s.v. " 'Ayyār," III, pp. 159-63.
144. *Justujū-yi dar taṣawwuf-i Īrān,* p. 197.

incidentally, Sulamī, having composed two books respectively on *malāmatiyya* and *futuwwat* as vital features of Sufism, cited as a *malāmatī,*[145]). The *malāmatī* mystic or follower of the 'path of blame', as described above, was a genuinely Khurāsānian phenomenon in which Abū Sa'īd played a central role. The importance of the *malāmatī* trend in Khurāsānian Sufism, constituting an evolutionary development of the pure asceticism of the earlier generation, goes back to the precedence of Ḥamdūn Qaṣṣār (d. 271/884), a master of Nīshāpūr, who put his stamp on the Sufi practice of the region, and stressed the importance of sincerity, declaring, "God's knowledge of you is better than people's."[146] Praised by Ḥujwīrī for his pious practice, his eloquent tongue and his religious knowledge, ranking him with the great clerics of Nīshāpūr,[147] he was called upon by the community to preach from the pulpit. Declining the honor, he explained that his words had no value for the heart, because his heart was still in the world, not having the station to make his words fruitful, so as to affect the hearts of others.[148]

Abū Sa'īd himself said, "*Malāmatī* means that in loving God, you have no anxiety or fear concerning whatever befalls you and that you do not ever worry about incurring blame or reproach from others."[149] In his introduction to the *Asrār al-tawḥīd,* Shafī'ī-Kadkanī states that in the presentation of the principles of his teachings, "Abū Sa'īd has shown that in activities and sayings he holds one issue to be fundamental and that is 'detachment from the passions *(nafs)*', and 'struggle with hypocrisy'. It has been said that this principle is one of the fundamentals of the teachings of the incurrers of blame *(ahl-i malāmat).*"[150]

---

145. Abū 'Abd al-Raḥmān Sulāmī, *La Lucidité Implacable: Épître des Hommes du Blâme,* French translation of Sulāmī's *Risālat al-malāmatiyya* by R. Deladrière (Paris 1991), *passim,* and biographical note, pp. 114-15. The fifteenth-century Sufi master Sayyid Muḥammad Nūrbakhsh, in his treatise *Silsilat al-awliyā',* even went so far as to describe Abū Sa'īd as one who "enjoyed gnosis of the realities of Divine Unity *(tawḥīd)* through being *malāmatī."* – *Silsilat al awliyā',* edited by Muḥammad Taqī Dānishpazhūh, in S.H. Nasr (ed.) *Mélanges offerts à Henry Corbin* (Tehran 1977), s.v. "Bāyazīd."
146. Hujwīrī, *op. cit.*, p. 206.
147. *Ibid.*
148. *Ibid.*
149. *Asrār al-tawḥīd,* ed. Shafī'ī-Kadkanī, p. 288.

Shafī'ī-Kadkanī goes on to say that the *malāmatīs* hide their virtues and make a display of the negative side of things, such as might offend the sensibilities of conventional society or orthodoxy. He gives the example of Abū Sa'īd's wearing of silk—or was it, he suggests, merely a cloth that looked like silk, which is forbidden by the religious law? Report of this travelled to the other end of the Islamic world, raising a hue and cry as far West as Andalusia, where Ibn Ḥazm attacked him virulently in a treatise, *Al-Faṣl fī'l-milal.*[151] The generation of a reputation for this sort of thing is typical of the *malāmatī* method, according to Shafī'ī-Kadkanī.

Now, some might argue that Abū Sa'īd's sporting of silk garments typified the *qalandariyya* rather than the *malamātiyya* outlook, the difference between the two attitudes being that whereas the former hides his devotion, the latter externalizes it, even exploits it, going out of his way to incur blame.[152] Describing the former term, Shihāb al-Dīn 'Umar Suhrawardī, writing in the thirteenth-century *'Awārif al-ma'ārif,* remarked that "the term *qalandar* is applied to people so possessed by the intoxication of 'tranquillity-of-heart', that they respect no custom or usage and reject the regular observances of society and mutual relationship."[153] The *qalandariyya* had also long been powerful in Khurāsān and through Abū Sa'īd and his immediate spiritual forebears this current became integrated into Sufism in general.[154]

The object to be striven for according to Sufi doctrine is indicated in Abū Sa'īd's cardinal principle: "Until you have become an unbeliever *(kāfir)* in your *nafs* ('self-identity'), you cannot become a believer *(mu'min)* in God."[155] The point is that when one has become entirely consumed in God, one acts *through* God, and those most perfectly in union, like Ḥallāj or Bayazid or Abū Sa'īd, often evince eccentric *qalandariyya* behavior, inwardly in accord with

---

150. *Asrār al-tawḥīd,* ed. Shafī'ī-Kadkanī, introduction, p. xcv.
151. *Asrār al-tawḥīd,* ed. Shafī'ī-Kadkanī, introduction, p. xciv.
152. Zarrinkub, *op. cit.*, p. 363.
153. Trimingham, *op. cit.,* p. 267, quoting Suhrawardī's *'Awārif al-ma'ārif* (Beirut 1966), p. 56-57.
154. An explicit reference to *qalandariyya* in the *Asrār al-tawḥīd* occurs in Shafī'ī-Kadkanī's edition, p. 73.
155. Nafīsī, *op. cit.*, p. 101, quatrain no. 688.

God, even if it be outwardly in discord with a person or a community's subjective conceptions of convention.

While Anṣārī was quite explicit about his disapproval of Abū Sa'īd's *malāmatī* temperament, Qushayrī preferred the discretion of simply omitting any mention of him in his otherwise broadly comprehensive *Risāla* of Sufi doctrine and its exponents. In the case of both of these Sufi critics, as with others, like Ibn Bākūya (Bābā Kūhī) Shīrāzī, the grounds for objection were institutional. These critics had conventional ideas about how Sufis should behave, seeing them as models of spiritual conduct for the average Muslim believer and, at the very least, masking their ecstatic side with the protective veneer of socially and canonically acceptable behavior. It is no coincidence that they were in the ranks of those who had reservations about Ḥallāj, while Abū Sa'īd was among those who wholeheartedly approved of him, declaring, "There was no one east or west who was as well versed in the sciences of [mystical] states."[156]

Abū Sa'īd's possession of the *qalandariyya* character and *malāmatī* temperament is illustrated by the manner in which he received his enemies. When he heard that the Karrāmite Abū'l-Ḥasan Tūnī was making a point of avoiding the neighborhood of his *Khānaqāh,* cursing and anathematizing the master, he replied, "He was not cursing me. He fancied that I was against God and he was for Him. What he was actually cursing was that 'being against God'—for the sake of God!"[157] However, if the meaning of *qalandar* is inwardly defined by such detachment, the outward expression of the condition is chivalry, *jawānmardī,* a trait which so profoundly characterized Abū Sa'īd that one of his most famous definitions of Sufism is really none other than a description of *jawānmardī:* "Put away what you have in your head; give away what you have in your hands, and do not shy away from what befalls you"[158] In fact, he is so steeped in spiritual chivalry that, unlike Qushayrī, Anṣārī and other Sufi authors, he hardly ever defines it as such. On the other hand, his definitions of other terms and his teachings in general are

156. Ibn Munawwar, *op. cit.,* p. 80.
157. Ibn Munawwar, *op. cit.,* pp. 101-2.
158. *Ibid.,*.p. 297.

redolent of the meaning of *jawānmardī,* such as his prescription on the most direct way to reach God "to bring ease to someone else," to which he adds, "I have travelled this way, and I commend everyone to it."[159]

***

The plain of Khāwarān, lying between a staging post on the Silk Road to China, the metropolis of Merv, and the town of Sarakhs, was also famous as a spawning ground for the free-spirited "free-booters," the chivalrous brigands or *'ayyār*s—those Robin-Hood-like rogues and brigands, whose bold and magnanimous character influenced esoteric trends of thought in the region in general, and Abū Sa'īd's Sufism, in particular. This pre-Islamic Persian tradition of the *'ayyār,* or *yār* in the New Persian, may be understood as linked semantically with the Arabic term *'ayyār,* or "knight errant."[160] This current had already spawned a great Sufi in the region, Fuḍayl ibn 'Iyāḍ (d. 187/803), from the neighboring territory of Ṭālāqān in Khurāsān, had been a brigand preying upon the caravans traversing this land, though in the conscience-guided spirit of the *'ayyār*s. Eventually, Fuḍayl became not only a great Sufi but also a distinguished traditionist, or *muḥaddith.*[161] Fuḍayl's approach was exemplary of the *'ayyāriyya* of this period, making in-roads within this cultural tradition which Abū Sa'īd would later in-corporate into his own mystical thought.

An encounter which Hujwīrī quotes Qaṣṣār as relating illustrates something of the *qalandariyya* strand of Sufism, providing an in-sight into the background of Abū Sa'īd's personal spiritual method. It also involves an *'ayyār,* whose presence (most notably in Abū Sa'īd's native Dasht-i Khāwarān, where Avicenna was deprived of his books by a robber sage) did so much to determine the character of the culture of the area. As Qaṣṣār tells it:

---

159. *Ibid.*, p. 302.
160. C. Cahen, "Tribes, Cities and Social Organization," *Cambridge History of Iran,* (Cambridge 1975), IV, p. 322.
161. Background on Fuḍayl ibn 'Iyāḍ can be found in 'Aṭṭār's *Tadhkirat al-awliyā',* ed. Este'lamī, pp. 89-101; and Hujwīrī, *Kashf al-maḥjūb,* ed. Zhukovskii, pp. 122ff.

> One day as I was walking along the riverbed in the Hira district of Nīshāpūr, I encountered a certain Nūḥ, an *'ayyār* famous for his chivalry *[futuwwat];* indeed, all the *'ayyārs* of Nīshāpūr were under his command. I asked him the meaning of chivalry *[jawānmardī].*[162] He asked, "Do you mean my chivalry or yours?" "Tell me of both," I replied. He said, "My chivalry is that I take off this cloak of a brigand and put on the patched Sufi mantle, then conduct myself in such a manner that I become a Sufi, avoiding sin out of shame before society in wearing that dress; whereas your chivalry lies in divesting yourself of the same patched cloak, so as not to deceive yourself with people's attention to you being a mystic and also not to mislead others about yourself. So, my chivalry involves outer observance of the religious law *(sharī'a)* while yours means inward observance of Reality *(ḥaqīqat).*[163]

It was this matter of outward actions versus inward state that posed a problem for Anṣārī when he visited Abū Sa'īd. (This was clearly before he met Abū'l-Ḥasan Kharaqānī [d. 426/1034], in whose presence the eye of insight was opened within him,[164] this visitation occurring most likely in 424/1033).[165] When Anṣārī first traveled to Nīshāpūr from his native Herat in 417/1026, he visited Abū Sa'īd, giving this account:

> I spent time with Abū Sa'īd on two occasions, and he tore off his turban, presented me his Egyptian carpet, and popped a boiled turnip into my mouth. When I first came in, he stood up and bowed to me with great respect, despite the fact that I object to him in point of doctrine and about his not observing the convention of masters. A number of the masters of the time did not approve of him.[166]

Abū Sa'īd's chivalry was such that he treated his severest Sufi critic with not only grace but warm affection. Other examples of Abū Sa'īd's *jawānmardī* include a delightful fictitious anecdote from 'Aṭṭār in his *Ilāhī-nāma,* demonstrating how Abū Sa'īd's compassion extended to animals, as well as humans. In the story

162. *Mystical Dimensions of Islam*, p. 86.
163. Hujwīrī, *op. cit.*, p. 228.
164. *Mystical Dimensions of Islam,* p. 90.
165. Ibn Munawwar, *op. cit.*, ed. Shafī'ī-Kadkanī, p. xli, no. 13.
166. *Ibid.*, p. xli.

recounted in verse a would-be Sufi, brushing against a dog, strikes it with his staff, badly wounding the dog in the paw. The dog rushes to Abū Sa'īd to seek recourse. When Abū Sa'īd confronts the miscreant Sufi with his deed, the latter accuses the dog of having defiled his clothes. At this the dog protests that, having seen that the man was dressed in Sufi clothes, the "garments of kindness," it felt that it could associate with the man with impunity. Abū Sa'īd takes the dog's part, asking the creature how he should punish the man. The dog replies, "Strip him of his Sufi cloak. That will be punishment enough for him till the Day of Judgment."[167]

Abū Sa'īd was a model practitioner of *jawānmardī,* famous for his encouragement of *ithār*, selfless generosity, examples of which are his giving of his horse to itinerant Turkmans;[168] his doffing his cloak in the bitter cold of winter and giving of it to a needy person;[169] his policy of forgiving, if not simply turning a blind eye to, offense;[170] his instruction that service to a pauper was better than a hundred rounds of supererogatory prayer;[171] his humble service of those in need, even those who scorned him, who came to wash in the public bath maintained by his *khānaqāh,* an example of which being his giving of a fine silk turban, just given him by a devotee, to a poor man invited to a wedding[172] his byword of "rejection of making objections" *(i'rāḍ az i'tirāḍ)* to anything, however unpleasant, that befell one;[173] his policy of looking with a kind eye upon everyone and of assuming the burdens of others as beholden upon one;[174] and his action, after seating a girl devotee beside himself and being accused by the parents of violating the Prophet's custom of accepting the presence of women only if they were properly covered, in removing his own cloak to cover her, whereupon she attained a high spiritual state.[175]

---

167. Aṭṭār, *Ilāhi-nāma,* ed. H. Ritter, (Tehran 1980), p. 46.
168. Ibn Munawwar, *op. cit.*, p. 230.
169. *Ibid.*, p. 235.
170. *Ibid.*, p. 260.
171. *Ibid.*, p. 264.
172. *Ibid.,* pp. 143-46.
173. *Ibid.*, p. 280.
174. *Ibid.*, p. 274 .
175. *Ibid.*, p. 282.

VII. EPILOGUE

The clearest effects of Abū Sa'īd's personality are his integration of *jawānmardī* into the context of Sufism and his pioneering role on the establishment of the *Khānāqah* as the Sufi center *par excellence.* Abū Sa'īd, as noted above, has been hailed by many as the founder of the *Khānāqah* as an institution in Sufism. An interesting side-effect of the humble service and generous hospitality embodied in the *khānaqāh* institution through Abū Sa'īd was his influence on the popular acceptance of Islam among non-Muslims. Sufi refugees from the Mongol invasion of Khurāsān and Transoxiana, pouring into Anatolia and other regions of the Islamic West, "manifesting a fervor and spirit quite different from that of legalist Islam, a spirit which also expressed itself in practical social aspects, such as hospitality to travellers and care for the sick and poor, were mediators of Islam to the Christians of the region."[176]

Abū Sa'īd's spiritual chivalry and charisma brought a tempering of passions in the Islamic community. When representatives of the four warring sects in Nīshāpūr came before him, he enjoined harmony upon them, an effect of which was the government-sponsored founding of *Madrasa*s for each of the four by a certain Abū'l-Qāsim 'Alī ibn Muḥammad related to the prominent families of Nīshāpūr and vice-governor of the province.[177] Domestic peace reigned until the Ghuzz erupted into Khurāsān, slew Sanjar, the last Seljuk Sultan, and destroyed the tomb of Abū Sa'īd in Mayhana, unleashing internal violence so great that Nīshāpūr became a virtual Beirut of its day, well-gutted before the Mongols even set foot on Khurāsānian soil.

A final sign of Abū Sa'īd's positive impact was the conversion of the orthodox clergy to formal acceptance of Sufism as an integral part of Islam. As Zarrīnkūb points out, whereas in the pre-Seljuk Ghaznavid period, "Abū Sa'īd and his associates were accused of heresy and apostasy by the clerics and jurisprudents of Nīshāpūr, "the *'ulamā'* came to be attracted to Sufism" in the Seljuk period

---

176. Trimingham, *op. cit.*, p. 24.
177. R.W. Bulliet, s.v. "'Abū'l-Qāsim 'Ali b. Muḥammad," *Encyclopædia Iranica,* I, p. 357.

"where the likes of Imām al-Haramayn Juwaynī along with his father Abū Maḥmūd and Imām Ghazālī ended up as Sufis."[178]

178. Zarrīnkūb, *op. cit.,* p. 56.

Sultan Maḥmūd of Ghazna with his Favourite Slave Ayāz. From a *Kulliyyāt-i Sa'dī*. Shiraz, Safavid Period. Copied 974/1566. B.L. Add. 24944, f. 51b. (Courtesy of the British Library).

Historical Conditions of Persian Sufism during the Seljuk Period

Hamid Dabashi

"A man has come here from Mayhana." The story is told about Shaykh Abū Sa'īd ibn Abī'l-Khayr (357/967–440/1048), one of the greatest Sufi masters of all ages who flourished towards the end of the Ghaznavid (reg. 366/977–582/1186) and early Seljuk (reg. 429/1038–590/1194) periods. Early in his career he had moved from his native Mayhana to Nīshāpūr, the great urban center of Khurāsān. "He claims to be a Sufi." His detractors were concerned that his ecstatic popularity was a threat to matters of public piety:

> He holds Sufi gatherings. He recites poetry on the pulpit. Commentary upon the Koran is not what he preaches. Nor does he tell of prophetic traditions. He makes grandiloquent claims. He sings and his young followers dance. They eat roasted chicken and cake, and then he claims to be an ascetic. This is not the manner of the ascetics, nor is it the belief of the Sufis. The masses are all attracted to him. They will be led astray. Most of the ignorant populace are already committing vices. If something is not done immediately, very soon public unrest will ensue.[1]

The custodians of public piety send their letter to Ghazna, the Ghaznavid capital, for the attention of the Sultan. The letter is returned with the royal command on it that the local leaders of the Shāfi'ite and Ḥanafite schools of jurisprudence, the followers of

1. Ibn Munawwar, *Asrār al-tawḥīd fī maqāmāt al-Shaykh Abī Sa'īd,* 2 vols.; ed. Muḥammad Riḍā Shāfi'ī-Kadkanī (Tehran: Āgah 1366 A.Hsh./1987), I, pp. 68-73.

Imam Abū Ḥanīfa and Imam Shāfi'ī, should consult and decide what is to be done with the Sufis. The Nīshāpūrī Sufis are frightened; the two local leaders of the Ḥanafiyya and the Karrāmiyya, Qāḍī Ṣā'īd and Abū Bakr Isḥāq, are determined. But Shaykh Abū Sa'īd is omniscient and confident. He arranges for a public feast to be given for his followers, the expenses for which are provided by a miraculous deed. Through other miraculous deeds Shaykh Abū Sa'īd convinces Qāḍī Ṣā'īd and Abū Bakr Isḥāq of his supreme spiritual powers, of his knowledge of the hidden, of people's unspoken thoughts. The local jurists are silenced, forced to recognize the superior authority of Shaykh Abū Sa'īd, the Sufi novitiates are properly admonished not to be easily frightened out of their wits. Shaykh Abū Sa'īd is established as a power to be reckoned with in the local affairs of Nīshāpūr; and Muḥammad Munawwar, the author of *Asrār al-tawḥīd,* the storyteller, consolidates the key feature of his narrative device, that the knowledge of the hidden, the unspoken truth, is known to the mystics, chief among them the hero of his enchanting narrative, Shaykh Abū Sa'īd ibn Abī'l-Khayr.

THE HISTORICAL SET-UP

Composed late in the third quarter of the sixth/twelfth century, 574/1178 to be exact, Muḥammad ibn Munawwar's recollection of stories about his great great grandfather is indicative of much about the history of Sufism under the Seljuks.

In the year 429/1038 the Seljuk warlord Rukn al-Dunyā wa al-Dīn Tughrïl (reg. 429/1038–455/1063) defeated the Ghaznavids, who had ruled over eastern Iran since 366/977, and proclaimed himself Sultan in Nīshāpūr. This started the great Seljuk reign over much of the Iranian plateau up until 590/1194. Between 429/1038 and 447/1055, when Tughrïl triumphantly entered Baghdad, relieved the Abbasid caliphate of effective obedience to the Būyids, and secured for himself the official title of "Sultan," the Turkish warlord allied himself emphatically with Sunni orthodoxy against sectarian Shi'ism. Along with Shi'ism, other non-orthodox versions of Islam—in sectarian, theological, philosophical, and mystical domains—entered into a compromising phase of their history.

The fifth/eleventh century in Islamic history evinced a rigid consolidation of all previously established and legitimated discourses of the sacred. The rapid systematization of various modes of authority in juridical, philosophical, mystical, and political domains was perhaps best represented in the radical hostility among their respective proponents. Persecution of ideological rivals, political opponents with a claim to an opposing discourse of legitimacy, was rampant in this period and the Seljuk warlords were always ready to exploit these hostilities for their own political ends. As in most other periods in Persian history, the juridical authorities had the greatest share of political ambition, very closely followed by the mystics and philosophers. The consolidation of political power proper, through various instrumentalities of legitimate authorities at the disposal of the court, put it in a favorable negotiating position with the other powerful centers of legitimacy and control.

The domination of the Seljuk Turks in the fifth/eleventh century acted as a potent catalyst to reactivate the latent elements of hostility among the competing discourses of Islamic legitimacy, gradually active and dominant from the earliest period. The nomocentricity of Islamic law and dogma, or the primacy of principle and action, and the logocentricity of philosophy, or the primacy of reason and knowledge, came into direct and active opposition to the counternarrative of Sufism, or the primacy of being-in-love. The political force, the relentless will-to-power, continued to act as the crucial catalyst in reengaging these forces against each other. The Muslim dogmatists and doctors of law continued to dominate the Islamic *Madrasa* system in the fifth/eleventh century.[2] As in earlier centuries, the study of philosophy and the practice of Sufism were both sources of constant suspicion by the ecclesiastical authorities. The study of philosophy, the course and the limited rule of reason in Islamic intellectual history, continued to be haphazard and subject to the whimsical vicissitudes of the Seljuk warlords. One of the most important institutional bases of Islamic philosophy, the court, continued to be ever more tangential and compromising in its support

2. See George Makdisi, *The Rise of Colleges: Institutions of Learning in Islam and the West* (Edinburgh: Edinburgh University Press 1981), pp. 35-75.

of the philosophical quest. Ghazālī's *Tahāfut al-falāsifa* gave considerable ammunition to the nomocentric forces in Islamic societies to oppose the independent judgment of reason in the pursuit of experimentally and/or logically verifiable claims on reality.[3]

By 465/1072, under Jalāl al-Dīn Malikshāh (reg. 465/1072-485/1092), the Seljuks reached the zenith of their territorial expansions.[4] Khwāja Niẓām al-Mulk, the Persian vizier *par excellence,* presided over a vast and thriving empire. But the radical Sunni orthodoxy of the Seljuk warlords was much more congenial to the theological and juridical disputations of the Ash'arites than to the philosophical concerns of either the Aristotelian tradition in the Avicennan philosophy or the gnostic discourses of post-Hallājian Sufism. The Niẓāmiyya colleges, as a result, were principally a network of loosely connected law schools exclusively concerned with juridical, jurisprudential, and, at best, (Ash'arite) theological issues. Whatever philosophical or gnostic issues were discussed, they remained mostly at the periphery of the Niẓāmiyya *Madrasa* System, in which the Shāfi'ite school of Islamic law found the zenith of its historical growth. The principal concern of the Shāfi'ites was their rivalry with the Ḥanbalites, who shared their penchant for claiming the exclusive legal right to determine and dictate not only the material course of Islamic intellectual and practical concerns but also the very spirit of 'Islam Itself'.

The dominant force of the nomocentric dogmatists, fully supported by the politically necessitated orthodoxy of the Seljuk warlords, found its way into the otherwise counter-dogmatic discourse of Persian Sufism. The radical dogmatism of Khwāja 'Abdullāh Anṣārī (d. 481/1089) in his excessive defense of Ḥanbalism has

---

3. See 'Abd al-Ḥusayn Zarrīnkūb, *Farār az madrasa: dar bāra-yi zindigī wa andīsha-yi Abū Ḥāmid Ghazālī* (Tehran: Amīr Kabīr 1364 A.Hsh./1985), pp. 117-20; Jalāl al-Dīn Humā'ī, *Ghazālī-nāma* (Tehran: Furūghī 1317 A.Hsh./1938), pp. 240-51; Jamīl Ṣalībā', *Ta'rīkh al-falsafa al-'arabiyya* (Beirut: Dār al-kitāb al-kubnānī 1986), pp. 363-80.

4. See Rashīd al-Dīn Faḍullāh, *Jāmi' al-tawārīkh,* 2 vols., edited by Aḥmad Ātash (Tehran: Dunyā-yi kitāb 1362 A.Hsh./1983), pp. 288-300; Hamdullāh Mustawfī, *Ta'rīkh-i guzīda,* edited by 'Abd al-Ḥusayn Nawā'ī (Tehran: Amīr Kabīr 1364 A.Hsh./1985), pp. 434-40; Muḥammad ibn 'Alī ibn Sulaymān al-Rāwandī, *Rāḥat al-ṣudūr wa 'āya al-surūr dar tārīkh-i Āl-i Siljūq,* edited by Muḥammad Iqbāl & M. Minuwī (Tehran: Amīr Kabīr 1364 A.Hsh./1985), pp. 125-38.

been singled out[5] as a significant mark in Persian Sufism in the late fifth/eleventh century. "Khwāja 'Abdullāh Anṣārī...," it has been reported by one historian, "was devoid of the liberalism and freedom of intellect expected of the Sufi masters. He considered the path of attaining truth as subservient to obedience to the artificial aspects of the Ḥanbalīte school. In enjoining the good and prohibiting the evil, in harassing the mystics and the Sufis, and even in accusing of corruption and blasphemy those mystics who fell short of performing their religious rites according to the Ḥanbalīte mandates, he surpassed all legal and religious authorities."[6]

The Sunni-Shi'ite hostility extended the sectarian divisions of early Islamic history into the fifth/eleventh century and much beyond. Within Shi'ism in general, sub-sectarian movements of the Zaydīs and the Ismā'īlīs further divided the Muslim communities.[7] These sectarian hostilities, aggravated by the continued presence of proto-Kharijite sentiments, were further extended into theological debates centered around the Mu'tazilī-Ash'arī controversies in any number of issues concerning the essence and attributes of God. Theological issues, in turn, were translated into juridical and jurisprudential debates among the Ḥanbalites, Ḥanifites, Malikītes, and Shāfi'ite. The practice of philosophy was, of course, the primary target of all suspicion by theologians and jurists alike. The mystics also joined in this collective suspicion of reason as a *bona fide* medium for any grasp of reality. These hostilities were not merely matters of intellectual debates. Physical harassments, bodily injuries, outright execution and murder of opponents, and, of course, book-burning were their common manifestations.

PATTERNS OF MYSTICISM

Beginning with the fifth/eleventh century, a number of typogeneric trends in Islamic mysticism, which had started earlier, began to

5. See Qāsim Ghanī, *Baḥth dar āthār wa afkār wa aḥwāl-i Ḥāfiẓ*, 2 vols. (Tehran: Zawwār 1322 A.Hsh./1943), II, p. 467.
6. *Ibid.*, II, pp. 467-68.
7. See Farhad Daftari, *The Ismā'īlīs: Their History and Doctrines* (Cambridge University Press 1990), pp. 91-143.

come to fruition and consolidation. The iconoclastic and defiant ecstasy of the Hallājian tradition, despite the violent retribution it caused, continued in such mystics as Shaykh Abū'l-Ḥasan Kharaqānī (d. 426/1034), who, his solitary life notwithstanding, managed to be surreally represented in Sufi hagiographical sources. In opposition to Kharaqānī stands Abū Nu'aym al-Iṣfahānī (d. 430/1038), whose monumental composition of the *Ḥilyat al-awliyā'* is a valiant attempt to renarrate and thus reconstruct a respectable and self-legitimizing genealogy for Islamic mysticism whereby the earliest generations of Muslim mystics are traced back to the Four 'Rightly Guided' Caliphs (who reigned from 11/632 to 40/661); and thus Abū Bakr, 'Umar, 'Uthmān, and 'Alī are considered among the first Sufis. Abū Nu'aym's construction of this sacred genealogical narrative ought to be seen as a pious endeavor to lend orthodox legitimacy to the more ecstatic concerns of the mystical practice proper.

The presence of Ḥāfiẓ Abū Nu'aym Iṣfahānī in the late fourth/tenth and early fifth/eleventh centuries is a good indication of the general condition of mysticism during that period. His principal work, the *Ḥilyat al-awliyā' wa ṭabaqāt al-aṣfiyā'*, follows a long tradition of post-Ḥallājian mysticism, where the initial ecstatic utterances of the Sufis in Baghdad and Khurāsān give way to cooler codifications and systemic classifications of doctrines and traditions. On a par with Abū Naṣr al-Sarrāj's (d. 378/988) *Kitāb al-Luma'*, Abū Ṭalib al-Makkī's (d. 386/988) *Qūt al-qulūb fī mu'āmalāt al-maḥbūb,* and Abū Bakr Kalābadhī's (d. 385/995) *Kitāb al-Ta'arruf li-madhhab ahl al-taṣawwuf,* Abū Nu'aym Iṣfahānī's *Ḥilyat al-awliyā'* sought to quell the vigorous scholasticism of the juridical doctrines that, while an end unto themselves, also reached for political power against the Sufi Orders. Encyclopedic in its scope and magnitude, the *Ḥilyat al-awliyā'* went a long way in appropriating, systematizing, and renarrating all the preceding generations of scattered mystical sentiments and ideas. That Abū Nu'aym Iṣfahānī took his manuscript to Nīshāpūr and sold it for four hundred dinars[8]

8. Zarrīnkūb, *Justijū dar taṣawwuf-i Īrān* (Tehran: Amīr Kabīr 1357 A.Hsh./1978), p. 186.

could be a further indication of Khurāsān's significance in relation to Western Persia. The *Ḥilyat al-awliyā'* is a recuperative reconstruction of the history of Sufism. Abū Nu'aym was a distinguished scholar of prophetic traditions; and already present in his version of Sufi history is an attempt to wed the nomocentricity of law and a more mystical, existentially nuanced, conception of faith and the individual. Abū Nu'aym was so adamant in his Ash'arite affiliation—necessary to give credence to his mystical narrative—that his fellow Iṣfahānīs of the Ḥanbalī persuasion condemned him for his radical literalism.

In the same vein of a relatively more sober re-imagination of the mystical tradition, we must consider Abū'l-Qāsim Qushayrī's (d. 467/1074) *Risāla,* in which we read one of the most conscious and articulate systematizations of gnostic ideas. The deliberate sobriety that Qushayrī demonstrates in this text is an excellent example of how Islamic mysticism has had to respond cautiously and conservatively to the violent reactions of jurists and dogmatists to their ecstatic indiscretions. Khwāja 'Abdullah Anṣārī is the most radical example of nomocentric reaction to mystical ecstasy.[9] In his *Manāzil al-sā'irīn,* he becomes more of a Ḥanbalīte than Imam Ḥanbal himself in defending the cause of a radical literalism in the routine observance of rituals. The same pious expression of doctrinal orthodoxy is found in Shaykh al-Islām Aḥmad Nāmiqī Jāmī, known as Zhinda Pīl (d. 536/1141), who was particular in his designation of the mystical path as that of retribution and punishment for the slightest act of ritual transgression. "Aḥmad-i Jām," it has been comparatively suggested, "was a Persian saint who was the opposite of Abū Sa'īd in almost every respect: stern, proud of his mystical power, drawing people to repentance, not to love, and often using his spiritual strength for revenge and punishment."[10]

Shaykh Abū Sa'īd ibn Abī'l-Khayr and Shaykh Aḥmad Ghazālī (d. 520/1126), on the other hand, are two joyous and ecstatic masters of their mystical experiences who positively celebrate and enjoy every aspect of the physical world as an expression of Divinity they

9. Cf. Ravān Farhādī's study of Anṣārī in the present volume.–Ed.
10. Annemarie Schimmel, *Mystical Dimensions of Islam* (Chapel Hill: University of N. Carolina Press 1975), p. 244.

so dearly love and remember. During the same period the stunning simplicity of Bābā Ṭāhir ʻUryān's (early fifth/eleventh century) poetry successfully supersedes both the experiential and the epistemological leaps of faith that Sufism proper necessitated. In the compelling plainness of his poetic imagination, Bābā Ṭāhir achieved an autonomous access to a vision of being that could keep him and his followers happy and content for generations.

EXCEPTIONS TO PATTERNS: TWO MAVERICK INTELLECTUALS

The two giant intellectual forces of this period, Abū Ḥāmid Muḥammad Ghazālī (450/1058–505/1111) and ʻAyn al-Quḍāt Hamadhānī (d. 525/1131), are distinct phenomena unto themselves. Despite their massive appropriation into the history of Islamic mysticism, the magnitude and intensity of their intellectual achievements should not and cannot be reduced to mysticism. They are exceptions in their respective ages, one succeeding the other. Ghazālī first mastered and then surpassed all the dominant discourses of authority of his time. From jurisprudence to theology to philosophy to mysticism and even to political theory, he mastered the best that was possible in these sub-paradigmatics of the Islamic intellectual universe and then surpassed them all and attained that rarest of all achievements in Islamic intellectual history—a personal voice above and beyond all that he had most successfully represented before. This rare historical accident was repeated in ʻAyn al-Quḍāt Hamadhānī, who read Ghazālī vociferously, mastered what the former had mastered and then proceeded to achieve his own distinct personal voice, one deeply and thoroughly vibrant with the best of the Islamic intellectual universe of imagination and yet specifically that of an individual, not of an archetype. These individual voices, Ghazālī's and ʻAyn al-Quḍāt Hamadhānī's, are few and far between in both Persian and Islamic intellectual history. Although the Koranic and the *ḥadīth* metanarratives had already decided the terms and limits of their intellectual engagements and although the coalition between the juridical and the political powers had also since divided what texts and documents could historically survive and reach us, there is still much evidence in their respective works to indicate that these men thought for themselves and tried to reach an understanding of their metaphysical conditions in terms constitutional to their existential realities.

By far the most influential intellectual figure of the second half of the fifth/eleventh century, al-Ghazālī defies categorization.[11] Any attempt to label him as a theologian, a jurist, a philosopher, a political theorist, or a mystic is false and futile. He was one of those rare intellectuals who achieved an independent voice beyond particular sectarian and doctrinal discourses. By virtue of any one of his many texts, he, of course, can be claimed by jurists, theologians, philosophers, or mystics. But the combination of his texts tells a different story: the story of one historical person in search of a truth that individually made sense and mattered. The domain of Ghazālī's influence also extends far beyond his native Khurāsān or Baghdad, where he taught at the Niẓāmiyya college. His writings on Koranic exegesis, theology, jurisprudence, political theory, philosophy, and also mysticism ought to be seen in light of his later, mature, and radically individual voice, which transcends all the trappings of the dominant discourses of his time. The attention Khwāja Niẓām al-Mulk, perhaps the greatest statesman of mediæval Persia, paid to Ghazālī gave him the unique political position of having as much intellectual power as the possibility of searching for a vision of reality truthful to his own unique individual sensibilities. The unique and unprecedented *doubt,* that rarest of all moments in the Muslim intellectual tradition, that characterizes Ghazālī's intellectual odyssey led him above and beyond the perfunctory regurgitation of the received modalities of conventional wisdom. He achieved a serenity and a solitude, a safe and safeguarding distance, that allowed all conventionalities of formal and politically correct wisdom to fade away into the more compelling emergence of a sustained individual narrative, most strikingly achieved in his semi-autobiography, *al-Munqidh min al-ḍalāl*. Ghazālī's abandonment of his distinguished teaching position at the Niẓāmiyya college in Baghdad and his

11. See Zarrīnkūb, *Farār az madrasa;* Jalāl al-Dīn Humā'ī, *Ghazālī-nāma;* Montgomery Watt, *Muslim Intellectual: A Study of Al-Ghazali* (Edinburgh University Press 1963).

subsequent solitary travels throughout the Islamic lands were deliberate occasions of leaving behind all societies of communal attachments and the attainment of an existential and individual certitude. Although the final texts that resulted from this solitary journey into the domain of an unmitigated self-consciousness—namely *al-Munqidh min al-ḍalāl, Iḥyā' 'ulūm al-dīn,* and its Persian version, *Kīmīyā-yi sa'ādat*—could distance themselves only so far from the dominant discourses of Ghazālī's time, they still achieve something beyond any ordinary text in theology, philosophy, or mysticism.

Sufism and theology, as well as jurisprudence and Koranic exegesis, took full and equal advantage of Ghazālī's writings. The obvious loser in the entire Ghazālī phenomenon was philosophy. His *Maqāsid al-falāsifa* set the stage for and then his *Tahāfut al-falāsifa* launched the most successful attack yet on the legitimacy and efficacy of the logocentric language of inquiry into the state of being. It was not until Averroes (520/1126–595/1198) wrote his celebrated defense of philosophy, *al-Tahāfut al-Tahāfut,* that the grip of Ghazālī's condemnation of philosophy was effectively unlocked and the course of Islamic philosophy resumed a healthy and thriving history. All these intended or unintended consequences of Ghazālī's writings, however, were, and are, tangential to phases of delivery towards that unique and rare accident of a mediæval Muslim intellectual surpassing the debilitating grip of conventional modes of wisdom, reaching a healthy and invigorating state of doubt, and then achieving that independence of judgment and autonomy of language which is so rare in the Muslim intellectual history.

The character and significance of Ghazālī's brother, Shaykh Aḥmad Ghazālī, are dwarfed next to his far superior brother, and rightly so. Shaykh Aḥmad's exclusively mystical discourse, best evident in his treatise, *Sawāniḥ-i 'ishq,* "Aphorisms on Love," is matched by his practical concerns with Sufism. He was a practising and proselytizing Sufi. There are even reports that he may have been instrumental in attracting his brother to the mystical possibilities of their faith. But the most significant cause of attraction to Shaykh Aḥmad Ghazālī's career as a Sufi is his personal contact with another great accident in Islamic and Persian intellectual history, 'Ayn al-Quḍāt al-Hamadhānī. Although the tragic end of 'Ayn al-Quḍāt is very much reminiscent of that of Manṣūr Ḥallāj (martyred 309/

922)[12] and Suhrawardī, 'Shaykh al-Ishrāq', his achievement of a personal voice, a unique discourse of self-discovery, is identical to that of Abū Ḥāmid Muḥammad Ghazālī. 'Ayn al-Quḍāt was perhaps the most radical voice of self-discovery in mediæval Persia, from whom we have an elegant, beautiful, and stunningly candid record. He was born in 492/1098 in Hamadān. His family had migrated to Hamadhān from Azerbaijan. His father was a religious judge who educated his son in his prestigious profession. But the intellectual passion of the young 'Ayn al-Quḍāt drew him away from law and jurisprudence and towards philosophy, mysticism, and then beyond. His relentless theological preoccupations were matched by a conscious and deliberate attention to the beauty and grace of his elegant prose. By the time he was in his early twenties, he was already an accomplished theologian and philosopher, having written treatises on a number of critical issues.

'Ayn al-Quḍāt's attraction to Abū Ḥāmid Ghazālī must inevitably be considered in light of a central moment of doubt that linked these two exceptional men. Both men, one in the space of twenty years following the other, approached their intellectual lives with complete seriousness and confronted the questions of their skeptical minds with utmost sincerity. Both were harassed, one of them brutally executed, by their incomparably inferior, and thus extremely dangerous, contemporaries. As is all but inevitable in such cases, the brutal sincerity of both men, combined with their superior minds, angered their contemporaries. But whereas, upon the moment of his paralyzing doubt, Ghazālī had the shrewd political awareness to leave the public life of a teacher and to reach for a personal voice beyond his doubts in solitude, 'Ayn al-Quḍāt had the youthful audacity of thinking his skepticism publicly. His attraction to mysticism, encouraged by his friendship with Shaykh Aḥmad Ghazālī, went far beyond both the practical asceticism and the reckless ecstasy of the Sufis. He journeyed to mysticism through theology and philosophy. Like Ghazālī, he turned to mysticism as a possible epistemic breakthrough in his debilitating doubts. 'Gnosis' *('irfān)* and 'certitude' *(yaqīn)* were the ultimate concerns that drew

12. On whom, see H. Mason's essay in this volume. –Ed.

him from theology to philosophy, to mysticism, and then ultimately towards the realization of a personal voice that could speak with the unmitigated (un)certainty of being-in-the-world. At the conclusion of their paradigmatic excursions, 'Islamic' theology and philosophy, despite their innate multiplicities of discourses, reached an epistemic dead-end beyond which a skeptical mind could attain no measure of self-ascertaining certitude.

Throughout all his writings he clung steadfastly to an extremely proud, boastful even, self-consciousness, ridiculing and dismissing his accusers as inferior minds. 'Ayn al-Quḍāt was in doubt. In his mind and judgment, Islamic theology and philosophy suffered from an epistemic rupture. In its gnostic preoccupation with a knowledge that surpasses all others in its certitude, Islamic mysticism promised—it is by no means clear that it actually delivered to 'Ayn al-Quḍāt's satisfaction—much beyond that rupture. A close reading of the *Tamhīdāt*[13] (among his other works) reveals 'Ayn al-Quḍāt's persistent attempt to cross the rugged boundaries of legitimate discourses of inquiry in Islam and reach for a more immediate and unmitigated language of discovery.[14] Why was he attracted to Sufism? We have an almost full knowledge, based on his writings which have reached us, of the course of his movement away from theology and philosophy towards Sufism. Was he content with Sufism? His brilliant life was cut too short, his last works are too full of a conscious and deliberate *will* which is anything but annihilated, too confident in itself and too determined to know, for us to be able to give an unequivocally affirmative answer. The succession and combination of the *Tamhīdāt, Shakwā'l-gharīb* and his *Letters* indicate that Islamic theology, philosophy, and Sufism are terms of engagement, modes of self-discovery, which 'Ayn al-Quḍāt uses with similar ease to reach for a truth that he personally sees and confronts. Theology, philosophy, *and* mysticism offer occasions of reflection, not spaces of confinement, to 'Ayn al-Quḍāt.

---

13. See 'Ayn al-Quḍāt Hamadhānī, *Tamhīdāt,* edited with an introduction by Afif Osseiran (Tehran 1962).

14. See Arberry's introduction to 'Ayn al-Quḍāt's ideas, *A Sufi Martyr: The Apologia of 'Ain al-Quḍāt al-Hamadhānī* (London: Allen & Unwin 1969), pp. 9-19, and Osseiran's introduction to the *Tamhīdāt,* pp. 1-102.

Crossing the boundaries of politically successful discourses of legitimacy inevitably angers both political and the juridical authorities. The theologians accused 'Ayn al-Quḍāt of heresy. Qawām al-Dīn Daragazīnī, the treacherous Seljuk vizier, had him detained and jailed in Baghdad where he wrote his famous *Shakwā'l-gharīb*[15] with compelling sincerity and a sustained sense of self-justification. The defence was useless. He was sent back from Baghdad to Hamadān and then executed right at the entrance of the school where he used to teach. The year was 525 of the hegira, 1130 of the Christian era, and 'Ayn al-Quḍāt was barely thirty-three years old. His body was wrapped in a cloth and set on fire. His ashes were scattered in the air. This was the punishment for a man whose mere physical presence was a testimony to the mental and intellectual indecencies of the politically correct jurists, theologians, philosophers, and mystics.

The execution of 'Ayn al-Quḍāt Hamadhānī is one of many indications of an active hostility between the opposing claims of the legal and mystical versions of Islam for absolute metaphysical and political authority. 'Ayn al-Quḍāt was a victim of that hostility. He was killed not because he was a Sufi. There were many politically correct Sufis wandering around Hamadān and Baghdad in his time. He was killed because he assimilated the Sufi discourse into his personal narrative and reached for a personal account of a truth with which he could live—others could not.

The deeper roots of this hostility between the legal and the mystical Islam has scarcely anything to do with either a supposedly "revolutionary" predilection in 'Ayn al-Quḍāt, as Bertel's would have us believe,[16] or anything inherently "blasphemous" in his teachings, as Zarrīnkūb seems to suggest.[17] Both "revolutionary" in the merely political sense of the term, and "blasphemous" in the

---

15. A critical edition of the Arabic text of this treatise was edited and published by Afif Osseiran: *Muṣannafat-i 'Ayn al-Quḍāt Hamadhānī* (Tehran: Dānishgāh 1341 A.Hsh./1962). For an English translation, see A.J. Arberry, *A Sufi Martyr*. For a discussion of the ideas in this treatise, see the author's "'Ayn al-Quḍāt Hamadhānī wa *Risāla-i Shakwā'l-gharīb-i* ū," *Iran Nameh*, XI/1 (1993), pp. 57-74.

16. Y.E. Bertels, *Taṣawwuf wa adabiyyāt-i taṣawwuf,* translated from Russian by Sīrūs Īzadī (Tehran: Amīr Kabīr 1356 A.Hsh./1971), pp. 424-25.

17. Zarrīnkūb, *Justujū dar taṣawwuf-i Īrān,* p. 193.

merely religious sense of the term fail to grasp 'Ayn al-Quḍāt's significance. This hostility, which dates back to the earliest period of Islamic history, is, instead, a reflection of two fundamentally opposed interpretations of the Koranic revelation and the Muḥammadan legacy. The positive nomocentricity of Islamic law found the language of Islamic mysticism as quintessentially flawed in nature and disposition. The feeling was mutual. The Sufis, too, rejected the rigid and perfunctory nomocentricity of the jurists as quintessentially misguided and a stultification of the Koranic message and the Prophetic traditions. The metaphysical bipolarity had, of course, an active political component with both the mystics and the jurists seeking to manipulate the powers-that-be in their respective interests and advantage. The political powers could, and would, alternate between the jurists and mystics as the culprits of effective legitimacy for their own rule. Muslim philosophers and other men of science, the mostly quiet advocates of the rule of reason, the logocentric forces in the course of Islamic intellectual history, had to manoeuver their limited ways through these troubled and dangerous lands. Once, successfully appropriated out of their individual voice and into the powerful mystical tradition, figures such as 'Ayn al-Quḍāt Hamadhānī represent dangerous implications in the culminations of the mystical potentialities of Islam, coming very close to negating the metaphysical authority of the jurists and thus substituting the rule of mystics. The widespread popularity of mystical Orders had particularly alarming effects for both the religious and the political authorities of the jurists. At strategic points in Islamic history, when the culmination of public sentiments towards mystical sensibilities appeared to undermine their authority, the jurists have reacted swiftly and effectively in eliminating their religious and political rivals.[18]

18. That Zarrīnkūb (*Justujū dar taṣawwuf-i Īrān,* pp. 193-94) suggests a possible Sunni-Shi'ite element in the hostility expressed by the mostly Sunni jurists to the possibly Ismā'īlī-influenced ideas of 'Ayn al-Quḍāt does not in any significant way modify the larger hostilities between the jurists and the mystics in general—whether Sunni or Shi'ite.

'Ayn al-Quḍāt's unmistakably personal voice is marked by a distinct passion, a relentless drive to convince, a noble disdain for the vulgar and the conventional. His entire corpus of writings is a hermeneutics of the novel, staccatos of unconventional discoveries. His conceptions and articulations of both philosophical and gnostic ideas are crystal clear, delivered in a voice of sustained dispassion. His was a courageous soul that could not hold back, conceal, or convolute what it saw and perceived. At times there is a unity, a harmony, a perennial design that he detects in being, and he decodes and systematizes that being in analytical detail. At times he de-systematizes that design, challenges that perenniality, and most fascinating of all de-narrates himself. He was merciless in his attacks against those he considered to be the perfunctory dogmatists of the normative routinizing of the faith, of the act of knowing. His innate superiority of intellect created anger and jealousy among his older, inferior, and threatened contemporaries. The multidimensionality of his intellectual disposition, perhaps the core reason for this jealousy, is such that, exactly like Ghazālī, his conscious champion and model, without grave injustice to the unfolding totality of his ideas, he cannot be categorically and exclusively identified as a mystic, philosopher, or a theologian. 'Ayn al-Quḍāt was a metaphysician of uncommon brilliance, mastering all languages of inquiry available in his time. In the span of a brutally short life, he produced a body of work unsurpassed in the clarity and precision of its conceptions and articulations. The range of issues, concerns, and problems addressed therein draw on a number of dominant Islamic discourses including theology, philosophy, mysticism, and Persian and Arabic literary traditions.

He was the most prominent authority on Ghazālī's writings and an outspoken and unusually articulate propagator of his ideas. Appropriating a discourse which, from its very inception, was persecuted and harassed and which, as a result, had developed a veiled and concealed language of deliberation, he dared to test the limits of his adversaries by writing and speaking in an unusually clear and eloquent diction. He was deliberate and emphatic in his defense of Manṣūr Ḥallāj, the legendary mystic whose martyrdom in 310/922 left an indelible mark on the historical legacy of mystical Islam. His open advocacy of Ḥallāj, who had uttered the impermissible counterclaim that "I am the Truth," meant implicit, if not explicit, repetition of what the theologians and legalists would consider to be blasphemous. Claims to divinity were one of major charges brought against him. This charge must be considered in light of the quintessential discrepancy between the language of mystical expressions, which 'Ayn al-Quḍāt appropriated, and the fundamental concerns of the jurists. Whereas for the Muslim mystic there is a pervasive existential presence of the Divine in all aspects of the material and immaterial realms, for the jurist the basis of human existence is absolute obedience to an all-powerful, distant, and quintessentially Other, God. The Sufi's self-perception includes the divine presence. The jurist's self-perception, exactly to the contrary, is predicated on the Other-perceptions of God. Whereas these Other-perceptions of God are doctrinal to the jurist, they are antithetical ('blasphemous', if we could use the term here) to the Sufi. Any Other-perception distinct from God, the conception of anything but God having an ontological reality, what the bifocal ontology of the jurist entails, is fundamentally opposed to the mystic's self-negating perception. And that is precisely the root of the opposition of the discourse between the mystic and the jurist.

The brutal execution of 'Ayn al-Quḍāt in the year 525/1131 in Hamadān was the result of a deliberate process of accusation, trial, indictment, and sentencing. The principal charge was that he had claims to divinity, which is the most serious charge in Islamic law. The indictment was brought against him, and an edict was issued, sentencing him to death. The actual order for his brutal execution, however, was issued by Qawām al-Dīn Abū'l-Qāsim ibn Ḥasan Daragazīnī, a Seljuk vizier. The apocryphal quatrain that has been attributed to 'Ayn al-Quḍāt posthumously has an emphatic reference to this execution:

We have asked for death and martyrdom from God
And that in exchange for three worthless things:
If the friend does as we wish
We have asked for fire, gasoline, and wool.[19]

19. Quoted by Dhabīḥullāh Ṣafā, *Tā'rīkh-i adabiyyāt dar Īrān,* 5 vols. (Tehran: Amīr Kabīr 1953-85), II, p. 228.

The deliberate tone of this quatrain, useful for a mystical reading of 'Ayn al-Quḍāt's execution, seems to have a suicidal ring to it which is not true of his articulate, defiant, sober, and conscious defense of his ideas. As is perfectly evident in his crystal-clear writings, particularly his apologia, *Shakwā'l-gharīb,* he was a brilliant and articulate systematizer of his ideas. He was vastly erudite, unusually deliberate and clear-headed in his ideas, and in full control of his intellectual pursuits.

THE POLITICS OF PIETY

The occasional violent harassment of mystics in the sixth/twelfth century should not be taken as an indication of a general condition of adversity for the Sufis. On the contrary, it is perfectly evident that the mystics by and large enjoyed a very prestigious and favorable position. Both the Mongol warlords and the less fanatic members of the clerical establishment were not only tolerant of the mystics but, in fact, paid them the highest respect. The mystics travelled, taught, and engaged in their mystical exercises rather freely. Sufi gatherings for the purpose of ecstatic exercises were equally common and popular. In fact, it was precisely this popularity and prestige of the mystics which often aroused the jealousy and hostility of some members of the clerical establishment. The Seljuk conquerors of the Persian territories realized the popularity of the mystics and used it for their own immediate political benefit. Sultan Tughrïl (reigned 429/1038-455/1063) himself and a number of his viziers are reported to have been devotees of various Sufi masters.[20]

The great Seljuk warlords are reported to have paid their highest respects to the mystic masters.[21] If the reports of the *Asrār al-tawḥīd,* written towards the end of the sixth/twelfth century, are to be accepted, the Sufis' greatest advocate in this period was no lesser

20. See Muḥammad ibn 'Alī ibn Sulaymān al-Rāwandī, *Rāhat al-ṣudūr wa āyat al-surūr dar tārīkh-i Āl-i Siljūq,* pp. 98-99.
21. See Muḥammad ibn Munawwar ibn Abū Sa'īd Mīhanī, *Asrār al-tawḥīd fī maqāmāt al-Shaykh Abū Sa'īd,* pp. 58-59. Ibn Munawwar reports on the authority of his uncle how Niẓām al-Mulk had seen Shaykh Abū Sa'īd in his childhood and how the great Sufi Shaykh had predicted the political grandeur awaiting the future Seljuk vizier.

authority than Niẓām al-Mulk himself. He is even reported to have been a devotee of Shaykh Abū Sa'īd ibn Abī'l-Khayr. He was as diligent in the establishment of his famous *Madrasas* as he was of the Sufi quarters *(Khānaqāh)*.[22] A particularly poignant feature, which is witnessed repeatedly in this period, is the public expression of humility by Seljuk warlords towards the mystics. The Seljuk sultans would publicly kiss the hand or even the feet of the Sufi masters. Another common expression of humility and obedience was to hold two hands as a step for the Sufi Shaykh to mount a horse. This latter gesture was considered a particularly powerful indication of the humility and obedience of the sultans towards the mystics.[23]

In the fifth/eleventh century, the mystics began to cultivate a greater role in the political reconfiguration of power. The story of Sultan Maḥmūd's encounter with Shaykh Abū'l-Ḥasan Kharaqānī is a typical example of the increasing prestige and status of the Persian mystics. Sam'ānī's *Kitāb al-ansāb* has given a full account of this encounter.[24] Sultan Maḥmūd's rather submissive portrayal in Shaykh Abū'l-Ḥasan Kharaqānī's presence indicates the political significance that the mystics had assumed. Shaykh Abū'l-Ḥasan al-Kharaqānī receives Sultan Maḥmūd as a superior monarch receives an inferior warlord. When Sultan Maḥmūd offers Shaykh Abū'l-Ḥasan Kharaqānī gold, the Sufi master dismisses the offer with great indignation. A similar encounter is reported between the Seljuk Sultan Tughrïl and Bābā Ṭāhir 'Uryān. In Rāwandī's *Rāḥat al-ṣudūr*, which was composed in 599/1202, there is a detailed account of this encounter.[25] Other than Bābā Ṭāhir, there are two Sufi Shaykhs who are reported to be present at this historical encounter: Bābā Ja'far and Shaykh Hamshad Kuhakī. When Tughrïl sees these three Sufi masters, he stops his royal entourage, descends from his horse, approaches them, and, as a sign of his humility towards them, kisses their hands. Tughrïl's vizier, Abū Naṣr al-Kundurī, follows

22. See *ibid.*, pp. 177-180. Ibn Munawwar reports on a Sufi *Khānaqāh* established by Niẓām al-Mulk in Iṣfahān. For other indications of Niẓām al-Mulk's devotion to the Sufis, see *ibid.*, pp. 90, 365-66.
23. Rāwandī, *op. cit.*, p. 99.
24. As reported in Ghanī, *op. cit.*, II, p. 474.
25. See Rāwandī, *op. cit.*, pp. 98-99.

him in this gesture of obedience. At this point, Bābā Ṭāhir is reported to have put a blunt question to Tughrïl: "What will you do with God's people?" The mere posing of the question and putting Tughrïl in a position of responsibility to answer further amplifies the political relation of power that now submits the Turkish warlord to the Sufi Shaykh. This question, rhetorical and accusatory, amplifies the already established relation of obedience vividly expressed in Tughrïl's kissing the hands of Bābā Ṭāhir and his fellow Sufis. Tughrïl is quoted as having answered that he would do as Bābā Ṭāhir commands. Bābā Ṭāhir commands him to do as God says: treat his subjects with justice and kindness. Bābā Ṭāhir's quoting the Koran for Tughrïl is a clear indication of what and who the supreme figures of authority are in that legitimate political culture to which both Bābā Ṭāhir and the Turkish warlord belong. Tughrïl obeys Bābā Ṭāhir. By speaking through the Koran, which is the voice and word of God, Bābā Ṭāhir, in effect, creates and legitimizes a universe of sacred imagination from which Tughrïl, as the ruler of a Muslim land, cannot escape. Whether this story is true or not, its historical memory serves as the prototypical model for subordinating the political to the mystical. Far from being apolitical mystics, these legendary Sufi Shaykhs are indeed great conduits of political power, figuring very prominently in any configuration of power that holds the Islamic polity together.

There are many stories in the *Asrār al-tawḥīd* which testify to the political power of the Sufi Shaykhs, particularly, in this case, that of Shaykh Abū Sa'īd.[26] Khwāja Abū Manṣūr Waraqānī, a vizier to Tughrïl, is reported to have asked both Shaykh Abū Sa'īd and Abū'l-Qāsim al-Qushayrī to come and pray on his grave when he dies, so that both the living people and the angels of death would recognize him as a pious and God-fearing man.[27] In another story, Ibrāhīm Ïnāl, a brother of Tughrïl, is reported to have been a particularly evil tyrant in Nīshāpūr. Despite his insistence, Shaykh Abū Sa'īd never praised him in public. Finally, one day he paid a visit to Shaykh Abū Sa'īd and begged him for a statement approving

26. On such stories, see also the essay by Terry Graham above, pp. 83-135 .–ED.
27. *Asrār al-tawḥīd,* II, pp. 115-16.

of his character. Shaykh Abū Sa'īd refused. Ibrāhīm Ïnāl insisted. After three refusals, Abū Sa'īd finally said, "You will lose all your fortune!" "That would be fine," the tyrant prince responded. "You will lose your reign!" Ibrāhīm Ïnāl consented. "You will lose your life!" Abū Sa'īd warned him for the third time. "That would be fine," Ibrāhīm said. Abū Sa'īd took a piece of paper and wrote on it, "Ibrāhīm is one of us!" and signed his name. Soon after this incident, Ibrāhīm Ïnāl rebelled against his brother and was captured. Before he was to be put to death, he asked for Abū Sa'īd's statement to be put in his hand and buried with him. "If his statement be with me," Ibrāhīm Ïnāl is reported to have said of Shaykh Abū Sa'īd, "tomorrow [that is, upon Judgement Day] I can seek his protection!"[28]

There is a story, similar to that reported in Rāwandī's *Rāḥat al-ṣudūr* between Tughrïl and Bābā Ṭāhir, in the *Asrār al-tawḥīd* between Tughrïl, his brother, Chaghrī Beg (d. 452/1060), and Shaykh Abū Sa'īd. The two Seljuk warlords come to pay their respects to the Sufi Shaykh in Mayhana. They come to Abū Sa'īd's *Khānaqāh* and, in front of his entire audience, kiss his hand and ask for his blessings. "As was his habit," Muḥammad ibn Munawwar reports of Shaykh Abū Sa'īd, "the master lowered his head in silence for a while, and then he raised his head and told Chaghrī, "We give thee the reign of Khurāsān," and told Tughrïl, "the kingdom of Iraq, we give thee." The two warlords pay their respects and leave. This is all *before* they ultimately defeat the Ghaznavids and come to power.

In another story, the same Khwāja Abū Manṣūr Waraqānī, Tughrïl's vizier, is reported to have excused himself one day when summoned by his Turkish warlord. "I have not said my daily prayer yet," the vizier tells the royal messenger. When he finally comes to Tughrïl's court, the vizier Waraqānī finds the Turkish prince rather angry. "Whenever I send for you," Tughrïl is reported to have said, "they tell me you are reading the Koran or saying your prayers; and then I cannot do anything." Vizier Waraqānī responds, "It is as your Majesty says. But you must know that I am the slave of God (first)

28. *Ibid.*, I, pp. 116-17; for other, similar, stories about this Ibrāhīm Ïnāl in the *Asrār al-tawḥīd,* see *ibid.*, I, p. 234.

and your obedient servant (next). Until I have performed my rightful duties, as a servant to Almighty God, I cannot attend your services. If your Majesty can find a vizier who is not a slave of God and totally obedient to him, I shall immediately retire." Tughrīl is properly admonished and permits his vizier to perform his duties to God first before he comes to his service. The story goes on to say that Shaykh Abū Sa'īd hears of this incident. "Prepare my horse! We wish to pay him a visit." As Shaykh Abū Sa'īd rides toward vizier Waraqānī, a dervish is sent in advance to inform him of the pending visit of the Sufi master. When Shaykh Abū Sa'īd reaches vizier Waraqānī's place, his entourage is begged to haste because, "as soon as he heard that the master is coming to pay him a visit, he has remained standing and refuses to sit down." When the vizier is told to sit down, he responds that, "It is not right for such a great master to be on his feet to come to visit us and then for us to be seated." Shaykh Abū Sa'īd finally enters and blesses the vizier with his words. "We were afraid, master," vizier Waraqānī confides to Shaykh Abū Sa'īd, "that this Sultan is a Turk and one cannot be too impertinent with him." Shaykh Abū Sa'īd consoles and encourages him and then teaches him a verse to recite when in the presence of any Sultan, and he will be protected.[29]

The collective sentiments of these stories indicate a very pronounced relation of power, wished for or attained, between the Persian mystics and the world conquerors who came their way. As is perfectly evident in the behavior of Shaykh Abū Sa'īd, he is quite conscious of the political power invested in him by virtue of having a massive group of followers. Figures of absolute political authority, whether Tughrīl himself or his brother or his vizier, also recognize this power and try to tame it to their own advantage. When vizier Waraqānī asks Shaykh Abū Sa'īd and Imam Qushayrī to pray on his grave when he dies, he is quick to point out to them that "I have loved you both and spent considerable money for you, and now I need you."[30] Whether in fear of the hereafter or the political necessity of here and now, the political authorities catered attentively to

29. *Ibid.*, I, pp. 319-21. For other stories about Shaykh Abū Sa'īd and vizier Abū Manṣūr Waraqānī, see *ibid.*, I, p. 338.
30. *Ibid.*, I, p. 115.

the needs of the Sufi Shaykhs. In his treatment of Ibrāhīm Ïnāl, Shaykh Abū Sa'īd exudes an air of disgust and intolerance. He praises vizier Waraqānī for standing up to Tughrïl himself. In his own treatment of Tughrïl, Shaykh Abū Sa'īd leaves no room for conjecture as to who is really in charge. "We give thee dominion over Iraq!" That is a political statement, an indication of a power that, rooted in an ethic of world-rejections although it might be, fully recognizes the terms of worldly authority.

This emerging pattern of authority for the Sufi masters creates a dual rivalry between them and the jurists who claim a similar relation of power between God's voice and the political figures. Tughrïl is reported to have wept in awe and obedience and then promised Bābā Ṭāhir to do as he says, upon which Bābā Ṭāhir puts onto Tughrïl's finger the holding-ring of a jug from which he had been using water for ritual ablutions. "Royal authority over the world," Bābā Ṭāhir is reported to have said, "I thus put into your hands. Be just."[31] Tughrïl kept that ring, so the story goes, among his most cherished possessions and put it on his finger whenever he was engaged in a battle.

Both these examples, those of Sultan Maḥmūd and Sultan Tughrïl in relation to Shaykh Abū'l-Ḥasan Kharaqānī and Bābā Ṭāhir, respectively, are good indications that during the fourth/tenth, the fifth/eleventh, and the sixth/twelfth centuries, the Sufi masters began to claim and assume considerable social significance that was effectively translated into political power. The emergence of this social and political significance must be attributed at least in part to both the systematization and codification of mystical doctrines, which began to provide Sufism with a measure of doctrinal stability, as well as to the apparently dismissive attitude towards political power adopted by the Sufi Shaykhs. This apparently dismissive attitude, more than anything else, created an aura of spiritual and emotional self-sufficiency which was particularly conducive to fostering sentiments of popular devotion.

---

31. See Rāwandī, *op. cit.*, p. 99.

The mystical discourse and practice in the fifth/eleventh century also had the added advantage of remaining distant from the dominant sectarian, dogmatic, and juridical disputes that divided Islamic societies into opposing and hostile camps. The mystical preaching of the primacy of being-in-love and of individual existential experiences made the Sufi alternative particularly appealing to a wide range of ordinary or powerful Muslims. This increasing popularity and prestige of the Sufis should not, of course, be considered by any means as an indication of the decline of the *'ulamā*'s authority. The predominance of the juridical discourse never relaxed its domineering control of the Islamic creedal and political cultures. Nevertheless, throughout the fourth/tenth, the fifth/eleventh, and the sixth/twelfth centuries we witness the institutional emergence of mystical authority over an ever-increasing body of followers. Shaykh Abū 'Alī Daqqāq (d. 407/1016) became incredibly popular and powerful in Nīshāpūr. Abū'l-Qāsim al-Qushayrī, his student and son-in-law, immortalized his teacher's thoughts in his famous *Risāla*. Through another great Sufi master, Abū Sa'īd ibn Abī'l-Khayr, we know of his teacher, Pīr Abū'l-Faḍl al-Sarakhsī. For generations this master-disciple relationship continued to institutionalize the historically anchored memory of mystical lore. Usually a particularly powerful but reclusive Sufi master is matched by an equally powerful yet more articulate student, and then the combination would result in a generation of successful repoliticization of the mystical orders. The relationship between Pīr Abū'l-Faḍl and Abū Sa'īd Abī'l-Khayr, as well as that between Shaykh Abū Alī Daqqāq and Abū'l-Qāsim al-Qushayrī, are of this nature.

Of particular importance in this period is the increasing tendency of the Seljuk warlords to enter into political dialogue with the jurists and mystics in the interests of legitimizing their authority. Philosophers by and large practiced their discourse at the court. As potential viziers, physicians, and astronomers, they had an established a courtly connection which needed the royal patronage for its survival. Given the historical hostility of both the juridical and the mystical discourses to the independent rule of reason, the philosophical discourse was increasingly limited to the domain of political protection. While the *Madrasa* system continued to function as the institutional basis of the juridical discourse and the *Khānaqāh* emerged as that of the mystical, the royal court—with its functional extension into the practical needs of the royalty, such as astronomical observatories, libraries, hospitals, and the administrative apparatus of the state—became the social framework of tolerated, if not legitimate and permissible, engagement with philosophy. The institutional and functional consolidation of these multiple discourses of authority in the fifth/eleventh century necessitated a more active dialogue between the political establishment and its respective counterparts in the juridical, mystical, and philosophical domains.

The reign of Sultan Maḥmūd the Ghaznavid (reigned 388–421/998–1030) marks perhaps the most pronounced period in the growth of active dialogue between the political and the juridical languages of legitimacy, whereby Maḥmūd would characterize his military conquest of India and western Persia as primarily religious missions on behalf of the Sunni orthodoxy of the central caliphate.[32] Following the reign of the Ghaznavids (366/977–582/1186), the same progressive composition of the political and juridical conceptions of legitimate discourse continued well into the Seljuk period (429/1038–590/1194). The Seljuks' juridical affiliation with the Ḥanafites put them in close alliance with the central caliphate and made them the staunchest enemies of not only their sectarian rivals, namely the Twelve Imamī Shi'ites and the Ismā'īlīs, but also of their rivals in the mystical and philosophical discourses. Tughrïl was a particularly pious Ḥanafite who lost no opportunity to please the central caliphate.

The relationship between Tughrïl and the Abbasid caliph al-Qā'im (reigned 422/1031–467/1075), although of a primarily political nature, reflecting the oscillating factor of legitimacy between the central caliphate and the eastern provinces, had a catalytic effect on the Seljuk warlord's attitude towards the non-juridical elements in his own realm. The more the Seljuk warlords were in need of political legitimacy by the central caliphate, the less their

32. See Niẓām al-Mulk, *Sīyāsatnāma,* edited by H. Darke (Tehran: B.T.N.K. 1340 A.Hsh./1961), pp. 64-65, for an example of a story characterizing Sultan Maḥmūd as a pious Muslim warrior. See also Abū'l-Faḍl Muḥammad ibn Ḥusayn Bayhaqī, *Tārīkh-i Bayhaqī,* edited by 'Alī Akbar Fayyāḍ (Mashad: Firdawsī University Press 1350 A.Hsh./1971), p. 92.

level of tolerance for the unorthodox concerns of their subjects for mystical or philosophical issues became. They invariably had a harsh and dismissive attitude towards both the sectarian (Shi'ites) and the discourse-based (Sufis and philosophers) enemies of their local *'ulamā'*, who, in effect, were the native representatives of the distant caliphatal orthodoxy. Thus, the famous encounter between Tughrïl and Bābā Ṭāhir must be considered in its implications for practising mystics in light of these more institutional developments. 'Aḍad al-Dawla Alp Arslān (reigned 455/1063–465/1072), who succeeded Tughrïl, extended this orthodox hostility against unorthodox tendencies into inter-religious domains and fought against the Christian enemies of the central caliphate. The clear winners in these political arrangements were the *'ulamā'*, the most successful custodians of the sacred lore. The Ḥanafite jurists, in particular, enjoyed increasing authority; and their juridical discourse was successfully established as the language of doctrinal legitimacy at the expense of both the mystical and the philosophical alternatives. The Shi'ites, the Qarmatians, the Sufis, and the Mu'tazilites, as well as the sectarian, political, mystical, and theological opponents of the Ḥanafite doctors, were the obvious losers in this state of affairs.

Among the four schools of Sunni law, the Shāfi'ites and the Ḥanafites were most successfully represented in the eastern Persian provinces. In the northern and western parts of Iran, however, Shi'ism had a strong historical hold. The sectarian hostilities between the Sunnis and Shi'ites in the eastern and western parts of Iran further consolidated their respective orthodoxies because these hostilities were in essentially dogmatic and doctrinal terms. The more the Sunnis and the Shi'ites fought each other's doctrinal positions, the more they consolidated their respective orthodoxies against both mysticism and philosophy. Mystics and philosophers, whether Sunni or Shi'ite, were the clear losers in this situation. Outside the sectarian preoccupations of the Sunni and Shi'ite dogmatists, the conceptual concerns of the philosophers and mystics were increasingly isolated in their libraries and *Khānaqāh*s, with their constituency always in a position of political compromise.

The Seljuk viziers were significant conduits of continuity and change during this period. 'Amīd al-Mulk Abū Naṣr al-Kundurī (murdered in 456/1063) was a staunch Ḥanafite and thus fully supported the Turkish warlords in their anti-heterodoxical policies. However, the most influential vizier of the Seljuks was Khwāja Niẓām al-Mulk, by far the most significant political theorist of mediæval Persia. He was a Shāfiʻite, and his pious orthodoxy is best expressed by a story reported in later sources. He is believed to have asked for a statement testifying to his justice and piety to be signed by all juridical authorities of his time. Imam Abū Isḥāq Fīrūzābādī, a prominent jurist of that time, is reported to have written on the statement, "Ḥasan was the best among the tyrants," and then signed it. Khwāja Niẓām al-Mulk liked this statement more than any other. That he is later reported to have appeared in someone's dream and said that precisely by that phrase his salvation was guaranteed[33] is an indication of the power of implication such stories had over many generations.

Niẓām al-Mulk's greatest contribution to mediæval Islamic intellectual history was the construction of the Niẓāmiyya *Madrasa* System. These dominant centers of juridical learning were dedicated exclusively to the cause of Shāfiʻite jurisprudence. It is reported in the *Tajārib al-salaf*[34] that when Sultan Jalāl al-Dawla Malikshāh (reg. 465/1072–485/1092) wished to establish a school in Iṣfahān, he was not particular that only the Ḥanafite Law, which he personally followed, be taught. Ultimately both the Ḥanafite and the Shāfiʻite Law, to which Niẓām al-Mulk subscribed, were to be taught simultaneously. This is a remarkable indication of the power that great viziers such as Khwāja Niẓām al-Mulk exerted in propagating not only their particular brands of juridical dogmas but the nomocentric orthodoxy of the faith in general.

Khwāja Niẓām al-Mulk was a crucial figure in the Persian political culture. On the ancient model of the Persian philosopher/vizier, he crafted a political discourse and practice above and beyond the dominant discourses of legitimacy operative in a Muslim empire. His *Siyāsatnāma* must be considered as a crucial text in achieving two significant objectives. First, as a 'mirror for princes', it advances, perhaps more than any text before it, the claim of

---

33. Hindūshāh ibn Sanjar ibn Ṣāḥibī Nakhjiwānī, *Tajārib al-salaf*, edited by ʻAbbās Iqbāl (Tehran: Tāhārī 1344 A.Hsh./1965), p. 277.
34. *Ibid.*, pp. 277-78.

Persian political discourse to independent autonomy. Second, it effectively enters into a sustained and mutually legitimizing dialogue with the juridical discourse. The ultimate result of the *Siyāsatnāma* in Persian political culture is that it effectively puts the significant political implications of both the Islamic philosophical and mystical discourses into an eclipse. What Niẓām al-Mulk achieves in the *Siyāsatnāma,* and indeed practises under the Seljuk warlords, is an autonomous political discourse and praxis which considers the act of political authority as a reality *sui generis,* independent of Islamic legitimacy. The Persian narrative of the *Siyāsatnāma,* its frame and form of references to pre-Islamic Persian sources, and its full recognition of political power as a historical and institutional authority all contribute to the effective legitimacy of a political discourse which is no longer reducible to Islamic (that is, Koranic and *ḥadīth)* sources. Both the theoretical and institutional discourses of Islamic legitimacy—from jurisprudence to theology, philosophy, and mysticism—are consequently rendered subordinate to the primacy of the Persian political narrative and administration of power.

Khwāja Niẓām al-Mulk's attention was never exclusively focused on the jurists and theologians. While he was adamant in his establishment of law schools for his preferred juridical discourse, he also paid attention to the mystical dimension of Islam and built a number of Sufi *Khānaqāh*s. He supported the jurists and the Sufis simultaneously—both to keep them in balance as well as to keep his political options open—as to which one was more popularly successful in the legitimation of his Seljuk warlords. There is no accurate way of ascertaining the relative powers of the jurists and the mystics. While the jurists had far-reaching power over political leadership, the urban elite and the merchant class, the mystics shared considerable power in all these areas, had an inroad into the artisan guilds, and then extended their influence well into the peasantry. Their habits of constant travel gave them an added advantage over the sedentary and urban *'ulamā'*. The number of clerics in the fifth/eleventh and sixth/twelfth centuries, which are given in the thousands only in the Persian provinces, could very well have been matched by the number of mystics.

There are a number of stories in the *Asrār al-tawḥīd* about the relation of the Sufi masters with Niẓām al-Mulk which can shed light on this aspect of his administration. According to one story, Kamāl al-Dīn Abū Sa'īd, the uncle of Muḥammad ibn Munawwar, along with his father and grandfather, once visited Niẓām al-Mulk in Sarakhs. The famous vizier recounts to his guests the story of his encounter with Shaykh Abū Sa'īd Abī'l-Khayr in his childhood:

> I was a child when Shaykh Abū Sa'īd (may his gracious tomb be sanctified!) came to Ṭūs. I was just a child. With a group of children I was playing in the Christian quarter. The master approached with a large group of his followers. When he reached us, he turned to his entourage and said, "Whoever wants to see the master of the whole world, he is standing right here!" And he pointed towards us. We were all looking in confusion at each other, wondering whom he meant, because we were all innocent children. Forty years have passed since that day. Today it is evident that he meant me.[35]

Forty years after the reported story, the incident still carried enough power for Niẓām al-Mulk to remember and remind his Sufi guests. In another audience with Niẓām al-Mulk, another group of Sufi masters was told by the Persian vizier how he owed everything he had achieved to Shaykh Abū Sa'īd. In another encounter with Shaykh Abū Sa'īd, Khwāja Niẓām al-Mulk reminisces with his Sufi audience how the great Sufi master had predicted that soon four thousand men would stand in his service, with four hundred of them having golden belts. And this had come to pass exactly, as Shaykh Abū Sa'īd had predicted it.[36]

In yet another story, Khwāja Niẓām al-Mulk is reported to have built a *Khānaqāh* for the Sufis in Iṣfahān. Every year, right before the month of Ramaḍān, he would attend to all the needs and expectations of the dervishes gathered in that *Khānaqāh*. One year the group of expectant Sufis is gathered in this *Khānaqāh;* and all through the months of Rajab, Sha'bān, and Ramaḍān Khwāja Niẓām al-Mulk does not lift a finger to attend to the needs of the Sufis, so used to the Persian vizier's generosity. They are baffled and confused as to what might be the explanation for this until, in the month

---

35. *Asrār al-tawḥīd,* I, pp. 58-59.
36. *Ibid.,* I, p. 90.

of Shawwāl, Niẓām al-Mulk sends word to the custodian of the *Khānaqāh,* a certain Sayyid Muḥammad, to come and pay him a visit and bring along ten of the Sufis. When the Sufis enter, they see Niẓām al-Mulk sitting at prayer, with a candle lit in front of him. In that condition, the Seljuk vizier tells his Sufi visitors the story of how, when he was a young man, he had asked his father to send him to Merv where he could pursue his studies more seriously. His father had agreed, given him a slave and a donkey, and sent him to Merv. But "when you reach Azhjāh," his father had stipulated, "ask your fellow-travellers to wait for you for a day and then you go to Mayhana to Shaykh Abū Sa'īd Abī'l-Khayr. Pay him your respects and listen to what he says. Whatever he says, listen carefully and do as he says, and then ask him to pray for you." Khwāja Niẓām al-Mulk did as his father had said. Early in the morning he reached Mayhana and was utterly surprised when he saw crowds of Sufis in their dark clothes gathered around the road leading to the town. He asked what so many Sufis were doing there so early in the morning. He was told that that morning Shaykh Abū Sa'īd had informed them after sunrise prayer that "whoever wants to see a young man blessed in this and the other world should go to the road to Azhjāh and welcome him." Khwāja Niẓām al-Mulk's eyes filled with tears. He went up to Shaykh Abū Sa'īd:

> I expressed my obedience and humbly greeted him, kissing the master's hand. The master looked at me and said, "Greetings and good tidings, young man! You will one day rule the whole world. Be steadfast because yours is that position. Nothing can prevent you from your destiny. But it will not be too late when seekers of knowledge will be in your need. Do you promise me to take good care of them?"[37]

Niẓām al-Mulk had promised to do as he was told by Shaykh Abū Sa'īd. Then he paused and asked if there was a sign as to how long he would be given the honor of providing for the Sufis. "Yes, there is," Shaykh Abū Sa'īd had answered. "Whenever the honor is taken from you, that will the end of your life."

At this point Niẓām al-Mulk turns to his Sufi guests and regret-

37. *Asrār al-tawḥīd,* I, pp. 178-79

fully informs them that for a month he had intended to attend to their needs at the *Khānaqāh,* and yet God Almighty has not given him the opportunity. He reports that he has been praying for three days and nights asking God to grant him the honor of once again attending to the Sufis' needs. "I know," he further adds, "that I have reached the end of my life, as the blessed words of the master said." Khwāja Niẓām al-Mulk is reported to have managed to attend to the material needs of the Sufis that year too but he soon left for Nahāwand, and there he was killed by the Ismā'īlīs.[38]

The power of these stories, and the act of their remembrance, cannot be overstated. Despite their pious exaggeration and hagiographical hyperbole, these stories, precisely in their fictional and narrative power, convey the historical dimensions of Sufi institutional authority in this period. As the greatest political mind of the Seljuk period, Niẓām al-Mulk undoubtedly recognized the power of the mystical language, the institutional organization of the Sufis, their popularity, and the impact of their predictive narrative. By repeatedly putting himself at the self-fulfilling end of Shaykh Abū Sa'īd's prophetic voice, he appropriates that predictive power for his own benefit and, in turn, by appropriating the political might of his own power into the mystical narrative of the *Asrār al-tawḥīd,* effectively demonstrates the moral and institutional superiority of Sufism over both its political and juridical counterparts. In fact, according to another story, Khwāja Niẓām al-Mulk is believed to have once been admonished by a Shi'ite for his support of the Sufis. "You make your means available," the Shi'ite scholar is reported to have admonished Niẓām al-Mulk, "to a bunch of people who cannot even do their ritual ablution properly according to the tradition. They cannot even say their minimum prayers right. They know nothing of religious sciences. A gang of ignoramuses, handmaidens of Satan himself!" Niẓām al-Mulk defends the Sufis and argues that the mystic masters are, indeed, very learned in religious sciences. Knowledge of the religious sciences, he argues, purifies one's conduct; and the Sufis are indeed very particular in conducting their lives properly. But the Shi'ite detractor does not give up easily. "Is

38. For the full text of this tale, see *ibid.*, I, pp. 177-80.

it not commonly believed that Shaykh Abū Sa'īd Abī'l-Khayr is the leader and master of all the Sufis of the world?" the Shi'ite man asks. "That is true," responds Niẓām al-Mulk. "Is it not," the Shi'ite interlocutor continues, "also commonly believed that after him his son is the best of all contemporary Sufis and that Shaykh Abū Sa'īd has said that Khwāja Abū Ṭāhir is a pillar of mysticism?" Niẓām al-Mulk again agrees. "Khwāja Abū Ṭāhir does not know the Koran," the Shi'ite raises his accusatory finger. "He knows the Koran!" Niẓām al-Mulk refuses to believe. "He does not," the Shi'ite insists. "He does!" the Persian vizier is adamant. "We are going to call him right away. You choose a verse from the Koran and I will ask him to recite it verbatim."

Khwāja Abū Ṭāhir, totally oblivious to what is happening, is summoned. "What verse do you want him to recite?" Khwāja Niẓām al-Mulk asks the Shi'ite man. "Ask him to recite, 'Lo! We have given'..."[39] Khwāja Abū Ṭāhir begins to recite the whole chapter in a loud and clear voice, moving his audience to tears and ecstasy. Khwāja Niẓām al-Mulk is delighted. The audience is ecstatic. The Shi'ite man is "greatly broken to have been proven a liar in such a gathering, in front of such a great man. In utter humiliation, he rose and left."[40] Khwāja Abū Ṭāhir subsequently reveals to his Persian patron that he really does not know the Koran, and that it was only due to the insistence of his great father, Shaykh Abū Sa'īd, that years ago he memorized only this passage of the Koran. The entire audience takes this episode as yet another indication of Shaykh Abū Sa'īd's exceptional premonition that he knew that his son would one day be put to a test and thus saved him from embarrassment and humiliation. From that point forward, "Niẓām al-Mulk became one thousand times more obedient" to the memory of Shaykh Abū Sa'īd.

In the remembering and creative imagination of Muḥammad ibn Munawwar, the author of *Asrār al-tawḥīd,* the supreme political authority of Khwāja Niẓām al-Mulk, as well as the accusatory charges of all Sufi detractors, are thus assimilated and subjected to

39. Koran XLVIII: 1. The full verse is "Lo! We have given thee (O Muḥammad) a signal victory..."
40. *Asrār al-tawḥīd,* I, p. 366.

the supreme memory and the predictive power, of the Sufi master. Through these narratives, the presiding figure of Shaykh Abū Sa'īd becomes a *sui generis* reality which, beyond time and space, determines the course and outcome of events. Evident in this story, however, is also the relentless rivalry between the mystical and the nomocentric readings of Islam to reach for the sympathy and support of political power. The Shi'ite detractor, Khwāja Abū Ṭāhir, and Khwāja Niẓām al-Mulk here represent and personify the nomocentric, mystical, and political representations of 'Islam', or 'Islam-in-history', in actual and institutional rivalry with each other. The political authority, however, the man with his hand on the sword, is always in the central position of power.

The rivalries and hostilities were not only between various readings of 'Islam' but also within them. The legal, nomocentric, reading had its own particular inner tensions. Throughout the fifth/eleventh and sixth/twelfth centuries, the two prominent schools of law in Iran, Ḥanafism and Shāfi'ism, were in hostile confrontation with each other. The extension of this legal hostility into the political realm, whereby the representatives of each school presented their opinion in the presence of sultans and viziers, had the unintended consequence of lending religious legitimacy to the powers that be. By the same token, Muslim jurists claimed to be the sole representatives of 'Islam', custodians of the sacred. This close proximity between the *'ulamā'* and the sultans, despite the immediate hostility it generated among various factions of the juridical discourse, led to the exclusive claim to legitimacy by the nomocentric forces. The more violent the expression of hostility among the juridically based arguments of the Shāfi'ites and the Ḥanafites, the stronger would emerge the cause of the nomocentric Islam. In fact, when these juridical arguments were extended into the arena of doctrinal hostilities among the Sunnis and the Shi'ites, the level of disputations still remained literal and dogmatic. The immediate political implications of these arguments put the entire juridical class, irrespective of its particular jurisprudence, in a favorable position of power against both philosophers and mystics.

During the sixth/twelfth century, the consolidation and institutionalization of mysticism required a conscious attention to the juridical requirements. The Persian mystics in the eastern part of the land, for example, were emphatic in their acceptance of the Shāfi'ite school of jurisprudence. Thus, according to the *Asrār al-tawḥīd,* Shaykh Abū Sa'īd was a pronounced Shāfi'ite,[41] and Muḥammad ibn Munawwar further reports that many other mystics were Shāfi'ite in their jurisprudence. However, he makes a point of not offending the Ḥanafites of his time and gives a full apologetic account of Imam Abū Ḥanīfa's piety and perspicacity.

THE POETICS OF PIETY

While effectively checked and balanced by the jurists and their legal/political power, the Persian mystics of the Seljuk period took full advantage of an entirely different opportunity. It has already been noted by historians of Persian Sufism[42] that, beginning with the fifth/eleventh century, mystical terms and ideas began to find their way into the fertile soil of the Persian poetic imagination. The metempsychosis of mystical love into physical love and vice versa forever changed and confused the clarity and reality of physical love most immediately accessible to the poetic imagination. When poetry qua poetry—not poetry as versified occasion for mystical reflection—forfeited its autonomous address/access to a truth coexistent with its own reality, it lost precious territory to Sufi ideas. Poetry became subservient to the mystical cause and almost forgot that it had an independent claim on reality. But Sufism benefitted greatly from this subservience of the poetic imagination. The attempt to argue that poetry and mysticism have something quintessentially in common with each other[43] does not reduce the autonomy of one to the authority of the other. The intrusion of Sufism into poetry is a simultaneous provision of a ready-made answer to enduring questions that must and does constantly animate poetry. When poetry propagates and celebrates the answers that Sufism, as a body of established and self-evolving doctrines, has independently reached outside poetry, it robs itself of its own possible access to its own answers. A considerable space in Persian poetic

41. *Asrār al-tawḥīd,* I, p. 20.
42. Ghanī, *op. cit.,* II, p. 472.
43. *Ibid.,* II, pp. 472-74.

imagination yielded obediently to the comforting certainties of Sufism and thus lost its own animating sense of wonder about the world.

In this vein, great Persian poets lend their poetic imagination to the mystical cause. Abū'l-Majd Majdūd ibn Ādam Sanā'ī (d. 525/1131),[44] author of the 'Enclosed Garden of the Truth' *(Ḥadīqa al-ḥaqīqa),* was one of the greatest poets of this period, with a particular penchant for mysticism.[45] He was a court poet of exceptional poetic gifts who served the Ghaznavid rulers. After a spiritual conversion, he put his poetic gifts at the disposal of mystical ideas. Following the tradition of Manūchihrī and Farrukhī, Sanā'ī had contributed immensely to the Persian court poetry before he submitted to the magnetic force of the mystical imagination. His *Ḥadīqa al-ḥaqīqa* is one of the earliest and most successful mystical *Mathnawīs*, which provided exemplary models for both 'Aṭṭār and Rūmī.[46]

With Sanā'ī, the Persian poetic imagination is successfully, but never completely, appropriated by mysticism. Prior to Sanā'ī, Shaykh Abū Sa'īd's occasional poems did provide a vehicle for certain mystical ideas. But Shaykh Abū Sa'īd was a Sufi, not a poet, whereas Sanā'ī was a full-fledged poet, with a magnificent creative imagination, who subsequently converted to Sufism.[47] Historians of Persian poetry consider him "the first Sufi poet" in the language.[48] For the first time, he gives full poetic expression to the range of mystical ideas the Sufis had developed. His impact on, in effect his mystification of, the Persian poetic discourse has even been identified as "revolutionary."[49] Prior to Sanā'ī, the Persian poetic

---

44. On Sanā'ī, see also the essay by J.T.P. de Bruijn above, pp. 361-79.–ED.
45. Bertel's argues against the notion of Sanā'ī as a Sufi poet; many other historians do consider him a mystic. See Jan Rypka, *History of Iranian Literature* (Dordrecht, Holland: D. Reidel Publishing Co. 1968), p. 243, n. 47.
46. See Rypka, *op. cit.*, pp. 236-37; see also Furūzānfar, *Sharḥ-i aḥwāl wa naqd wa taḥlīl-i āthār-i Shaykh Farīd al-Dīn Muḥammad 'Aṭṭār Nishābūrī* (Tehran: Diḥkhudā Publications 1353 A.Hsh./1974), pp. 70-72, 147-48, and *passim*.
47. For the most recent and comprehensive study of Sanā'ī's poetry, see De Bruijn, *Of Piety and Poetry: the Interaction of Religion and Literature in the Life and Works of Ḥakīm Sanā'ī of Ghazna* (Leiden: E.J. Brill 1983).
48. See Abū'l-Majd Majdūd ibn Ādam Sanā'ī, *Ḥadīqa al-ḥaqīqa,* edited and annotated by Mudarris Raḍawī (Tehran: University Press 1360 A.Hsh./1981), p. KJ.

discourse can be identified as a reality *sui generis,* after its own material or ideal interests. With Sanā'ī's mystification of this discourse, Sufism to a considerable degree, but never completely, subordinates the Persian poetic imagination. He, in effect, establishes a poetic convention, systematizes a range of poetic terms, which thenceforth paradigmatically anticipates much of Persian poetry of subsequent generations—from his own *Ḥadīqa al-ḥaqīqa,* to 'Aṭṭār's *Manṭiq al-ṭayr,* to Rūmī's *Mathnawī* and then beyond. As indeed realized by Rūmī, Sanā'ī was the key poetic cornerstone upon whom 'Aṭṭār and Rūmī themselves were made possible.

'Aṭṭār was the spirit, Sanā'ī the two eyes
And I tread in the tracks of Sanā'ī and 'Aṭṭār [50]

Sanā'ī's systematization of the Sufi poetic narrative becomes so successful that even during his lifetime his contemporary Sufis begin to quote him as a source of mystical authority. Aḥmad Ghazālī, his contemporary, quotes him frequently in his *Sawāniḥ*. Sanā'ī himself was quite conscious of his achievements in putting his poetic gifts in the service of a mystical purpose. In the final chapter of his *Ḥadīqa al-ḥaqīqa,* he asserts:

Of all the poets major and minor
Only I know the words of the Prophet.
My poetry is a commentary on the religion and the law,
And that is what the truthful poet does.
Of all the poets, only I
am the Prophet's, by Almighty God...
I am the slave of the religion, obedient to piety,
A truth-telling poet am I, nothing coveting.[51]

TEXTS THAT AUTHORIZE

Beyond the appropriation of the poetic imagination, the mystical discourse sought another significant narrative. A particularly important mode of continuity and self-legitimacy in Persian Sufism of this

49. *Ibid.*
50. Rūmī, cited *ibid.*
51. *Ḥadīqa al-ḥaqīqa,* pp. 725-26.

period is the textual authority of the biographical/hagiographical dictionaries which the mystics began to compose. The model of this biographical/hagiographical discourse was, of course, that of the Prophet's immediate companions, which was later appropriated by the *'ulamā'* and the jurists to provide a genealogical narrative of self-legitimacy for their own class. Other social groupings, such as philosophers and physicians and even poets, also used this powerful self-legitimizing tool to construct a history of sustained institutional continuity and authority for themselves. The same self-legitimizing force was also behind the mystics' construction of a genealogical narrative, such as Shaykh Abū 'Abd al-Raḥmān Sulamī's (d. 412/1021) *Ṭabaqāt al-ṣūfiyya* and Ḥāfiẓ Abū Nu'aym Iṣfahānī's *Ḥilyat al-awliyā'*, in which generations of Sufis began to trace their origins back to the immediate companions of the Prophet and ultimately to the Prophet himself. The legitimizing force of their genealogical narrative can scarcely be overestimated. In the post-Ḥallājan crisis of mystical legitimacy in which a full and critical view of the powerful ecstatic utterances of some mystics began to be taken, it became particularly necessary to take full advantage of this powerful legitimizing device. Since the construction of a sense of sustained continuity bred authority and legitimacy, these hagiographical dictionaries became the very institutional basis of the historical continuity and doctrinal legitimacy of the mystical discourse. When Sulamī wrote his *Ṭabaqāt al-ṣūfiyya,* he could claim the entire gamut of Islamic mystical tradition all the way back to the Prophet's own time. This same *Ṭabaqāt al-ṣūfiyya* later reaches Khwāja Abdullāh Anṣārī, who renders it from Arabic into the Herātī dialect of Persian and adds additional material to it. It is this text that later reaches 'Abd al-Raḥmān Jāmī (d. 898/1492), who produces a Persian text—the *Nafaḥāt al-uns*—from it and adds some new material. This succession of genealogical narratives from one patristic generation to another becomes a central discourse of self-legitimacy that provides one group of Sufis after another with a sustained and uninterrupted sense of tradition and history.

THE ECSTATIC INTERLUDES

Although the systematization of Sufi doctrines and its formal approximation to the established and hegemonic discourse of the theological and juridical discourses went quite far in legitimizing the mystical narrative, by no means did the ecstatic and intoxicated utterances *(shaṭḥiyyāt)* in the spirit of Ḥallāj cease in the brutal aftermath of that martyred mystic. In the sporadic utterances of Bāyazid Basṭāmī (d. 261/875), Shaykh Abū'l-Ḥasan al-Kharaqānī (d. 425/1033), and, ultimately, Abū Sa'īd ibn Abī'l-Khayr, the ecstatic counternarrative continued well into the fifth/eleventh century. The forceful and uncompromising nature of this ecstatic counternarrative was in radical opposition not only to the predominant nomocentricity of the juridical discourse but, in effect, it even took to task the sobriety of the mainline mystical orthodoxy. Although Khurāsān initially appears to have been a particularly fertile ground for such intoxicated statements, later, in the sixth/twelfth century, 'Ayn al-Quḍāt Hamadhānī seems to have extended it into the northwestern Seljuk territories. The proclivity of this intoxicated counternarrative towards ecstatic utterances should not necessarily be considered a sign of anti-institutional tendencies. Shaykh Abū Sa'īd Abī'l-Khayr, for example, is credited with having been one of the most authoritative sources of formal etiquette in Sufi gatherings.[52]

During the reign of the Ghaznavid Sultan Maḥmūd (reg. 388/998–421/1030), Sultan Muḥammad (reg. 421/1030–421/1031), and Sultan Mas'ūd (reg. 421/1031–432/1041), Shaykh Abū Sa'īd Abī'l-Khayr, as noted above, became the most famous and prominent Sufi of his time. Even allowing for the obvious hyperbolic language of *Asrār al-tawḥīd* which is dedicated to a pious remembrance of this Sufi master's sayings and doings, Shaykh Abū Sa'īd represents the extreme case of ecstatic acts during this period. He gave the jurists of his time much excuse to plot his murder. He went so far as to openly sing and dance in a mosque, preventing his followers from performing their obligatory religious duties. He was the complete opposite of Khwāja 'Abdullāh Anṣārī, who was emphatic about the importance of a Muslim's religious obligations. Caught between the ritual aspects of his faith and a mystical concern with inner sensibilities beyond such manifestations, Anṣārī sought refuge in the

52. See Ghanī, *op. cit.*, II, p. 477.

humble piety of his simple but compelling invocations.

Such ecstatic interludes, however, did not effectively disrupt the course of the Persian Sufism during the Seljuk period. From the Ghaznavid to the Seljuk periods, devoted mystics managed to maintain a sustained level of engagement with ideas and sentiments constitutional to Persian mysticism. The most prominent mystic of the early fourth/tenth century in Fars, Abū ʻAbdullāh Muḥammad ibn Khafīf Shīrāzī, known as the 'Grand Master' *(Shaykh-i kabīr,* d. 371/981), tried to maintain a careful balance between law and ecstasy, between strict ritualist dogma and ecstatic freedom. A generation later, Shaykh Abū Isḥāq Kāzarūnī known as the 'Master Guide' *(Shaykh-i murshid,* d. 426/1034) was one of those Sufis whose direct connection to his Zoroastrian ancestry points to the continuing evidence of a thematic link between the mystical dimensions of Zoroastrianism and Persian Sufism. But it is also because of this Zoroastrian connection that *Shaykh-i murshid* was particularly observant of Islamic *Sharīʻa* and, in fact, engaged in a kind of 'crusade' against the Zoroastrians of Fars.[53]

Thus, against all odds, turning disadvantage to benefit, persistently expanding its territorial claims on the Islamic sacred imagination, Persian Sufism emerged triumphantly from the formative Ghaznavid and the Seljuk periods and waited upon its more victorious institutional achievements during the Mongol era.

---

53. See Zarrīnkūb, *Justijū dar taṣawwuf-i Īrān,* p. 186.

Early Sufism in Eastern Anatolia

Ahmet T. Karamustafa

I. INTRODUCTION

The present study focuses on aspects of Sufism in Asia Minor during the sixth and seventh/twelfth and thirteenth centuries. Since the religious dimensions of this period of Islamic history are particularly difficult to trace, it may be advantageous first to give a brief survey of the existing scholarship on the subject.

The Islamization of Asia Minor started with the first major Turkish incursions that took place following the battle of Manzikert in 463/1071. In the course of the following two centuries, to about the death of Rūmī (671/1273), the frontiers between Islamdom and Byzantium were transferred West from Eastern Anatolia to a line that ran roughly from Kastamonu to Nicaea in the north, to Antalya in the south, while the newly conquered territories in between were rapidly Turkicized and Islamized through the immigration of largely, though not exclusively, Turkish Muslims throughout this period.[1]

The religious dimension of this process of Islamization is usually understood in terms of what may be called 'the great and little

1. Detailed studies of the process of Islamization of Asia Minor are Claude Cahen, *Pre-Ottoman Turkey: A General Survey of the Material and Spiritual Culture and History, c. 1071-1330,* trans. J. Jones-Williams (New York: Taplinger Publishing Company 1968), and S. Vryonis, Jr., *The Decline of Medieval Hellenism in Asia Minor and the Process of Islamization from the Eleventh through the Fifteenth Century* (Berkeley: University of California Press 1971).

traditions paradigm'. In this view, the spread of Islam took place on two levels that displayed a peculiar relationship to one another. One level consisted of the 'great tradition' of the sophisticated urban elites, which flourished with the formation of traditional Islamic towns in the peninsula. Another was the 'little tradition' of the rural masses, peasants and nomads, which remained subject, though largely immune, to influences originating from the great tradition. Applied to the Anatolian case, this paradigm produces the following picture with respect to Sufism:

On one hand, the growth of traditional Islamic communities in urban centers like Erzurum, Tokat, Sivas, Kayseri, Malatya, and Konya prepared the spaces within which sophisticated Sufism, expressed in the respectable linguistic channels of Arabic and Persian, could breathe and develop. The most notable feature of this particular phase of the 'great' Sufi tradition in Asia Minor was its incredibly creative synthetic power, as evidenced by the geniuses of Jalāl al-Dīn Rūmī and Ibn al-'Arabī (d. 638/1240). On the one hand, one encounters the Persian culture, exemplified by such Sufis as Najm al-Dīn Rāzī (d. 618/1221), 'Azīz al-Dīn Nasafī (d. circa 680/1282) and Bahā' al-Dīn Walad (d. 627/1230)—and, on the other, the Arab intellectual background, incarnate in the philosophical pedigree of Ibn al-'Arabī. These focal movements in the history of Sufism, as well as the later development of the Mevlevī Order and the School of Ibn 'Arabī, rightly have been, and continue to be, at the center of scholarly research on this Anatolian phase of the great Sufi tradition.

In the countryside, on the other hand, the process of Islamization manifested itself most clearly in the rise to prominence of a new class of holy men generally known as *bābā*s (Turkish for 'father'). The *bābā*s, representatives of the 'little' Sufi tradition, are depicted in the scholarly literature as thinly Islamized versions of the ancestral shamans of the non-Muslim Turkish nomadic tribes. Mostly lacking any formal education and without a working knowledge of either Arabic or Persian, these itinerant preachers, we are told, often had at best a deficient understanding of the different currents of the great tradition. Their Sufism, therefore, sat like a layer of veneer on the hardwood of their essentially non-Islamic belief-systems. Devoid of interest in and of itself, the Sufism of the *bābā*s has attracted scholarly attention chiefly on account of the significant roles these holy men played in the social and political history of the period.[2]

The great and little traditions paradigm suggests, therefore, that both the elite and the folk currents of early Anatolian Sufism coexisted side by side as discrete religious trends without any noticeable interaction. The great tradition, Arabic and Persian in medium, and urban in orientation, was superimposed upon the little tradition, Turkish in medium and rural in outlook—a pale and distorted reflection of its refined counterpart. The former grew directly out of mainstream Arab and Persian Sufism, while the latter remained at the very margins of Islamic mysticism as, at best, a Sufi-colored religious phenomenon. The Sufi-coloring of the latter is then explained as the legacy of a crucial early encounter between the Turkish tribal mind and mainstream Sufism, namely the disciple-master relationship between Aḥmed Yesevī (d. 562/1166) and Yūsuf Hamadānī (441-535/1049-1140). In this view, the master architect of which was the Turkish historian M. F. Köprülü,[3] the origins of the little tradition in early Anatolian Sufism are to be traced back to a Khurāsānian milieu, where, it is postulated, the nascent Yesevī movement was the point of contact with Sufism for the majority of Turkish-speaking Muslim peoples. The *bābā*s of Asia Minor are

2. On the close relations between political rulers and popular religious figures, see I. Beldiceanu-Steinherr, "Le règne de Selim Ier: Tournant dans la vie politique et religieuse de l'Empire Ottoman," *Turcica* 6 (1975), p. 36; Claude Cahen, "Baba Ishaq, Baba Ilyas, Hadjdji Beḳtash et quelques autres," *Turcica* 1 (1969), p. 1; and M. F. Köprülü, "Anadolu'da Islāmīyet: Türk istilāsından soñra Anadolu tārīḫ-i dīnīsine bir naẓar ve bu tārīḫiñ menba'ları,' *Dārü'l-fünūn Edebiyāt Fakültesi Mecmū'asi* 2 (1922-23), p. 293. The relationship between the Ottoman Orḫān Ġāzī and Geyikli Bābā (see below) provides an excellent example. On the alliance between the Karamanoğlu dynasty and an Ilyāsī trend, see Cahen, "Baba Ishaq," p. 61; and H. Z. Ülken, "Anadolu tārīḫiñde Dīnī rūhīyāt müşāhedeleri," Medḫal: I. Burak Baba. II. Geyikli Baba. III. Ḥācī Bektāş Velī,' *Mihrāb* 1 (1923), pp. 444-445.
3. M.F. Köprülü developed his views in "Anadolu'da İslāmīyet," (pp.281-311; 385-420; 457-486) and *Türk Edebiyatında İlk Mutasavvıflar,* 2nd ed. (Ankara: Diyanet İşleri Başkanlığı Yayınları 1966), Part I, pp. 21-153. This latter should be read in conjunction with the article on Yesevī by the same author in *İslam Ansiklopedisi,* s.v. "Aḥmed Yesevī," which contains some important revisions of the earlier work. On Abū Ya'qūb Yūsuf b. Ayyūb al-Hamadānī, see *İlk Mutasavvıflar,* pp. 51-58, and W. Madelung, "Sufism and the Karrāmiyya," in *Religious Trends in Early Islamic Iran* (Albany: Bibliotheca Persica 1988), pp. 49-51.

The Mausoleum of Aḥmed Yesevī. (Photo by Mehmet Yalcin)

thus rendered direct spiritual descendants of the great Turkish Sufi master Aḥmed Yesevī.

It is not my intention here to evaluate the above-outlined trends in existing scholarship on early Anatolian Sufism as a whole. I would, instead, like to identify several areas in which the great and little traditions paradigm should be modified in order to render it more flexible and incisive. My observations will be based on specific case studies, and with this purpose in mind, I now proceed to present brief biographies of several prominent Turkish Sufis of the period under consideration.

II. BĀBĀ İLYĀS

The most informative source on the life of Bābā İlyās is the *Menāḳıbu'l-ḳudsiyye fī menāsıbi'l-ünsiyye* (760/1358-59, in Turkish) written by Elvān Çelebi.[4] The author, a great-grandson of Bābā İlyās and the son of the more famous 'Āşıḳ 'Alī Paşa (d. 733/1332, who composed the first major Sufi work written in western Turkish entitled the *Ġarībnāme),* devotes the second chapter of his six-chapter work to Şücā'eddīn Ebū'l-Baḳā Bābā İlyās-ı Ḫorāsānī (d. 638/1240). The latter mystic came from Khurāsān to Anatolia during the time of the Anatolian Seljuk Sultan 'Alā al-Dīn Kayqubād I (reg. 618-634/1200-37) settling in the village of Çat near Amasya. Although he was on good terms with Kayqubād I, he fell out of favor during the reign of the latter's son Ghiyāth al-Dīn Kaykhusraw II (reg. 634-643/1237-45) and had to take refuge in the castle of Amasya in order to escape persecution. It was at this juncture that one of his prominent disciples, namely Bābā İsḥāḳ, revolted against the Seljuks in Syria and travelled to Amasya to join his Shaykh against the wishes of the latter, who had asked İsḥāḳ to stay clear of

4. İ. Erünsal and A. Y. Ocak, eds., *Menāḳıbu'l-ḳudsiyye fī menāsıbi'l-ünsiyye: Bābā İlyas-ı Horasānī ve Sülālesinin Menkabevi Tarihi* (Istanbul: İstanbul Üniversitesi Edebiyat Fakültesi Yayınları 1984). Earlier studies on the text are A. Y. Ocak, "Les *Menakib'ul-Ḳudsīya fī Menāsib'il-Unsīya:* une source importante pour l'histoire religieuse de l'Anatolie au XIIIe siècle," *Journal Asiatique* 267 (1979), pp. 345-56; M. Önder, "Eine neuentdeckte Quelle zur Geschichte der Seltschuken in Anatolien," *Wiener Zeitschrift für die Kunde des Morgenlandes* 55 (1959), pp. 83-88. Cahen also refers to it in his "Baba Ishaq," p. 58.

Amasya. When İlyās refused to see him, İsḥāḳ moved with his mostly nomadic supporters, who had by then increased significantly in number, to the vicinity of Kırşehir where he engaged in a pitched battle with a Seljuk army containing Georgian, Kurdish, and 'Frankish' contingents. It is said that after this battle, which saw the total destruction of İsḥāḳ's army, Bābā İlyās mounted his white horse and ascended to the sky; no trace of him could be found after this point.

The official Seljuk historian Ibn Bībī gives an account of the Babā'ī uprising in his *al-Awāmīr al-'Alā'iya* (written in 680/1281, in Persian). Surprisingly, however, Ibn Bībī's account revolves around the figure of Bābā İsḥāḳ, and no mention is made of Bābā İlyās. According to Ibn Bībī, Bābā İsḥāḳ was from the Kafarsūd region in Syria. He was gifted in jugglery as well as magic and preached among Turkish tribes. Eventually growing afraid that he would start to be perceived as an impostor, he disappeared into the common folk and re-emerged in Amasya as a righteous and pious holy man absorbed in devotion and prayer. It is said that he acted as an arbiter of conflicts and disagreements among his followers by preparing talismans for them. For a while, he travelled around southeast Anatolia and preached against Sultan Ghiyāth al-Dīn. The latter reacted by dispatching troops against him under the command of a certain Muẓaffar al-Dīn, who was defeated twice by İsḥāḳ and his followers; the rebels thus gained control over Tokat and Sivas. Soon afterward, Bābā İsḥāḳ was captured and executed by the Seljuk commander Ḥājjī Armaghānshāh, who was himself later killed by İsḥāḳ's followers. The forces of İsḥāḳ, which were apparently not shaken by their leader's death, could only be suppressed by a special army (which contained a sizeable 'Frankish' contingent) summoned from the eastern borders of the Anatolian Seljuk empire. The Seljuk victory was followed by an extensive massacre, in which all the supporters of İsḥāḳ were killed, women and children included.[5]

In a third source contemporary with these events, the history of Gregory Bar Hebraeus (Ibn al-'Ibrī, d. 685/1286, in Syriac), Bābā İlyās appears under the title 'Papa.' Bar Hebraeus writes that Bābā

5. Ibn Bībī, *Die Seltschukengeschichte des Ibn Bībī,* trans. H. W. Duda (Kopenhagen: Munksgaard 1959), pp. 216-220. The Persian original of this work was not available to the author for this study.

İsḥāḳ was a disciple of an old ascetic Turkmen in Amasya known as 'Papa' who claimed to be the messenger, *rasūl,* of God. It was Papa who dispatched Bābā İsḥāḳ to the eastern borders of the land of Rum, where İsḥāḳ gathered many supporters among the Turkmens and defeated the forces of the *amīr* of Malatya sent against him. In the meantime, however, Papa died in Amasya, whereupon İsḥāḳ and his immediate entourage began to spread the rumor that their spiritual leader ascended to the sky in order to recruit the angels to his cause. Turkmen rebels, numbering around six thousand, then moved westward towards Amasya, inflicting serious blows to Seljuk forces on their way. Such was their devotion and strength that an army of six thousand could not attack them; they could be beaten only when around one thousand Frankish horsemen, who were placed in the front ranks of the Seljuk army, charged upon them without fear and the rebels were massacred to the last man.[6]

In other sources Bābā İlyās is mentioned only in passing. In the *Tevārīḫ-i Āl-i 'Osmān* (written 889/1484-85, in Turkish), 'Āşıḳpaşazāde confirms the lineage of Bābā İlyās as given by Elvān Çelebi and gives the additional information that he was the deputy, *khalīfa,* of a certain Seyyid Ebū'l-Vefā as well as the Shaykh of Geyikli Bābā. 'Āşıḳpaşazāde also states that Ḥācī Bektāş and his brother Menteş paid homage to Bābā İlyās when they travelled to Rum from Khurāsān.[7] In the Arabic *al-Shaqā'iq al-nu'māniyya fī 'ulamā' al-dawlat al-'uthmāniyya* (965/1558) of Aḥmed Taşköprīzāde, Bābā İlyās is only mentioned once as the Shaykh of Geyikli Bābā.[8] The Turkish translation of this work by Edirneli Mecdī (995/1586), however, has a separate entry under the title 'Bābā İlyās-i 'Acemī,' where it is related that he came from Khurāsān during the time of Chingiz Khān, settled in Amasya and

6. Abu'l-Farac Tarihi, trans. Ö. R. Doğrul (Ankara: Türk Tarih Kurumu Yayınları 1950), pp. 539-540.
7. The edition of *Tevārīḫ-i Āl-i 'Osmān* used here is that of N. A. Çiftçioğlu in *Osmanlı Tarihleri* (İstanbul: Türkiye Yayınevi 1949), pp. 77-319. References to Bābā İlyās are found on pp. 91, 122, 234, and 237. Ebū'l-Vefā (Muḥammad Abū'l-Wafā' Tāj al-'Ārifīn), Geyikli Bābā and Ḥācī Bektāş are dealt with later in this essay.
8. Aḥmed Taşköprīzāde, *al-Shaqā'iq al-numāniyya fı 'ulamā' al-dawlat al-'uthmāniyya* (Beirut: Dār al-Kitāb al-'Arabī 1390/1970), p. 11.

gathered many supporters around himself. Most of his followers, however, were destroyed by Sultan Ghiyāth al-Dīn, who had become suspicious of their aims, and soon Bābā İlyās himself was killed at the hands of his followers. Mecdī also adds that İlyās had a son called Muḫliṣ Bābā.[9] Two later sources, the *Bahjat al-tawārīkh* (composed in 861-63/1455-58, in Persian) of Şükrullāh and Müneccimbaşı Aḥmed Dede's *Ṣaḥā'if al-akhbār fī waqāyi' al-a'ṣār* (1083/1673, in Arabic) recapitulate the information already given above, yet contain the additional report that Bābā İlyās was involved in the uprising led by Bābā İsḥāḳ, but was granted a pardon by the Sultan after the supression of the rebellion.[10]

Several additional sources mention a certain Bābā Resūl without giving the proper name of this figure. One of these, the history of Bar Hebraeus, where Bābā Resūl is depicted as an old ascetic Turkoman who claimed to be an apostle of God, *rasūlallāh,* has already been noted. The Dominican missionary Simon of Saint-Quentin, who crossed through Anatolia shortly after the Bābā'ī revolt, refers to a certain "Paperoissole" who presented himself as the messenger of God as the leader of the uprising.[11] Ṣibt b. al-Jawzī, writing shortly before 653/1255, also mentions a Bābā Rasūl in his *Mir'āt al-zamān.*[12] Finally, Bābā Resūl appears in the *Vilâyetnāme* (composed possibly late 9th/15th century, in Turkish) as one of the prominent disciples of Ḥācī Bektāş and conversely, as the Shaykh of this latter in the *Manāqib al-'ārifīn* (718/1318-19—754/1353-54, in Persian) of Shams al-Dīn Aḥmad Aflākī.[13]

On the basis of the information presented above, it is difficult to reconstruct the history of the Babā'ī revolt. The central puzzle concerns the identity of Bābā Resūl. If it is kept in mind that the active

9. Mecdī Efendi, *Şaḳâyıḳ Tercümesi* (İstanbul: n.p. 1269/1853), pp. 32-33.
10. These references are cited in Köprülü, *İlk Mutasavvıflar,* pp. 177-178, no. 35.
11. Simon de Saint-Quentin, *Histoire des Tartares (Historia Tartarum),* ed. J. Richard (Paris: Paul Geuthner 1965), pp. 62-63.
12. Reference cited in Cahen, "Baba Ishak," p. 55.
13. *Vilâyet-nâme: Manâkıb-ı Hacı Bektāş-ı Veli,* ed. A. Gölpınarlı (İstanbul: İnkilap Kitabevi 1958), pp. 58-59, and Shams al-Dīn Aḥmad Aflākī, *Manāqib al-'ārifīn,* 2 vols., ed. T. Yazıcı (Ankara: Türk Tarih Kurumu Yayınları 1976-1980), vol.1, pp. 381-383 (anecdote number 3/312). In the same place, Aflākī also refers to a chief disciple of Ḥācī Bektāş named İsḥāḳ, though it is not possible to know if this figure bore any relation to Bābā İsḥāḳ, the disciple of Bābā İlyās.

leader of the Babā'ī uprising was not İlyās but İsḥāḳ, and more significantly, that Ibn Bībī specifically mentions the reputation of Bābā İsḥāḳ among his followers as the 'messenger of God', then it is tempting to think that it was İsḥāḳ who was also known as Bābā Resūl.[14] On the other hand, if Bar Hebraeus' account is to be believed, it might seem more plausible that the old ascetic Turkoman mentioned by him who claimed to be *rasūlallāh* was in reality no other than Bābā İlyās.[15] In this respect, it is significant that Bābā İlyās's great grandson Elvān Çelebi supplies us with a third alternative, namely that Bābā İlyās himself did not claim to be the prophet of God but was alleged to have made such a claim by his detractors who desired to incite the Seljuk Sultan against him.[16] Whatever the truth, it can be asserted with some degree of certainty that there were at least two different *bābā*s who were involved in the uprising, namely İlyās and İsḥāḳ, and that the latter was probably a disciple of the former.

14. Köprülü is the most consistent exponent of this view. He believes that Bābā İsḥāḳ was the real initiator of the rebellion and that he exploited the reputation of Bābā İlyās for his own political purposes. See his "Anadolu'da İslāmīyet," pp. 305-306, and *İlk Mutasavvıflar*, pp. 177-178. Cahen also seems to think that Resūl is to be identified with İsḥāḳ, see 'Baba Ishaq', p. 55, and "A propos d'un article récent et des Babâ'is," *Journal Asiatique* 268 (1980), pp.69-70.
15. This is the position of the foremost scholar of this episode in Seljuk history, Ahmet Yaşas Ocak, *Babaīler İsyanı* (Istanbul: Dergāh Yayınları 1980); see also the published version of his doctoral dissertation, *La Révolte de Baba Resul ou la Formation de l'Hétérodoxie Musulmane en Anatolie au XIIIe Siècle* (Ankara: Türk Tarih Kurumu 1989). Ocak holds that Bābā İlyās was identical with Bābā Resūl and that Bābā İsḥāḳ was his disciple.
16. *Menāḳıbu'l-ḳudsiyye,* pp. 42-44 (verses 477-501). Ocak thinks that Elvān Çelebi is here merely trying to absolve his great-grandfather of objectionable allegations. However, there seems to be little reason to discard Elvān Çelebi's account as a clever attempt to clear his ancestor's name.

III. GEYIKLI BĀBĀ

Information on Geyikli Bābā is found in several sources, the earliest among them being the history of ʻĀşıḳpaşazāde and the anonymous *Tevārīḫ-i Āl-i ʻOsmān.* As the *al-Shaqā'iq al-nuʻmāniyya* by Taşköprīzāde contains the most comprehensive account of this *bābā* and is in agreement with the reports of the earlier sources, it is this account which is presented below.

Taşköprīzāde mentions Geyikli Bābā among the Shaykhs who flourished during the reign of the Ottoman Orḫān Ġāzī (r. 726-761/ 1326-59). He was called Geyikli Bābā (in Turkish, literally meaning the 'Bābā with deer'), because he used to ride deer, which were also very fond of him. His real name was not known to Taşköprīzāde. Originally from the town of Khoy in Iran, he was a disciple of Bābā İlyās, and the master of his initiatic lineage *(pīr* of the *silsila)* is identified as Ebū'l-Vefā el-Baġdādī. Geyikli Bābā participated in the conquest of Bursa by Orḫān (726/1326), then settled in a village in the vicinity of that city where he spent the rest of his life. He was highly cherished by Turgut Alp, Orḫān's close friend and a military commander under him. The following anecdotes reveal Orḫān's deep reverence for Geyikli Bābā.

After the conquest of Bursa, Orḫān wanted to donate the nearby town of İnegöl along with its surroundings to Geyikli Bābā. The holy man first refused the offer, saying that property was the due of rulers only, but later conceded to the persistent demands of Orḫān and accepted a piece of land for his dervishes. On another occasion, Geyikli Bābā uprooted a tree and, carrying it all the way to Bursa, planted it right beside Orḫān's residence, an act to which Orḫān reacted with the greatest joy. When Geyikli Bābā died, the Sultan had a mausoleum, and, according to Mecdī also a mosque and a *zāwiya,* built over his grave.

Taşköprīzāde reports that Geyikli Bābā was a man of ecstasy *(jadhba),* possessing miraculous powers *(karāma);* he was cut off from worldly interests, always facing the divine presence. In one entry in *al-Shaqā'iq* one of his miraculous deeds is recorded which gives information on another famous dervish of the same period, Abdāl Mūsā. The latter, who also resided in Bursa, sent a piece of burning coal wrapped in cotton to Geyikli Bābā as a sign of his miracle-working powers. Yet he had to acknowledge the superiority of Geyikli Bābā's sanctity when he received a bowl of deer's milk from him in return. Abdāl Mūsā explained that it was more difficult to enchant living beings *(ḥayawān)* than plants.[17]

A somewhat different version of this account is found in an undated document of the Ottoman Imperial Council, *Dīvān-i Hümāyūn.*[18] There, it is reported that Geyikli Bābā had, all by himself, conquered a church with three hundred and sixty doors called Ḳızıl Kilise (in Turkish, 'the crimson church'). When this fact was reported to Orḫān Ġāzī, he sent Geyikli Bābā two loads of wine and two loads of rakı (a kind of alcoholic drink distilled from grape juice), thinking that the latter was a wine-drinker. However, when these were taken to him, Geyikli turned to a friend who happened to be with him and said, "The Sultan has sent me two loads of honey and two loads of butter." These words were confirmed when the loads were opened in the presence of Orḫān's envoy. Thereupon, Geyikli Bābā cooked a sweet dish, *zerde,* with the honey and butter, and sent some of it to Orḫān along with an ember from the fire

17. *Al-Shaqā'iq,* pp. 11-12; the additional information taken from Mecdī is on p. 32 of the translation.

18. The document from the Dīvān-i Hümāyūn is reproduced in A. R. Altınay, *Türkiye Tārīḫi* (İstanbul: Kütübḫāne-i Ḥilmī 1923), p. 349; also partially in Ülken, p. 447. Neither Altınay nor Ülken identify or date the document. Ülken reports further that two stanzas in Turkish which he thinks could be ascribed to Geyikli Bābā are found on the back of the document. These verses, reproduced by Ülken on p. 448, are simple in style and language and reveal an ascetic tendency. The second stanza in particular calls for renunciation of this world in favor of the "world of truth."

On the other hand, Gölpınarlı, *Yunus Emre: Hayatı,* (Istanbul: Bozkurt Basimevi 1936), pp. 59-60; *Yunus Emre ve Tasavvuf,* (Istanbul: Remzi Kitabevi 1961), p. 11; and "'Āşık Paşa'nın şiirleri," *Türkiyat Mecmuası* 5 (1935), pp. 99-100), noting that Geyikli is mentioned in a poem of Yūnus Emre, reads the relevant line from this poem to imply that Geyikli Bābā's proper name was Ḥasan. If his ascription of this name to Geyikli Bābā is justified, Gölpınarlı argues, then it is possible that a certain poem attributed to 'Āşıḳ Paşa should instead be attributed to Geyikli Bābā. In this connection, it may be observed that a contrary reading of Yūnus Emre in this case is just as possible, if not more so, and further that the mentioned poem (cited in "'Āşık Paşa'nın şiirleri," pp. 98-99), replete with Persian words and betraying a definite literary and religious learning, could hardly have been composed by the same person who was responsible for the verses in Turkish cited by Ülken. Whether Geyikli Bābā was the composer of any of this poetry remains, however, an open question.

wrapped in cotton. In response, Orḫān ordered Ḳızıl Kilise to be bestowed upon Geyikli Bābā as a pious endowment.

IV. ḤĀCĪ BEKTAŞ

The earliest work in which Ḥācī Bektāş is mentioned is the *Manāqib al-'ārifīn* by Aflākī, who refers to him in two different stories. In the first, Ḥācī Bektāş appears as one of the disciples of Bābā Resūl. He had an enlightened heart, says Aflākī, but did not abide by the *Sharī'a.* His antinomian tendencies are also emphasized in another story, where it is specifically mentioned that Ḥācī Bektāş neglected the *Sharī'a* and did not perform the daily prayers.[19]

More extensive information is provided by 'Āşıḳpaşazāde. This author relates that Ḥācī Bektāş came to Sivas from Khurāsān with a brother named Menteş. The two brothers then went to Kayseri, where they parted. Menteş returned to Sivas and was soon killed under unknown circumstances. Ḥācī Bektāş, on the other hand, ended up in the small village of Karahöyük, where he settled down and adopted a woman called Ḫatun Ana as his daughter. 'Āşıḳpaşazāde categorically rules out the possibility that Ḥācī Bektāş might have ever conversed with anyone from the house of 'Os̱mān Ġāzī. He asserts that Ḥācī Bektāş was an ecstatic holy man, far from being a Shaykh or a disciple. Further down, however, he writes that Ḥācī Bektāş had a disciple through Ḫatun Ana, whose name was Abdāl Mūsā.[20]

Taşköprīzāde mentions Ḥācī Bektāş among the Shaykhs of the reign of Sultan Murād I (762-792/1362-89), yet does not give any information on him. His translator Mecdī, although he enlarges the entry on Ḥācī Bektāş, fails to add anything of value.[21]

---

19. Aflākī, *Manāqib al-'ārifīn,* vol.1, pp. 381-383 (anecdote 3/312) and 497-498 (anecdote 3/476).
20. *Osmanlı Tarihleri,* pp. 237-238. There is no positive connection between Menteş, the brother of Ḥācī Bektāş, and the principality of Menteşe which came to flourish in the late 7th/13th and early 8th/14th century; see P. Wittek, *Das Fürstentum Mentesche: Studie zur Geschichte Westkleinasiens im 13.-15. Jh.* (Istanbul: Istanbuler Mitteilungen herausgegeben von der Abteilung Istanbul des Archäologischen Institutes des Deutschen Reiches 1934), pp. 24-57.
21. *Al-Shaqā'iq,* p. 16; Mecdī's translation, pp. 44-35.

One additional piece of information which we can adduce is that Ḥācī Bektāş most probably died before 691/1291, and possibly in the year 669/1270-71. A *waqfiyya* seen by John K. Birge demonstrates that Ḥācī Bektāş was certainly dead before the year 697/1297. Another *waqf* deed reported by Ali Emiri takes this date back to 695/1295-96. A third deed consulted by Hüseyin Hüsameddin Yaşar puts the date still further back to 691/1291-92.[22] To this information, however, Abdülbaki Gölpınarlı adds that in a collection of manuscripts bound in Sivas in 691/1291, and less significantly, in a late copy of the *Vilāyetnāme* (1179/1765) as well as in the *Silsilenāme* (1291/1874-75) of Meḥmed Şükrü, the date of Ḥācī Bektāş's death is given as 669/1270-71.[23] It is, therefore, safe to conclude that Ḥācī Bektāş probably died at around the same time as Jalāl al-Dīn Rūmī (in 673/1273), or soon thereafter.

A significant document relating to Ḥācī Bektāş's thought is the Turkish translation, in both verse and prose, of an Arabic work attributed to him. The Arabic original, presumably entitled *Maqālāt,* has so far been located only in defective fragments. The Turkish translation in verse, by a certain Ḫaṭīboğlu, bears the date 812/1409, whereas the translation in prose by someone called Sa'īdeddīn cannot be dated. The chief merit of this work, which is a learned exposition of the four stages of the mystic way *(sharī'a, ṭarīqa, ma'rifa,* and *ḥaqīqa),* as well as of the different categories of people belonging to these four stages *('ābid, zāhid, 'ārif,* and *muḥibb* respectively), is that it proves, contrary to 'Āşıḳpaşazāde's assertion, that Ḥācī Bektāş was a learned Sufi.[24]

Finally, there is the legendary biography of Ḥācī Bektāş, generally known as the *Vilāyetnāme.* The oldest copy of this prose work dates back to 1034/1624. The oldest extant copy in verse, however,

---

22. The first two deeds are reported in J. K. Birge's *The Bektashi Order of Dervishes* (Hartford, Conn.: Hartford Seminary Press 1937), p. 41; the third deed by Köprülü in his *İlk Mutasavvıflar,* p. 95.
23. *Vilāyet-nāme,* Introduction, pp. xix-xx.
24. On the *Maqālāt,* see *Maḳālāt,* ed. E. Coşan (Ankara: Seha Neşriyat, n.d.), and the popular edition by S. Aytekin, *Makalât-i Hacı Bektāş Veli* (Ankara: Emek Basım-Yayımevi 1954). Also see Birge, *op. cit.,* pp. 44-45; Gölpınarlı, *Yunus Emre: Hayatı,* pp. 17-19, especially note 1 on p. 18; Köprülü, "Anadolu'da İslāmīyet," p. 406, note 1; and Ülken, p. 442.

was written at an earlier date in the late 9th/15th or early 10th/16th century, most probably between 886/1481 and 906-7/1501. Judging from a number of references in some later copies, in both prose and verse, this early version of the *Vilāyetnāme* in verse was written by a certain Firdevsī, mentioned in the biographical dictionaries as Firdevsī-i Rūmī or as Uzun Firdevsī.[25] We possess, however, no indication of the identity of the original author of the prose *Vilāyetnāme.* While Bektāşī tradition has it that this latter was the work of a certain 'Alī b. Mūsā, it is conceivable that Firdevsī was responsible for the prose version as well.[26] It is clear that even if there was a version that preceded Firdevsī, it could not have been written any earlier than the beginning of the ninth/fifteenth century, since the stories told in the *Vilāyetnāme* definitely presuppose the formation of a well-developed Bektāşī tradition, which must have certainly taken a considerably long time in the making after the death of Ḥācī Bektāş in the late seventh/thirteenth century. It is plausible to conclude, therefore, that the legendary biography of Ḥācī Bektāş was written after the full-scale development of Bektāşī legend and lore during the eighth/fourteenth and the first half of the ninth/fifteenth centuries, but before the definitive establishment of the order by Pīr Bālım Sultan, who is considered to be the second pīr of the Bektāşī Order, in the first two decades of the tenth/sixteenth century.

Can we extract any reliable historical information on Ḥācī Bektāş from the *Vilāyetnāme?* Although the work is replete with stories of supernatural deeds and achievements of several holy men which do not yield any hard historical facts, it seems to have a surprisingly sound historical basis when compared with contemporary historical sources. Most of the characters mentioned in the narrative can be identified with historical personages of the seventh/thirteenth century so that it remains within the realm of possibility that Ḥācī

---

25. *Hacī Bektāş Velī Velāyetnāmesi,* ed. B. Noyan (Ankara: Doğuş Matbaacılık 1986). On Uzun Firdevsī, and the controversy surrounding his proper name, works, and true identity, see the introduction to his *Ḳuṭbnāme,* eds. İ. Olgun and İ. Parmaksızoğlu (Ankara: Türk Tarih Kurumu Yayınları 1980).
26. *Vilāyet-nāme,* Introduction, pp. xix-xxv. Cahen ("Baba Ishaq," p. 56) thinks that the *Vilāyet-nāme* is anonymous and that it was written around 1400.

Bektāş might in reality have been acquainted with many of the characters whom he is said to have met in his biography. Thus, for instance, he may well have conversed with Taptuḳ Emre, Seyyid Maḥmūd-i Ḥayrānī, Ṣarı Ṣaltuḳ, Aḫī Evrān and Emīr Cem Sultan, or may have sent one of his disciples to Jalāl al-Dīn Rūmī.[27] On a similar note, the few identifiable historical events, such as the Mongol invasion of Anatolia and the capture of Baghdad in 656/1258, which find an echo in the work, also serve to place the historical life of Ḥācī Bektāş firmly within the seventh/thirteenth century. A number of other facts about Ḥācī Bektāş which can be deduced from the *Vilāyetnāme* with the help of other sources do not add much of significance to the already available body of material on him, but merely serve to strengthen and support the more reliable information

---

27. Taptuḳ Emre was the Shaykh of the more famous Yūnus Emre and himself the disciple of Baraḳ Bābā, according to several poems by Yūnus. The most thorough account on him is in Gölpınarlı, *Yunus Emre ve Tasavvuf,* pp. 41-43.

We possess almost no information on the life and character of Aḫī Evrān. Two *waqfiyas*, dated 706/1306 and 676/1277 respectively, which were previously thought to belong to Aḫī Evrān, were proven to be forgeries and are thus of no value. See Gölpınarlı, *Vilâyet-nâme,* p. 120, and *The Encyclopedia of Islam,* new edition, s.v. "Akhi Ewrān" (F. Taeschner). On the other hand, sources for the early Ottoman times permit us to establish only that he lived during the time of Orḫān Ġāzī and that probably did not survive to the period of Murād I (r. 760-791/1359-1389). See *al-Shaqā'iq,* p. 12; Mecdī, p. 33; and Āşıḳpaşazāde's *Tevārīḫ-i Āl-i 'Osmān* in *Osmanlı Tarihleri,* p. 235. It is not certain when he came to be recognized as *Pīr* of the tanners, for which he is best known. Taşköprīzâde, Āşıḳpaşazāde, and Gülşehrī, who wrote a Turkish *mathnawī* on Aḫī Evrān shortly after 717/1317 (published in Taeschner's *Gülschehrī's Mesnevī auf Achi Evran, den Heiligen von Kirschehir und Patron der türkischen Zünfte* (Wiesbaden: Deutsche Morgenländische Gesellschaft, Kommissionsverlag Franz Steiner 1955), do not refer to Aḫī Evrān in this capacity; but already in the *Vilāyet-nāme* (p. 52) and Mecdī's translation of *al-Shaqā'iq,* he is mentioned as *pīr-i ṭarīqa* of the tanners. Other than these sources, there also exists a manuscript titled *Hāẕā fütüvvet-i Aḫī Evrān,* bearing the date 876/1471, which reports that Aḫī Evrān was contemporary with Geyikli Bābā, Ḥācī Bektāş, and Abdāl Mūsā and died at the age of 93 during the reign of Orḫān Ġāzī. See R. Soykut, *Ahi Evran* (Ankara: San Matbaası 1976), p. 7. For the present, there is no reason to reject this information.

The correct form of the name of Emīr Cem Sultan was probably Emīrci Sultan. He was a Yesevī Shaykh who resided in the province of Bozok in Central Anatolia and died during the Babā'ī uprising. For more information, see Ocak, "Emirci Sultan ve zāviyesi. XIII. yüzyılın ilk yarısında Anadolu (Bozok)'da bir Babâi şeyhi: Şeref'üd-Din İsmail b. Muḥammed," *Tarih Enstitüsü Dergisi* 9 (1978), pp. 129-208.

contained in different works. Such, for instance, are the facts that Ḥācī Bektāş was originally from Khurāsān, that he settled in the village of Sulucakaraöyük in Kırşehir when he came to Anatolia, and that he did not fully conform to the *Sharīʻa.* Perhaps a more detailed analysis of the text in the light of all the relevant historical information available might reveal additional material of some significance.

V. ṢARI ṢALTUḲ

The earliest reference to Ṣarı Ṣaltuḳ in the sources appears in the second quarter of the 8th/14th century. Ibn Baṭṭūṭa (the dates of his travels are 726-755/1325-54), having twice visited the town of Bābā Ṣaltuḳ in Dobruja, depicts Ṣaltuḳ as "an ecstatic devotee, although things are told of him which are reproved by the Divine Law."[28] At around the same time, the history of Birzālī (up to 738/1338) and the *Aʻyān al-ʻaṣr wa aʻwān al-naṣr* of al-Ṣafadī refer to a certain "Ṣarīq" (Eastern Turkish for 'Ṣarı') as the Shaykh of Baraḳ Bābā.[29] These reports do not give any positive information on the life or personality of Ṣarı Ṣaltuḳ; they do establish, however, that he was well known as a historical personage by mid-8th/14th century.

The first source to relate the story on Ṣarı Ṣaltuḳ and Baraḳ Bābā, which was later repeated with some variations by Seyyid Loḳmān in his *Oġuznāme* and by Müneccimbaşı in the *Ṣaḥā'if al-akhbār,* is the *Selçuknāme,* alternatively called the *Oġuznāme,* of Yazıcıoğlu 'Alī, written in Turkish early in the reign of the Ottoman Sultan Murād II (r. 824-855/1421-51).[30] Yazıcıoğlu 'Alī reports that Ṣarı Ṣaltuḳ crossed to Dobruja from Anatolia shortly after 660/1261 with the nomad families of the army of the Seljuk Sultan 'Izz al-Dīn

28. *The Travels of Ibn Battūta, A.D. 1325-1354,* vol. 2, transl. H. A. R. Gibb (Cambridge: Cambridge University Press 1961), pp. 499-500.
29. Cited in Gölpınarlı, *Yunus Emre: Hayatı,* p. 39, and *Yunus Emre ve Tasavvuf,* p. 27.
30. The following summary of the information on Ṣarı Ṣaltuḳ contained in the Oğuznāme of Yazıcıoğlu 'Alī is taken from P. Wittek, "Yazijioughlu 'Alī on the Christian Turks of the Dobruja," *Bulletin of the School of Oriental Studies* 14 (1952), pp. 639-668, especially pp. 648-651, and from Gölpınarlı, *Yunus Emre: Hayatı,* pp. 37-39.

Kaykā'ūs II, who had received permission for this migration from the Byzantine basileus. Later, the Tatar Berke Khān of the Crimea transferred the Turks of Dobruja, and with them Ṣarı Ṣaltuḳ as well, into the steppes. These nomadic people soon gained permission to return to their abode in Dobruja and were sent back there under the leadership of Ṣarı Ṣaltuḳ. Meanwhile, one of the sons of 'Izz al-Dīn Kaykā'ūs II, who was held captive in the hands of the Byzantine emperor, tried to escape and was imprisoned. The patriarch asked for this prince from the basileus, baptized him and made him a monk. After serving in the Hagia Sophia for some time, the prince was then sent to Ṣarı Ṣaltuḳ upon the latter's request; the patriarch knew Ṣarı Ṣaltuḳ to be a holy man, whose demands he was thus ready to meet. Ṣarı Ṣaltuḳ converted the prince back to Islam and, bestowing upon him the name 'Baraḳ' as well as his own supernatural powers which he himself had received from Maḥmūd-i Ḥayrānī of Akşehir when he was still a shepherd, sent him to the village of Sulṭāniyya, presumably in Azarbaijan.[31] Ṣarı Ṣaltuḳ himself died in Dobruja shortly after 700/1300.

Other than this early account by Yazıcıoğlu 'Alī, there also exists a legendary biography of Ṣarı Ṣaltuḳ entitled *Ṣaltuḳnāme,* which was written by Ebū'l-Ḫayr Rūmī between 878-885/1473-80 for Meḥmed the Conqueror's son Cem Sultan.[32] In this work, the real name of Ṣarı Ṣaltuḳ is said to be Şerīf Ḫıżır; he is depicted as a

31. Maḥmūd-i Ḥayrānī is mentioned in the *Manāqib al-'ārifīn* (vol. 2, pp. 605-606, anecdote 3/593) as a contemporary of Jalāl ad-Dīn Rūmī much favored by the patron-saint of the Mevlevîs, and also in the *Vilāyetnāme* (pp. 49-50), where he comes to meet Ḥācī Bektāş riding a lion and using a snake as a whip, but acknowledges the latter's greatness when he sees Ḥācī Bektāş riding a "lifeless rock" and becomes his disciple. The inscription on his wooden coffin preserved in Türk ve İslam Eserleri Müzesi in Ankara gives the date of his death as 667/1268-69. See Gölpınarlı, *Yunus Emre: Hayatı,* p. 38, note 1, and *Yunus Emre ve Tasavvuf,* pp. 45-46; and Wittek, p. 658, note 1. Also Köprülü, *İlk Mutasavvıflar,* p. 219, note 1, where the date of Ḫayrānī's death is given as 655/1257-58, yet the source, said to be a *waqf*-deed, is not specified.

32. Ebū'l-Ḫayr Rūmī, *Ṣaltuḳ-nāme,* ed. F. İz, 7 vols., Sources of Oriental Languages and Literatures 4, Turkish Sources 4 (Cambridge, Mass.: Harvard University, Office of the University Publisher 1973-84); summaries in K. Yüce, *Saltukname'de Tarihī, Dinī ve Efsanevī Unsurlar,* Kültür ve Turizm Bakanlığı Yayınları, 832, Kaynak Eserler Dizisi, 9 (Ankara: Kültür ve Turizm Bakanlığı 1987), 331-379 and Gölpınarlı, *Yunus Emre ve Tasavvuf,* pp. 33-38.

devout Sunni who fought against heretics *(rāfiḍīs)* and gave a *fatwā* to the effect that Ḥanafiyya was the strongest of the Sunni sects *(madhhab)*. At the same time, however, he is said to have stayed in mourning for three days in the month of Muḥarram, to have conversed with 'Alī in the same well in which 'Alī was buried and finally, to have made brothers with the famous *qalandar* Sufi Jamāl ad-Dīn al-Sāwī (d. ca. 630/1232), in whose *zāwiya* he stayed for seventy days. In addition, he was a disciple of Maḥmūd-i Ḥayrānī and was on very good terms with all the Turkmen *bābā*s of his time. He travelled widely in the Islamic world waging holy war against infidels while he remained particularly attached to Adrianople, which he adopted as his land, and also to the Crimea, where he spent much of his time. The *Ṣaltuḳnāme* gives the date of Ṣarı Ṣaltuḳ's death as 696/1296 and the location of his tomb as Bābādağı, where he was supposed to have spent his last days.[33]

In the *Vilāyetnāme,* Ṣarı Ṣaltuḳ appears as a disciple of Ḥācī Bektāş. Originally only a shepherd, Ṣarı Ṣaltuḳ was transformed into a holy person by Ḥācī Bektāş who granted him a sword, a bow with seven arrows, and a prayer-rug, and sent him off to the land of Rūm. Accompanied by two other dervishes and working miracles of all sorts, Ṣarı Ṣaltuḳ wandered from place to place, fighting infidels and converting them to Islam. It is not possible to extract any historical information from this legendary account.[34]

Among the later reports on Ṣarı Ṣaltuḳ, the most extensive one is that of Evliyā Çelebi,[35] who gives Ṣarı Ṣaltuḳ's name as Meḥmed Buḫārī, and claims, as the name implies, that he was a Yesevī dervish from Turkistan. Evliyā Çelebi's account includes many stories

33. This last piece of information on Ṣarı Ṣaltuḳ's death and the place of his tomb is also cited from the *Ṣaltuḳnâme* by Y. Z. Yörükan in "Bir Fetva Münasebetiyle: Fetva Müessesesi, Ebussuud Efendi ve Sarı Saltuk," *Ankara Üniversitesi İlahiyat Fakültesi Dergisi* 1/2-3(1952), pp. 152-153. It should be added that the history of Birzālī reports the date of Ṣarı Ṣaltuḳ's death as c. 690/1291, which confirms the view that Ṣarı Ṣaltuḳ was certainly dead before the turn of the century; see Gölpınarlı, *Yunus Emre ve Tasavvuf,* pp. 42-43.
34. *Vilâyet-nâme,* pp. 45-58.
35. A good summary of Evliyā Çelebi's account of Ṣarı Ṣaltuḳ is supplied by Gölpınarlı, *Yunus Emre ve Tasavvuf,* pp. 39-40. For further extensive information on Ṣarı Ṣaltuḳ, along with profuse references, see Yüce, *Saltukname'de Tarihī, Dinī ve Efsanevī Unsurlar.*

on Ṣarı Ṣaltuḳ not attested in any earlier source. These, however, are all legendary in nature and contribute little to our knowledge of Ṣarı Ṣaltuḳ as a historical figure.

VI. BARAḲ BĀBĀ

There are two conflicting traditions on the origins of Baraḳ Bābā. The first tradition, the best account of which was summarized in the above section on Ṣarı Ṣaltuḳ as it is given by Yazıcıoğlu ʻAlī, claims Baraḳ Bābā as one of the sons of the Seljuk Sultan ʻIzz al-Dīn Kaykāʼūs II. According to the second tradition contained in Mamlūk sources of the 8th/14th and 9th/15th centuries, however, Baraḳ Bābā is a native of a village of Tokat in Central Anatolia; his father is one of the local chieftains *(umarāʼ)* and his uncle a clerk.[36]

Nevertheless, all sources agree that Baraḳ Bābā was a disciple of Ṣarı Ṣaltuḳ. The history of Birzālī, and quoting from it, *Aʻyān al-ʻaṣr,* note that Baraḳ Bābā was a dervish of a Shaykh named Sartuk from the Crimea, who almost certainly was identical with Ṣarı Ṣaltuḳ.[37] The Arab authors report that Baraḳ Bābā ate of Ṣarı Ṣaltuḳ's vomit, who then gave him the name Baraḳ.[38] The account in Yazıcıoğlu ʻAlī's *Oġuznāme* is closely reminiscent. There, it is written that when Ṣarı Ṣaltuḳ was still a shepherd, Maḥmūd-i Ḫayrānī had placed a morsel of food mixed with yoghurt into his mouth, which stayed stuck unto his palate. When Ṣarı Ṣaltuḳ finally spat it out one day, his young disciple ate it in an attack of ecstasy.

36. The Mamlūk sources are (1) the history of Birzālī (up till 736/1335-36), (2) *Aʻyān al-ʻaṣr wa aʻwān al-naṣr* of al-Ṣafadī (d. 764/1363), (3) *al-Durar al-kāmina fī aʻyān al-miʼat al-thāmina* of Ibn Ḥajar al-ʻAsqalānī (up till c. 832/1428-29), (4) *ʻIqd al-jumān fī tāʼrīkh ahl al-zamān* of al-ʻAynī (d. 855/1451), and (5) *al-Manhal al-ṣāfī waʼl-mustawfī baʻd al-wāfī* (up until 862/1458) by Ibn Taghrībirdī. The relevant passages from these works are summarized by Gölpınarlı in his *Yunus Emre: Hayatı,* p.40. All Arabic sources agree on the points noted, except for *al-Manhal,* which seems to combine the reports on Baraḳ Bābā's father and uncle by writing merely that his father was a clerk; it omits the uncle altogether. See Gölpınarlı, *Yunus Emre: Hayatı,* p. 40.

37. Gölpınarlı, *Yunus Emre ve Tasavvuf,* p. 27.

38. Gölpınarlı, *Yunus Emre: Hayatı*, p. 39.

Apparently pleased with this act, Ṣarı Ṣaltuḳ stroked his disciple and called him "my *baraḳ.*"[39] That Baraḳ Bābā was a disciple of Ṣarı Ṣaltuḳ is further confirmed by an extant corpus of ecstatic sayings *(shaṭḥiyya)* by Baraḳ Bābā himself, in which Ṣarı Ṣaltuḳ is the only person, besides Baraḳ, who is mentioned by name.[40]

Almost all of what is known about the life and character of Baraḳ Bābā is derived from the Arabic sources mentioned above. The story of his life, as it is told in these works, can be summarized as follows. He came to Syria in 705/1305-6 or 706/1306 as an envoy of the Īlkhān Ghāzān Khān (an anachronism, since Ghāzān Khān is known to have died in 703/1304), visited Jerusalem and also possibly Aleppo at least once, but was refused entry to Egypt, possibly because he was the envoy of the Īlkhāns. At this time, he was about forty years old. In 707/1307-8, he was sent by Sultan Muḥammad Khudābanda to Gīlān, where he was killed within the same year—"boiled to death," "torn to pieces," or "impaled," according different accounts—either because he was perceived to be a non-believer, or because he was at the service of the infidel Mongols. This informa-

---

39. Wittek, p. 659, and Gölpınarlı, *Yunus Emre ve Tasavvuf,* pp. 18-19. It should be added that the word Baraḳ meant 'hairy' and "was a favorite descriptive word for Turkic shamans and shamanic animals," especially for dogs. See R. Dankoff, "Baraq and Burāq," *Central Asiatic Journal* 15 (1971), p.111.

40. This *shaṭḥiyya* survives in a the form of a commentary *(sharḥ)* written on it in Persian by a certain Quṭb al-'Alawī in the year 756/1355. The Persian original of the commentary and its Turkish translation are given by Gölpınarlı in *Yunus Emre ve Tasavvuf,* pp. 457-472 and 252-275, respectively. The reference to Ṣarı Ṣaltuḳ is on p. 265 of the translation. At another place in the same work, p. 17, Gölpınarlı quotes a couplet from Yūnus Emre which also demonstrates the close relation between Baraḳ Bābā and Ṣarı Ṣaltuḳ. See also *Yunus Emre: Hayatı,* p. 54. Later Bektāşī tradition also has it that Baraḳ Bābā was a disciple of Ṣarı Ṣaltuḳ; see Köprülü, "Anadolu'da İslāmīyet," p. 308.

Baraḳ Bābā's *shaṭḥiyya* itself deserves some attention. Arguing that most of Baraḳ Bābā's words can be grouped to form rhyming couplets of seven-syllable lines, Gölpınarlı *(Yunus Emre ve Tasavvuf,* pp. 275-278) suggests that Baraḳ Bābā must have uttered these couplets in moments of ecstasy. He compares them to similar utterances of shamans and soothsayers in general and finds it only natural that most of Baraḳ Bābā's words should be nonsensical. Such indeed is the character of the *shaṭḥiyya* which consists of a set of cryptic sentences held togeher by repetition and a certain musicality. The commentator Quṭb al-'Alawī, who as Gölpınarlı rightly observes *(ibid.,* pp. 253-254), apparently had a very sound knowledge of both religious and literary writings, shows exceptional skill and insight in his interpretation which has an unmistakable *bāṭinī* character.

tion is complemented by Aflākī, who in his *Manāqib al-'ārifīn* cites Baraḳ Bābā as one of the Sufi Shaykhs in the immediate entourage of Sultan Ghāzān Khān.[41]

More important for our purposes is the description of Baraḳ Bābā contained in these sources. It is said that he was naked from his waist up, with a red cloth wrapped around his middle. On his head he wore a reddish turban with two buffalo horns attached at each side. His hair, beard, and moustache were all very long, though some accounts assert that he shaved his beard or even both his beard and moustache. He always carried with a him a very large and long pipe or horn, *nafīr,* and a black bowl (the famous dervish *kashkūl).* He went around with a large number of disciples who resembled him in outlook, carrying long staffs with bells on their shoulders, and with painted anklebones and molar teeth hanging on strings from their necks, tambourines and large drums in their hands. Wherever they went, the disciples played and Baraḳ Bābā danced like a bear and sang like a monkey, and especially enjoyed entertaining children. He never accumulated any wealth. When, on one occasion, Ghāzān Khān gave him a large sum of money—ten or thirty thousand dirhams according to different accounts—because Baraḳ Bābā was not afraid of a wild tiger set upon him but instead approached and mounted him, the dervish distributed the money to the poor the same day. On another occasion, in the presence of Afram, the Amīr of Damascus, he rode a wild ostrich, rising from the ground on the animal's back, and while still in the air cried down to Afram, asking him if he should fly more.

He made it mandatory for his disciples to perform the daily prayers; if any of them failed in this task, he was given a certain number of blows with the long staff. Despite this show of pietism, Baraḳ Bābā and his disciples were well-known for their antinomian ways, such as not fasting in the month of Ramaḍān, eating of what was forbidden to eat (presumably hashish), and gazing at what is beautiful, that is to say, women. Moreover, they reportedly believed in metempsychosis and denied the existence of the next world. Baraḳ Bābā supposedly once said that the only real religious

41. Aflākī, *Manāqib al-'ārifīn,* vol. 2, p. 848 (anecdote 8/20).

obligation was the love of 'Alī. For all these reasons, Barak̤ and his disciples were generally perceived to be libertines *(ibāḥī*s).[42]

To this account of Barak̤ Bābā, it only remains to be added that in the *Vilāyetnāme* he appears among the disciples of Ḥācī Bektāş.[43]

VII. CONCLUSION

The above survey of the available historical information on certain prominent Turkish Sufis of early Islamic Asia Minor directly leads to the following observations concerning existing scholarship on this phase of Sufism as reviewed at the beginning of this essay.

1. To begin with, one can hardly fail to notice the presence of strikingly close ties of either discipleship and/or friendship between these different *bābā*s who are all distinctly famous in their own ways. Ḥācī Bektāş and Geyikli Bābā were disciples of Bābā İlyās. The celebrated Yūnus Emre was connected through Taptuk̤ Emre to Barak̤ Bābā. Barak̤ Bābā was a disciple of Ṣarı Ṣaltuk̤, who in turn was initiated by Maḥmūd-i Ḫayrānī. Maḥmūd-i Ḫayrānī was apparently dear to both Ḥācī Bektāş and Rūmī. The mere existence of such a well-established network of relationships among prominent Turkish Sufis indicates that these latter functioned well within the

42. This description is based on the translations of the relevant passages in the above-mentioned Arabic works contained in the following Turkish works: Gölpınarlı, *Yunus Emre: Hayatı,* pp. 39-47, and *Yunus Emre ve Tasavvuf,* pp. 20-26; Köprülü, "Anadolu'da İslāmīyet," p. 393; and H. H. Yaşar, Amasya Tarihi, 4 vols. (İstanbul: Aydınlık Basımevi 1912-1935), III: 460-464. Ibāḥa, literally 'permission' in Arabic, was a term generally applied to antinomian teachings; see the *Encyclopedia of Islam,* new edition, s.v. "Ibāḥa."

43. *Vilāyetnāme,* pp. 81 and 90. A. Bodrogligeti, in his "Ahmad's Baraq-Nāma: A Central Asian Islamic Work in Eastern Middle Turkic," *Central Asiatic Journal* 18 (1974), pp. 83-128, publishes in transcription and English translation a *Baraqnāma* in Eastern Middle Turkic, possibly dating from the first half of the 8th/14th century. If Bodrogligeti is justified in identifying Baraq in this work with Barak̤ Bābā—he states, "Indeed, Baraq in our story was to all indications a certain Barak Bābā, a distinguished personality in early Turkic Sufism," p. 86—this would be sufficient proof that the fame and popularity of Barak̤ Bābā had very early spread into Central Asiatic Turkish folk culture as well. For more information and further references on Barak̤ Bābā, see *The Encyclopaedia of Islam,* new edition, s.v. "Barak̤ Baba" (B. Lewis); D. P. Little, "Religion under the Mamlūks," *Muslim World* 73 (1983), pp. 175-176; and *Encyclopedia Iranica,* s.v. "Barāq Bābā" (H. Algar).

matrix of mainstream Sufism where the concept of the spiritual lineage of initation *(silsila)* reigned supreme. The Turkish *bābā*s in question were not tribal religious figures but full-fledged Sufis who functioned beyond narrow ethnic/tribal identities. For this reason alone, it would not be proper to consider them shamans in Islamic disguise. For these Turkish holy men at least, the process of conversion to Islam had long been completed.

2. Though not as rich as one would like it to be, our evidence suggests that Turkish Sufis of the little tradition were not at all ignorant of the great tradition. Ḥācī Bektāş is credited with an Arabic prose work that bears distinct affinities with the thought of the Persian Sufi ʻAzīz-i Nasafī; the *shatḥiyyāt* of Baraḳ Bābā attracted a very learned commentary in Persian by a certain Quṭb al-ʻAlawī in the mid-eighth/fourteenth century; and the lineage of Bābā Ilyās produced learned authors such as Elvān Çelebi, ʻĀşıḳ Paşa, and ʻĀşıḳpaşazāde. The works of Yūnus Emre, and somewhat later, those of Ḳāyġūsuz Abdāl, the disciple of Abdāl Mūsā, display comfortable competence in all aspects of contemporary elite Sufism. The separation between the great and little traditions was not watertight; indeed, insofar as the period under consideration marks the birth of Anatolian Turkish Sufism, it may be more fruitful to view the relationship between the two traditions not as one of mutual indifference and exclusion but of mutual affinity and attraction. Emphasis should be placed not on the continuation of pre-Islamic Turkish beliefs and practices but on the emergence of a new Turkish voice within mainstream Sufism.

3. The theory that Anatolian Turkish Sufism bears an indelible Yesevī imprint should be revised. The clearest indication for the necessity of such a revision lies in the prevalence of a Wefā'ī Order in early Turkish Asia Minor which can be traced back to Abū'l-Wafā' Tāj al-ʻĀrifīn (d. 501/1107), an Iraqi Sufi of partially Kurdish origin. In the primary sources, Abū'l-Wafā' appears as the spiritual master of the circle of Turkish Sufis around Bābā İlyās, including one who was later attributed a legendary role in the formation of the Ottoman Empire, Şeyẖ Edebālī. This 'Iraqi' connection not only challenges the theory of Yesevī origins by directing our attention to Arab Sufism of Iraq contemporary with Abū'l-Wafā' (a milieu later dominated by the figures of ʻAbd al-Qādir al-Gīlānī and Aḥmad al-

Rifāʻī). It also demonstrates that Turkish Sufis had, naturally, more points of contact with Arab and Persian mainstream Sufism than hitherto suspected. Aḥmed Yesevī was not the only 'real' Turkish Sufi in a time period of two centuries, and Sufism did not sit like a veneer on the thinly disguised ancestral religious practices of shamanist Turks in early Turkish Anatolia: by this time, Sufism was, rather, the natural color of the hardwood of Turkish religious culture.[44]

44. Presumably Shaykh Abū'l-Wafā' Sayyid Muḥammad Baghdādī, commonly known as Tāj al-ʻĀrifīn. On this person, see A. Krupp, *Studien zum Menāqybnāme des Abu l-Wafā' Tāǧ al-ʻĀrifīn: Das historische Leben des Abu l-Wafā' Tāǧ al-ʻĀrifīn* (Munich: Rudolf Trofenik 1976). The most extensive account on Abū'l-Wafā' is found in Taqī al-Dīn ʻAbd al-Raḥmān Abū'l-Faraj al-Wāṣitī (d. 744/1343), *Tiryāq al-muḥibbīn fī ṭabaqāt khirqat al-mashāyīkh al-ʻārifīn* (Cairo: Maṭba'at al-Miṣr 1305/1887), pp. 41-44. See also Gölpınarlı, *Yunus Emre: Hayatı,* pp. 56-58; idem, *Yunus Emre ve Tasavvuf,* pp. 46-49; J. S. Trimingham, *The Sufi Orders in Islam* (Oxford: Oxford University Press 1971), pp. 49-50, note 6. Since this Tāj al-ʻĀrifīn died in 501/1107, he could hardly have been the Shaykh of Bābā İlyās, who died in 638/1240, but probably was merely his *pīr;* see Gölpınarlı, *Yunus Emre: Hayatı,* pp. 58-59.

IV

Ideas of Time in Persian Sufism

Gerhard Böwering

For more than a millennium, mysticism—Sufism in particular, but also Ismā'īlī and Imāmī gnosis—has shaped the vision of Islam. In the realm of mysticism, more dominantly than in many other domains of Islamic culture, the Persians[1] have been at work creating the inner religious sphere of Islam. To this day Persian images are anchored in the minds of Muslims throughout the world as a goad to poetic inspiration, and Persian ideas are stored in the inner recesses

1. In this article, "Persia" and "Persian(s)" are used as general terms for what are also called "Iran" and "Iranian(s)." The terms "Persia" and "Persian(s)" are not restricted to their linguistic or geographical connotations, but are understood in their full ethnic and cultural extension. The abbreviations of journal titles follows J.D. Pearson, *Index Islamicus,* (London 1958). *EI* (reprint 1987) stands for *The Encyclopaedia of Islam* (ed. M.T. Houtsma *et al.,* Leiden 1913-38; repr. Leiden 1987), *EI (new edition)* for *The Encyclopædia of Islam* (ed. H.A.R. Gibb *et al.,* Leiden 1960), *EIr* for *Encyclopædia Iranica* (ed. E. Yarshater, New York 1982-), *ER* for *The Encyclopedia of Religion* (ed. M. Eliade, New York 1987) and *ERE* for *The Encyclopedia of Religion and Ethics* (ed. J. Hastings, Edinburgh 1908-26; reprint New York 1980). Koran quotations are inserted into the main body of the text, with chapter and verse placed in brackets and separated by a colon. For convenient reference, the Arabic definite article and the Persian *iḍāfa* have been omitted before the *nisba* (names of persons denoting descent or origin) by which a person is principally quoted. This article grew out of four lectures given in the United States during 1992, one on the occasion of the Thirteenth Levi della Vida Conference honoring Professor Ehsan Yarshater at UCLA, another at the invitation of the Committee of Religious Studies at Washington University in St. Louis, a third before the Department of Religion at Amherst College, and a fourth at a conference on Persian Sufism at The George Washington University in Washington, D.C.

ها روز عرفه است زیرا که حجاج جمله به عرفات حاظر شوند یعرف به هم بعضا

ی روز عید است در این روز ابراهیم اسمعیل را علیه السلام قربان کرد خواست

باری جل و علا کبشی بفدای اسمعیل علیه السلم فرستاد و است این ایام را اایام

نشرین خواند زیرا که کوشتهای قربانی در این روزها ثواب قدید کند

و عده عذر بر خم نیز خواند که پمینبر صلعم با امیر المومنین علی علیه السلام برادری

در این روز نزل الاستغفار علی داود علیه السلام و اسد الموفق للصواب

خاتمه فی معرفه اوایل الشهور

اگر خواهی که اوایل شهور معلوم کنی که کدام روز است از ماهای

کذشته یا آینده طریق آن است که ماهای کذشته را از هجرت پیغمبر صلی الله

علیه و سلم جمع کنی تا آن سال که روز و ماهی از آن سال میخواهی وضع

بران فزایی آنکه هشت هشت می انداز تا آنکه که کمتر از هشت بماند پس در این قول

طلب کن آن روز که عدد بده و رسد اول آن ماه بود و اگر پسیج نماند اول ماه

آن روز بود که در پیت آخر است و هذا لدا یر

Diagram of the Twelve Months. From Qazwīnī's *'Ajā'ib al-makhlūqāt* Timurid Period, Herat, dated 909/1503-4. BL. Or. 12220 f.45r. (Courtesy of the British Library).

of Muslim hearts as a source of spiritual aspiration. Even the stridently puritanical reductionism of some contemporary Muslims acknowledges, albeit in oblique ways, the strength which Persian mysticism has injected into the hearts of many Muslim men and women. Indeed, Islamic fundamentalism, from Morocco to Mindanao, lives in fear of a resurgent Sufi religiosity displacing its own hold on the future of Islam.

It has become customary in the scholarly world to celebrate the spirit of Persian mysticism by citing innumerable examples of beautiful Persian verse from the glorious *dīvāns* and by tracing fascinating symbols of Iranian religions in the profundity of Persian prose. I suggest that one might also follow another approach based mainly on Sufi sources written in Arabic, that other linguistic medium which the Persian authors controlled with such consummate skill. It may be appropriate to take a fresh look at the beauty of Persian mysticism and to select a new road into the depth of Persian religiosity by examining the idea of time that propelled Sufism throughout the history of Islam. In its conception of time, Persian mysticism manifests an astonishing capability of integrating a wide spectrum of cultures and an uncanny aptitude for articulating its own vision of the world.

Time strikes us as mysteriously slipping away and continually eluding the grasp of our consciousness. Time makes us feel that the present is real while the past and the future are not. The past has ceased to exist and the future has not yet come to be. Then again, here and now, we observe one thing beside the other and experience one event after another. We have come to accept a flux of time from the past to the future flowing through the elusive 'now' of the moment. Although able to affect the future, we cannot change the past. We neither possess the power to capture the presence in the instant nor have the skill to snare duration by reaching into eternity. Educated in a culture formed by Christianity, we have a legacy of our own thinking about time. In it we find Augustine's puzzle about time and its measure as well as the widespread perception of time as a myth of passage, as a stream that flows or as an ocean over which we advance. Some of us may be familiar with the notion of space-time and Einstein's relativity, others may be attracted by theories of infinity and the continuum, and again others may be aware of the antinomy Kant constructed about time. More recently, some have come to think about time as the fourth dimension or to envision the apparent temporal asymmetry of the universe, while others are attracted by ideas of big bang, black holes and string theory.[2] Yet even as heirs of a different cultural tradition, we share the common human experience of time with the world of Islam and the mystics which it generated. Like our culture, Islamic culture developed its own theories about time over a long history.[3] The world of Islam advanced a great variety of theories explaining time, and Muslim mysticism in particular blended seemingly contradictory conceptions of the temporal into an integrated understanding of human experience. In examining some of these conceptions, our focus will be on the Persian mystics of the Islamic world and their thinking within the wider framework of Islamic ideas of time.[4]

---

2. There are numerous studies on time from philosophical and historical perspectives as well as from cross-cultural points of view. Entries on "time" can of course be found in any standard encyclopedia. The list that follows enumerates only a very small number of studies that have been consulted for the background of this paper. M. Eliade, *Cosmos and History: The Myth of the Eternal Return* (New York 1954); *Man and Time: Papers from the Eranos Yearbooks,* edited J. Campbell, Bollingen Series XXX.3 (Princeton 1957); S.J. Samartha, *The Hindu View of History* (Bangalore 1959); S.G.F. Brandon, *History, Time and Deity* (Manchester 1965), J.T. Fraser, *The Voices of Time* (New York 1966; 2nd ed. Amherst 1981); R.M. Gale (ed.), *The Philosophy of Time* (Sussex 1968); H.I. Marrou, *Théologie de l'histoire* (Paris 1968); S. Sambursky and S. Pines, *The Concept of Time in Late Neoplatonism* (Jerusalem 1971); J.T. Fraser (ed.), *The Study of Time,* 4 vols. (New York 1972-81); *Cultures and Time* (Paris 1976); *Time and the Philosophies* (Paris: Unesco Press 1977); P. Ricoeur, *Time and Narrative* (Chicago 1984); J.T. Fraser, *Time: The Familiar Stranger* (Amherst 1987); S. Hawking, *A Brief History of Time* (London & New York 1988). A good select bibliography is found at the end of J.J.C. Smart's article "Time" in *The Encyclopedia of Philosophy,* edited by P. Edwards, Vol. 8 (New York 1967), pp. 133-4. A rather exhaustive bibliography is J.T. Fraser, "A Report on the Literature of Time 1900-1980" in *The Study of Time IV,* edited by J.T. Fraser (New York 1981), pp. 234-70.

3. A good example of a contemporary Muslim's combining of Western ideas on time with certain Islamic notions is A. Ahmad, *Change, Time and Causality, with Special Reference to Muslim Thought* (Lahore 1974).

4. See p. 203—›

When the Arabs conquered Iran, bringing the pre-Islamic Arab tradition of the *jāhiliyya,*[5] the message of the Koran and the customs of the Medinan community with them, the Persians met a people with a conception of time rooted in the experience of *dahr,* the infinite extension of time, which, like the desert wind, erases footprints in the sand that stretches to the horizon. In old Arab poetry this *dahr,* also called the "days" or the "nights," is seen as an almost mythical being of all-devouring time, the cause of earthly happiness and especially of earthly misery. It is doom of death *(himām, maniyya)* and measure of destiny *(qadar, qaḍā').* Time is always shifting; it changes everything, and nothing resists it. Time is a manifestation

4. There is no scholarly monograph on time in Islam or on time in Islamic mysticism. F. Rosenthal, *Sweeter than Hope* (Leiden 1983), pp. 1-58, S. Pines, *Beiträge zur islamischen Atomenlehre* (Gräfenhainichen 1936) and *Nouvelles Etudes sur Awḥad al-zamān Aby-l-Barakāt al-Baghdādī* (Paris 1955), include ground-breaking observations on 'time' in Islam. E. Behler, *Die Ewigkeit der Welt* (München 1965), offers a thorough historical analysis of the controversy on the beginnings of the world and its eternity in Arabic and Jewish mediæval philosophy. Some additions to Behler's analysis can be found in two articles of F. Rahman, "The Eternity of the World and the Heavenly Bodies in Post-Avicennan Philosophy" and "The God-World Relationship in Mullā Ṣadrā," in G. F. Hourani (ed.), *Essays on Islamic Philosophy and Science,* (Albany 1975), pp. 222-37 and 238-53. Some helpful specific articles on aspects of 'time' in Islam are: L. Massignon, "Le Temps dans la pensée islamique," *Eranos-Jahrbuch* XX (1951), (Zurich 1952), pp. 144-8, repr. in *Opera Minora,* ed. Y. Moubarac (Beirut 1963), vol. 2, pp. 606-12, and tr. into English by R. Manheim, "Time in Islamic Thought," in *Man and Time, Papers from the Eranos Yearbooks,* ed. J. Campbell, Bollingen Series XXX.3 (Princeton 1957), pp. 108-14; H. Corbin, "Le Temps Cyclique dans le Mazdéisme et dans l'Ismaélisme," *Eranos-Jahrbuch* XX (1951); tr. into English by R. Manheim, "Cyclical Time in Mazdaism and Ismailism," in *Man and Time, Papers from the Eranos Yearbooks,* pp. 115-72; repr. in H. Corbin, *Cyclical Time and Ismaili Gnosis* (London 1983), pp. 1-58; L. Gardet, "Moslem Views of Time and History," in *Cultures and Time* (Paris 1976), pp. 197-214 and L.E. Goodman, "Time in Islam," *Asian Philosophy,* 2 (1992), pp. 3-19. An ethnological perspective is offered by D. Eickelmann, "Time in a Complex Society: A Moroccan Example," *Ethnology* 16 (1977), pp. 39-55. Only limited information can be culled from L. Gardet, "The Prophet," in *Time and the Philosophies* (Paris 1977), pp. 197-209; A. Hasnaoui, "Certain Notions of Time in Arab-Muslim Philosophy," in *ibid.*, pp. 49-79; and S.L. Goldman, "On the Beginnings and Endings of Time in Medieval Judaism and Islam," in vol. 4 of *The Study of Time,* ed. J.T. Fraser (New York 1981), pp. 59-72.

5. The term *jāhiliyya,* used as the opposite of the word *islām,* refers to the life and lore of the Arabs before Muḥammad's mission as Prophet; cf. T. Nöldeke, "Arabs (Ancient)," *ERE,* 1, pp. 659-73; Ed., "D̲jāhiliyya," *EI (new edition),* II, pp. 383-4.

of fate *(manūn)* whose destructive power the Meccans wished on Muḥammad: "He is a poet for whom we await fate's uncertainty *(rayb al-manūn)*" (LII: 30; cf. XXIII: 25). As the assigned lot of destiny approaching the inescapable hour of death, time expressed the transience of everything, brought good tribal fortune or caused the death of a relative or friend.[6] Like a sure arrow, *dahr* never missed the mark. However, *dahr* was punctuated by the Days of the Arabs *(ayyām al-'Arab)*,[7] the days of vengeance in combat and tribal prowess, when memorable events placed markers in the recollection of the course of events, good and bad. While *dahr* held sway like fate, it could be transcended by a moment marked out in tribal memory, often preserved in poetry as one of the days that captured the minds of men. The *jāhiliyya* view of time is rejected in the Koran and branded as an expression of Arab disbelief: "There is nothing but our present life; we die, and we live, and nothing but time *(dahr)* destroys us" (XLV: 24). In the *jāhiliyya* there was neither resurrection nor life after death.

The Koranic message opposed this fatalistic view and explained time from the perspective of a transcendent monotheism promising paradise and warning of hell. The Koran countered the Days of the Arabs with the Days of God *(ayyām Allāh)*. Moses, sent with "Our (God's) signs *(bi-āyātinā)*," was commanded, "bring forth your people from the shadows to the light and remind them of the Days of God" (XIV: 5). Muḥammad's own followers, the believers, are bidden to forgive "those who do not look for the Days of God

---

6. W.M. Watt, "Dahr," *EI (new edition)*, II, pp. 94-5; T. Nöldeke, "Vorstellungen der Araber vom Schicksal," *Zeitschrift für Völkerpsychologie und Sprachwissenschaft*, 3 (1885), pp. 130-5; W.L. Schrameyer, *Über den Fatalismus der vorislamischen Araber* (Bonn 1881); C.J. Lyall, *Translation of Ancient Arabian Poetry, Chiefly Pre-Islamic, with an Introduction and Notes* (London 1885); J. Wellhausen, *Reste arabischen Heidentums* (Berlin 1897); W. Caskel, *Das Schicksal in der altarabischen Poesie* (Leipzig 1926); J. Pedersen, "The Islamic Preacher: wā'iẓ, mudhakkir, qāṣṣ," *Goldziher Mem.*, Vol. I, (Budapest 1948), pp. 226-51; H. Ringgren, *Studies in Arabian Fatalism* (Uppsala 1955); *idem*, "Islamic Fatalism," in *Fatalistic Beliefs*, ed. H. Ringgren (Stockholm 1967); H. Ritter, *Das Meer der Seele* (Leiden 1955), pp. 43-4.

7. E. Mittwoch, "Ayyām al-'Arab," *EI (new edition)*, I, pp. 793-4; W. Caskel, *"Aijām al-'Arab," Islamica* 3, supplement (1930), pp. 1-99.

(ayyām Allāh)" (XLV: 14). Just as the old Arabs had their days of vengeance, so God had His days of punishment.[8] The Koran also revealed God's creative command *(amr),* His *kun* ("Be!"): "When He decrees a thing He but says to it 'Be!', and it is *(kun fa-yakūn)"* (II: 117; III: 47; XIX: 35; XL: 68; cf. XVI: 40;XL; XXXVI: 82). God gave this command of creation when He formed the first human being (III: 59) and made the heavens and the earth (VI: 73), fashioning them in six days (VII: 54; X: 3; XI: 7; XXV: 59; XXXII: 4; L: 38; LVII: 4).[9] "His are the creation *(khalq)* and the command *(amr)"* (VII: 54). God is not only Creator at the beginning of creation and at the origin of a person's life, He also is Judge at the end of the world and at the individual's death when mankind will hear "the Cry in truth" (L: 42). In the final 'Hour' *(sā'a),* the only perfect moment that there is, the divine command is revealed in "the twinkling of an eye" *(lamḥ al-baṣar,* LIX: 50; cf. XVI: 77) and "the whole earth shall be His handful and the heavens will be rolled up in His right hand" (XXXIX: 67).

There is no place in the Koran for impersonal time; man's destiny is in the hands of God who creates male and female, gives life and brings death, and grants wealth and works destruction (LIII: 44-54). God is active even in a person's sleep, for "God takes the souls unto Himself *(yatawaffā al-anfus)* at the time of their death, and that which has not died, in its sleep. He keeps those on whom He has decreed death, but looses the others till a stated term *(ajal musammā)"* (XXXIX: 42). Unless He has decreed a person's death, God sends back the soul and man wakes up. The divine command rules all of human life and resembles a judicial decision, proclaiming God's decree *(ḥukm)* with authority and stating the instant that releases the acts which humans perform. Man's life (and hence human action) begins with the announcement of the divine *kun* and comes to an end at the "stated term" *(ajal,* XL: 69; *ajal musammā,* XXXIX: 42),[10] as

8. These days of divine punishment were the Arabicized "Wars of the Lord" *(milḥamōt Yhwh)* of the Old Testament (Num. 21:14), see J. Horovitz, *Koranische Untersuchungen* (Berlin-Leipzig 1926), p. 22.
9. The same imperative in the feminine form *kūnī* ("Be!") is used when God commanded the fire to be coolness for Abraham (XXI: 69).

the irrevocable period of life assigned by God comes to an end at the moment of divine sanction. This appointed term of man's life is fixed, it can neither be anticipated nor deferred: "No one has his life prolonged and no one has his life cut short except as [it is written] in a book [of God's decrees]" (XXXV: 12). The image-rich promise of man's new creation beyond time in paradise heightened the awareness that nothing escapes the grasp of God's perpetual presence. From the *kun* of his creation to the *ajal* of his death, man's existence falls under the *ḥukm* of God, which occurs instantaneously in time-spans expressed in the Koran by the terms of *ḥīn* and *ān* (*ḥīn:* XXI: 111; XXVI: 218; XXXVII: 114 & 178*; ān:* XVI: 22). *Ḥīn* appears more frequently and is set explicitly in relation to *dahr* in the rhetorical question of the Surah called *al-Dahr,* "Wasn't there a time-span *(ḥīn min al-dahr)* for man when he was as yet nothing to be mentioned?" (LXXVI: 1) In the Koran, Allāh is the Lord of the instant; what He has determined happens.

Islamic tradition *(ḥadīth)* amplified the notion of divine determination included in the Koran, and tended to transform Muḥammad's stress on divine omnipotence into a rigid predeterminism, while also identifying time, *dahr,* with God. This identification of Allāh and *dahr* can be traced back to an important *ḥadīth* report in which God is the speaker *(ḥadīth qudsī)*, "God said: Man insults Me in blaming time *(dahr)*; I am time *(Anā al-dahr)*. In My hands is the command *(amr),* and I cause the alternation of night and day."[11] The Prophet warned against blaming disappointment on time: "Do not say, what a disappointment of time *(lā taqūlū khaybata al-dahr)*, because God

---

10. I. Goldziher and W. M. Watt, "Adjal," *EI (new edition),* I, p. 204; cf. G. Weil, *Maimonides über die Lebensdauer* (Basel 1953); R. Eklund, *Life Between Death and Resurrection According to Islam* (Uppsala 1941).

11. A.J. Wensinck, *Concordance et indices de la tradition musulmane,* 8 vols. (Leiden 1936-88), I, pp. 50,101; II, p. 155; (Bukhārī, *Tafsīr,* 45:1; *Tawḥīd,* p. 35; Muslim, *Ṣaḥīh, Alfāẓ,* pp. 2, 3; Dārimī, *Adab,* p. 169; Aḥmad b. Ḥanbal, *Musnad,* II, pp. 238, 272). This tradition is very old and exemplifies the merger of the Koranic with the *jāhiliyya* world-view in *ḥadīth,* cf. Ḥumaydī (d. 219/834), Abū Bakr 'Abdullāh b. al-Zubayr, *al-Musnad,* ed. Ḥabīb al-Raḥmān al-A'ẓamī (Beirut 1409/1988), no. 1096; see also R. A. Nicholson, *Studies in Islamic Poetry* (Cambridge 1921), p. 155.

Himself is time *(fa-inna Allāha huwa al-dahr).*[12] Later, the Ẓāhirī school interpreted time *(dahr)* as an actual attribute of God.[13] A tradition going back to Abū Idrīs Khawlāmī (d. 80/699) may conceal the roots of this strand of *ḥadīth* in God's address to Moses, "O Moses, the first thing I created is that in which I resolved within Myself the decree and determination of all things: time *(dahr).*"[14]

Another strand of *ḥadīth* literature records that everything that happens is written in a heavenly book: "God wrote down the decrees *(maqādīr)* regarding the created world fifty thousand years before He created the heavens and the earth."[15] According to other *ḥadīth,* God commanded the Pen *(qalam),* the first thing He created, to write down the destinies of all things, thus establishing His unalterable decree. While the embryo is still in the womb, an angel writes down the child's daily sustenance, its works, its hour of death, and its misery or happiness (in this life and/or life to come?).[16] God's decree is invariably fulfilled; though prayer may ward it off for a while, no human effort can change it.[17] Combining pre-Islamic notions of all-pervading time with the idea of God's decree in the Koran, the *ḥadīth*[18] saw time as a series of pre-determined events binding divine omnipotence to the certain occurrence of each instant in a person's life span. Though such occurrence was as unavoidable as fate

---

12. Wensinck, *Concordance,* II, pp. 92, 155 (Bukhārī, *Ṣaḥīh, Adab,* p. 101; Muslim, *Saḥīh, Alfāẓ,* 4; Mālik b. Anas, *Muwaṭṭa', Kalām,* p. 3; Aḥmad b. Ḥanbal, *Musnad,* II, pp. 259, 272, 275, 318, 934); Abū Muḥammad al-Ḥusayn b. Mas'ūd Baghawī, *Miṣbāḥ al-Sunna,* 4 vols. (Beirut 1407/1987), III, p. 305 (no. 3700); J. Robson, *Mishkāt al-maṣābīḥ* (Lahore 1975), p. 996; the variant, "time itself is God" *(fa inna al-dahra huwa Allāh)* is also quoted by Abū Ḥayyān Tawḥīdī, *al-Baṣā'ir wa'l-dhakhā'ir,* ed. W. Qāḍī (Beirut 1408/1988), V, p. 141.

13. I. Goldziher, *Die Ẓāhiriten, ihre Lehrsystem und ihre Geschichte* (Leipzig 1884), pp. 153-4; W.M. Watt, *Free Will and Predestination in Early Islam* (London 1948), p. 31.

14. 'Abd al-Jabbār Khawlānī, *Ta'rīkh Darāyā,* ed. Sa'īd al-Afghānī (Damascus 1975, repr. 1984), p. 65.

15. Ringgren, *Studies,* p. 117.

16. *Ibid.*, pp. 117-18.

17. *Idem.*, "Islamic Fatalism," in *Fatalistic Beliefs,* pp. 57-9.

18. For the implications of these strands of *ḥadīth* and their *isnāds* on Islamic doctrines of predestination, see J. van Ess, *Zwischen Ḥadīṯ und Theologie* (Berlin 1975), pp. 75-81.

and as irreversible as time, it happened through God's very own action alone.

Islamic law *(fiqh)* captured time in the stipulations of ritual precision while adopting its measure from old Arab custom as sanctioned in the Koran. The Koran expressly confirmed the moon as the measurer of time: "It is He (God) who made the sun a radiance, and the moon a light. And He determined it (the moon) by stations that you may know the number of the years and the reckoning *(ḥisāb)*" (X: 5). The day began at nightfall, when the sun set, going to its resting place *(mustaqarr,* XXXVI: 38; cf. XVIII: 86), and the month was reckoned from the actual sighting of the new moon *(hilāl).*[19] The appearance of the crescent in the sky determined the date of the pilgrimage *(ḥajj)* and the end of the month of fasting (II: 183-184, 189). The exact times of prayer *(ṣalāt),* however, were fixed after Muḥammad's death by times of the day determined by the sun, such as the night prayer when the twilight disappeared, the morning prayer at daybreak, the midday prayer when the sun began to decline from the zenith, the afternoon prayer when the shadows matched their objects, and the evening prayer immediately after sunset.[20]

While dependence on the lunar calendar and the times of ritual prayer provided rhythm to a Muslim's daily life, the law followed the Koranic summons to give witness *(shahāda)* to the divine signs *(āyāt)* that established events in time. On account of this strong sense of witness, the law favored methods of measuring time by observation over calculation. It was crucial for legal procedure that testimony be given by a free and mentally able Muslim with a record of moral rectitude *('adāla)* who was an actual eye- or ear-witness *(shāhid)* to the evidence of a crime at the time of its occurrence. Documentary evidence was generally disregarded as testimonial proof.[21] The law *(sharī'a)* as a system of religious duties with its framework of five basic categories *(aḥkām),* ranging from

---

19. W. Hartner. "Zamān," *EI* (reprint 1987), VIII, pp. 1209-12; J. Schacht and R. Ettinghausen, "Hilāl," *EI (new edition),* III, pp 379-85; D. Pingree, "Ḳamar," *EI (new edition),* III, pp. 517-8.
20. A.J. Wensinck, "Mīḳāt," *EI* (reprint 1987), V, pp. 492-3.
21. J Schacht, *An Introduction to Islamic Law* (Oxford 1964).

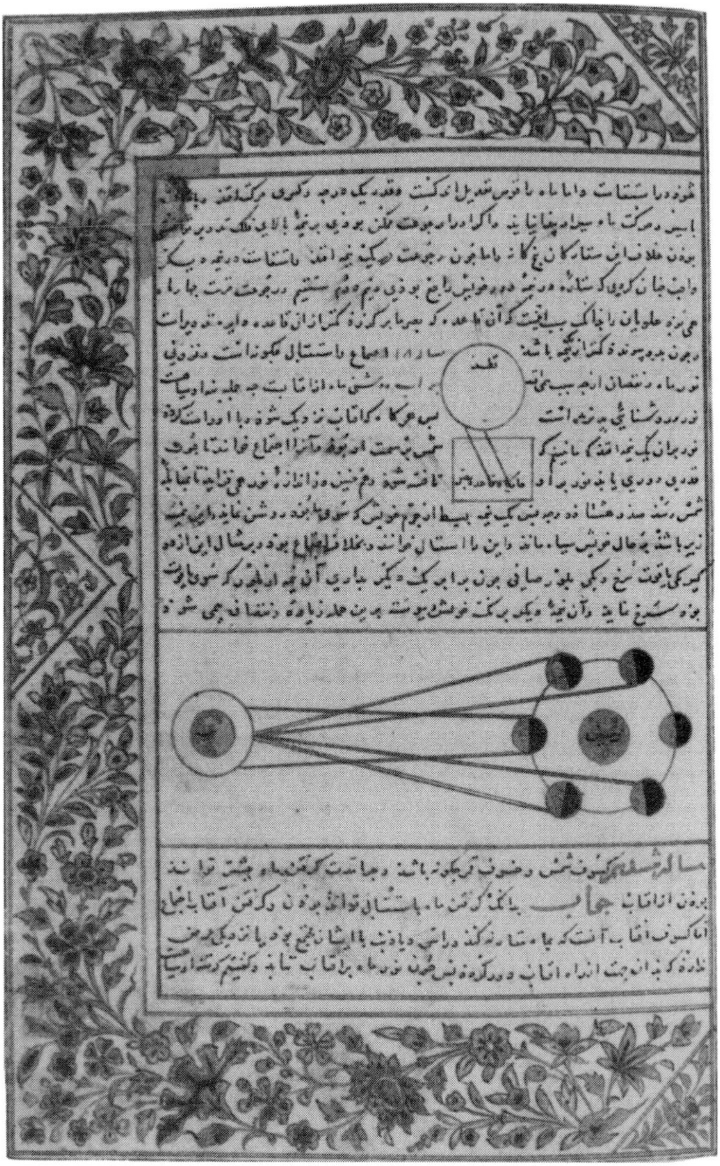

Diagram of Eclipses of the Sun and the Moon, from a Treatise on Astrology in a Miscellany written for Jalāl al-Dīn Iskandar ibn ʻUmar Shaykh. Shiraz, Timurid School. Copied 813/1410. BL. MS. Add. 27261, f. 410a. (Courtesy of the British Library).

obligation through indifference to prohibition, derived its validity from its timeless existence but elaborated many rules by a casuistical method over a long period of time. Time played an important role with regard to legal terms, as seen in one example. Divorce in its strict three-fold form was an irrevocable legal act, but in its simple form it could be revoked within a specified time. On a widow or a divorced woman the law imposed a waiting-period *('idda)* of abstention from sexual relations (three menstrual periods, an interval of similar duration in months and days, or the actual childbirth) as the term of expiry.

The Koranic concept of history revolved around prophetic figures, from Adam to Muḥammad. It was a typological view of history with a recurring pattern of events focused on the prophets of old, such as Noah, Abraham, Moses and Jesus, as well as heroes of Arab lore.[22] And religion itself, active submission to God *(islām)*, had its peaceful pace ruptured by the struggle for dominion *(jihād)* in the path of God. With the establishment of an empire by conquest, Islam acquired a dynamic sense of history and began dating events from the *hijra*, Muḥammad's emigration from Mecca to Medina in A.D. 622,[23] thus placing the record of history *(ta'rīkh)*[24] under God's continually sustained direction. Although other calendars, such as the Coptic, the Persian and the Turkish calendars, and other world eras, such as those of creation, the deluge, and Alexander, were known to Islam,[25] it was *ta'rīkh*, embracing annalistic and biographical history, that formed the heart of Muslim historical writing

---

22. The basic framework of the Koranic view of typological history has been surveyed by R. Paret, *Mohammed und der Koran* (Stuttgart 1957), pp. 81-92.
23. H. M. Watt, "Hidjra," *EI (new edition)*, III, pp. 366-7.
24. H. A. R. Gibb, "Ta'rīkh," *EI* (reprint 1987), Suppl., pp 231-45; for a thorough analysis of Muslim views of history, see F. Rosenthal, *A History of Muslim Historiography* (Leiden 1968; 2nd revised ed.), especially pp. 3-197.
25. The standard reference to Muslim calendars is B. Spuler and J. Mayr, *Wüstenfeld-Mahler'sche Vergleichungs-Tabellen* (Wiesbaden 1961). For general remarks on Muslim views of world eras, see B. Carra de Vaux, "Ta'rīkh," *EI* (reprint 1987), VIII, p. 672. The Muslim belief in the "good old times, the golden age of the past," is cxamined by R. Gramlich, "Vom islamischen Glauben an die 'gute, alte Zeit'," in R. Gramlich (ed.), *Islamwissenschaftliche Abhandlungen Fritz Meier zum sechzigsten Geburtstag* (Wiesbaden 1974), pp. 110-17.

and replaced the legends and popular traditions of an earlier age.

Islam not only began to develop a sense of genuine history and to embody a great variety of images of time in its literatures,[26] it also adopted a philosophy of time by integrating the legacy of the Greeks and the Persians. The general term for time, used in Arabic translations from Pahlavi, is *zamān*.[27] The term corresponds to Zurwān, the name of a deity who is father of twins, "luminous and perfumed" Ohrmazd and "dark and malodorous" Ahriman. The first was born of the sacrifice which Zurwān performed in order to have a son, who would create heaven and earth; the second was born of the doubts with which Zurwān was assailed while performing the rite. Ahriman, the first who saw the light of day, was given sovereignty for a limited time. At its end Ohrmazd, the son for whom Zurwān had offered the sacrifice, would assume absolute rule.[28] This myth

---

26. The scope of 'time' in Arabic and Persian poetry and *belles lettres,* which cannot be analysed here, is wide. It ranges from the tyranny of time in the *Thousand and One Nights* (see Ringgren, *Studies,* pp 201-3; E.W. Lane, the *Arabian Nights Enertainments* (New York 1927) to the *carpe diem* of the *Quatrains* of 'Umar Khayyām (d. 526/1132), who challenged the great chess player Heaven with the attitude, "I never worried about two days, the day that has not yet come and the day that has gone by" (see A. Christensen, *Recherches sur les Rubā'iyāt de 'Omar Ḫayyām* [Heidelberg 1905] p. 112). A divergent example is the time concept of Abū'l-'Alā' Aḥmad b. 'Abdullāh Ma'arrī (d. 449/1058) as explained by Nicholson, "Time, being independent of the revolutions of the celestial spheres, does not affect the course of events, which (indirectly, at any rate) is determined by the ever-changing position of the planets relatively to one another. Time brings nothing to pass; it is, so to speak, the neutral, unconscious atmosphere of all action and suffering;" see his *Studies in Islamic Poetry* (Cambridge 1921), p. 156; see also p. 59, note 1. Abū'l-'Atāhiya (d. 210/825), the early exponent of Arabic ascetic poetry, is an excellent example for early expressions of time in Arabic poetry. See G. Schoeler, "Bashshār b. Burd, Abū'l-'Atāhiyah and Abū Nuwās," in J. Ashtiany *et alii* (eds.), *The Cambridge History of Arabic Literature*: *'Abbasid Belles-Lettres* (Cambridge 1990), pp. 275-99, esp. p. 289; Sezgin, *GAS,* vol. II, pp. 534-5.
27. T. DeBoer, "Zamān," *EI* (reprint 1987), VIII, pp. 1207-9.
28. H.S. Nyberg, "Questions de cosmogonie et de cosmologie mazdéennes," *JA* 214 (1929), pp. 193-310; *JA* 219 (1931) pp. 1-134, 193-244; H.H. Schaeder, "Der iranische Zeitgott und sein Mythos," *ZDMG* 95 (1941), pp. 268-99; A. Christensen *L'Iran sous les Sassanides* (Copenhagen 1944, 2nd ed.); R. C Zaehner, *Zurvan: A Zoroastrian Dilemma* (Oxford 1955); M. Molé, "Le problème zurvanite," *JA* 247 (1959), pp. 431-69; G. Gnoli, "L'évolution du dualisme iranien et le problème zurvanite," *RHR* 201 (1984), pp. 115-38; G. Monnot, *Penseurs musulmans et religions iraniennes* (Paris 1974).

captured the concept of time in Mazdaism that distinguishes between eternal time without origin *(zurwān ī akanārag)* and bounded or finite time *(zurwān ī derang khwadāy).* It implied, as Corbin has argued, the essential Mazdean view of time as the time of a gnostic return to an eternal origin, not as that of an eternally returning time.[29] In a detailed analysis, Ringgren has shown the large extent to which the Persian epics, and with them Persian culture since before the Arab conquest, are permeated by the idea of all-pervading time and irreversible fate. In the epics, time plays a central role as the course of events determined by the revolving sky *(āsmān, sipihr, charkh, falak, gunbad, gardūn),* the power of human destiny *(rūzgār, zamān, zamāna, dahr)* and the lot of man's fortune *(bakht).*[30] Both the Persian lore of the epics and the religion of Mazdaism, the only non-Biblical tradition in substantial contact with Islam in its early centuries, affected ideas of time formed by Islam in later centuries.

The most common Islamic term for time, *zamān,* remained unknown to the Koran, as did *qidam,*[31] its counterpart for eternity. The Arab lexicographers, however, had a great variety of terms for time. In general, they distinguished *dahr,* time from the beginning of the world to its end, from *zamān,* a long time having beginning and end; *'aṣr,* a span of time; *ḥīn,* a period of time, little or much; *dawām,* duration; *mudda,* a space of duration; *waqt,* a moment in time; *ān,* present time; *awān,* time or season; *yawm,* a time, whether night or day; and *sā'a,* a time of night or day, a while. *Abad* was duration without end, and *azal* duration without beginning, to which *qidam,* time without beginning, corresponded in its primary sense as distinct from *sarmad,* incessant continuance, whereas *khulūd,* perpetual existence, was implicit in the Koranic *yawm al-khulūd,* day of eternity (L: 34), the entrance to *dār al-khulūd,* paradise. It is obvious that these distinctions do not reflect a quasi-technical usage

29. Corbin, "Cyclical Time," in *Man and Time,* pp. 115-72.
30. H. Ringgren, *Fatalism in Persian Epics* (Uppsala 1952), see also I. Scheftelowitz, *Die Zeit als Schickalsgottheit in der indischen und iranischen Religion (Kāla und Zurvān)* (Stuttgart 1929).
31. R. Arnaldez, "Ḳidam," *EI (new edition),* V, pp. 95-9.

of each term to the exclusion of others, but rather an approximately predominant meaning that often blends with the neighboring terms in the actual literary use.[32] When it came to translating Greek philosophical texts into Arabic, the most commonly employed correspondences were *chrónos,* translated by *zamān, aión* by *dahr, kairós* by *waqt,* and *diástasis* by *mudda.*[33]

Through exposure to Greek thought, the philosophers of Islam became familiar with two powerful and mutually opposed philosophical notions of time. Those who followed the Aristotelian view (beginning with Ya'qūb b. Isḥāq Kindī, d. about 252/866) saw time as an accident of motion and defined it as the number, measure or quantity *('adad, miqdār, kamiyya)* of motion according to 'before' and 'after' (in the first place as a number of movement of the celestial spheres). On the basis of this definition, Aristotle had attempted to prove the eternity of the universe from the nature of time. In the Plotinian concept (going back to Plato's image of time as emblem of eternity and espoused by the *Rasā'il* of the *Ikhwān al-ṣafā',* written about 350-75/961-86), time has no extra-mental reality since it is viewed as the stream of consciousness of a thinking mind and defined as a duration *(mudda, imtidād, maḍā')* that exists independently of motion as a quality of mind. That also meant that time did not come into existence with the creation of the universe, but existed from eternity as the duration of God's infinite consciousness.[34]

The Muslim philosophers adopted the term *abad* for eternity *a parte post* (Middle Persian *a-pād,* 'without foot', i.e. end; Greek *atéleuton,* 'without end'), in opposition to *azal,* eternity *a parte ante* (Pahlavi *a-sar,* "without head," i.e. beginning; Greek *ánarchon,* 'without beginning'), cognizant of the parallel philosophical usage of Greek, *áphtharton* (incorruptible) versus *agéneton* (ungenerat-

32. For details on these terms, see e.g. E.W. Lane, *An Arabic-English Lexicon* (London 1863-93).

33. S. Pines, *Beiträge zur islamischen Atomenlehre,* pp. 49-51. (Ibn Sina [d. 428/1037] refines the terminology by the distinction of *zamān, dahr* and *sarmad.*) See also E. Schmitt, *Lexikalische Untersuchungen zur arabischen Übersetzung von Artemidors Traumbuch* (Wiesbaden 1970), pp. 13-19.

34. DeBoer, "Zamān," *loc. cit.*

ed). They followed the Aristotelian maxim that *azal* and *abad* imply each other, that what has a beginning must have an end, and what has no beginning cannot have an end; thus time is eternal in both directions. The theologians of Islam, on the other hand, acknowledged only one assumption: an eternal God and a temporal world. They argued that time came into existence with the creation of the universe. Since God is absolutely incorporeal, He existed alone in timeless eternity prior to creation and has no relation to motion and consequently none to time. They offered a convoluted argument for the temporal creation of the world. If the world were without a beginning, at the present moment an infinite past would have been traversed—this is impossible. There is no such impossibility in the future since no infinite will ever be traversed. Parallel forms of argumentation would assert that a series of integers needs a first term but no final one, and a man may have eternal remorse although his remorse must have a beginning. Muslim theologians detected no rational proof for the incorruptibility of the world or its opposite and deemed it possible that the universe would be annihilated. This world *(dunyā)* will be destroyed but not heaven and hell.[35]

While Muslim notions of time oscillated between Aristotelian motion and Plotinian duration, it was the atomism of Democritus that appealed most strongly to the creators of normative Islamic theology. Atomism offered a concept of time which conceived of it as composed of a finite number of time-atoms or instants which are real entities. These atomic instants *(ānāt, awqāt)*, are not mental states but a constellation or galaxy of instants, paralleling an atomistic concept of space existing only of mathematical points. Atomism describes reality as consisting of indivisible and irreducible

---

35. S. van den Bergh, "Abad," *EI (new edition)*, I, p. 2. A controversial attitude to physical time and space is also included in the conceptions of motion *(ḥaraka)* and rest *(sukūn)* advanced by Muslim philosophers and theologians (see R. Arnaldez, "Ḥaraka wa-Sukūn," *EI [new edition]*, III, pp. 169-72). The difference of views between Mu'ammar b. 'Abbād (d. 215/830; motion in reality is rest), and Naẓẓām (d. between 220/835 and 230/845; motion is identical with being or existence and can be explained by the idea of the "jump," *ṭafra)* is highlighted by H. Daiber, *Das theologisch-philosophische System des Mu'ammar Ibn 'Abbād as-Sulamī* (Beirut 1975), pp. 294-306.

atoms with concomitant accidents. The atoms and their accidents exist for only an instant. In every instant, God is thus creating the world anew; there are no intermediate causes, and God can be thought of as continually creating the universe from nothing.[36] Turning Greek 'materialistic' atomism upside down (the Greeks defined nature through the monad, while the theologians anchored creation in God's persistent power), the Mu'tazila and Ash'ariyya made atomism an instrument of divine omnipotence and providence and held that each moment within time is the direct creation of the eternally active God.[37] Of itself, creation is discontinuous; it appears continuous only because of God's compassionate consistency. Atomism was not only most congenial to a vision of God acting instantaneously in the world as a sole true cause, it also proved most closely akin to Arabic grammar. In Arabic, verbal tenses are not understood as states but as verbal aspects—complete *(al-māḍī)* and incomplete *(al-muḍāri')*—marking, outside of time, the degree to which the action has been realized. These verbal aspects are qualified by the subjective consciousness of the moment expressed by the modality of circumstance *(ḥāl),* while nontemporal statements are normally made without any copula.[38]

In stark contrast to atomism stood the conception of the Dahriyya, a group who divinized duration.[39] This conception appeared to be compatible with notions of physical time that distinguished past *(māḍī),* present *(ḥāḍir)* and future *(mustaqbal).* It seemed to overcome the paradox that the present moment is the only real one in time. It placed time over space since space could be visualized by the point at the end of a line at rest, while time as a measure of motion flowed always on. Because Muslim belief deems only God

---

36. S. van den Bergh, "Djawhar," *EI (new edition),* II, pp. 493 4; S. Pines, *Beiträge zur islamischen Atomenlehre;* Massignon, "Time in Islamic Thought," in *Man and Time,* pp. 108-14; R.M. Frank, *The Metaphysics of Created Being according to Abū'l-Hudhayl al-'Allāf* (Istanbul 1966); C. Baffioni, *Atomismo e antiatomismo nel pensiero islamico* (Naples 1982).
37. H. S. Nyberg, "Mu'tazila," *EI* (reprint 1987), VI, pp. 787-93; J. van Ess, "Mu'tazilah," *ER,* X, pp. 220-9; R.M. Frank, "Ash'arīyah," *ER,* I, 449-55.
38. Massignon, "Time in Islamic Thought," *loc. cit.*
39. E. Goldziher and A.M. Goichon, "Dahriyya," *EL (new edition),* II, pp. 95-7.

as absolute, infinite and eternal, the Dahrī view of time was condemned as heresy. However, it left traces in the hermetic tradition of Islam, especially among the Ismā'īlīs. Time figured as one of the highest principles of the world in the pentad speculations of Abū Bakr Muḥammad b. Zakariyyā Rāzī, the physician (d. 313/925): God-Creator, World-Soul, Original Matter, Absolute Space and Absolute Time. This metaphysical pentad was mirrored by five things in the system of physics: matter, form, space, motion and time.[40] In this way Rāzī maintained a distinction between time *(zamān)* as finite and limited *(maḥṣūr),* and duration *(mudda, dahr)* as infinite and absolute *(muṭlaq).*[41] Since space was seen as an accident of the body and time as proceeding from the soul Abū Ḥayyān Tawḥīdī (d. 414/1023) answered the question, "Which is better, space or time?" with "Time is better, for space is of the senses but time is spiritual; space is in the world but time surrounds it."[42]

Perhaps the most prominent Islamic thinker on time was the Jewish convert Abū'l-Barakāt Baghdādī (d. ca. 560/1165) who defined time as "the measure of being" *(al-zamān miqdār al-wujūd),* not of motion, and held that the apperception of time is anterior in the soul to any other perception.[43] Ibn 'Arabī (d. 638/1240), who had been a Ẓāhirī for some time, was influenced by the thought of the Ẓāhirī school which interpreted time *(dahr)* as an attribute of God.[44] Ibn 'Arabī described God as time *(dahr),* defined as a single day *(yawm wāḥid)* without night-time or daytime, yet divided into many days,

40. DeBoer "Zamān," *loc. cit.;* Pines, *Beiträge,* pp. 34-93.
41. P. Kraus and S. Pines, "Al-Rāzī," *EI* (reprint 1987), VI, pp. 1134-6.
42. Abū Ḥayyān 'Alī b. Muḥammad Tawḥīdī, *Muqābasāt,* ed. H. Sandūbī (Cairo 1929), pp. 172-3, cf. pp. 154, 278; DeBoer, "Zamān," *loc. cit.;* M. Berge, *Pour un humanisme vécu: Abū Ḥayyān al-Tawḥīdī* (Damascus 1979). It is not possible to develop the rich legacy of Shi'ite ideas on 'time' in the framework of this article. Some basic Shi'ite notions are discussed by H. Corbin, *En Islam iranien,* 4 vols. (Paris 1971- 2); for references, see IV, pp. 556-7.
43. S. Pines, *Nouvelles études sur Awḥad al-zamān Abu-l-Barakāt al-Baghdādī* (Paris 1955); S. Pines, "Abu 'l-Barakāt," *EI (new edition)*, I, pp. 111-13; DeBoer, "Zamān," *loc. cit.*
44. Ibn 'Arabī, *al-Futūḥāt al-Makkiyya,* 4 vols. (Bulaq 1329 A.H.; repr. Beirut n.d., ca. 1970), III, pp. 315, 411; Goldziher, *Die Ẓāhiriten,* pp. 153-4; W.M. Watt, *Free Will and Predestination,* p. 31; A.E. Affifi, *The Mystical Philosophy of Muhyid Din Ibnul Arabi* (Lahore 1964), pp. 44, 111-12, 186.

the "Days of God," by the properties of the divine names and attributes.[45] "Each name has days which are the time *(zamān)* of the ruling property of that name. But all names are the Days of God *(ayyām Allāh),* and all are the differentiations of time *(dahr)* in the universe by virtue of the ruling property."[46] Telescoping the technical vocabulary into one phrase, 'Alī b. Muḥammad Jurjānī (d. 816/1413) offered the simplified definition, "duration *(dahr)* is the permanent moment *(ān)* which is the expansion *(imtidād)* of the divine presence and the innermost part of time *(zamān),* in which eternity *a parte ante* and *a parte post (azal* and *abad)* are united."[47]

In this rich cultural mix of contradictory conceptions of time and notions of history, the Persian mystics felt in their element. They tackled the paradox of the temporal and the eternal that had been left at the doorsteps of their meditation chambers by the old-Arab *dahr* and Koranic *ḥukm,* the Persian myth of time and the gnostic return to eternal origin, motion and rest, and time-atoms and divinized duration. Sufi knowledge inherited a kaleidoscope of time that merged themes culled from literature, philosophy, theology, law, scripture and poetry. Absorbing these themes, they discovered solutions to the paradox of time by refracting it through the prism of mystical experience. In the Sufi looking-glass, time became a pattern with its pivot in ecstasy and its course of spiritual time suspended between pre-existence and post-existence. The philosophers had explained time; the mystics set out to conquer it.[48]

It may be helpful for the analysis that follows to separate the

---

45. Ibn 'Arabī, *Futūḥāt,* III, pp. 198, 202; Cf. W.C. Chittick, *The Sufi Path of Knowledge* (New York 1989), p. 395.

46. Ibn 'Arabī, *Futūḥāt,* III, p. 201; cf. Chittick, *Sufi Path, loc. cit.,* and G. Böwering, "Ibn 'Arabī's Concept of Time," in *God is Beautiful and He loves Beauty: Festschrift for A. Schimmel,* ed. J.C. Bürgel and Alma Giese (Leiden 1994).

47. 'Alī b. Muḥammad Jurjānī, *Kitāb al-ta'rīfāt (A Book of Definitions)* (Beirut 1969), p. 111: *al-dahr huwa al-ān al-dā'im alladhī huwa imtidād al-haḍrat al-ilāhiyya wa-huwa bāṭin al-zamān wa-bihi yattaḥidu al-azal wa'l-abad.* A great variety of Muslim notions of time are enumerated in Muḥammad 'Alī Taḥānawī, *Kashshāf iṣṭilaḥāt al-funūn,* ed. Muḥammad Wajīn, 'Abd al-Ḥaqq and Ghulām Qādir (Calcutta 1862, repr. photo-offset Istanbul 1404/1984), pp. 61-2 *(abad),* pp. 84-5 *(azal, azalī),* pp. 393-4 *(ḥīn),* pp. 479-80 *(dahr),* pp. 619-23 *(zamān),* pp. 1211-15 *(qidam),* p. 1327 *(mudda, imtidād),* pp. 1449-50 *(waqt).*

classical from the mediæval period of Persian mysticism with the death of Muḥammad Ghazzālī (d. 505/1111). Sufi ideas of time in the classical period will be illustrated, first, by a case study of select mystics and, second, by an examination of crucial terms employed by the mystics for their conceptions of time. Bāyazīd Bisṭāmī (d. 234/848 or 261/875), a descendant of a Zoroastrian family converted to Islam, was the first to employ ecstatic utterances consistently as expressions of Sufi experience. The most frequently cited examples are *Subḥānī! mā a'ẓama sha'nī* ("Glory be to Me! How great is My majesty!") and *Anā Huwa* ("I am He").[49] Unlike the babbling of one possessed or blasphemy intended to scandalize others, Bāyazīd's utterances are in fact vividly phrased expressions of the experience of temporal consciousness merging with the eternal. Bāyazīd compares himself to God, claims the praise of angels in God's stead, turns the direction of prayer from God to himself, and declares that the Ka'ba walks around him.[50] He becomes God's rival, finding God's throne empty and ascending it in recognition of his own true being: "I am I and thus am 'I'."[51] Bāyazīd claims to be without beginning or end, and without morning or evening.[52] With his claim, "I am I; there is no God but I; so worship me!",[53] the monotheist Bāyazīd has reached a consciousness so thoroughly infused with the eternal that there is room neither for the human self nor for God but only for the ultimate and absolute "I", called God as

---

48. For a general description of 'orthodox' and 'heterodox' (Shi'ite) views on the beginning of creation and the world to come, see F. Meier, "The Ultimate Origin and the Hereafter in Islam," in *Islam and its Cultural Divergence,* ed. C.L. Tikku (Urbana 1971) pp. 96-112.
49. G. Böwering, "Besṭāmī (Basṭāmī), Bāyazīd," *EIr,* IV, pp. 183-6; H. Ritter, "Die Aussprüche des Bāyezīd Bisṭāmī," in *Westöstliche Abhandlungen,* ed. F. Meier (Wiesbaden 1954), pp. 231-43; "Abū Yazīd al-Bisṭāmī," *EI (new edition),* I, pp. 162-3.
50. Abū'l-Faḍl Muḥammad b. 'Alī Sahlajī, *Kitāb al-nūr min kalimāt Abī Ṭayfūr,* in *Shaṭaḥāt al-ṣūfiyya,* ed. 'A.R. Badawī (Cairo 1949) pp. 88, 108; Abū'l-Faraj 'Abd al-Raḥmān b. 'Alī Ibn al-Jawzī, *Talbīs Iblīs* (Cairo: n.d.), p. 332; Farīd al-Dīn 'Aṭṭār, *Tadhkirat al-awliyā',* ed. R.A. Nicholson, 1-2 (London-Leiden 1905-7), I, p.161.
51. Sahlajī, *Kitāb al-nūr,* p. 128.
52. Ibn al-Jawzī, *Talbīs Iblīs,* p. 332; Sahlajī, *Kitāb al-nūr,* p. 70.
53. *Ibid.*, p. 122.

the object of faith but "I" as the subject of mystical experience. Time and eternity have coalesced in the human psyche and the temporal has merged with the eternal in ecstatic consciousness.

Bāyazīd's sense of ecstatic time may be likened to an hourglass whose two conical chambers, time and eternity, connect at the narrow neck of the ecstatic "I." Sahl b. 'Abdullāh Tustarī (d. 283/896), living in another corner of Persia, envisioned time as an arch anchored in eternity at its origin and end, yet reaching its apex in the mystic's memory and mind. Tustarī's sense of time can be visualized as a boomerang traveling to the target and returning to the point of its release.[54] Passing from the picture to the paradigm, one might say that God is envisioned by Tustarī as both the transcendent mystery and the immanent secret of man's existence. Though inaccessible in absolute mystery, God manifests Himself in two fundamental events antecedent and subsequent to the temporal existence of man, the Day of Covenant *(yawm al-mīthāq)* and the Day of Resurrection *(yawm al-qīyāma).* In the act of recollection, *dhikr,*[55] which Tustarī was the first to put on a firm theoretical basis,[56] the mystic reactualizes his pre-existential past and anticipates his post-existential future, drawing the two antipodal events into his temporal existence and realizing the direct and certain presence of the Eternal within his inmost being. Through existential Koran interpretation, Tustarī understands the act of *dhikr* from the "Day of *Alast*"[57] as an act of anamnesis. God reveals Himself as the Lord of the primordial covenant in the inmost recesses of the human soul *(sirr al-nafs)* as the mystic recollects the Koranic phrase, *alastu bi-rabbikum* ("Am I not your Lord?", VII: 172). In this covenant, the pre-existing souls of all humanity had acceded to the lordship of God before the beginning of time. Through anamnesis the mystic

---

54. G. Böwering, *The Mystical Vision of Existence in Classical Islam* (Berlin 1980); *idem,* "The Islamic Case," in *The Other Side of God,* ed. P. Berger (New York 1981), pp. 131-53; L. Massignon, "Sahl al-Tustarī," *EI* (reprint 1987), VII, p. 63.
55. L. Cardet, "D̲hikr," *EI (new edition),* II, pp. 223-7; G. Böwering "D̲ekr," *EIr,* V (forthcoming).
56. Böwering, *Mystical Vision,* pp. 45-9, 201-7.
57. R. Gramlich, "Der Urvertrag in der Koranauslegung (zu Sure 7, 172-3)," *Der Islam* 60 (1983), pp. 205-30.

rediscovers this moment of his beginnings before creation in Pharaoh's blasphemous proclamation of his own lordship *anā rabbukum al-a'lā* ("I am your Lord Most High," LXXIX: 24). Listening to God, the true speaker of the Koranic word, the mystic ironically perceives the actual essence of belief flowing from Pharaoh's tongue of unbelief and remembers in his experience the moment when God, in pre-existence affirmed His lordship for human consciousness: there is only One who can truly say "I."[58] As the mystic speaks these very words of the Eternal, either uttering them perceptibly on the tongue or recollecting them imperceptibly in the heart, his memory returns to his origin before time, his primal moment with God. The eternal beginning of his being, drawn out of his distant past on the Day of Covenant, is captured here and now, in the light of certitude *(yaqīn)* with which he beholds his future and ultimate destiny, the vision of God's face and the sounds of God's voice on the Day of Resurrection.[59] For Tustarī, time is memory of the eternal past and certitude of the eternal future drawn into the present moment.

While Bāyazīd touched eternity in the "I" of his ecstasy and Tustarī drew eternity from infinity into the moment of memory, Abū Bakr Shiblī (d. 334/945) used the paradox of the mystic moment, the "now" *(waqt,* "time, instant"), to express lasting timelessness experienced in temporality. Shiblī adopted Junayd's (d. 298/910) basic principle of trust in God,[60] "that you are before God as you were before you were while God is before you as He always is,"[61] and approved the equation of "I am You and You are I *(anā anta wa-anta anā)".*[62] In mystical experience, his own "I" could not co-exist with the divine "I," for "if I were with Him, I would be 'I'[63] *(fa-innanī*

58. Böwering, *Mystical Vision,* pp. 185-201.
59. *Ibid.*, pp. 207-16.
60. Abū Bakr Muḥammad b. Isḥāq Kalābādhī, *Kitāb al-Ta'arruf li-madhhab ahl al-taṣawwuf,* ed. A.J. Arberry (Cairo 1934), p. 72, tr. *idem, The Doctrine of the Sufis* (repr. Cambridge 1977), p. 92.
61. Abū Naṣr 'Abdullāh b. 'Alī al-Sarrāj, *Al-Luma' fī al-taṣawwuf,* ed. R.A. Nicholson (London-Leiden 1914), p. 52: tr. R Gramlich, *Schlaglichter über das Sufitum* (Stuttgart 1990), p. 99.
62. Sarrāj, *Luma',* p. 360; Gramlich, *Schlaglichter,* p. 498.

anā); but I have passed away in Him." "It has been my life-long desire to be alone with God, without Shiblī's being there at this being alone."[64] Shiblī overcame the dichotomy of God's claim on every moment and the mystic's self-awareness in time through the paradoxes of the everlasting moment and the ocean without shore. He coined the verse, "My moment lasts forever in You; it is everlasting *(musarmad).* You made me pass away from You, and so I was made bare *(mujarrad),"*[65] and phrased the two paradoxes, "My moment is without two ends, and my ocean is without shore *(waqtī laysa lahu ṭarafān wa-baḥrī bi-lā shāti').*"[66] Expressing his conviction that the present is only real through the past and future that exist compressed into it, he produced the aphorism of "a thousand past years in a thousand coming years, that is the moment. Let the phantoms *(ashbāh)* not deceive you!"[67] Beyond the moment, everything past or future is phantom; what the moment holds, it alone is like cash in hand.[68] "I am on my way to the 'without-beyond', but I see only 'beyond' *(amurru ilā mā lā warā'a fa-lā arā illā warā').* I go right and left to the 'without-beyond', but I see only 'beyond'. Then I return and behold, everything is in a hair of my little finger."[69] Other accounts have Shiblī exclaim, "I am the moment!" "My moment is glorious!" and "Nothing but I is in the moment!"[70] "I am the point under the 'bā'," that is to say, the diacritical mark under the Arabic "b", the first letter of the Koran.[71] Since God demands each moment for Himself in His divine jealousy,[72] Shiblī prays, "O God,

---

63. Sarrāj, *Luma',* p. 395; Gramlich, *Schlaglichter,* p. 493.
64. 'Aṭṭār, *Tadhkirat,* II, p. 165.
65. Sarrāj, *Luma',* p. 365; Gramlich, *Schlaglichter,* p. 502.
66. Sarrāj, *Luma',* p. 365; Gramlich, *Schlaglichter,* p. 502.
67. Sarrāj. *Luma',* p. 404-5; Gramlich, *Schlaglichter,* p. 546.
68. 'Aṭṭār, *Tadhkirat,* II, p. 179.
69. Sarrāj, *Luma',* p. 365; Gramlich, *Schlaglichter,* p. 544.
70. Sarrāj, *Luma',* p. 405; Gramlich, *Schlaglichter,* p. 546.
71. Abū'l-Qāsim 'Abd al-Karīm b. Hawāzin Qushayrī, *al-Risāla al-Qushayriyya,* ed. 'Abd al-Ḥalīm Maḥmūd and Maḥmūd b. al-Sharīf, 1-2 (Cairo 1385/1966), p. 345; tr. R. Gramlich, *Das Sendschreiben al-Qušayrīs über das Sufitum* (Wiesbaden 1989), p. 218, (on which, see the review by G. Böwering, in *Orientalia* 58 [1989], pp. 569-72).
72. Sarrāj, *Luma',* p. 228; Gramlich, *Schlaglichter,* p. 346; Qushayrī, *Risāla,* p. 515; Gramlich, *Sendschreiben,* p. 355; 'Aṭṭār, *Tadhkirat,* II, p. 179.

if you notice that there is any room left in me for someone else than You, then burn me in Your fire!"[73] For Shiblī, then, the paradox of time holds the past and future in the moment, capturing eternity as if in a fleeting instant that cannot cease.

A subjective view of time was also reflected in the mystical speculation on *tawḥīd,* the oneness of God, the eternal and true reality, the One without partners, beside whom the mystic's temporal existence has no claim to reality and his self no right to selfhood.[74] Realizing *tawḥīd*, the mystic has to abandon any trace of temporal consciousness so that his self is blotted out in actual non-existence and the Eternal alone in truth subsists. In the words of Abū'l-Ḥasan Kharaqānī (d. 425/1033), "One is a Sufi who is not. The Sufi is a day that has no need of sun, a night that needs neither moon nor star, and a non-existence that needs no existence."[75] This non-existence equals the state of primordial existence at the "Day of *Alast"* prior to creation when, at the moment of his standing *(waqfa)* in the presence of God, man received his own intellect by virtue of his first act of consciousness. Throughout his life the Sufi has the task of dying to his temporal existence and returning to his only true existence (i.e. his non-existence), being "as he was, when he was before he was" (Dhū'l-Nūn Miṣrī, d. 245/860)[76] or "returning to the beginning" (Junayd).[77] The fundamental experience of passing away from temporal existence and subsisting in eternal existence was couched in the language of *fanā'* and *baqā'* by Abū Sa'īd Kharrāz (d. 286/899).[78] He saw the transition from temporal to eternal existence not as a total annihilation, since the self is not reduced to pure nothingness, but as a purification of the self which is drawn to higher forms of being and ultimately absorbed in God—in Abū'l-

73. Sarrāj, *Luma',* p. 405; Gramlich, *Schlaglichter,* p. 547.
74. G. Böwering, *"Baqā' wa Fanā',"* *EIr,* III, pp. 722-4.
75. Nūr al-Dīn 'Abd al-Raḥmān b. Aḥmad Jāmī, *Nafaḥāt al-uns min ḥaḍarāt al-quds,* ed. M. Tawḥīdīpur (Tehran 1336 A.Hsh./1957), p. 298; Böwering, *"Baqā' wa Fanā',"* *EIr,* III, p. 722.
76. Kalābādhī, *Ta'arruf,* p. 105.
77. Khwāja 'Abdullāh Harawī Anṣārī, *Ṭabaqāt al-ṣufiyya,* ed. 'Abd al-Ḥayy Ḥabībī (Kabul, 1340 A.Hsh./1961), p. 168.
78. Böwering, *"Baqā' wa Fanā',"* *EIr,* III, p. 722.

Ḥusayn Nūrī's (d. 295/908) words, "fashioned in the attributes of God" *(al-ṭakhalluq bi-akhlāq Allāh).*[79] In the passing-away, one's own self is stripped off, like a snake shedding its skin, and self-identity is obliterated. As the mystic loses the identity with his own self, he experiences identity with God, as exclaimed by Abū Sa'īd b. Abī'l-Khayr (d. 440/1049), "When you see me you see Him, and when you see Him you see me."[80]

When it came to theory, the Persian mystics of the classical period coined their spiritual conceptions of time in a variety of terms, prominent among them *waqt,* often used interchangeable with *ḥāl,* "state"[81] and *ān,* "here and now."[82] Abū Sulaymān Dārānī (d. 215/831) was one of the earliest Sufis to define *waqt* in mystical terms as "the preservation of one's state *(ri'āyat-i ḥāl).*"[83] 'Alī b. Muḥammad Dīnawarī (d. 330/941-2) compared these states to bolts of lightning *(al-aḥwāl ka 'l-burūq).*[84] The mystics understood *waqt* as the present moment, "that which dominates the mystic" and "that time *(zamān)* in which he is."[85] Abū Bakr Wāsiṭī (d. 320/932) described it as an experience, lasting less than an hour that comes unexpectedly, brings its own experience of blessings and hardships, and neutralizes experiences preceding it. "The moment *(waqt)*[86] is less than an hour. Whatever blessing or hardship attained you before that moment, you are unencumbered by it. However, you do not know whether or not what occurs in that moment or after it will be

79. 'Aṭṭār, *Tadhkirat,* II, p. 54-5.
80. Muḥammad b. Munawwar, *Asrār al-tawḥīd,* ed. Dh. Ṣafā (Tehran 1332 A.Hsh./1953), p. 259; G. Böwering, "Abū Sa'īd b. Abi-l-K̲ayr," *EIr,* I, pp.377-80.
81. R. Gramlich, *Die schiitischen Derwischorden Persiens. Zweiter Teil: Glaube und Lehre* (Wiesbaden 1976), p. 352.
82. For a lengthy discussion of this term, see A.R. Arasteh, *Growth to Selfhood* (London 1980), pp. 107-33.
83. Abū'l-Ḥasan 'Alī b. 'Uthmān Hujwīrī Jullābī, *Kashf al-maḥjūb,* ed. V. Zukowsky (photo-repr. Tehran 1336 A.Hsh./1957), p. 139; tr. R.A. Nicholson, *The "Kashf al-Maḥjūb," the Oldest Persian Treatise on Sufism* (repr. London 1976), p. 112.
84. Qushayrī, *Risāla,* p. 142; Gramlich, *Sendschreiben,* p. 86.
85. Qushayrī, *Risāla,* p. 188; Gramlich, *Sendschreiben,* p. 107.
86. Abū 'Abd al-Raḥmān Muḥammad b. al-Ḥusayn Sulamī, *Ṭabaqāt al-ṣūfiyya,* ed. J. Pedersen (Leiden 1960), p. 306; ed. Nūr al-Dīn Sharība (Cairo 1389/1969), p. 304.

within your reach." *Waqt* is a liberating moment that makes the mystic independent of the past and the future and so collected *(mujtami')* that he has no memory of the past and no thought of what has not yet come.[87] With a particularly striking image, the Sufis likened *waqt* to the sharp edge of a sword.[88] "The moment is a cutting sword *(sayf qāṭi')*"[89] cutting the mystic to the quick and separating the "two non-existents" of whatever was before and after. In Junayd's image, the moment is the breath "between two breaths," the one before and after, that cannot be overtaken again once it is gone.[90] The same is expressed by Kharrāz's statement that *waqt* is the precious moment "between the past and the future."[91] For Abū 'Alī Daqqāq (d. 405/1015) *waqt* was "a file *(mibrad)* that abrades but does not erase you."[92] In a phrase of 'Abdullāh b. Khubayq Anṭāki (d. 200/815-16), the Sufi was a person standing "under the decree of the moment" *(bi-ḥukm al-waqt).*[93] *Waqt* also provided the shortest definition of a Sufi, "son of his moment" *(ibn waqtihi).*[94] In Anṣārī's (d. 481/1089) view, *waqt* compressed one's whole lifetime into the present moment which alone, in being captured, gave the mystic a hold on past and future: "in reality extended time is the moment" *(az rūy-i ḥaqīqat zamān waqt ast).*[95] The moment dominates the mystic with violent, irresistible force—its attribute is *qahr,* compelling force[96]—because the divine action overpowers the mystic,

---

87. Jullābī, *Kashf,* p. 480; Nicholson, *Kashf al-Maḥjūb,* p. 368.
88. Qushayrī, *Risāla,* p. 189, Gramlich, *Sendschreiben,* p. 108.
89. Qushayrī, *Risāla,* p. 189; Gramlich, *Sendschreiben,* p. 108; Jullābī, *Kashf,* p. 482; Nicholson, *Kashf al-Maḥjūb,* p. 369; see also G. Böwering, "The Ādāb Literature of Classical Sufism: Anṣārī's Code of Conduct" in *Moral Conduct and Authority,* ed. B.D. Metcalf (Berkeley 1984), pp. 84-5.
90. Sarrāj, *Luma',* p. 342; Gramlich, *Schlaglichter,* p. 479.
91. Jullābī, *Kashf,* p. 480; Nicholson, *Kashf al-Maḥjūb,* p. 368.
92. Qushayrī, *Risāla,* p. 190, Gramlich *Sendschreiben,* p. 108.
93. Sarrāj, *Luma',* p. 61; Gramlich, *Schlaglichter,* p. 112; Kalābādhī, *Ta'arruf,* p. 69; Arberry, *Doctrine,* p. 89.
94. Böwering, "The Ādāb Literature," *loc. cit.;* Qushayrī, *Risāla,* p. 188; Gramlich, *Sendschreiben,* p. 107. The phrase appears to have been coined by Abū'l-Ḥasan 'Alī b. Ja'far Shīrwanī, see Anṣārī, *Ṭabaqāt,* p. 484; Jamī, *Nafaḥāt,* p. 272; B. Reinert, *Die Lehre tawakkul in der klassischen Sufik* (Berlin 1968), pp. 191-2.
95. Böwering, "The Ādāb Literature," *loc. cit.*
96. Jullābī, *Kashf,* p. 482; Nicholson, *Kashf al-Maḥjūb,* p. 482.

independently of his own volition.[97] In Ḥusayn b. Manṣūr Ḥallāj's (d. 309/922) words, "It is a breeze of joy blown by pain" and "a pearl-bearing shell sealed at the bottom of the ocean of a human heart."[98] In Massignon's interpretation, it is both a moment of anguish and a divine touch of hope that transfigures human memory. It can survive like a germ of immortality buried at the bottom of the heart as a hidden persistence oriented towards the future, to "the final stoppings of the pendulum of our vital pulse."[99] Anṣārī defines *waqt* as the moment containing only God, which can be of three kinds. It can come like a bolt of lightning *(barq),* stay for a long while *(pāyanda)* or be overpowering *(ghālib).* The moment coming like lighting springs from meditation *(fikrat);* it purifies and makes one forget this world. The moment that perdures is the result of recollection *(dhikr);* it focuses the person and makes him forget the world to come. The one that overpowers originates in auditions and visions *(samā' wa naẓar);* it wipes out all traces of human awareness so that only God remains.[100] Later, Ibn 'Arabī called the most perfect human being, the pole *(quṭb)* and mirror of God *(mir'āt al-ḥaqq),* "the possessor of the moment *(ṣāḥib al-waqt),* the eye of time *('ayn al-zamān)* and the mystery of destiny *(sirr al-qadar)".*[101]

The character of both a sudden impact of grace and an instant of anguish, endowed with emotions ranging from consolation *(basṭ)* to desolation *(qabḍ),* were the marks of ecstasy, a condition for which the mystics used the term *wajd* which carries two connotations, *wajada,* "to find," and *wajida,* "to suffer." *Wajd* is an inner event, it comes according to Junayd as "an unexpected occurrence *(muṣādafa).*"[102] Nūrī[103] describes it as "a flame flaring up in the hearts *(asrār)* and rising out of longing so that the limbs are stirred

97. Jullābī, *Kashf,* p. 480; Nicholson, *Kashf al-Maḥjūb,* p. 480.
98. Massignon, "Time in Islamic Thought," in *Man and Time,* p. 113.
99. *Ibid.*, p. 114.
100. S. De Laugier de Beaurecueil, *Khwādja 'Abdullāh Anṣārī* (Beirut 1965), pp. 192-5. For Abū Sa'īd b. Abī'l-Khayr's views on *waqt* as the mystic moment, see F. Meier, *Abū Sa'īd-i Abu l-Ḫayr, Wirklichkeit und Legende* (Leiden 1976), pp. 105-9.
101. *Futūḥāt,* II, p. 573; cf. Böwering, "Ibn 'Arabī's Concept of Time."
102. Sarrāj, *Luma',* p. 301; Gramlich, *Schlaglichter,* p. 431.
103. Kalābādhī, *Ta'arruf,* p. 82; Arberry, *Doctrine,* p. 106.

to joy or grief at that visitation." Ecstasy is an act of finding something that has been lost, a moment between a loss *(faqd)* that preceded it and a loss that followed it. In theory it is divided into two acts, *wajd,* ecstasy that is as yet longing, and *wujūd,* finding in ecstasy what one longed for (while *tawājud* is the mere affectation of yearning). In a picture, *tawājud* is looking at the ocean, *wajd* traveling on it and *wujūd* being immersed in it.[104]

In mediaeval Persia, three lesser-known Persian mystics, all active before Ibn 'Arabī's impact on Persian mysticism, may be singled out for their original conceptions of time. The brilliant mystical philosopher and Sufi martyr, 'Ayn al-Quḍāt (d. 526/1131) of Hamadān,[105] was a highly original thinker known for the excellence of his language and admired or reproached for his daring thought. His conception of time can be viewed against the background of the Persian dualism of light and darkness which he neither rejects nor avows. "The Divinity is two: one is Yazdān, Light, the other Ahriman, Darkness. Light is that which commands the Good, Darkness that which commands Evil. Light is the primordial Time of Day, Darkness the final Time of Night. Unbelief results from one, belief from the other."[106] Transcending the dualism of light and darkness, 'Ayn al-Quḍāt transposed the dichotomy into God and combined it with the figures of Muḥammad and Iblīs. "When the point of divine Magnitude expanded from the one divine Essence to the horizons of pre-eternity and post-eternity, it did not stop anywhere. So it was in the world of the Essence that the range of the attributes unfolded, namely divine beauty, homologue of Muḥammad, and divine majesty, homologue of Iblīs."[107] Adopting the opaque notion of the black light *(nūr-i siyāh)* that lies beyond the divine throne, 'Ayn al-Quḍāt fused the dualist tends of his thought into a

104. Qushayrī, *Risāla,* pp. 201-6; Gramlich, *Sendschreiben,* p. 108.
105. G. Böwering, "'Ayn-al-Qożāt Hamadānī," *EIr,* III, pp. 140-3.
106. 'Ayn-al-Quḍāt Hamadānī, *Tamhīdāt,* ed. Afif Osseiran (Tehran 1341A.Hsh./1962), p. 305.
107. *Ibid.,* p. 73. Cf. M. 'Abdū'l-Ḥaq, "'Ayn al-Quḍāt Hamadānī's Concept of Time and Space in the Perspective of Sufism," *Isl. Qtly.*, XXXI (1987), pp. 5-37, N. Pourjavady, "Selfhood and Time in the Sufism of Aḥmad Ghazzālī," *Sophia Perennis,* IV (1981).

paradoxical unity. The black light is both "the shadow of Muḥammad" whose nature is pure luminosity and "the light of Iblīs" conventionally called "darkness" only because of its sharp contrast to God's light.[108] Taken from a quatrain of Bustī, qualified as "well-known and difficult" by Nūr al-Dīn Jāmī (d. 898/1492),[109] the image of the black light is "higher than the point of no *(lā)"* beyond which "there is neither this nor that."[110] As if in a nutshell, Ayn al-Quḍāt expressed the paradox of time and eternity by the black light, the unthinkable conjunction of opposites.

The work of Shams al-Dīn Daylamī (d. *ca.* 593/1197),[111] a contemporary of *Shaykh al-Ishrāq* Yaḥyā Suhrawardī (d. 587/1191), escaped scholarly notice except for Jāmī, who calls him "a great master and scholar whose teachings on the true reality of time, as set forth in his writings, are rarely found in the works of others."[112] His ideas on time are not only recorded in the *Ghāyat al-imkān fī ma'rifat al-zamān wa'l-makān,*[113] a work of his disciple Maḥmūd Ushnuhī who paraphrases his master's words, but also in his many other works that provide a framework of thought in which he anchors the world of his visions. The visionary world of the mystic is seen as totally real and fully identical with the spiritual world of the invisible realm. The twins of the inner world of man and the upper world of the unseen provide a mirror for the bipolarity of divine nature, eternal time and space, and intuitive knowledge and direct vision of the Eternal. In tackling the controversial problem of the time possessed by God, Daylamī defines it as a totally present moment

---

108. *Ibid.*, pp. 118, 248.
109. Jāmī, *Nafaḥāt,* p. 413.
110. Hamadānī, *Tamhīdāt,* pp. 119, 248; Ritter, *Meer,* p. 541. Cf. Pourjavady, *Zindagī wa āthār-i Shaykh Abū'l-Ḥasan Bustī,* (Tehran 1985).
111. G. Böwering, "Deylamī, Šams ud-dīn," *EIr,* V, (forthcoming, with a list of his works); "The Writings of Shams al-Dīn al-Daylamī," *Islamic Studies* 26 (1985), pp. 231-6; A. J. Arberry, "The Works of Shams al-Dīn al-Dailamī, *BSOAS* 29 (1966), pp. 49-56.
112. *Nafaḥāt,* p 355.
113. For the attribution of this work, see Böwering, "'Ayn-al-Qożat Hamadānī," p. 141; the work was edited as *Ghāyat al-imkān fī dirāyat al-makān* by R. Farmanish (Tehran 1339 A.Hsh./1960), and re-edited by N.M. Harawī, *Majmū'ah-i āthār-i farsī-yi Tāj al-Dīn-i Ushnuwī* (Tehran 1368 A.Hsh./1989), pp. 47-82.

without past or future, since "time" may be defined as the present moment that is both continuous in nature, and past plus future compressed into that very presence. Daylamī finds the proof for his view of time in the possibility of the beatific vision of God and in his own visionary ability to reduce long time spans to single moments.

In a recent monograph, Fritz Meier has chiseled out of the extant sources the magnificent image of Bahā'-i Walad (d. 628/1231),[114] the father of Mawlānā Jalāl al-Dīn Rūmī (d. 672/1273). Bahā'-i Walad emerges in his *Ma'ārif*[115] as a man who erases the gulf between God's transcendence and immanence and actually integrates, rather than ascetically sublimates, man's temporal reality into life with God. God is in no direction and in all directions: He is above, below or on the same plane; far away or intimately close; neither within nor outside the world; here and beyond; neither in things nor in nothingness; nowhere and everywhere; in short, in an "additional dimension" beyond any dimension. God is without locus and beyond description, and yet has a core of divine essence covered by the mantle of attributes through which He performs His acts, extending Himself as far as their effects. Despite the total break in dimension between God and His creation, God is intimately related to the world. His *ma'iyyat* ("being-with") accompanies all that is and all that becomes, be it on the intellectual, spiritual or physical plane. *Ma'iyyat* is time matched with eternity, the penetrating nearness of the impenetrable Other. God permeates all things on the level of being, remains present to them through His act of creation, and intertwines with them through His knowledge, will and perception. The world is made of atoms, the ultimate components of all things, created by God at each moment. As God is present to each of these atoms, each atom is conscious of facing God with its alert countenance *(wajh)* and turning away its dark back. All things down

114. F. Meier, *Bahā'-i Walad: Grundzüge seines Lebens und seiner Mystik,* Acta Iranica 27, troisième série textes et mémoires, vol. 14 (Leiden 1989); see the review by G. Böwering in *JAOS* 111 (1991), pp. 801-2.

115. Ed. Badī' al-Zamān Furūzānfar, vol. I (Tehran 1333 A.Hsh./1955), and vol. II (Tehran 1338 A.Hsh./1959); see also Sulṭān Walad, *Ma'ārif,* ed. N.M. Harawī, (Tehran 1367 A.Hsh./1988).

to their tiniest particle have this mental relationship to God, being aware of Him explicitly (or implicitly, as if in stupor or indifference). Reflecting on the atomistic structure of the universe and the divine coexistence with it in continuous conscious symbiosis, Bahā'-i Walad seeks a return to God whose image he mirrors, yet not a reversion to the nothingness from which he was created. This type of total 'cosmic' mysticism, based on atomism and the Eternal's coexistence, seeks the "lust" *(maẓa)* of drawing matter and body into the embrace of eternity.

Adopting this spiritual mode of time and eternity in poetry, the Persian mystics of the mediæval period discovered the true self in the depth of one's personality as the divine secret of the eternal I-ness taking the place of the temporal self. Realizing this secret, the *Bīsarnāma* of pseudo-'Aṭṭār exclaims, "I am God, I am God, am God!" *(man khudā-yam, man khudā-yam, man khudā),* and Nasīmī's *Dīvān* takes up a theme of Rūmī's *Mathnawī,* "I beheld that I am God from top to toe," *(sar tā pā-qadam wujūd-i khwud ḥaqq dīdam).*[116] Rūmī catches this secret in the image of a ruby permeated by the rays of the sun and transformed as if into sunlight. As long as the ruby is ruby, there are as yet two, ruby and sunlight, but when the penetration of sunlight is complete there is only one brilliance.[117] The old "I" *(anā)* has become the "no" *(lā)* that is denied by the new "I": *man man nī-am* (I am not I) as Rūmī says.[118] Rūmī also was inspired by a *ḥadīth,* often linked with the Prophet's heavenly journey *(mi'rāj),* "I have a moment with God *(lī ma'a Allāh waqt)* to which no created being has access, not even Gabriel who is pure spirit."[119] The angel remained outside the Divine Presence, stopping at the "lote-tree of the boundary" *(sidrat al-muntahā,* 53:14) where reason ends, without scorching his veils, while Muḥammad entered into an intimate time with God, the secret

---

116. Ritter, *Meer,* p. 590.
117. Jalāl al-Dīn Muḥammad Rūmī, *Mathnawī-yi ma'nawī,* ed. R. A. Nicholson (London-Leiden 1925-40), repr. by N. Pourjavadi (Tehran 1363 A.Hsh./1984), III, pp. 129-30 (bk.V: vv. 2025-35).
118. *Ibid.*, I, p. 193 (bk. I: vv. 3124-6).
119. See p. 230—›

discourse of love between lover and Beloved.[120] Taken out of created time, the Prophet touched God's eternity, foreshadowing the Sufis' own mystical moment with God, as Sanā'ī (d. 526/1131) had exclaimed: "Love is higher than reason and soul — 'I have a moment with God' belongs to the true man."[121] Persian mystical poetry, in particular, interiorized the Koranic history of prophetic types by transforming the Prophet's *mi'rāj,* his ascent through the heavens to God, into the soul's journey from the world of temporality to the height of mystical union with the Eternal.[122]

The Persian mystics not only composed beautiful poetry, they also related wondrous legends about the miracles *(karāmāt)* which they claimed to have worked. One kind of miracle was their ability to pull large time spans into short moments or draw out time to inconceivably long durations, rolling up time *(ṭayy al-zamān)* or expanding time *(nashr al-zamān).* Awḥad al-Dīn Kirmānī (d. 635/1238) had the ability of rolling up time when he called to mind his

---

119. Badī' al-Zamān Furūzānfar *Aḥādīth-i mathnawī* (Tehran 1334 A.Hsh./1955), p. 39 (no 100). This *ḥadīth* is not cited in the canonical *ḥadīth* literature and is thus absent from Wensinck's *Concordance,* but it is frequently quoted in Sufi literature in the variant and earlier form, "I have a moment with God *(lī ma'a Allāh waqt)* in which no angel drawn near *(malak-i muqarrab)* or prophet sent *(nabī-yi mursal)* rivals me." The earliest references in Persian Sufi literature are found in the Persian commentary on Kalābādhī's *Ta'arruf* by Abū Ibrāhīm Ismā'l b. Muḥammad Mustamlī Bukhārī (d. 434/1042-3), *Nūr al-murīdīn wa-faḍīhat al-mudda'īn,* ed. M. Rawshān (Tehran 1363 A.Hsh./1984), pp. 613, 767, 777, 879, 887, 902, 906, 1329, 1423; then also in Jullābī (d. 465/1072–469/1077), *Kashf,* p. 480; Nicholson, *Kashf al-Maḥjūb,* p. 368; 'Ayn al-Quḍāt Hamadānī, *Tamḥīdāt,* pp. 79, 123, 131, 203, 317. Rashīd al-Dīn Abū'l- Faḍl Sa'īd Maybudī (d. 530/1135), *Kashf al-asrār wa 'iddat al-abrār,* ed. 'Alī Aṣghar Ḥikmat, 10 vols. (Tehran 1363 A.Hsh./1984), I, pp. 269, 683; II, p. 328; III, p. 187; VI, p. 460; VII, pp. 172-3; IX, p. 238; X, p. 432; Maybudī also records another significant variant, I, p. 614. If Ibn Sīnā's (d. 428/1037) *Mi'rājnāma* is authentic, then its quotation of the *ḥadīth* would be the earliest found in *mi'rāj* literature: see Abū 'Alī al-Ḥusayn b. 'Abdullāh b. Sīnā, *Mi'rājnāma,* ed. N.M. Harawī (Tehran 1365 A.Hsh./1986), p. 92.

120. A. Schimmel, *Mystical Dimensions of Islam* (Chapel Hill 1975), p. 220; *eadem, The Triumphal Sun* (London 1978), pp. 285-6; *eadem, And Muḥammad is His Messenger* (Chapel Hill 1985), p. 169. In this century Iqbāl (d. 1938) took up the theme forcefully in his poetry and prose, see G. Böwering, "Iqbal–Poet between India and Europe," *Islam and the Modern Age,* 9 (1978), pp. 57-70.

121. Abū'l-Majd Majdūd b. Ādam Sanā'ī, *Ḥadīqat al-ḥaqīqat wa sharī'a al-ṭarīqat,* ed. Mudarris Raḍawī (Tehran 1329 A.Hsh./1950), p. 328.

122. G. Böwering, "Mi'rāj," *ER,* vol. IX, pp. 552-6.

seventy thousand disciples at night one by one. In a dream, Rūzbihān Baqlī (d. 606/1209) taught Abū Ḥafṣ Suhrawardī (d. 632/1234) ways in which time could be rolled up. Sufis were observed reciting the Koran from beginning to end, with every letter clearly pronounced, while walking a few steps around the Ka'ba in Mecca —a feat of time expansion *(basṭ al-zamān)* in 'Umar Suhrawardī's view.[123] Next to speed recitation of the Koran, called *ṭayy al-ḥurūf*, there were examples of bilocation or uncanny locomotion. Tustarī was seen with the pilgrims at 'Arafāt outside Mecca and leaving his home in Iraq on the same day. Abū'l-Ḥasan Kharaqānī went five times a day from his home to the Lebanon mountains to lead a group of men in prayer. 'Uthmān b. Marzūq Qurashī (d. 564/1169) and his servant made the round trip Cairo–Mecca–Medina–Jerusalem–Cairo in a single night. One night, Rūmi left Konya in secret to be with a dervish in the Ka'ba and, before dawn, showed Meccan sand on his feet as proof for his wife. At Baghdad, Ma'rūf Karkhī (d. 200/815) explained a scar in his face by a fall at the well Zamzam in Mecca during the night.[124] Another story has it that one of them took off his clothes, plunged into the Tigris river, but came up in the Nile. He walked ashore, started a family and went about his business for seven years. One day, while bathing in the Nile, he stuck his head under water, found it pop up in the Tigris, picked up his clothes and went about his job. Some Sufis hid their face in their robes and found themselves transported to distant places in no time. Others traveled in a split second from India to Arabia, taking one step from east to west, or had mountain peaks and river banks move towards each other allowing them to step across. Last but not least, Muḥammad Shirbīnī (d. 927/1520) had children in Morocco, Iran, India and Sub-Saharan Africa and, in the span of a single hour, looked after all

123. R. Gramlich, "Zur Ausdehnung der Zeit und Verwandtem," in *Die islamische Welt zwischen Mittelalter und Neuzeit,* ed. U. Haarmann and P. Bachmann (Beirut 1979), pp. 180-92; Tāj al-Dīn Abū Naṣr 'Abd al-Wahhāb b. 'Alī Subkī, *Ṭabaqāt al-Shāfi'iyya al-kubrā,* ed. Maḥmūd Muḥammad al-Ṭanāḥī and 'Abd al-Fattaḥ al-Ḥulw (Cairo 1383/1964), p. 340, uses the terminology *ṭayy al-zamān* and *nashr al-zamān,* wheras Jamī uses the nomenclature *qabḍ al-zamān* and *basṭ al-zamān,* see his *Nafaḥāt,* pp. 563-4.
124. R. Gramlich, *Die Wunder der Freunde Gottes* (Wiesbaden 1987), pp.287-91

of them so that everybody thought he was always with them.[125] Bāyazīd cautioned, however, that "even Satan moves from east to west in the twinkling of an eye".[126] The mystics did not interpret these stories of contracting or expanding time and space along with other tales about flying through the air, walking on water or predicting the future *(firāsa)* in a flat-footed, literalistic way. Instead they used them as pedagogical devices, perceiving them to be fitting metaphorical expressions of their own capacity to pass beyond time into eternity.

The Persian mystics also incorporated their sense of time in their religious practices and hagiographies. In writing their religious history the Persian mystics used a variety of approaches. They recorded their history by creating accounts of spiritual itineraries rather than relating chronicles of events. They wrote *tadhkira,* memories of their encounters with God, and diaries of their inner *jihād* to that goal. With the emergence of the Sufi orders *(ṭarīqa)* and the social organization of Sufism, the Persian mystics achieved an increasing awareness of their history as a spiritual quest beginning with the origins of Islam. They saw themselves in a genealogical chain *(silsila)* of spiritual ancestors connecting them, frequently through Junayd, with a tradition traced back to Muḥammad's companions as represented by 'Alī or Abū Bakr. By adopting the idea of *walāya* as the very principle of Sufism itself, according to Hujwīrī (d. between 465/1072 and 469/1077), they expressed their awareness of being chosen as God's friends *(awliyā' Allāh).*[127] Soon this idea became associated with the belief in an invisible hierarchy of saints continuing the cycle of prophethood *(nubuwwa)* that had come to an end with Muḥammad, the Seal of the Prophets *(khatm al-anbiyā').* On the strength of divine inspiration, rather than revealed scripture and divine law, they continued the aeon of the prophets with a new cycle, that of *walāya.* This new cycle reaches out into the future when the Seal of the Saints *(khatm al-awliyā')* would appear, either

---

125. Gramlich, "Zur Ausdehnung," in *Die islamische Welt,* pp. 188-92.
126. Ibn 'Arabī, *Mawāqī' al-nujūm wa-maṭāli' ahillat al-asrār wa'l-'ulūm* (Cairo, 1325/1907), p. 134.
127. H. Landolt, "Walāyah," *ER,* XV, pp. 316-23.

physically concealed here and now, or, in Sufi circles favoring Shiʿite ideas, apocalyptically expected as the leader *(mahdī)* of the end-times.

The journey through the world of time in Persian mysticism led from Bāyazīd's ecstasy, Tustarī's recollection of primordial time, Shiblī's paradox of the eternal moment and Kharrāz's annihilation of temporality and subsistence in eternity through theoretical notions of *waqt* and *wajd* and such select mediaeval expressions of time as ʿAyn al-Quḍāt's black light, Daylamī's past and future compressed into the present and Bahā'-i Walad's co-being of the Eternal with time expressed in the images of poetry, miracle stories and social institutions. It may be appropriate to conclude with that ritual in which the Persian Sufis gave physical expression to their perception of time and ecstasy: the practice of *samāʿ* (literally, 'audition'). The Mawlawī Order in particular drew music and dance into this liturgical practice.[128] The harmony between the leader *(shaykh),* the dancers and the musicians, the repeated movement of the dance in a number of rounds *(dawra),* synchronizing the movements of the group as a whole and integrating the steps of each individual, capture in the dance the choreographed expression of ecstasy. The dance gave Persian mysticism its 'body language' of time. It may not be far-fetched, therefore, to espy in the Mawlawī *samāʿ* a rhythm of time and history become ritual in the whirling around the still-point of one's heart where time and eternity are blended in silent music.[129]

---

128. H. Ritter, "Der Reigen der 'Tanzenden Derwische'," *Zeitschrift für vergleichende Musikwissenschaft* 1 (1933), pp. 28-40.

129. This article is reprinted with minor changes from *Iran: Journal of the British Institute of Persian Studies* 30, (1992), pp. 77-89 by kind permission of the editors.

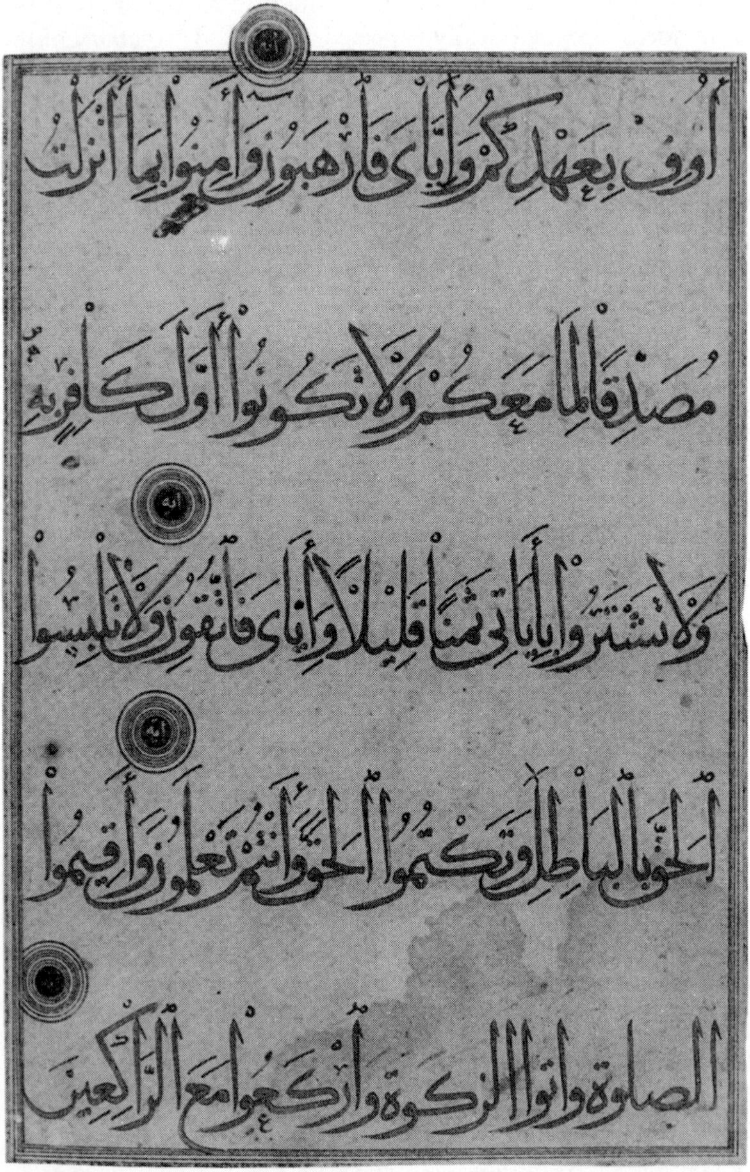

Page from a Manuscript of the Holy Koran. Surah II: 40-43. In *muhaqqaq* script. Egypt, ca. 1320.

Abū Ḥāmid al-Ghazālī's Esoteric Exegesis of the Koran

Nicholas Heer

Ghazālī is reported in a number of sources to have written a commentary on the Koran in some forty volumes. If, in fact, he did write such a commentary, no copy of it appears to have survived to the present day.[1] Nevertheless, many of Ghazālī's other works, such as his *Iḥyā' 'ulūm al-dīn, Mīzān al-'amal, Mishkāt al-anwār, Iljām al-'awāmm 'an 'ilm al-kalām, Jawāhir al-Qur'ān,* and *Qānūn al-ta'wīl,* contain passages and sections which deal extensively with the esoteric interpretation of the Koran,[2] and Ghazālī's theory of Koran interpretation can be readily derived from them.

This essay attempts to deal with the various aspects of Ghazālī's theory. It is divided into four sections: The first section deals with Ghazālī's assertion that the Koran has many levels of meaning. The second takes up Ghazālī's concept of exoteric interpretation and his claim that it is inadequate to explain fully all the levels of meaning in the Koran. In the third section Ghazālī's theory of esoteric interpretation is discussed along with his belief that such interpretation must be based on knowledge acquired through contact with the intellectual or spiritual world. The final section takes up Ghazālī's views concerning the different levels of understanding exhibited by human beings, and concludes with his admonition against the divulgence of esoteric interpretations to those who may not be capable of understanding them.

---

1. Jāmī in his *Nafaḥāt al-uns min ḥadarāt al-quds,* ed. M. Tawḥīdīpur (Tehran: 1336 A.Hsh./1957) lists as one of Ghazālī's works *Tafsīr Yāqūt al-ta'wīl* in 40 volumes (see *Nafaḥāt,* p. 371). Al-'Aydarūs and Ḥājjī Khalīfa both list *Yāqūt al-ta'wīl fī tafsīr al-tanzīl* also in 40 volumes (See al-'Aydarūs, *Ta'rīf al-aḥyā' fī faḍā'il al-Iḥyā'* , printed on the margin of *Iḥyā' ulūm al-dīn* [Cairo 1352/1933], I, 35; Ḥājjī Khalīfa, *Kashf al-ẓunūn an asāmī al-kutūb wa-al-funūn,* 2 vols. [Istanbul 1310], II, 658), and Ismā'īl Bāshā al-Baghdādī, *Hadīyat al-'ārifīn,* 2 vols. (Istanbul 1951-55), II, 81. Murtaḍā al-Zabīdī, on the other hand, lists two commentaries: *Tafsīr al-Qur'ān al-'aẓīm* as well as *Yāqūt al-ta'wīl fī tafsīr al-tanzīl* (See his *Itḥāf al-sāda al-muttaqīn bi-sharḥ asrār Iḥyā' 'ulūm al-dīn,* 10 vols. [Cairo 1311; reprinted Beirut: Dār Iḥyā' al-Turāth al'Arabī, n.d.], I, 41, 43). See also Bouyges, *Essai de chronologie* (Beirut 1959), pp.67-68; and Badawī, *Mu'allafāt al-Ghazālī,* 2 vols. (Cairo 1961), p.199.

2. I should like to acknowledge here my indebtedness to W.H.T. Gairdner, Nabih Amin Faris and Muḥammad Abul Quasem, previous translators of many of the passages quoted in this paper. Koranic passages cited in English are based on the translation of Mohammed Marmaduke Pickthall.

I. THE LEVELS OF MEANING IN THE KORAN

The Koran as the Speech of God

The Koran is God's speech, and as such is an eternal attribute of God's essence. Since human beings are incapable of fully understanding any of God's attributes, how is it possible for them to understand the meanings of the Koran? Ghazālī deals with this question in a passage in his *Kitāb ādāb tilāwat al-Qur'ān* (rules for the recitation of the Koran), the eighth book of the first volume of his *Iḥyā' 'ulūm al-dīn*. A reciter of the Koran, Ghazālī says,

> should consider how God showed kindness towards human beings in delivering to their understanding the meanings of His speech, which is an eternal attribute subsisting in His essence. [He should also consider] how that attribute is revealed to human beings under the cover of letters and sounds which are human attributes, because human beings are unable to arrive at an understanding of the attributes of God except by means of their own attributes. If the essence *(kunh)* of the majesty of His speech were not concealed under the garment of letters, neither throne nor ground would remain steady upon hearing His speech, and all that is between the two would be reduced to nothing because of the greatness of His authority and the majesty of His light. If God had not strengthened Moses he could not have endured hearing His speech, just as the mountain could not endure the beginnings of His manifestation, and so became level ground.[3] It is not possible to make the magnificence of [divine] speech intelligible to human beings except through examples on the level of their understanding.[4]

To explain more fully how it is possible for human beings to understand God's speech Ghazālī goes on to recount the following story:

> A wise man invited a certain king to [embrace] the law *(sharī'a)* of the prophets. The king questioned him concerning several

3. A reference to Koran VII: 143.
4. *Iḥyā' 'ulūm al-dīn,* 4 vols. (Cairo 1352/1933), I, 252; Muḥammad Abul Quasem, *The Recitation and Interpreation of the Qur'ān: al-Ghazālī' Theory* (Kuala Lumpur: University of Malaysia Press 1979), pp. 56-57.

matters, and the wise man answered in such a way that the king was able to understand. Then the king asked him, "Tell me, how can man understand what the prophets bring, when they claim that it is not the speech of a human being but rather the speech of God?" The wise man replied, "We have seen that when people wish to make some of the animals and birds understand what they want them to do, such as to proceed, or to wait, to move forward, or to back up, and they realize that the discernment *(tamyīz)* of these animals falls short of understanding their speech, which proceeds in all its beauty, adornment and marvelous order from the lights of their intellects, they then descend to the level of the discernment of the animals and convey their intentions to the souls *(bawāṭin)* of these animals through sounds to which they will pay attention and which are suitable for them, such as whistling, the snapping of fingers, and other sounds similar to their own sounds, so that they can understand them. In like manner human beings are unable to understand the speech of God in its essence *(kunh)* and in the perfection of its attributes. Thus [God's speech] has become, through the sounds which human beings use among themselves and through which they have heard [divine] wisdom, like the sound of snapping fingers and whistling which animals have heard from humans."[5]

The Multiple Levels of Meaning in the Koran

In the two passages cited above Ghazālī, following Ash'arite doctrine, makes a clear distinction between God's speech as one of His eternal attributes and His speech as manifested in the form of letters and sounds which can be understood by human beings. One may also infer that Ghazālī believes there is more to be understood from God's speech than is apparent from the literal meaning of the sounds and letters in which it is expressed. In fact, in the fourth chapter of *Ādāb tilāwat al-Qur'ān,* Ghazālī argues that there are, indeed, multiple levels of meaning in the Koran. Ghazālī's argument is made in the form of a reply to an objection based on a tradition of the Prophet which states: "Whoever interprets the Koran in accordance with his own opinion shall take his place in the Fire."[6] Ghazālī asserts that

5. *Iḥyā',* I, 252; Abul Quasem, *Recitation,* pp. 58-59.

because of this tradition "scholars in the exoteric interpretation [of the Koran] have reviled the Sufi interpreters for their metaphorical interpretation *(ta'wīl)* of certain words in the Koran [in a sense] contrary to what was transmitted on the authority of Ibn 'Abbās[7] and other interpreters, and took the position that it amounted to unbelief."[8] This position is refuted by Ghazālī as follows:

> The man who claims that the Koran has no meaning except that which the exoteric exegesis has transmitted is acknowledging his own limitations. He is right in his acknowledgment, but is wrong in his judgement that puts all people on the level to which he is limited and bound. Indeed, reports and traditions [of the Prophet and others] indicate that for men of understanding there is great latitude *(muttasa')* in the meanings of the Koran. Thus, 'Ali said, "[The Messenger of God did not confide to me anything which he concealed from people], except that God bestows understanding of the Koran upon a man."[9] If there were no meaning *(tarjama)* other than that which has been transmitted, what, then, is [meant by] that understanding of the Koran? The Prophet said, "Surely, the Koran has an outward aspect *(ẓahr),* an inward aspect *(baṭn),* an ending *(ḥadd)* and a beginning *(maṭla').*"[10] This [tradition] is also related as being from Ibn Mas'ūd[11] on his own authority, and he was one of the scholars of exegesis *('ulamā' al-tafsīr)*. What, then, is the meaning of the outward aspect, inward aspect, end and beginning?
>
> 'Alī said, "If I wished I could load seventy camels with the exegesis of the Opening Surah *(al-Fātiḥa)* of the Koran." What is the meaning of this, when the exoteric interpretation [of this surah] is extremely short? Abū al-Dardā'[12] said, "A man does not

---

6. Al-'Irāqī, in his *Mughnī,* I, 33, cites al-Tirmidhī, Abū Dāwūd, and al-Nasā'ī for this tradition.
7. 'Abd Allāh ibn al-'Abbās (d. 68/688), a cousin of the Prophet, is usually considered the first exegete of the Koran. See Brockelmann, *Geschichte der arabischen Litteratur,* 2nd ed., 2 vols. (Leiden 1943-49; 3 supplementary vols., Leiden 1937-42), S. I, 331; and *Encyclopaedia of Islam,* I, 40-41
8. *Iḥyā',* I, 260.
9. The complete tradition has been cited earlier by Ghazālī. See *Iḥyā',* I, 254.
10. Al-'Irāqī, in his *Mughnī,* I, 88, cites Ibn Ḥibbān's *Ṣaḥīḥ* (also known as *Kitāb al-taqāsīm wa-al-anwā')* for this tradition. Several editions of this work have been published in the arrangement of 'Alī ibn Balabān ibn 'Abdallāh al-Fārisī (d. 739/1339) under the title *al-Iḥsān fī taqrīb (bi-tartīb) Ṣaḥīḥ Ibn Ḥibbān*.
11. 'Abdallāh ibn Ghāfil ibn Ḥabīb ibn Mas'ūd, a companion of the Prophet. See *Encyclopaedia of Islam,* 2nd edit. (Leiden 1960-19-), III, p. 875

[truly] understand until he attributes [different] perspectives *(wujūh)* to the Koran." A certain scholar said, "For every [Koranic] verse there are sixty thousand understandings *(fahm),* and what remains to be understood is even more." Others have said, "The Koran contains seventy-seven thousand two hundred sciences *('ilm),*[13] for every word [in it] is a science, and then that [number] can be quadrupled, since every word has an outward aspect, an inward aspect, an end and a beginning."

The Prophet's repetition of [the phrase] "In the name of God, the merciful, the compassionate" twenty times was only for the purpose of pondering *(tadabbur)* its esoteric meanings *(bāṭin ma'ānīhā).*[14] Otherwise its explanation *(tarjama)* and exegesis *(tafsīr)* are so obvious *(ẓāhir)* that someone like him would not need to repeat it. Ibn Mas'ūd said, "He who desires the knowledge of the ancients and the moderns should ponder the Koran," and that is not something that can be attained merely by its exoteric interpretation *(tafsīrihi al-ẓāhir).*[15]

In the passage above Ghazālī makes the claim that the Koran has both an outward and an inward aspect and that there is an exegesis or interpretation for each of these aspects. Ghazālī's position on the exoteric exegesis of the Koran is dealt with in Section II, immediately below. His treatment of the esoteric interpretation of the Koran is discussed in Section III.

II. THE EXOTERIC EXEGESIS OF THE KORAN

The Linguistic Interpretation of the Koran

In a passage in the fourth chapter of the *Ādāb tilāwat al-Qur'ān* in the *Iḥyā'* Ghazālī asserts that the exoteric interpretation of the Koran involves primarily the study of what he calls *gharā'ib al-Qur'ān,*

12. Abū al-Dardā' 'Uwaymir (or 'Āmir) al-Anṣārī al-Khazrajī, a companion of the Prophet. See *Encyclopaedia of Islam,* I, pp. 113-114.
13. A reference to the number of words in the Koran. See Jalāl al-Dīn 'Abd al-Raḥmān ibn Abī Bakr al-Suyūṭī, *al-Itqān fī 'ulūm al-Qur'ān,* 2 vols. (Lahore 1400/1980), I, 70 *(naw'* 19). I am indebted to my colleague, Aron Zysow, for this reference.
14. Al-'Irāqī, in his *Mughnī,* I, 254, cites the *Mu'jam* of Abū Dharr al-Harawī for this tradition.
15. *Iḥyā',* I, 260; Abul Quasem, *Recitation,* pp. 87-88.

that is, the strange words and figures of speech which appear throughout the Koran. Such interpretation, Ghazālī maintains, requires a thorough familiarity with the Arabic language in the form in which it existed at the time of the Prophet, including such peculiarities of usage as ambiguous and substituted words *(al-alfāẓ al-mubhama wa-mubdala),* abridgement *(al-ikhtiṣār),* omission, *(al-ḥadhf),* ellipsis *(al-iḍmār),* preposition and postposition *(al-taqdīm wa al-ta'khīr),* inverted transmission *(al-manqūl al-munqalib),* repetition which breaks the continuity of speech *(al-mukarrar al-qāṭi' li-waṣl al-kalām),* and explanation by stages *(al-tadrīj fī al-bayān).*[16] For each of these figures of speech Ghazālī cites examples from the Koran. He asserts that knowledge of such linguistic usage can only be acquired by study of what has been transmitted by previous scholars concerning the Arabic language as it existed at the time of the Prophet. At the conclusion of this passage he says:

> In this and similar [questions] only knowledge which has been transmitted and heard *(al-naql wa al-samā')* is of any use. The Koran, from its beginning to its end, is not lacking in [rhetorical figures of] this kind, and, because it was revealed in the language of the Arabs, it includes such figures of their speech as conciseness *(ījāz),* prolixity *(taṭwīl),* ellipsis *(iḍmār),* omission (*ḥadhf*), substitution *(ibdāl),* and preposition and postposition (*taqdīm wa-ta'khīr*), all of which served to dumbfound the Arabs and render them unable to imitate it. Anyone who is satisfied with an understanding of the outward aspect alone of the Arabic language, and who then hastens to explain the Koran without having recourse to that knowledge which has been transmitted and heard *(al-naql wa al-samā')* in these matters, is to be counted among those who explain the Koran by their personal opinions. For example, a person may understand the term *umma* in its most widely known meaning, and in his nature and opinion he may incline towards that meaning. However, if he then encounters the term in another place, he may still incline in his opinion towards that widely-known meaning which he has previously heard, and he will ne-

16. These figures of speech are dealt with by a number of classical authors. See, for example, Abū al-Ḥusayn Aḥmad Ibn Fāris, *Al-Ṣāḥibī fī fiqh al-lugha wa-sunan al'arab fī kalāmihā,* edited by Muṣṭafā al-Shuwaymī (Beirut 1382/1963), pp. 198-273; and al-Suyūṭī, *al-Muzhir fī 'ulūm al-lugha,* edited by Muḥammad Aḥmad Jād al-Mawlā, Muḥammad Abū al-Faḍl Ibrāhīm and 'Alī Muḥammad al-Bukhārī, 2 vols. (Cairo: n.d.), I, 321-345.

> glect to pursue what has been transmitted with respect to that term's many other meanings. It is possible that this is what is prohibited [in the aforementioned tradition][17] and not the understanding of the secret meanings [of the Koran], as has previously been mentioned. When, on the other hand, one acquires [the requisite transmitted knowledge] *(al-samā')* in such matters, one has then mastered the exoteric exegesis [of the Koran]. This, however, is merely the translation *(tarjama)* of its words, and is not sufficient for an understanding of the realities of its meanings *(ḥaqa'īq al-ma'ānī)*.[18]

In summary, Ghazālī asserts that the exoteric exegesis of the Koran deals with the peculiar features of the Arabic language as it was spoken at the time of the Prophet. It relies on knowledge about the language that has been transmitted from that time to later generations. Such exegesis can be carried out only by someone who is thoroughly familiar with that transmitted knowledge. Exoteric exegesis, however, is not sufficient to explain fully all the levels of meaning in the Koran.

The Inadequacy of the Exoteric Exegesis of the Koran

One reason why the exoteric exegesis of the Koran is inadequate is that there are verses in the Koran, such as the one cited in the passage quoted below, which on the surface do not make sense rationally and which require further explanation. In a passage immediately following the passage cited above, Ghazālī states:

> The distinction between the realities of the meanings [of the Koran] and its exoteric exegesis can be understood from the following example: God said, "You did not throw when you threw, but God threw."[19] The exoteric exegesis of this verse is clear. Its real meaning, however, is obscure, because it both affirms throwing and denies it, and these appear to be contradictory statements, unless one understands [from them] that in one respect he threw, but in another respect he did not throw, and that in the respect in which he did not throw, it was God who threw.[20]

---

17. I.e., "Whoever interprets the Koran in accordance with his own opinion shall take his place in the Fire."
18. *Iḥyā'*, I, 263; Abul Quasem, *Recitation*, p. 101.
19. Koran VIII: 17

Another reason is that there are verses which, although not self-contradictory, are in apparent contradiction with propositions known to be true through reason. One such verse is: "The Merciful seated Himself on His throne."[21] Reason declares that God is not a body, and that if He is not a body, He cannot be in a place. It is, therefore, not possible for Him literally to seat Himself on His throne, since that would imply that He was a body occupying a specific place.

Although the human faculty of reason is capable of pointing out which passages in the Koran do not make sense rationally, it is not, at least in Ghazālī's opinion, capable of providing an explanation or interpretation of such passages. The various Islamic schools of thought took different positions on the question of whether reason was capable of providing a metaphorical interpretation *(ta'wīl)* of those verses in the Koran which had little or no meaning if taken in their literal sense. Ghazālī discusses these different positions in a passage of the *Iḥyā'* to be found in the *Kitāb Qawā'id al-'aqā'id* (Foundations of the Articles of Faith), and at length in a separate essay entitled *Qānūn al-ta'wīl* (Principles of Metaphorical Koranic Interpretation). In the passage in the *Iḥyā'* he says:

> The masters of the exoteric sciences *(arbāb al-ẓawāhir)* inclined towards closing the door [of metaphorical interpretation]. What is believed about Aḥmad ibn Ḥanbal is that, although he knew that sitting *(al-istiwā')* did not imply being established *(al-istiqrār)* [in a place] and that descending *(al-nuzūl)*[22] did not imply movement *(al-intiqāl)* [from place to place], he nevertheless forbade metaphorical interpretation *(al-ta'wīl)* in order to close its door and to safeguard the welfare of the people, for should the door be opened, disruption would spread, and the situation would get out of control and exceed the limits of moderation, because the limits of moderation cannot be precisely determined. Thus, there is nothing wrong with this restriction, and the practice of the predecessors

20. *Iḥyā'*, I, 263; Abul Quasem, *Recitation*, pp. 101-102.
21. Koran, XX: 5. Other verses using the same terms are: VII: 54; X: 3; XIII: 2; XXV: 59; XXXII: 4; LVII: 4.
22. A reference to the well-known *ḥadīth*, "God descends each night to the heaven closest to the earth." See Wensinck, *Concordance et indices de la tradition musulmane*, 7 vols. (Leiden 1936-69), II, 548, 16 (s.v. *al-samā'*).

> *(sīrat al-salaf)*[23] attests to it. They used to say [referring to the ambiguous verses of the Koran], "Let them pass as they have come [i.e. without interpretation]." Mālik [ibn Anas], when asked about [God's] sitting *(istiwā')* [on His throne], said, "The sitting is known, but [its] modality is not. Faith in it is obligatory, and inquiry about it is an innovation."
>
> Another group believed in moderation *(al-iqtiṣād)* and opened the door of metaphorical interpretation to everything pertaining to God's attributes, but left the verses pertaining to the afterlife in their apparent meanings *('alā ẓawāhirihā)* and prohibited their interpretation. These were the Ash'arites.
>
> The Mu'tazilites went further than the Ash'arites and, with respect to His attributes, interpreted metaphorically His visibility as well as His being 'hearing' and 'seeing'. They also interpreted the Prophet's ascension *(mi'rāj)* and claimed that it did not occur in the body. They interpreted metaphorically the torment in the grave, the Balance *(al-mīzān),* and the Bridge *(al-ṣiraṭ),* and a number of propositions regarding the afterlife. On the other hand, they affirmed the gathering of bodies *(ḥashr al-ajsād),* the Garden *(al-janna)* with the foods, fragrances, carnal relations, and other sensual pleasures contained in it, as well as the Fire *(al-nār),* comprising a sensible, burning body that scorches skin and melts fat.
>
> The philosophers went even further than the Mu'tazilites and interpreted metaphorically everything pertaining to the afterlife, reducing it to intellectual and spiritual pains and pleasures. They denied the resurrection of bodies, but affirmed the immortality of souls, believing that they were either tormented or gratified with a pain or pleasure not perceptible to the senses. These [philosophers] were the extremists.[24]

Having indicated the areas of exegesis in which metaphorical interpretation has been practised by various groups in the past, Ghazālī continues in the next few lines to point out that such interpretation is successful only when carried out by persons who are guided by the divine light of certainty. He says:

---

23. The predecessors *(al-salaf),* according to Ghazālī, are the companions of the Prophet *(al-ṣaḥāba)* and their followers in the next generation *(al-tābi'ūn).* See his *Iljām al-'awāmm 'an 'ilm al-kalām.* (Cairo 1309), p.3. Ghazālī deals at length with the school of the predecessors *(madhhab al-salaf)* in this work.
24. *Iḥyā',* I, 92; Nabih Amin Faris, *The Foundations of the Articles of Faith, Being a Translation with Notes of The Kitāb Qawā'id al-'Aqā'id of al-Ghazzālī's 'Iḥyā' 'Ulūm al-Dīn* (Lahore: Sh. Muhammad Ashraf 1963), pp. 50-52.

> The determination of what is moderate, that is, what lies somewhere between the complete flexibility [of the philosophers] and the rigidity of the Ḥanbalites, is something obscure and subtle. It is achieved only by those to whom God grants success, who perceive things not by hearing but by means of a divine light *(nūr ilāhī)*. If the secrets of these things, as they really are, are then revealed to them, they look at scripture *(al-sam')* and the words appearing in it and affirm that which agrees with what they have witnessed by the light of certainty *(nūr al-yaqīn)* and interpret metaphorically that which differs from what they have witnessed.[25]

To understand why, in Ghazālī's opinion, reason is often incapable of interpreting the Koran correctly, one must turn to what he has to say in his *Qānūn al-ta'wīl*.[26] In this short essay Ghazālī explains that metaphorical interpretation is necessary because of the apparent contradictions between scripture and reason. He then proceeds to make three recommendations with respect to the questions of how such interpretation should be carried out and why reason may be unable to determine what the correct interpretation is:

> The first recommendation is that one not aspire to know all of that,[27] and this was the purpose to which I was directing my discourse. Such knowledge is not something to be aspired to, and one should recite [the verse from the Koran in which] God says, "And of knowledge you have been given but little."[28]
>
> The second recommendation is that one should never deny the testimony of reason *(burhān al-'aql)*, for reason does not lie. Were reason to lie, it might lie in establishing scripture *(al-shar')*, for it is by reason that we know scripture to be true. How can the

---

25. *Iḥyā'*, I, 92; Faris, *Foundations*, p. 52.
26. Or *al-Qānūn al-kullī fī al-ta'wīl*, edited by Muḥammad Zāhid al-Kawtharī (Cairo: 1359/1940). This work is listed by Brockelmann *(Geschichte*, I, 539, no. 21) as having been edited by A.J. Casas y Manrique (Uppsala 1937). This appears to be a misprint. The work edited by Casas is No. 24 in Brockelmann's list, *Jāmi' al-ḥaqā'iq bi-tajrīd al-'alā'iq*, which, as Brockelmann states, should correctly be attributed to Ibn 'Arabī, as it is identical with Ibn 'Arabi's *Tuḥfat al-safarah ila ḥaḍrat al-bararah*. See *Geschichte*, I, 575, No. 25. An article on Ghazālī's *Qānūn al-ta'wīl* was published by M. Şerafeddin under the title "Gazalī, nin Te'vil Hakkında Basılmamış bir Eseri" in *Darülfünun İlahiyat Fakültesi Mecmuası*, vol. 4, No. 16 (Teşrinievvel 1930), pp. 46-58.
27. That is, that one not aspire to a complete understanding of the Koran.
28. Koran, XVII: 85.

truthfulness of a witness be known through the testimony *(tazkiya)* of a lying character witness *(al-muzakkī al-kādhib)*. Scripture is a witness for the details, and reason is the character witness for scripture. If, then, it is necessary to believe reason, one cannot dispute [the fact that] location *(jihah)* and form *(ṣūra)* must be denied to God. If you are told that works are weighed,[29] you will recognize that works are an accident that cannot be weighed, and that metaphorical interpretation *(ta'wīl)* is therefore necessary.

If you hear that death is brought in the form of a fat ram *(kabsh amlaḥ)* which is then slaughtered,[30] you will know that [such a statement] requires interpretation. The reason for this is that death is an accident, and as such it cannot be brought, for bringing *(ityān)* constitutes movement *(intiqāl)*, which is impossible for an accident. Moreover, death does not have the form of a fat ram, since accidents cannot be transformed into bodies. Nor is death slaughtered, for slaughtering involves separating the neck from the body, and death has neither a neck nor a body. Death is an accident, or the absence of an accident in the opinion of those who believe that it is the absence of life. Therefore, metaphorical interpretation [of this statement] is inescapable.

The third recommendation is that one refrain from specifying an interpretation when the possibilities are in conflict. Judgement concerning the intention of God or of His prophet by means of supposition *(ẓann)*, and guessing *(takhmīn)* is dangerous. One knows the intention of a speaker only when he reveals his intention. If he does not reveal his intention, how can one know it, unless the various possibilities are limited, and all but one of them is eliminated. This one [intention] is then demonstrably specified. Nevertheless, the various possibilities in the speech of the Arabs, and the ways of expanding upon them are many, so how can they be limited? Refraining from interpretation is therefore safer.

For example, if it is clear to you that works cannot be weighed, and the tradition concerning the weighing of works comes up, you must interpret either the word "weighing" or the word "works." It is possible that the word used metaphorically *(al-majāz)* is "works," and that it was used in lieu of the register of works *(saḥīfat al-'amal)*, in which they are recorded, and it is these reg-

---

29. A reference to the weighing of men's works in the Balance as an indication of who will be the inhabitants of the Garden and who the inhabitants of the Fire. See Koran, VII: 8-9; XXIII: 101-104; CI: 6-11.
30. A reference to a well-known tradition. See Wensinck, *Concordance,* V, 517 (under *kabsh)*.

isters of works which are weighed. On the other hand, it is also possible that the word used metaphorically is "weighing," and that it was used in lieu of its effect, that is, the determination of the amount of work, since that is the utility of weighing, and weighing and measuring are ways of determining [amounts]. If you conclude at this time that what is to be interpreted is the word "works" rather than the word "weighing" or "weighing" rather than "works" without relying either on reason *('aql)* or scripture *(naql)*, you are making a judgement about God and His intention by guessing, and guessing and supposition are tantamount to ignorance *(jahl)*.

Guessing and supposition are permitted as necessary for the performance of acts of worship *('ibādāt)*, piety *(ta'abbudāt)* and other works *(a'māl)* that are ascertained by *ijtihād*. Nevertheless, matters unrelated to any action belong in the same category as abstract sciences and beliefs, so on what basis does one dare to make judgements in these matters by supposition alone? Most of what has been said in the way of interpretation consists of suppositions and guesses. The rational man has the choice either of judging by supposition or of saying: "I know that its literal meaning is not what is intended, because it contains what is contrary to reason. What exactly is intended, however, I do not know, nor do I have a need to know, since it is not related to any action, and there is no way truly to uncover [its meaning with] certainty. Moreover, I do not believe in making judgements by guessing." This is a safer and more proper choice for any rational man. It also provides more security for the day of resurrection, since it is not improbable that on the day of resurrection he will be questioned [about his judgements] and held accountable for them and be told, "You made a judgement about Us by supposition." He will not, however, be asked, "Why did you fail to discover Our obscure and hidden meaning [in a verse] in which there was no command for action? You have no obligation with respect to belief in it except absolute faith and general acceptance of its truth." This means that one should say, "We believe therein. The whole is from our Lord."[31]

III. THE ESOTERIC INTERPRETATION OF THE KORAN

The Science of Disclosure

Although reason is capable of pointing out which passages in scrip-

31. Koran, III: 7. *Qānūn al-ta'wīl*, p.10-12.

ture must be interpreted metaphorically, it cannot itself be the source of any such interpretation. The only source of such interpretation is what Ghazālī calls *'ilm al-mukāshafa,* the science of disclosure. Rather than being based on sense perception and reason, as are the ordinary sciences, the science of disclosure is a type of knowledge that is acquired through revelation *(waḥy)* and illumination *(ilhām)*[32] and has as its source the Preserved Tablet *(al-lawḥ al-maḥfūẓ)*.[33] It is by means of this science of disclosure that the hidden meanings of the Koran become known, and the interpretation of the Koran without resorting to guesses or supposition becomes possible. Ghazālī describes this science in the second chapter of *Kitāb al-'ilm* from the first volume of the *Iḥyā':*

> It is tantamount to a light which appears in the heart when it is cleansed and purified of its blameworthy attributes. Through this light are disclosed many things for which names had been previously heard, and for which only general and vague meanings had been imagined, but which now become clear. Eventually one acquires true knowledge of God's essence, of His abiding and perfect attributes, of his acts, of His reasons for creating this world and the next, and of the way in which He has arranged the other world with respect to this world. One gains knowledge of the meaning of prophecy and the prophet, and of the meaning of revelation *(al-waḥy)*.[34]

---

32. The distinction between revelation and illumination according to Ghazālī, is that in revelation the recipient of the knowledge is aware of and sees the angel who introduces the knowledge into his heart. In illumination, on the other hand, the recipient of the knowledge is unaware of the manner in which the knowledge has entered his heart. Revelation is, of course, peculiar to the prophets, whereas illumination is the special characteristic of the saints *(al-awliyā')* and the pure *(al-aṣfiyā')*. See *Iḥyā'*, III, 16.
33. Ghazālī asserts that the philosophers identify *al-lawḥ al-maḥfūẓ* with the souls and intelligences of the heavens. See *Maqāṣid al-falāsifa,* III: 67, and *al-Tahāfut al-falāsifa,* edited by Maurice Bouyges (Beirut 1927), pp. 254-255; *al-Tahāfut al-Falāsifa,* translated by Sabih Ahmad Kamali under the title: *Al-Ghazali's Tahafut al-Falasifah [Incoherence of the Philosophers],* (Lahore 1958), p. 172-173. The reader familiar with the works of Ibn Sīnā will be struck by the similarity between Ghazālī's *'ilm al-mukāshafa* and Ibn Sīnā's doctrine concerning the contact of the human soul with the active intellect.
34. *Iḥyā',* I, 18; N.A. Faris, *The Book of Knowledge, Being a Translation With Notes of the Kitāb al-'Ilm of al-Ghazzālī's Iḥyā' 'Ulūm al-Dīn* (Lahore: Sh. Muhammad Ashraf 1962), p.47.

Ghazālī continues with a lengthy list of subjects which can be known in this way. He concludes the passage by saying:

> We mean by the science of disclosure *('ilm al-mukāshafa)* that the veil is lifted, so that the pure truth *(jalīyat al-ḥaqq)* in these matters is made as clear as eyesight *(al-'iyān),* which allows no doubt. This is something possible in the nature of a man, but for the rust *(sada')* and tarnish *(khabath)* which have accumulated on the mirror of his heart[35] because of the defilements of the world. We mean by the science of the otherworldly path *('ilm ṭarīq al-ākhira)* the way in which this mirror is polished of these impurities, for they constitute a veil concealing God and the knowledge of His attributes and acts. The purification and cleansing of the mirror can only be achieved through the renunciation of desires and by following the prophets in all their states. Then, to the extent that [the tarnish] is removed from the heart, and the heart is faced in the direction of God *(al-Ḥaqq),* His truths will shine within it.[36]

The Preserved Tablet, Ghazālī asserts, is the source of this knowledge which shines into the mirror of the heart. In a passage in *Kitāb Sharḥ 'ajā'ib al-qalb* from the third volume of the *Iḥyā'* Ghazālī says that the Preserved Tablet:

> is inscribed with everything that God has decreed up to the day of resurrection. The revelation *(tajallī)* of the truths of the sciences *(ḥaqā'iq al-'ulūm)* from the mirror of the Tablet into the mirror of the heart is like the imprinting of an image existing in one mirror in a second mirror facing the first.[37]

The Preserved Tablet makes up part of what Ghazālī calls the spiritual world *(al-'ālam al-rūḥānī).* The spiritual world, together with the corporeal world *(al-'ālam al-jismānī),* constitute the entirety of the universe. The spiritual world is hidden from most

---

35. The image of the heart as a polished mirror in which are reflected the truths inscribed in the Preserved Tablet is a favorite of Ghazālī. See, for example, *Mīzān al-'amal,* pp. 218-219; *Iḥyā',* I, 256; III, 11-12; IV, 119; *Maqāṣid al-falasifa,* I, 6-7; III, 11-12. Ibn Sina uses the same image. See his *al-Ishārāt wa al-tanbīhāt* with the commentaries of Naṣīr al-dīn al-Ṭūṣī and Quṭb al-Dīn al-Rāzī, 3 vols. (Tehran 1369 A.Hsh./1980), II, 365; III, 386.
36. *Iḥyā',* I, 17-18; Faris, *Knowledge,* p.48-49.
37. *Iḥyā',* III, 16.

people, who are aware only of the corporeal world. In his *Mishkāt al-anwār* Ghazālī describes these two worlds in some detail:

> The world is two worlds, spiritual *(rūḥānī)* and corporeal *(jismānī),* or if you will, sensual *(ḥissī)* and intellectual *('aqlī),* or again, if you will, superior *('ulwī)* and inferior *(suflī).* All [of these expressions] are close to one another [in meaning], and the difference between them is merely one of viewpoint. If you view the two worlds in themselves, you say "corporeal" and "spiritual"; if you view them in relation to the eye which apprehends them, you say 'sensual' and 'intellectual'; and if you view them with respect to their relationship to each other, you say 'superior' and 'inferior.' You may also, perhaps, call one of them the world of dominion and sense-perception *('ālam al-mulk wa'-l-shahāda),* and the other the world of concealment and sovereignty *('ālam al-ghayb wa'-l-malakūt).*[38] One who directs his attention to the realities underlying these words may be puzzled by the multiplicity of the terms and imagine a [corresponding] multiplicity of meanings. But he to whom the realities underlying the terms have been disclosed makes the meanings basic and the terms subordinate. An inferior mind takes the opposite course and seeks the realities from the terms themselves.[39]
>
> The world of sovereignty *(al-'ālam al-malakūtī)* is a world of concealment *('ālam ghayb),* since it is hidden from most people. The sensual world *(al-'ālam al-ḥissī),* however, is a world of perception *('ālam shahāda),* since it is perceived by all. The sensual world, moreover, is the point of ascent to the intellectual world, and were it not for a connection *(ittiṣāl)* and a relationship *(munāsaba)* between the two, the path of ascent to the intellectual would be barred. And were this path of ascent impossible, then the journey to the Presence of Lordship *(ḥaḍrat al-rubūbīya)* and the near approach to God would also be impossible.[40]

---

38. Ghazālī also describes these two worlds in the introduction to his *Jawāhir al-Qur'ān* (reprinted, Beirut: 1401/1981); see especially pp. 11, 28, 33. See also the study of A. J. Wensinck, "On the Relation Between Ghazālī's Cosmology and His Mysticism" in *Mededeelingen der Koninklijke Akademie van Wetenschappen,* Afdeeling Letterkunde, Deel 75 (1933), Serie A, No. 6, pp.183-209; and al-Tahānawī, *al-Kashshāf iṣṭilāḥāt al-funūn* (Calcutta 1278/1861), p.1339 (s.v. *malakūt).*
39. *Mishkāt al-anwār,* edited by Abū al-'Alā 'Afīfī (Cairo 1383/1964), pp. 65-66; W.H.T. Gairdner, *Al-Ghazzali's Mishkat Al-Anwār ("The Niche for Lights"),* translation with introduction (Lahore: Sh. Muhammad Ashraf 1952; a reprint of the edition published by the Royal Asiatic Society, London 1924), pp.122-23.
40. *Mishkāt,* p. 66; Gairdner, *Mishkāt,* pp.123-24.

> The world of perception *('ālam al-shahāda)* is a point of ascent to the world of sovereignty *('ālam al-malakūt),* and progress on the straight path *(al-ṣirāṭ al-mustaqīm)* is an expression for this ascent, which may also be expressed by the terms "religion" or "the stages of guidance." Thus, were there no relationship and connection between the two, ascent from one of them to the other would be inconceivable. For this reason the divine mercy gave the world of perception a correspondence *(muwāzana)* with the world of sovereignty. Thus, there is nothing in this world which is not a symbol (*mithāl)* of something in that other world. Sometimes one thing [in this world] is a symbol for several things in the world of sovereignty, and sometimes one thing in the world of sovereignty has many symbols in the world of perception. A thing is considered a symbol of something only if it resembles it or corresponds to it in some way.[41]

Because there is a correspondence between the spiritual world and the corporeal world and because everything in the corporeal world symbolizes something in the spiritual world, all verses in the Koran have an esoteric interpretation, even those that make good sense when understood literally. Thus Ghazālī by no means limits esoteric interpretation to those verses which do not make sense rationally. Verses which can be understood literally also have an esoteric interpretation.

Esoteric Exegesis is Never in Conflict with Exoteric Exegesis

Although each verse in the Koran has an esoteric meaning, the esoteric meaning is never in conflict with a rationally acceptable exoteric meaning. Ghazālī explains his position fully in another passage in his *Mishkāt al-anwār:*

> The rejection of exoteric meanings *(al-ẓawāhir)* is the opinion of the Bāṭiniyya,[42] who, being one-eyed, looked only at one of the two worlds and did not recognize the correspondence between the two and did not understand its significance. Similarly, the rejection of the esoteric meanings *(al-asrār)* is the position of the

41. *Mishkāt,* p. 67; Gairdner, *Mishkāt,* pp.125-26.

42. According to Ghazālī this is one of the names by which the Isma'ilis are known. Ghazālī's refutation of their position may be found in his *Faḍā'iḥ al-bāṭiniyya,* edited by 'Abd al-Raḥmān al-Badawī (Cairo 1383/1964); for an explanation of the various names by which they are known see pp.11-17.

> Ḥashwiyya.[43] Whoever takes only the outward meaning *(al-ẓāhir)* is a Ḥashwi, and whoever takes only the inward meaning *(al-bāṭin)* is a Bāṭinī, but whoever combines the two of them is perfect. For this reason the Prophet said, "The Koran has an outward aspect *(ẓāhir),* an inward aspect *(bāṭin),* an ending *(ḥadd)* and a beginning *(maṭla').*"[44]

Ghazālī explains further by taking an example from the story of Moses in Sūrat Ṭāhā. When Moses reached the fire which he had seen from afar, God called to him and said, "Indeed, I am thy Lord; so take off thy shoes. Indeed, thou art in the holy valley of Ṭuwā."[45] According to Ghazālī:

> Moses understood from the command "take off thy shoes" the renunciation *(iṭṭirā)* of the two worlds *(al-kawnayn).* He obeyed the command outwardly by taking off his shoes, and inwardly by renouncing the two worlds *(al-'ālamayn).* This is what heeding an example *(al-i'tibār)* means: The crossing-over *(al-'ubūr)*[46] from one thing to another, from the outward aspect to the inner secret *(al-sirr).*[47]

Similarly in *Ādāb tilāwat al-Qur'ān* Ghazālī says:

> [This esoteric exegesis is] not in conflict with exoteric exegesis *(ẓāhir al-tafsīr);* rather it is its completion and the attainment of its innermost meaning *(lubāb)* from its outward aspect. What we have presented here is for the purpose of understanding the inner meanings [of the Koran] *(al-ma'ānī al-bāṭina),* not what is in conflict with its outward aspect.[48]

Not only does esoteric exegesis not conflict with exoteric exegesis, but exoteric exegesis must be mastered first before anyone

43. Or Ḥashawiyya. Ghazālī uses this term for the anthropomorphists *(mujassima* and *mushabbiha),* who give a literal interpretation to the Koranic verses and traditions which mention God's hand, foot, descent, motion, etc. He attacks their position throughout his *Iljām al-'awamm 'an 'ilm al-kalām.*
44. *Mishkāt al-anwār,* p. 73; Gairdner, *Mishkāt,* p.137. See above, note 10.
45. Koran XX: 12.
46. Ghazālī is here tying the concept of heeding an example or warning *('ibra)* with the root meaning of the verb *'abara,* which means to cross over or traverse. He apparently has in mind the Koranic verse (LIX: 2): *Fa-i'tabirū yā uwlī al-ābṣār:* "So take heed, O ye who have eyes."
47. *Mishkāt al-anwār,* p.73; Gairdner, *Mishkāt,* p. 138.
48. *Iḥyā',* I, 264; Abul Quasem, *Recitation,* p. 104.

should attempt to practise the esoteric exegesis of the Koran. In the fourth chapter of *Ādāb tilāwat al-Qur'ān* Ghazālī says:

> One should not neglect the learning of outward exegesis first, for there is no hope of reaching the inward aspect [of the Koran] before having mastered the outward. One who claims to understand the secrets of the Koran *(asrār al-Qur'ān)* without having mastered its outward exegesis, is like a man who claims to have reached the main room of a house *(ṣadr al-bayt)* without having passed through its door, or who claims to understand the intentions of the Turks from their speech without any understanding of the Turkish language. Outward exegesis is like learning the language that is required for understanding [the Koran].[49]

IV. THE DIFFERENCES AMONG HUMAN BEINGS WITH RESPECT TO KNOWLEDGE AND UNDERSTANDING

Ghazālī believes that human beings differ greatly not only in their understanding of the Koran but also in the amount and variety of knowledge which they possess and are capable of acquiring. Although all human beings are equal in their grasp of certain *a priori* rational principles, such as the impossibility of a thing's being in two different places at one and the same time, they are by no means equal in the knowledge they may have acquired beyond these a priori principles as a result of their education and experience. In the *Kitāb sharḥ 'ajā'ib al-qalb* from the third volume of the *Iḥyā'*, Ghazālī says:

> People differ with respect to the abundance or paucity of knowledge, and with respect to its nobility or baseness. They differ also in the method of acquiring it, for knowledge occurs to some hearts through divine illumination *(ilhām ilāhī)* by means of [divine] initiative *(mubāda'a)* and disclosure *(mukāshafa)*, whereas to others it occurs through learning *(ta'allum)* and study *(iktisāb)*. Moreover, its acquisition can be quick or slow. It is at this stage *(maqām)* [of knowledge, i.e. beyond that of the knowledge of *a priori* principles] that the ranks *(manāzil)* of the scholars, philosophers, prophets, and saints are differentiated, for

49. *Iḥyā'*, I, 262; Abul Quasem, *Recitation,* p.94.

> the degrees of ascent *(darajāt al-taraqqī)* at this stage are unlimited, owing to the infinitude of God's knowledge. The highest of the ranks *(rutab)* is that of the prophet, to whom all or most truths are revealed not by study or effort, but by divine revelation *(kashf ilāhī)* in the quickest of time.[50]

The Inability of Most to Understand the Esoteric Meanings of the Koran

Unfortunately most believers are unable to understand the inner meanings of the Koran and are thus incapable of its esoteric exegesis. In the third chapter of *Kitāb Ādāb tilāwat al-Qur'ān* Ghazālī states that the cause of their inability is that Satan has veiled their minds and they therefore have no access to the world of sovereignty *(al-malakūt)* and the Preserved Tablet on which the inward meanings of the Koran are inscribed.[51] In support of this position he quotes the following tradition of the Prophet: "Had it not been for the satans hovering round the hearts of the sons of Adam, they would have gazed at the world of sovereignty." Ghazālī then describes four veils which prevent one from understanding the Koran. The first of these, he says, is:

> one's attention being diverted to the exact pronunciation of the letters *(taḥqīq al-ḥurūf bi-ikhrājihā min makhārijihā)*. This [diversion] is undertaken by a satan assigned to Koran reciters to distract them from understanding the meanings of God's speech. He continually induces them to repeat a letter, making them imagine that it has not been correctly pronounced. When the concentration of a

---

50. *Iḥyā'*, III, 7. An almost identical passage may be found in Ghazālī's *Mīzān al-'amal,* (Cairo 1964), pp.206-07

51. A more extensive treatment of the veils which prevent people from acquiring true and complete knowledge of reality may be found in the third chapter of *Mishkāt al-anwār* in which Ghazālī gives his interpretation of the Prophetic tradition concerning the seventy thousand veils of light and darkness. See *Mishkāt,* pp. 84-93; Gairdner, *Mishkāt,* pp. 154-75. See also *Iḥyā'*, III, 111-12 where Ghazālī lists five reasons why images may not be reflected in a mirror and why the knowledge contained in the Preserved Tablet may not be reflected in the mirror of the heart. They are: 1) imperfection in the form of the mirror, 2) tarnish *(khabath),* rust *(sada')* and grime *(kudūra)* on its surface, 3) the mirror's not being placed facing the object to be reflected in it, 4) there being an obstruction between the object and the mirror, and 5) ignorance as to the position of the object to be reflected in the mirror, so that the mirror can be faced in its direction.

> Koran reciter is confined to the pronunciation of the letters of the Koran, how can its meanings be disclosed to him?[52]

The second veil is blind adherence to a particular school of thought *(taqlīd li-madhhab)*[53] which prevents a person from consideration of any ideas with which he is not already familiar. Concerning this veil Ghazālī says:

> If a flash of lightning shines in the distance, and there appears to a reader one of the meanings [of the Koran] which differ from what he has heard, then the satan of blind adherence *(shayṭān al-taqlīd)* attacks him severely, saying "How can this occur to your mind, seeing that it is at variance with the belief of your fathers?" So he thinks that [the flash of lightning] is a deception from Satan, and distances himself from it and guards himself against the like of it.[54]

The third veil which prevents the understanding of the meaning of the Koran is:

> a man's insistence upon sin, or his being characterized by pride, or his being, in general, afflicted with a worldly passion which he obeys. This [veil] is the cause of the darkness of the heart and its rust *(ṣada')*. It is like tarnish *(khabath)* on a mirror and prevents the clear truth from becoming manifest in the heart. It is the greatest of the heart's veils, and the majority of people are veiled by it. As the accumulation of [worldly] desires *(shahawāt)* increases, the more hidden the meanings of [divine] speech become, but as the burdens of the world upon the heart lessen, the revelation of its meaning in the heart draws closer. Thus, the heart is like a mirror, and desire is like rust. The meanings of the Koran are like the images which are seen in a mirror, and disciplining *(riyāḍa)* the heart by removing desires is like polishing the lustre of the mirror.[55]

As for the fourth veil, it is the belief that the only valid exegesis of the Koran is its exoteric interpretation. It exists whenever someone:

> has read an exoteric exegesis of the Koran and has come to believe

---

52. *Iḥyā'*, I, 255; Abul Quasem, *Recitation,* p. 69-70.
53. Ghazālī speaks of his own lack of adherence to a school of thought at the end of his *Mīzān al-'amal,* pp. 405-409.
54. *Iḥyā'*, I, 255; Abul Quasem, *Recitation,* p.70
55. *Iḥyā'*, I, 255-256; Abul Quasem, *Recitation,* p. 71.

that the words of the Koran have only those meanings which have been passed down from Ibn 'Abbās,[56] Mujāhid,[57] and others, and that whatever goes beyond that is an interpretation of the Koran by personal opinion *(tafsīr bi-al-ray')*, and that "whoever interprets the Koran in accordance with his personal opinion has taken his place in the Fire."[58] This too is one of the great veils.[59]

Esoteric Meanings Should not be Divulged to the Common Man

Ghazālī asserts that most believers remain veiled from the understanding of the inner meanings of the Koran and would be unable to understand such meanings even if they were revealed to them. It is, therefore, incumbent upon those to whom the hidden meanings have been revealed not to divulge those meanings to anyone incapable of understanding them. In the fifth chapter of the *Kitāb al-'ilm* Ghazālī warns against teaching anything to students that is beyond their comprehension and understanding. Among the ten duties of the teacher listed by Ghazālī in this chapter,[60] the seventh duty requires that he:

> should give his less competent students only such things as are clear and suitable for them, and should not mention to them that there is anything more complex to follow which he is [for the present] withholding from them. To do so would weaken their desire for what is clear, muddle their minds, and make them imagine that he is stingy in imparting his knowledge, since everyone believes himself capable of every science no matter how complex. Thus there is no one who is not pleased with God for the perfect intellect he possesses, for the most stupid of men and the weakest in intellect is the most pleased with the perfection of his mind.
>
> For this reason one should not confuse the belief of anyone of the common people *(al-'awāmm)* who has bound himself to the religion, and in whose heart the articles of faith handed down from the predecessors *(al-salaf)* are firmly established without anthropomorphisms *(tashbīh)* or metaphorical interpretations *(ta'wīl)*,

56. See above, note 7.
57. Mujāhid ibn Jabr al-Makkī, one of the 'Successors', studied Koran interpretation under Ibn 'Abbās. See *Encyclopedia of Islam*, VII, p. 293.
58. See above, note 6.
59. *Iḥyā'* I, 256; Abul Quasem, *Recitation*, p. 72.
60. A similar list of seven duties may be found in Ghazālī's *Fātiḥat al-'ulūm* (Cairo 1322), pp. 60-63.

> and whose conscience is clear, but whose intellect is not capable of anything beyond that. On the contrary such a person should be left to mind his own business, because if the metaphorical interpretations *(ta'wīlāt)* of the literal [verses] *(al-ẓāhir)* should be mentioned to him, his bonds as a common man [to religion] would be loosened, and it would not be easy to bind him with the bonds of the elite *(al-khawāṣṣ)*. The barrier which has prevented him from acts of disobedience will cease to exist, and he will turn into a rebellious Satan who will destroy both himself and others.
>
> In fact, the common people should not be brought into a discussion on the realities which underlie complex sciences, but rather should be confined to instruction in the acts of worship and in the practice of reliability in the crafts they are involved in. Their hearts should be filled with yearning for the Garden and fear of the Fire as the Koran has articulated. They should not be exposed to doubts, lest such doubts take root in their hearts, and they will find them difficult to resolve. They will then be miserable and perish. In short, the door of discussion should not be opened to the common people, because that keeps them from working at their crafts, on which the sustenance of the populace as well as the continued livelihood of the elite depend.[61]

V. CONCLUSION

Ghazālī's theory of Koran interpretation may be summarized as follows: The Koran is the speech of God, one of God's eternal attributes. As an attribute of God, however, the Koran can be understood by human beings only as manifested in the form of letters and sounds. In this form, however, the Koran has many levels of meaning. Some of these levels pertain to the outward aspect of the Koran, and these levels of meaning are often obvious and apparent to all. Other levels pertain to the inward aspect of the Koran, and at these levels the meaning of the Koran may be hidden from all but a few.

The exoteric exegesis of the Koran is concerned with those levels

61. *Iḥyā'*, I, 51; Faris, *Knowledge*, pp.151-152. A quite similar passage may be found in Ghazālī's *Mīzān al-'amal*, pp. 369-370. See also the second chapter of *Kitāb qawā'id al-'aqā'id, (Iḥyā'*, I, 88-92; Faris, *Foundations*, pp. 39-49) in which Ghazālī lists five types of secrets which should not be divulged to the common man. Ghazālī devotes his *Iljām al-'awāmm 'an 'ilm al-kalām* to this topic. See particularly pp. 3-23.

of meaning which pertain to the outward aspect of the Koran. These are the levels of meaning which can be understood through the study of the Arabic language and the many rhetorical figures in use at the time of the Prophet. Reason may be of assistance in determining which of the passages in the Koran are expressed in metaphorical language but is not capable of interpreting them with certainty. Exoteric exegesis is thus of little use in explaining the inward aspect of the Koran. This can be done only through esoteric exegesis, which is based on knowledge gained through revelation and illumination.

The ability to understand the various outward and inward levels of meaning in the Koran differs from person to person. Those with little education or spiritual development may understand only those clear and obvious passages which pertain to the outward aspect of the Koran. Others may in rare instances come close to the level of understanding of the prophets and be able to comprehend most of the inward aspect of the Koran.

Various 'veils' prevent most believers, however, from such exalted levels of understanding. By removing these 'veils' believers may, nevertheless, advance from lower levels of understanding to higher levels, but such advancement requires great effort in the form of study, contemplation, and spiritual discipline and exercise. Finally, because most believers are incapable of understanding the Koran on all but its most obvious levels of meaning, esoteric interpretations of the Koran should be divulged only to those who are well advanced on the path of spiritual development and are truly capable of understanding the inward aspect of the Koran.

The village of Suhraward. From Suhrawardī, *Oeuvres Philosophiques et Mystiques,* III, ed. S.H. Nasr & H. Corbin (Tehran: 1970)

The Significance of Suhrawardī's Persian Sufi Writings in the Philosophy of Illumination

Mehdi Aminrazavi

The history of Islamic philosophy provides an excellent representation of how divine wisdom (*theosophy*)[1] manifests itself in various intellectual tendencies. The diversity of intellectual inquiries in Islam ranges from the rationalistic philosophy of the Peripatetics *(mashshā'*īs) and the intellectual intuition of the 'illuminationists' *(ishrāqiyyān)*,[2] to the asceticism and inner journey of the Sufis. However, there have been very few philosophers who have dared to synthesize these diverse schools of thought into a unified philosophical paradigm.

In what follows I discuss the centrality of Suhrawardī's Persian Sufi narratives in so far as *ishrāqī* epistemology is concerned. To do so, I first present an outline of Suhrawardī's philosophical epistemology and then allude to his *ishrāqī* epistemology. I then demonstrate that the understanding of how one can come to know the truth is only possible through a correct understanding of the place and the content of Suhrawardī's Persian Sufi writings in the rest of his

1. I am using the word 'theosophy' in its original and etymological sense and meaning of 'Divine Wisdom'. This is not to be mistaken with the eighteenth/nineteenth-century theosophical movement in England. Some scholars of Suhrawardī such as Mehdi Ha'iri are opposed to the use of this term and feel that 'illuminative philosophy' is a more appropriate term. I have used both theosophy and illumination interchangeably and consider both of them to be adequate translations for *ḥikmat* in Islamic philosophy.
2. For more information on *ishrāqiyyān* see: S.H. Nasr, "The Spread of the Illuminationist School of Suhrawardī," *Islamic Quarterly,* 14, July-Sept. pp. 111-121, and S.H. Nasr, "The School of Isfahan" in *A History of Muslim Philosophy,* ed. by H.M. Sharif (Wiesbaden: O. Harrassowitz 1966), II, pp. 904-32.

corpus. Finally, a brief illustration of some of the more important Sufi narratives of Suhrawardī is offered to provide further textual support for my argument.

Shiḥāb al-Dīn Yaḥyā ibn Amīrak ibn Abū'l-Futūḥ Suhrawardī, the Persian philosopher of the 6th/12th century,[3] was the founder of the school of illumination *(ishrāq)* and an advocate of what he called ancient wisdom *(Ḥikmat al-'atīq).* He understood the necessity to show the truth that lies at the heart of all divinely revealed religions. It is in this context that one should see his celebrated attempt to create a bridge between Islam and the pre-Islamic philosophies of Hermeticism, Pythagoreanism, neo-Platonism, and in particular between Islam and the wisdom of the ancient Persians.[4]

He, like al-Fārābī,[5] lived at a time when there was a need to re-unify the Islamic sciences by bringing about a synthesis of the different and often contradictory schools of thought. Suhrawardī's achievements can only be appreciated when his attempt to bring about a new theory of knowledge is paralleled with his critique of the Peripatetics. Unlike some of the earlier sages and gnostics in Islam, Suhrawardī maintained that philosophical discourse was a

3. For further information on Suhrawardī's biography and his short but prolific career see: Abi 'Uṣaybiah, *'Uyūn al-anbā' fī ṭabaqāt al-aṭibbā',* ed. Muller (Konigsberg Press 1884), and Ibn Khallikān, *Wafayāt al-a'yān,* ed. I. 'Abbās (Beirut 1965), pp. 268-274.; Shams al-Dīn Shahrazūrī, *Nūzhat al-arwāḥ wa rawḍāt al-afrāḥ fī tārīkh al-ḥukamā wa'l-falāsifa,* edited by Khūrshīd Aḥmad (Haydarabad 1976), vol. 2, pp. 119-143; Ghulam-Ḥusayn Dinānī, *Shu'a'i andīsha wa shuhūd dar falsafa-yi Suhrawardī* (Tehran: Ḥikmat Publ. 1985). In recent years a number of works have been done on specific aspects of Suhrawardī's philosophy; some of them include: Aminrazavi, "Suhrawardī's Theory of Knowledge" (Ph.D. Diss., Temple University 1989); M. Bylebyle, "The Wisdom of Illumination: A Study of the Prose Stories of Suhrawardī" (Ph.D. Diss., University of Chicago 1976); K. Tehrani, "Mystical Symbolism in Four Treatises of Suhrawardī" (Ph.D. Diss., Columbia University 1974); Gisella Webb, "Suhrawardī's Angelology" (Ph.D. Diss., Temple University 1989); H. Ziai, "Suhrawardī's Philosophy of Illumination" (Ph.D. Diss., Harvard University 1976).

4. For more information on the relationship between the *ishrāqī* doctrine and the wisdom of ancient Persia see: H. Corbin, *Les motifs zoroastriens dans la philosophie de Sohrawardī* (Tehran: Publication de la Société d'Iranologie, vol. 3, 1946) and *Terre céleste et corps de résurrection: de l'Iran mazdéen à l'Iran shî'ite* (Paris 1978).

5. For more information on this see S.H. Nasr, "Why Was Fārābī Called the Second Teacher" (translated by M. Aminrazavi), *Islamic Culture,* 59 (1985), p. 4.

necessary part of one's spiritual path. This was quite revolutionary since Sufis usually rejected rationalistic philosophy—as exemplified by the Peripatetics—who in turn rejected Sufism.

The significance of Suhrawardī becomes more clear when he is viewed as a gnostic who advocates philosophical discourse and asceticism at the same time. In order to determine the place and the significance of Suhrawardī's Sufi writings, one should first briefly consider his works. Traditionally, Suhrawardī's works have been classified into five different categories: [6]

1. Suhrawardī wrote four large treatises of a philosophical nature: a*l-Talwīḥāt* (The Book of Intimations), *al-Mūqāwamāt* (The Book of Opposites), *al-Muṭāraḥāt* (The Book of Conversations) and finally *Ḥikmat al-ishrāq* (The Philosophy of Illumination). The first three of these works were written in the tradition of the Peripatetics although there are criticisms of certain Peripatetic thinkers in them.

2. There are shorter works, some of which are also of a doctrinal nature, but should be viewed as further explanations of the larger doctrinal treatises. These are: *Hayākīl al-nūr* (Luminous Bodies), *Alwāḥ al-'Imādiyya* (The Tablets of 'Imād al-Dīn), *Partaw-nāma* (Treatise on Illumination), *Fī i'tiqād al-ḥukamā'* (On the Faith of the Adepts), *al-Lamaḥāt* (Flashes of Light), *Yazdānshinākht* (Knowledge of the Divine), and *Būstān al-qulūb* (The Garden of the Heart). Some of these works are in Arabic and some in Persian. His works in Persian are among the finest literary writings in the Persian language. Suhrawardī himself may have translated some of these treatises from Arabic into Persian.[7]

3. Suhrawardī also wrote a number of treatises of a purely esoteric nature in Persian. These are initiatory narratives which contain

---

6. For more information on L. Massignon's classification see: *Recueil des textes inédits concernant l'histoire de la mystique en pays d'Islam* (Paris 1929), p. 113. For S.H. Nasr's classification see: *Three Muslim Sages* (New York: Caravan Books 1966), p. 58. For H. Corbin's classification see his "Prolegmenis instructa" to Suhrawardī, *Opera Metaphysica et Mystica,* I (Istanbul: Bibliotheca Islamica, vol. 16, 1945), p. 16ff.
7. See page 262—›

a highly symbolic language, most of which incorporate Zoroastrian and Hermetic symbols as well as Islamic ones. These treatises include: *'Aql-i surkh* (The Red Intellect), *Awāz-i par-i Jibra'īl* (The Chant of the Wing of Gabriel), *al-Qiṣṣa al-ghurbat al-gharbiyya* (Recital of the Occidental Exile), *Lughāt-i mūrān* (Language of the Termites), *Risāla fī ḥalāt al-ṭufūliyya* (Treatise on the State of Childhood), *Rūzī bā jamā'at-i ṣūfiyān* (A Day among the Community of the Sufis), *Ṣafīr-i sīmurg* (The Song of the Griffin), and *Risāla fī'l-mi'rāj* (Treatise on the Nocturnal Journey). These treatises are intended to demonstrate the journey of the soul toward unity and the inherent yearning of man toward gnosis *(ma'rifa).* As will be seen, without the help of the above works *ishrāqī* doctrine cannot be fully understood.

4. There are also a number of treatises of a philosophic and initiatic nature. These include his translation of *Risāla al-tayr* (Treatise of the Birds) of Ibn Sīnā and the commentary in Persian upon Ibn Sina's *al-Ishārāt wa'l tanbīḥāt.* There is also his treatise *Risāla fī ḥaqīqat al-'ishq* (Treatise on the Reality of Love) which is based on Ibn Sina's *Risāla fī'l-'ishq* (Treatise on Love) and his commentaries on verses of the Koran and the *ḥadīth*. It is also said that Suhrawardī may have written a commentary upon the *Fuṣūṣ* of al-Fārābī, which has been lost.[8]

5. Finally, there is the category of his liturgical writings, namely prayers, invocations and litanies. Shaḥrazūrī calls them *al-Wāridāt wa'l-taqdīsāt* (Invocations and Prayers).[9] Despite certain extracts which appear in Henry Corbin's *L'Archange*

---

7. The authenticity of some of these works remains disputable. For example, his work *Yazdān-shinākht* is said to have been written by 'Ayn al-Quḍāt Hamadhānī and the *Būstān al-qulūb,* which has appeared as *Rawḍāt al-qulūb,* may have been written by Sayyid Sharīf Gurgānī. S.H. Nasr argues that on the basis of the unity of style between the *Būstān al-qulūb* and his other works, it can be concluded that this work does belong to Suhrawardī himself. For more information on this see: M.M. Sharif, *A History of Mulsim Philosophy,* p. 375 and Dr. Nasr's introduction to *Opera Metaphysica et Mystica,* III, p. 40; see below, no. 55.
8. S.H. Naṣr, *Three Muslim Sages* (Cambridge 1973), p. 150, no. 16.
9. The invocations and prayers were published by M. Mu'īn in the *Majāla-yi amūzish wa parvarish* (Tehran: Ministry of Education Press 1924), p. 5ff.

empourpré, these important writings of Suhrawardī have received the least amount of attention.[10] They are of a liturgical nature and represent Suhrawardī's angelology and its relationship to the spiritual entities of the planets.

In his Peripatetic writings, Suhrawardī addresses a number of traditional philosophical themes[11] and offers extensive commentaries on them. One of the central issues that he discusses is the problem of knowledge and how knowledge is attained. Suhrawardī maintains that philosophical analysis is a proper mode of cognition if one is to gain knowledge of the existent beings within the corporeal world. I have called this epistemological system 'philosophical epistemology' as opposed to *'ishrāqī* epistemology', which is the knowledge of those things that are attained through illumination.

SUHRAWARDĪ'S PHILOSOPHICAL EPISTEMOLOGY

It is difficult to identify Suhrawardī's epistemological system with any particular paradigm (i.e. empiricism, rationalism, etc.). While he argues that ultimately one can attain certainty only through the knowledge which is realized by illumination, he does not discard the possibility of attaining partial knowledge through other modes of cognition. Suhrawardī's philosophical epistemology is primarily made up of the following three elements: (1) Definition, (2) Sense Perception, and (3) Innate Ideas.

1) He maintains that knowledge by definition is problematic because it has to include not only the essentials of a thing in question, as Aristotle indicates, but all its attributes and accidents as well which for all practical purposes is impossible. Suhrawardī says this problem exists because:

10. *L'Archange empourpré: Quinze traités et récits mystiques* (Paris: Fayard 1976).
11. For a discussion of Suhrawardī's philosophical themes see: M. Aminrazavi, "Suhrawardī's Metaphysics of Illumination," *Hamdard Islamicus,* XV/1 (1992).

> All definitions inevitably lead to those *a priori* concepts which themselves are in no need of being defined; if this were not the case there would result an infinite succession.[12]

Even if the above were possible, Suhrawardī tells us that there are those elements that are beyond definition such as sound, smell, etc. He says: "Sound cannot be defined by something else and generally simple sensations cannot be defined."[13] To Suhrawardī, therefore, definition should be taken for what it is worth and its value in disclosing the truth should not be overemphasized:

> Therefore, it became clear that limits and definitions in the manner presented by the Peripatetics will never be attained.[14]

2) In contrast to the less significant place which definition plays in Suhrawardī's philosophical epistemology, sense perception is much more important. This is partly because most things that cannot be defined may be known through the senses. For this reason he says: "Thus, knowledge and recognition of some affairs becomes a task of the senses." [15]

The senses, Suhrawardī tells us, will be able to distinguish between the simple and compound entities. The compound ones are defined in terms of the simple entities and not vice versa. Despite this, our senses cannot escape the same problem that definition faced. That is, when faced with an existent being, the compound entities can be known by the simple, but how do we know the simple? It is at this point that an axiomatic principle is required in terms of which everything can be defined; otherwise we, again, face the problem of knowing one thing through another, *ad infinitum*. Concerning this, Suhrawardī states:

> There is nothing more apparent than that which can be sensed... since all our knowledge comes from the senses; therefore, all that is of the senses is innate and cannot be defined.[16]

---

12. *Ḥikmat al-ishrāq,* translated into Persian by Sayyid Ja'far Sajjādī (Tehran: Tehran University Press 1357 A.Hsh./1978), p. 194.
13. *Ḥikmat al-ishrāq,* trans. Sajjādī, p. 194.
14. *Ḥikmat al-ishrāq,* trans. Sajjādī, p. 36.
15. *Ḥikmat al-ishrāq,* trans. Sajjādī, p. 35.
16. *Ḥikmat al-ishrāq,* trans. Sajjādī, p. 195.

Hence, sense-perception ultimately faces the same shortcoming as definition. However, Suhrawardī does not discard this mode of cognition altogether and considers it useful in so far as it allows us to know those things that cannot be defined.

3) Finally, there are the innate ideas which provide the necessary link between Suhrawardī's view of knowledge by definition and sense-perception. This, enables him to offer a coherent and consistent theory of knowledge. The nature of these ideas and their structure, be it Kantian or Platonic, remains somewhat unclear in his philosophical writings, and it is not until one considers his *'ishrāqī* principles that this matter is clarified.

Suhrawardī's concept of philosophical epistemology, therefore, is based on the idea that while different modes of cognition and schools of epistemology are useful in some domains, ultimately, certainty cannot be attained through philosophically-based epistemological models. Thus, while the rationalistic context of Suhrawardī's theory of knowledge is important, his philosophical epistemology has to be viewed as a prelude to his *ishrāqi* and other esoteric works.[17]

ISHRĀQĪ EPISTEMOLOGY

The cornerstone of Suhrawardī's theosophical epistemology is that any epistemological relationship can take place if, and only if, we know ourselves first. For Suhrawardī, when we say "I know P" or "I do P," we have implicitly stated that we know ourselves. According to Suhrawardī this is the underlying axiom upon which cognition can take place and which the Peripatetics have ignored.

According to Suhrawardī, the question which is of utmost importance is how does the self know itself? It is precisely the answer to this question which constitutes the core of his theosophical or *ishrāqī* epistemology. His answer might be formulated as follows: there is a special mode of cognition which attains knowledge directly and without mediation and thereby goes beyond the

17. For a complete discussion of Suhrawardī's epistemology, see: H. Ha'iri, *The Principles of Epistemology in Islamic Philosophy: Knowledge by Presence* (New York: SUNY Press 1992).

traditional subject/object distinction.

It can be said that the first step in Suhrawardī's *ishrāqī* epistemology is to argue that there exists a self which is an immaterial and immutable substance.[18] The proof for the existence of the 'I' is a task that discursive philosophy ought to deal with, and one which Suhrawardī fulfills in a masterly fashion.

Having proved that there exists an 'I' which has an independent existence from the body, he then offers very complex arguments to show how this self knows itself. Although a thorough discussion of his arguments[19] would require a separate study, suffice it to say that Suhrawardī demonstrates that if the self does not know itself by itself, it then implies that the self cannot know itself. For the self, clearly knowing itself necessitates the existence of a special mode of cognition often referred to as 'knowledge by Presence' *(al-'ilm al-ḥuḍūrī)* [20]

So far, we have relied on a purely philosophical method to analyze Suhrawardī's arguments for the existence of the 'I'. It is precisely here that without the aid of Suhrawardī's Persian Sufi writings, one is apt to misinterpret the *ishrāqī* doctrine. Let me examine this further.

Having argued for the existence of the 'I', Suhrawardī then mentions that this self has many attributes that are attached to it. Whereas the proof for the existence of the metaphysical 'I' requires philosophical arguments, the attributes of the self are all too obvious to argue for. They include its worldly desires, which he alludes to in his Persian Sufi writings. Therefore, in the *ishrāqī* doctrine, philosophy is useful insofar as it is able to separate the attributes of the self from the 'I'. Just as sweetness can be separated from sugar only through conceptual means, such is the case with the self and its attributes.

The second stage is that in order for the self to be able to reveal itself, the 'veiling' attributes of the self should be removed. To do so, Suhrawardī prescribes practicing asceticism, and goes on to illustrate in great detail the type and nature of these practices—

18. Ha'iri Yazdi, *The Principles of Epistemology in Islamic Philosophy*, pp. 90-92.
19. For more information see: *ibid.*, pp. 69-92.
20. *Ibid.*, pp. 43ff.

which are intended to destroy the individual ego so that the attributes of the self begin to vanish one by one. As the process goes on, the self, whose relation to its attributes was like the relationship between the accidental qualities of sugar (i.e. whiteness, etc.) to sweetness, begins to reveal its 'I-ness'. This process will have to continue until the complete annihilation of the attributes of the self is completed, and once this process has been finished, the self will remain in its purity without being veiled from itself.

> When you have made a careful inquiry into yourself you will find out that you are made of 'yourself' which is nothing but that which knows its own reality. This is your own 'I-ness' (*ana'iyyātūkā*). This is the manner in which everyone is to know himself and in which everyone's 'I-ness' is common with you.[21]

The methodology employed by Suhrawardī in order to bring the self to its fullness and to restore the dignity of the self to its original state can be formulated into four steps or journeys, as follows: realization, separation, destruction and annihilation. The first two, that is, the realization that there is an 'I', and that it is separate from its attributes, is the task of philosophy. Destruction of the accidental qualities of the self, that is to say, worldly desires and finally, annihilation, is the task of the ascetic practices and Sufism.

It is in regard to the above epistemological scheme that philosophy and asceticism have their own place in the *ishrāqī* doctrine and, in fact, are able to become part and parcel of a tradition of wisdom that brings about a synthesis between discursive philosophy, intellectual intuition and practical wisdom.

THE CENTRALITY OF SUHRAWARDĪ'S SUFI WRITINGS

We now may turn to the place and the centrality of Suhrawardī's Persian Sufi writings in light of the foregoing discussion and the existing interpretation of them. There are three contemporary interpretations of the *ishrāqī* doctrine, none of which completely explains how the actual experience of *ishrāq* is attained. As mentioned

21. *Opera Metaphysica et Mystica,* II, p.112 (trans. M. Ha'iri).

above, this is because his Persian Sufi narratives are regarded either as literary works or non-doctrinal works. Let us briefly examine some of these interpretations.

The first and the least convincing of these interpretations is put forward by H. Ziai.[22] He argues that the notable part of Suhrawardī's philosophy is his views on logic and goes so far as to identify the *ishrāqī* doctrine itself with Suhrawardī's logic. This is perhaps the reason why the title of his doctoral dissertation, "Suhrawardī's Philosophy of Illumination," and his latest book, entitled *Knowledge by Illumination*, both entirely concern Suhrawardī's logic. Ziai's view completely disregards the Persian Sufi writings of Suhrawardī and their doctrinal significance. For Ziai, Suhrawardī's Persian Sufi narratives have merely literary value and are not to be counted amongst his doctrinal works. Suhrawardī's Sufi narratives therefore, should be regarded as literary addenda to his philosophical works. I will presently allude to the shortcomings of this view.

The second view—and a much more valid one—is that of a number of Iranian philosophers, in particular Mehdi Ha'iri Yazdi, who is a proponent of theoretical Sufism (*'irfān-i naḍarī*) but who rejects the practical and ascetic dimension of Sufism. Ha'iri argues that the study of 'illuminative philosophy' alone leads to the experience of illumination.[23] Once an individual has mastered illuminative philosophy, he will experience the 'unity of being' which has been attained through his intellectual insight. This, according to Ha'iri, is what Suhrawardī calls the experience of *ishrāq*.

The above view, however, also ignores the Persian Sufi writings of Suhrawardī. This omission is symptomatic of the fact that Ha'iri and Ziai both separate Suhrawardī's Sufi writings from his philosophical works. It is true that the style in these writings are quite different, but nonetheless one should treat his entire corpus as a single unity. If philosophy by itself, as Ha'iri says, and logic, as Ziai states, could lead to the experience of *ishrāq*, then how do we account for

22. For more information on H. Ziai's interpretation of Suhrawardi see his "Suhrawardī's Philosophy of Illumination," and his *Knowledge and Illumination* (Atlanta: Scholars Press 1990).
23. H. Ha'iri, *The Principles of Epistemology in Islamic Philosophy,* pp. 5-26

those who claim to have mastered the illuminative philosophy or who are logicians, and yet maintain that they have not experienced illumination? There are, for example, many learned orientalists who have mastered what Ha'iri calls 'illuminative philosophy' and yet, by their own admission, are not 'enlightened'. To say that one would experience illumination if one did master illuminative philosophy sufficiently is quite inadequate as well. Furthermore, throughout his Persian Sufi writings, Suhrawardī himself advocates asceticism, not to mention that in the beginning and end of the *Ḥikmat al-ishrāq*[24] Suhrawardī tells us that only those who have fasted for forty days and are vegetarians can understand the text.

The third interpretation of Suhrawardī's *ishrāqī* doctrine is offered by S.H. Nasr and H. Corbin.[25] Despite minor differences, both scholars acknowledge that asceticism and discursive philosophy are part and parcel of the *ishrāqī* doctrine. Their view takes into consideration both Suhrawardī's philosophical and Sufi writings and offers a single interpretation of Suhrawardī's philosophy which is a rapprochement between discursive philosophy, ascetic practices and intellectual intuition.

Although I accept the above to be an accurate interpretation of Suhrawardī, it has one shortcoming. This view neither addresses the order in which asceticism and philosophy come into play, nor explains which of these two is the principle element: discursive philosophy or asceticism. S.H. Nasr would respond by saying that both asceticism and philosophy are simultaneously necessary, the former refines the character and the latter prepares the mind. While the above answer is reasonable, it is not what Suhrawardī tells us is the case. Let me elaborate on this. In the beginning of the *Ḥikmat al-ishrāq* Suhrawardī summarizes his view in this regard and states:

> We observe the sensible world through which we gain certainty of its state of affairs; we then base a thorough and precise science on this foundation (mathematics, astronomy). By analogy, we observe certain things in the spiritual domain and then use

---

24. *Ḥikmat al-ishrāq,* trans. Sajjādī, p. 222.

25. For S.H. Nasr's view see his *Three Muslim Sages,* pp. 63-64. For Corbin's view see his introduction to his annotated translation of Suhrawardī's *Kitāb Ḥikmat al-ishrāq: Le livre de la sagesse orientale* (Paris: Verdier 1986).

> them as a foundation upon which other things can be based. He whose path and method is other than this will not benefit from it and soon will be plunged into doubt." [26]

In this statement Suhrawardī informs us that he had first gained knowledge of the world through his senses, and then had observed things in the spiritual domain. Following this observation he then measures the verity of his other findings. This and many other quotations establish not only the superiority of the experience of illumination over philosophy, but also the chronological order in which they occur. In the *Ḥikmat al-ishrāq* he makes revealing statements that indicate his experience of illumination came about independently of his philosophical endeavors. Thus, in the introduction to the *Ḥikmat al-ishrāq* he states:

> The truth and the content of that *[Ḥikmat al-ishrāq]* for me was not realized through intellection but through a separate means. Finally, having realized their truths [through illumination], I then sought to find their rational justification, however, in such a fashion that even were I to ignore [the rational basis of] these demonstrated propositions, no skeptic could ever cause me to fall into doubt concerning the truth of these things.[27]

The above passage clearly demonstrates how the experience of *ishrāq* can be induced by following a non-rational methodology, that is, by ascetic practices. He states this clearly at the end of *Ḥikmat al-ishrāq* by saying:

> Before beginning [to read] this book one should fast for forty days, practice asceticism and refrain from eating meat. The seeker of truth should eat very little, etc.[28]

In these and many other statements Suhrawardī leaves no doubt that asceticism and the Sufi path are the necessary conditions for having an experience of *Ishrāq*. How one ought to pursue the spiritual path is then elaborated in some detail in his Persian Sufi writings.

---

26. *Ḥikmat al-ishrāq,* trans. Sajjādī, p. 22.
27. *Ḥikmat al-ishrāq,* trans. Sajjādī, p. 18.
28. *Ḥikmat al-ishrāq,* trans. Sajjādī, p. 403.

To summarize the foregoing discussion the following conclusions can be drawn:

1- Suhrawardī's Persian Sufi writings should be regarded as an integral part of his doctrinal work and not merely as a sublime example of Persian literature. They are both philosophically and esoterically important.

2- Asceticism, to which Suhrawardī often alludes in his Persian Sufi writings, is an integral part of the *ishrāqī* doctrine .

Whereas in the *Ḥikmat al-ishrāq* he presents a doctrinal analysis of *ishrāqī* thought, in his Persian writings he discloses the practical aspect of his *ishrāqī* doctrine, without which his *ishrāqī* system would be incomplete. Suhrawardī's epistemological system ultimately relies on the type of wisdom that is attained through practicing the *ishrāqī* discipline, and this is precisely what he is trying to demonstrate in his mystical narratives. In fact, his instructions for the attainment of truth in some of these works are very direct and specific. They range from dietary matters to how one should stay up all night. Let me now briefly offer an exposition of some of these Sufi writings to provide further support for my argument.

1. TREATISE ON THE BIRDS *(RISĀLA AL-ṬAYR)*

This work was originally written by Avicenna and was translated and restated by Suhrawardī into Persian.[29] It discloses a number of esoteric doctrines through the language of the birds, a theme which 'Aṭṭār and Aḥmad Ghazālī also found useful to adopt. The story is about a group of birds who, having fallen into a hunter's trap, describe how their attempt to free themselves is faced with a number of setbacks and how they overcome these obstacles through inner purification. The work depicts the spiritual journey of man from his original abode into the world of form and how the attachments of the material world obstruct his desire to reunite with his spiritual origin. In one passage, having stressed spiritual death and rebirth,

29. *Opera,* III, p. 198.

Suhrawardī reminds us of the hardships of the ascetic path. In symbolic language he states:

> Oh, brothers in truth, shed your skin as a snake does and walk as an ant walks so the sound of your footsteps cannot be heard. Be as a scorpion whose weapon is on his back since Satan comes from behind. Drink poison so you may be born. Fly continuously and do not choose a nest in that all birds are taken from their nests, and if you have no wings, crawl on the ground... Be like an ostrich who eats hot sand, and the vulture who eats hard bones. Like a salamander be in the midst of fire so no harm can come upon you tomorrow. Be as a moth who remains hidden by day so he may remain safe from the enemy.[30]

Suhrawardī uses the above symbols as a set of practical instructions for those who are on the spiritual path. For example, the shedding of one's skin refers to the abandoning of one's ego, and walking like an ant alludes to the way one ought to walk on the path of truth so that no one will know it. Drinking poison symbolically indicates spiritual death and rebirth, and so on. By using the prophetic *ḥadīth,* "Love death so you may live,"[31] Suhrawardī refers to spiritual death. The gnostic concept of annihilation is the death and rebirth that Suhrawardī himself describes in a poem:

> *If you die before the natural death*
> *you have placed yourself in eternal heaven.*
> *O you who have not set foot on this path,*
> *shame upon you that you brought suffering upon yourself.*[32]

Suhrawardī illustrates the various hardships of the path by alluding to the eating of hot sand by the ostrich or the eating of sharp bones by the vulture. Enduring such pain is necessary if one is to progress and achieve higher stations on the spiritual path. Suhrawardī's use of a salamander has different levels of interpretation. The salamander is the symbol of gold in alchemy and gold is the

---

30. *Ibid.,* p. 199.
31. This is a *ḥadīth* of the Prophet used by Suhrawardī in various places to defend the doctrine that 'spiritual death' is the necessary condition for spiritual birth. It was also espoused by 'Ayn al-Quḍāt Hamadhānī (d. 525/1131) before him (cf. the essay below by L. Lewisohn, pp. 285-336).
32. *Opera,* III, p. 395.

symbol of the divine intellect. He might be referring not only to Abraham who was thrown into fire, but also to the fire within man. The popular myth maintains that if a salamander goes through fire and does not burn, it becomes resistant to everything. Therefore, those who are consumed by divine fire have cast their impurity into fire. They have swallowed this fire and become purified.

Finally, Suhrawardī tells us that we ought to be like a moth that flies at night and remains hidden by day. Night represents the esoteric, the hidden aspect, and day the exoteric dimension. In this way Suhrawardī uses symbols of traditional Sufi literature, with night symbolizing the esoteric and the spiritual milieu, providing the sacred space which allows man to fly.

In this treatise Suhrawardī describes the spiritual journey of man by recounting the tale of a number of birds who were 'flying freely' but fell in the trap of the hunters. 'Flying freely' here symbolizes the condition in which man lived in the eternal state prior to creation, and falling into the trap denotes coming into the domain of material existence. Having become the prisoner of the material world (often identified in Persian literature as the 'prison of the body'), those who are conscious of this imprisonment can begin their journey towards their origin.

The bird who finds himself a prisoner symbolizes the worldly man, who, because of the forgetfulness of human nature, becomes used to the attachments of the material world. This adaptation and the acceptance of the condition of imprisonment is the greatest danger on one's spiritual journey according to Suhrawardī. In the language of the birds, Suhrawardī tells us:

> We focused our attention on how we can free ourselves. We were in that condition for a while until our first principle (freedom) was forgotten and we adapted to these chains, giving into the constriction of the cage.[33]

Suhrawardī's description of the spiritual journey in the "language of the birds" continues with the flight of the birds as they free themselves from some of the bondages and yet are not able to free themselves entirely. To translate this into theosophical

---

33. *Ibid.*, p. 200.

language, it can be said that men who have fallen into the world of forms can partly free themselves through their own willpower. However, to remove all the chains of attachments requires the guidance of a master. While the potential for man to become 'illumined' exists, this process will not take place without the inner yearning and will to make the journey. This point becomes clear when the main character of the story begs the other birds to show him how they freed themselves.

Having pursued the path of asceticism and hardship, the birds arrive at different states and stations of the path where they think it is time to rest. Suhrawardī warns us against this desire to rest in one place, although the beauties of the path—which he describes as the "attractions that remove the mind *('aql)* from the body"—are extremely tempting.[34] Finally, their desire to stay is overcome by divine grace, which is manifested by a voice calling upon them to continue. Suhrawardī then describes their encounter with God, whose presence he describes as a blinding Light. The Light-of-Lights tells the birds that he who has placed the chains must remove them as well. God then sends a messenger to oversee the removal of these chains.

The following principles can be inferred from the *Risāla al-ṭayr:*[35]

1- The earthly human state is a prison for the human soul.
2- The soul by necessity has a yearning to journey towards the Light-of-Lights.
3. The grace attained through such an experience helps the spiritual wayfarer *(sālik)* to remove the final attachments to this world.
4.-The experience of the Light-of-Lights can be realized if one is able to free oneself from the prison of the corporeal world.

---

34. *Ibid.,* p. 202.
35. *Ibid.*, p. 198-205.

2. THE CHANT OF GABRIEL'S WING
(ĀWĀZ-I PAR-I JIBRA'ĪL)

This is one of the most esoteric and well-known works of Suhrawardī, in which a seeker of truth visits a *khānaqāh* (Sufi house) which has two doors, one facing the city and the other one to the desert. Having gone to the desert, he meets ten spiritual masters and questions them in regard to the mystery of creation, the stages of the path and the dangers thereon.[36]

The conversation which follows reveals the essential elements of the *ishrāqī* doctrine and the significance of the initiation rite and ascetic practices in the *ishrāqī* system. In this highly symbolic work Suhrawardī discusses the essential elements of his *ishrāqī* epistemology. Suhrawardī makes full use of the traditional Sufi symbols of gnosis as well as a number of other symbols in this treatise which are employed uniquely by him and cannot be found elsewhere in classical Persian Sufi literature. The thrust of the work is stated in the beginning:

> Abū Alī Fārmadī, peace be upon him, was asked, "How is it that those who wear the blue robes[37] name certain sounds 'the chant of Gabriel's wing'?" He replied, "Know that most things which your faculties observe derive from the chant of Gabriel's wing."[38]

One can say that the entire theory of 'knowledge by presence', which is at the core of Suhrawardī's epistemology, is expressed in this mystical tale. Using metaphorical language Suhrawardī provides us with precise directions for the development of a inner faculty capable of gaining knowledge directly and without mediation. Relying on the traditional symbolism of Sufi poetry and prose, Suhrawardī elaborates on the contention that exists between empiricism, rationalism and the gnostic mode of cognition.

---

36. Numerous commentaries have been written on this work, the most famous of which is by an anonymous author who lived in India around the 15th century (cf. M. Qāsimī. "Sharḥ-i āwāz-i par-i Jibrā'īl," *Ma'ārif,* 1, March-May (1984).
37. I.e. the Sufis, whose traditional robes were blue.
38. *Opera,* III, pp. 208-209.

3. THE RED INTELLECT
('AQL-I SURKH)

In this treatise[39] the tale opens with the question of whether or not birds understand each other's language. The eagle, who initially says yes, is later captured by the hunters and her eyes are closed only to be opened gradually. The eagle meets a red-faced man who claims to be the first man created. The red color signifies the divine intellect and that is the reason why he appears both young and old at the same time. He is old because he represents the 'perfect man' who existed in a state of perfection before creation[40] in the form of the archetype of man, and he is young since divine light has illuminated his being and thereby he is 'born again' by becoming illumined.

Suhrawardī then uses the Zoroastrian symbolism of Mt. Qāf, the story of Zāl, Rustam and other epic heroes exemplified in the *Shāhnāma*.[41] Qāf is the name of the mountain on whose peak the Sīmurgh (Griffin), symbol of the divine essence, rests. Zāl, who was born with white hair, representing wisdom and purity, was left at the bottom of Mt. *Qāf.* The *Sīmurgh* bore Zāl to his nest and raised him until he grew up and married Taḥmīna; from their union, Rustam was born. Rustam, the hero of the *Shāhnāma,* who is often perceived as the soul of epic Persia, is a man who has ultimately overcome his own ego.

Using a new set of symbols, Suhrawardī brings forth some of the classic issues of Islamic philosophy and mysticism, such as the distinction between the rational faculty which he calls the 'particular intellect' *('aql-i juz'ī),* and the Intellect which he calls 'universal intellect' *('aql-i kullī)*. In doing so he relies heavily on Zoroastrian symbolism and ancient Persia sources. It is precisely the interaction between the particular and universal intellect that is the basis upon which one can gain knowledge within different domains.

---

39. *Opera,* III, pp. 226-39.
40. *Ibid.,* p. 228.
41. Suhrawardī employed the symbolism of Firdawsī's *Shāhnāma* to formulate his angelology. Some scholars argue that the *Shāhnāma* is a profoundly mystical work and make an esoteric reading of this book.

Like other works of a theosophical nature, Suhrawardī hides his theory of knowledge behind a maze of myth and symbols which can only be disclosed if one is familiar with traditional Persian sacred symbolism.

In this tale, an eagle appears who asks the 'eternally young' master Khiḍr, how the spiritual path can be traversed. Khiḍr's response reveals a profoundly esoteric and yet very practical theory of knowledge. In narrating the dialogue with Khiḍr, Suhrawardī uses the following symbols to expound the seven stages of the spiritual path experienced by the seeker:

> I asked, "What of the wonders of the world have you seen?" He said, "Seven things. First, Mt. Qāf, which is my abode. Second, the night-illumining pearl. Third, the Ṭūbā tree. Fourth, the twelve workshops. Fifth, David's chainmail. Sixth, Balārak's sabre. And seventh, the Fountain of Life.[42]

Suhrawardī then informs us how the perennial truth, which he equates with drinking from the Fountain of Life, can be realized by interpretation of the above symbols. Mt. Qāf symbolizes the eternal Utopia or 'nowhere' which was the abode of man in the Adamic state. The night-illumining pearl symbolizes reason, and in top of the Ṭūbā tree is the nest of the Sīmurgh, symbol of the divine Essence. The twelve workshops are the hierarchies of beings, each of which is emanated by its previous level and ultimately they all proceed from the Light-of-Lights *(nūr al-anwār).*

How does one come to know of the above cosmological principles, asks Suhrawardī? By liberating oneself from the bonds of the sensory realm (David's chainmail) through the use of the power of the spiritual will which is Balārak's sabre, the blow of which is, however, often extremely painful. Only by finding the Fountain of Life (divine knowledge) which lies in land of Darkness (the senses) and bathing in its *aqua vita,* can the pain of severing David's chainmail with Balārak's sabre be lessened.

Once again, in a mystical narrative written in a highly symbolic language, Suhrawardī makes the cognition of metaphysical

---

42. *Opera,* III, p. 229.

principles contingent on spiritual practice rather than upon comprehension of the theoretical sciences.

4. A DAY AMONG THE COMMUNITY OF THE SUFIS *(RŪZĪ BĀ JAMĪʻAT-I SŪFIYYĀN)*

The story begins in a *Khānaqāh,*[43] where the disciples speak of the status of their masters and their views with regard to creation. Suhrawardī, who speaks as a master, objects to such questions which merely seek to explain the nature of the universe and the structure of the heavens. Suhrawardī considers them to be shallow and maintains that there are those who see through the appearance and understand the science of the heavens.

Finally, he argues that those who attain the mastery of the celestial world are the true men of knowledge. Suhrawardī then goes on to give specific instructions regarding ascetic practices which can bring about an experience of illumination, stating:

> All that is dear to you: property, furniture, worldly pleasures and such things...(throw them away)...if this prescription is followed, then your vision will become enlightened.[44]

In this work, amid a mixture of myth, symbolism and traditional Islamic metaphysics, Suhrawardī elaborates on the relationship between the pursuit of esoteric knowledge and the practice of asceticism. Practicing asceticism will open the inner eye, which for Suhrawardī is an unmeditated and direct mode of knowledge. As he states:

> Once the inner eye opens, the exterior eye ought to be closed. The lips must be sealed and the five external senses should be silenced. Interior senses should begin to function so the person, if he attains anything, does so with the inner being *(bāṭin)*, and if he sees, he sees with the inner eye, and if he hears, he hears with the inner ear... Therefore, when asked what would one see

43. *Opera,* III, p. 242.
44. *Ibid.,* p. 248.

(the answer of the inner self is): it sees what it sees and what it ought to see.[45]

Therefore the closure of the five external senses for Suhrawardī is a necessary condition for the opening of the internal senses essential for the attainment of the Truth.

This work alludes to different stages of the spiritual path and how the spiritual elite can achieve purity of heart and clarity of vision. Also, it is in this work that the relationship between asceticism and epistemology is discussed by employing specifically Sufi symbolism.

5. TREATISE ON THE STATE OF CHILDHOOD *(RISĀLA FĪ ḤALĀT AL-ṬUFŪLIYYA)*

In this work,[46] Suhrawardī describes having met a master who reveals the divine secrets to him which he in turn disclosed to men of an exoteric nature who lacked the aptitude to understand such mysteries. The master punishes him for 'casting pearl before swine.' Suhrawardī also alludes to the difficulty of communicating the esoteric message to those who stand outside of the tradition. Then the spiritual wayfarer *(sālik),* having repented, finds the master again who tells him a number of secrets relating to such things as the ethics of the spiritual path, and certain rituals, such as the Sufis' practice of *samā'* (audition to musical concerts in which mystical poetry is sung).

Suhrawardī expresses this in a symbolic conversation between a bat and a salamander, whose passage through fire is supposed to have protected it against all harm. The bat is describing the pleasure of drinking cold water in winter, while the salamander is suffering from a cold. Each one could provide a different interpretation of 'cold water' in accordance to their knowledge through experience.

So far Suhrawardī has drawn an outline of the esoteric instructions needed for a seeker to pursue the spiritual path, which begins by an inner yearning and continues with ascetic practices under the

45. *Ibid.,* p. 249.
46. *Opera,* III, p. 252.

guidance of a master. This rather traditional path that Suhrawardī describes through the use of so many myths and symbols has been the cornerstone of Sufism since its inception. The treatise thus intends to illustrate the journey of the seeker *(sālik)* from its beginning, which Suhrawardī symbolically identifies as childhood. The significance of having a spiritual master to avoid the dangers on the path, as well as different stages of inner development, are among some of the issues that Suhrawardī discusses. Once again, it is obvious that a practical guide as to how the spiritual path has to be pursued constitutes the core of the teachings of Suhrawardī in this treatise.

6. TREATISE ON THE REALITY OF LOVE *(RISĀLA FĪ ḤAQĪQAT AL-'ISHQ)*

This work not only represents a most sublime specimen of Persian literature, but also contains some of Suhrawardī's most profound philosophical views. The *Risāla fī ḥaqīqat al-'ishq* is a mixture of prose and poetry in which Suhrawardī offers an esoteric commentary on such Koranic tales as Jacob's longing for his son Joseph, and Zulaykhā's intense love of him as well as to illustrate man's separation from God. In doing so, he again tells us of the value and place of practical wisdom in the understanding of the secrets of creation.

He begins by quoting a verse from the Koran and then goes on to discuss knowledge and its relationship with the Intellect.

> Know that the first thing God, praise be upon Him, created was a luminous substance, which he called intellect *('aql),* for (according to the *ḥadīth]* "God first created Intellect." And he gave this substance three features: knowledge of God, knowledge of self and knowledge of that which was not and then was.[47]

From the 'knowledge of God', says Suhrawardī, sprang 'Beauty', from the 'knowledge of self' came 'Love', and from that which did not exist and then existed, arose 'Sorrow'. In one of the most beautiful and lucid examples of Persian Sufi literature, Suhrawardī tells us the Koranic story of creation using the trinity of Beauty,

47. *Opera,* III, p. 208-209.

Love and Sorrow to illustrate three distinct dimensions of creation:

> Once Sorrow was separated from Beauty, he said to Love, "Together you and I were at the service of Beauty and received our *khirqa* from him, and he is our master *(pīr).* Now that we have been sent into exile, the right course is that each of us set out in a different direction, and undertake a journey by way of ascetic self-restraint. For a while, let us remain constant and steadfast, braving Fate's hard knocks, bowing our heads into the yoke of submission, and prostrating ourselves on this parti-coloured prayer-carpet of Providence and Destiny. Maybe through the kind efforts of the seven hidden masters who are the guardians of this world of growth and decay, we will be reunited with our Shaykh...[48]

Chapter six of the treatise is an exposé of esoteric psychology, devoted to discussion of the 'City of the Soul' *(sharistān-i jān),* entrance into which, Suhrawardī stresses once again, is only to be attained by various ascetic practices:

> He who would reach this city must loosen the six ropes which are suspended over these four arches, and making a lasso of love, set the saddle of intuitive spiritual taste *(dhawq)* on the mount of ardent yearning *(shawq),* and with the bodkin of hunger paint his eyelids with the collyrium of wakefulness, and taking in hand the sword of knowledge, so seek out the microcosm...[49]

The treatise reaches its climax in this chapter where Suhrawardī presents his own unique mystical psychology and offers us a spiritual map of the universe.[50]

---

48. *Opera,* III, pp. 273-4.
49. *Ibid.,* p. 279.
50. S.H. Naṣr, *Three Muslim Sages,* p. 59. It has been argued that this work was written on the basis of Ibn Sīnā's *Risāla al-'ishq.* However, it should be noted that this work is different both in form and content.

7. THE LANGUAGE OF THE TERMITES *(LUGHĀT-I MŪRĀN)*

In this treatise[51] Suhrawardī describes the nature of the knowledge needed by the seeker to know God, himself and all creation. Citing the words of classical Sufi masters such as Abū Ṭālib Makkī, Ḥallāj and Ḥusayn ibn Ṣāliḥ to buttress his argument, Suhrawardī notes that "all agreed that as long as the veil is not removed, vision of Reality will not be attained."[52] Suhrawardī also uses the ancient Persian symbol—a favorite topos of the Persian Sufi poets—of the "World-revealing Cup of Kay-khusraw" *(jām-i gītī-namā-yi Kay-Khūsraw),* in this treatise to denote the illuminated gnosis of the heart "wherein all the lines and forms of the world appear reflected."[53]

In the penultimate chapter Suhrawardī provides us again with a practical set of guidelines for realization of the experience of inner illumination *(ishrāq),* observing:

> Whatever hinders good is evil and whatever blocks the [spiritual] Path is infidelity *(kufr)* for men. To be contented with whatever one's sensual self *(nafs)* presents and to adapt oneself to it, is impotence on the path of mystical progression *(dar ṭarīq-i sulūk).* To look with delight upon oneself – even if one have God in mind – is ruination. Salvation is to turn one's face utterly towards God.[54]

***

51. *Opera,* III, pp. 294-311.
52. *Ibid.,* p. 297.
53. *Ibid.,* pp. 298-9.
54. *Ibid.,* p. 310.

In the above discussion, I have briefly analysed the central themes in seven of Suhrawardī's mystical narratives. However, these by no means exhaust his Persian Sufi writings, and other of his works such as the *Būstān al-qulūb* or *Rawḍāt al-qulūb*[55] and *Yazdān shinākht*[56] are quite significant. What has been discussed so far nonetheless suffices to demonstrate that Suhrawardī's *Persian writings,* be they of philosophical orientation or in the Sufi style, are of a *doctrinal nature* and should be regarded as such. To divide and separate Suhrawardī's mystical narratives from his doctrinal works simply because of the former's different literary and symbolic style leads to a grave misinterpretation of the entire *ishrāqī* doctrine. While Suhrawardī prescribes mastery of discursive philosophy, 'illumination' can ultimately only be experienced through following the Sufi path—which is none other than engagement in austere forms of ascetic practices whose primary purpose is to destroy the ego and, ultimately, realize annihilation of the finite self in the Divine Being.

55. S.H. Nasr *(Opera,* III, p. 55) indicates that this work has been attributed to a number of authors including Sayyid Sharīf Gurgānī, Ibn Sīnā, Khwāja Naṣīr al-Dīn Ṭūsī, Bābā Afḍal Kāshānī and finally, 'Ayn al-Quḍāt Hamadhānī. However, it is his opinion that on the basis of the form and content of the book, it belongs to Suhrawardī.

56. *Opera,* III, p. 403.

Illuminated Frontpiece from the *Tamhīdāt* of ʻAyn al-Quḍat Hamadhānī. MS. Ethé 1793, f. 1v.; n.d. (Courtesy of the India Office Library).

In Quest of Annihilation: Imaginalization and Mystical Death in the *Tamhīdāt* of ʻAyn al-Quḍāt Hamadhānī

Leonard Lewisohn

PROLOGUE

In the annals of twelfth-century Persian Sufism ʻAyn al-Quḍāt Hamadhānī is renowned for his daring and eloquent expression of the most esoteric elements of Sufi doctrine. A paragon of the paradoxical position, he was at once an authority in the sphere of the religious law *(sharīʻa)* and one of the most famous of the apparent antinomians, or 'shatterers' of the mould of that law. His name also calls to mind Manṣūr Ḥallāj (martyred 922), whose tradition he followed and whose passion-to-the-death became to him a constant preaching and living practice. Indeed, it was that very fire of Ḥallājian love that drove ʻAyn al-Quḍāt inward from the shell of legal convention to penetrate the kernel of the Truth embodied therein, inspired by his master Aḥmad Ghazāli (brother of the illustrious theologian, Muḥammad Ghazālī), famed as the 'Sultan of the Sufi Path' among other towering spiritual figures of this period.

ʻAyn al-Quḍāt flourished in the age of the great founding fathers of Sufism; he was a contemporary of the founder of the Qādirī Order, ʻAbd al-Qādir Jīlānī (d. 561/1166), as well as the founder of the Suhrawardī *silsila* (known as the 'Mother of the Orders', *umm al-salāsil),* Abū'l-Najīb al-Suhrawardī (d. 563/1168, who was also ʻAyn al-Quḍāt's fellow disciple under Aḥmad Ghazālī) and of Abū Yaʻqūb Yūsuf Hamadānī (d. 535/1140), his fellow townsman and founder of the chain which was to lead to the establishment of the Naqshbandī Order. He breathed in the same heady fragrance of poetic mysticism which his contemporary giants in Persian mystical poetry, Sanā'ī (d. between 525/1131 and 545/1150) and Niẓāmī (d.

598/1202) had absorbed, and was swept up in the same wave of ecstatic spirituality whose *élan* intoxicated and then dashed down to early martyrdom the brilliant 'Master of the Philosophy of Oriental Illumination' (Shaykh al-Ishrāq) Shihāb al-Dīn Yaḥyā Suhrawardī (d. 587/1191).

Insofar as the key to the spiritual attainments of 'Ayn al-Quḍāt lay in his exceptional attitude to death, that is to say, his conscious 'pursuit of annihilation', the present study[1] focuses on the concept of *fanā'* in his Persian writings. Since no philosophical doctrine may be properly analyzed in isolation from other ideas which infiltrate its inspiration, five or six other—outwardly extraneous but inwardly intimately related—themes will also hold our attention.

In the first part of the essay, 'Ayn al-Quḍāt's youth, spiritual affiliations and early intellectual development are discussed, followed by a brief look at the inspiration of his longest Persian book, the *Tamhīdāt,* in the second part. Part three analyses the nature of 'annihilation' in 'Ayn al-Quḍāt's thought. Annihilation of the self is the basis of the Sufi *via purgativa,* so extensive treatment of the various forms in which this doctrine appears in his writings is given. Part four discusses the type of consciousness which the adept realizes in the realm of annihilation, presenting 'Ayn al-Quḍāt's views on mystical anthropology, the reality of death and the science of 'imaginalization' which enables the aspirant to attain mystical death. Lastly some conclusions are presented on 'Ayn al-Quḍāt's views of the relationship between physical and mystical death, between the orthodox and the mystical view of the hereafter, and why one must transcend formal Islam to understand any of these matters.

I. FROM MULLA TO SUFI: THE DISCIPLESHIP OF 'AYN AL-QUḌĀT

Abū al-Ma'alī 'Abdullāh ibn Abī Bakr Muḥammad ibn 'Alī ibn al-Ḥasan ibn 'Alī al-Miyānjī, better known as 'Ayn al-Quḍāt

1. The author would like to acknowledge his gratitude to Dr. Jeffrey Rothschild, Dr. Muhammad Isa Waley, Dr. Merida Blanco, Phillip Edmundson and Paul Weber for providing invaluable comments on initial drafts of this article.

Hamadhānī, was born in Hamadān, Iran in 492/1098.[2] Miyānjī, the city of his family's origins, is located between Tabriz and Maragheh in the province of Azerbaijan in northwestern Iran. 'Ayn al-Quḍāt's grandfather Abū al-Ḥasan 'Alī ibn al-Ḥasan migrated with his family from Miyānjī to Hamadān where he settled, gaining an established reputation as a Judge *(Qāḍī),* as well as some renown as a poet in the Arabic language. He died a martyr. His son, the father of 'Ayn al-Quḍāt, also became a judge, passing on the family profession to his son, 'Ayn al-Quḍāt.

'Ayn al-Quḍāt received the normal education in the traditional sciences of his day: Mathematics, Logic, Jurisprudence *(fiqh),* Tradition *(Ḥadīth),* prosody and the *belles-lettres* (both Arabic and Persian). He particularly excelled in scholastic theology *(Kalām),* and in his Arabic-language *Apologia*, the only work of his translated today into English,[3] he demonstrates a formidable mastery of grammar, linguistics, mathematics, logic, and prosody.

'Ayn al-Quḍāt's childhood and early years were pervaded by the mystical milieu and spiritual ideals of Sufism. His father habitually brought him to attend local Sufi seances[4] and at age sixteen or seventeen he became a disciple of a certain Baraka, a Sufi Shaykh whose lack of exoteric learning did nothing to impede the youth's devotion to his gnostic 'wisdom of the heart'. Concerning him 'Ayn al-Quḍāt recalled that

> He had memorized no more than the Surah *al-Ḥamd,* that is, the Opening Surah of the Koran *(Fātiḥa),* and a few other short Surahs. He could only recite these in special circumstances, himself unaware of any of the learned discussions and debates surrounding these texts. Actually, if one were to probe deeply into his learning, he could not even recite any of the *Ḥadīth*s in our local Hamadānī dialect. Despite this, I know that it is he who understands the Koran correctly and not me – except for some of it – and even that I do not know through the science of hermeneutical exegesis *(tafsīr).* Aside from this, and that which

2. See 'Ayn al-Quḍāt Hamadhānī, *Tamhīdāt*, edited with an introduction by Afif Osseiran (Tehran 1962), introduction, p. 45. [Abbreviated hereafter as "T"]
3. A.J. Arberry, trans., *A Sufi Martyr: The Apologia of 'Ain al-Quḍāt al-Hamadhānī* (London: Allen & Unwin 1969).
4. T 250-52.

> I realized through service to him, I understood nothing of the Koran.[5]

In a letter to one of his disciples written a decade later, 'Ayn al-Quḍāt also recalled his profound attraction to this saint and the agonizing efforts he underwent during his period of discipleship under him:

> I spent seven years visiting Baraka, but never once did I dare to touch the thongs of his sandals.[6] Do you think that the Men do not realize what the sign of a Man is? If one of the heart's sovereigns *(ṣāḥib dil)* were to take you into his heart, and you were to lay a finger on one of the Men's sandals, Satanic arrogance would have prompted you to this. In order that one of the heart's sovereigns may accept you into his heart the first stage and requirement is that your heart remain on fire in his love for several years. If you remain constant in this devotion, he will then seize the 'you' from 'yourself'.[7]

'Ayn al-Quḍāt's attitude here reflects the overwhelming influence of the Khurāsānī tradition of Persian Sufism during the early twelfth century in which it was customary for the disciple to treat his master with the same awe and veneration exacted by absolute temporal sovereigns from their subjects. The truth of Hermann Landolt's observation that "the presence of a living master and not the study of books was the First condition of the mystic life of Hamadānī"[8] is borne out in all of his later writings.

The agony of 'Ayn al-Quḍāt's novitiate is also painfully expressed in another letter addressed to a notable disciple, employed

---

5. From one of 'Ayn al-Quḍāt's Epistles, cited by Afif Osseiran, T 63, introduction.
6. The author refers to the custom of removing one's shoes on entering the Sufi *khānaqāh,* where, as a form of service, novice dervishes were often employed as doorkeepers responsible for organizing and setting in orderly pairs the sandals and shoes of the dervishes. The 'doorkeeper' is considered to be very high position in many of the Iranian *ṭarīqa*s. For instance, it is not uncommon today for novices of the Qādiriyya Order in Iran to wait many years before being granted permission by their Shaykh to arrange the dervishes' shoe rack. (Hence, Sa'dī's dictum: "Service to people is the whole of worship," cited above, p. xxvi).
7. T, introduction, pp. 61-62.
8. 'Two Types of Mystical Thought in Muslim Iran: An Essay on Suhrawardī Shaykh al-Ishrāq and 'Aynulquẓāt-i Hamadānī' in *The Muslim World,* vol. 68 (1978), p. 194.

at the royal court, who questioned him about pursuit of the Spiritual Path:

> You still have no awareness. Even after you free yourself from being a servant of Sultan Maḥmūd, you must spend many years serving the Men of the Way, until they either wrest 'you' from yourself or abandon you. Then you will fathom the agony and ecstasy of the disciple.
>
> What have you to do with tales of devotion *(irādat)* to a master? You have not tasted yet of the joy of union nor suffered the pain of separation from him; neither have you experienced the awesome majesty and grandeur of his presence. You have not wished to die every day, a thousand times.... You have not yet experienced infinite remorse, have not been swept under the sea and drowned in its depths, losing yourself in the tributaries and vales flushed with the blood and the grief of your love. You have not piled dust and ashes on your own head a thousand times over, letting that cruel hand leave unwashed your ashen brow, wailing with none to watch.
>
> Nor have you bound a cincture about yourself a million times – sometimes with your own hand and sometimes by the hand of the master, being cast headlong into a pool of blood and dust. You have not sunk the razor-sharp tooth of the shark of voluntary failure into your heart! You have not dug up an entire mountain with your fingernails! Why concern yourself with these tales? How should they mean anything to you?[9]

Stressing the indispensability of a living spiritual master in the training both of the Sufi disciple and the religious scholar, 'Ayn al-Quḍāt told another disciple:

> What do you know and what does most of the world know what the Koran is? Your Koranic recitation, your prayers, your fasting, your almsgiving, your *Ḥajj* and *jihād* is that you seek to attain closeness to the sandals of a Man, so that you may make the earth on which he walks day and night your eye's collyrium, so that perhaps – after you have spent fifty years of your life in his service – one day he may cast his glance upon you and you will be blessed by fortune.
>
> But what can you understand of this which you hear – that

9. T, introduction, pp. 87-88.

> by one glance the beloved bestows myriad favors? No. "One who has not tasted it does not know its flavor." I wait for the time when I may be favored by this glance.[10]

Despite Baraka's lack of formal education, 'Ayn al-Quḍāt always was in awe of his high spiritual stature:

> When I sat in Baraka's company I always felt myself to be little more, in fact much less, than a fresh convert to Islam who knows nothing of its religious or intellectual history. *Vis-à-vis* Baraka this was actually my condition, but still I had the power within me to compose the *Zubdat al-ḥaqā'iq* in two or three days.[11]

The book referred to in this passage was 'Ayn al-Quḍāt's first philosophical composition[12] written in 516/1122 at age twenty-four—apparently in order to resolve, through visionary insight, *(kashf)* both his own spiritual crisis and certain intellectual enigmas confounding him in scholastic theology. When he was twenty years old (in 512/1118), he had begun to study the *Iḥyā' 'ulūm al-dīn,* the monumental encyclopedia of Islamic piety by Abū Ḥamīd al-Ghazālī (d. 505/1111), which he continued to read with intense interest, for four years, until 516/1122. 'Ayn al-Quḍāt describes himself as having been led to study the science of *Kalām* "like a drowning man trying to save himself,"[13] and the *Iḥyā 'ulūm al-dīn,* with its elaborate defence and advocacy of the truths of Sufism and reconciliation of the Sufis' views with those of nomocentric theologians,[14] proved the proper palliative for the scholar's pain, as he wrote:

> Whilst afflicted by this crisis, confused and perplexed, my life was in tatters, until the Guide of those bewildered in the Vale of Confusion set me on the right path and graciously assisted me. Thus, by God's grace, through study of the books of *Shaykh al-Islām* Muḥammad Ghazālī, I was delivered from falling headlong from this horrifying precipice. I spent nearly four years

10. *Ibid.*
11. T, introduction, p. 61.
12. According to Prof. Landolt, an unpublished English translation and analytical study of the *Zubdat al-ḥaqā'īq* by Dr. 'Umar Jah exist in the library of the Institute of Islamic Studies, McGill University, Montreal.
13. T, introduction, p. 48.
14. A.J. Arberry, *A Sufi Martyr,* p. 14.

studying his works, during which time my complete preoccupation with [religious] learning *('ulūm)* caused me to behold many marvels which delivered me from heresy, error, blindness and perplexity.[15]

Another significant factor in 'Ayn al-Quḍāt's early spiritual development was his encounter, in 512/1118 at age 21, with Abū Ḥāmid's less famous but equally celebrated brother, Aḥmad Ghazālī. Although intellectually already a follower of Abū Ḥāmid Ghazālī, 'Ayn al-Quḍāt's emotional temperament was deeply affected by the 'school of love'[16] advocated by Aḥmad. And as he confesses in the *Zubdat al-ḥaqā'īq,* his encounter, in the flesh, with this spiritual teacher rivalled in importance the study of all the religious textbooks of the other Ghazālī:

> Little by little, the eye of inner vision *(chashm-i baṣīrat)* opened. While this process was going on, I began to look for a way which would bring me to that which transcends science. I spent nearly one year in this condition, without being able to realize inwardly the actual reality which I had discovered. Then I encountered my spiritual guide and master *(pīr)* and venerable guide to the divine Reality *(ḥaqīqat),* Abū'l-Fatḥ Aḥmad ibn Muḥammad Ghazālī (may God preserve the Islamic community through his life and reward him for his goodness to me!) whom destiny had brought to Hamadān, my hometown and birthplace.
>
> I had spent no more than twenty days in his company when all the veils of perplexity mentioned above were lifted and an experience was vouchsafed me during which the actuality of things became apparent to me and a Reality revealed to me so that nothing remained of 'me' or 'my desires', except what God had willed. For many years now I have had no other occupation but the quest for annihilation and absorption in this Reality[17]—may God assist me in accomplishing this aim... Were I to be granted the lifespan of Noah and to pass it entirely in this quest

15. Cited in T, introduction, p. 48.
16. See N. Pourjavady's translation of Aḥmad Ghazālī's *Sawāniḥ,* under the title of *Inspirations from the World of Pure Spirits* (London: KPI 1986), introduction, p. 15.
17. Hence, our title; the original Arabic of this phrase in the *Zubdat al-ḥaqā'iq* (ed. Afif Osseiran [Tehran 1341 A.Hsh./1962], p. 7) reads: *Laysa lī shughlun illā ṭalab al-fanā' fī dhālīka'l-shay'.*

> it would be of no significance, for, in relation to this Reality, all life is worthless. It is a Reality which encompasses the whole world. My eye has never beheld anything without first seeing that Reality manifested therein. May Fortune frown upon every moment of my life which does not cause my absorption in this reality to increase![18]

The above passage, penned in the light of his overwhelming vision of the 'beauty of the spiritual guide' which appeared to 'Ayn al-Quḍāt in the form of Aḥmad Ghazālī, was to make an even more illustrious entrance into the annals of Persian Sufi poetry when Jāmī (d. 898/1492) later versified the original Arabic prose in his *Subḥat al-abrār* (under the rubric, "The Tale of 'Ayn al-Quḍāt Hamadānī, who could split many a hair of knowledge, yet was still was no more than a hair wrapped around himself, for until he sought out the society of Aḥmad Ghazālī, he was unable to thread the needle of this Work") in eloquent Persian *mathnawī* verse.[19]

Probably from the earliest days of his association with Baraka, it had become clear to his contemporaries that 'Ayn al-Quḍāt's dry juridical gown and turban harbored a fiery prodigy of the spirit. Even before his composition of the *Zubdat* he had recounted his "abhorrence for the pursuit of knowledge" which he felt to be due to his preoccupation with the 'affairs of the heart'—meaning the pursuit of the spiritual discipline and Path of Sufism. "I even wondered how I could ever find leisure to write anything again," he noted,[20] admitting that if his friends, who hung on his words, had not prevailed upon him he would never have put pen to paper.[21]

The depth and extent of his absorption in God were also revealed

---

18. T, introduction, pp. 51-52.
19. Jāmī, *Mathnawī-yi Haft awrang,* ed. Murtaḍā Mudarris-Gīlānī, 2nd edit. (Tehran: Sa'dī 1366 A.Hsh./1987), p. 461. As Aḥmad Mujāhid points out *(Majmū'a-yi āthār-i fārsī-yi Ahmad Ghazālī,* Tehran: Intishārāt-i Dānishgāh-i Tihrān 1370 A.Hsh./1991, 2nd edit., p. 116), Jāmī's poetic gloss on 'Ayn al-Quḍāt's encounter with the *'Sulṭān-i ṭarīqat'* Aḥmad Ghazālī exemplifies the truth that intellectual knowledge and scholarly investigation alone—however profound, sincere or dedicated—are ultimately doomed to spiritual failure without the intercessionary 'company' *(ṣuḥbat)* with and 'service' *(khidmat)* to the spiritual guide. And here Jāmī reaffirms the totally 'Sufi' context of 'Ayn al-Quḍāt's thought.
20. *Zubdat,* p. 2; cited in T, introduction, p. 66.
21. *Ibid.*

through certain remarkable charismatic powers *(karāmāt),* such as one ability, through mastery of the powers of certain divine Names and supplications, to slay and revive a man (the circumstances of which are recounted in great detail in the *Tamhīdāt).*[22] Reflecting back, a decade later, on this incident—which had, of course, aroused the jealousy of the weak-spirited, ignorant common people and evoked the wrath of the theocrats of Hamadān—'Ayn al-Quḍāt was very emphatic that wisdom is self-known, openly admitting his conscious awareness and acceptance of the existence of such 'miracles' worked through (rather than *by)* him:

> But people just do not listen to me. They think I am a magician. However, just as Jesus worked miracles and with his breath made birds come to life, made the blind into seers and the dead to rise[23]...so the Friend of God *(walī-yi khudā)* has [similar] charismatic powers, and this destitute wretch [i.e. 'Ayn al-Quḍāt] also possesses these powers.[24]

Placing himself under the tutelage of Aḥmad Ghazālī, 'Ayn al-Quḍāt progressed more rapidly than ever in his spiritual quest. Recounting his encounter with Aḥmad Ghazālī, he wrote:

> The majesty of the pre-eternal dominion became radiantly clear to me and my own reason and knowledge were shattered and dissolved in its glory. I was left as an author incognizant of himself. His Real Existence supplanted and embraced my being and garbed my illusory being in Himself.[25]

With such charismatic gifts and mystical visions, 'Ayn al-Quḍāt soon became known as a sage in his own right, and gained considerable popularity as a lecturer.[26] In 517/1123, at age 25, he began to write a series of epistles, actually letters of spiritual counsel, to

22. T 250-52.
23. The author refers to part of the Koranic account of the miracles of Jesus, found in Surah V: 110.
24. T 250, no. 327.
25. T introduction, p. 55.
26. In one of his epistles he states: "Every day I teach seven or eight classes in different fields of knowledge to diverse types of people. In each class—God knows best—I do not ever discourse in less than a thousand words. I do not know whether I will lose my life because of my tongue or my pen!" Cited in T, introduction, p. 77.

disciples and close friends. Two bulky volumes of these letters have been published by 'Ayn al-Quḍāt's indefatigable Persian editor, Afif Osseiran.[27] These volumes, however, represent only a third of the entire correspondence of the young visionary![28] As 'Ayn al-Quḍāt wrote at the time: "For some time now I have been so wrapped up in this passion that I compose four or five different letters every day and night. Each letter contains some eighty lines and every word therein is a priceless gem." It would seem that by the time he was twenty-eight years old, 'Ayn al-Quḍāt had reached full intellectual maturity, and from then on the epithet *'Ayn al-Quḍāt* (Cynosure of Judges) appears in the letters addressed to him by Aḥmad Ghazālī,[29] who also habitually addressed this brilliant disciple as his own "son" and the "light of my eyes."[30]

Although 'Ayn al-Quḍāt's writing is intimately bound up with his life as a practising *Qāḍī* and public lecturer in Hamadān, there are several passages in his epistles where he describes his daily life in the Sufi cloister *(Khānaqāh).* The main emphasis of his literary efforts was to advance the course of his many Sufi disciples on the mystical path. His writings may be seen as a pedagogical device for those same disciples, the study of the *Tamhīdāt* revealing how inseparable the spiritual experiences and the Path *(ṭarīqat)* of Sufism were from the philosophical thought of the sage.[31]

The following section is devoted to examining the literary style and inspiration of the *Tamhīdāt,* the longest Persian prose work and most mature composition of 'Ayn al-Quḍāt on mystical theology, followed by three other sections which discuss the leitmotifs of mystical death, imaginalization *(tamaththul),* annihilation *(fanā'),* selflessness and obliteration *(maḥw),* which appear in the *Tamhīdāt.*

---

27. *Nāmahā-yi 'Ayn al-Quḍāt Hamadānī,* vol. 1, edited by 'Alīnaqī Munzawī and Afif Osseiran (Tehran: Intishārāt-i bunyād-i farhang-i Īrān # 73, 1969); vol. 2, edited by 'Alīnaqī Munzavī and Afif Osseiran (Tehran: Intishārāt-i bunyād-i farhang-i Īrān # 138, 1971)
28. See T, introduction, p. 80.
29. T, introduction, p. 46.
30. These letters have been published by N. Pourjavady: *Mukātabāt-i Khwāja Aḥmad Ghazālī bā 'Ayn al-Quḍāt Hamadānī* (Tehran: Intishārāt-i Khānaqāh-i Ni'matullāhī 1356 A.Hsh./1977), introduction, p. 9.
31. T, introduction, pp. 79-80.

II. ECSTASY IN A SEA OF MEANING: THE INSPIRATION OF THE *TAMHĪDĀT*

Four years before his execution, at age thirty-three in 525/1131, at the hands of the powerful Seljuk vizier Abu'l-Qāsim al-Darguzīnī, 'Ayn al-Quḍāt composed his longest work: *Tamhīdāt*. The prose style of this work, written nearly nine hundred years ago, is very straightforward—one might even say 'modern in form'[32]—and devoid of conscious ornament. Nevertheless, owing to the great number of outwardly unrelated allusions to the Koran and *Ḥadīth* and the generally ecstatic disposition of the author, the language is often dense and difficult to follow. His literary style, aside from his original analytical approach to theology, most resembles that of his master, Aḥmad Ghazālī, concerning whose difficult writings Nasrollah Pourjavady has observed that "the literal meanings of his words acted as mere husks for the symbolic allusions contained within them; such expressions were intended to be understood only by mystics endowed with intuitive 'taste', 'heart-savour' *(ahl-i dhawq).*"[33] "L'esthétique soufie, chez 'Ayn al-Quzāt," observes Christiane Tortel , commenting upon the *Tamhīdāt*'s original literary style, "est construite sur une vision sans stéréotype, totalement subjective. C'est une esthétique non normative."[34]

In the *Tamhīdāt* 'Ayn al-Quḍāt basically confines himself to a discussion of the essential principles of Sufism rather than incidental corollaries. So esoteric and startling were its contents, however, that the author, when arrested, deliberately attempted to hide the fact that he had composed it, not even giving it a final title.[35] Nonetheless, he clearly intended the work to serve as a lasting monument to

---

32. As Majd al-'Alā Khurāsānī pointed out, "'Ayn al-Quḍāt," in *Armagān* (1306/1926), pp. 31-41
33. N. Pourjavady, *Mukātabāt-i Aḥmad Ghazālī,* introduction, p. 9. The notion of 'taste' is also fundamental's to Abū Ḥāmid's epistemology; see E.L. Ormsby, "The Taste of Truth: the Structure of Experience in al-Ghazālī's *Al-Munqidh min al-ḍalāl*" in W.B. Hallaq & D. Little, *Islamic Studies Presented to Charles J. Adams* (Leiden: Brill 1991), pp. 133-52
34. *'Ayn al-Quzāt Hamadāni: Les Tentations Métaphysiques (Tamhīdāt),* Présentation, traduction du persan et de l'arabe, et notes par Christiane Tortel (Paris: Les Deux Océans 1992), introduction, p. 25.
35. T, introduction, p. 15.

his mature theosophical speculation rather than as a treatise merely composed for his own generation, as he explicitly stated at the end of the book.[36]

As shown above (pp. 287ff.), the writings of ʿAyn al-Quḍāt cannot be understood without recourse to the mystical terminology and spiritual disciplines of Sufism. In his Arabic language treatise *Shakwā'l-gharīb,* 'Complaint of a Stranger in Exile', after providing an extensive discussion of the history of Sufism,[37] ʿAyn al-Quḍāt notes that just as each field of academic study has its own technical language, the words of the Muslim mystics likewise cannot be understood without recourse to the terminology *(iṣṭilāḥāt)* of the Sufis. And after defending his thought as directly belonging to the classical Sufi tradition—he even indexes his own utterances by reference to the pre-eminent Islamic mystics[38]—and giving his unqualified support to the 'science of Sufism' *(ʿilm-i taṣawwuf),* he states unequivocally: "Every expression of mine occurring in these anecdotes requires the preparation of rules and the laying down of fundamentals of the science of Sufism, so that its meaning may be fully realized."[39] The *Tamhīdāt,* likewise, which was written shortly before the *Shakwā'l-gharīb,* and many passages of which are meditations upon the dicta of the Sufis, also ardently pleads the cause of the Sufi tradition.[40]

In the first few pages of the book, interpreting the famous *ḥadīth* used by many Islamic esotericists to defend their right to freedom of

36. "Come forth from selfhood if you can, that you may hear this mystery and be worthy of these words. I know that you will say, 'Yes,' and although I have said that the person being addressed [in this book] is you, my intent was to address not those present today, but those who are to come after me and who will gain extraordinary profit from the study of this book." –T 327.
37. For the Arabic text, see Afif Osseiran, *Muṣannafat-i ʿAyn al-Quḍāt Hamadhānī* (Tehran: Dānishgāh 1341 A.Hsh./1962). For an English translation, see A.J. Arberry, *Apologia.* For an extensive discussion of the ideas in this treatise, see Hamid Dabashi's article "ʿAyn al-Quḍāt Hamadhānī wa *Risāla-i Shakwā'l-gharīb*-i ū," *Iran Nameh,* 11/1 (1993), pp. 57-74. My analysis here draws on some of the conclusions of Dr. Dabashi's study.
38. Even adducing 13 pages of definitions of Sufism to support his arguments, on which, see Arberry, *Apologia,* pp. 43-56
39. Arberry, *Apologia,* pp. 57-8.
40. Cf. T, p. 300, for instance, where the highest mystical adept is defined as "a *ḥulūlī* who is a Sufi."

expression: "Speak to people according to their intellectual capacities," 'Ayn al-Quḍāt observes that the bewilderment and incomprehension of some non-mystics in the face of his exposition betray their own intellectual limitations, rather than any deficiency in his own powers of expression:

> In these pages certain sayings will be related which are not meant for that dear friend,[41] but rather for others among the lovers who were absent during its composition. The latter should also receive some benefit – so do not imagine that you were my sole object in its composition. All that one hears which does not correspond to one's spiritual station or is beyond one's intellectual capacity will always be misunderstood and rejected anyway. My friend, do you imagine that the Koran was addressed to just one group of people, or to one hundred tribes, or to one hundred thousand tribes? No, each verse, each word, is addressed to a different person, intended for another individual – or rather, for another universe. In the same way, each sentence written in these pages possesses its own particular spiritual station and state; each word has its own peculiar purpose and unto each aspirant a different discourse will be directed.[42]

He also clearly felt, prophetically, the immense importance of his opus in the history of Sufism, boasting:

> To extol these words it befits you to surrender yourself utterly to them. After all, do you not realize that among all the possible styles of literary expression, nothing can be uttered with greater precision and clarity than this? You must transcend both worlds[43] – then you will be able to give a proper reckoning of these words and commune with them. From the two worlds, the world of the soul *(malakūt)* and the world of divine Sovereignty *(jabarūt),* no more than this can ever be brought into this world. Alas! How can you understand how many thousands of spiritual stations which we have passed beyond in this one chapter alone! And from each spiritual realm beheld we have proffered the reader the main features and highlights *(zubda)* of its gnosis in

---

41. An unknown correspondent.
42. T 6-7.
43. Meaning: Earth and heaven, this world and the next.

the garb of the mysteries inscribed herein.[44]

Although the more sober nomocentricity of certain mediæval Islamic theological writings such as Muḥammad Ghazālī's *Iḥyā' ulūm al-dīn* does not appear in the *Tamhīdāt,* its intensely autobiographical style does, in a way, resemble Ghazālī's own autobiography, *al-Munqidh min al-ḍalāl.* And as in *al-Munqidh,* the author's personality haunts every paragraph with sighs, cries and confessions of human impotence, somewhat reminiscent of Descartes' *Discourse on Method.*[45] The Persian penchant for flamboyant expression hardly appears in the book: 'Ayn al-Quḍāt's prose is intimate and spontaneous, while also quite complex, combining oracular utterance, passionate rapture and the weighty symbolic diction of poetic inspiration, with philosophical depth, prolix theological lore and rich mystical anagogy. Commenting on the poetic polysemy and multi-leveled complexity of 'Ayn al-Quḍāt's use of language, T. Izutsu remarked,

> In Hamadānī's view, nothing could be further from the truth [than]... that there is a one-to-one correspondence between a word and its meaning. The world of meanings is something of a infinitely delicate, flexible and flowing nature. It has no such rigid stability as corresponds to the formal or material rigidity of words... Compared with the vast field of meaning that lies behind each word, the latter is nothing more than a tiny, insignificant point. The word is but a narrow gate through which the human mind steps into a boundless *sea of meaning.* ...By simply observing from outside the word thus employed, one could hardly judge the width and depth of the meaning that is intended to be conveyed by it. This is particularly true when the meaning that has been poured into the mold of a word happens to be backed by a profound mystical experience.[46]

Some of the following quotations from the *Tamhīdāt* actually

44. T 309, no. 406.
45. Here again, his style reflects Muḥammad Ghazālī, who, as Watt reflected, "introduces his discussions in a manner reminiscent of Descartes." W.M. Watt, *The Faith and Practice of Al-Ghazālī* (London: Allen & Unwin 1953), p. 12.
46. "Mysticism and the Linguistic Problem of Equivocation in the Thought of 'Ayn al-Quḍāt Hamadānī," *Studia Islamica,* XXXI (1970), pp. 157-58. Italics mine.

seem to trace the form of the waves in this 'sea of meaning' – to use Professor Izutsu's analogy. Here we behold the writer adrift and anchorless in God's shoreless ocean, exposing himself as one intoxicated and bereft of self:

> There was once a time when the heart of this love-intoxicated author attended and audited his tongue, such that the tongue became the orator and the heart listener. Formerly, I often set out to write things, but for some time now my tongue has been listening to the heart, the heart being orator and the tongue listener. Strange and wondrous are the mystical states and metaphysical 'moments' *(awqāt)* which have, for some time, been revealed to this wretch![47]

> Love's vehement fury *(sawdā)* has made me so bereft-of-self and in passion so enrapt *(bīkhwud wa shīfta)* that I don't even know what I am saying. Suddenly the thread of my discourse snaps. Yet I still come out on top, more upright than before. He wrestles with me – until it becomes clear which of the two of us has been thrown down to the ground. But I know that it will be I who will be thrown down – as so many others just like me have been also hurled to the earth. The lovers and those afflicted with love-fervor shall pass away; love-fervor and Love are eternal.[48]

> Ah me! That night, the night of the festival, I attained to a place in which I saw everything that was in pre-eternity and all that will be in post-eternity within the letter *alif.* Ah! I need to find someone who can understand what I am saying![49]

> However much I try to flee from the realm of writing, writing pursues me and grabs me by the hand, not allowing me either to abide in what I have written nor to relinquish the act of writing.[50]

In encountering passages such as these it is useful to remind ourselves that ultimately, only the author and his Muse know the truth and meaning of such inspiration. No matter how much we try to analyze and dissect the words of any God-intoxicated mystic, much of

47. T 16.
48. T 237
49. T 347, no. 459.
50. T 324.

what they pronounce will not be within reason's capacity to grasp. Many passages in the *Tamhīdāt* underline the fact that only readers having direct experience of selflessness, and consequently, of 'annihilation', will be able to follow fully the thread of 'Ayn al-Quḍāt's exposition. In one place in the text the author boasts that his "utterances can be contained neither in this world, or the next;"[51] in another place (an epistle) he tells his correspondent:

> What you understand of this epistle depends upon your own reason and intelligence. To comprehend it deeply would take you many days and require a perfect development *(sulūk)* [in the disciplines of Sufism]. For these writings are the fruit of fifteen years of my own esoteric training *(sulūk)* and what it took me *fifteen years* to understand will not be fathomed by someone else in *fifty years!*[52]

Elsewhere, explaining the doctrine of welcoming adversity (see below, pp. 325-8) through which the Sufi's 'mystical death' is realized, 'Ayn al-Quḍāt tells us that only direct experience of adversity and tribulation can convey his ideas to the aspirant:

> Only one who has been wrenched out of selfhood by grief and fear can relish the taste of these words. Did you not hear what one of those Sufis, who attained Union with God, said: "One who knows God is made to suffer extended misfortune and adversity." Ah! it was for this reason that I mentioned above my master's saying, "None knows God but God."
>
> O friend! He alone knows Himself. When the moth *becomes* the candle's flame, what benefit then does flame gain from flame? What joy, what profit comes to it? And yet, when separate from fire, how can it enjoy itself—for how should it endure the company of aught but fire? Reason can never reach this place! If you have [understood] something of that which transcends reason, you will grasp for yourself what we say.[53]

Stressing the universal truth known to all mystics that (in Blake's words) "the light of the sun when she unfolds it/depends upon the eye that beholds it,") 'Ayn al-Quḍāt often reminds readers that

51. T 209.
52. T, introduction, p. 82.
53. T 282-83, no. 367.

understanding his writing depends more on their spiritual sensitivity rather than any philosophical breadth of learning.

> Ah! you still are fettered by the passions of your lower soul *(nafs-i ammāra)* and so cannot hear the recital of these mysteries except with the ear of discursive reason *(gūsh-i qāl)*. Wait till your soul converts, becomes Muslim—"My satan became Muslim by my will"[54]—and takes on the heart's hue: then your heart will communicate to you in the language of direct intuition *(ḥāl)* all that it could not tell you in the tongue of dialectical discourse *(qāl)*. Then you will understand how true is the adage that 'the language of *ḥāl* speaks with superior reason to the language of *qāl*'. Whatever you read [in this book] and cannot comprehend, beg for forgiveness and seek a way to realize its truth. But if you do understand, I wish you good fortune![55]

This supralrational dimension of 'Ayn al-Quḍāt's thought is particularly evident in his exposition of the 'more-than-mortal' Reality of the Prophet Muḥammad. He conceives of the Prophet as having possessed a body in merely a figurative sense, and being, in truth, a spirit totally abstracted from matter. Here, following a complex and esoteric exposition of prophetology in the *Tamhīdāt*, he reiterates the natural incapacity of the non-mystic to analyze his doctrine:

> These words are beyond your capacity to understand. What suits your capacity is that you realize that the entire world is but a shadow of Muḥammad. When the sun vanishes, what do you think, does the shadow remain? No, it never remains. "The Day when We shall roll up the heavens as a recorder rolleth up a written scroll." [Koran XXI: 104] Alas! When the body is placed beside divine Reality *(ḥaqīqat)*, and takes on its hue, this occurrence portends the extinction of the world. When the Sun of divine Reality sinks into nonexistence, the light of the body is extinguished. I am an infidel if I myself know what I am saying! Alas! If the speaker does not know what he is saying, how can the listener know what he hears?[56]

* * *

54. Badī' al-Zamān Furūzānfar, *Aḥadīth-i Mathnawī* (Tehran: Dānishgāh-i Tihrān 1335 A.Hsh./1956), no. 459.
55. T 196-97.
56. T 239, nos. 326-27.

All those writings of our author—the *Tamhīdāt* in particular—composed during the final five years of his life (between the death of Aḥmad Ghazālī in 1126 and his own execution in 1131) are filled with the consciousness and anticipation of death. There are several places in the *Tamhīdāt* [57] where 'Ayn al-Quḍāt directly predicts his death, or invokes his future martyrdom, lamenting, with precognizant vision, his own execution. Near the end of the ninth chapter of the *Tamhīdāt,* he relates how a certain bigoted jurisprudent in Baghdad had signed a decree and issued a *fatwā* for his execution (although his imprisonment was still some four years away).[58] In accordance with his belief in the virtue of resignation to adversity *(balā)* and view of misfortune as God-given grace, 'Ayn al-Quḍāt accepted his fate as enjoined in this unjust legal edict with eloquent irony:

> If they ask for a *fatwā* from you, my friend, deliver them one. Let them have your personal adjudication in respect of me. Personally, my will is that anyone asked for their legal pronouncement should write this Koranic verse in response: "To God belongs the Names Most Beautiful/so call to Him by them/and leave the crowd of them who blaspheme His Names." [VII: 180] As for myself, I pray for such a death *[qatl:* execution] but alas! the time is still distant! When will it happen? Ah! "That is surely no great matter for God." [XIV: 20][59]

In order to understand 'Ayn al-Quḍāt's obsession with death and to grasp the intellectual foundations of his doctrine of annihilation, it is necessary to summarize the antecedents of the doctrine of *fanā'* in the Sufi tradition, which we take up below.

57. Cf. T 236; 250-51; 309, no. 407; 327, n. 428.
58. On which, see also Carl Ernst's study, *Words of Ecstasy in Sufism* (Albany: SUNY Press 1985), p. 111.
59. T 251, no. 329.

III. IN QUEST OF ANNIHILATION: THE SPIRITUAL PRACTICE AND PATH OF DEATH

'Tis love, not years nor limbs, that can
Make the martyr or the man

– Richard Crashaw

The essence of the doctrine of annihilation, as it was generally understood by Sufis from the earliest days down to the fifth/eleventh and sixth/twelfth centuries when 'Alī Hujwīrī (d. 463/1071) and 'Ayn al-Quḍāt flourished, is summed up in the description by Junayd (d. 298/910) of Sufism as "a quality in the mystic which takes up residence." Pressed to elucidate this quality, Junayd explained, "In essence, it is a quality of God, but outwardly of the Sufi himself. That is, its being demands the annihilation *(fanā')* of the servant's attributes, which in turn implies subsistence *(baqā')* of God's attributes. So Sufism is a quality of God even though outwardly it demands constant striving on the Sufi's part, which is an attribute of the servant."[60]

The Sufis were careful to guard against advocating "the un-Islamic idea of identifying the human ego with God...and denied both the incarnation of God in man and the total mergence of the individual and finite human ego in God."[61] Hujwīrī complained that many Sufis grossly misinterpreted the doctrine of *fanā'*, "wrongly imagining that annihilation signifies loss of essence and destruction of personality, and that subsistence indicates the subsistence of God in man" and noted that, "both these notions are absurd."[62] On the contrary, states Hujwīrī, annihilation is experienced by the mystic "through vision of the majesty of God and through the revelation of Divine omnipotence to his heart, so that in the overwhelming sense of His majesty this world and the next world are obliterated from his mind, and 'states' and 'stations' appear contemptible in the sight of his aspiring thought...he becomes dead to reason and passion alike,

60. Cited by J. Nurbakhsh, *Sufism: Meaning, Knowledge and Unity* (New York), p. 19.
61. Fazlur Rahman, in EI^2, s.v. *Bakā*.
62. *Kashf al-Maḥjūb*, abridged trans. R.A. Nicholson (London 1936), p. 243.

dead even to annihilation itself, and in that annihilation of annihilation his tongue proclaims God, and his mind and body are humbled and abased."[63] He also cautions that "whoever explains these terms otherwise, i.e. annihilation as meaning 'annihilation of substance' and subsistence as meaning 'subsistence of God (in Man)', is a heretic and a Christian."[64] To Hujwīrī, annihilation is a means to knowledge and higher consciousness. Those today who would mistakenly equate *fanā'* with world-weariness, brokenness of spirit, suicidal neurosis or some sort of crude Freudian *thanatos,* will find no evidence to support their interpretation in the *Kashf al-maḥjūb.*[65]

The traditional doctrine of annihilation as it is expressed, more or less universally, by Semitic mystics, Christian and Muslim alike, mainly refers to the annihilation of the individual self. In his essay on the 'Intellectual Fraternity' between the European and Asiatic cultures, Ananda K. Coomaraswamy quotes these verses of William Blake:

> *I will go down to self annihilation and eternal death*
> *Lest the Last Judgement come and find me unannihilate*
> *And I be seiz'd and giv'n into the hands of my own Selfhood.*[66]

Coomaraswamy remarks that the 'quest for annihilation' is a universal aspiration found in all religious traditions, for "one could not find in Asiatic scripture a more typically Asiatic purpose than is revealed in his [Blake's] passionate will to be delivered from the bondage of division." In the *Book of Thel,* William Blake himself has a cloud preach the doctrine of *fanā'* in words as one would expected to have heard from a Rūmī or an Ibn 'Arabī: "O maid, I tell thee, when I pass away/ It is to tenfold life, to love, to peace and raptures holy."

---

63. *Kashf al-Maḥjūb,* p. 246.
64. *Ibid.*
65. *Ibid.,* pp. 242-3. Traditional interpreters of the doctrine of *fanā'* explicitly reject such pseudo-psychological reductionism. See, e.g. Javad Nurbakhsh, "The Psychology of Annihilation and Subsistence" in Nurbakhsh, *Sufism: Fear and Hope* (New York: KNP 1982), pp. 90ff. Also cf. the remarks of Ḥakīm Tirmidhī concerning the dynamic nature of *fanā'* below, p. 490.
66. A. Coomaraswamy, *The Dance of Siva: Fourteen Indian Essays* (New York 1924), p. 113. The verses belong to Blake's epic poem *Milton,* XIV: 21, in G. Keynes (ed.) *Blake: Complete Writings* (London: Oxford University Press 1972), p. 495.

Similar expressions of this doctrine occur in the English metaphysical poets: in particular John Donne and Richard Crashaw, as well as in the Catholic mystical poet, San Juan de la Cruz. According to this Spanish friend of God, the spiritual method of the Christian mystic "demands only the one thing necessary: true self-denial, exterior and interior, through surrender of self both to suffering for Christ and to *annihilation in all things.*" Thus the mystic should realize that "the greatness of the work he accomplishes will be measured by his annihilation for God in the sensory and spiritual parts of his soul. When he is brought to nothing, the highest degree of humility, the spiritual union between his soul and God will be effected. This union is the most noble and sublime state attainable in this life."[67]

If 'selflessness' is chamberlain to vision of God, it is the 'self' which is the main obstacle on the path of annihilation.[68] It is also in terms of transcendental doctrines such as annihilation that mystics of diverse religions unite on common ground. R.A. Nicholson's observation, that "the Moslem's conception of personality is different from ours. In Islam God, not man, is the measure of things"[69] — although true in respect to Western humanist thought, in respect to *Western mysticism,* as the above quotations show, is obviously quite mistaken, for the realization of 'annihilation of self' is the true "measure of things" in all mysticism, whether Oriental or

67. "The Ascent of Mount Carmel" translated by K. Kavanaugh & O. Rodriguez, *The Collected Works of St. John of the Cross* (Washington: ICS 1979), pp. 124-25. (Italics in the above passage are mine). For a good exposition of San Juan de la Cruz's ideas about mystical death, see George Tavard, *Poetry and Contemplation in St. John of the Cross* (Ohio University Press 1988), pp. 203-207. For a discussion of the influence of Persian Sufism on his thought, see Luce López Baralt, *San Juan de la Cruz y el Islam: Estudio sobre las filiaciones semíticas de su literatura mística.* (Puerto Rico 1985).

68. In the words of the modern Catholic mystical thinker Simone Weil: "Humility is the refusal to exist outside God. The self is only the shadow which sin and error cast by stopping the light of God, and I take this shadow for a being. ...All the things that I see, hear, breathe, touch, eat; all the beings I meet—I deprive the sum total of all that contact with God, and I deprive God of contact with all that in so far as something in me says 'I'."– *Gravity and Grace,* translated by E. Craufurd (London: ARK 1987), pp. 35-36.

69. *The Idea of Personality in Sufism* (Cambridge University Press 1922, reprinted Lahore 1970), p. 100.

Occidental.

'Ayn al-Quḍāt's doctrine of annihilation is likewise based on the destruction of the lower soul. Without annihilation of the ego, spiritual consciousness cannot exist. In the language of theology, one cannot be said to possess a soul unless one passes beyond the level of "There is no god…" *(Lā ilāha)* and reaches the level of "but God" *(illā'llāh).* Thus, the process of 'raising consciousness' consists paradoxically in negating selfhood. This path of negation, like the Pseudo-Dionysian *via negativa* or the *noche oscura* of San Juan de la Cruz, is fraught with danger, for, as our philosopher pronounces, the "whole world is caught up in the realm of negation *(Lā ilāha),* wherein a hundred thousand souls have been bereft of their soul. On this Path, only one who reaches affirmation *(illā 'llāh)* possesses a soul; one barred from this degree possesses none of the soul's perfections."[70]

Emphasizing the centrality of Sufi discipline in his thought, 'Ayn al-Quḍāt notes that such annihilation and self-effacement is purely the product of discipleship. Thus, "the highest blessing for the seeker of Truth," he declares in the *Zubdat,* "is to exert himself wholeheartedly in the service of a man who has *annihilated* himself in God and the vision of God. And when he has passed his life serving his master, God will quicken him with a pure life; nothing of this is known to the rest of the *'ulamā'* aside from an empty name and a hollow form."[71]

In bringing the disciple to realize and to accept this 'annihilation of self', the part played by the spiritual master is similar to that of the Koran. Here, one is reminded of Rūmī's advice to aspirants to "inquire as to the meaning of the Koran solely from the Koran itself, or else from one who has set fire to his selfish passions. One who has immolated himself upon the Koran, and become abased, so that his spirit in essence has *become* the Koran."[72] In the following passage, 'Ayn al-Quḍāt even goes so far as to describe the ideal disciple as one who "loses himself in the master." If, in his exposition below,

---

70. T 75.
71. T introduction, p. 71.
72. R.A. Nicholson (ed.,)*The Mat̲hnawí of Jalálu'ddín Rúmí* (London & Leiden 1925-40; repr. London 1982), Bk. V̄: 3128-29.

the verbs may differ (that is, 'to lose oneself' is used in lieu of 'to annihilate oneself'), the meaning is still the same: the mystic must die to selfhood through love of God—a love which is beheld in the mirror of the spiritual guide:

> The more I write about it, the more complicated the issue becomes [yet there is no alternative]: know that, in general terms, the disciple *(murīd)* is one who loses himself in the master *(dar pīr bāzad).* First, he loses his religion and then, himself. Do you know the meaning of 'losing one's religion'? It means that if the spiritual master commands him to contradict and disregard the dictates of his own religion, the disciple obeys. If the disciple, in order to conform with his master's directives, does not act contrary to his own religion, he is still a disciple of his own personal religion, not his master's disciple.
>
> If the disciple pursues the course of his own desires, he is a self-worshipper and an egotist. Discipleship is to adore the master *(murīdī pīr parastī buwad)* and to gird oneself with the cincture of Almighty God and his Prophet (peace be upon him!)
>
> ...This writing is so extremely complicated that finding someone who understands it on the face of the earth is extremely rare, for among the thousands of spiritual aspirants who wholeheartedly pursue the Path of God, only one is ever brought into the narrow straits of disciplic devotion *(irādat).*
>
> ...In the whole world I seek one disciple whose skin I can stuff with straw and then yoke it up and hang him from the sun's round disc so that the folk of the world may take heed. ...If I find an aspirant [on the Sufi Path] to suit my heart's wishes, and if he lives according to my rule for two or three years—no less—I can reveal to him the verity of these spiritual truths.[73]

The mysticism of the 'Light of Muḥammad' as it was espoused by Sahl al-Tustarī (d. 896) and his disciple Ḥallāj (d. 922) also appears fully developed in the *Tamhīdāt:* the entire book is very much in the tradition of Ḥallāj's esoteric *imitatio Muhammadi,*[74] and could be described as one long love poem elaborating the Judge of Hamadān's passionate love for the spiritual reality of the Prophet. The book is full of descriptions of his visions of Muḥammad, and it

73. T, introduction, pp. 98-99.
74. See A. Schimmel, "The Light of Muhammad" in *And Muhammad is His Messenger* (Chapel Hill: University of North Carolina Press 1985), pp. 32, 124-29.

is rare to find a passage whose essential ideas or whose outer expressions do not focus on the *Ḥadīth.* According to 'Ayn al-Quḍāt, all self-knowledge depends upon knowing 'the soul of Muḥammad'. Whoever desires to acquire gnosis *(ma'rifa)* of the Divine Essence, must make the "soul of his reality *(nafs-i ḥaqīqat-i khwud)* into a mirror and gaze therein," where, he explains, "the mystic will recognize the soul of Muḥammad."[75] So behind all epistemology lies prophetology.

Weaving the metaphors of annihilation and intoxication into the warp of the Koranic tapestry while expounding the mystical doctrine that 'the Kingdom of Heaven is within you', the following passages expound the oft-reiterated idea that 'Sufism is selflessness', and are particularly good examples of the densely Koranic style of the *Tamhīdāt:*

> O friend! When the wayfarer settles down in the city of servanthood *('ubūdiyyat)* which is his own heart, he enters Paradise. "Enter thou among My servants! Enter thou My paradise" [Koran LXXXIX: 29-30]. In this Paradise he is asked, "Do you desire anything from Me?" He replies, "O Lord, we desire annihilation and selflessness from you." So a wine from the liqueurs of divine Union and intimacy is poured into his inner being so that every place it spills, its alchemical transformation works upon him. The Koranic expression "a pure wine" [LXXVI: 21] alludes to this.[76]
>
> * * *
>
> When God wills that we view ourselves within His Light— "Have they not considered the dominion of the heavens and the earth" [Koran VII: 185]— His light invades and ravages the soul of the spiritual pilgrim. "Lo! Kings, when they enter a township, ruin it." [XXVII: 34] Laying hand onto the raft of God's Being, the pilgrim's soul tries to save itself. "Doth not thy Lord suffice, since He is Witness over all things? How is it? Are they still in doubt about the encounter with their Lord? Lo! does He not encompass everything?" [XLI: 53-54] So our being is entirely absorbed and swallowed in the omnipresence of His Light. "Vision comprehendeth Him not, but He comprehendeth all

75. T 58.
76. T 291-92, no. 383.

> vision." [VI: 103]
>
> In this station a man realizes what it means to behold his own being [reflected] in the mirror of the Light of the Eternal *(nūr-i ṣamadī).* Call me an infidel if I have not seen it myself. The exposition of this mystical state by the Prophet Muḥammad in saying "Whoever has seen me, has seen God," becomes apparent at this sublime spiritual station. And do not the exclamations of Ḥallāj and Bāyazīd[77] have the same significance?[78]

As in all traditional Sufism, the Koran and Koranically-based contemplative disciplines[79] also play a central role in 'Ayn al-Quḍāt's mystical theology. The following passage, in which the numinous rhythms of Koranic Arabic accompany the melodious Persian as a kind of chorale, reads as a virtual 'hymn to annihilation'. Employing theological language in interpreting the esoteric meaning of the ritual prayer, 'Ayn al-Quḍāt describes his experience of 'annihilation in prayer':

> Have you ever seen the existence of both the terrestial and celestial worlds *(mulk u malakūt)* obliterated in [the recitation of] *Allāh akbar?* Have you ever witnessed 'establishment' (*ithbat*) after 'obliteration' *(maḥw)* in the act of magnifying God *(takbīr)?* Have you ever given thanks for the grace of 'establishment-after-obliteration' in uttering "Boundless Praise belongs to God" *(al-ḥamdu'lillāh kathīran)?* ...When a man becomes effaced in "and I am not one of the idolaters," [Koran VI: 79] what meaning at this point can polytheistic dualism have? How can one who understands that "All that dwells upon the earth is perishing" [Koran LV: 26] ever be a polytheist?[80]

Elsewhere 'Ayn al-Quḍāt describes the experience of being encompassed by the Koran, becoming the point under the *bā'* of the *basmala,* which leads him to elaborate, with forceful lucidity, a theory of 'annihilation in the Koran':

> Alas! In the Koran we see nothing but black letters upon white paper. As long as you are 'in existence' *(dar wujūd),* nothing but

77. "I am the Truth" and "Lord, how great is my glory." See above, p. xvii.
78. T 273-74, nos. 357-359.
79. On which, see Muhammad Isa Waley's study below, pp. 497-552.
80. T 84-85.

> black and white is seen; when you depart from 'existence' the Word of God *(kalām Allāh,* i.e. the Koran) will obliterate you in its own being and then will bring you forth from obliteration into consolidation *(ithbāt).* Having realized consolidation you will see no more blackness – all you behold is white. So read the verse: "With God is the source of the Book." [XIII: 39] O Chevalier, the Koran was sent down to mankind swathed in many thousands of veils. If the majesty of the dot under the *bā'* of the *basmala* were to fall upon the earth or the heavens, both would immediately disintegrate and melt away, for "If We had caused this Koran to descend upon a mountain, you would have seen it humbled, rent asunder by the fear of God." [LIX: 21][81]

Only when "obliterated in beauteous *lumen gloriae* of the Koran," says 'Ayn al-Quḍāt in the introductory chapter of the *Tamhīdāt,* can the Sufi realize that there is a 'Reality-beyond-Humanity' *(juz īn bashariyyat ḥaqīqatī dīgar[ast])* which is the goal of his devotion:

> One who confesses [his faith in] the Scripture beholds the bride of the Koran's spiritual beauty... perceiving with pure translucence its seven layers of meaning and while having attained to "With Him is the source of the Scripture," [XIII: 39] he understands the Koran's meaning. He becomes so drowned and effaced in its light that neither the Koran is left nor its reciter; rather, all that remains is the [transcendent] recitation and inscription.[82]

So central is the Koran's revelation to 'Ayn al-Quḍāt's inspiration, that his consciousness often appears entirely immersed in the sacred text, from which he quotes as often as five times in one sentence. Thus, in an account of another experience of 'annihilation in the Koran', the contemplative is described as envisioning the Sacred Scripture being re-composed from *within* his soul. The Divine Calligrapher, he says, inscribes the verse, 'Nūn. By the Pen...' upon the 'slate of the heart' of the adept. Both gnosis of and faith in the Koranic revelation depends on the mystic's interior attainment to 'the Library' of the pre-eternal 'Light of Muḥammad.' At that point, says 'Ayn al-Quḍāt, will "The Instructor of 'God taught me

81. T 172-73.
82. T 3-4.

courtesy, so how beauteous is my courtesy' *[Ḥadīth]* write the Koran without intermediary upon the slate of your heart."[83]

Of course, there is no such thing as annihilation for its own sake, for the purpose of following the *via negativa* is to realize a transcendental knowledge beyond the veils of selfhood. Using a poetic simile, first popularized by Ḥallāj, of the passionate self-immolation of the moth upon the candle, 'Ayn al-Quḍāt describes this type of annihilation as a 'love unto death':

> My friend, the moth's nourishment is provided by his love for the flame, for without fire the moth is distraught. The moth does not obtain life through fire until fire so completely transfigures him that he beholds the entire world to be fire. ... When the moth hurls itself into the fire, it is totally consumed, becoming itself all fire. Of self what awareness could it possess? As long as the moth abided with its 'self' it was fettered and 'hung-up'. Now, it beholds 'love' and love possesses such an [attractive] power that when love is commingled with the Beloved, the Beloved draws the lover to herself and devours him. The fire of love gives both power and nutriment to the moth. The lover is the moth and the beloved is the candle which bestows such power and nutriment to it [the moth]. Seeking these things, the moth hurls itself upon the flame. The candle-flame, that is, the beloved, commences to burn the moth, until the entire candle becomes fire: neither love nor moth remains.[84]

Having dissolved itself in fire, the lover realizes like Rūmī

> *I have tested it: death is in life*
> *When I die, arrives Eternal life.*

At this juncture it is necessary to digress slightly, from the sublimity of mystical annihilation to the lowlands of common religious faith, because to understand the zenith of the doctrine of *fanā'* one must first comprehend 'Ayn al-Quḍāt's doctrine of 'real infidelity', which is the substratum of his concept of 'annihilation in spiritual poverty'. Our discussion here will be restricted in scope because his writings on this theme have already been extensively analyzed by

83. T 174.
84. T 99-100.

scholars elsewhere.[85]

The common cleric, 'Ayn al-Quḍāt asserts, is inwardly but an infidel. Citing Koran XII: 106, "And most of them believe not in God except that they attribute partners unto Him," he concludes, "So you see, God says that most believers are infidels."[86] 'Ayn al-Quḍāt believed that most so-called Muslims who styled themselves 'believers' were, in fact, infidels in their hidden hearts. By 'infidels' here he wishes to imply that their confession of 'faith' is a mere formality, based upon imitation and reason rather than vision and revelation, and, as far as the external letter of the Law goes, although they may pass as 'believers', *vis-à-vis* the Spirit and Reality they are but 'infidels':

> If a single religion *(madhhab)* could guide a man to God, it would be the religion of Islam, but if this religion [Islam] provides no higher consciousness to the aspirant, then such a religion is worse than infidelity *(kufr)* in God's eyes. *According to the wayfarers on the Sufi Path, 'Islam' signifies that which brings a man to God and 'infidelity' refers to that which impedes the seeker and causes him to be perfunctory in his quest.*
>
> Beware! Do not think that the Judge of Hamadān is saying that infidelity is good and Islam is not so. God forbid! *I praise neither infidelity or Islam! O friend, whatever brings a man to God is Islam and whatever debars a man from the way to God is infidelity.* And the truth is that the mystical wayfarer can never put either infidelity or Islam behind him, for infidelity and Islam are two mystical states from which the seeker never escapes so long as he is 'with himself'. When liberated from selfhood, however, neither infidelity nor Islam will never catch up with you should they come running after you![87]

From this visionary standpoint, as Carl Ernst points out, 'infidelity' becomes something "all-pervasive, the process of spiritual *takfīr,* i.e. the recognition of *kufr* in oneself and the consequent self-accusation, has an inherent momentum towards transcendence, a longing

85. See Carl Ernst, *Words of Ecstasy in Sufism* , Part II, C, and Peter Awn, *Satan's Tragedy and Redemption: Iblīs in Sufi Psychology* (Leiden: E.J. Brill 1983), pp. 134-50.
86. T 204, no. 263.
87. T 23, 25.

for completion analogous to Platonic *eros* or Aristotelian *orexis*... Thus the path of infidelity is the path of progressive self-annihilation."[88] The subject of infidelity is treated extensively in the ninth chapter of the *Tamhīdāt,* entitled "Elucidation of the Reality of Faith and Infidelity"—a kind of critique of formal religion from the transcendent perspective of visionary Sufism, and perhaps the most daring attack on religious reductionism, dogmatism and clerical exotericism in the whole history of Islamic Sufism.

The Judge of Hamadān here discerns four different levels of infidelity beheld as visions the soul has of itself in its ascent towards Faith. When the all-pervasive *existential* actuality of infidelity becomes apparent to the gnostic, all the negative charge and connotation of *kufr* is dissolved, so that infidelity loses its pejorative significance and becomes inverted in meaning to connote the pure sincerity of heart held by the true lover. 'Infidelity', thus turned inside out, becomes transfigured and exalted into a sublime spiritual rank. Here 'Ayn al-Quḍāt asks rhetorically, "Do you think it insignificant or a small thing to become conscious of infidelity? Did you never hear that Muḥammad always supplicated, 'O Lord, I seek refuge in Thee from hidden polytheism'?"[89] According to his doctrine, infidelity is a spiritual fact of life, escape from which is only possible once one admits its presence within the psyche. 'Ayn al-Quḍāt's formulation of the theory of the four hierarchical levels of infidelity, demonstrating the intimate connection between infidelity, spiritual poverty and annihilation in God, is based on this paradoxical view of the relativity of faith and infidelity.

> Among the worlds through which the wayfarers [on the Sufi Path] pass, one type of infidelity is termed 'majestic' *(jalālī)* and another type is said to be 'beautiful' *(jamālī).* Ah! my friend! Now hear the description of the 'divine infidelity' *(kufr-i ilahī).*
>
> Look carefully, until the first infidelity[90] becomes manifest

---

88. Ernst, *op. cit.,* p. 81.

89. T 213. 'Hidden polytheism' *(shikr-i khafī)* alludes to *kufr-i nafs,* on which, see below.

90. The author's reference here is to the fourfold hierarchical division expounded earlier on, of the 'types of infidelity;' these are, respectively: outer infidelity *(kufr-i ẓāhir),* the soul's infidelity *(kufr-i nafs),* the heart's infidelity *(kufr-i qalb),* and the infidelity of the divine Reality *(kufr-i ḥaqīqat).*

> to you. Proceed on until you find Faith *(īmān).* Then renounce yourself until you perceive the second and third types of infidelity.[91] Next, rend your soul to shreds until you attain the fourth type of infidelity. Here you become a true believer *(mū'min).*[92] At this point the verse "And most of them believe not in God except that they attribute partners to Him," [Koran XII: 106] will show you what true Faith is. Here the verse, "Lo! I have turned my face towards Him who created the heavens and the earth, as one by nature upright, and I am not one of the idolaters,"[93] will be displayed to you. The 'self' of yourself will then be hurled against the 'Self' of Himself, until you become all Him. Here spiritual poverty *(faqr)* appears to you, and the truth of the adage: "When poverty is complete, God is present" becomes apparent—meaning that you become entirely Him.
>
> Is this 'infidelity', or not? What do you say? This experience is what the Prophetic tradition: "Poverty approaches the point of infidelity"[94] alludes to. Here Divine Oneness *(tawḥīd)* is realized. And is this not the meaning of Ḥallāj's verse:
>
> *In the religion of God I have become an infidel.*
> *But upon me infidelity is incumbent,*
> *Even if unto the Muslims it be hateful.*[95]

Thus, the summit of the mystic's aspiration is to attain the level of 'real infidelity' where the duality of the human and divine personalities are dissolved, and 'annihilation in spiritual poverty' is realized. Obviously, because this doctrine would appear as heretical to Muslim exotericists and Mullas, it was best characterized as a 'divine infidelity.'

Although 'Ayn al-Quḍāt did recognize that his religion of 'real infidelity' could not present a credible public face, nor gain for itself a place in the hearts of the fanatic clerics of his day, notwithstanding

---

91. I.e. Infidelity of the soul and infidelity of the heart.
92. I.e. When Selfhood is obliterated in God, one realizes the 'Reality-of-infidelity'; belief in the true sense of the word, beyond all taint of self-centeredness and hypocrisy, only begins here.
93. The words spoken by Abraham in the act of repenting from star-worship.
94. For a comprehensive analysis of these and other traditions cited in this passage concerning *faqr,* see Dr. Javad Nurbakhsh, *Spiritual Poverty in Sufism* (transl. Leonard Lewisohn), (London: KNP 1984), chap. 1.
95. T 214-15.

his avowed despair of the limited intellectual scope of twelfth-century Academe, he dared to compose the ninth chapter of the *Tamhīdāt* as an "Exposé of the Reality of Faith and Infidelity." In the first few pages of this chapter he predicts his own martyrdom, laments the necessity for sobriety and temperance in love, and explains why sincerity requires the Sufis, or at least the bolder visionaries amongst them, to acknowledge their inner infidelity *(shirk-i khafī)* before God and confess their religious hypocrisy. The Sufi descends into 'infidelity' voluntarily because the journey from 'false Islam' to the land of Faith can only be made upon the road of Infidelity:

> There is a group of spiritual wayfarers who are driven crazy by [contact with] the divine Reality *(diwāna-i ḥaqīqat)*. Now the founding father [the Prophet Muḥammad] of the religious Law *(sharī'a)* perceived through the Light of Prophecy that madmen must be chained and fettered, so he made the Law their chain. Ah! did you never hear of that great mystic who directed his disciple, "You may behave with God as one demented, but act straight and sober with Muḥammad"?
>
> ...The wayfarers to the Supernal Presence are of diverse types and arts. Some realized their religion through direct vision: beholding the reality of things and themselves, they saw that in fact they were girded with a cincture.[96] They desired that their outer and inner being should be in concordance, so they girded that same cincture around their bodies as well. Their idea was this: since their inner being – the locus of Divinity – is filled with infamy and error, what substantial difference would it make if their outer being or body – the focus of society's attention – were to don the cincture as well?
>
> Still another group, the drunkards, arose. They bound the cincture about themselves, discoursing with words of intoxication. Some were slain, others afflicted by His jealousy, as I myself, alas, will be! I know not when it will come to pass. As yet the hour is distant."[97]

96. *Zunnār:* this may mean here both the cord which Zoroastrians tied around their waist as well as the cord which Christians, as an officially protected minority under Muslim rule, were formerly required to wear to distinguish themselves from the Muslim majority. For the exoteric Mullas, it was a symbol of religious infidelity.
97. T 204-06.

To recapitulate our discussion above, 'Ayn al-Quḍāt's doctrine of annihilation is based on several key principles which work simultaneously to effect within the Sufi a state of 'unveiling' and selflessness.

First, Ayn al-Quḍāt exhorts his reader to serve a master who has annihilated himself in God, losing his ego in a life of service on the Spiritual Path. Discipleship, in 'Ayn al-Quḍāt's understanding, leads to effacement in God and annihilation in the spirit of the Koran's inspiration.

Second, there is 'annihilation in the Prophet': Muḥammad being visualized as a sun, and all creation as the shadow of the light of his inspiration.

Following this adherence to the Prophet comes 'annihilation in prayer': at this level certain Koranic verses ravish the mystic with their supra-formal meanings, intoxicating him with the divine vision within the "Paradise of the heart."

Lastly, the stage of 'annihilation in spiritual poverty' supervenes. This is the level of 'real infidelity' where the temporal self and the duality of the human and divine personalities are obliterated. Since 'infidelity' is a higher form of faith and the perfection of spiritual poverty is the final goal of Sufism, the Sufi finds himself absorbed in God, and although utterly poor and annihilated, subsists in a pure emptiness wherein nothing remains to veil him from the Beloved.

IV. IMAGINALIZATION OF DEATH IN THE REALM OF ANNIHILATION

Special attention has been given so far to 'Ayn al-Quḍāt's concept of the relativity of faith and his doctrine of 'real infidelity', his immersion in the sacred text of the Koran and his belief that all knowledge depends upon knowing the "soul of Muḥammad." In this section, we examine the interiorized view of the Afterlife found in the *Tamhīdāt* in order to explore the 'realm of annihilation' wherein the Sufi realizes the reality of death.

Five basic concepts are found in 'Ayn al-Quḍāt's doctrine of mystical death. Once these are expounded, his theopathic statements on the matter appear somewhat more comprehensible, even if, ultimately, what he says will always be 'over our heads', because

Sufism must be experienced through 'unveiling'; mere intellectual analysis brings us only to the threshold, not across it.

i. 'Ayn al-Quḍāt views human beings as essentially different in spiritual capacity from one another. Thus, according to his mystical anthropology, only the most advanced adepts among the Sufis will ever attain the 'Realm of Annihilation'.

ii. Epistemologically speaking, annihilation can only be realized through 'selflessness': that is, through enravishment from self by the divine Essence.

iii. Annihilation and death are spiritual, not corporeal, facts. God, says the Judge of Hamadān, does not fix His regard on the body, but only on the soul.

iv. Pain born of divine love is preferable to pleasure experienced by the soul estranged from the Beloved (this was the doctrine of *balā*, 'adversity', formulated two centuries earlier by Junayd).

v. The reality of death and the circumstances of *fanā'* are comprehensible to the mind only through the 'science of similitudes' and analogies – what 'Ayn al-Quḍāt calls 'imaginalization'.

These concepts will be discussed below in the order mentioned above:

i. In the *Tamhīdāt* 'Ayn al-Quḍāt speaks of a certain experience of death which overwhelmed him, describing how he was caught up in the 'highest heaven', the 'Paradise of Sanctity', for an entire month. Everyone imagined that he had died and then

> They sent me forth from that Paradise, with great aversion, to another spiritual station. In this second station, a sin came into being through me, the chastisement for which will be that in a few seasons you will see me killed. What do you say? See what adversity is visited upon the head of someone who hinders a lover from reaching his beloved![98]

98. T 232.

The rival whom 'Ayn al-Quḍāt here rails against is quite obviously his own carnal nature or *ṭab'*, whose interference he bemoans. Musing on this experience, he reflects that it is like being caught between two jealous mistresses—if he attends to one, the other will murder him. He introduces these two metaphysical mistresses as the 'Light of Muḥammad' and the 'Light of Iblīs', both of which continually accompany the Sufi wayfarer, unto the very end of the Path.[99]

> Whoever is subjected to affliction and left half-dead in the world of Satan will be revived and cured in the world of Muḥammad. This is because infidelity *(kufr)* has annihilation *(fanā')* as its hallmark whereas Faith carries the emblem of Subsistence *(baqā')*. Without the presence of annihilation, there is no subsistence. The more annihilation there is on the Spiritual Path, the greater and more perfect is the mystic's subsistence.[100]

Both Carl Ernst and Peter Awn have shown that 'Ayn al-Quḍāt viewed Iblīs as a complementary rather than a polar reality to God. This Satanic-Divine complementarity which pervades all creation underlies 'Ayn al-Quḍāt's unique anthropology, according to which humankind is divided into three basic types.[101] The threefold hierarchy is traced back to the Koran, all three groups being mentioned in Koran XXXV: 32 according to his exegesis. On the first, the lowest, level appears 'animal man and woman';[102] those at this level are endowed with the form and shadow of humankind but lack the reality and substance on humanity. Being unable to fathom the meaning of divine Revelation, Faith or Prophecy,[103] such people inhabit the 'animal realm' *('ālam-i ḥayawānī)* [104] and know neither faith nor infidelity.[105]

The second tier is inhabited by spiritual men/women, also referred to in various places in the Koran,[106] who possess both the

99. T 30, no. 43. See also, Awn, *op. cit.*, p. 139.
100. T 233, no. 302.
101. T 39. *Ādamiyān bar sih gūna fiṭrat āfarīda shuda-ānd.*
102. T 47
103. According to the author, mention of this lower class appears in the Koran in various places, e.g. VII: 179; XLIII: 83; LXX: 42; LXXXIII: 14-15; X: 41; XI: 188; II: 6; VI: 25.
104. T 39.
105. T 47.

human form and the spiritual reality of humanity. These are the "chosen elect of God" and being endowed with gnosis, "priceless and precious is the pearl of their humanity."[107] Despite their exalted station, they are still among the devotees the Koran calls "lukewarm *(muqtaṣidūn)*" among God's bondsmen. These are the 'infidels of the spirit,' as 'Ayn al-Quḍāt explains:

> "And of them are some who are lukewarm" [XXXV: 32] – for the infidel *(kāfir)* is called 'lukewarm'. Ah! How can you understand this? Infidelity *(kufr)* is the intermediate station [on the path] of Devotion *('ubūdiyyat),* a mystical state experienced at the midpoint of the Way. The ultimate point in [divine] Guidance *(hidāyat)* is but midway in relation to [the divine] Misguidance *(ḍilālat).* Misguidance is juxtaposed to Guidance, insofar as God "guides whom He wills and misguides whom He wills."
>
> One day our master was saying his prayers and during the statement of his intention *(niyya)* exclaimed, "I have become an infidel and girded myself with a cincture. God is Most High!" When he finished his prayers, he remarked, "O Muḥammad, you have not yet attained to the midpoint of Devotion; they have not yet let you enter behind the curtain of 'By Thy Might, I will surely beguile them every one' [Koran XXXVIII: 82]. Wait, until the veil is lifted!"
>
> ...I don't know what you have understood about infidelity! There are many different types of infidelity, for many are the stages which the wayfarer must traverse. Each moment of the spiritual path it is necessary and required that the traveller face faith and infidelity. For as long as the wayfarer is conscious of himself and is still some 'thing' to himself, he will not be liberated from the hand of "and surely I will lead them astray." [the words of Iblis to God, Koran IV: 119] ...On this Path there is no more distressing adversity than your existence *(wujūd-i tū)* and no poison more deadly than the desires of disciples.[108]

Of the inhabitants of the third tier of humanity, 'Ayn al-Quḍāt admits that only symbolic allusions can be made, for although they have realized the kernel *(lubb)* of religion, they are protected by divine Jealousy. "Of this saintly company," he remarks, "people

---

106. E.g. XVII: 7; XXXV: III: 29; II: 87.
107. T 41-42.
108. T 48-50.

comprehend no further portion than a simile *(tashbīh)* and an analogy *(tamthīl);"*[109] only the mystic who fathoms the spiritual level and station of Muḥammad is can comprehend the sublime level of this company.[110] The three signs of Prophecy (the power to break natural laws and work miracles; direct vision of the Hereafter and its affairs; and vision, in the waking state, of the imaginal realm beheld by the mass of humankind only in dreams) are possessed by the adepts of the third tier in the form of *karāmat, futūḥ,* and *wāqi'a.*[111] Here, in the most exalted level of his hierarchy, says the Judge of Hamadān, also lies 'the Realm of Annihilation':

> When God's pre-eternal favour wills that the wayfarer be engaged in the heart's ascension *(mi'rāj-i qalb),* He sends a ray from the flame of "It is the fire of God kindled, which leaps up over the hearts..." [Koran CIV: 6-7] to strike him. Struck by this flaming ray the wayfarer sloughs the skin of humanity and exits from the domain of humankind. The experience of this mystical state makes the wayfarer realize the significance of [the verse] "Every soul will taste of death" [III: 185; XXI: 35; XXIX: 57) and the meaning of death on the *via mystica.* Then the truth of "All that dwells upon the earth is in annihilation" [cf. LV: 26] is revealed to him and he passes beyond the place where "upon that day the earth shall be changed to other than the earth," [XIV: 48] and reaches the frontier of the *Realm of Annihilation.* Here the solace of death is presented to him. As he is subjected to this experience, quite without his volition, he renounces all hope and severs his connection with all creation and people. At this juncture the circumstances of the Resurrection are shown to him.[112]

'Ayn al-Quḍāt makes an interesting observation concerning this third and highest tier of humanity. Having realized the meaning of the verse "and [they] have certainty in the Hereafter," (Koran II: 4) such mystics understand why God said to Muḥammad, "Thou knewest not what the Scripture was, nor what the Faith." (XLII: 52). According to 'Ayn al-Quḍāt:

---

109. T 43.
110. T 45, no. 62.
111. Y 46.
112. T 51-52.

The Prophet was brought with aversion into the realm of the Scripture and Faith for the benefit and grace of people... else, how wide the gap between him and absence from that [Transcendent] Presence [which entailed] the duties of apostleship and [instruction of people in] the Scripture.

Alas, in the realm of Certitude the wayfarer beholds himself as utterly obliterated and sees God as 'the Terminator.' He has surpassed "God obliterates what He wills" [Koran XIII: 39] and has confirmed the truth of "He establishes what He wills" [XIII: 39], so that Subsistence [in God] *(baqā')* is vouchsafed to him as this station. Then the people of establishment and obliteration *(ahl-i ithbāt wa maḥw)* display Reality to his sight. One who has realized this knows 'establishment' *(ithbāt)* rather than obliteration, and he leaves those characterized by obliteration trailing far behind.

Herein one discovers the infinite and interminable nature of all these spiritual stations and degrees, each individual ending up at the particular degree which befits him. The verse, "No soul knows what land it shall die in" [XXXII: 34] expresses this. Ah! – What horror this verse brings to me! Hear what Muḥammad said concerning this: "Many are the valleys and ravines in the heart of man, and in each of these lie gorges. Whoever lets himself follow and course down the paths into the gorges, God cares not in which valley he perishes." And in another place *[Ḥadīth]* he said, "The heart is like a feather in the desert which the wind wafts hither and thither."[113]

The wind of the Mercy of pre-eternal Love spins the heart about in its own domain until at last it finds peace in one place and abides therein. For the heart itself is 'an alternator' *(mutaqallib-ast ya'nī gardanda-ast)* which never ceases its rotation. Dear friend! Whenever God wishes to seize the spirit of a wayfarer [i.e. cause him to die] at a certain place, He causes him to need and desire that place. Whenever the wayfarer's nostalgic heart is brought to halt in a certain domain, his spirit is taken away from him and he is made to need and desire that land and station so that he stoops to it and contents himself with it."[114]

In the realm of annihilation *('ālam-i fanā')* all wayfarers are

---

113. Badī' al-Zamān Furūzānfar *(Aḥadīth-i Mathnawī,* no. 219) provides four versions of this *Ḥadīth.* See also R.A. Nicholson's commentary on the *Mathnawī,* III 1643.
114. T 53-54.

> fellow travellers and companions for "all that dwells upon the face of the earth is in annihilation *(fān)."* [Koran LV: 26] But what is the situation of those brought to the world of subsistence *('ālam-i baqā)?* How will they find themselves again [after experiencing annihilation] and where will each of them settle down? The verse, "Yet still abides the Face of thy Lord, in Might and Glory" [LV: 27] has such a meaning. The verse: "And none of us is there but has a known station" [XXXVII: 164] may be presented as an [acceptable] apology on behalf of all the wayfarers, for it demonstrates the extreme limit of each aspirant's spiritual realization.
>
> Dear friend, what of this "earth" *(arḍ)*[115] have you understood? "The earth is God's and He bequeaths it to whom He will" [VII 128]. This "earth" is not this terrestrial ground, for this ground shall suffer annihilation *(fanā dārad)* and annihilation does not besuit the Creator and the Eternal Being. The "earth" intended here is the ground of Paradise and the Heart... When the Ground of Perishable Annihilation *(fanā')* and bodily form *(qālib)* is transformed into the Ground of the Heart and Eternity, a man attains to the degree wherein he beholds the glorious earth in a single atom and within every atom a glorious and wondrous earth.[116]

Hence, when the mystic attains to the third tier of sainthood, the Realm of Annihilation is revealed to him and the veil over the Hereafter is lifted.

ii. The conceptual framework of 'Ayn al-Quḍāt's epistemology here is based on the doctrine of 'visionary unveiling' *(kashf)* expounded by the Muslim mystics. From the exoteric perspective of Islamic theology, the Muslim is defined as one who adheres unquestioningly to certain religious tenets, *viz.* the existence of the angels, the Resurrection, the vision of God in the Hereafter, the questioning by the two recording angels in the grave, etc. However, the Sufis, who introduced themselves as the 'brethren of visionary unveiling and direct perception' *(ahl-i kashf wa shuhūd),* felt a more intimate understanding and realization of their faith to be indispensable to the

---

115. The allusion here is to Koran LV: 29 – "All that are in the heavens and the earth *(arḍ)* entreat Him" – following the two verses (26, 27) from Sura LV quoted above.
116. T 53-55.

development of the spiritual life. Interpreting Surah III: 18, "Allah Himself is Witness that there is no God save Him, and the angels and the men of learning (too are witness), maintaining His creation in justice," 'Ayn al-Quḍāt exclaims:

> Do you imagine that faith *(īmān)* is in the Unseen *(ghayb)?* No, the faith of the unitarians is in the direct vision of the Seen. In Faith the lineaments of extrinsic difference *(ghayriyyat)* in respect to the angels and the men of learning are discarded. Everything becomes "God is Witness..."[117] It becomes apparent to the wayfarer that [the verse of Koran IV: 136]: "O ye who believe! Believe in Allah and His Messenger" states that besides this [exoteric] faith, one must have another type of faith. Now, what would be the inverse of this statement? It would be that beyond this infidelity, exists another infidelity. That is [the meaning of]: "And whosoever has faith in God, He guides his heart." [LXIV 11] When a man still lives with his heart, although he is a believer, one of 'the faithful', still, he lacks Guidance. When a man becomes selfless, Guidance presents itself."[118]

In the following passage, commenting on the *Ḥadīth,* "Meditate on all things but do not meditate on God's Essence," selflessness also appears as the foundation of 'Ayn al-Quḍāt's epistemology:

> "Reflect on God's attributes but do not reflect on His Essence." Here the world of the religious Law *(shar')* is turned topsy-turvy. Do you understand what I am saying? I am saying that the light of God Almighty can be seen by oneself and at this level a man is with himself. But the Essence of God may be seen only *through* God and this experience takes 'the man' out of a man, rendering him selfless. This is the meaning of "Vision comprehendeth Him not" [Koran VI: 103] which ravishes the wayfarer from himself; "but He comprehendeth all Vision" [VI: 103] implies that *all is God.*[119]

iii. Another essential part of 'Ayn al-Quḍāt's doctrine of mystical death is his emphasis on spiritual development over concern with the physical body. He believed that God's grace and attention are

117. That is, under the aegis of God's omnipresent vision, the creature – whether angel or savant – ceases to be veiled by its own temporality from its Creator.
118. T 324, no. 425.
119. T 303-04, no. 399.

not directed towards the body but the Spirit, God's regard for the body being purely illusory and figurative *(majāzī).* The real development occurs in the heart and the soul. It is only the heart which can direct God's attention to the flesh, resulting in immortality:

> God's regard and love is never directed at the body *(qālib)* but rather is directed at the soul *(jān)* and heart *(dil),* for "Verily, God does not look at your forms nor your deeds. Rather God's attention is focused on your hearts." *[Ḥadīth]* The heart, as delegated by God, directs a figurative attention *(naẓar-i majāzī)* toward the bodily frame so that the body may remain a brief moment in the world until the advent of death. When death arrives, if the heart had directed its attention towards the body, the body does not die, for "Verily, We shall quicken him with a good life" [Koran XVI: 97), but if the heart had disregarded the body, then total death ensues.[120]
>
> * * *
>
> If a man perishes totally at death, why then did Muḥammad say [about death] on his deathbed, "The best friend, the purest delight, the most faithful perfection!"? Why did he remark that, "The tomb is a garden among the fields of Paradise, or else, a pit among the holes of hell"–?
>
> ...But a complete exposition of this idea is found in the verse: "Think not of those who are slain in the Path of God that they are dead. No, they are living with their Lord." [III: 169] If this were not so, why would Muḥammad have said, "The believer is alive in both the worlds [i.e. here and Hereafter]," or elsewhere have stated, "The friends of God do not die but are transported from realm to realm"–?
>
> All of this is an exposition of the truth that when the body dies, the soul lives on and subsists; if the body descends into the grave, the soul is brought "firmly established [in the favour of a mighty King]" [LIV: 55].[121]

Earlier in the *Tamhīdāt*, 'Ayn al-Quḍāt had commented on this same verse, offering more of an anagogic interpretation, again supporting his argument with *Ḥadīth:*

> The meaning of "firmly established in the favour of a mighty

120. T 163, no. 219.
121. T 161-62.

> King" is the throne of the innermost consciousness upon which lovers seat themselves. Listen to what Muḥammad (peace be upon him!) said to Jābir ibn 'Abdullāh on the day when his father, 'Abdullāh ibn Rawāh was slain during the battle of Uḥud, thus becoming a martyr. He stated, "God has brought your father to life and has established him on the Divine Throne with the Prophet Moses."[122]

Furthermore, anyone who considers the Prophet as a 'body' is an infidel, 'Ayn al-Quḍāt asserts, citing verses LXIV: 6 and LIV: 24 from the Koran, which describe how disbelievers derided the pre-Islamic Prophets of monotheism for being "mere mortals." On the other hand, the Prophet Muḥammad was

> a soul purified of the fleshly human condition *(bashariyyat)* and beyond this world. The verse, "Say: I am only a mortal like you," [Koran XVIII: 10, in reference to the Prophet Muḥammad] concerns the [Prophet's] body alone and the body is not of Yonder World. Alas! The Jews and the Christians said, "We are sons of God and His loved ones" [V: 18] and received in the Scripture a brusque rebuttal: "Say: Why then does He chastise you for your sins? Nay, you are but mortals of His making." [V: 18] You are still caught up in humanity. How could you ever be Our friend? The friends of God are not human *(bashar),* yet your entire makeup consists of *la condition humaine (bashariyyat).*[123]

From 'Ayn al-Quḍāt's visionary perspective, neither death nor life have ultimate value in itself. What matters for the lover is not the body's estate but the heart's state. Such a vision of life is indeed at odds with the outlook of modern man, yet is hardly alien to traditional Western Christendom, and was even expressed by Shakespeare:

> *Men must endure*
> *Their going hence, even as their coming hither.*
> *Ripeness is all.*[124]

---

122. T 132.
123. T 164-65, no. 220.
124. Shakespeare, *King Lear* V, 2.

To 'Ayn al-Quḍāt, what constitutes the "Perfection of the life" (that "heavenly mansion, raging in the dark," to use W.B. Yeats' image[125])—is nothing but this very "ripeness" of divine Love. Love is worshipped in the religion of love and 'life' and 'death' are but incidental to this immortal passion:

> For the lover's reckoning is with love: of what account is the Beloved to him? His aim is Love and his life is Love and without Love he dies. ...From Love he experiences so much grief, pain and rue that he ceases to be tied down by Union nor afflicted by the torments of separation. For Union gives him no joy, nor separation any pain or suffering. He has surrendered up his will to Love.[126]

iv. Given this relativity of physical existence, death may even become an object of desire to the love-intoxicated mystic—did not the Judge claim he prayed for death? The Sufi may court calamity, even befriend adversity:

> The bread and butter of men is calamity and pain and adversity. Their meals are set for lunch and dinner at the door of Iblis. By the Almighty Majesty of Eternity, you do not understand what you are reading! How could these accounts ever be related to the likes of you? ...It requires a man who is detached from both the worlds and has become uniquely isolated in his contemplation *(fard),* to be able to eat pain in place of bread and water.[127]

In his quest for annihilation and purification from selfhood, 'Ayn al-Quḍāt was led to accept and to acknowledge, in Blake's words, the truth of the maxim "Listen to a fool's reproach, it is a kingly title." Indeed, many of Blake's 'Proverbs of Hell' (from which the above adage is drawn) accord with the spirit of the Judge of Hamadān's pursuit of the fate of Iblīs, accursed by God in this world, but beloved on the 'Day of Judgement'—the day when Love rules and the 'Law of Unity' reigns over all.[128] So Truth in the guise of pain is far preferable for the seeker of Transcendental Unity to

---

125. N. Jeffares (ed.) *W.B. Yeats, Selected Poetry* (London 1962), "The Choice", p. 153
126. T 101.
127. T introduction, p. 91. From one of the epistles.
128. See T 226-27, no. 295; T 122-23, no. 171. Awn, *op. cit.,* p. 141.

vanity bedecked in temporal 'grace'. This is the spirit of many of 'Ayn al-Quḍāt's utterances concerning the high spiritual level of "those who embrace adversity." The following passage is typical:

> Ah! Do you think that calamity *(balā)* is given to just anyone? What do you know of calamity? Be constant until you reach a point where you would willingly purchase calamity at the price of your own soul. Did not Shiblī refer to this experience by saying: "O God, all people seek You for Your grace and comfort, but I seek you for the sake of calamity." So wait until the alchemy of "an attraction from the Divine attraction"[129] begins to transform you. Then you will know what calamity is! Is not this then the true context of the Prophet's saying: "Just as gold is tried by being placed in a crucible over fire, so is the believer tried through disasters and calamities."
>
> The believer must endure so much calamity that he becomes one with it and calamity becomes one with him. Then he becomes calamity in essence and calamity becomes in essence, him. Thenceforth, he ceases to be conscious of calamity. Alas! This is the meaning of the verse "Lo! Kings, when they enter a township, ruin it." [Koran XXVII: 34]
>
> ...Alas, have you not heard the saying of that great master, "The lover's claim to love is insincere unless he enjoys the rebuke of the Beloved"? ...Whoever does not endure separation from the Beloved will not attain the pleasure of Union; whoever does not consider the Beloved's insult as a Grace is alien from the Beloved.[130]

Hence, one of the highest degrees of divine love, according to 'Ayn al-Quḍāt, is to enjoy the Beloved's rebuke more than the beneficence of others;[131] here, the true lover stakes his life upon the 'truth of pain':

> Every day, a thousand times over, the friends of God become intoxicated with the wine of Union and then, in the end, are abased and trampled beneath the feet of separation from him. The lover is still a disciple, and in this world the lover is hung

---

129. An allusion to a well-known Prophetic tradition: "There is a kind of attraction which comes from God and is comparable to the sum of all the acts of devotion of man and angel."– Furūzānfar, *Aḥadīth-i Mathnawī,* p. 119)
130. T 244-45, nos. 318-19.
131. T 221.

> from the cross of separation. Have you not heard the address which is directed at the seekers of Him in That world?
>
> *Many there are who are seekers of Us in this town;*
> *Ah! How wretched is the labor of all who seek Us.*
> *Ten thousand gallows have been raised*
> *at the door to Our court and upon each gallows*
> *another miserable disciple is strung up.*
>
> From within the souls of the seekers of the Divine Presence, each day a myriad times the cry goes up: "We well know that our Beloved is fond of wrath and calamity *(qahr wa balā),* but unto His wrath and calamity we have submitted ourselves. From Him comes calamity *(balā),* but from us contentment *(riḍā);* from Him comes wrath *(qahr)* but from us love *(mihr).* ...For, alas, it is such a love which declares, "Eternal suffering we have chosen for ourselves and have given over mercy and grace to be the portion of others."
>
> ...That chivalrous man Iblis says, "If others flee from the blow, I will take it upon my own neck." ...Since my Beloved considered me worthy of commemoration, whether the warp and woof of my fate's carpet be woven black or white is all one to me." Whoever distinguishes between these two [i.e. between fortune and misfortune] is still raw in matters of love. Whether one is given poison or honey, sugar or colocynth, wrath or grace by the Friend's hand, what difference does it make? Whoever is a lover of grace or a lover of wrath is in love with himself, not with the Beloved. Alas! When a prince bestows a honorary robe or hat upon someone, the giving of the gift itself suffices; the rest, the substance and kind of the gift, is not a lover's concern.[132]

Hence, the fruit of this conscious cultivation of adversity and calamity is detachment from all temporal ties and spiritual habits, the inner 'heart's Beloved' taking precedence over external religious ties. Describing Uways Qaranī's physically 'distant', although spiritually intimate, love of the Prophet, 'Ayn al-Quḍāt observed: "He did not behold the Prophet's outer form. His only object of interest in the body [i.e. physical presence] of the Prophet was to behold the Prophet's inner meaning *(ma'nā).* When at last he contemplated that

---

132. T 222-224.

meaning, the Prophet's form *(ṣūrat)* had become a veil for him."[133] Likewise, the relationship enjoyed by Abū Bakr with the Prophet was one of 'the soul and the heart' rather than of the physical body and material presence; in a similar manner, the physical absence or presence *(ghaybat wa ḥuḍūr)* of the spiritual master makes little difference to the advanced disciple.[134]

v. At this point, the question arises as to the true reality of the after-death state. According to 'Ayn al-Quḍāt, the reality of death and the condition of the Next world are only comprehensible by analogy, by way of 'making a similitude' or *tamaththul,* that is, by the method of 'imaginalization'. "Vision of the Hereafter and the spiritual world *('ālam-i malakūt)* is all dependent on imaginalization," he writes, adding that "it is no small thing to gain true cognizance of imaginalization."[135] Understanding the reality of imaginalization, or gaining awareness of the similitudes which bridge the material world and the supraformal realm, all depend on realizing *mystical death.* On this, he pronounces:

> Don't you realize that [physical] death is not real death? True death is annihilation *(fanā').* Whoever does not realize this [real] death has no life. Do you understand what I say? I say that as long as 'you' are 'you' and caught up in your 'self', you do not really exist. When 'you' cease to be 'you' then you [truly] become yourself.
>
> Alas! What do you hear? According to us, death is that an individual die from everything except the Beloved, so that he finds life through and in the Beloved. Then you will realize, within yourself, how death occurs.[136]

'Ayn al-Quḍāt goes on to explain that the present state of mortal humanity *(bashariyyat)* is itself a tomb; all the torments of the grave are actually with us in the present life. Man' body is itself a tomb, and the torments of the afterlife are all experienced owing to his subjection to passions and lusts in the present life:

---

133. T 34 no. 48.
134. T 33 no. 47.
135. T 287, no. 374.
136. T 287-88, no. 374.

> The first thing which the spiritual pilgrim becomes aware of concerning the realm of the Hereafter is the condition which prevails in the tomb, and the first imaginal similitude which the mystic sees is the tomb. For example, all of the things promised [in the Koran] as appearing in their tombs to the inhabitants of hell – such as snakes, scorpions, dogs and fire, are shown to him through imaginalization. These things are all in the interior of the spiritual man, for they all arise from him and are, therefore, always by his side.[137]

All the worlds of the spirit and divinity lie "within the human heart,"[138] and the wondrous events of the Hereafter are all visions enjoyed by the Sufi through his realization of the analogical or imaginalized *(tamaththul)* nature of Reality, says the author of the *Tamhīdāt.*

Just as the lover's religion is the Love of God, so his paradise is nearness and his hellfire distance from the Beloved.[139] 'Ayn al-Quḍāt's radical interiorization of Islamic eschatology leads him to assert that "the foundation of the existence of the state of the hereafter is upon imaginalization." The science of imaginalization involves strenuous inner labor, and described as the highest of all spiritual sciences:[140]

> There are myriad mystical states and stations *(maqāmhā)* within imaginalization *(tamaththul).* One of the stations which pertain to imaginalization is that the one who experiences it, even in a minute portion, if he remains at that station, will be totally bereft of himself, and is enabled to transcend his 'self'. If deprived of this station, he becomes beside himself with loneliness and grief. Contemplative thought *(tafakkur)* stems from this station.
>
> ...Ah! How can you comprehend how this station transforms a person? I am an infidel if all that has been vouchsafed to me [of divine graces] has not solely been for the sake of this station. Wait until one atom of this spiritual station through similitude shows its outermost degree to you.[141] Then you will understand the condition of a poor wretch like me![142]

---

137. T 288-89, no. 376.
138. T 291.
139. T 292, no. 384.
140. T 293, no. 385.
141. Translation uncertain.

'Ayn al-Quḍāt and four others outside a Metal-workers Shop. From a manuscript of the *Majālis al-'ushshāq*. MS. Ouseley, Add 24, f. 46r. (Courtesy of the Bodleian Library, Oxford).

V. CONCLUSION – THE LAWS OF ETERNITY BEYOND SEPARATION AND UNION

Nothing in his life
Became him like the leaving of it: he died
As one that had been studied in his death,
To throw away the dearest thing he owed.

Shakespeare, Macbeth I, 4[143]

In his monumental three-volume history of Sufism, the *Ṭarā'iq al-ḥaqā'iq,* Ma'ṣūm 'Alī Shāh describes 'Ayn al-Quḍāt's tragic career as "Christian in death and Ḥallājian by orientation."[144] and Y.E. Bertel's, in his classic Russian study of Persian Sufism, notes that 'Ayn al-Quḍāt's ultimate aspiration and longing, expressed throughout the *Tamhīdāt* was "to enjoy the fate of Ḥallāj."[145]

The physical facts of his execution tell us that by the order of the Seljuk vizier of Iraq, Abu'l-Qāsim Qiwām al-Dīn Nāṣir ibn 'Alī al-Dargazīnī on May 6-7, 1131 (Jumādā II 525) at the age of 33, 'Ayn al-Quḍāt was skinned alive and strung up on a gibbet at the entrance of the college at which he taught.[146] The political circumstances of his death, as recent studies have demonstrated,[147] show that his execution was not the outcome of "an anti-mystical trend, but because of a personal vendetta in Saljuq politics," and that owing to this vendetta, "he received the full impact of the fears and frustrations of the *'ulamā'.*"[148] But his death, in spiritual terms, by no means concluded the biography of the mystic Judge of Hamadān, for his death was also a mystical one—the fruit of the soul's tree, as Rūmī put it —as well as physical martyrdom. His was a death, which rather, "reencloses [life] in the divine origin of its potentiali-

142. T 295, no. 386.
143. Malcolm, reporting to Duncan the execution of the Thane of Cawdor.
144. Edited by Muḥammad Ja'far Maḥjūb, (Tehran 1940), II, p. 568.
145. *Taṣawwuf wa adabiyyāt-i taṣawwuf,* translated from Russian into Persian by Sirūs Īzadī (Tehran 1977), p. 418.
146. Arberry, *A Sufi Martyr,* p. 14; Maṣūm 'Alī Shāh, *op. cit.,* II, p. 571.
147. See Ernst, *op. cit.,* pp. 110-15 and Raḥīm Farmanish, *Aḥwāl wa āthār 'Ayn al-Quḍāt Abū'l-Mu'ālī 'Abdullāh ibn Muḥammad ibn 'Alī ibn al-Ḥasan ibn 'Alī al-Miyānjī al-Hamadānī* (Tehran: Mullā 1360 A.Hsh./1981), pp. 55-81.
148. Ernst, *op. cit.,* p. 115.

ties, forever, through a kind of spiritual 'upward curve' of time."[149]

Massignon's view of Ḥallāj as one of the immortal "Witnesses of the Eternal" whose "posthumous 'survival' on earth through chains of suffering and sacrificed witnesses involves us and draws us away from earth toward 'temples' *(hayākil)* of the eternal City of souls raised up from the transfigured holocaust of their earthly bodies,"[150] recalls 'Ayn al-Quḍāt's own Sufi 'religion of love', according to which the believer's "bread and butter" is adversity, whose submission to God *(islām)* is the joyous embrace of the lover who is "hung from the cross of separation in this world" (T 223), and whose 'death' is actually 'Life' gained through realization of the meaning of (the Sufic version of the Delphic maxim) 'spiritual poverty' (cf. Koran XXXV: 15): annihilation. Indeed, the ecstatic spirit of Ḥallāj haunts the rhythmical Persian prose of the *Tamhīdāt,* with the Judge of Hamadān often comparing his own career to that of Ḥallāj—whom he praises as "the master of lovers, chief of gnostics."[151] Scorched by the passion of that enigmatic martyr from Shiraz, in the *Tamhīdāt* 'Ayn al-Quḍāt had likewise predicted his own martyrdom, invoking his own death in aspiration for relief from the bondage of division:

> Do you imagine that being slain on the Path of God is a calamity? No, on our Path, to be slain is to gain a soul."[152] ...We [God] gave him [Ḥallāj] the key to the Arcanum of Mysteries. He revealed Our mystery. So We placed adversity *(balā)* in his way that others might take heed and keep our secrets. Not everyone is capable of keeping such a secret – alas! Tomorrow—or after a few days—may it come to pass that you too will see how 'Ayn al-Quḍāt has attained this blessing, having forsaken his own head to obtain headmastership![153]

In the light of the above discussion of the inner reality of *fanā',* had not 'Ayn al-Quḍāt already died before his own martyrdom—died to

---

149. L. Massignon, *The Passion of al-Ḥallāj: Mystic and Martyr of Islam,* trans. H. Mason (Princeton University Press, 1982), vol. I, p. lxviii.
150. *Ibid.,* p. lxiii.
151. T 235.
152. T 235.
153. T 236.

his own desire, and like the magicians in the Koran who converted to the religion of Moses, been quickened in the realm of annihilation.

> *Pharoah imagined that the magicians*
> *felt terror, suffered abasement and fear for their lives;*
> *Little did he know that they were free,*
> *reclining in comfort upon the doorway*
> *of the light of the heart.*[154]

Pursuit of union and flight from separation, thought 'Ayn al-Quḍāt, were illegitimate desires for advanced Sufis to harbor... he had even written in reproach to one of his own disciples:

> The beginning of the end of divine love is that the lover forget the Beloved—what concern has the lover with the Beloved? ...A man must be so subjected and disciplined through the experience of union and separation with the Beloved that neither is his joy increased through union nor is his pain amplified by separation. If such is the farthest stage of beginners, it is but the point of departure for adepts near the end of the mystical way. You have not even come out of your father's loins![155]

"You must realize," wrote 'Ayn al-Quḍāt—as if describing his death which indeed transcended all martyrdom of the flesh—"that there is a type of death above and beyond corporeal death and another type of life beyond that of the corporeal and physical frame." In this second type of life, "in Yonder world," he states, "all is life within life, whereas in this world, all is death within death. Until you transcend death, you'll never attain life. 'Lo! the abode of the Hereafter - that is Life, if they but knew" [XXIX: 64].[156] There are two births, pronounced the Judge, and quoting the saying of Jesus on being 'born again', he comments that the second birth for the Sufi is "to be born *from* oneself, so that he *sees* the realm of Eternity and

154. Rūmī, *Mathnawī,* III 1721.
155. T, introduction, p. 90.
156. T 319, no. 418. Cf. Massignon's remarks on Ḥallāj's martyrdom: "We are propounding here the absolute transcendence of the humblest of heroic acts as sole cornerstone of the eternal City. The history of religions thus conceived envisages it as the axis and the apex of the world in motion towards the next life, even if the author of this act forgets it." *The Passion,* p. lxv.

God."[157]

Admittedly, here the exposition of 'Ayn al-Quḍāt deserts the realm of common sensory experience and theoretical theology, and propounds a completely visionary theology, leading the author to bluntly admit that he is now outside the pale of formal Islam.[158]

> I know that these words do not hail from the realm of your religious conventionalism—which is, anyway, but spiritual conventionalism (*'ādat-parastī,* i.e. idolatrous attachment to habits). Spiritual conventionalism belongs to the realm of the *Sharī'a,* and practicing the *Sharī'a (sharī'a-warzī)* is all spiritual conventionalism.. Unless you abandon spiritual conventionalism you can never be a minister of the Truth *(ḥaqīqat-warz).*[159]

According to this viewpoint, faith and infidelity in their formal sense—of a purely non-existential commitment to, or confession of, the dogmas of monotheism—become meaningless. All that is not Divinity is Infidelity: the existence of the state of 'humanity' is but rust corroding the spiritual heart, to be burnished away by recitation of the Koran and meditation upon death.[160] When the rust of humanity is dissolved, 'annihilation' is attained, and the state of 'indwelling' *(ḥulūl)* in which the divine and the human are united, is realized. Knowing, however, that his readers will perceive him as being an advocate of 'incarnationism'—the heretical aspect of *ḥulūl,* of which doctrine Ḥallāj was accused, against which Hujwīrī and Sarrāj had warned and railed—'Ayn al-Quḍāt comments:

> Alas! Here 'indwelling' will appear. O friend, if you wish to obtain eternal bliss, spend one hour in the company of a *ḥulūlī* who is a Sufi so that you can realize who the *ḥulūlī* really is. Did not a Sufi master at this juncture exclaim, "The Sufi is God"? 'Abdullāh Anṣārī says that "the scholar vaunts his knowledge and the ascetic prides himself on his austerities; of the Sufi what can be said for the Sufi is all Him." If the Sufi is Him, then the

157. T 319.
158. On 'Ayn al-Quḍāt's concept of religious faith, see L. Lewisohn, "From Islamic Falsity to Real Infidelity: Interiorization of Faith in the Writings of 'Ayn al-Quḍāt Hamadhānī and Maḥmūd Shabistarī," forthcoming.
159. T 320, no. 419.
160. T 299, no. 392.

> Sufi is not an 'indweller' *(ḥulūlī).* Whatever is God implies that his indwelling is also unification. In this station, whatever you have heard from him, you have really heard from God.
>
> Ah! Whoever desires to hear the divine mysteries without any mediation, may say 'Hear them from 'Ayn al-Quḍāt Hamadānī"—which has the meaning [of the *ḥadīth)* "God speaks from the tongue of 'Umar." If it were possible for anything among created, living beings to be excluded from the hearing, sight, knowledge, and power of God Almighty, it would be possible that it also be excluded from the hearing, vision and power of such a wayfarer.[161]

In this imaginal realm envisioned by 'Ayn al-Quḍāt, a life spent in 'quest of annihilation' is not in vain, for the worst misfortune or calamity a man or woman may suffer is neither corporeal death nor physical adversity, but imprisonment in selfhood. 'Ayn al-Quḍāt's description of mystical death leads him far beyond conventional Islam, for when denuded of 'selfhood', the dictates of the religious law no longer apply to the mystic. Faith becomes vision and the outer letter of the Scripture becomes a vividly interiorized audition. This is the 'Christian death' of which Ma'ṣūm 'Alī Shāh spoke, the passion for which pervades mystics of every denomination and religion.

> *Such are the laws of Eternity, that each shall mutually*
> *Annihilate himself for others' good, as I for thee.*
> *Thy purpose & the purpose of thy Priests & of thy Churches*
> *Is to impress on men the fear of death, to teach*
> *Trembling & fear, terror, constriction, abject selfishness.*
> *Mine is to teach men to despise death & to go on*
> *In fearless majesty annihilating Self... & put off*
> *In Self annihilation all that is not of God alone...:*[162]

161. T 300, nos. 393-94.
162. William Blake, *Milton* 38: 35-41, 47-48.

V

The Myth of Adam's Fall in Aḥmad Sam'ānī's *Rawḥ al-arwāḥ*

William C. Chittick

INTRODUCTION

Sufi literature is still largely unexplored. Many texts have long been recognized as classics and many others have been brought to light by contemporary scholars, but still others are lying neglected in manuscript libraries or private collections waiting to be discovered. The fact that these works are unknown does not mean that they are unimportant. A case in point is *Rawḥ al-arwāḥ fī sharḥ asmā' al-malik al-fattāḥ* by a contemporary of Ghazālī and Sanā'ī, Aḥmad Sam'ānī, who died in 534/1140. Manuscripts of this book of more than 600 pages exist in several libraries. Some of the great contemporary scholars of Persian literature, such as Badī' al-Zamān Furūzānfar and Muḥammad Taqī Dānishpazhūh, have noticed the work, but no one paid much attention to it until it was published in 1989 by Najīb Māyil Hirawī.[1] Now that the text is readily available, anyone can see that it deserves to be counted as a major classic of Persian Sufi literature.

Although Aḥmad Sam'ānī is unknown to most contemporary scholars, information on his life is not difficult to find. He was a member of a famous family of Shafi'ite scholars from Marv. His father, Abū'l-Muẓaffar Manṣūr ibn Muḥammad (422-489/1031-

1. *Rawḥ al-arwāḥ fī sharḥ asmā' al-malīk al-fattāḥ* (Tehran: Shirkat-i intishārāt-i 'ilmī wa farhangī 1368). See pp. xv-xxii for the remarks of Furūzānfar (from his *Sharḥ-i Mathnawī-yi sharīf* [Tehran: Dānishgāh 1346-48 A.Hsh./1967-69], vol. 3, pp. 915-17) and Dānishpazhūh, *Majalla-yi dānishkada-yi adabiyyāt wa 'ulūm-i insānī* (Tehran) 5/2-3, pp. 300-312 (as cited in *Rawḥ al-arwāḥ,* pp. xvii-xxii).

1096), was the author of a commentary on the Koran and a number of books on *Ḥadīth,* jurisprudence, and *Kalām.* Aḥmad studied with his father and with his eldest brother, Abū Bakr Muḥammad ibn Manṣūr (d. 510/1116-17). This brother was in turn the father of the most famous member of the family, 'Abd al-Karīm ibn Muḥammad Sam'ānī (d. 562/1166-67), the author of the well-known genealogical work *al-Ansāb.* In this work 'Abd al-Karīm describes his uncle Aḥmad as an eloquent preacher, a good debater, and a fine poet—qualities that are apparent in *Rawḥ al-arwāḥ.* In the year 529/1134-35, 'Abd al-Karīm tells us, the two of them traveled together from Marv to Nishapur to hear the *Ṣaḥīḥ* of Muslim.[2]

Commentaries on the divine names were common in Arabic,[3] but *Rawḥ al-arwāḥ* seems to be the first detailed and systematic work of its kind in Persian. Sam'ānī discusses 101 names under seventy-four headings. In each case, he begins by explaining the literal meaning of the name or names in question. Then he lets the inspiration of the moment take his hand. The result is a series of extraordinary meditations on basic themes of Islamic spirituality.

Rawḥ al-arwāḥ shows that Sam'ānī was a master of all the religious sciences. But it is the Sufi dimension of Islam that shines most clearly in the form and content of his work. Sam'ānī frequently quotes Sufi poetry (including verses from Sanā'ī) and composes many verses and ghazals himself. However, his prose is often more poetical than the poetry, and he must be considered one of the truly great prose writers of the Persian language. He writes with utter spontaneity and joy, while illustrating all the techniques of a first-rate stylist. His writing is not particularly simple—certainly it is more difficult than the Persian of the Ghazālī brothers or 'Ayn al-Quḍāt Hamadānī. But the musical qualities and the beauty of the text are astounding. Without doubt he wrote the book to be read aloud. When his nephew tells us that his uncle was an eloquent preacher, one can easily imagine him reciting passages of this work and

---

2. On the return journey, 'Abd al-Karīm parted from his uncle at Ṭūs and returned to Nishapur for a year, and then went on to Isfahan and Baghdad. He did not see his uncle again. *Rawḥ,* pp. xxvii-xxviii.
3. See Daniel Gimaret, *Les noms divins en Islam* (Paris: Cerf 1988), a work that lists twenty-three Arabic works on this topic up to Ghazālī.

producing in his listeners ecstatic states of the type that are often described in the hagiographic literature.

Sam'ānī's work can best be compared with that neglected classic of Sufi literature *Kashf al-asrār,* the ten-volume Koran commentary by Maybudī, which was begun in 520/1126, some ten years before Sam'ānī wrote *Rawḥ al-arwāḥ.* But Maybudī's commentary reaches the heights of eloquence only in the third sections of the work, which deal with the Koran's inner meaning. Sam'ānī maintains the same high level of inspiration and beauty from the beginning to the end of his text, descending into ordinary prose only at the outset of each section. In fact, I know of no other prose text with such originality, freshness, rich use of poetic imagery, and sense of humor.

Rawḥ al-arwāḥ, like *Kashf al-asrār,* is a detailed early source for Sufi theoretical teachings. Sam'ānī makes important contributions to many topics, including Islamic anthropology. He was certainly influenced by *Kashf al-asrār* and the *Rasā'il* of the Brethren of Purity *(.Ikhwān al-Ṣafā').*[4] In turn, he must have inspired many of those who followed him. In all likelihood, Rūmī was familiar with his work. Rūmī's *Mathnawī,* written about 120 years later, is as close in style and spirit to *Rawḥ al-arwāḥ* as any work in Persian literature.

Some of the qualities of Sam'ānī's book may be illustrated through the examination of one of its major themes. The basic, underlying idea of the text is that human beings were created for the sake of love, and that all pain and suffering play the positive role of increasing people's desire for God. Like most Sufi theoreticians, Sam'ānī stresses God's mercy, love, and compassion rather than His wrath and vengeance. The central idea of his work is summarized by the famous *ḥadīth,* "God's mercy predominates over His wrath."

Much of Sam'ānī's discussion of God's mercy focuses on the

---

4. These works seem to be more important in forming the background of Sam'ānī's teachings than the sources cited by Māyil Hirawī—such as Mustamlī Bukhārī's *Sharḥ-i ta'arruf (Rawḥ,* p. xxiii). For example, *Rawḥ,* pp. 63-64, is based on *Kashf al-asrār* (ed. 'A. A. Ḥikmat [Tehran: Dānishgāh 1331-39/1952-60]), vol. 8, p. 545. Cf. *Rawḥ,* pp. 292-293 and *Kashf,* vol. 8, pp. 374-375. For a passage that is probably based on the Ikhwān al-Ṣafā's *Fī qawl al-ḥukamā' annā'l-insān 'ālam ṣaghīr (Rasā'il* [Beirut: Dār Ṣādir/Dār Bayrūt 1957], vol. 2, pp. 456ff.), see *Rawḥ,* pp. 177-181.

Adam with Joseph, Jonnah and Noah. *Dīwān-i Ḥāfiẓ*. Kashmīr, 18th-century. B.L. Add. 7763, f. 19v. (Courtesy of the British Library).

key mythic event of human existence, the fall of Adam. Given the Koranic version of Adam's fall, Islam has never stressed its negative consequences as much as Christianity. Nevertheless, many Muslim authorities have seen the fall as a result of God's wrath and have stressed the rupture of equilibrium with the divine Reality that resulted. Sam'ānī does not forget that God is wrathful and severe in punishment, but he tends to leave the explication of this part of the divine message to others. He would not have stressed the positive sides to Adam's fall if opinions to the contrary were not common. Clearly, he has set out to counteract the idea that the primary motive for obeying God should be fear.

Sam'ānī's insistence that Adam's fall was rooted in God's mercy and forgiveness may appear surprising to some readers. One might immediately object that Sam'ānī makes sin into a virtue and encourages disobedience to the divine command. But this would be to forget Sam'ānī's own social and religious context and to read his text in terms of our own contemporary situation, in which institutionalized forms of religious discipline are looked upon as constrictions of freedom. Sam'ānī lived in a society where observance of the *Sharī'a* was taken for granted. He is not suggesting that people should sin and be happy about it. Rather, he is asking them to look carefully at their own motivations for activity. Is it correct to follow the *Sharī'a* simply because God tells us to, or because we want to avoid punishment? No, says Sam'ānī. Human activity must be motivated by love for God, just as God was motivated by love when He created the universe ("I was a Hidden Treasure, and I loved to be known"). In short, Sam'ānī writes in order to give his listeners a good impression of God. He wants to stir up love for Him in their hearts. He knows full well that such love will not lead to disregard for the *Sharī'a,* but rather to a more serious and profound understanding of the *Sharī'a* and a renewed dedication to putting it into practice. As the Koran puts it, "Say [O Muḥammad]! 'If you love God, follow me, and God will love you and forgive you your sins; God is Forgiving, Compassionate'" (Koran III: 31). The *sine qua non* of following Muḥammad is observing the *Sharī'a* that he himself observed.

In order to illustrate Sam'ānī's theoretical orientation and stylistic peculiarities, I provide a few examples of his interpretation of Adam's fall, often with quotations from his own words. Unless close attention is paid to the details of his text, it is easy to overlook the fact that his rhetoric is at least as important as his theory. One always has to remember that he wrote *Rawḥ al-arwāḥ* to be recited aloud and that its sound and imagery provide a good deal of its power. Although this imagery cannot be reproduced in English, much will be lost if no attempt is made to do so.

ADAM'S FALL

Sam'ānī's views on Adam's fall need to be understood in the context of the Koranic story, which I summarize here, stressing the details that Sam'ānī finds especially important:

God decided to place a vicegerent or representative in the earth. Before creating the vicegerent, He informed the angels about His decision. They seemed to be taken aback, for they said, "What, will You place therein one who will do corruption there, and shed blood, while we glorify You in praise and call You holy?" (Koran II: 30). God simply replied that He knew something that the angels did not.

Having created Adam, God taught him all the names. These are the names of everything, or the names of God, or both, depending on various interpretations. God asked the angels the names, but they admitted their ignorance. God told Adam to teach the angels the names, and He reminded the angels that He had said that He knew something that they did not know. Then God commanded the angels to prostrate themselves before Adam, and all did so, except Iblis.[5] When God asked Iblis why he refused, he said, "I am better than he. You created me of fire, and You created him of clay" (Koran VII: 12; XXXVIII: 76).

5. There is of course a good deal of discussion among theologians and other scholars as to whether or not Iblis was an angel. The position they take depends largely on how the terms 'angel' *(malak)* and 'jinn' are defined. Those who distinguish clearly between jinn and angels maintain that he was a jinn, on the basis of Koran XVIII: 50. But others do not draw lines so clearly and consider him one of the angels, or a certain kind of angel. Sam'ānī does not bother with the distinction between angel and jinn, so he commonly refers to Iblis as an angel.

According to a *ḥadīth,* God kneaded Adam's clay for forty days with His own two hands.[6] Then He breathed from His own spirit into him. Perhaps at this point He offered the Trust to the heavens, the earth, and the mountains, but they all refused. The human being—here the term *al-insān* rather then *ādam* is employed—carried the Trust, and, the Koran tells us in concluding the verse, "He is a wrongdoer, ignorant" (Koran XXXIII: 72). Within the same mythic time frame, God takes all of Adam's descendants out from his loins and addresses them: "Am I not *(alastu)* your Lord?" They all acknowledge His Lordship (Koran VII: 172). This is the "Covenant of *Alast,*" a well-known theme in Sufi literature.

By this time God has created Eve as Adam's companion and placed the two of them in Paradise to roam freely wherever they desire. However, they are told not to approach 'this tree,' which the tradition identifies as wheat. Hence Sam'ānī frequently alludes to Adam's selling Paradise for "one grain of wheat." When Adam and Eve eat the forbidden wheat, the cry goes up, "Adam disobeyed" (Koran XX: 121). This is a key event, Adam's "sin," if you like. But in keeping with the general Islamic perspective, Sam'ānī never refers to this event as a "sin" *(gunāh, ithm, dhanb)*, but rather as a "slip" *(zillat)*. Having slipped, Adam and Eve repent, saying to God, "Our Lord, we have wronged ourselves" (Koran VII: 23). God forgives them, and, the Koran tells us, "His Lord chose him" (Koran XX: 122). In other words, God appointed Adam as a prophet. In the same way, the Koran tells us that "God elected Adam" along with Noah and other prophets (Koran III: 33). Finally Adam and Eve are told, "Fall down out of it" (Koran II: 38). This is 'the Fall' proper, through which Adam and Eve go down to the earth.

It is important to note that Sam'ānī almost never refers explicitly to Eve,[7] not because women are unimportant, but rather because he

---

6. Clearly, this is a great deal of attention for God to pay to a single creature, since in creating everything else, including the heavens and the earth, God simply says "Be," and the thing comes into existence. Moreover, as Sam'ānī reminds us, the Koran tells us that a day with God is equivalent to a thousand of our years (Koran XXII: 47), so this forty days devoted to Adam is an extraordinary length of time.
7. Sachiko Murata quotes the only passage in which Sam'ānī mentions (in passing) Eve in *The Tao of Islam: A Sourcebook on Gender Relationships in Islamic Thought* (Albany: SUNY Press 1992), p. 35.

is not interested in those elements of the myth that allow for a differentiation of gender roles.[8] When Sam'ānī says "Adam," he follows the Koran and much of the Islamic tradition by understanding the word to refer to the first or archetypal human being, whose fundamental qualities are shared by all human beings.[9] Since Sam'ānī is dealing with the question of what it means to be human, he can ignore the question of what it means to be a man or a woman. Adam's fall is the fall of everyone.

ADAM'S CREATION

The first question that naturally arises is why God created Adam in the first place. In explaining this, Sam'ānī keeps in view two basic categories of divine names that are frequently discussed in Islamic texts: names that refer to God's gentleness, beauty, mercy, and nearness, and names that refer to His severity, majesty, wrath, and distance.[10]

Unique among all created things, human beings can know God and His whole creation, since they alone were taught all God's names, both the names of majesty and the names of beauty. However, people do not come into the world knowing these names in any conscious way. Sam'ānī points out that when Adam was in Paradise, he still had not yet fully actualized the knowledge of these names. He had come to know the meaning of the names of beauty and mercy, but he did not know the significance of the names of majesty and wrath. In order to gain this understanding, he first had to come

---

8. As soon as Eve is distinguished from Adam, a relationship is set up between them, and then one needs to discuss the nature of this relationship. From Sam'ānī's point of view, this is a secondary matter, subordinate to the question of God's relationship with all human beings. The divine-human relationship is the focus of the myth, not the man-woman relationship.

9. This usage of the term Adam is of course Koranic. Note, for example, the following passage, which is addressed to all human beings. God is speaking: "We established you in the earth, and there appointed for you a livelihood; little thanks you show. We created you, then We shaped you, then We said to the angels, 'Bow yourselves to Adam'" (Koran VII: 10-11). Sam'ānī frequently refers to Adam and then quotes relevant Koranic verses in which the dual form of the verb is being employed, since both Adam and Eve are at issue.

10. On the fundamental significance of these two categories of names for much of Islamic thought, see Murata, *Tao of Islam.*

down to the earth.

> God brought Adam into the garden of gentleness and sat him down on the throne of happiness. He gave him cups of joy, one after another. Then He sent him out, weeping, burning, wailing. Thus, just as God let him taste the cup of gentleness at the beginning, so also He made him taste the draught of pure, unmixed, and uncaused severity in the end.[11]

Since God is infinite, the possible modes in which the knowledge of His names can be realized are also infinite. This means that it is not enough for Adam himself to know God's names. Each of his children must also know the names in his or her own unique way. Only then can every potentiality of the original human constitution come to be actualized. One implication of this perspective is that Hell itself demands human existence in this world. Hell is nothing but a domain that is ruled almost exclusively by the names of wrath and severity, just as Paradise is ruled by the names of mercy and gentleness, while the present world is governed by the effects of both kinds of names. The fact that God is merciful and wrathful demands that there be both Paradise and Hell. Hence, Sam'ānī tells us, God addressed Adam as follows when He wanted to explain to him why it was necessary for him to leave Paradise:

> Within the pot of your existence are shining jewels and jet-black stones. Hidden within the ocean of your constitution are pearls and potsherds. And as for Us, We have two houses: In one We spread out the dining-cloth of good-pleasure... In the other We light up the fire of wrath... If We were to let you stay in the Garden, Our attribute of severity would not be satisfied. So leave this place and go down into the furnace of affliction and the crucible of distance. Then We will bring out into the open the deposits, artifacts, subtleties, and tasks that are concealed within your heart.[12]

God's gentleness and severity are reflected in the two dimensions of Adam's nature, dimensions that the tradition calls 'spirit' and 'clay'. The attribute of gentleness is connected to spirit, while

11. *Rawḥ,* p. 199.
12. *Rawḥ,* p. 297, also cf. *Rawḥ,* p. 199, where Sam'ānī makes the same point in more detail.

the attribute of severity is more closely bound up with clay. But to say this is not to devalue clay, for severity is also a divine attribute. Without clay, Adam would have been an angel, not a human being, and then he could not have performed the function for which he was created.

> If there had been only spirit, Adam's days would have been free of stain and his acts would have remained without adulteration. But undefiled acts are not appropriate for this world, and from the beginning he was created for the vicegerency of *this* world.[13]

This last point is important, and Sam'ānī often refers to it. The Koran states explicitly that God's purpose in creating Adam was to place a vicegerent in the earth. Adam could not have been the vicegerent if he had remained in Paradise.

> Adam was not brought from Paradise into this world because of his slip. Even if we suppose that he had not slipped, he still would have been brought into this world. The reason for this is that the hand of vicegerency and the carpet of kingship were waiting for the coming of his foot. Ibn 'Abbās said, "God had taken him out of the Garden before putting him into it."[14]

If God created Adam to be a vicegerent in the earth, why did He not place him there immediately? Sam'ānī offers several answers to this question. In the present context, he replies by having recourse to the nature of Paradise, which is dominated by God's attributes of mercy and gentleness. When Adam was first created, he was like a child, so he did not have the strength to bear God's wrath and severity. Hence God caressed and nurtured him for a while until he gained strength. Then He sent him down to this world, where the attributes of severity and wrath are displayed openly.

> Adam was still a child, so God brought him into the path of caresses. The path of children is one thing, the furnace of heroes something else. Adam was taken into Paradise on the shoulders of the great angels of God's kingdom. Paradise was made the cradle

13. *Rawḥ,* p. 420.
14. *Rawḥ,* p. 313.

> for his greatness and the pillow for his leadership, since he still did not have the endurance for the court of severity.[15]

One of the several virtues of Adam's fall is that it paved the way for his descendants to enter Paradise. Sam'ānī tells us that God sent Adam out of Paradise with the promise that He would bring him back with all his children.

> Then the creatures will all come to know that, just as We can bring Adam's form out of Paradise through the attribute of severity, so also We can bring him back through the attribute of gentleness.
>
> Tomorrow, Adam will go into Paradise with his children. A cry will rise up from all the particles of Paradise because of the crowding. The angels of the world of the dominion will look with wonder and say, "Is this that same man who moved out of Paradise a few days ago in poverty and indigence?" Adam, bringing you out of Paradise was a curtain over this business and a covering over the mysteries... Suffer a bit of trouble, then in a few days, take the treasure![16]

LOVE

Like Rūmī and many other Sufis, Sam'ānī finds the key to human existence in God's Love for human beings and human love for God. He frequently comments on the Koranic verse, "He loves them and they love Him" (Koran V: 54). Nothing other than human beings can love God with full love, since nothing else is made in God's own image.

> God created every creature in keeping with the demand of power, but He created Adam and his children in keeping with the demand of love. He created other things in respect of being the Strong, but He created you in respect of being the Friend.[17]

Although the manifestation of Adam's greatness depends upon the outer dimension of his self known as 'clay' *(gil)*, the true locus of his glory lies in the innermost dimension of his self known as 'heart' *(dil)*, for the heart is where God looks and love for Him is born.

---

15. *Rawḥ,* p. 262.
16. *Rawḥ,* p. 91-92.
17. *Rawḥ,* p. 223.

> The place of Love is the heart, and the heart is pure gold, the pearl of the breast's ocean, the ruby of the innermost mystery's mine. ...The divine majesty polished it by gazing upon it, and the burnisher of the Unseen placed its mark upon it, making it bright and pure. ...The traces of the lights of the beauty of unqualified Love appear in the mirrors of pious hearts. Human love subsists through God's Love.[18]

Love, it needs to be remembered, can never be separate from pain and anguish. Lovers yearn for their beloved, and the more difficult the beloved is to reach, the greater the lovers suffer. The goal of love is union, and the divine attributes that bring about union are those of mercy and gentleness. But just as love demands union, so also it demands separation. There can be no love without testing and trial. True love proves itself by becoming more intense when the beloved is far away. Hence the lover must experience the effects of the names of wrath and severity, since it is these names that manifest God's distance. In this world and in Hell, the effect of these divine names is affliction, pain, and suffering.

> From the Throne down to the earth, no love whatsoever is sold except in the house of human grief and joy. Many sinless and pure angels were in the Court, but only this handful of dust was able to carry the burden of this body-melting, heart-burning verse: ["He loves them, and they love him"].[19]

Love is a divine quality that correlates with God Himself, who is both beautiful and majestic, merciful and wrathful, gentle and severe, near and distant. The angels are cut off from God's love because they cannot taste true distance, while the beasts are far from Love because they cannot experience true nearness. Human beings are woven from nearness and distance. All conflicting attributes are brought together within them. Only they can truly love God, within whom all opposites coincide.

> In the eighteen thousand worlds, no one drank down the cup that holds the covenant of "They love Him" except human beings.[20]

---

18. *Rawḥ,* p. 223.
19. *Rawḥ,* p. 488.
20. *Rawḥ,* p. 488.

Human beings are the crown of God's creation, since they manifest the full range of the divine attributes. Without them the world would be a drab place indeed.

> Before Adam was brought into existence, there was a world full of existent things, creatures, formed things, determined things—but all of it was a tasteless stew. The salt of pain was missing. When that great man walked out from the hiding-place of nonexistence into the spacious desert of existence, the star of Love began to shine in the heaven of the breast of Adam's clay. The sun of loverhood began to burn in the sky of his innermost mystery.[21]

What made Adam great was the fact that he carried the burden of the Trust. For Sam'ānī, that Trust is love for God. Only Adam knew the secret of love, for it was the underlying cause of his own existence. He knew that his love could not be nurtured and strengthened until he tasted the pain of separation and severity. Hence he ate the forbidden fruit.

> In keeping with God's munificence and generosity Adam was sent into Paradise, where he sat on the pillow of mightiness. The whole of Paradise was put under his command, but he did not look at it, because he did not see a speck of grief or of Love's reality. He said, "Oil and water don't mix."[22]

God was party, of course, to Adam's disobedience, because He had created him for the vicegerency, which is inseparable from Love. And the essence of Love is yearning and heartache. As Sam'ānī remarks,

> That Lord who was able to protect Joseph from committing an ugly act could have prevented Adam from tasting of the tree. But since the world has to be full of tumult and affliction, what could be done?[23]

When God offered the Trust to the heavens, the earth, and the mountains, they all refused, since they did not know the secret of Love. But Adam, as a lover, thought only about his Beloved. Hence

21. *Rawḥ,* p. 295.
22. *Rawḥ,* p. 237.
23. *Rawḥ,* p. 296.

he did not bother to look at his own incapacity, even though the Trust was a heavy burden that was feared by all of creation.

> The poor polo-ball in the field! Caught in the bend of the stick, it runs on its own head, sent by the hands and feet of the players. If it reaches this one—a stick. If it reaches that one—a stick. A frail handful of dust was placed in the bend of the polo-stick—the Almighty's severity. The ball rushes from the beginning of the field—the beginningless divine will—to the end of the field—the endless divine desire. At the front of the field, a banner is set up: "He shall not be questioned as to what He does, but they shall be questioned" [Koran XXI: 23]. At the back of the field stands a second banner: "He does what He desires" [Koran LXXXV: 16].
>
> But a bargain was struck with the ball: "You look at the gaze of the Sultan, not at the striking of the stick." Those who looked at the striking of the stick fled from the court. "They refused to carry it" [Koran XXXIII: 72]. Then Adam, with a lion's liver, lifted up that burden. As a matter of course, he reaped the fruit... The heaven and the earth saw today's burden *[bār]*. But Adam saw tomorrow's royal court *[bār]*. He said, "If I do not carry this burden, I will not be shown into the court of Majesty tomorrow." Like a man, he jumped at the task. Hence he became the point of the compass of mysteries. In truth, the seven heavens and the earth have not smelt a whiff of these words.[24]

ASPIRATION

The mark of lovers is their high aspiration. They strive only for their beloved, who is God. In order to reach Him, they must turn their gaze away from everything in the created universe, even Paradise.

> Adam had aspiration in his head. He took and gave through his own aspiration. Whenever human beings reach something, they reach it through aspiration. Otherwise, they would not reach anything at all through what is found in their own constitution. When Adam was first brought into existence... the angels prostrated themselves before him, and the name of kingship and vicegerency was recorded in the proclamation of his covenant. The eight paradises were given to him alone. "O Adam, dwell, you and your spouse, in the Garden" [Koran III: 35]... His boundless aspiration placed him like a Sultan on the horse of Love. He took the arrow

24. *Rawḥ*, 186-187.

> of uniqueness from the quiver of detachment and stretched the bow to its limit. He shot the beautiful peacock of Paradise, which was strutting in the garden of Everlastingness. He knew that this was the path of the detached, the work of those with high aspiration, the court of those brought near to God. Time, space, entities, effects, traces, shapes, existent things, and objects of knowledge must be erased completely from in front of you. If any of these cling to your skirt, the name of freedom will not stick to you. As long as you do not become free, you can never be a true servant of God.[25]

Love, then, means to be free of everything in the created world for the sake of God. It is to serve God, nothing else. And only human beings are given a constitution that allows them to serve God in His infinite, all-comprehensive reality, embracing the attributes of both beauty and majesty, gentleness and severity. Sam'ānī tells us that God addresses the angels and human beings as follows:

> O Riḍwān, Paradise belongs to you! O Mālik, Hell belongs to you! O Cherubim, the Throne belongs to you! O you with the burnt heart, you who carry the seal of My love! You belong to Me, and I belong to you.[26]

If human beings are to aspire to God, they need to be able to differentiate between God and everything else. Hence the key to human love and perfection is a discerning heart, one that sees God in the midst of the confusing multiplicity of creation. Adam provides the model for God's lovers, since he was not deceived even by Paradise.

> In reality Love has taken away the luster of both worlds. In the world of servanthood, Paradise and Hell have value. But in the world of Love, the two are not worth a speck of dust. They gave the eight paradises to Adam, the chosen. He sold them for one

---

25. *Rawḥ,* p. 120.
26. *Rawḥ,* p. 598, compare the following, where Sam'ānī begins by alluding to Iblis's claim to be better than Adam, because he was created of fire: "O accursed one, are you proud of fire? You belong to fire, and fire belongs to you. O Korah, are you proud of treasures? You belong to your treasures, and they belong to you. O Pharaoh, are you proud of the Nile? You belong to the Nile, and the Nile belongs to you! O you who declare My Unity. Are you proud of Me? You belong to Me, and I belong to you." *(Rawḥ,* p. 420).

> grain of wheat. He placed the wares of aspiration on the camel of good fortune and came down to the world of heartache.[27]

Adam had to go to Paradise in order to see the best in creation. Having seen it, he could measure its worth against his own Beloved.

> The root of every business is the discernment of value. The sultan of Adam's aspiration sat on the horse of his majestic state. Then it rode into the Garden to measure its worth. [In jurisprudence] there is a difference of opinion as to whether or not a person can buy what he has not seen. But no one disagrees that you cannot judge the value of something without having seen it.
>
> "O Adam, what is entering Paradise worth to you?" He replied, "For someone who fears Hell, Paradise is worth a thousand lives. But for someone who fears You, Paradise is not worth a grain." Hence the wisdom in taking Adam to Paradise was to make his aspiration manifest.[28]

When Adam saw that Paradise had no value, he naturally decided to leave. But God had given it to him as his own domain. The only way to get out quickly was to break God's commandment and suffer His displeasure.

> When Adam reached for the grain of wheat, it is not that he did not know what it was. On the contrary, he knew, but he made his own road short.[29]

POVERTY AND NEED

Human love grows up out of need *(niyāz)* which Sam'ānī calls "a fire in the heart, a pain in the breast, and dust on the face"[30] If you have something, you do not need it. God possesses all perfections in Himself and has no needs. Only those who possess no perfections whatsoever can love God fully. To the degree that people find wealth and independence in themselves and see themselves as positive and good, they will be empty of love for God. The secret of Adam's love was that he saw himself as nothing. This helps explain

27. *Rawḥ,* p. 170.
28. *Rawḥ,* p. 314.
29. *Rawḥ,* 198, compare *Rawḥ,* p. 90, translated in Murata, *Tao,* p. 65.
30. *Rawḥ,* p. 186.

why the Sufis call their way the path of "poverty." As the Koran puts it, "O people, you are the poor toward God; and God—He is the Wealthy, the Praiseworthy" (Koran XXXV: 15). Sam'ānī quotes a great Sufi on the question of poverty and need:

> Sahl ibn 'Abdallāh Tustarī said, "I looked at this affair, and I saw that no path takes one nearer to God than need *[iftiqār],* and no veil is thicker than making claims *[da'wā]."*...
>
> Look at the path of Iblis, and you will see nothing but making claims. Then look at the path of Adam, and you will see nothing but need. O Iblis, what do you say? "I am better than he" [Koran VII: 12]. O Adam, what do you say? "Our Lord, we have wronged ourselves" [Koran VII: 23]. God brought all the existent things out from the cover of nonexistence into the open plain of His decree, but the plant of need grew only in earth. When this handful of earth was moulded, it was moulded with the water of need. It had everything, but it had to have need as well, so that it would never cease weeping before God's court.
>
> Adam's constitution was moulded of need, and he received help from need. The angels had to prostrate themselves before him, and he was placed on the throne of kingship and vicegerency, while the angels near to God were placed next to him. But his need did not decrease by a single mote of dust. He was taken to Paradise, and this proclamation was made: "Eat thereof easefully, you two, wherever you desire" [Koran II: 35]. "The eight Paradises belong to you; wander freely as you wish." But his poverty did not disappear.[31]

Adam's need distinguishes him sharply from all other creatures, who are satisfied with what they have. Adam can never be satisfied, since he desires the Infinite.

> They say that on the Guarded Tablet it is written, "Adam, do not eat the wheat." And in the same place it is written that he ate it. "Surely the human being was created grasping" [Koran LXX: 19]. The greed of Adam's children goes back to the time of Adam himself. Whoever is not greedy is not a human being. As much as a person eats, he has to have more. If someone eats something and says, "I'm full," he's lying. There is still more space.[32]

---

31. *Rawḥ,* p. 90.
32. *Rawḥ,* p. 156.

Adam's need for God grows up out of his recognition that he himself is nothing. This recognition of his own unreality distinguishes him from the angels, who think of themselves as something.

> Before Adam, it was the time of the rich and the possessors of capital. As soon as Adam's turn arrived, the sun of poverty and need arose and indigence made its appearance. There was a group of creatures sitting on the treasure of glorification and calling God holy. They were auctioning off their own goods—"We glorify Thee in praise" [Koran II: 30]. But Adam was a poor man who came from the hut of need and the corner of intimate prayer. He had dressed himself in indigence and destitution. Poverty was his means, so in regret he raised up a cry in the court of the Almighty—"Our Lord, we have wronged ourselves" [Koran VII: 23].
>
> O dervish! They take the rejected coin from beggars in place of good cash; they close their eyes to the transaction. But when it comes to the rich, they are very careful. No doubt, the angels of the dominion had many capital goods, but among these was a certain amount of self-praise. They had written down the notation of 'we-ness' *[nahnīyyat]* on the wares of their own obedient acts. Adam had no capital, but his breast was a mine for the jewel of need and an oyster for the pearl of poverty...
>
> O angels of the dominion, O inhabitants of the precincts of holiness and the gardens of intimacy! You are all wealthy and possessors of riches, but Adam is a poor man, and he looks upon himself with contempt. Your good coin is adulterated, since you turn your attention and vision toward yourselves. Now you must place the good coin of your own works into the furnace of Adam's need. He is the assayer of the divine presence. 'Prostrate yourselves before Adam' [Koran II: 34].[33]

HUMILITY

Adam's need implies that he recognizes his own incapacity and worthlessness. Need demands humility, which is the acknowledgement of human weakness and nothingness in face of the divine reality. Humility sees all good as coming from God, and all evil as coming from self.

---

33. *Rawḥ,* pp. 294-295.

> Alms are given to the needy, and we are the needy. Our "good" is in fact slipping, while evil is our own attribute. Our father Adam was given the hat of election and the crown of being chosen. Then he fell prisoner to a grain of wheat. What then is the state of us children who have been left in the church of this world? "When the beginning of the bottle is dregs, what do you think its end will be?"[34]

But if our wine is all dregs, this is not our loss but our gain.

> You should know for certain that the grain of wheat that Adam placed in his mouth was the fortress of his lifetime. Human nature demands looking, and whoever looks at himself will not be saved... That grain of wheat was made into Adam's fortress. Whenever Adam looked at himself, he looked in shame. He comes forward asking forgiveness, not in pride. In order for a person to be a traveler on the path to God, he must say, "Praise belongs to God," whenever he looks at God's giving success. And whenever he looks at his own actions, he must say, "I ask forgiveness from God."[35]

Because of his slip, Adam recognizes that his own shortcomings are the dominant reality of his own existence. He is nothing but dirt. Anything else comes from divine providence. Hence, far from being a fault, Adam's fall is his salvation and glory. When the Koran says that the human being was "a wrongdoer, ignorant" while recounting how he carried the Trust, this is not a criticism but a statement of his saving virtue. Likewise, the "soul that commands to evil" *(al-nafs al-ammāra bi'l-sū'),* which every human being must confront, makes possible the ascent beyond the heavens to God.

> If a palace does not have a garbage pit next to it, it is incomplete. There must be a garbage pit next to a lofty palace so that all the refuse and filth that gather in the palace can be thrown there. In the same way, whenever God formed a heart by means of the light of purity, He placed this impure soul next to it as a dustbin. The black spot of 'ignorance' flies on the same wings as the jewel of purity. There needs to be a bit of corruption so that purity can be built

---

34. *Rawḥ,* p. 261-62.
35. *Rawḥ,* pp. 205-206, also compare *Rawḥ,* p. 624.

> upon it. A straight arrow needs a crooked bow. O heart, you be like a straight arrow! O soul, you take the shape of a crooked bow…!
>
> When they place the dress of purity on the heart, they show the heart that black spot of wrongdoing and ignorance so that it will remember itself and know who it is. When a peacock spreads out all its feathers, it gains a different joy from each feather. But as soon as it looks down at its own feet, it becomes embarrassed. That black spot of ignorance is the peacock's foot that always stays with you.[36]

The lesson that people need to learn from all this is that imperfection is part of human nature, that God knows this full well, and that no one should despair of God's mercy. At the same time, they have to take a lesson from the angels and never be proud of their own good works, for seeing oneself as good is to see wrongly, since all good goes back to God.

> The angels had no slips, neither in the past nor in the future. But there would be a slip on Adam's part in the future, for God said, "And Adam disobeyed" [Koran XX: 121]. However, there is a secret hidden under this, for the angels saw that they were pure, while Adam saw that he was indigent. The angels were saying, "We call You holy" [Koran II: 30], that is, we keep our own selves pure for Your sake. Adam said, "Our Lord, we have wronged ourselves." God showed him that the slip of him who sees the slip is better in His eyes than the purity of him who sees the purity. That is why God gave Adam the honor of being the object before whom prostration was made, while He gave the angels the attribute of being the 'prostrators'. Hence no obedient person should be self-satisfied, and no disobedient person should lose hope.[37]

GOD'S FORGIVENESS

Human imperfection leads to the perfection of love. Awareness of imperfection keeps people from gazing upon themselves and allows them to turn all their aspiration toward the Beloved. At the same time, imperfection allows God to manifest His perfections. Without sinners, how could He be the Forgiver? Hence God's forgiveness

36. *Rawḥ,* p. 288.
37. *Rawḥ,* p. 406.

demanded Adam's fall. Sam'ānī sometimes quotes a sound *ḥadīth* of the Prophet that alludes to the role of God's forgiveness in bringing sin into existence: "If you did not sin, God would bring a people who do sin, so that He could forgive them."

> The angels were honored by the Divine Presence. Each of them worshiped while wearing a shirt of sinlessness and an earring of obedience. But as soon as the turn of the earth arrived, they called out from the top of their purity and began to boast in the bazaar of 'me, and no one else'. They said, "We glorify Thee in praise" [Koran II: 30].
>
> "O angels of the celestial dominion! Although you are obedient, you have no blind passion in your souls, nor do you have any darkness in your constitution. If human beings disobey, they have blind passion and darkness. Your obedience along with all your force is not worth a mote of dust before My majesty and tremendousness. And their disobedience along with all their brokenness and dejection does not diminish My domain. You hold fast to your own sinlessness, but they hold fast to My mercy. Through your obedience, you make manifest your own sinlessness and greatness, but through their disobedience, they make manifest My bounty and mercy."[38]

In one long passage, Sam'ānī cites accounts of several great prophets to show that each of them performed certain blameworthy acts. But this is not a sign of their imperfection, but rather of God's mercy. God wanted to provide human beings with excuses for their weaknesses. Sam'ānī begins with the prophet Adam:

> The perfection of divine gentleness caused a mote to fall into the eye of every great person's days. Hence those who come after will have something to cling to. Adam fell on his head in the Abode of Sinlessness. The Almighty Lord had decreed a slip at first so that that abode would be an abode of sinners. Then if a weak person should fall on his head, he will not lose hope. He will say, "In the abode of subsistence, in the house of bestowal, in the station of security, and in the place of honor, Adam fell on his head, and the Almighty Lord accepted his excuse. In the abode of annihilation, in the house of affliction, and in the world of grief and trouble, it will not be strange if a weak person falls on his head and the

38. *Rawḥ,* p. 300.

> Almighty Lord does not take him to task, but instead accepts his excuse."[39]

In short, Sam'ānī sees the whole drama of the fall in terms of God's kindness and mercy. God desires to make human beings aware of their own nothingness so that they will put aside claims and open themselves up to His gentleness, love, and forgiveness.[40] I quote a final passage that summarizes his views:

> Dervish, I will tell you a secret... In the row of purity they gave Adam, the chosen, a cup full of the unmixed wine of love. From the distant Pleiades to the end of the earth they set up the hat of his good fortune and the mirror of his magnificence. Then they commanded the angels of the celestial kingdom to prostrate themselves before him. But his magnificence, honor, eminence, good fortune, high level, and purity did not appear in that prostration. It appeared in "Adam disobeyed" [Koran XX: 121]. In certainty and in truth, these words extend higher than the Throne of God's majesty. Why? Because being treated kindly in the time of conformity is no proof of honor. Being treated kindly in the time of opposition is the proof of honor.
>
> The chosen and beautiful Adam sat on the throne of majesty and perfection with the crown of prosperity on his head and the robe of bounty across his breast. The mount of beneficence was at the door, the pillars of his good fortune's seat were higher than the Throne, the umbrella of kingship was opened above his head, and he himself had raised the exalted banner of knowledge in the world. If the angels and the celestial spheres should kiss the ground before him, that is no surprise. What is surprising is that he fell into the pit of that slip. His straight stature, which had been pulled up by "God elected Adam" [Koran III: 33], became bent because "Adam disobeyed." Then from the heaven of eternal gentleness the crown of "Then He chose him" [Koran XX: 122] took wing. O dervish, if God had not wanted to accept him with all his defects, He would not have created him with all those defects...
>
> Do not think that Adam was brought out of Paradise for eating some wheat. God wanted to bring him out. He did not break any commandments. God's commandments remained pure of being

39. *Rawḥ,* p. 309.
40. For Sam'ānī's explanation of what was going on behind the scenes when Adam ate the forbidden fruit, see *Rawḥ,* p. 312, translated in Murata, *Tao,* p. 35. For his explanation of how God's mercy and forgiveness determine human existence, see *Rawḥ,* pp. 224-225, translated in Murata, *Tao,* pp. 138-139.

broken. Tomorrow, God will bring a million people who committed great sins into Paradise. Should He take Adam out of Paradise for one small act of disobedience?[41]

41. *Rawḥ,* pp. 150-151.

Sanā'ī Leaving his Shoes Outside a Butcher's Shop. From the *Majālis al-'ushshāq*. Or. 11837, f. 61b.(Courtesy of the British Library).

Comparative Notes on Sanā'ī and 'Aṭṭār

J.T.P. de Bruijn

I. INTRODUCTION

It is a commonplace to mention Ḥakīm Sanā'ī (d. 525/1131) and Farīd al-Dīn 'Aṭṭār (d. c. 618/1221) together as early highlights in a tradition of Persian mystical poetry which reached its culmination in the works of Mawlānā Jalāl al-Dīn Rūmī and those who belonged to the early Mawlawī circle. There is abundant evidence available to prove that the founders of the Mawlawiyya in the thirteenth and fourteenth centuries regarded these two poets as their most important predecessors. This was acknowledged by Rūmī's son Sulṭān Valad when he wrote:

'Aṭṭār was the soul and Sanā'ī his two eyes;
We have come as a qibla *to Sanā'ī and 'Aṭṭār.*

His words express both a sense of superiority and of indebtedness towards these older masters of mystical poetry.[1]

In an introduction she wrote to the French translation of one of 'Aṭṭār's works, the mystical epic *Muṣībat-nāma,* Prof. Annemarie Schimmel ascribed "une certaine qualité 'terrienne'"—the quality of earth to Sanā'ī—while she compared Rūmī to fire, and 'Aṭṭār, the poet in the middle, to water: to "a river springing from a small

1. *Dīwān-i Sulṭān Valad,* edited by S. Nafīsī, (Tehran 1338 S.Hsh./1959), p. 240. On the variations of this statement, to be found in Sulṭān's Valad's *Dīwān* and elsewhere, see the present writer's "Sanā'ī and the Rise of Persian Mystical Poetry," in *Actes du 8me Congrès de l'Union Européenne des Arabisants et Islamisants* (Aix-en-Provence 1978), p. 35.

source and flowing slowly through mountains and valleys." Amīn-i Rāzī, the author of the sixteenth century anthology *Haft iqlīm,* relates that he heard an anonymous mystic say that 'Aṭṭār was like an ant, "travelling along the Path at a slow pace," in contrast to Rūmī, who like "a royal falcon reached the *qibla* of Truth from the platform of the Path in a twinkling of the eye."[2]

These similes provide parallels to the 'eyes,' 'the soul' and 'the *qibla*' of Sulṭān Valad in as far as they all imply a gradual development of Persian mystical poetry toward a fulfilment reached finally with Rūmī. However, the question remains to be answered whether this relationship between Sanā'ī and 'Aṭṭār was only established in hindsight or whether it can indeed be accepted as a reality of literary history. Can Sanā'ī indeed be considered as an important influence on 'Aṭṭār? Did the two poets really participate in a single strain of mystical poetry as it was seen by the Mawlawī tradition?

A meaningful comparison between Sanā'ī and 'Aṭṭār can only be made through a detailed search for contrasts and similarities of both form and content in their works. In the present essay only a few notes can be presented by way of a reconnaissance of the field. Out of the various genres of mystical poetry to which each poet contributed, their respective didactical *mathnawī*s will be considered most closely.

II.

First, however, a few facts about Sanā'ī and 'Aṭṭār should be mentioned. Sanā'ī was born in the last quarter of the 5th/11th century in Ghazna, a city in the eastern parts of present-day Afghanistan which was then the residence of the Ghaznavid Sultans. He died in the same city in 525/1131, but we know that he spent a part of his life in the great cities of Khurāsān. We are less certain about the dates of 'Aṭṭār's life. It is generally accepted that he died in his home-town Nishapur at the hands of the Mongol invaders of Khurāsān as it is asserted in an early source. This means that he died about 618/1221, presumably at a great age, so that his earliest works

2. *Le Livre de l'épreuve (Muṣībatnāma),* traduit du persan par Isabelle de Gastines; introduction par Annemarie Schimmel (Paris 1981), p. 11.

were probably written towards the end of the preceding century.

In neither case do we have anything like a reliable biography, independent from data which can be gathered from their own works. Quite early, as it seems, pious phantasy began to weave legends around the personality of Sanā'ī which, eventually, grew into a small hagiography. Already in 674/1275-76, the geographer Zakarīyā al-Qazwīnī described him as a sage and mystic who lived in "ruined places" *(kharābāt)* in self-imposed poverty and wandered around on his bare feet. Such picturesque details were clearly inferred from the imagery Sanā'ī himself used in his poems without having the intention to be taken literally. Most celebrated is the story of his conversion to the mystical path as the result of an encounter with a tramp who led a miserable life in the basement of a bathhouse. This man scolded him for squandering his talents on such unworthy goals as soliciting the rewards of his royal patron. These words affected Sanā'ī so deeply that he changed his life and became a mystical recluse.

If one follows the clues contained in Sanā'ī's poetry a rather different picture emerges. He began his career as a minor poet in Ghazna, dependent on patrons among the local elites surrounding the Sultan's court, apparently without much success. After having left his home town for Khurāsān, he found there a more congenial environment with religious personalities in the various cities of that eastern Iranian province. Many of those clerical patrons were also active as preachers and it is very likely that the turn towards a religiously inspired poetry which took place in Sanā'ī's career about that time was caused by the demands for that kind of literature on the part of these patrons. At the end of his life when he had returned to Ghazna, he wrote his major work, the didactical poem *Ḥadīqat al-ḥaqīqat*, which he dedicated to the Ghaznavid Sultan Bahrām-shāh, thus showing to what extent he still was attached to the old ways of Persian court poetry

In the case of 'Aṭṭār, we also have some legends of little historical value, but there is, on the other hand, hardly any evidence to be drawn from his own works to compensate for this. In none of his works can any reference be found to a worldly patron of his art nor, for that matter, to a spiritual master whose guidance he would have followed. On rare occasions he speaks about himself in little stories which depict him as a pharmacist who ran a shop in the bazaar of Nishapur.[3]

III.

If we would have to judge only on these external facts, there would be very little ground for a comparison between the two poets. It must be added that the younger poet hardly ever refers to Sanā'ī in his works. The latter's name is only mentioned twice by 'Aṭṭār; both references occur moreover in a single work, the *Book of Afflictions (Muṣībat-nāma).*

There are also noticeable differences as far as their works are concerned. Sanā'ī left us, besides three *mathnawī* poems, a huge *Dīwān* of lyrical poems containing specimens of all the forms and genres familiar from the secular tradition of Persian poetry as it had developed up to his time. However, there are a number of important new elements to be noted in his lyrical poetry. One of these is a substantial number of *ghazal*s, in fact the first sizable collection of this kind of poetry known in the history of Persian literature. This does not mean, of course, that Sanā'ī invented the Persian *ghazal*. It is certain that the *ghazal* had already been a common form for a very long time among the poets of the court. Up to the time of Sanā'ī, however, it had existed mainly as a form of oral poetry about love and wine, reflecting the frivolous atmosphere at the Persian courts. Sanā'ī's contribution was to give a different meaning to this form by loading its anacreontic themes with a new, religious content. Remarkable also was his use of the *qaṣīda* as a didactical poem. In some early manuscripts of his *Dīwān* these poems have been collected in a special section headed *zuhdiyyāt,* that is, poems on ascetic themes. Another characteristic genre are the so-called *qalandariyyāt,* poems distinguished by a cluster of themes relevant to antinomian mysticism. They were of great important to the subsequent development of Sufi poetry.

The collected lyrics of 'Aṭṭār show a greater amount of specialization. The majority of these poems are either *ghazal*s or quatrains. The latter have been collected separately in the *Mukhtār-nāma*—

3. See further B. Reinert, *Encyclopaedia Iranica,* s.v. 'Aṭṭār.

actually a selection from a much larger number of poems—which has been arranged according to subject-matter.[4] 'Aṭṭār also wrote a few *qaṣīdas*, all of the didactical type known already from Sanā'ī's work.[5] Unlike Sanā'ī he also wrote a major prose work, the *Tadhkirat al-awlīyā'*, a collection of the lives and sayings of the early Sufi Shaykhs. The best known part of his collected works are the *mathnawīs*, at least five of which are generally considered to be authentic. There can be no doubt that 'Aṭṭār's entire work is much more homogeneous than is that of Sanā'ī, as it contains exclusively mystical poetry and prose.

IV.

In a recent study on Sanā'ī,[6] I had a chance to indicate some traces of the influence of Sanā'ī on 'Aṭṭār as far as the use of *qalandarī* motifs is concerned. In the present essay I would like to concentrate on the use they made of the *mathnawī*, one of the most characteristic forms of Persian poetry, which the mystical poets made into an effective instrument of their teaching.

The *mathnawī* was probably created in early Islamic times on the basis of a pre-Islamic Iranian type of narrative and didactic verse about which we know little more than the fact that it did not yet have a regular pattern of rhyme. As the use of rhyming couplets became its most distinctive feature, the *mathnawī* as we actually know it from the Islamic period must have been adapted at a very early date to the principles of Arabic metrics. As far as their contents are concerned, *mathnawīs* were marked from the very beginning by a combination of narrative and didactical elements, even in poems dealing chiefly with heroic or romantic stories. Hardly any *mathnawī* was ever composed without at least some sections which properly should be classified as 'wisdom lit-

---

4. Edited by M.R. Shafī'ī Kadkanī (Tehran 1358 A.Hsh./1979); see also the analysis of this collection by H. Ritter, *Oriens* 13-14 (1961), pp. 195-228.
5. *Dīwān-i ghazaliyyāt wa qaṣā'id*, edited by T. Tafaḍḍulī (Tehran 1341 A.Hsh./1962), pp. 645-767.
6. "The *Qalandariyyāt* in Persian Mystical Poetry, From Sanā'ī Onwards" in Leonard Lewisohn (ed.), *The Heritage of Sufism II*, pp. 75-86.

erature'.[7]

As an early instance of this the heroic poem *Garshāsp-nāma* may be mentioned. It was written in the second half of the fifth/eleventh century by the poet and lexicographer Asadī who dedicated the poem to a local ruler in Azarbaijan.[8] The story is a chivalrous novel in the style of the *Shāh-nāma*. Garshāsp is presented as an ancestor of Firdawsī's hero Rustam, living in a primeval period. His adventures bring him to India and Sri Lanka where, like Alexander, he meets with wise Brahmans who disclose to him their ancient wisdom. More interesting for our purpose, however, are the sections which Asadī added to the obligatory praise to God and the Prophet, and the dedication to his patron in the introduction of his poem. They deal respectively with 'religion' *(dīn),* 'the world' *(jihān),* 'the heavens' *(āsmān),* 'the natural elements' *(ṭabāyi'-i chahārgāna),* 'humankind' (*mardum)* and 'the soul and the body' *(tan wa jān)*. Together they sketch a coherent doctrine about the role of religion as the guiding principle of man's life on earth.

In this world, Asadī argues, man is permanently threatened by oppressive armies of demons, that is by the forces of the passions generated by his lower soul. The only way towards salvation is through religion and wisdom. The former provides him with a key to paradise and should prepare him to stand through the final judgement after the Mahdi has come to establish the realm of peace on earth. The latter, wisdom, should help him to understand the meaning of his earthly existence.

My purpose in referring to Asadī's poem here is to show how a *mathnawī* which in itself could not possibly be characterized as a religious work could be given an extra meaning. Through the addition of this doctrine of salvation the poet made it possible for his reader to read the adventures of Garshāsp as an emblem a man's journey through this world. From a literary point of view, this early example of religious didacticism in the *mathnawī* also demands our attention because Asadī clothed some of his ideas in an allegorical form. Most remarkable is the image of the human body which he

7. See further *Encyclopedia of Islam*. New Edition, VI, s.v. *Mathnawī*.

8. Ḥakīm Abū Naṣr 'Alī b. Aḥmad Asadī Ṭūsī, *Garshāsp-nāma,* ed. by Ḥabīb Yaghmā'ī, 2nd ed. (Tehran 1354 A.Hsh./1975).

evokes in the following passage:

> *The body should be seen as a house which contains a garden.*
> *It is lighted by the lamp of the soul, life is its pillar.*
> *Four chains are hanging down from its ceiling.*
> *The lamp is attached to them like a chandelier.*
> *Whenever the ties to these chains become weak,*
> *Suddenly damage appears from all sides:*
> *The house disintegrates, the garden withers;*
> *The pillar falls down, the lamp is extinguished.*[9]

V.

Sanā'ī's use of the *mathnawī* provides an almost exact parallel to the course of his literary and spiritual career. Early in his life he wrote a short *mathnawī* entitled *Kārnāma-i Balkhī,* an entirely secular work. There is no didacticism of any kind, not even any narrative fiction in it. The contents consist merely of panegyrics and satire directed towards patrons, fellow-poets and other contemporaries of the author. The only point which is of any interest to the present discussion is the fact that it faithfully reflects the stage of Sanā'ī's career where the turn towards religious poetry had not yet been made.

His second *mathnawī,* which received the eloquent Arabic title *Sayr al-'ibād ilā'l- ma'ād* (The Journey of the Faithful to the Place of Return), is of a quite different nature. The only feature it has in common with the *Kār-nāma* is that it also contains a panegyrical section. Roughly one-third of the less than 800 lines of the poem contain the praise of a certain Muḥammad ibn Manṣūr, a chief justice *(qaḍī'l-quḍāt)* and renowned preacher in the Khurāsānian city of Sarakhs. This person must have played an important role in the change-over in Sanā'ī's career to the writing of religious poetry by providing him with the social protection he needed. The really interesting part of the poem, however, is its long introduction which has the form of an allegory of the cosmic journey: Sanā'ī describes the development of his own soul up to the spiritual level occupied by his patron, who seems to have been to him a spiritual guide and a

9. *Garshāsp-nāma,* p. 12, 11-14.

Maecenas at the same time. The literary importance of this little work is considerably greater than its topical purpose alone would suggest. Even if it is an exaggeration to compare it with Dante's *Divina Commedia* (as Reynold Nicholson has done)[10] the poem is indeed a striking specimen of Sanā'ī's use of the allegorical technique. See, for example, how he pictured the animal soul which, according to medieval psychology, humans share with demons and animals. The animal soul controls the perception through the five sense organs corresponding to five 'inner' senses in the mind. At the same time, the instincts which prompt the animal being to feed, defend and procreate have all their foundation in this part of the soul which, in its turn, is subjected to physical forces, that is, the four material elements. At this level, therefore, psychic health can only subsist as long as these forces are in equilibrium:

A ruler with two faces and ten heads,
The offspring of two fathers and two mothers.
Five heads were looking out over the plain;
Five heads provided news about the Heavens.
Of noble origin, based on perception;
Endowed with knowledge, sprung from equity.
Clothed in images, greed, hate and lust.
A soul for demons, cattle and wild beasts.
Outwardly shining, but inside a fire.
One body, but divided into four:
These four survived as long as kept in balance,
But killed their children through inequity.[11]

VI.

The *Ḥadīqat al-ḥaqīqa* ('The Garden of Truth') is a product of Sanā'ī's old age. The poem has for centuries been a favorite of Muslim readers who were interested in Sufi poetry, but from a philological point of view the text is extremely problematic. It has been transmitted in a number of versions differing greatly as far as the arrangement of the text and the number of the verses are concerned.

---

10. In his short appraisal of the poem: *A Persian Forerunner of Dante* (Towyn-on-Sea, N. Wales 1944).
11. *Sayr al-'ibād ilā'l-ma'ād,* MS. Bağdatli Vehbi (Istanbul), No. 1672, fol. 181a.

The main cause of this confusion seems to have been the untimely death of Sanā'ī which prevented him from preparing a final version of the poem. Later editors have added material to which the poet himself had not yet assigned its proper place. It is quite obvious, however, that, in the process, many unauthentic passages have been inserted as well.

Fortunately, a very ancient copy of the poem has been preserved in a manuscript of the Süleymaniye Library, Istanbul. The copy was made in 552 of the Hijra calender (or 1157 A.D.) at Konya for a goldsmith by the name of 'Alī al-Ḥasan Ghāzī. The date is remarkable because it was only two decades after Sanā'ī died. The text of this version is much shorter—little more than 5000 distichs—than all other versions known to exist. It carries, moreover, a different title, namely *Fakhrī-nāma,* which refers to one of the honorary names of Sultan Bahrām-shāh. To all appearances, the Vehbi manuscript contains a form of the poem which brings us as close to the original design of Sanā'ī as we may ever hope to get.[12]

The *Fakhrī-nāma* can best be characterized as a continuing homiletic discourse. There is no leading story to guide the reader. Didacticism is the only discernible principle in the poem. At the most, one can divide its contents into three major sections:

1– An introductory section discusses the general aspects of religious life, such as man's relationship with and obligations to God, the urgency of his awakening from the slumber of neglect to prepare himself for the hereafter, the central significance of the Koran to the spiritual life and the examples of the great men of Islam: not only the Prophet and the four 'rightly-guided' Caliphs, but also Ḥasan and Ḥusayn and the Imāms of the most important school of Sunnite law, al-Shāfi'ī and Abū Ḥanīfa, are included among them. Sanā'ī strongly denies that there could be any contradiction between the pious reverence he paid to the 'People of the House' and his adherence to Sunni Islam. The doctrine of salvation expounded implies more than Muslim piety

12. For further details on the textual history of Sanā'ī's works, see the present writer's *Of Piety and Poetry: the Interaction of Religion and Literature in the Life and Works of Ḥakīm Sanā'ī of Ghazna* (Leiden 1983).

alone: there is much emphasis on the need for gnostic knowledge of the metaphysical structure of the universe and the constitution of the human soul.

2–The transition to the second section is made through the introduction of a brief allegory: the poet meets with a spiritual Guide who probably is to be identified with the *Intellectus Agens* ('the Active Intellect') of the philosophers, as this is the interpretation specified in a quite similar passage of the *Sayr al-'ibād.* The discourse then continues to deal with the particular demands made on the followers of Sanā'ī's path. He talks about matters of everyday life, such as sexual morality, the ethics of the profession of poetry, the equal rights of Persian and Arabic as far as religion is concerned, old age and death, family life and rules for eating, speaking and laughing. There is no apparent ordering in this catalogue of prescriptions except for the repeated warning given concerning the power of the lower soul (which stimulates lust, greed, aggression and jealousy), the condemnation of this world, and admonitions concerning the approaching end of earthly life. Finally, the ultimate goal becomes evident in a description of nature in springtime symbolizing the state of the purified human being. This confusing plurality of subjects appears to be the track of a 'Pilgrim's Progress'.

3–At this point another transition is made which brings the reader back to the concrete world in which Sanā'ī was living. He starts to praise the Sultan by means of an exposition of the ethics of the Islamic ruler as they are familiar from works of the 'mirror-for-princes' tradition. The poem closes with a lengthy plea by the poet to be excused from a close connection with the Ghaznavid court as he has opted for a secluded life.

This description of the contents of Sanā'ī's major work is by no means adequate but in its very incompleteness it may give one an idea of its great complexity. If, in spite of all this, the poem has indeed exerted a very pervasive influence it should be realized that the numerous small sections and even single lines lent themselves very easily for being selected from the whole of the text.

The force of Sanā'ī's discourse appears best in his art of

formulation. An attentive reading of his text brings to light a fine texture of abstract themes and subsidiary themes on the one hand, and illustrative elements like images, parables and anecdotes on the other, each layer performing its proper function within the exposition. To give an example I translate one of the earliest sections of the *Fakhrī-nāma*, where Sanā'ī broaches the theme of *tanzīh*, the purification of the concept of the Divine from anthropomorphic representations:

If what you search for is not in any place,
How can you ever start upon this journey?
The Royal Road leading your soul to God
Is nothing but the cleansing of the heart's mirror.
To him whose heart is free from any doubt
The image and the mirror are not one:
The mirror, which is form, remains behind,
For it only receives its forms through light.
But light itself can never leave the sun;
The fault lies with your mirror and your eyes.
To him who lives forever behind veils
Applies the parable of owl and sun:
If owls do not support the light of day,
The cause of this is weakness, not their nature.
You only look with phantasy and senses,
When unaware of lines, surfaces and points.
It is mere boasting to speak out here, at this stage,
If you can't tell the 'manifest' from the 'unified'.
Do you want Him to show Himself to you,
Don't hold the mirror oblique, keep it shining!
Likewise the sun, though not in want of light,
Appears to be of glass behind the clouds.
Joseph, who had more beauty than an angel,
Looked, mirrored in a dagger, like a demon.
The more your heart becomes a cleansed surface,
The better it reflects manifestations.
As Abū Bakr's faith was the sincerest,
So many things to him were manifest![13]

His treatment of this central theme of Islamic theology is entirely practical. The problem of *tanzīh* is reduced to the proper understand-

13. *Fakhrī-nāma,* MS. Bağdatli Vehbi (Istanbul), No. 1672, ff. 4a-b.

ing of the reflection of the Divine light in the mirror of the mystic's heart. In fact, it is the light which travels, not the mirror. The light remains essentially attached to its source, the sun, and can therefore never be united with the mirror. The point is further illustrated by a scientific example: the right view is comparable to that of the mathematician who would never be able to discern true geometrical proportions if he regarded things solely with his senses and his phantasy. In this way Sanā'ī puts the approach to God he is going to teach in his poem safely within the framework of the orthodox vision on the unbridgeable distance between man and his Creator.

VII.

Whatever importance Sanā'ī may have had for the early development of mystical poetry, there can be no doubt that 'Aṭṭār surpassed him as a writer of *mathnawī*s. Several important changes can be noticed in his works which helped the genre to mature. First of all, the relative prominence of the *mathnawī* should be noted. Even if we do not take into account that a great number of the works ascribed to 'Aṭṭār in the manuscripts were forgeries of a much later time, the output is very impressive indeed. The panegyrical references which determined the structure of both the *Sayr al-'ibād* and the *Ḥadīqa* have disappeared completely, which can be interpreted as a reflection of the conditions of 'Aṭṭār's personal life.

Most important of all, the narrative has become a major feature in his poems. It is, moreover, present in a variety of forms. His stories are also much more developed than those of Sanā'ī, where they were most often little more than very brief sketches. In his best known *mathnawī*s—the *Manṭiq al-ṭayr, Ilāhī-nāma,* and *Muṣībat-nāma*—he introduced the principle of the 'leading story' which he borrowed from a secular tradition, the 'mirrors-for-princes' in prose, such as *Kalīla wa Dimna* and *Sindbād-nāma*. With the exception of the *Asrār-nāma* all his major poems have a clearly and easily recognizable structure, strikingly in contrast with the often confusing line of thought followed by Sanā'ī in the *Ḥadīqa.*

The *Muṣībat-nāma,* which was mentioned above as the one text containing references to Sanā'ī by name, is much less known than the *Manṭiq al-ṭayr,* the famous 'Conference of the Birds' which has often been translated into Western languages.[14] Of the *Muṣībat-nāma* only one translation in French exists, but the poem is certainly not less interesting than the *Manṭiq al-ṭayr.* The subject-matter and allegorical technique which dominate the structure of the poem can tell us something about possible affinities with Sanā'ī's *mathnawīs*.[15]

The poems tells the allegorical story of the *fikrat-i sālik,* the human mind which travels through the cosmos and the spiritual world in search of self-knowledge. In his introduction to the story 'Aṭṭār explained to his readers the nature of his allegorical technique which he called *zabān-i ḥāl,* 'the language of spiritual feeling':[16]

> *That Traveller converses with the Angels,*
> *And brings to speech the Heavens and the Earth,*
> *Or goes beyond both Pedestal and Throne,*
> *Or puts his questions to so many things;*
> *That he seeks the opinion of the Prophets*
> *And queries every atom about its state.*
> *Consider that to be 'the language of spiritual feeling'*
> [zabān-i ḥāl],
> *It is not meant as plain and actual speech* [zabān-i qāl].
> *In actual speech this would be a deception,*
> *But in the language of spiritual feeling it is true.*
> *If this expression still seems strange to you,*
> *You may as well call it: 'the language of thought'.*[17]

'Aṭṭār devised a most ingenious plan for this journey. The track mainly goes downwards along various paths each of which represents a different sphere of existence. It starts in the metaphysical realm with the four archangels Jabrā'īl, Asrāfīl, Mīkā'īl and 'Azrā'īl; then follow the various places distinguished by the religious tradition as pertaining to the other world: from the Throne

14. For instance, by Dick Davis and Afkham Darbandi: Penguin Books (Harmondsworth 1984).
15. The *Muṣībat-nāma* was edited by Nūrānī Wiṣāl (Tehran 1338 A.Hsh./1959); for a detailed summary of its contents, see H. Ritter, *Das Meer der Seele* (Leiden 1955), pp. 18-30.
16. On the meaning of this rhetorical term see H. Ritter, *op. cit.,* p. 4, who translated it in German as "sprache des zustandes;" the archaic form *zafān* is still used instead of *zabān* in early manuscripts of 'Aṭṭār's works.
17. *Muṣībat-nāma* , p. 56.

of God down into Hell. Subsequently, the physical cosmos is explored when the mind visits the astral world, the natural elements and the main features of the terrestrial sphere (the Mountains, the Seas), until he reaches the composite beings, ranging from the minerals to man. From there the mind seeks help with the Prophets. Finally he reaches the Prophet Muḥammad who shows him the way into his own soul where he finds the reflection of God's light and the 'light of Muḥammad.' During this quest, the mind resorts to forty different entities from whom he receives answers which are explained to him by his spiritual Guide whom he had encountered when he was setting out on his journey.

Various sources have been mentioned for this structure. One is the well-known concept of *shafā'a,* the mediation by the Prophets and Muḥammad in particular on behalf of the believers at the Day of Judgement. There is also a very close link with the forty days vigil of the Sufis.[18] The text leaves several possibilities for an interpretation and this was undoubtedly the intention of the poet.

Apart from the leading stories mentioned earlier, the use of a great amount of small anecdotes filling these frameworks is one of the most attractive features of 'Aṭṭār's poems. In this respect he also surpasses Sanā'ī, with whom the didactical material always predominates. In the *Muṣībat-nāma,* 'Aṭṭār inserted the following story picturing Sanā'ī as an itinerant dervish who comments on the people he observes in the course of his travels:

Sanā'ī, in his wanderings without end,
Once saw a sweeper busy with his job.
When looking to the other side, his eye
Fell on a muezzin who called to prayer.
"The latter's work," he said, "is in no way better;
In fact, they carry out a similar task.
They do not know what they are really doing,
Performing only duties for a living.
Both immature, merely earning their bread,
I do not see what difference there is.

18. B. Radtke, in his article "Die älteste islamische Kosmographies. Muḥammad-i Ṭūsī's *'Ağā'ib ul-mahlūqāt," Der Islam,* 64 (1987), p. 286, points to the close resemblance between 'Aṭṭār's concept of the cosmos and the scientific views of his age.

Only: the sweeper does the honest labor;
The pious task deludes the muezzin."[19]

VIII.

Following an established convention, already referred to in our discussion of Asadī's poem above, 'Aṭṭār prefaces the poem with a very long introduction. The subjects he deals with are partly determined by this convention. Relatively new in his time was the addition to the latter section of the description of the *mi'rāj,* the heavenly journey of Muḥammad. An interesting parallel to Sanā'ī's poem is present in the praise addressed to the holy figures of both the Shi'ites and the Sunnis. 'Aṭṭār added a paragraph in which he strongly condemns the fanaticism *(ta'aṣṣub)* of those who despise what is holy to the other side. His defence of tolerance is quite similar to the attitude taken by Sanā'ī against sectarianism within the unity of Islam.

One of 'Aṭṭār's sections in this part of the poems deserves our special attention. This is the section on 'poetry' in which he responds to a statement made by Sanā'ī in the *Fakhrī-nāma.* Sanā'ī had made use of a wordplay on the words *shi'r* (poetry) and *shar'* (the Law) which are built on the same three letters of the Arabic alphabet: *shīn, 'ayn,* and *rā'*. The word *shar'* (practically synonymous to the better known *sharī'a)* refers to the religious Law of Islam and, in a wider sense, to a pious attitude of obedience to God's will. By poetry, the craft of the court poet is meant, which Sanā'ī had practised himself in his early years but now had come to detest as being equivalent to begging and dishonesty:

Sanā'ī, you have now approached the Law,
Put all this craft of poetry aside!
You saw the Law. Abandon poetry!
It merely brings your heart to beggary.
However pure a poet's talents be,
Sacred Tradition makes it into mockery.
At first, when Body still rules sovereign,
Poetry shows its face like a false dawn.
It caters to the impudent, the mean,
But leads muezzins and watchmen astray.

---

19. *Muṣībat-nāma,* p. 240.

Then Law reveals its glorious true dawn,
Increasing light to you which never wanes.[20]

With the help of another wordplay Sanā'ī contrasts the values of literature and religion:

The words of poets are nothing but coquetry (ghamz);
The niceties of Prophecy contain true symbols (ramz).[21]

Sanā'ī's severe censure of poetry implies a rejection of the profession of the court poet, but not necessarily of the use of poetic language for other purposes. This was correctly understood by 'Aṭṭār when he reacted to this statement in the *Muṣībat-nāma.* To make himself clear 'Aṭṭār added another transposition of the same three Arabic letters to Sanā'ī's pair: *'arsh,* meaning 'the Throne of God'. The symbolism inherent in the common elements of the three words reveals their fundamental unity:

Poetry, Throne and Law, all from one root:
Three letters lending beauty to both worlds.
One source of light pervades the entire earth;
Three letters bind together all there is.
Although the sun belongs only in heaven,
Its 'splendor' (sanā) *can be seen in 'Sanā'ī'.*[22]

Literary art, obedience to the Law and the mystical search for the nearness of God, all spring from a single source. Elaborating his reference to the literal meaning of his predecessor's pen name (Sanā'ī='the man of splendour') 'Aṭṭār goes on to point to similar celestial associations implied in the names of other Persian poets, such as Azraqī ('the blue one'), Anvarī ('the most luminous one') and Firdawsī ('the paradisical one'). His intention, however, goes far beyond such verbal plays. He continues to discuss at length the position of poetry in Islam, especially with regard to the problem of making the proper distinction between the words of Prophets and poets. Far from rejecting poetry 'Aṭṭār claims that, in his age, it has

20. *Fakhrī-nāma,* MS. Bağdatli Vehbi (Istanbul), no. 1672, fol. 79b.
21. *Loc. cit.*
22. *Muṣībat-nāma,* p. 46.

received a new dispensation:

As poetry acquired a bad name in our time,
The best minds turned away, the weak remained.
No wonder that discourse has lost all esteem.
Praise is outdated; now is the time for wisdom.
I do not care for the outdated panegyric;
It is deprived of all splendor in my mind.
Forever praising wisdom will suffice me.
This sole ambition occupies my heart.[23]

IX. CONCLUSION

In the course of this brief search for similarities and contrasts between the two poets we found that, as far as their works are concerned, the outcome is different according to the genre which is considered. There can be no doubt that Sanā'ī's example was a decisive influence on 'Aṭṭār's lyric poetry. The similarities of the *qalandarī* poems and the ascetic *qaṣīda*s which they both wrote are too obvious to require comment.

It is certainly more difficult to find common traits in their *mathnawī*s. On the surface, Sanā'ī's homiletic discourse in the *Fakhrī-nāma* has little in common with 'Aṭṭār's emphasis on storytelling as his most important illustrative device. Even the *Asrār-nāma,* which lacks a 'leading-story', is characterized by the same orientation towards the narrative element as the other poems of 'Aṭṭār. Only the *Muṣībat-nāma* can be shown to be a poem in which 'Aṭṭār, probably intentionally, followed some of the elements Sanā'ī had added to the tradition of the didactic *mathnawī.* This can be deduced both from the theme of the poem—the cosmic journey of the mind—and from its allegorical technique. The difference in scope as well as in aim between the *Muṣībat-nāma* and Sanā'ī's small poem *Sayr al-'ibād ilā'l-ma'ād* however must not be overlooked. The former poem also contains 'Aṭṭār's reply to Sanā'ī's denunciation of secular poetry.

The biographical facts reflect another important contrast

23. *Ibid.,* p. 47.

between the two poets. The relative abundance of extra-literary references in the works of Sanā'ī not only allows us to sketch the history of his life, at least in its main outlines, but they do also provide the opportunity to define his place in the social history of Persian mystical literature. The period in which he wrote was one of transition in Persian literature: up to that time the poets' art had been limited in scope by its ties to the environment of the courts. It is quite evident that Sanā'ī exerted himself to break these bonds.

The great impact he made on his contemporaries, who already during his lifetime began to use his poetry as a rich mine for citations, bears witness to the originality of these attempts which rightly gained him the reputation of a pioneer of mystical poetry in the Persian language. Yet, in spite of that, he was never entirely free from those ties of patronage and social protection which in his day were still the necessary conditions of a literary career, whether secular or spiritual.

The virtual absence in 'Aṭṭār's poetry of such references to the circumstances of his life is equally telling. It makes it clear that, by the end of the sixth/twelfth century, it had become possible to exist as an independent mystical poet and produce an extensive *oeuvre* without having to turn to the mighty of this world for material support. On the other hand, it is most regrettable that, for the same reason, we know absolutely nothing about the audience for whom 'Aṭṭār wrote.

In the composition of his *Mathnawī-yi ma'nawī,* Rūmī made a synthesis of the different forms of the didactical *mathnawī* which we find in Sanā'ī and 'Aṭṭār. Rūmī's poem is also really a continuing homily, just like the *Fakhrī-nāma,* but at the same time the poem is based on a sequence of 'leading stories' and subsidiary tales forming a network of considerable complexity if compared with the clarity to be found in the poems of 'Aṭṭār.

Finally, if one were to remark on their relationship to Persian literature in general, the boundaries of the tradition in which these poets participated could be described as two concentric circles. The widest circle encompassed Persian classical poetry as a whole. The mystical poets did not create an entirely new poetical idiom. Most of the means of expression at their disposal, whether poetical forms, images, rhetorical devices or motifs were derived from the conventional apparatus of early Persian court poetry as we know it from the fourth/tenth century onwards. The inner circle consists of the adaptation of the available forms to a new use as a means of expression for mystical ideas.

Khwāja ʻAbdullāh Anṣārī with Four Disciples. From ʻAlī Shīr Nawā'ī's *Ḥayrat al-abrār.* Copied 890/1485. MS. Elliot 287 f. 24r. (Courtesy of the Bodleian Library).

The *Hundred Grounds* of 'Abdullāh Anṣārī of Herāt (d. 448/1056)

The Earliest Mnemonic Sufi Manual in Persian

A.G. Ravān Farhādī

I. INTRODUCTION: THE WORKS OF ANṢĀRĪ

The life of Khwāja 'Abdullāh Anṣārī of Herāt (396/1006–481/1089) is divided into childhood, student life, and a fifty-six year career as a spiritual guide and teacher.[1] Serge de Beaurecueil, after many decades of Anṣārīan studies, has reminded us how much teaching and guiding novices on the spiritual path constituted the pivot of a life full of trials for this great master.[2]

To illustrate the importance of the *Hundred Grounds,* Anṣārī's mnemonic manual of Sufism and the subject of our essay, it is necessary to provide a brief survey of some of his other works. Due caution should be exercised in compiling an index of Anṣārī's genuine works. Amateurs interested in Sufi literature among the Persian-speaking peoples, whether Sufi or not, and whether Sunni or Shi'ite in sectarian affiliation, are usually united in their admiration for his

1. For general overviews of Anṣārī's life and works, see A. Schimmel, *Mystical Dimensions of Islam* (Chapel Hill: University of N. Carolina Press 1975), pp. 89-90; S. de Laugier de Beaurecueil, in *Encyclopædia Iranica,* I, s.v. "'Abdallāh Anṣārī," pp. 187-90. The author highly appreciates the assistance of Dr. Leonard Lewisohn. As a result of long and patient reading of this article, he presented valuable proposals welcomed by the author and included in the text, especially in the English translations of selected passages of *The Hundred Grounds.* A slightly modified version of the original Persian text of this article appeared in *Ṣūfī: Faṣlnāma-yi Khānaqāh-i Ni'matullāhī* (London 1993), issue 18, pp. 26-35.

2. Page 382—›

'Intimate Prayers' or *Munājāt.*[3] However, many readers of these inspiring invocations will be disappointed to know that their printed texts are not authenticated by the earliest extant manuscripts.[4] Having said this, it is imprudent to reject outright these popular collections as spurious, insofar as their style is not far removed from the texture of Anṣārī's genuine *munājāt,* found in his *Kashf al-asrār* and *Tabaqāt al-ṣūfiyya* (concerning which, see below). Although one might well speculate that, somewhere, a lost manuscript of the 'real' *munājāt* not available to the compilers of the last two books does exist—in the meantime, the fact remains that these popular *munājāt* of Anṣārī have had and continue to exert a great impact on devotees of Sufism throughout all lands in which the Persian tongue is known.

---

2. See S. de Laugier de Beaurecueil, *Khawādja 'Abdullāh Anṣārī (396-481 H./ 1006-1089), mystique ḥanbalite* (Beirut: Recherches d'Institut de lettres orientales de Beyrouth, XXVI: 1965); *idem.,* "al-Anṣārī al-Harawī" in EI[2]. Beaurecueil has translated into French and edited the original Persian text of the *Ṣad maydān,* in *Mélanges islamologiques,* t. 2, (Cairo: IFAO 1954), pp. 1-90; the *Kitāb manāzil al-sā'irīn,* avec étude de la tradition textuelle, traduction, lexique et 6 planches (Cairo: IFAO 1962); *Kitāb 'ilal al-maqāmāt,* (éd et trad.) in *Mélanges Massignon* (Damacus 1956), pp. 153-71. Beaurecueil's fully annotated French translation of the last three texts later appeared as *Anṣārī: Chemin de Dieu,* trois traités spirituels: *Les Cent Terrains (Sad Maydān), Les Étapes des Itinérants vers Dieu (Manāzil al-sā'irīn),* traduits du Persan et de l'Arabe, presentés et annotés (Paris: Sindbad 1985). He has also translated into French the *Munājāt* as *Anṣārī: Cris du coeur* (Paris: Sindbad 1988). (Cf. p. 153 of the last work for a long bibliography of his other Anṣārīan studies).
3. For English translations, see L. Morris & R. Sarfeh, *Munajat: The Intimate Prayers of Khwajih 'Abd Allah Ansari* (New York: Khaneghah Maleknia Naseralishah1975); Sir Jogendra Singh, *The Invocations of Shaikh Abdullah Ansari* (London: John Murray 1939); Wheeler M. Thackston, *Kwaja Abdullah Ansari: Intimate Conversations* (New York: Paulist Press 1978).
4. Muḥammad Āṣaf Fikrat has compiled a relatively genuine version of the *Munājāt* in a volume published in celebration of the millenary of Anṣārī's birth (Kabul 1355 A.Hsh./1976), which is drawn from three sources: 1) the *dicta* ascribed to the *Pīr-i ṭarīqat* in the *Kashf al-asrār;* 2) *munājāt* found in the *Ṭabaqāt al-ṣūfiyya;* 3) *munājāt* in the Anṣārī's treatises *(rasā'il).* Fikrat's edition, however, needs to be updated by reference to Muḥammad Jawād Sharī'at's *Fihrist-i tafsīr-i Kashf al-asrār* (Tehran 1363 A.Hsh./1984) and the recent edition of the *Ṭabāqāt al-ṣufiyya,* ed. by Muḥammad Sarwar-Mawlāyī (Tehran: Sahāmī 'ām 1362 A.Hsh./1983). A collection of Anṣārī's invocations and other sayings, as extracted from the *Kashf al-asrār,* has been published by Muḥammad Jawād Sharī'at (ed.), *Sukhanān-i Pīr-i Herāt* (Tehran, 1st ed. 1355 A.Hsh./1976; 3rd ed. 1361 A.Hsh./1982), pp. 77-188.

In studying his other works, it is useful to recall that Anṣārī's normal manner of literary composition, mentioned in the introductions to many of his books and treatises, was not usually to write his books by hand, but rather to dictate them to his students. A case in instance is the *Unveiling of Mysteries (Kashf al-asrār),* his Koranic commentary compiled and edited in an unfinished form by one or more of the Master's students, and which has only reached us today in the greatly expanded version of his disciple Rashīd al-Dīn Maybudī (d. 520/1126).[5] In the introduction to this work, Maybudī recounts the background of his redaction of the Master's text as follows:

> I read the book, unique in its day and age, by Abū Ismā'īl 'Abdullāh ibn Muḥammad ibn 'Alī Anṣārī, which is an exegesis and elucidation of the meanings of the Koran. Although I found it marvelously eloquent in syntax of expression, penetrating in its profoundity and beauty, yet it was too succinct and concise. Thus, it was hardly suited the purposes of students and wayfarers [on the Sufi Path]. Therefore, I undertook the task of providing a commentary and detailed exposition of its contents, gathering together the 'realities of exegesis' *(ḥaqā'iq al-tafsīr)* and the 'subtleties of commemoration' *(laṭā'if al-tadhkīr).*[6]

Each chapter of Maybudī's exegesis contains one or more Koranic passage(s) interpreted on three different 'levels' or 'semantic shifts' *(nawba),* each of which constitutes a separate section:

Shift 1) the literal Persian translation of the Arabic Koranic text;

Shift 2) the exoteric commentary: incorporating linguistic, grammatical, historical, juridical, ethical and general exegetical matters, being a summary of earlier Arabic commentaries which discussed similar themes, as well as of the teachings of Anṣārī himself. Portions of this section, which take up between eight to ten pages in the published text, are in Arabic.

---

5. Maybudī, *Kashf al-asrār wa 'uddat al-abrār,* edited by 'Alī Aṣghar Ḥikmat, 10 vols. (Tehran: Intishārāt-i Dānishgāhī 1952-60).
6. *Ibid.*, I, p. 1.

> Shift 3) Sufi (esoteric) commentary: being an exposition of selected verses of the Koranic passage in question, constituting approximately three printed pages in the published edition, portions of which are also written in Arabic. Here, however, the commentary is entirely mystical and includes sayings, poetry and stories of the Sufi masters which Anṣārī's marshals up to aid his exegesis. Many of the original *munājāt,* poetry and prose of the Master also are found in this section.[7]

This last 'Sufi' section deserves a systematic comparison with the *Ḥaqā'iq al-tafsīr* of Abū 'Abdullāh Raḥmān Sulamī (d. 412/1021) an Arabic Sufi commentary on the Koran (unfortunately still unpublished) compiled a century earlier, between 360/970 and 370/980.[8]

The text of the *Kashf al-asrār* is dotted with Anṣārī's axioms, exhortations and aphorisms; in utilizing these its author, Maybudī, makes it quite clear that he is providing a precise quotation of the very words uttered by the 'Master of the Path' *(Pīr-i ṭarīqat).* Aside from such quotations, there also appear poems, both in Arabic and Persian, some of which are by Anṣārī himself. The remarkable alteration of literary styles of this commentary—from the pedantically didactic and scholarly to the enthusiastically ecstatic and lyrical, accompanied by a sudden changing of subjects—immediately reminds us of the style found in certain Surahs of the Koran itself.[9]

---

7. In the later history of Persian Sufism, this section of Anṣārī's commentary greatly influenced Ḥusayn Wā'iẓ Kāshifī who incorporated selected texts of it into his Persian commentary on the Koran, entitled *Mawāhib-i 'Aliyya* (completed in 899/ 1493-4), generally known as the *Tafsīr-i Ḥusaynī.*

8. See G. Böwering, "The Qur'ān Commentary of al-Sulamī," in W.B. Hallaq & Donald Little (eds.), *Islamic Studies Presented to Charles Adams* (Leiden: Brill 1991), pp. 49.

9. An interesting example of this is Surah LXV *(al-Ṭalāq),* verses 2, 5, 7, 10, 11, 12). If one examines Anṣārī's mystical interpretation, in his "shift 3" section, of verses 2-3 of this Surah, one finds many sublime mystical pronouncements, and intensely esoteric descriptions of various mytical states and stations, little of which has any apparent relevance to the central exoteric theme ("divorce" [from women]) of this Chapter *(Kashf al-asrār,* X, pp. 148-51).

Anṣārī's *Ṭabaqāt al-ṣūfiyya* (Generations of the Sufis),[10] which has reached us only in the form of a student's notes, is also characterized by the same alternation of literary styles, from dry and abstruse historical accounts to sudden leaps of mystical lyricism, found in the *Kashf al-asrār*. The Persian text of the *Ṭabaqāt* is based on an Arabic book of the same name by Sulamī. In fact, it reads as though Anṣārī had read selected passages from Sulamī's book to his students and then delivered his own extemporaneous commentary upon them, many sections of which are in the form of his students' concise notes which often update their original source. Thus, the book is not simply a Persian translation of Sulamī's work, but a fresh recapitulation with significant additions and annotation. However, the Persian prose style is quite archaic, and in the phonetics, morphology and vocabulary of the *Ṭabaqāt al-ṣūfiyya* one can find many traces of what Jāmī (whose *Nafaḥāt al-uns,* written four centuries later, is an updated and greatly expanded version of Anṣārī's book in classical Persian) was to call "the old language of Herāt." Until 883/1478 when Jāmī composed his *Nafaḥāt,* Anṣārī's *Ṭabaqāt* remained unrivalled in its own language as a source of Sufi biography. Nearly half of Jāmī's opus is a summary redaction, in plain literary Persian, of Anṣārī's work, the other half being a mise-à-jour of the subject illustrating mystical figures of the latter days after Anṣārī.

For students and lovers of the Persian *Munājāt* of Anṣārī it is fortunate that, scattered through the *Kashf al-asrār* and *Ṭabaqāt,* appear authentic texts of his famous 'Invocations'. These invocations, which function as spiritual 'intermissions', although they have little or no direct relation to the flow of the rest of the text, do have a peculiar and interesting artistic function to fufill. Their main purpose seems to disperse the pieces of these *Munājāt* in the course of exhausting scholarly texts as a kind of mental and spiritual recreation. The stylistic similarity between the Maybudī/Anṣārī Koran commentary and the *Generations of the Sufis* originates from this common method of compilation which Anṣārī encouraged his

---

10. There are two published editions: ed. 'Abd al-Ḥayy Ḥabībī (Kabul 1961, reprinted in Tehran 1980), and the greatly improved edition of Muḥammad Sarwar Mawlāyī (Tehran: Sahāmī 'ām 1362 A.Hsh./1983).

student-editors to adopt—almost as if the Master had deliberately instructed them to plant green oases all along the ardous academic trail of their theological studies.

Another work of great significance by Anṣārī, which unfortunately still remains unpublished, is his polemical *Critique of Scholastic Theology and its Practitioners (Dhamm al-kalām wa ahlih)*[11] which assails these theologians for being enemies of the Prophetic Sunna. For many years of his long career he had suffered persecution from Seljuk officialdom for his virulent denunciation of the *Kalām* theologians. As we know, after his death in 481/1089, it was the Ash'arite sect which prevailed as the officially acceptable theological doctrine in the state-sponsored Niẓāmiyya *madrasas*. While Anṣārī considered Sufism and the *Sharī'a* as integral elements of a single Islamic whole, he was vehement in his rejection of both philosophy and scholastic theology *(Kalām),* including Ash'arism. His opposition to *Kalām*-inspired speculation, and his conception of the simultaneous pursuit of the *ṭarīqa* of Sufism and adherance to the regulations of the *Sharī'a* as non-contradictory components of Islam, resembles the mature views of the great Abū Ḥāmid Ghazālī (d. 505/1111, who eventually came to spurn his own long career as a professor of Kalām theology, and to assert the superiority of Sufism. Under the intellectual leadership of Ghazālī a century later, the stand taken by Anṣārī on these issues appears as vindicated—and the fact remains that, whereas Anṣārī's tomb at Gāzargāh, a few kilometers north of Herat, remains a site of pilgrimmage for all and sundry today, the whereabouts of the tomb of Ash'arī are still virtually unknown.

11. British Museum Add. 27520, Catalogue no. 1571; Damascus Library, Om. 24/587; also cf. Beaureceuil's summary of this treatise in *Encyclopædia Iranica,* I, p. 188.

II. ANṢĀRĪ'S *HUNDRED GROUNDS*

The *Hundred Grounds (Ṣad maydān)* is prefaced as being a *tarājim-i majālis-i 'aqīda:* "Introductory Notes[12] to Lectures concerning the Articles of Faith." The book was taken down by students of Anṣārī in Herāt on the first of Muḥarram, 448/1056 (= 21 March 1056, the first day of the Persian New Year *[naw-rūz])* in his fiftieth year.[13] A quarter of a century later, in 475/1082, having been appointed to the post of 'Shaykh al-Islām', he dictated his *Manāzil al-sā'irīn (Stations of the Wayfarers)*[14] in the same style as the *Hundred Grounds*, but in the Arabic language. In this later text—upon which Anṣārī's subsequent reputation in the annals of Sufism primarily rests—he revised the priorities and the ordering of the chapters (these being ten chapters with ten 'stations' apiece) and provided more elaborate commentary on each of the one hundred spiritual stations. His *Hundred Grounds,* however, retains its importance as the first didactic treatise on Sufism to be written in Persian, and specifically intended to serve as a mnemonic manual for mystics.

Stylistic Features of the *Hundred Grounds*

Anṣārī's method of composition in this treatise seems entirely practical. Its essential purpose was didactic and homiletic, designed to guide his student-novices in the memorization of difficult subjects. The peculiar tripartite distinction of subjects used for didactic and

---

12. The word *tarājim* has two meanings: 1) translation and 2) introduction, foreword or exposition. It is possible that the text of the *Ṣad maydān* originally was translated from Arabic to Persian, in which case, one should read "Translation of Lectures..."

13. Selected sections translated from the original Persian, taken from the beginning, middle and end of the *Hundred Grounds,* are provided in section III of this study. We hope to publish in the future the full Persian text and the English translation of this concise Sufi manual. The English translation of the *Ṣad maydān* by Munir Ahmad Mughal, entitled *The Hundred Fields Between Man and God* (Lahore: Islamic Book Foundation 1983) lacks accuracy and fidelity to the Persian original.

14. See the present writer's edition of the Arabic text of this treatise, with a Persian translation: *Manāzil al-sā'irīn: matn-i 'arabī bā muqāyasa bā matn-i 'Ilal al-maqāmat wa Sad maydān, tarjama-yi darī-yi Manāzil al-sā'irīn wa 'Ilal al-maqāmat wa sharḥ-i kitāb az rūyi āthār-i Pīr-i Herāt* (Kabul 1350 A.Hsh./1971; rprt.Tehran: Mawlā 1361 A.Hsh./1982)

mnemonic purposes both in the *Hundred Grounds* and in the *Stations of Wayfarers* does not mean that the theme is completely exhausted by such detailing. Nor does the number 100 (=10x10), in the numeration of the Grounds and Stations in each treatise, necessarily indicate any finite delimitation in their quantity. The spelling out of each subject in three items, as well as the exposition of the entire matter in 10x10 chapters, is meant only as *aide-mémoire,* and was not intended to be mathematically concretized.[15] The master favoured and selected three components or aspects of a subject as being the most important and the easiest for the purposes of memorization, adopting an order of priorities in his mind in each case, before giving expression to the three items.

Often the same subject items elaborated in Anṣārī's various works *(The Hundred Grounds, Stations of the Wayfarers,* and *The Unveiling of Mysteries)* do not completely coincide with each other. The details of these differences have been analyzed by Serge de Beaurecueil in his French translation of *The Hundred Grounds.*[16] Certainly Anṣārī's didactical priorities were not rigidified during the course of his long years as a mentor. The differences arose from distinct assessments made in different social circumstances, his awareness of the aptitudes and the varying dispositions of the student-novices surrounding him and of the ever-widening group of his readers in the Islamic world of his time.

The Mnemonic Tradition of the *Hundred Grounds*

We may recognize three main techniques classically known and employed in the East to facilitate the memorization of texts and to make them attractive and engaging:

I. *Eloquent and vigorous expression* in the forms of aphorisms, adages, maxims, and precepts. The prophetic *Ḥadīth* has this characteristic, following the revealed text of Koran and parts of earlier scriptures. We find this method used by Anṣārī in his *Dhamm al-*

15. For Anṣārī's own views on this, cf. *ibid.,* pp. 13-15.
16. *Chemin de Dieu,* pp. 36-46.

kalām and in *Ṭabaqāt al-ṣūfiyya.* In this connection, the sayings of Abū Sa'īd ibn Abī'l-Khayr (d. 440/1049), later collected by his grandson Ibn Munawwar in the *Asrār al-tawḥīd,* many passages of the *Kashf al-maḥjūb* of Hujwīrī (d. 463/1071), and especially the *Sawāniḥ* of Aḥmad Ghazālī (d. 520/1126), deserve to be mentioned as far as the early Sufi Persian literary tradition is concerned.

II. *Parallel end and internal rhyme,* a rhetorical technique also found in the Koran. The literary device known as *saj'* (rhymed prose with rhymes recurring, by way of consonance or assonance, at parallel points in a sentence) was used to great effect by Anṣārī in *Munājāt,* and a century later by Ḥakīm Sanā'ī (d. 525/1131) in his *Makātīb.*[17] The use of poetry as a mnemonic device, with its precise metres and elaborate system of prosody, and especially the popular *mathnawī*'s metric form (couplets consisting of two end-rhyming hemistiches, in many cases of eleven sylables each) was also common. Sanā'ī's *Ḥadīqa,* Farīd al-Dīn 'Aṭṭār's (d. 618/1221) *Illāhi-nāma, Manṭiq al-ṭayr* and other *mathnawī*s, each in a different meter, and the thoroughgoing, encyclopædic *Mathnawī* of Mawlānā Jalāl al-Dīn Muḥammad Rūmī, are among the most influential and prestigious works of Sufi teachings in the Persian language which exemplify this genre.

III. *Itemization into ternary form* of a treatise's subject-matter or ideas was also a common mnemonic device. In Anṣārī's work, especially the *Hundred Grounds,* and the *Stations of the Wayfarers,* this ternary system is usually employed, his ideas being generally arranged in ternate form, in sets of three, as can be seen below (see pp. 393ff.).

This tripartite division of subjects for mnemonic purposes has many precedents in the ancient cultures of the Middle East. One of the earliest didactic works versified in Persian was the *Dānish-nāma* of Ḥakīm Maysarī, a manual of medicine[18] which chronologically

---

17. *Makātīb Sanā'ī,* edited Nadhīr Aḥmad (Tehran 1362 A.Hsh./1983); and Kabul 1976.
18. Edited Barāt Zanjānī (Tehran 1987).

speaking seems to precede Anṣārī's *Hundred Grounds.* Another mnemonic work is the *Niṣāb-e al-ṣibyān (Children's Lexicon)*[19] of Abū Naṣr of Farāhī (d. 618/1221), a versified *aide-mémoire* translated from Arabic into Persian rhyme to facilitate the study of Arabic vocabulary and prosody. Each chapter is composed in a different metre in order to teach Arabic prosody, the poetry also serving to acquaint a child with the elementary scientific and historical knowledge of Abū Naṣr Farāhī's time. Another well-known mnemonic poem is the *Nām-i ḥaqq (The Name of the Truth*)[20] by Sharāf al-Dīn Bukhārī (d. 682/1283), a Muslim 'Manual of Devotion', written for followers of the Sunnī Ḥanafite rite, consisting of 170 Persian couplets. The *Khulāṣat al-alfiyya* ('The Thousand-verse Compendium')[21] is also a famous mnemonic summary of Arabic grammar by Abū 'Abdullāh Muḥammad Ibn Mālik (d. 672/1247), upon which some forty-five commentaries have been written in Arabic and Persian for students of advanced Arabic grammar.

Needless to say, the *Khulāṣat al-alfiyya* in Arabic and the *Niṣāb-i al-ṣibyān* and the *Nām-i ḥaqq* in Persian are all treatises composed after Anṣārī's time, and thus cannot have influenced his style. However, there is one mnemonic work in the field of Sufism which preceded Anṣārī and probably influenced his literary style. This is the 'Path of the Elect' *(Risāla-yi nahj al-khāṣṣ)* by Abū Manṣūr Iṣfahānī (d. 418/1027), a work organized into forty chapters (on 'Repentance', 'Devotion', 'Truthfulness', 'Sincerity', 'Self-examination', etc.), featuring *three* spiritual stations *(maqām)* each. Here, we may note the same ternary structure is employed which is found in the *Hundred Grounds.* It is evident that Anṣārī highly venerated the memory of Abū Manṣūr Isfahānī, calling him in the *Ṭabaqāt al-ṣūfiyya,*[22] "the Imam of the exoteric sciences and the sciences of divine reality, the paragon of his age, unique among the Masters, and

19. Lithographed text edited by 'Alī ibn Naẓar 'Alī (Tabriz 1308/1890), as well as the Tehran edition of 1942 and subsequent Tehran editions; Neval Kishor's Kānpūr edition of 1294/1877.
20. Lucknow 1889; Bombay 1915; periodically published in India (and later in Pakistan) for Afghan *madrasa* pupils.
21. Published with the 1912 Persian translation of Aḥmad Bahmanyār (Tehran: n.d.).
22. Ed. Sarwar Mawlāyī, pp. 624-25.

Khwāja 'Abdullāh Anṣārī and his Disciples. From the *Majālis al-'ushshāq*. Copied 959/1552. MS. Ouseley Add 24, f. 39v. (Courtesy of the Bodleian Library).

a Sunni of the Ḥanbalī sect." Anṣārī also makes mention of having read and admired the *Risāla-yi nahj al-khāṣṣ*.[23]

However, amongst all these various literary and religious genres of writing, none could have had a greater impact on the mind of Anṣārī of Herāt than the prophetic Traditions *(ḥadīth)*. As a child, Anṣārī possessed a marvelous memory, and later, as an assiduous student (attending the lectures of Ya'qūb al-Qarrāb of Sarakhs, d. 429/1038) he learned by heart a great number of *ḥadīth*, together with their chains of transmission *(isnād)*. We find numerous examples of tripartite itemization—employed by Anṣārī throughout the *Hundred Grounds*—in the *ḥadīth*.[24] The number three also has a special place in Islamic piety, being featured in its fundamental rituals, the performance of which is based on the imitation of the life of the Prophet.[25]

---

23. See S. de Laugier de Beaurecueil's edition of this treatise in *Mélanges Ṭaha Ḥusein,* (Cairo 1962).

24. Two examples of such ternate *Ḥadīth* texts deserves comparison with the ternary structure of the *Hundred Grounds* (and the *Stations of Wayfarers)*. First of all, we may consider the Prophet's famous *ḥadīth* concerning the hypocrites, which is found in all six authentic collections, and secondly, the *ḥadīth* on treachery and fraud:

1. "The signs of the hypocrite are three: When he speaks, he lies. When he promises, he breaks (it). When he is trusted, he commits treason."

2. God, the Most-Exalted, says: "There are three persons who will have Me as their foe on Day of Resurrection: the man who gave a promise in My Name and betrayed it. The man who sold a free man (as a slave) and took the money for himself. The man who employed a worker to perform a job, and did not pay his wages after the task was completed."

Both *ḥadīth* are quoted with references to the earliest authentic *(Ṣaḥīḥ)* collections by 'Izz al-Dīn Bliq in *Minhāj al-ṣalīḥīn* (Beirut 1978), pp. 99, 281. Many other ternate *aḥadīth* can be found in all the *Ṣaḥīḥ* collections.

25. Examples of this ternate structure in fundamental Islamic rituals include: the ninety-nine (3x33) Names of God; the washing of each part of the body three times during ablutions; the repetition of the 'magnification of God' *(tasbīḥ)* three times during the ritual bowing *(rukū')* and prostration *(sajda)* in the five daily prayers (likewise the pronouncing of the *tasbīḥ, taḥmīd,* and *takbīr* 33 times repectively after each of the five daily ritual prayers); the recitation of *talbiya* (reply [to the divine call]): *labbayk:* "Here I am, (O Lord), here I am," repeated three times in the beginning of the rite of pilgrimmage *(Ḥajj)* rituals, & etc.

As the above examples demonstrate, it is evident that the enumeration of ideas in ternary form, structured and modeled on traditional genres of Islamic practical and literary *adab,* had a fundamental affect on the inspiration of Anṣārī's *Hundred Grounds.*

III. READINGS FROM THE *HUNDRED GROUNDS*

1. The Ground of Repentance (tawba)

The first Ground is the stage of Repentance. Repentance is returning to God. In the words of God Almighty: "Turn unto God in sincere repentance."[26]

Know that Knowledge is life, Wisdom a mirror, and Contentment a fortification, Hope is divine intercession, Recollection (of God) is a medicine, and Repentance is an antidote (for all ills). Repentance is the signpost of the way, the chieftain of admittance[27] (to divine grace), the key to treasure, the Intercessor of Union, the major mediator, the condition for acceptance, and the secret of all joy.

The principles of repentance are three: compunction of the heart, begging apology on the tongue, and severing ties with wickedness and wrong-doers.

The types of repentance are three: the repentance of the obedient devotee, the repentance of the disobedient sinner, and the repentance of the knower.[28]

The obedient devotee repents of overestimating his own devotion; the disobedient sinner repents of underestimating his own insubordination and sin, and the knower repents of being oblivious of God's favours conferred on him.

1. Overestimating one's own devotion has three signs: considering oneself worthy of salvation through one's own acts (of devotion), regarding other seekers with disdain, and failing to investigate

---

26. Koran LXVI: 8.
27. "chieftain of admittance" if *bār* is understood as meaning 'audience, admittance'. Otherwise *bār* may signify 'cargo', in which case *sālār-i bār* would mean 'cargo-master (of the caravan)'; this is the meaning of this expression in the *Gulistān* of Sa'dī.
28. "knower *('ārif)"* means 'gnostic', but we do not use this word because of its connotation in *Kalām.*

the flaws of one's own acts (of devotion).

2. Underestimating one's own insubordination and sin has three signs: to consider oneself worthy of God's forgiveness, to be untroubled by persistence in acts of disobedience, and to keep company with bad companions.

3. Being oblivious of God's favour has three signs: ceasing to hold oneself in contempt, highly estimating one's own spiritual state, and ceasing to seek the joy of intimacy with God.[29]

69. The Ground of Unification (tawḥīd)

The sixty-ninth Ground is Unification. The Ground of Unification arises from the [sixty-eighth] Ground of Exile *(Ghurba).* Unification is [1] to say One, [2] to see One, and [3] to know One. As God Almighty says: "So know that there is no God but God."[30]

I. 'To say One' is the beginning of all science, the gateway to all worldly and spiritual knowledge, and the partition between friend and foe. The profession of faith [in divine Oneness=Unification] is the banner, Sincerity the foundation (it is set upon), and Faithfulness its precondition. The profession (of Unification) has three outward and inward aspects:

> 1. To bear witness that God, the Most Exalted, is Uniquely One in Essence, exempt from association with any spouse, progeny, partner or associate. May He be Magnified and Exalted!
>
> 2. To bear witness that God is Uniquely One in His Attributes, for in these no one bears Him any resemblance. They are *His* Attributes and beyond our reason; the manner and quality of His Attributes are incomprehensible, and cannot be encompassed [by rational thought], being beyond imagination. He has no associate or likeness (amongst created things) in these Attributes. May He be Magnified and Exalted!
>
> 3. To bear witness that God is Uniquely One in His pre-eternal Names. Whereas these Names can be ascribed to Him in reality, to others they are something borrowed and derivative.

---

29. *Ṣad maydān,* ed. A.G. Ravān Farhādī, pp. 252-53.
30. Koran XLVII: 19.

Although His created beings also have 'names', His Names are properly Real, being Eternal and anterior *a parte ante* to creation, and worthy of Him, while the names of created beings are temporal, in keeping with their contingent nature suitable to them. His truly proper Names are 'Allāh' and 'Raḥman' alone; by these (two) Names no other being may be addressed.

II. 'To see Him as One' is in (regard to) [1] His decrees, [2] His allotments, and [3] His bounties.

[1] 'To see Him as One and Unique in His decrees' is (the recognition) that, in the allotment of providence, He is One and Unique in His comprehensively infinite pre-eternal Knowledge and all-embracing pre-eternal Wisdom. None but Him has the knowledge and wisdom to realize this. Vision of this is the fruit of wisdom; true realization of this is the fruit of wonderment; the furtherance of this is the fruit of power—which none but Him possesses!

[2] 'To see Him as One and Unique in His allotments' is (the recognition) that His boons to creation are meted out each according to his proper share and best interest, and provided at the appropriate time.

[3] 'To see Him as One and Unique in His bounties' is (the recognition) that He alone, in His singularity, is the Provider. He is the Giver and none else. No one but Him is deserving of gratitude and acknowledgement; His is the Power and the Might, and none else but Him possesses the wherewithal to withhold or dispense bounty.

III. 'To know Him as One' is in one's [1] service, [2] 'spiritual interactions' and [3] will and aspiration.

[1] In service, it is to abjure leadership, to observe sincere truthfulness, and to control (stray) thoughts.

[2] In one's spiritual interactions, it to purify one's innermost consciousness, realize (the essence of) the recollection of God, and to steadfastly maintain one's confidence (in God's grace).

3. In will and aspiration, it is losing sight of everything but

Him, forgetting everything save Him, and gaining deliverance, through the heart's emancipation, from everything save Him.[31]

97. The Ground of Contemplation (mushāhada)

The ninety-seventh Ground is Contemplation. The Ground of Contemplation arises from the [ninety-sixth] Ground of Bedazzlement *(dahshat).* God Almighty says, "(Surely in that is a reminder) for one who harkens and contemplates."[32] Contemplation is the removal of obstacles between the devotee and God. The paths to contemplation are threefold: First of all, realization of the degree of Wisdom by means of the degree of Knowledge.[33] Second, attainment of the degree of Purity by means of the degree of Patience *(ṣabr).* Thirdly, realization of the degree of Reality through the degree of Knowing *(ma'rifat).*

I. Man attains the degree of Wisdom by means of the degree of Knowledge by means of three things:
[1] putting one's knowledge to good use,
[2] by venerating the divine Commands,[34] and
[3] faithful adherance to the Sunna (of the Prophet).
—This is the stage of the sages *(ḥakīmān).*

II. Man attains the degree of Purity through the degree of Patience by means of three things:
[1] by abandoning contention,
[2] by renouncing self-direction,
[3] by considering contentment as necessary.
—This is the stage of those who are content (with God's will).

III. Man may attain to the degree of Reality through the degree of Knowing by means of three things:
[1] by reverence (to God) in solitude,

---

31. *Ibid.,* pp. 520-22.
32. Koran L: 37.
33. I.e. by medium of the study of exoteric religious knowledge or theology*('ilm)* one advances to the higher degree of esoteric divine wisdom or theosophy *(ḥikmat).*
34. I.e. revering the Koranic directives concerning spiritual practice.

[2] by reproaching oneself for inadequacy in rendering due service (to God),
[3] by preferring one's friends above oneself *(ithār).*[35]

98. The Ground of Direct Observation (mu'āyana)

The ninety-eighty Ground is that of Direct Observation. The Ground of Direct Observation arises from the [ninety-seventh] Ground of Contemplation. God Almighty states: "Have you not observed how your Lord has spread out the shadow–?"[36] The meaning of Direct Observation is seeing something in its total perfection, and this consists in three things: [I] to regard Love with the eye of sympathetic compliance; [II] to regard the Unique (Being) with the eye of isolation ; [III] to regard the Everpresent One with the eye of presential consciousness.

I. Exposition of the first aspect ["to regard Love with the eye of compliance"] entails three things:
[1] responding affirmatively to the divine summons to make humble entreaty (to God);
[2] replying to the summons of divine Grace, by soliciting it,
[3] responding affirmatively to the divine summons to make firm one's resolve, and seeking a response to the divine summons made to one's innermost consciousness, by soliciting (that summons).

II. Exposition of the second aspect ["to regard the Unique Being with the eye of isolation"] entails three things:
[1] (through knowledge of the fact that) He is Unique (as an Agent) in Guidance, to maintain a strictly unitarian profession of faith;
[2] and (through knowledge of the fact that) He is Unique in Knowledge, to express one's gratitude to Him alone;
[3] and (through knowledge of the fact that) He is Unique in Protection, to keep oneself devoted to Him exclusively.

---

35. *Ṣad maydān,* p. 467-68. (On *īthār,* see above, pp. xxxii, 60-1 –ED.)
36. Koran XXV: 45.

III. Exposition of the final aspect ["to regard the Everpresent One with the eye of presential consciousness"] entails three things:

> [1] Through distance from one's 'self', to be near in His Nearness;
>
> [2] Through absence from one's 'self', to be present in His Presence;
>
> [3] He is not far from those who resolve to reach Him, nor lost to those who seek Him, nor absent from those who devotedly pursue Him.[37]

99. The Ground of Annihilation (fanā')

The ninety-ninth Ground is Annihilation. The Ground of Annihilation arises from the [ninety-eighth] Ground of Direct Observation (*mu'āyana*). God Almighty states: "All things perish except His Face. His is the Judgment and unto Him you shall be returned"[38] Annihilation is naughting, and this naughting occurs through three things in three things:

[1] Annihilation of seeking in the Found, [2] Annihilation of knowledge in the Known, [3] Annihilation of sight in the Seen. How can 'that-which-is-naught' ever find out anything about 'that-which-eternally-is'? How can Reality—Eternally Subsistent—ever be aligned with a merely nominal perishable phenomenon? What can bind the Worthy to the unworthy?

All save Him are juxtaposed betwixt three things: yesterday's non-existence, today which has gone astray and been mislaid, and tomorrow's nullity. Thus, all save He are non-existent, and yet existent by Him. So all existence is His. The raindrop reached the sea and found therein its mellowing, just as the star by daylight was effaced. Whoever reaches his Lord, has attained his 'self'.[39]

---

37. *Ṣad maydān,* pp. 470-71.
38. Koran XXVIII: 88.
39. *Ṣad maydān,* p. 497.

100. The Ground of Subsistence (baqā')

The hundredth Ground is the Ground of Subsistence. The Ground of Subsistence arises from the [ninety-ninth] Ground of Annihilation. God Almighty declares: "God is better, and more subsistent"[40]—God Almighty—and naught else: (for here) attachments are severed, secondary causes overturned, conventions and norms nullified, limitations naughted, understandings wrecked, history obliterated, allusions effaced, expressions negated, and God, One and Unique, abides by Himself, eternally subsistent.[41]

* * *

Now, these Hundred Grounds are all absorbed in the Ground of Love:

The Ground of Love (maḥabba)

The Ground of Love is the Ground of Friendship. God Almighty declares: "...a people whom He loves and they love Him"[42] and, "Say: If you love God..."[43] Love has three stages:

First of all, Uprightness;
at midway, Intoxication,
and finally, Annihilation.
—and praise be to God, the First and the Last![44]

---

40. Koran XX: 73.
41. *Ṣad maydān,* pp. 498-99.
42. Koran V: 54.
43. Koran III: 31.
44. *Ṣad maydān,* p. 413.

One of the First Folios from Rūmī's *Mathnawī* (Bk. I, vv. 29-71, in R.A. Nicholson's Edition). Copied 1656, MS. 1065 f. 3r. (Courtesy of the India Office Library, London).

The Concept of Knowledge in Rūmī's *Mathnawī*

Muhammad Este'lami

The definition of *'ilm* or knowledge in Rūmī's *Mathnawī* is both the same and not the same as the definitions of science, knowledge, philosophy, theology or mysticism in dictionaries. In Rūmī's view, *'ilm* is a concept which may partly include the meanings of these terms, but which is also different from all of them. In the historical tradition of Europe from mediæval to modern times, especially in the past two centuries with the establishment of modern academic institutions, we find specific definitions for these terms in scientific and scholarly works of reference, all of which are more or less different from Rūmī's definition of *'ilm.*

The modern world of the twentieth and twenty-first century is justifiably proud of its progress in science, industry, technology and also in the modernization of education and in social relations. In many parts of the world there are modern facilities for life, and natural resources have been harnessed by man in the service of civilization. The spiritual side of existence, however, does seem to be ignored by modern man. Here I am not referring to the side effects of industrial and technological progress, nor of the contamination of the natural environment. Neither am I speaking of the discoveries and inventions which were and are used to create destructive weapons. Rather I am alluding to the fact that there is another way of learning and understanding through which we may attain peace and spiritual satisfaction. Our civilized world has an urgent need to find such a way and in this respect Rūmī may serve as a guide and a master in this quest, and his *Mathnawī* can enlighten the travelers along this way. Rūmī's spiritual education opens a window upon an invisible school inside man's heart and upon the mysteries which are perceptible only through inner vision.

After many years of study at theological schools where he became well acquainted with the Koran, jurisprudence, prophetic traditions, Islamic philosophy and literature, Rūmī discovered that his scholastic knowledge did not fulfill his spiritual expectations. He realized that there is another pathway to revelation which is invisible to most scholastic scholars.

In a similar manner in our world today, one can list more than twenty famous books, all written and published in developed countries, most of them recognized as best-sellers, and all of which discuss, directly or indirectly, the problems of modern civilization. All of the writers concerned say or imply that over and above progress in science, technology and education, man needs a sense of spiritual elevation, or a power to direct this very progress toward humane, moral and spiritual satisfaction. But such an elevation is not accessible through sophisticated institutions of education and research.

Almost the same concept was frequently discussed by Rūmī more than seven hundred years ago. A very clear expression of his interest in the matter is a verse in the sixth volume of his *Mathnawī:*

Though you believe in the accuracy of the scholastic knowledge,
it will not open your inner eyes to invisible existence [1].

There are two main definitions for *'ilm* in the Mathnawī: in one of them *'ilm* is related to visible and material existence accessible through educational facilities. The other is not worldly, not taught in the schools and not accessible through books, laboratories or educational and academic facilities. This extraordinary *'ilm* testifies to a comprehension of Truth lying beyond common human understanding, or an awareness of the invisible world which is the only

1. See Jalāl al-Dīn Muḥammad Balkhī, *Mathnawī,* a critical edition by Dr. Muhammad Este'lami with an introduction, notes and indices; 6 vols. (Tehran: Intishārāt-i Zawwar 1370 A.Hsh./1991), M VI/263. In subsequent references to this text, "M" refers to the published text cited here, with Roman numerals referring to the *daftar* and Arabic numerals to its *bayt.*

real and eternal aspect of existence.

In the *Mathnawī* there are many tales and anecdotes by which Rūmī refers to the differences between the two concepts of *'ilm*. Perhaps the most famous is the story of a conceited grammarian, a *naḥwī,* who embarked on a boat and asked the boatman: "Have you ever studied *naḥw* ('grammar')?" When the boatman said that he had never studied grammar, the *naḥwi* said to him: "O! I feel so sorry for you, half your life has gone for naught." The boatman did not answer immediately and kept silent for a while, until the wind cast the boat into a whirlpool. Then the boatman shouted: "Do you know how to swim?" The proud grammarian said that he would never be able to swim. The boatman said: "O *Naḥwī!* Your whole life has gone for naught, because the boat is sinking in this whirlpool." Following this anecdote, Rūmī says:

> *Here what is needed is self-effacement* (maḥw), *not grammar*
> (naḥw).
> *If you're effaced from self, then plunge into the sea,*
> *and be not frightened of any peril or danger.*[2]

Being knowledgeable in any field of scholastic studies does not open a window to the invisible world. What is needed to achieve that end, is not *fiqh* or *ṣarf* or *naḥw.* We need the "jurisprudence of jurisprudence" *(fiqh-i fiqh),* the "morphology of morphology" *(ṣarf-i ṣarf),* and the "grammer of grammer" *(naḥw-i naḥw).* By these expressions, Rūmī means a knowledge which is received through a spiritual relation with the Divine world. Another expression for this relation is: a knowledge "from That Source" *(az ān sar)*, that is, a knowledge which grows from a Divine root.[3]

Another expression for such awareness is *fatḥ-i bāb az sīna,* or the opening of a gate in one's heart:

> *Everyone in whose breast [or heart] the gate is opened*
> *will behold the Sun from everywhere.*[4]

And for a man with a religious background, such a gate can be

---

2. M I/2853.
3. M III/1124.
4. M I/1409.

opened only by God. In this process, in Rūmī's view, a master, a *pīr* or *murshīd* must provide guidance and pave the way for disciples. In many verses of the *Mathnawī,* Solomon, the famous Jewish prophet and ruler, and also Noah are mentioned as masters, and in this comparison Rūmī implies that a *murshīd* must be obeyed as a prophet:

With Solomon put your foot in the Sea, that the water, David-like, may make a hundred suits of mail [to protect you].
That Solomon is present to all, but if we do not deserve his guidance, our inward eyes will not be opened by him.[5]

* * *

Keep silent, so that you may hear from the speakers,
that which may not come into utterance or into explanation.
Keep silent, so that you may hear from the Sun
that which may not come in books or into allocution.
Keep silent, so that the Spirit may speak for you.
In the Ark of Noah leave off swimming.[6]

To express the concept of that inward *'ilm,* or *'ilm-i bāṭin,* Rūmī uses many different words and expressions and in most cases, he uses the antonyms of the same words for worldly knowledge. A man who is aware of that Divine *'ilm* and of the mysteries of the invisible existence is a 'realizer' *(muḥaqqiq).* One who has studied the same subject through scholastic programs and discussions is called *muqallid* or imitator, because he imitates the words and expressions without awareness of their realities or inward meanings:

Between the realizer and the imitator,
there are many differences.
The former is like David and the imitator
is only an echo [not a song, not a singer].[7]

Some other of Rūmī's expressions of esoteric knowledge *('ilm-i bāṭin)* might here also be mentioned:

Taḥqīq or *'ilm-i taḥqīqī* or knowledge gained through spiritual realization is another expression for knowledge of the real and Eternal Existence and, on the opposite side, there is *'ilm-i taqlīdī* or

5. M II/3797-3798.
6. M III/1306-8.
7. M II/496.

imitative knowledge which refers to what is taught in the schools:

> *Conventional* 'ilm *is only for sale [or self-advertisement].*
> *When it finds a purchaser, it glows with delight.*
> *The purchaser of real knowledge is God*
> *And for such a knowledge, the market is always flourishing.*[8]

For *'ilm-i taḥqīqī,* Rūmī has also used the terms "the knowledge of real religion" *('ilm-i dīn),*[9] or "the knowledge of one who becomes aware through his heart" *('ilm-i ahl-i dil).*[10] Rūmī believes that worldly knowledge is an obstacle on the road to the real and divine knowledge:

> *The knowledge of followers of external sense is a muzzle,*
> *So that those believers in sense perception*
> *cannot drink the milk of that high knowledge* [11]

This high knowledge, in some other verses of the *Mathnawī* is mentioned as: *naẓar,*[12] *baṣar,*[13] *dīd,*[14] *dīd-i-ṣun'-bīn,*[15] *chishm-i rāst,*[16] *chishm-i dil,*[17] *chishm-i maḥramān,*[18] *nūr-i dil,*[19] *'ayān,*[20] *'aynu'l-'ayān,*[21] and *'ilm-i ladunī* or *'ilm-i min ladun.*[22] All of these are Rūmī's expressions for a spiritual vision which enables man to understand the eternal and invisible Being by medium of what Rūmī regards as the internal senses or *ḥawāss-i bāṭin.*[23]. On the other hand, as I said before, Rūmī takes the antonyms of these terms to indicate worldly and scholastic knowledge, for example:

---

8. M II/3276.
9. M I/1019.
10. M I/3461.
11. M I/1020.
12. M IV/422 673 & v. VI/1467-70, 3001.
13. M I/1476 & III/1224, 1727, VI/1469, 2627.
14. M I/925-8, 1416 & v. III/4353.
15. M VI/1667.
16. M II/452.
17. M VI/4419.
18. M VI/4659.
19. M III/727; VI/2141.
20. v. 2/177, 1825-30 & M III 4124, & VI 4031.
21. M VI/4419.
22. M I/817, 994 & VI/1849.
23. M I/3590.

– *'Ilmhā-yi ahl-i ḥiss,*[24] "the knowledge of those who believe in their material senses."

– *Ḥiss-i khuffāsh,*[25] "the bat's sense," meaning 'the sense of one who is unable to see the Sun of reality.'

– *Ẓann, Gumān or Shakk,*[26] "supposition," "mistrust" and "doubt" in the reality and existence of the invisible world.

In Rūmī's view, man was not created to satisfy the material side of his being; rather material being is a vehicle by which he should approach the frontier of Eternity. Rūmī believes that besides our five material senses, there are five internal ones by which the eternal and invisible world may be understood. We have to reduce little by little our dependency on our material senses and try to get rid of our material desires. Then our internal senses will start to work and enable us to understand what cannot be taught through educational programs and by means of the sophisticated and expensive equipment of modern schools and universities:

> *The ear of the head is as cotton-wool in the ear of conscience.*
> *To open the inner ear, the ear of the head must become deaf.*[27]

Such a transition from the material and sensual life into a spiritual understanding of the invisible existence, for most people, seems to be unbelievable or at least impossible, and indeed most people are not expected to elevate themselves to experience such a transformation. But in Rūmī's view, this elevation is accessible to everyone who deserves the favor of God and His support. Divine favour will enable man to change his external senses into inner senses or *ḥawāss-i bāṭin.* For such a change, Rūmī's expression is *guzāra shudan-i ḥawāss,* or "the passing of the senses through the veil of ignorance":

24. M I/1018.
25. M II/45-47.
26. M I/3456, v. 3/4120 & VI/2797, 4118.
27. M I/571.

When his senses have passed through the veil,
His vision and allocution from God will be continuous.[28]

Another expression for this change is *taqlīb-i rabb* or *taqlīb-i khudā,*[29] "a spiritual change made by God," by which Rūmī refers to a Prophetic tradition *(ḥadīth)* according to which "the hearts of human beings are all between two fingers of God as a single heart, and He turns that single heart as He likes."[30]

To explain the differences between a man who deserves favor and support from God and a man who does not have such a capacity, Rūmī has many different allegories and parables in the *Mathnawī.* One of them is the story of a domestic fowl who fostered a few ducklings, which she hatched under her wings. The ducklings came out of their shells and later walked toward the riverside with their foster mother. On the river they immediately began to swim, but the domestic fowl walked around and did not dare to go into the water. Following this parable, Rūmī says:

Leave the nurse on the dry land;
You sail into the sea of spiritual reality like ducks.[31]

Those who are able to swim in the sea of reality, are not slaves of their material desires or *hawā-yi nafs.* Their material needs and desires have been harnessed in the service of their immaterial life, and as Rūmī said, "They believe that man's original food is the Light of God."[32] Such food may not be eaten through our material mouths and throats. Their spiritual elevation gives them another mouth and another throat by which they can get immaterial food and drink,[33] and that food is nothing but the spiritual awareness of Absolute Existence *(hastī-yi muṭlaq).*

In conclusion, I would like to emphasize again that my purpose in this brief survey of Rūmī's conception of knowledge is not to

28. M VI/1929.
29. See: M/IV 3729, v. 6221, 3710.
30. See Badī' al-Zamān Furūzānfar, *Ahadīth-i Mathnawī* (Tehran: Amīr Kabīr 1361 A.Hsh.), p. 6.
31. M II/3786.
32. M II/1086.
33. See: M I/3890.

denigrate or deny the valuable results of progress in science and technology. Rūmī himself did not denigrate the values of scholastic and religious studies in his time. The main consideration is that the whole of knowledge, culture and civilization must serve as a ladder to the achievement of a spiritual and humane elevation, and all schools, universities and research centers must cooperate in the attainment of such a degree.

Contemporary man cannot, and does not need to close down schools, universities and research centers. Neither can he live all the time in a *Khānaqāh* or a monastery. He does not need to deprive himself of worldly pleasures and activities, but he urgently needs to take some courses in divine love, and to search for a resurrection which hopefully may lead us towards moral and spiritual stability, *In shā'Allāh.*

Rūmī and *Ḥikmat:* Towards a Reading of Sabziwārī's Commentary on the *Mathnawī*[1]

John Cooper

I. THE AGE OF RŪMĪ

Ages of great social and political upheaval often seem to provoke responses of a similiar strength in the world of literature, learning, philosophy, and spirituality. These responses may be directly related to the events with which they are coeval, and some of the greatest histories can be viewed as rewritings and reconstructions in the light of seismic disturbances in society. In some cases, however, the connection may seem to be rather fortuitous in nature, as when, for example, a work is produced which sets out for those of a later age a statement of the sum of a particular aspect of the knowledge of the time, a time when the face of the world is set to change irrevocably for its inhabitants. Such a work is the *Mathnawī* of Jalāl al-Dīn Rūmī, which became for subsequent generations an eloquent encyclopaedia of Sufi teaching from which they would mine the gems of its verses down to the present day. These gems naturally come to be set in new surroundings, and it is to one aspect of the way in which Rūmī has been read by subsequent generations of Persians, namely through the metaphysical tradition of 'wisdom', 'philosophical mysticism' *(ḥikmat),* that this study is devoted.[1]

There has probably been no period in Islamic history (at least until present times) quite so destabilizing as the invasion of its Asian heartlands in the seventh/thirteenth century by the Mongols: destabilizing, at first, on account of the fear and terror which the

---

1. I am extremely grateful to Dr. Leonard Lewisohn for his constructive comments on the first draft of this essay, and for tracing many of the poetic citations.

Portrait of Mawlānā Rūmī. Museum of the Deccan

immanent onslaught inspired in people, causing many to flee their ancestral homes, and then, by the devastation wreaked on city and countryside by the hordes, and, in the subsequent and prolonged aftermath, by the resettling of lives and boundaries (both geographical, as well as doctrinal, intellectual, and cultural).

The spiritual life of Islam was no less affected by these events than were other aspects of the community's life. It is not the place here to go into the post-Mongol history of Persian Sufism, except perhaps to look forward to remarks which will be made further on and draw attention in passing to one aspect of this history—the developing rapport between Sufism and Shī'ism (both Twelver and Ismā'īlī) that characterizes the period between the Mongol invasion and the establishment of the Safavid dynasty at the beginning of the tenth/sixteenth century.[2] The effects of the Mongol invasion on Persian Sufism are mirrored in a particularly close fashion in the life of the great Sufi master of that century Mawlānā Jalāl al-Dīn Rūmī, (604/1207–672/1273). Rūmī was born in Balkh, in northern Afghanistan, renowned in its fourth/tenth-century Sāmānid period of splendour as the "Mother of Lands" *(umm al-bilād)*. Before it was conquered for Islam, Balkh had been a centre of Buddhism, and subsequently it played an important role in the development of Persian Sufism and literature, as well as of later Islamic theology.[3] Although never quite to recover from its destruction at the hands of the Ghuzz Turks in 550/1155, it nevertheless continued to be important as a centre of learning; the great theologian Fakhr al-Dīn Rāzī, who resided there, died in 606/1210—just three years after Jalāl al-Dīn's birth. The city had been captured in bloody circumstances by Muḥammad Khwārazmshāh in 603/1206, but this was nothing in comparison to the complete leveling of the city and the massacre of its inhabitants by Genghis Khān fourteen years later. Only a matter of few years before this final catastrophe, however, Jalāl al-Dīn's father left with his family and a considerable entourage to journey

2. For a general overview of the religious history of Persia in the eighth/fourteenth century, see B.S. Amoretti, "Religion in the Timurid and Safavid Periods," in Peter Jackson and L. Lockhart (eds.) *The Cambridge History of Iran* (Cambridge University Press 1986), VI, pp. 610-40.
3. See EI², I, pp. 1000-2, s.v. "Balkh."

on *ḥajj*. Muḥammad ibn al-Ḥusayn Bahā' al-Dīn, Rūmī's father, better known as Bahā' Walad, was himself a noted theologian and mystic, and it is said that at the beginning of this journey he called upon the aging Farīd al-Dīn 'Aṭṭār (d. 617/1220) in Nīshāpūr, where the great Sufi poet foretold the pre-eminence his son was to achieve in mystical teaching.[4]

After visiting Mecca, Rūmī's father took the family to Syria and Anatolia, where they stayed for a few years, first moving to Lāranda (modern-day Larende or Karaman in Turkey), before taking up an invitation from the learned Seljuk Sultan 'Alā' al-Dīn Kayqubād to settle in Konya. Bahā' Walad was to die two years later, shortly after which, apparently upon the arrival in Konya of his father's foremost disciple in Balkh, Burhān al-Dīn Muḥaqqiq Tirmidhī, Rūmī began in earnest his journey along the spiritual path. It is also necessary to remind ourselves of the eruption into Rūmī's life in 642/1244 of the figure of Shams al-Dīn Tabrīzī, and the extraordinary effect this was to have not only on Rūmī, but on Persian literature as a whole.[5]

My hand always used to hold the Koran,
but now it holds Love's flagon.
My mouth was filled with glorification,
but now it recites only poetry and songs.[6]

Through the exceptional relationship between Shams and

---

4. See Badī' al-Zamān Furūzānfar, *Risāla dar taḥqīq-i aḥwāl wa zindagī-yi Mawlānā Jalāl al-Dīn Muḥammad* (Tehran 1315 A.Hsh./1936), pp. 17-18, referring to Dawlatshāh Samarqandī's *Tadhkirat al-shu'arā,* ed. E.G. Browne (Leiden/London 1901), p. 193. On the circumstances and date of Bahā' al-Dīn Walad's departure from Balkh, see Furūzānfar, *op. cit.,* pp. 9-16.
5. The biography of Rūmī can be found in many references, but the most thoroughly researched and argued is probably Furūzānfar, *op. cit.* (see also, 2nd ed., Tehran 1332 A.Hsh./1953). For a list of accounts in both Persian and European languages, see S.H. Nasr, *Islamic Art and Spirituality* (Ipswich: Golgonooza 1987), p. 130, note 2, and Annemarie Schimmel's *I am Wind, You are Fire: The Life and Work of Rumi* (Boston & London 1992).
6. *Dīwān-i Shams-i Tabrīz,* ed. B. Furūzānfar as *Kulliyyāt-i Shams yā Dīwān-i kabīr,* 10 vols. (Tehran: University Press 1957-67), vv. 24875-6; translation from W.C. Chittick, *The Sufi Path of Love: the Spiritual Teachings of Rumi* (Albany 1983), p. 3. References to Rūmī's *Dīwān* (=D) are given according to Furūzānfar's edition, and to his *Mathnawī* (=M) according to R.A. Nicholson (ed., trans, & comm.), *The Mat͟hnawí of Jalálu'ddín Rúmí* (London & Leiden 1925-40; repr. London 1982).

himself, Rūmī lived and expressed the reality of the spiritual stations of separation and union with the Divine.

> *Indeed, Shams-i Tabrīzī is but a pretext*
> *—it is I who display the beauty of God's Gentleness, I!*[7]

The life of Jalāl al-Dīn spanned almost the entire troubled period of the Mongol invasion from its beginning in the East, through the sack of Baghdad in 656/1258, up to the taking of Syria by Hülegü in 658/1260 and the check of the Mongol advance by the Syrian Mamluks in the same year. Anatolia was left disturbed by these events, and Seljuk power there became increasingly compromised by subservience to the Mongols and internal struggles and feuds, especially in the last years of Rūmī's life. Glimpses of these events are afforded us in his works.

The two works which, apart from the *rubā'iyyāt,* form the sum of Rūmī's poetic output are the *Dīwān-i Shams-i Tabrīzī*, containing some 40,000 verses,[8] and the *Mathnawī*, containing some 25,500 verses.[9] The *Mathnawī*, which, in contrast to the *Dīwān*, was conceived as a continuous work, was composed at the initial request of his favourite disciple, Ḥusām al-Dīn Chilibī.

The *Mathnawī* is a summa of Sufi teaching up to the time of Rūmī. Written in a style which follows the tradition of the great didactic Persian Sufi poems which preceded it, such as those of Sanā'ī and 'Aṭṭār, it incorporates material and imagery ranging over the whole spiritual spectrum of Islam. Not only can it be read as a commentary on the Qur'ān, but also as a commentary on the mystical states and spiritual stations *(aḥwāl* and *maqāmāt)* of the spiritual path; not only does it refer to and situate with respect to Sufi teaching, the various Islamic sciences from jurisprudence *(fiqh)* to philo-sophy *(falsafa),* but it also raids that vast storehouse of parables through which the art of story-telling had been employed by Sufis before him to illustrate the turns of the spiritual life, and

---

7. D 16533; trans. Chittick, *op. cit.,* p. 4.
8. See above, no. 5.
9. See above, no. 5. A new edition of the text with annotations has recently been published by Muḥammad Este'lami, *Mathnawī-yi Mawlawī,* 6 vols. (Tehran 1370 A.Hsh./1991).

which has remained vibrant in the spiritual and literary lives of Persians down to our times as a witness to the essentially oral character of spiritual teaching in Islam, not to say of the teaching of Islamic sciences in general. The *Mathnawī* is thus at the same time a guide *sans pareil* to the spiritual path, whose influence even beyond the Islamic world is attested by the numerous translations, renderings, and versions which now appear, and also what might properly be termed a work of great erudition. By this is meant a work through which it is possible to discover almost the entire spectrum of the religious life of the time, and in this case through which it is also possible to understand what may be called the 'spiritualizing' tendency so marked within Islam, whereby the teachings of the Islamic sciences, as well as the more accessible vehicle of literature, are transposed to a higher octave, as it were, and universalized so that their connection with spiritual realities is continuously re-established.

We should not leave this brief acount of Rūmī's work without a short mention of his poetic *silsila*. Rūmī evidently saw himself as the heir to, and the culmination of, his predecessors. Not only was he steeped in the poetry of Sanā'ī, the 'pre-eminent' *(fā'iq),*[10] and 'Aṭṭār, the 'lover'*('āshiq),*[11] to whom he had been introduced, but he was also familiar with other great works of Arabic and Persian literature up to his time—*Kalīla wa Dimna,* the *Shāhnāma, Vis u Rāmin,* the poetry of Niẓāmī, the *Kitāb al-aghānī*, Abū Nuwās, Mutanabbī, and the *Maqāmāt* of Ḥarīrī.[12]

Perhaps as a kind of compensation for the devastation and anguish of the times, the period of Rūmī's life also witnessed the arrival in the area of the person and the teaching of Shaykh al-Akbar, Ibn 'Arabī, who ended his days on earth in Damascus in 638/1240. A meeting between Shams-i Tabrīzī and Ibn 'Arabī is related, perhaps aprocryphally, and Shams is said not to have been too favourably impressed.[13] Whether this feeling carried over into

---

10. See Annemarie Schimmel, *The Triumphal Sun: a Study of the Works of Jalāloddin Rumi* (The Hague 1978), pp. 37-40.
11. *Ibid.*
12. *Ibid.,* pp. 40-42. See also Nasr, *op. cit.,* pp. 125-6.
13. Schimmel, *The Triumphal Sun,* p. 19 & n. 31, following Aflakī's *Manāqib al-'arifīn* and Jāmī's *Nafaḥāt al-uns.*

Rūmī's attitude or not, he can be seen from his work to have found the trappings of theoretical speculation in spiritual matters to have been to a certain extent inimical. Ibn 'Arabī's foremost pupil, and his chosen successor, was Ṣadr al-Dīn Qūnawī (d. 673/1274), a native of Konya. Although Rūmī initially entertained a certain hostility towards him,[14] the two subsequently became intimate friends, and it was Qūnawī who led the funeral prayers for Rūmī. Two other figures should be mentioned as a contemporary link between Rūmī and Ibn 'Arabī: Fakhr al-Dīn 'Irāqī, who attended Rūmī's mystical sessions and was also present at his funeral, and Awḥad al-Dīn Kirmānī, who reportedly met Shams-i Tabrīzī, again a meeting which left Shams unimpressed.[15] Both these figures were associated with Ibn 'Arabī. Awḥad al-Dīn was a favourite companion, and 'Irāqī studied his teachings with Qūnawī; and both, of course, contributed in no small measure to the body of Persian mystical literature.[16]

II. RŪMĪ AND THE PERSIAN *ḤIKMAT* TRADITION

These moments of Rūmī's biography, whether genuine or apocryphal, give anecdotal form to a tension which characterizes the relation between *taṣawwuf* and philosophy throughout Islamic history. The experience of unveiling or witnessing *(kashf)* which is central to the Sufi Path was also at the heart of much of philosophy. It is more explicitly so in the writings of Shihāb al-Dīn Suhrawardī and the *Ishrāqī* school, but is also to be discovered in the works of the Peripatetics. The antipathy that is displayed in the accounts of the meetings mentioned above between, on the one hand, Shams-i Tabrīzī and Rūmī, and on the other, Ibn 'Arabī and his disciples is one manifestation of this tension, underlying which is the fear that rationalization of the moment of unveiling can only serve to detract from, and weaken, it. But at the same time there is manifested in

14. Furūzānfar, *Risāla,* p. 119.
15. See Schimmel, *op. cit.,* p. 19n. 30.
16. Some sources also mention meeting or meetings between Rūmī and Ibn 'Arabī and several of his disciples in Baghdad when Rūmī was studying there in the 630/1230's, but there is reason to doubt the accuracy of this. See Furūzānfar, *op. cit.,* pp. 42-3, quoting Kamāl al-Dīn Ḥusayn Khwārazmī in his commentary on the *Mathnawī,* the *Jawāhir al-asrār,* and Schimmel, *op. cit.,* p. 16, quoting Sipāhsalār.

these meetings a conviviality which testifies to their sharing of this mystical moment.

It is in Persia some two centuries or so later that a philosophical movement set out to harmonize this tension. And it is also during this time—the Safavid period—that the term *'irfān,* 'gnosis' gains currency in a more specific sense as the expression of inward illumination in a philosophic or quasi-philosophic language. Moreover, this inward illumination is now increasingly attained through a spiritual affiliation to the Shi'ite *Imams*, most importantly to the Twelfth, al-Mahdī. Sufism or *taṣawwuf,* for the gnostics *('urafā'),* thus occasionally takes on a pejorative sense of charlatanry, while *'irfān,* for the Sufis, sometimes takes on a corrrespondingly pejorative sense of intellectual pretension. These two terms take on their various colourings from the political and religious contexts in which they are used.

The Safavid dynasty was born of the Sufi *ṭarīqa* of the same name which traced its lineage back to Shaykh Ṣafī al-Dīn in the Īl-khānid period. Centred in Ardabīl, it had, by the late ninth/fifteenth century, become one of several Turkmen Orders combining militant organization with Shi'ism of a radical nature more usually associated with the extremist tendencies of the *ghulāt*. Originally Sunnī in orientation, it was now represented by the radical scarlet head-dress of the Qizil-bāsh militias. Under the young Ismā'īl, they took Azarbaijan from the Aq-Qoyunlu dynasty; and, on entering Tabrīz, Ismā'īl proclaimed himself Shāh at the same time as declaring Twelver Shi'ism the official sectarian religion of his new state. He quickly established control over the whole of Persia, thus inaugurating for the first time in Islamic history a nation whose identity was fused with that of the followers of the Twelve Imams, Ismā'īl himself claiming an ancestry which stretched back to Mūsā al-Kāẓim, eighth in the line of *Imams*.

In the process of converting the newly forged nation to Shi'ism, the tendency to which was by no means absent previous to his accession, but which existed in a popular and unorganized form, he and his successors carried out a policy of attracting Shi'ite scholars from areas of the Arab world where Shi'ism had traditionally been strong, and setting up a network of teaching and legal institutions. In this process of consolidation, of both the Safavid dynasty and of

Twelver Shi'ism in a 'politically correct' form, the movement which had been taking place in Persia over the previous two centuries, and which has been variously described as the "Shī'itization of Sunnism"[17] and "*ṭarīqa* Shī'ism,"[18] moved into a new phase. Rival Shi'ified and non-Shi'ified Sufi *ṭarīqas* were at first ruthlessly suppressed (with one or two politically insignificant exceptions) by the Safavids, and the indigenous religious scholars, who seem to have embraced the new state religion with little resistance, found themselves having to compete with the Shī'ī *fuqahā'* newly arrived from such centres as Jabal 'Āmil in Lebanon, for posts in the now official state religious hierarchy.[19] During this period, Persia became the locus of a revival of philosophical learning, but one which differed remarkably from its forbears.

Some contemporary scholars have seen this philosophical development in terms of a reaction on the part of the indigenous Muslim clerical hierarchy (*'ulamā'*) against the newly arrived legalism of the Arab *'ulamā'*, but recent studies have indicated a far more complex state of affairs.[20] A particular case in point is provided by Shaykh Bahā' al-Dīn al-'Āmilī (953/1547–1030-1/1621), the subject of some recent research.[21] Shaykh Bahā'ī was born in Baalbek in 1547, but moved with his father to Iran when still a child. Although Iran remained his home throughout his life, and under Shāh 'Abbās I he held the position of *Shaykh al-Islām* in Isfahan, he was an inveterate traveller, and it is what is known of his life as a traveller which gives some indication of the complexity of his character

17. See Farhad Daftary, *The Ismā'īlīs: Their History and Doctrines* (Cambridge University Press 1990), p. 462, quoting Claude Cahen; also cf. pp. 461-6 *passim.*
18. *Ibid.,* p. 461, citing Marshall G.S. Hodgson.
19. For the suppression of *ṭarīqa* Sufism, see Said Amir Arjomand, *The Shadow of God and the Hidden Imam: Religion, Political Order and Societal Change in Shi'ite Iran from the Beginnings to 1890,* (Chicago and London 1984), pp. 112-19, and for the indigenous and immigrant scholars, see *ibid.,* chap. 5, pp. 122-59.
20. For the former view, see *ibid.,* pp. 144-59; for the latter, see Andrew Newman, "Towards a Reconsideration of the 'Iṣfahān School of Philosophy': Shaykh Bahā'ī and the Role of the Safawid 'Ulamā'," *Studia Iranica,* XV/ii (1986), pp. 165-99.
21. See C.E. Bosworth, *Bahā' al-Dīn al-'Amilī and His Literary Anthologies,* Journal of Semitic Studies Monograph, no. 10 (Manchester 1989); and Devin J. Stewart, "A Biographical Notice on Bahā' al-Dīn al-'Āmilī (d. 1030/1621)," *Journal of the American Oriental Society,* CXI/iii (July-Sept. 1991), pp. 563-71.

and makes it difficult to classify him along the normal *faqīh/ṣūfī/faylasūf* lines.[22] One of Shaykh Bahā'ī's works, the *Kashkūl,* an anthology which, in Bosworth's words, quotes extensively "from a vast range of knowledge, spanning the Greek ancients, the Jewish prophets, the Persian sages, the writers of the classical period of early and high Islam of the Caliphate, and then the authors of the period of the 'great empires' and Bahā'ī al-Dīn's own time,"[23] also provides information on his travels,[24] but, perhaps more importantly, reveals the range of erudition of this religious scholar of the early Safavid period. Shaykh Bahā'ī's Sufi sympathies and leanings are the subject of some dispute: Shi'ite scholars prefer to pass over them as a forgivable excess, Sufis like to claim him as one of their own,[25] and modern scholars remain skeptical. On the evidence of the *Kashkūl* and his considerable output of poetry, however, there can be no doubt that he was deeply attracted to, and a notable practiticioner of, the mystical path. The *Kashkūl* contains much material on the early Sufis, as well as numerous quotations from Persian and Arabic mystical poetry. Ibn Fāriḍ is the most often quoted Arabic poet, and Rūmī is the most quoted Persian poet, with quotations from the *Mathnawī* being "probable the most numerous of all Persian citations."[26] Moreover, Shaykh Bahā'ī is known to have clothed himself in Sufi garb on several of his journeys, although whether this was part of his strategy to disguise his Shi'ism, or a genuine sign of Sufi affiliation is unclear. What is important is that as a close friend of Mīr Dāmād, and as a teacher of Mullā Ṣadrā and Mullā Muḥsin Fayḍ Kāshānī (for both of whom see below), he stands firmly in the line of the newly emerging Shi'ite philosophers of the Safavid era, most of whom were also renowned scholars in other Islamic sciences, such as *fiqh* and *ḥadīth,* and many of whom had close ties with the court.

---

22. For the life of Shaykh Bahā'ī, see E.I.^{2}, III, pp. 429-30, art. "Bahā' al-Dīn 'Amelī," (E. Kohlberg). Bosworth, *op. cit.,* pp. 29-32, cites the sources for details of Shaykh Bahā'ī's journeys.
23. Bosworth, *op. cit.,* p. 23.
24. For the places visited by Shaykh Bahā'ī and recorded in the *Kashkūl,* see Bosworth, *op. cit.,* pp. 32-4.
25. See E. Kohlberg, *art. cit.,* E.I.^{2}.
26. Bosworth, *op. cit.,* p. 78; see also pp. 58-9.

Whatever the true nature of the relationship between this new school and the political changes of the time may have been, and despite the fact that the elucidation of this problem still awaits much careful and close study of the texts written by the scholars involved before a considered opinion can be given, there is no disagreement on the fact that the outstanding figure of the Safavid philosophical revival was Ṣadr al-Dīn Shīrazī, known as Mullā Ṣadrā.

Mullā Ṣadrā (979-80/1571-2–1050/1640) was born in Shīrāz into a well-established family of Persian scholars and officials, and was a near contemporary of Shah 'Abbās I. Having completed his elementary education in Shīrāz, he betook himself to Iṣfahān, then the centre, not only of philosophical studies, but also of all the traditional sciences—and now, of course, a Shi'ite centre. He studied there for certain with the above-mentioned Shaykh Bahā' al-Dīn al-'Āmilī, whose interests in *fiqh* and the other legal sciences, as mentioned above, were tempered by mystical interests, and Mīr Damād (d. 1040/1630), more famous as a philosopher, although also renowned for legal and theological studies. After some years spent mastering the intellectual sciences, Mullā Ṣadrā retired to the village of Kahak, near Qum, where he found the peace in which to devote himself to meditation and spiritual purification, far away from the intrigues in Iṣfahān, of which he seems now to have become a victim, for in several places in his writings there are not only complaints of the lack of understanding among the more outwardly oriented *'ulamā'*, but even somewhat violent outpourings against the obscurantism and pursuit of worldly ambitions to be found in the *Madrasa*s. After a period which is reported variously as being from seven to fifteen years, Mullā Ṣadrā was invited to return to Shīrāz, and he spent the rest of his years teaching in the Allāh-Wirdī Khān *Madrasa*, and writing most of his works, most notably completing *Al-Ḥikma al-muta'āliyya fī'l-asfār al-'aqliyya al-arba'a*, the *Asfār*, the work for which he is most famous.[27] It is impossible here to do

27. For the life and works of Mullā Ṣadrā, see S.H. Nasr, *Ṣadr al-Dīn Shīrāzī and His Transcendent Philosophy* (Tehran: Iranian Academy of Philosophy 1978); James Winston Morris, *The Wisdom of the Throne: An Introduction to the Philosophy of Mullā Ṣadrā* (Princeton University Press 1981); Fazlur Rahman, *The Philosophy of Mullā Ṣadrā* (Albany 1975).

justice to either the content of Mullā Ṣadrā's philosophy or the intellectual power of his vision. It is sufficient merely to remark upon the synthetic qualities of his output. The Peripatetic and *ishrāqī* schools of Islamic philosophy are combined with Shī'ite theology and the unitary existentialism of Ibn 'Arabī, all under the guiding principle—which is also enunciated by Suhrawardī—that intellectual endeavour uninformed by direct perception, or witnessing, of spiritual realities, is as insufficient as the confrontation with spiritual realities without the guidance of intellectual rigour.

The influence of Ibn 'Arabī had penetrated into the Safavid world through two avenues. We have already indicated the origins of one of these two lines in the figures of Qūnawī, 'Irāqī and Awḥad al-Dīn Kirmānī. This line leads mainly through the works of subsequent Sufis, most notably, of course, Jāmī, but also of note here is Shams al-Dīn Muḥammad Lāhījī, the author of the famous commentary on the *Garden of Mystery (Gushan-i rāz)* of Maḥmūd Shabistārī: the *Mafātiḥ al-i'jāz fī sharḥ-i Gulshan-i Rāz.*[28] Shabistārī himself lived in the early Mongol period in Tabriz, and was born some fifteen years after Rūmī's death. Lāhījī lived most of his life in Shīrāz, where he was the most outstanding disciple of Sayyid Muḥammad Nūrbakhsh, founder of the eponymous *ṭarīqa*, and where he died in 869/1507. He was apparently highly regarded by Jāmī, and lived just long enough to see the Safavid dynasty installed and to receive a visit from the new Shāh. The well-known reason he is said to have given for his black clothing (that it was in mourning for the martyrdom of the Imam Ḥūsayn), and the similarly celebrated passage of the *Gushan-i rāz* commentary in which he describes the black light associated with the ultimate stage of the mystic's perfection before his passing from *fanā'* to *baqā'*, is itself a component in the development of *"ṭarīqa* Shī'ism," and Lāhījī's position on the cusp of this movement from Sunnism to Shī'ism, and from Sufism to *ḥikmat* deserves further attention. His commentary is imbued with the intellectual tenor of the Persian Ibn 'Arabīan tradition, and the metaphysical doctrine of the Unity of Being *(waḥdat*

28. Ed. Kaywān Samī'ī (Tehran 1337 A.Hsh./1958), and more recently, the useful critical edition by Muḥammad Riẓā Buzurg Khāliqī and 'Iffat Karbāsī (Tehran 1371 A.Hsh./1992-3).

al-wujūd), but it is also worth remarking that he often quotes Rūmī and refers to him by name. The commentary's notable rational discourse make its composition a significant moment in the development of that intellectual mysticism for which Persian reserves the word *'irfān*.

The second line connecting Ibn 'Arabī to the Safavid philosophers passes most notably through the figure of Sayyid Ḥaydar Āmulī (719/1319–d. after 787/1385), of the generation following Shabistārī, but of a spiritual world very different from that of the Tabrīzī Sufi. After an education in Khurāsān and Iṣfahān, Ḥaydar Āmulī rose to a high position in the court of the Shi'ite Bāwandī ruler of Ṭabaristān, Fakhr al-Dawla Ḥasan ibn Shāh Kay-Khusraw ibn Yazdigird. At the same time as the murder of this king, and following a dream-revelation, Ḥaydar Āmulī abandoned "family and fortune, King and courtly honour, mother and father, brothers, friends, and companions,"[29] and left for the 'Atabāt of Iraq via Iṣfahān and a *Ḥajj*. In Iraq he is said to have studied under Fakhr al-Muḥaqqiqīn (682/1283–771/1370), the son of the famous Shi'ite theologian and *faqīh* the 'Allāma Ḥillī (648/1250–726/1326), and in the holy city of Najaf upon return from the *ḥajj* he composed the works which make him the most outstanding of the early scholars who 'Shi'ified' the teachings of Ibn 'Arabī. The core of this 'Shi'ification' was the concept of *walāya* and the holder of this station, which had to be transfered to the Imams, more particularly the Imam 'Alī and the Mahdī. Mention should also be made of Ibn Abī Jumhūr al-Āḥsā'ī (b. ca. 837/1433-4 d. after 904/1499), who constructed a thoroughly Shi'ite cosmology in which the Sufi sages or *ḥukamā'* also featured.

Mullā Ṣadrā is known to have written only one prose work in Persian, the *Sih aṣl*.[30] This short *risāla* on the purification of the soul from the obstacles which bar its progress towards full spiritual development was also a castigating critique of those *'ulamā'* and *fuqahā'* whose face is turned towards this world rather than the next,

29. Sayyid Ḥaydar Āmulī, *La philosophie shi'ite,* ed. Henry Corbin and Osman Yahya, Corbin's introduction, p. 17, citing Āmulī's autobiographic fragment in the introduction to his commentary on Ibn 'Arabī's *Fuṣūṣ al-ḥikam,* the *Naṣṣ al-nuṣūṣ*.
30. Ed. S.H. Nasr (Tehran 1340 A.Hsh./1961).

and who deny the possibility of the type of *'irfān* whose advocate Mullā Ṣadrā was. The fact that it is written in Persian rather than Arabic is perhaps an indication that it was addressed to a wider audience beyond the scholars of the *Madrasa*, an audience whose literature would be that of the Persian poets rather than or as well as that of the Arabic text-books, but which would also have included, one may suppose, the indigenous clerical classes. The work is replete with poetic quotations, used as 'proofs' *(dalīl)* for the propositions enunciated in the text, a common device in a long tradition of Persian philosophical-mystical writings running from Aḥmad Ghazālī's *Sawāniḥ,* through 'Ayn al-Quḍāt al-Hamadhānī's *Tamhīdāt,* Fakhr al-Dīn 'Irāqī's *Lama'āt,* and Jāmī's *Lawāyiḥ,* to the works of Mullā Ṣadrā himself. The quotations come from the whole range of mystically inspired Persian poetry, notably Shabistarī's *Gulshan-i rāz* and the *Dīwān* of Ḥāfiẓ, but the text demonstrates above all how Mullā Ṣadrā was steeped in the *Mathnawī* of Rūmī, which he frequently cites.[31] Three examples will suffice. In the eighth chapter on 'discovering the path to God',[32] he quotes a famous passage in which Rūmī sketches the progress of the individual mystic in parallel with that of the entire species upwards towards a divine 'non-existence', a passage which can, incidentally, be seen to illustrate Mullā Ṣadrā's own doctrine of transubstantial motion.

> *I died to inanimacy and was endowed with [the] growth [of plants],*
> *Then I died to [this] growth and attained to the animal.*

---

31. Shabistarī, *inter alia* (page and line nos. in Nasr's edition of the *Sih aṣl,* followed by line no. of the *Gulshan-i rāz* in Ṣamad Muwaḥḥid, *Majmū'a-yi āthār-i Shaykh Maḥmūd Shabistarī,* 2nd pr. (Tehran 1371 A.Hsh./1982): 9,9/923; 19,4-5/918; 46,11-16/668,680,682; 47,1-4/66-6; 73,8-12/263ff.; 76,1-7/582-5; 105,13/84; 113,1-6/185,182,184. Ḥāfiẓ, *inter alia* (page and line nos. of the *Sih aṣl* as above, followed by the ghazal no. and line no. in Parwīz Nātil Khānlarī's edition of the *Dīwān-i Ḥāfiẓ* (Tehran 1359 A.Hsh./1980): 5,8-9/373,1-2; 19,14-15/239,7; 34,17-18/154,3; 73,7/179,3. Rūmī, *inter alia* (page and line nos. of the *Sih aṣl* as above, followed by vol. and line nos. in Nicholson's edition of the *Mathnawī):* 12,7-8/III:1053; 30,2-5/IV:1500-1; 30,11-12/I:2436; 37,12-13/I:1028; 41,5-12/IV:475,472,470,478; 55,15-56,2/III:4209-10; 71,16-72,7/III:3901-3, 3905-6; 96,11-18/IV:3030-4; 109,15/V:463.

32. *Sih aṣl,* pp. 71-2.

I died from animality and became man,
So what should I fear? When have I diminished through death?
Another time I shall die to being human,
Till I soar up amongst the angels.
Again I shall be sacrificed from being an angel;
I shall become that which is not imaginable.
Then I shall become non-existence, which, like an organ,
Will say to me: 'Verily, unto Him shall we return.''[33]

Mullā Ṣadrā uses a second passage to illustrate what he means by the essence of the heart *(jawhar-i dil)*, which, he says, is the rational soul. In these lines Rūmī compares this essence to the butter in milk, awaiting the churning of a divine messenger in order to coagulate and manifest itself.[34]

Lastly, in a chapter[35] which begins with some verses on the mystical fire of love, Mullā Ṣadrā castigates those scholastic theologians *(mutakallim)* who confine themselves to the outward dimensions of theology and reject the beneficial influence which ascetic practices and company with the people of the heart *(ahl-i dil)* can, and indeed must, exert on the understanding of religion. He then quotes a *ḥadīth* from the Prophet on the necessity of having recourse to the people of insight and certainty *(ahl-i baṣīrat wa yaqīn),* over and above the study of the exoteric science of *ḥadīth,* in order to gain understanding of the ambiguous *(mutashābiḥ)* passages in the Koran and *ḥadīth.* The Prophet specifies these people of insight and certainty as the *ahl-i bayt,* that is, the Shī'ite Imams. Having thus stated how religious understanding can only be vouchsafed by combining the outward and the inward, Mullā Ṣadrā goes on to illustrate this by quoting a passage from the *Mathnawī* where Rūmī asserts that the understanding of the Koran without divine guidance leads many astray, and that it must be understood through the guidance of what Mullā Ṣadrā refers to as *āgāhī-yi ḍamīr wa ma'rifat-i bāṭin* "spiritual awareness and inward knowledge."

For many have been led astray by the Koran:
by [clinging to] that rope a multitude have fallen into a well.

---

33. M III: 3901-3, 3905-6
34. *Sih aṣl,* p. 96.
35. *Sih aṣl,* [Bāb 6], pp. 52-9.

There is no fault in the rope, O perverse man,
inasmuch as you had no desire to reach the top.[36]

This whole passage is particularly interesting as an illustration of the way Mullā Ṣadrā binds together the exoteric discipline of *Kalām,* the Persian Sufi tradition, and the Shī'ite belief in divine guidance through the Imams, in order to define what constitutes knowledge.

Mention should also be made here of Mullā Ṣadrā's pupil and son-in-law, Mullā Muḥsin Fayḍ Kāshānī (d. 1090/1679). S.H. Nasr has indicated the existence of a commentary (or a summary of) on the *Mathnawī* written by this prolific scholar,[37] who, in addition to works on theology, law, and, notably, *ḥadīth*, also wrote a fair-sized body of poetry in Persian, which he collected in a *Dīwān*. Incidentally, the introduction to this *Dīwān* also quotes and comments on a number of passages from Shabistārī's *Gulshan-i rāz.*

III. RŪMĪ AND ḤAKĪM SABZAWĀRĪ

The second flowering of this philosophical school originating in Safavid times occured in nineteenth century Qajar Persia, and one of its most important figures was Ḥajjī Mullā Hādī Sabzawārī (1212/1797-8–1289/1878). Ḥajjī Mullā Hādī was born in Sabzawār and completed his elementary education in Mashhad, before moving on to Iṣfahān where he studied with Mullā 'Alī Nūrī, the most celebrated philosopher of his time, and also, according to his son-in-law Mīrzā Sayyid Ḥasan, with Shaykh Aḥmad Aḥṣā'ī, the founder of the Shaykhī school of Shi'ism. His studies completed, he performed the *ḥajj*, and on his way back from Mecca spent some time in Kirmān, where he married, before returning to Sabzawār where the rest of his life was devoted to teaching and writing.[38] His most widely studied book is the *Sharḥ-i Manẓūma*, a complete cycle of philosophical teaching, including logic, the general matters of metaphysics (and

---

36. M III: 4209-10.
37. Unfortunately as yet unpublished. See S.H. Nasr, "The School of Isfahan," in M.M. Sharif, *A History of Muslim Philosophy,* (Wiesbaden 1966), II, p. 927.
38. For the biography of Sabzawārī, see S.H. Nasr, "Ḥājī Mullā Hādī Sabzawārī," in *A History of Muslim Philosophy,* pp. 1543-56, and Mehdi Mohaghegh and Toshiko Izutsu (transl.), *The Metaphysics of Sabzavārī* (New York 1977; 3rd repr. Tehran 1991), pp. 1-27.

بسم الله الرحمن الرحيم

وبه نستعين

نحمدك يا من تجلى لذاته بذاته على ذاته المبرّاة عن السمات وبصفاته واسمائه في صور الاسماء
والصفات من الصور العلميات والاعيان الثابتات الكامنة في الاسماء والصفات كمون
الشجرة في النواة وتجلى بفعله على الجواهر المفارقات من العقول القادسات والنفوس
الزاكيات وعلى الجواهر البرزخيات من المثل المعلقات وعلى الجواهر المقارنات من
القوى والطبايع والاجسام المتجددات المتصرمات والسيالات الداثرات ونشكرك
يا من اشرق بعد ختم القوس النزولي على القوس الصاعدات من الجماد والنبات والحيوانات
فعلى ما اسلفنا نعطف وعلى ما ابتدع ابهج وعلى ما افتتح اختتم سيما على القوس الاكمل
الاعم والصراط الاوسع الاتم صراط الكامل من بني ادم وهو اسمك الاعظم سيما المجلى
المكرم المقدس المقدم محمد سيد العرب والعجم صلى الله عليه وآله واصحابه المتأدبين
بادابه وسلم وبارك وتحنن وترحم ان هذا القرآن يهدي للتي هي اقوم وبعد فيقول الفقير الى الله
البارى الهادى بن المهدى الخراسانى السبزوارى تغمدهما الله بجلابيب رحمته ولاحظهما
بعين هدايته هذا شرح كالمترع المحنوي والمشرع المزنوي للكتاب العظيم والاسلوب الحكيم
المثنوى المعنوى لا بل للتفسير المنظوم والسر المكتوم اذ كله كما ترى بيان للآيات البينات
وتبيان للسنن النبويات وقبسات من نور القرآن اللامع وجذوات من شعاع مصباح الشاطع

Frontispiece of Sabzawārī's *Sharḥ-i asrār-i Mathnawī* Lithograph edition. Tehran: Sanā'ī Library, n.d.

ontology), theodicy, natural philosophy, theological questions such as prophecy and eschatology treated in the manner of the *ḥukamā'*, and ethics. This work consists of a poem, the *Manẓūma*, together with a commentary, and is still widely used in the *Madrasa*s as a beginner's text in philosophy. T. Izutsu and M. Mohaghegh have edited and translated into English a large part of this work, and a large later commentary by Mīrzā Mahdī Āshtīyānī has also been edited and published.[39] Its stucture again reminds us of the important oral component in the transmission of learning in the *Madrasa*s, where a poem assists the memorization of the subject and the commentary provides the text upon which the teacher will himself comment.

Sabzawārī's eminence in *Ḥikmat* is reflected not only in the continuing status of his work, but also by the significant number of his students, and the fact that he enjoyed a degree of royal attention, although his pious and ascetic lifestyle led him to refuse personal patronage. In addition to the *Manẓūma* he also wrote works on *fiqh,* rhetoric, and grammar; he has a Persian *Dīwān*, and commentaries on two of the most well-known prayers *(dū'ā*s) in Shī'ī piety, *al-Sabāḥ* and *al-Jawshan al-kabīr,* this latter being a litany comprising mention of the Names of God. He is also credited by his son-in-law with an unpublished work against the Shaykhī School of his former teacher Shaykh Aḥmad Aḥṣā'ī. Sabzawārī composed two important Persian works as well, and it is these with which we shall be concerned.

The first is a work composed for Naṣir al-Dīn Shāh by the name of *Asrār al-ḥikam fi l-muftataḥ wa-'l-mukhtatam*,[40] a work in which he elucidates the knowledge of eschatology *(mabda' wa ma'ād),* through expositions of theodicy, psychology and ethics, theology, and the *Sharī'a.* The work is replete with poetic quotations, used in a variety of different ways. Sometimes they are introduced in the

---

39. H.Sabzawārī, *Sharḥ-i Gawhar al-farā'id,* Part I, 'Metaphysics', ed. M. Mohaghegh and T. Izutsu (Tehran 1969, for its English translation, see *The Metaphysics of Sabzavārī;* cited above (n. 38), part II, 'Speculative Theology'; Mīrza Mehdī Modarris Āshtiyānī, *Commentary on Sabzawārī's Sharḥ-i Manẓūma,* ed. A. Falāṭūrī and M. Moheghegh (Tehran 1973).
40. Ed. Ḥ.M. Farzād (Tehran 1361 A.Hsh./1982-3). This work was first published in lithograph by Mīrzā Yūsuf Mustawfī al-Mamālik, who also had Sabzawārī's tomb constructed in Mashhad (see Mohaghegh & Izutsu, *The Metaphysics*..., p. 16.

way we saw poetry being used by Mullā Ṣadrā, as 'proofs' for theoretical propositions, sometimes these quotations stand at the head of a section which propounds upon them in the manner in which a teacher comments upon a text, and sometimes they just stand on their own to speak for themselves, yet are inserted into the text in order to give the reader occasion to pause and reflect on the contents. The pervasiveness of this use of poetry extends beyond the metaphysical and theological parts of the book into the section dealing with the realities behind the practices of the *Sharī'a*. This is an important genre of literature to which both Sufi and the Shi'ite gnostics *('urafā')* contributed and continue to contribute. In seeking to explain why the unbeliever is considered *najis* or impure in the eyes of Islamic jurisprudence *(fiqh)*, for example, Sabzawārī first gives a hemistich in Arabic to the effect that ordinary people *(al-nās)*, are as dead, while the people of knowledge are the 'quickened', the truly alive. Then he proceeds to give a passage from the *Mathnawī* which begins:

Hark! for the friends of God (awliyā')
are the Isrāfīls of the present time,
From them freshness and life come to the dead.[41]

The unbelievers are therefore, we are led to understand—but not told explicitly—the ignorant, that is: those whom the friends of God have not awakened from their metaphorical death, and by analogy with the impurity of corpses, the conclusion is reached.

The second Persian work of Sabzawārī is of even greater import in the present context, for it is a commentary on the *Mathnawī* itself and the object of the present study.[42] This work was written for the Qājār Prince Sultan Murād. It is not a continuous commentary, but, as the author describes it—recalling Rūmī's description of the *Mathnawī* in his own introduction to the first book as the immortal fountain of Paradise *(salsabīl)* at which travellers on the path may quench their thirst and where the righteous may drink—it is "like the

---

41. M I: 1930; *Asrār al-ḥikam,* pp. 442-4.
42. *Sharḥ-i asrār-i Mathnawī* (Tehran: lithograph, n.d.). This work is otherwise referred to by its full title: *Sharḥ-i ba'ḍ-i asrār-i mughlaqa-yi Mathnawī,* first published, Tehran 1275 A.Hsh. See the illustration on page 425.

vessel which fills up or the place where the water of *Mathnawī-yi Ma'nawī* runs."[43] He considers the entirety of "this great book" to be "an explanation of the clear signs, an exposition of the prophetic practices, and firebrands of the light of the lustrous Koran."[44] It is thus an explanation of the some of the more abstruse passages of Rūmī's text to enable the whole to be read correctly, an explanation which reveals the meaning of its words in the light of *Ḥikmat* and 'gnosis' or 'theosophy' (*'Irfān*). In its own turn, just as the *Mathnawī* was a summa of the knowledge of its time bound together by the spiritual teaching which it was used to set forth, Sabzawārī's commentary is a summa of the knowledge of this nineteenth-century theosopher put to the use of exegesis on the *Mathnawī.* Quotations inform the text from a very broad range of sources: the Hellenic and Islamic Peripatetic philosophers, the Persian Neo-Platonists or *Ishrāqī* philosophers, Arabic poetry (both pre-Islamic and Islamic), and Persian poetry. Grammatical explanations and justifications are given for obscure and confusing passages. *Ḥadīth* from the Prophet and the Imams are copiously cited. But above all, it is, as the author states in his introduction, a kind of exegesis of the Koran through an explanation of Rūmī's own commentary on the Holy Book.

The following summary of Sabzawārī's commentary on a section from the beginning of the second book of the *Mathnawī* gives some idea of both the wide range of the content and the punctuated style of the whole. The commentary concerns some verses describing the Spirit of the Perfect Man. (The actual words commented on and given in the text are here given in bold type: Sabzawārī's text does not quote the whole text of Rūmī's verse).[45]

> ***O you whose attributes*** *are [those of] the Sun of Gnosis,*
> *while the Sun of the Heavens is linked to a single attribute.*
>
> ***Now you become the Sun, now you become the Sea,***
> ***Now Mount Qāf, now the 'Anqā.***

---

43. *ka-'l-mutri' al-muḥtawā wa-'l-mashri' al-murtawā li-'l-kitāb al-'aẓīm. Sharḥ,* p. 1.
44. *Ibid.*
45. *Ibid.,* pp. 97-98.

In your essence ***you are neither this nor that,***
O greater than all that can be imagined, and more than 'more'.

The Spirit is a confidant of Science and Reason;
What has the Spirit to do with Arabic or Turkish?

O You who, despite your many forms, are still imageless;
Both ***the absolute unitarianian*** **(muwaḥḥid)**
and pantheist **(mushabbih)** *by you are bedazzled.*[46]

Sabzawārī comments on the first couplet above that, "since the Spirit is the theophanic receptacle *(maẓhar)* of *all* the divine Attributes, and cognizant of *all* the Divine Names *(asmā'-yi ḥusna),* its attributes are the 'Sun of divine Gnosis', for it is the temple of divine Unity *(haykal-i tawḥīd)* and presents a comprehensive exposition *(maẓhar-i jāmi')* [of these realities], in contradistinction to the sun of the physical heavens, which is the locus of manifestation of only a *few* of the divine Attributes.

The Sun, the Sea, Mount Qāf and the *'Anqā'* are glossed as follows. The Sun is illustrated by an Arabic verse by Ibn 'Arabī:

Truly my heart has become receptive to all forms,
a meadow for the grazing of gazelles, the monks' cloisters.

The "Sea" is interpreted as "the wide ocean of the divine Mercy and all-expansive existence, which like the Reality of Muḥammad *(ḥaqīqat-i Muḥammadiyya),* is a 'Mercy to all the worlds'." Mount Qāf indicates the "effective power of the divine activity *(qudrat-i fa'aliyya),* for the heart of the faithful believer is the divine Throne, insofar as the heart is one of the seven subtle organs *(laṭā'if).*" It also symbolizes the world of Image-exemplars *('ālam-i mithāl).*

Of the legendary supernatural bird, the *'Anqā',* Sabzawārī informs us that,

> By different people it is called various things: the Holy Spirit *(rūḥ al-qudus),* the Angel of Inspiration *(surūsh* [of Zoroastrian origin]), the Highest Law *(nāmūs-i akbar),* Active Intelligence *('aql-i fa''āl),* and many other names in different languages. ...It is also said to have many thousands of heads, wings, beaks, and

---

46. *Mathnawī,* II: 53-57.

> [to sing a myriad] beautiful melodies. Yes, these are all different interpretations used to describe its perfections and actions—all of which are the operation of the *Intellectus in actu.*

It is "the essence of the Spirit *(dhāt-i rūḥ)*..." says Sabzawārī, which is referred to by Rūmī in the next couplet as "neither this nor that," for this essence is beyond all determinations—in this context, he cites an anonymous mystic's saying, "Say of me no more than '[I am the] Existent [One]'." Deepening his exegesis of Rūmī's verse leads him to quote the opinions of "Shaykh Ishrāqī Shihāb al-Dīn Suhrawardī" (d. 587/1191), the founder of Islamic illuminationism, and "Ṣadr al-Muta'allihīn," that is to say, Mullā Ṣadrā, as well as others among the gnostic verifiers *(muḥaqqiqīn)* that the "rational soul *(nafs-i nāṭiqa)* is undifferentiated in its being *(wujūd-i basīṭī)* and has no quiddity." He concludes his exegesis of Rūmī's couplet with a quotation from Shaykh Ishrāq,

> Mind every determination *(ta'ayyunī)* and quiddity for which I give an intellectual indication, even though that quiddity be an immaterial essence *(jawhar-i mujarrad)* or a commanding spirit *(ruḥ-i amrī);* I myself explain with finality that Reality is other than these determinations and quiddites.

In other words, one should beware of every kind of conceptual particularization of the Spirit, even the most abstract, for it is the Reality which transcends all other realities, and is therefore ultimately inexpressible. The paradox of God's transcendence and immanence described in Rūmī's last couplet—which contrasts the believer who annuls all comparisons and eschews the use of metaphorical language to describe God *(muwaḥḥid)* with the one who readily institutes comparisons and sees God in everything *(mushabbih)*—is given ample philosophical commentary by Sabzawārī. Although neither of these theological perspectives express the whole truth, of course, the bewilderment of both those who describe God by human likeness and those who exalt God above such comparisons is due to "Spirit of the Perfect Man *(rūḥ-i insān-i kāmil)* who is the Supreme Sign of the Truth (May He be magnified!) and the Supreme Theophanic Exposition *(maẓhar-i a'ẓam)*. From head to toe he is a mirror and illustration of both types of divine Attributes, the transcendent and the immanent." The Perfect Man is thus a mirror of harmony, forming the temple of divine Unity. He then quotes two *ḥadīth,* "The Light rises from the morning of pre-eternity and its traces shine forth in the temples of divine Unity," and "The human soul is the Straight Path," in support of his exegesis, to conclude with a citation from the Koran: "...and in your souls, but you do not see."[47]

IV. CONCLUSION

The preceding synopsis of a couple of pages from Sabziwārī's commentary, however brief, hopefully gives some idea of the form and style of the text. It is not a work which lends itself readily to translation; the text is technical, highly condensed, often elliptical, and the commentary frequently seems to ask for more clarification than the poetry. It gives the impression of being the record of sessions during which Rūmī's poem was read, with pauses every now and then, to explain difficulties and to interpret certain passages, so as to open up the text for Sabzāwarī's audience. Whether this was the actual state of affairs or not, the commentary fills just over five hundred large lithograph pages, while the *Mathnawī* contains slightly more than 25,500 couplets, which gives an average of around fifty couplets per page of commentary. In actual fact an average page is likely to provide a commentary on a mere dozen words. How these dozen or so words came to be chosen for comment clearly reflects the expectations of Sabzawārī's audience, and the interest of the commentary lies thus to a great extent in the insight it gives us into the erudition of Sabzawārī and his audience, an erudition which, we have seen, includes metaphysics, the natural sciences, speculative mysticism, Koran and *ḥadīth,* the linguistic sciences, and literature.

What results can be drawn, then, from a comparison of the different intellectual worlds inhabited by Rūmī on the one hand and Sabzawārī on the other, in the light of the intervening seven hundred years? There is, first of all, the change from the Sufism of Rūmī and those Persian poets who followed him, to the more philosophically oriented *'irfān* of the Safavid period. The pre-Safavid Persians of Ibn 'Arabī's school, if we can call it that, were almost all Sufis

---

47. *Sharḥ,* p. 98.

within the prevailing *ṭarīqa* system. Even the Imāmī Sayyid Ḥaydar Āmulī was invested with a *khirqa* and a *dhikr* in a line of transmission from Shaykh ‘Umar Suhrawardī which he traced back to ‘Alī ibn Abī Ṭālib. The suppression of most Sufi *ṭarīqas* in Safavid lands and times is well-attested, and so it is not surprising to find little or no evidence of initiation into a formal *ṭarīqa* for figures such as Mullā Ṣadrā, although it is likely that his son-in-law Mullā Muḥsin Fayḍ did have such an affiliation. Shaykh Bahā’ al-Dīn al-‘Āmilī is known to have spent some time in Syria and the surrounding areas travelling in the garb of a Sufi, although whether this was a precaution to disguise his Shī‘ism, or the actual sign of initiation is unclear. However, from the text of the *Sih aṣl* it can be seen that much of the *ṭarīqa* culture survived for a figure such as Mullā Ṣadrā. The mystical vocabulary is largely taken over form the Persian Sufi tradition, and the corpus of Persian mystical poetry, and in particular, Rūmī’s *Mathnawī,* forms the literary stock from which he drew so much of his imagery. It is also clear that Mullā Ṣadrā’s mystical sensitivity is very close to that of Persian Sufism, which, by his time, had thoroughly incorporated the speculative mysticism of Ibn ‘Arabī: Mullā Ṣadrā’ extensive use of Shabistarī is a clear indication of this. There is no reason to doubt that what was true for Mullā Ṣadrā was also true for a great many of his circle and students.

Apart from the decline in *ṭarīqa* allegiance, the most notable differences between pre-Safavid Sufism and the *‘irfān* of the Safavid period lie thus in the religious domain, where Shī‘ism replaces Sunnism as the predominant framework, and in philosophy, where a synthesis of Peripatetic, Illuminationist and Akbarian philosophy is created. The figure of the Imam to a great extent replaces that of the Shaykh, and Sunni *ḥadīth* are largely replaced by Shī‘ite *ḥadīth,* although not altogether. It must be remembered that the purity of an *‘ārif*’s Shī‘ism continued to be open to criticism by the *‘ulamā’,* something which surfaced within the framework of the renewed Uṣūlī-Akhbārī controversy as well as in allegations concerning Sufi affiliation. *‘Irfān* was, and indeed still is, seen by some Persian *‘ulamā’* to dilute a person’s Shī‘ism and draw him towards Sunni sympathies, and the label ‘Sufi’ is sometimes used pejoratively in this sense; conversely it may be taken as a sign of extremism, a factor which has played its part in the development of the elusive language of Shī'ite mysticism. How, after all, can the aspirant mystic receive the guidance of the Imam, which must for him be something more substantial than the guidance attainable by any of the *'ulamā'* through the study of *ḥadīth,* and then express the event? If someone claims contact, or even, in extreme cases, some kind of identification, with the Imam, is this to be understood as purely imaginal or at the same time more literal and physical? How can he escape the misunderstandings of the exoteric scholars and the ignorant?

After the Safavid period, Shī'ism in Persia remained interwoven with the Persian Sufi tradition: many of the *'ulamā'* were *faqīh*s, philosophers and *'ārif*s at the same time. The figure of Sabzawārī in the late Qājār period stands as a particular example of how these strands of learning could be combined. He is unlikely to figure prominently in a list of *faqīh*s in a century in which legal learning rises to new heights, but he was a product of the *Madrasa* and was scrupulous in his observance of the *Sharī'a,* and several of his writings demonstrate his thorough knowledge of the legal sciences. He wrote prfound commentaries on two well-known Shī'ite supplications *(du'ā),* commentaries which reflect in their spiritual content the link between the Shī'ite *'ārif* and his Imam. He was the most outstanding philosopher of his time, continuing the *ḥikmat* tradition which was formed during the Safavid period by Mullā Ṣadrā and others. And his commentary on Rūmī's *Mathnawī* is testimony to the enduring legacy of Persian Sufism and mystical poetry within the world of Shī'ite learning. It also shows the outstanding importance of Rūmī in this legacy, an importance rivaled by no other Sufi poet.

The Tomb of Rūzbihān. Shiraz, Iran.

VI

The Stages of Love in Early Persian Sufism, from Rābi'a to Rūzbihān

Carl W. Ernst

Everyone acknowledges that love is hard to classify, but that has not kept people from trying to do so. Especially in a tradition like Persian Sufism, in which love is the subject of innumerable tributes, it has been impossible to resist the attempt to describe the character of love. The panorama of early Sufism in Persia offers many testimonies to love and its many moods and degrees. Mystical classifications of the stages of love differed from secular, legal, and philosophical analyses of love in that the Sufis consistently placed love in the context of their mystical psychology of 'states' and 'stations', with an emphasis on love as the transcendence of the self.[1] Moreover, love in its various forms was of such importance that it generally was recognized as "the highest goal of the stations and the loftiest summit of the stages," in Abū Ḥāmid al-Ghazālī's phrase.[2] The classifications of the stages of love according to the early Sufis differed in detail, but the fundamental emphasis throughout was on love as the most important form of the human-divine

1. For secular, mystical, and legal classifications of love, see the tables in Joseph N. Bell, *Love Theory in Later Ḥanbalite Islam* (Albany: SUNY Press 1978), pp. 157-60. Surveys of the literature are found in Hellmut Ritter, "Philologika VII: Arabische und persische Schriften über die profane und die mystische Liebe," *Der Islam 21* (1933); Hellmut Ritter, *Das Meer der Seele: Mensch, Welt und Gott in den Geschichten des Farīduddīn 'Aṭṭār,* 2nd ed. (Leiden 1978), esp. pp. 504-574; Lois Anita Giffen, *The Theory of Profane Love Among the Arabs: The Development of the Genre* (New York: NYU Press 1971); and 'Abd al-Raḥmān ibn Muḥammad al-Anṣārī al-ma'rūf bi-Ibn al-Dabbāgh, *Kitāb mashāriq anwār al-qulūb wa mafātīḥ asrār al-ghuyūb,* ed. H. Ritter (Beirut: Dār Ṣādir, Dār Bayrūt 1379/1959), Introduction, pp. ii-vi (in Arabic).
2. See page 436—›

relationship. We can trace the historical development of the classifications of love in Persian Sufism in an almost direct line from its origins through Rābi'a of Basra to the summa of love by the sixth/twelfth-century Sufi of Shiraz, Rūzbihān Baqlī. Throughout this development, we can see the gradual elaboration of many refinements, and even the intrusion of vocabulary from the secular philosophical tradition, but the fundamental emphasis is on love aspiring to union with God.

The problem of the classification of love's stages is inseparable from the larger theme of the states *(aḥwāl)* and stations *(maqāmāt)* in Sufism. Ultimately, the impulse to categorize goes back to the Koran, with its differentiation of souls in the eschaton, and the term *maqām* is fairly frequent in the Koran.[3] In Sufism, many commentators have noticed that this type of classification goes back at least to Dhū'l-Nūn the Egyptian (d. 246/861), who is credited with lists of nineteen or eight stages, while in Iran, Yaḥyā ibn Mu'ādh (d. 258/872) spoke of seven or four.[4] Paul Nwyia has traced the Sufi concern with the structure of mystical experience to the sixth Imam of the Shī'ites, Ja'far al-Ṣādiq (d. 148/765), whose Koran commentary formed the basis for the Sufi exegesis of Dhū'l-Nūn. Ja'far al-Ṣādiq compiled three lists of stages, which analyzed the spiritual itinerary toward the vision of the face of God: the twelve springs of gnosis, the twelve constellations of the heart, and the forty lights deriving from the light of God. As Nwyia pointed out, the order and selection of the terms included in the different lists vary considerably,

---

2. Abū Ḥāmid al-Ghazālī, *Iḥyā' 'ulūm al-dīn* (16 parts in 4 vols., Cairo: Dār al-Shu'ab, n.d.), p. 2570. Cf. Abū Ḥāmid Muḥammad Ghazālī Ṭūsī, *Kitāb-i Kīmīyā-yi sa'ādat*, ed. Aḥmad Ārām (2nd ed., Tehran: Kitābkhāna wa Chāpkhāna Markazī 1333 A.Hsh./1955; reprint ed., Istanbul: Waqf al-Ikhlāṣ 1408/1366 A.Hsh./1988), p. 850, where he calls love *(maḥabba)* "the greatest of the stages."

3. The term *maqām* occurs fourteen times in the Koran. It hardly seems necessary to suppose with Massignon that this concept is a "philosophical intrusion" of Stoic origin; cf. Louis Massignon, *La Passion de Husayn Ibn Mansûr Hallâj, martyr mystique de l'Islam exécuté à Baghdad le 26 mars 922,* new ed., 4 vols., (Paris: Gallimard 1975), I, 390, n. 3.

4. Massignon, Passion, I, 390, nn. 3-4; idem, *Essai sur les origenes du lexique technique de la mystique musulmane,* Études Musulmanes, 2, new ed., (Paris: Librairie Philosophique J. Vrin 1968), p. 41; Annemarie Schimmel, *Mystical Dimensions of Islam* (Chapel Hill: University of North Carolina 1975), p. 100.

indicating that the stages of the soul's progress were far from being fixed at this time.[5] Yet it is significant that stages of love occupied prominent positions in Ja'far al-Ṣādiq's lists: love *(maḥabba)* and intimacy *(uns)* are the eleventh and twelfth of the twelve springs of gnosis, while love *(maḥabba)*, longing *(shawq)*, and ravishing *(walah)* are the last three constellations of the heart. For the sake of illustration, Ja'far's second list reads as follows:

> Heaven is called "heaven" due to its loftiness. The heart is a heaven, since it ascends by faith and gnosis without limit or restriction. Just as "the known" [i.e., God] is unlimited, so the gnosis of it is unlimited. The zodiacal signs of heaven are the courses of the sun and moon, and they are Aries, Taurus, Gemini, Cancer, Leo, Virgo, Libra, Scorpio, Sagittarius, Capricorn, Aquarius, and Pisces. In the heart there are zodiacal signs, and they are:
>
> 1. The sign of faith *(īmān);*
> 2. The sign of gnosis *(ma'rifa);*
> 3. The sign of intellect *('aql);*
> 4. The sign of certainty *(yaqīn);*[6]
> 5. The sign of submission *(islām);*
> 6. The sign of beneficence *(iḥsān);*
> 7. The sign of trust in God *(tawakkul);*
> 8. The sign of fear *(khawf);*
> 9. The sign of hope *(rajā');*
> 10. The sign of love *(maḥabba);*
> 11. The sign of longing *(shawq);*
> 12. The sign of ravishing *(walah).*
>
> It is by these twelve zodiacal signs that the heart remains good, just as it is by the twelve zodiacal signs, from Aries and Taurus to the end, that the evanescent world and its people are good.[7]

---

5. Paul Nwyia, *Exégèse coranique et langage mystique, Nouvel essai sur le lexique technique des mystiques musulmanes* (Beirut: Dar el-Machreq Éditeurs 1970), pp. 170-73.
6. The Berlin MS has here instead "soul *(nafs),*" corresponding to no. 8 on the list of Ḥallāj, given below.
7. See page 438—›

If it is correct to see a progression or ascent in this early classification, then the stages of love occupy an important, not to say preeminent, position in the spiritual experience of the soul.

The elevation of the love of God to a supreme level in Sufism has most often been connected to Rābi'a al-'Adawiyya (d. 185/801), the famous woman saint of Basra. An early Sufi ascetic of the so-called school of Basra, 'Abd al-Wāhid ibn Zayd in the seventh century, had introduced the non-Koranic term *'ishq* or 'passionate love' to describe the divine-human relationship.[8] Another Basran, Rabāḥ al-Qaysī, used the Koranic term *khulla* or 'friendship.'[9] But it is especially Rābi'a who has gained fame as the one who distinguished between the selfish lover of God who seeks paradise and the selfless lover who thinks only of the divine beloved. For her, love *(ḥubb* or *maḥabba)* meant concentration on God to the exclusion of all else. When Sufyān al-Thawrī asked Rābi'a what was the reality of her faith, she replied, "I have not worshipped Him from fear of His fire, nor for love of His garden, so that I should be like a lowly hireling; rather, I have worshipped Him for love of Him and longing for Him."[10] Her oft-quoted distinction between the 'two loves,' a selfish love seeking paradise and a selfless love seeking God's pleasure, is the fundamental beginning point in the understanding of the stages of love.[11] She wrote,

---

7. Paul Nwyia, "Le Tafsīr Mystique attribué à Ǧa'far Ṣādiq: Édition critique," *Mélanges de l'Université Saint-Joseph,* XLIII/4 (1968), pp. 35-36, commenting on Koran XXV: 61; Nwyia has summarized the text in his *Exégèse coranique,* pp. 171-72. The Arabic text is also given by Rūzbihān al-Baqlī, *Tafsīr 'Arā'is al-bayān* (Lucknow: Nawal Kishōr 1301/1883-4), II, 98; Rūzbihān al-Baqlī, *'Arā'is al-bayān,* MS. 864 Sprenger, Staatsbibliothek, Berlin, fol. 272a. I am indebted to Alan Godlas for supplying these references.
8. Massignon, *Essai,* p. 214.
9. *Ibid.*, p. 217.
10. Rābi'a, in Ghazālī, *Iḥyā'*, IV, 2598.
11. Schimmel, *Dimensions,* pp. 38-40; Massignon, *Essai,* p. 216; Marijan Molé, *Les mystiques musulmans* (Paris: Les Deux Océans 1982), p. 41; Roger Arnaldez, *Réflexions chrétiennes sur la mystique musulmane* (Paris: O.E.I.L. 1989), p. 233; G.-C. Anawati and Louis Gardet, *Mystique musulmane, Aspects et tendances - Expériences et techniques,* Études Musulmanes, VIII, 4th ed. (Paris: Librairie Philosophique J. Vrin 1986), pp. 26-7, 162-70.

I love You with two loves:
a selfish love and a love of which You are worthy.
That love which is a selfish love
is my remembrance of You and nothing else.
But as for the love of which You are worthy
Ah, then You've torn the veils for me so I see You.
There is no praise for me in either love,
but praise is Yours in this love and in that.[12]

Although she did not go into detail regarding the analysis of love beyond this basic distinction, the great Andalusian Sufi Ibn al-'Arabī remarked of Rābi'a, that "she is the one who analyzes and classes the categories of love to the point of being the most famous interpreter of love."[13] The poems and anecdotes that have come down to us concerning her are related by authors of later periods; however, it is striking that the Sufi tradition unanimously credits Rābi'a with these insights into love and regards her as the example of the pure lover of God.[14] Regardless of the difficulty of ascertaining her exact formulations, we may still invoke Rābi'a as the figure who stands for the first intensive meditations on the nature of mystical love in Islam.

The earliest Persian Sufis developed further the distinction between the selfish love of God that seeks paradise and the love of God for his own sake. Shaqīq al-Balkhī (d. 194/810), an early Sufi of

---

12. Rābi'a, in Ghazālī, *Iḥyā',* IV, 2598. Gardet, p. 165, n. 20, cites Kalābādhī (d. 385/995) and Abū Ṭālib al-Makkī (d. 386/996) as transmitters of this poem with a variant reading in the second half of the third line: "Would that I see no more creatures, but see You!"

13. Ibn 'Arabî, *Traité de l'amour,* trans. Maurice Gloton (Paris: Albin Michel 1986), p. 247 (from *al-Futūḥāt al-Makkiyya,* chapter 115).

14. Rābi'a was the subject of a biography by the Ḥanbalī scholar Ibn al-Jawzī (d. 597/1200) (Massignon, *Essai,* p. 239), and her story was told by European Christians in the thirteenth and seventeenth centuries as a model of true charity (Gardet, p. 167, nn. 25-26; Schimmel, p. 8). Modern tributes to her include the well-known monograph by Margaret Smith, *Rābi'ah the Mystic and Her Fellow-Saints in Islam* (Cambridge: Cambridge University Press 1928); 'Abd al-Raḥmān al-Badawī, *Shahīdat al-'ishq al-ilāhī, Rābi'a al-'Adawiyya,* Dirāsāt Islāmiyya, no. 8 (Cairo: al-Nahḍa 1946); a hagiography by Widad el Sakkakini, *First Among Sufis:The Life and Thought of Rabia al-Adawiyya, the Woman Saint of Basra,* trans. Nabil Safwat (London: The Octagon Press 1982); and reworkings of English translations of her poetry by Charles Upton, *Doorkeeper of the Heart: Versions of Rābi'a* (Putney, VT: Threshold Books 1988).

Khurāsān, was especially interested in psychological classification. Of him Sulamī (d. 412/1021) remarked, "I believe that he was the first to speak of the sciences of mystical states *(aḥwāl)* in the districts of Khurāsān."[15] In a small treatise on worship, *Ādāb al-'ibādāt* ("The Manners of Worship"), Shaqīq gave one of the earliest descriptions in Sufi literature of the progress of the soul through different abodes *(manāzil)*. These abodes are four: asceticism *(zuhd)*, fear *(khawf)*, longing for paradise *(shawq ilā al-janna)*, and love of God *(maḥabba li'llāh)*. This classification is evidently very archaic. Shaqīq describes each stage in terms of a forty-day retreat, and for the first two abodes he gives details of the discipline of appetite and emotion, and of the illuminations of divine grace bestowed on the aspirant. The third abode calls for meditation on the delights of paradise to such an extent that by the fortieth day one has forgotten about the previous stages and possesses a happiness that no misfortune can disturb.[16]

Although many enter the abodes of asceticism, fear, and longing for paradise, according to Shaqīq, not all enter the abode of love, which is the highest station. Those purified ones whom God brings to this abode have their hearts filled with the light of love and forget the previous stations; the light of divine love eclipses the other experiences, as the rising sun makes the moon and stars invisible. The essence of the experience of the love of God is that it is absolute and exclusive devotion, leaving room for nothing else in the heart.[17] It is especially noteworthy that in this classification, the term longing *(shawq)* is here reserved for longing for paradise, while in later discussions of love it is another mode of the soul's desire for God. It seems that the early Sufis' concern with establishing the primacy of the love of God succeeded in excluding the desire for paradise as a

---

15. Abū 'Abd al-Raḥmān al-Sulamī, *Ṭabaqāt al-ṣūfiyya*, ed. Nūr al-Dīn Sharība (Cairo: Maktabat al-Khānjī 1406/1986), p. 61.
16. Shaqīq al-Balkhī, *Ādāb al-'ibādāt*, in *Trois œuvres inédites de mystiques musulmans: Šaqīq al-Balkhī, Ibn 'Aṭā, Niffarī,* ed. Paul Nwyia, Recherches, Collection publiée sous la direction de la Faculté des Lettres et des Sciences Humaines de l'Université Saint-Joseph, Beyrouth, Série I: *Pensée arabe et musulmane,* vol. 7, 2nd ed. (Beirut: Dar el-Machreq Éditeurs SARL 1982), pp. 17-20. Nwyia has analyzed this passage at length in his *Exégèse,* pp. 213-31.
17. *Ibid.*, pp. 20-21.

legitimate goal of mysticism; henceforth, longing can only be directed toward God.

It is difficult to trace out the precise development of Sufi teachings about love's stages from this point, but it is clear that the Baghdadian Sufis in the third/ninth century devoted much attention to this topic. As we can tell by his nickname, 'the Lover,' Sumnūn al-Muḥibb (d. 287/900) is reported to have raised love to the highest position in his teaching. In a testimony preserved by the Ghaznavid master 'Alī Hujwīrī (d. 465/1072), Sumnūn described love as the highest and most comprehensive of spiritual states. "Love is the principle and foundation of the Path to God Most High. The states and stations are abodes [all related to love]; in whichever abode the seeker resides, it is appropriate that it should end, except for the stage of love. In no way is it appropriate that this should come to an end, as long as the Path exists."[18] Hujwīrī comments that all other Shaykhs agree with Sumnūn in this matter, though they may use a different terminology out of prudence.

Among the Baghdadian Sufis, Ḥallāj (d. 309/922) also placed a particular emphasis on love as a quality of God, with what some have perceived as a philosophical emphasis.[19] Louis Massignon pointed out that Ḥallāj, in a passage recorded by Sulamī, had described a list of psychological states and stages in which the final items are clearly related to love; this list is evidently based on Ja'far al-Ṣādiq's list of 'constellations of the heart,' described above. In this passage, Ḥallāj proposes a test for the sincerity of spiritual claims, juxtaposing each moment *(waqt)* of inner experience with

18. Sumnūn al-Muḥibb, in Abū'l-Ḥasan 'Alī ibn 'Uthmān al-Jullābī al-Hujwīrī al-Ghaznawī al-Lāhawrī, *Kashf a-maḥjūb,* ed. 'Alī Qawīm (Islamabad: Markaz-i Taḥqīqāt-i Fārsī-i Īrān wa Pākistān 1398/1978), pp. 269-70. The phrase in brackets is missing from the Islamabad edition, but an old lithograph edition reads "the states and stages are abodes equally related to it [i.e., love]"; cf. *Kashf al-maḥjūb-i fārsī,* ed. Aḥmad 'Alī Shāh (Lahore: Ilāhī Bakhsh Muḥammad Jalāl al-Dīn 1342/1923), p. 240. 'Aṭṭār preserves a similar reading of this saying: "The states and stages all are related to love-play;" cf. Farīd al-Dīn 'Aṭṭār Nīshāpūrī, *Kitāb tadhkirat al-awliyā',* ed. Muḥammad Khān Qazwīnī (2 vols., 5th ed., Tehran: Intishārāt-i Markazī, n.d.), II, 69.

19. I have briefly discussed this problem in "Rūzbihān Baqlī on Love as 'Essential Desire'," in *God is Beautiful and Loves Beauty: Essays presented to Annemarie Schimmel,* ed. J.-C. Bürgel and Alma Giese (Leiden: Peter Lang 1994).

the practices and qualities that are required of one who claims it:

> And among their manners is striving in the gnosis of claims *(da'āwī)*[20]and seeking [to attain] every moment with the manners [of the state] announced by the one who claims that moment. Ḥusayn ibn Manṣūr said,
>
> 1. One who claims *(dā'ī)* faith *(īmān)* needs *(yad'ū ilā)* guidance *(rushd).*
> 2. One who claims submission *(islām)* needs morals *(akhlāq).*
> 3. One who claims beneficence *(iḥsān)* needs witnessing *(mushāhada).*
> 4. One who claims understanding *(fahm)* needs abundance *(ziyāda).*
> 5. One who claims intellect *('aql)* needs taste *(madhāq).*
> 6. One who claims learning *('ilm)* needs audition *(samā').*
> 7. One who claims gnosis *(ma'rifa)* needs spirit, peace, and fragrance *(al-rūḥ wa al-rāḥa wa al-rā'iḥa).*
> 8. One who claims the soul *(nafs)* needs worship *('ibāda).*
> 9. One who claims trust in God *(tawakkul)* needs confidence *(thiqa).*
> 10. One who claims fear *(khawf)* needs agitation *(inzi'āj).*
> 11. One who claims hope *(rajā')* needs quietude *(ṭama'nīna).*
> 12. One who claims love *(maḥabba)* needs longing *(shawq).*
> 13. One who claims longing *(shawq)* needs ravishing *(walah).*
> 14. One who claims ravishing *(walah)* needs God *(allāh).*
>
> And one who has nothing remaining *(dā'iyya)* from these claims will fail; he is among those who roam in the deserts of astonishment. And God is with the one who does not worry."[21]

---

20. The term *da'wā* has been defined as follows: "The claim *(da'wā)* is the relationship of the soul with something that is not its station. But in reality, it is the manifestation of boldness *(jur'at)* with the quality of discovering reality." (Rūzbihān Baqlī Shīrāzī, *Sharḥ-i shaṭḥīyyāt,* ed. Henry Corbin, Bibliothéque Iranienne 12 [Tehran: Departement d'iranologie de l'Institut Franco-iranien 1966], p. 572).

21. Ḥallāj, in 'Abd al-Raḥmān al-Sulamī, *Jawāmi' Ādāb al-ṣūfiyya,* ed. Etan Kohlberg, Max Schloessinger Memorial Series, Texts 1 (Jerusalem: Jerusalem Academic Press 1976), p. 61, para. 156; also reproduced from an Istanbul MS. by Massignon, *Essai,* pp. 428-9, no. 8, omitting the eighth category and miscopying some words. Oddly, Massignon hastily described the remaining thirteen terms as twelve, stating that they are identical to the list of twelve psychological constellations enumerated by Ja'far al-Ṣādiq. Massignon speculated *(Passion,* I, 394, n. 4) that this text was transmitted by Ibn 'Aṭā'.

Massignon rightly observed that Ja'far al-Ṣādiq's list partially duplicates that of Ḥallāj; the last six terms in both lists are identical, and the first six terms in Ja'far's list are (with one exception) duplicated in a different order in Ḥallāj's list.[22]

In comparing the lists of Ja'far's constellations and Ḥallāj's spiritual claims, one may ask how similar their purposes are. In terms of Sufi terminology, both lists belong largely to the category of states *(aḥwāl)* rather than stations *(maqāmāt)*.[23] Ḥallāj's list seems more clearly to represent an ascending series, since it culminates in God. It complicates the basic list of states by making each state that one claims dependent on other attainments. The last terms in the series link up, so that the twelfth, *maḥabba,* depends on the thirteenth, *shawq,* which in turn depends on the fourteenth, *walah.* In contrast, Ja'far's list of states is structured in a simpler form in terms of the zodiacal signs. Each of these states is a constellation in the heaven of the heart, and forms a mode of relation to God. The states are essentially unlimited, since the object to which they are related (God) is unlimited. Like the zodiacal constellations in heaven, the states of the heart are the means of regulating order, in this case in the psychic microcosm, conceived of as orbiting around God. Ḥallāj's fourteen spiritual claims appear to be a kind of commentary and expansion on the earlier list, explaining the human efforts or divine gifts that are prerequisites for these spiritual states. The two categories that he added to Ja'far al-Ṣādiq's list are *'ilm* and *fahm,* religious knowledge and understanding, both of which pertain to the realm of knowledge. But Ḥallāj recognized the extraordinary character of the last three stages relating to love; they are linked together, and the last stage, ravishing *(walah),* depends only on God. In this articulation of the stages of love, Ḥallāj adapted the scripturally based formulation of Ja'far al-Ṣādiq to illustrate and further emphasize the supreme position that love holds among the spiritual degrees.

---

22. If the Berlin variant is followed, all of the first six terms in Ja'far's list occur in that of Ḥallāj.

23. E.g., Sarrāj lists four of these terms *(maḥabba, khawf, rajā', shawq)* as nos. 2-5 of the nine *aḥwāl* that he enumerates, while only one *(tawakkul)* occurs in his list of stages. Cf. Abū Naṣr 'Abdullāh b. 'Alī al- Sarrāj al-Ṭūsī, *Kitāb al-Luma' fi'l-Taṣawwuf,* ed. R.A. Nicholson, E. J. W. Gibb Memorial Series, vol. 22 (London 1914; reprint ed., London: Luzac 1963), pp. 41-71, esp. pp. 51-2, 57-64.

Chronologically the next well-known analysis of love that pertains to Persian Sufism is that of Abū al-Ḥasan al-Daylamī, a scholar of the late fourth/tenth century who followed the tradition of the Sufi Shaykh Ibn al-Khafīf of Shiraz (d. 371/981).[24] At the same time, however, Daylamī participated in the Greco-Arabic philosophical tradition, probably through the circle of the philosopher Abū Ḥayyān al-Tawḥīdī. Daylamī is the author of the *Kitāb 'aṭf al-alif al-ma'lūf 'alā'l-lām al-ma'ṭūf* ("The Book of the Inclination of the Familiar *Alif* toward the Inclined *Lām*"), a treatise on love, known from a unique manuscript, that draws on Sufism, philosophy, and Arabic court culture *(adab)*. In the course of this treatise, Daylamī has produced a list devoted exclusively to the stages of love, using the distinctive Sufi term 'station' *(maqām)* to describe them. He describes these stages as ten, as follows:

1. *ulfa* or familiarity;
2. *uns* or intimacy;
3. *wudd* or affection
4. *maḥabba ḥaqīqiyya dūna al-majāziyya* or real love without metaphorical (i.e., physical) love;
5. *khulla* or friendship;
6. *sha'af* or excessive love;
7. *shaghaf* or infatuation;
8. *istihtār* or recklessness;
9. *walah* or ravishing;
10. *hayamān* or bewilderment

These ten categories are completed by an eleventh, *'ishq* or passionate love, as a comprehensive term for exclusive devotion to the beloved.[25] Daylamī succeeds in fine-tuning the gradations of love with an unmistakable increase in energy and intensity in the progression of ten stages. He preserves terms central to the Sufi vocabulary

24. Ibn al-Khafīf evidently wrote two treatises on love, a *Kitāb al-Wudd* and a *Kitāb al-Maḥabba,* but these are lost; see Abū al-Ḥasan Daylamī, *Sīrat-i Shaykh-i kabīr Abū 'Abdullāh ibn Khafīf Shīrāzī,* Persian trans. Rukn al-Dīn Yaḥyā ibn Junayd Shīrāzī, ed. Annemarie Schimmel (Ankara 1955; reprint ed., Tehran: Intishārāt-i Bābak 1363 A.Hsh./1984), Introduction, p. 28.

25. Abū'l-Ḥasan 'Alī b. Muḥammad al-Daylamī, *Kitāb 'Aṭf al-alif al-mā'lūf 'alā'l-lām al-ma'ṭūf* [sic], ed. J. C. Vadet, *Textes et Traductions d'Auteurs Orientaux,* vol. 20 (Cairo: Institut Français d'Archéologie Orientale 1962), pp. 20-24.

of love, such as *maḥabba, uns,* and *walah,* and he has also put the hitherto controversial term *'ishq* at the heart of the discussion. Daylamī in fact credits Ḥallāj with being the Sufi who was closest to the philosophers in speaking of *'ishq* as being the essence of God.[26] Another spirit breathes through this classification, however, recalling the court poetry of the 'Abbāsid age; not only are some of the terms unfamiliar in Sufi contexts, but in every instance, Daylamī also gives learned etymologies and specimens from classical Arabic poetry, including several attributed to Majnūn, to illustrate the overtones of each of the ten terms. The title of his treatise, with its learned reference to the calligraphic properties of the letters *alif* and *lām,* further indicates the literary character of his approach. In addition, by separating the stations of love from the rest of the spiritual stations, Daylamī has removed love from its Sufi context. His list of definitions and categorizations of love resembles instead the learned discussions that commonly took place in philosophical circles.[27] While this admittedly eclectic and partially secular work does not appear at first sight central to Persian Sufism, its sections on Sufi attitudes to love preserve some important testimonies, and it survived in the Shiraz tradition and was appropriated by Rūzbihān Baqlī, as we shall see.[28] The significance of Daylamī's arrangement is as a systematic classification of love uniting the tendencies of Sufism, philosophy, and court culture.

The important apologetic works and instruction manuals of Iranian Sufis in the fifth/eleventh century continued to elaborate on love in terms of the states and stations. Abū al-Qāsim al-Qushayrī (d. 465/1072), in his famous handbook on Sufism, listed love *(maḥabba)* and longing *(shawq)* as the forty-ninth and fiftieth of his fifty stations.[29] Qushayrī's understanding of longing was complex;

---

26. Daylamī, *op. cit.,* p. 25. See my previously cited article (above, n. 19) for more on this topic.

27. Joel L. Kraemer, *Philosophy in the Renaissance of Islam: Abū Sulaymān al-Sijistānī and his Circle* (Leiden: E. J. Brill 1986), pp. 52-53.

28. See especially Daylamī, pp. 32-36, 42-45, 68-71, 84-88 for quotations from Sufi authorities on love.

29. Abū'l-Qāsim 'Abd al-Karīm al-Qushayrī, *al-Risāla al-Qushayriyya,* ed. 'Abd al-Ḥalīm Maḥmūd and Maḥmūd ibn al-Sharīf, 2 vols. (Cairo: Dār al-Kutub al-Ḥaditha 1972-74), II, pp. 610-33.

it was not simply a deprivation from the presence of the beloved. Longing for the vision of the divine countenance, in his view, was so intense that it could only continue in the encounter with God.[30] 'Abdullāh Anṣārī (d. 481/1089), in his early Persian work *Ṣad maydān* (One Hundred Fields), regarded love as the comprehensive principle of spiritual progress. He concluded that "These one hundred 'fields' are all submerged in the field of love *(maḥabba)*."[31] Love itself he divided into the three degrees of uprightness *(rāstī)*, intoxication *(mastī)*, and nothingness *(nīstī)*.[32] In his later treatise on one hundred stations, *Manāzil al-sā'irīn* (Abodes of the Wayfarers), he downgraded the stations of love somewhat, for the purposes of instruction; love *(maḥabba)* was now number sixty-one, longing *(shawq)* was number sixty-three, and bewilderment *(hayamān)* number sixty-eight. This shift of emphasis has been convincingly explained as a result of Anṣārī's strong insistence that the beginner focus on the annihilation *(fanā')* of the ego and the incomparability of the divine unity *(tawḥīd)*. Love and longing are stages which still imply the existence of the lover, at least as far as the novice is concerned.[33] For the elite, however, "their love is their annihilation in the love of the Real, because all loves become invisible in the love of God, by His loving *(iḥbāb)*."[34]

The Seljuk era also saw the emergence of treatises especially devoted to love or placing great emphasis on it, although these works were often poetic and diffuse, in contrast to the more systematic Sufi handbooks. The best-known of these is the *Sawāniḥ* of Aḥmad Ghazālī (d. 520/1126), brother of the famous theologian. Ritter described this as one of the most original writings on love produced in the Islamic world, yet he also confessed that its content was

30. *Ibid.*, II, 627.
31. A translation of this section of Anṣārī's work is given in A.G. Ravān Farhādī's essay in this volume, above, p. 399. –Ed.
32. 'Abdullāh Anṣārī, *Manāzil al-sā'irīn,* Arabic text ed. with Persian trans. by A.G. Ravān Farhādī (Tehran: Intishārāt-i Mawlā 1361 A.Hsh./1982), p. 413.
33. Anṣārī clarified this point in his *'Ilal al-maqāmāt* ("The Flaws of the Stations"), a text written in response to questions concerning the *Manāzil al-sā'irīn;* cf. *'Ilal al-maqāmāt,* quoted in *Manāzil al-sā'irīn,* pp. 413-14, and Bell, pp. 171-72.
34. Farhādī describes this passage as "from the end of the treatise about love;" cf. *Manāzil al-sā'irīn,* p. 415, remark no. 4 (appended to the Persian translation of the section on *maḥabba* from *'Ilal al-maqāmāt).*

remarkably obscure.[35] Pourjavady, who translated and commented on this text, remarked with some understatement that Ghazālī "does not express his ideas in a very systematic fashion."[36] The *Sawāniḥ* is in fact of a highly refined and allusive character, intended for a restricted audience, and it makes no attempt to analyze love in terms of a system of stages. It is, rather, a kind of phenomenology and psychology of the human-divine love relationship, expressing that love with a rich symbolism; it presupposes the density of the Sufi literary and mystical tradition, but without ostentation.

Ghazālī's disciple 'Ayn al-Quḍāt Hamadhānī (d. 525/1131), the Sufi martyr, devoted several memorable passages in the sixth chapter of his *Tamhīdāt* to meditations on love, which are worth noting as an example of this freer style of expression. He identifies love as a religious requirement *(farḍ)*, since it brings humanity to God.[37] Like earlier Sufis, he makes a distinction between seeking heaven and seeking the love of God. He maintains that heaven as a separate state is a prison for the spiritual elite; properly speaking, God is himself the highest heaven.[38] Not a systematizer, 'Ayn al-Quḍāt divides love *('ishq)* into only three categories:[39]

> 1. the lesser love *('ishq-i ṣaghīr),* which is our love for God;
> 2. the greater love, *('ishq-i kabīr),* which is God's love for Himself—it has no trace by which it can be recognized, and because of its surpassing beauty it is describable only by cypher and parable *(ba-ramzī wa mithālī);*[40]

---

35. *Aḥmad Ghazālī's Aphorismen über die Liebe,* ed. Hellmut Ritter, Bibliotheca Islamica 15 (Istanbul: Staatsdruckerei 1942), Introduction, pp. i-ii.
36. Aḥmad Ghazzālī, *Sawāniḥ, Inspirations from the World of Pure Spirits, The Oldest Persian Sufi Treatise on Love,* trans. Nasrollah Pourjavady (London: KPI 1986), p. 6. One may note that a number of Indian Sufis wrote commentaries on the *Sawāniḥ,* including Ḥusayn Nāgawrī, as cited in 'Abd al-Ḥaqq Muḥaddith Dihlawī al-Bukhārī, *Akhbār al-akhyār fī asrār al-abrār,* ed. Muḥammad 'Abd al-Aḥad, (Delhi: Maṭba'-i Mujtabā'ī 1332/1913-4) p. 177; and 'Abd al-Karīm Lāhawrī, *Sharḥ-i Sawāniḥ,* MS. 218 Persian, Jamia Millia Islamia, New Delhi.
37. Abū al-Ma'ālī 'Abdullāh ibn Muḥammad ibn 'Alī ibn al-Ḥasan ibn 'Alī al-Miyānjī al-Hamadānī mulaqqab ba-'Ayn al-Quḍāt, *Tamhīdāt,* ed. Afif Osseiran, Intishārāt-i Dānishgāh-i Tihrān, 695 (Tehran: Chāpkhāna-i Dānishgāh 1341 A.Hsh./1962), pp. 96-97.
38. *Tamhīdāt,* pp. 111, 135-37.
39. *Tamhīdāt,* p. 101.
40. *Tamhīdāt,* pp. 123-25.

> 3.the in-between or mutual love *('ishq-i miyāna),* which he also despairs of describing—in it one at first finds a difference between witnesser and witnessed, until it reaches the limit, when they become one.[41]

The various manifestations of the beloved's face, symbolized by Koranic passages, should be considered as many stations, not one.[42] But 'Ayn al-Quḍāt is not interested in giving a detailed account of these stations. He only mentions that the first station of love is astonishment *(taḥayyur).*[43] 'Ayn al-Quḍāt's main concern is the state of mutual love between God and human, when the Koranic phrase "He loves them and they love Him" *(yuḥibbuhum wa yuḥibbūnahu,* Koran, V: 54) becomes fulfilled. Experiencing this mutuality of love is like basking in the splendor of the cosmic sun, which is revealed in Koranic phrases that become seclusion retreats for the meditating soul.[44] At that point the essence of the intimate relationship between God and the soul is revealed to be love: "Did you know that the unique Essence of Might has a characteristic, and that characteristic *('araḍ)* is nothing but passionate love? …God's love becomes the substance *(jawhar)* of the [human] soul, and our love becomes the characteristic of His existence."[45]

But it is with Rūzbihān Baqlī (d. 606/1209) that we meet perhaps the most striking articulation of the stages of love in early Persian Sufism. Rūzbihān composed his Persian treatise *The Jasmine of the Lovers* '*(Abhar al-'āshiqīn)* at the request of a female interlocutor, to decide the question of whether it is legitimate to describe God in terms of passionate love *('ishq);* modern scholars like Corbin have speculated that this woman may have been the beautiful singer with whom Rūzbihān is supposed to have fallen in love during a sojourn

---

41. *Tamhīdāt,* p. 115.
42. *Tamhīdāt,* p. 127.
43. *Tamhīdāt,* p. 109.
44. *Tamhīdāt,* p. 128, where the following verse summarizes this state:

Last night my idol placed his hand upon my breast,
seized me hard and put a slave-ring in my ear.
I said, "My beloved, I am crying from your love!"
He pressed his lips on mine and silenced me.

45. *Tamhīdāt,* p. 112.

in Mecca.[46] There are many aspects of this treatise deserving of comment and analysis, but for purposes of this discussion, two passages stand out. The first is Rūzbihān's brief recapitulation of Daylamī's list of the stages of love, with some alterations; the second section is the lengthy description of Rūzbihān's own list of the stations of love. As Takeshita has shown, Rūzbihān incorporated a little less than one-sixth of Daylamī's *'Aṭf al-alif* into the *'Abhar al-'āshiqīn,* and this list of ten stations occupies a couple of pages in Rūzbihān's sixth chapter, on the nature of human love.[47] Actually Rūzbihān has abridged Daylamī's list considerably, leaving out the samples of Arabic poetry for six of the ten terms, and omitting one term *(istihtār)* altogether. Then, almost as an afterthought, he has added, with minimal explanation, three extra terms not employed by Daylamī: *hayajān* or agitation, *'aṭsh* or thirst, and *shawq* or longing. As we have already seen, Daylamī's list of ten terms belongs more to the philosophical and courtly tradition than to Sufism. What is the significance of its presence here, in this form? The context indicates that Rūzbihān is using Daylamī's list to illustrate the character of mundane human love.

The list of the stages of love follows on a somewhat obscure cosmological discussion, in which Rūzbihān describes four principles of love analogous to the four elements of nature. These principles appear to be:[48]

> 1) the natural capacity of the body to receive spiritual influence;
> 2) uniting with the spiritual light;
> 3) love being constituted as the capacity of the lover to perceive beauty; and

46. Rūzbihān Baqlī Shīrāzī, *'Abhar al-'āshiqīn,* ed. Henry Corbin and Muḥammad Mu'īn, Bibliothèque Iranienne, 8 (Tehran: Institut Français d'Iranologie de Téhéran 1958; reprint ed., Tehran: Intishārāt-i Manūchihrī 1365 A.Hsh./1981), Introduction, p. 109, citing the report of Ibn al-'Arabī, *Kitāb al-Futūḥāt al-Makkiyya* (Cairo 1329), II, 315.

47. *'Abhar,* pp. 40-41; cf. Masataka Takeshita, "Continuity and Change in the Tradition of Shirazi Love Mysticism – A Comparison between Daylamī's *'Aṭf al-Alif* and Rūzbihān Baqlī's *'Abhar al-'āshiqīn,*" *Orient* XXIII (1987), pp. 113-31, esp. p. 118-19.

48. *'Abhar,* pp. 38-39. Although Takeshita remarks that Rūzbihān does not name these four "elements" in this admittedly obscure passage, the anonymous Persian commentary *('Abhar,* p. 154) helps to clarify it along the lines suggested here.

4) beauty coming into actual relation with the lover's eye to create the unity of love, differentiated into lover and beloved.

The result of these four principles is that the lover seeks the beloved through the senses and then slowly ascends through the stations of love until reaching perfection. Now, the eleven stations of love that Rūzbihān has elaborated on the basis of Daylamī's are only the beginning of the lover's progress; Rūzbihān describes them as rivulets leading to the sea of love. Then comes presence and absence, sobriety and intoxication, and a multitude of qualities for which love is the overarching rubric. But all this is still in the realm of human love, contemplating the works of the Creator, in the beginning of love. The philosophical categories of love borrowed from Daylamī are still unpurified and contain the flaws *('ilal)* of the carnal self. Natural love, the lowest form, can nonetheless be first spiritualized and then divinized.[49] The context indicates that Rūzbihān has reinserted Daylamī's philosophical categories into a Sufi teaching.[50] Like Platonic eros, philosophical *'ishq* provides the energy that can transformed and purified by the spiritual path. But that will come later.

In the last quarter of the *'Abhar al-'āshiqīn,* from chapters nineteen to thirty-two, Rūzbihān describes the mystical ascent to perfect love. This progress consists of twelve stations:

1. *'ubūdiyyat* or servanthood
2. *wilāyat* or sainthood
3. *murāqabat* or meditation
4. *khawf* or fear
5. *rajā'* or hope

49. *'Abhar,* pp. 42-43.

50. Rūzbihān has appropriated philosophic views on love from Daylamī into another of his writings. In his treatise on one thousand and one spiritual states, Rūzbihān quoted the pre-Socratic philosopher Heraclitus (via Daylamī) on the nature of *'ishq:* "The Creator makes space for the souls in all creation so that they gaze on His pure light, which emerges from the substance of the Real. And at that time their passionate love *('ishq)* and longing becomes intense and does not ever cease." Cf. Abū Muḥammad Rūzbihān al-Baqlī al-Shīrāzī, *Kitāb mashrab al-arwāḥ,* ed. Naẓīf Hoca (Istanbul: Üniversitesi Edebiyat Fakültesi Yayinlari, no. 1876. Edebiyat Fakültesi Matbaasi 1974), p. 135, corrected according to Daylamī, *'Aṭf,* p. 25.

6. *wajd* or finding
7. *yaqīn* or certainty
8. *qurbat* or nearness
9. *mukāshafa* or unveiling
10. *mushāhada* or witnessing
11. *maḥabbat* or love
12. *shawq* or longing

These twelve stations are followed by "the highest rank, universal love *('ishq-i kullī)*, which is the goal of the spirit."[51] Rūzbihān has elaborated on the meaning of each station in a comprehensive and even practical way, although he often complicates his points with his distinctive style of metaphoric overflow. His explanations invoke specific Koranic verses that are seen as the loci of particular spiritual experiences. We may briefly summarize his descriptions of these stations as follows. Servanthood consists of the practices of spiritual discipline such as *dhikr,* prayer, silence, and fasting, in order to purify one's character. Sainthood includes such qualities as repentance *(tawba),* piety *(wara'),* and asceticism *(zuhd).* Meditation is based on control of random thoughts and seeing one's true nature. Fear is a kind of purifying fire that instills the manners of the prophets, although it is a deception if it alienates one from the beloved. Then hope is the cure, leading to the springtime of the soul. Finding is encountering the nearness of the beloved (Rūzbihān notes that he has explained its varieties in a work for novices, the *Risālat al-quds* or 'Treatise on the Holy'). The certainty of the elite is something beyond the unshakeable faith that is the certainty of the ordinary person; it is a direct perception of divine attributes in the heart. Nearness is an ascent to the divine presence in an increasingly intensive transcendence, which Rūzbihān describes in a characteristic image as the burning of the wings of a bird in flight.[52] Unveiling operates on the levels of intellect, heart, and spirit to reveal the different forms of love; it joins love and beauty in the soul and reveals divine lordship as the wine of love. Witnessing is a category that Rūzbihān divides into two parts corresponding to sobriety and in-

51. *'Abhar,* p. 100. The stations are described on pp. 101-48.
52. I have translated a section of this passage in "The Symbolism of Birds and Flight in the Writings of *Rūzbihān Baqlī,"* in *The Heritage of Sufism II,* p. 363.

toxication (a division that can be made in every station); the sober part of witnessing is clothing with divinity *(iltibās)*, a trait of Abraham, while the intoxicated part is effacement *(maḥw),* a characteristic of Moses—yet Muḥammad united both experiences in his witnessing.[53]

After the ten stations just described, Rūzbihān expands on the nature of the eleventh, love *(maḥabba).* This love can naturally be divided into two phases corresponding to the common folk and the elite. The love of the common folk is based on the manifestation of beauty in creation, and while it is indeed miraculous, its degrees are those of faith rather than direct witnessing. The elite love is based on three kinds of witnessing. The first of these occurred in the precreational state, when the disembodied spirits of humanity made a covenant with God by acknowledging Him as their Lord (Koran, VII: 171).

> They asked the Real for beauty, so that gnosis would be perfect. The Real removed the veil of might, and showed them the beauty of majesty's essence. The spirits of the prophets and saints became intoxicated from the influence of hearing [the divine speech and seeing] the beauty of majesty. They fell in love with the eternal beloved, with no trace of temporality. From that stage, their love began to increase with degrees of divine improvement, because when the holy spirits entered earthly form, from their prior melancholy they all began to say "Show me!" (Koran, VII :143). They found the locus of delight, so that whatever they saw in this world, they saw all as Him.[54]

This is followed by a second stage of witnessing in which the substance of the spirit is not veiled at all by human characteristics, and the divine beloved is encountered without any intervening me-

---

53. At the beginning phase of witnessing, Rūzbihān invokes some terms from Daylamī's list of the stations of love: "In the beginning, in witnessing the soul experiences no duration, because the assaults of the Essence violently cast it into universal intoxication from the vision [of God]. In that ravishing *(walah),* the eye has no power to see. When it reaches the witnessing of knowledge and union, it remains long in witnessing, but the bewilderment *(hayamān)* and agitation *(hayajān)* of its ecstasy *(wajd)* disturb it from the sweetness of beauty." *('Abhar,* p. 130).
54. *Ibid.,* p. 132. The Koranic reference (VII: 143) is to Moses' demand to see God face to face.

dium. The third stage of witnessing perfects the second, as the unimpeded vision of God takes place in eternity. Each attribute of the beloved inspires a different kind of love, and the lover is transformed into a mirror of God, so that whoever looks upon the lover becomes in turn a lover of God. Even at this level of love, there are additional distinctions, depending on the degree of knowledge of the divine unity.

With the twelfth stage, longing *(shawq),* Rūzbihān brings us so close to the divine unity that the distinctions implied by love and longing become paradoxical. He connects longing to prayers of Muḥammad that ask for "the pleasure of gazing on your face, and the longing for meeting with you." He describes longing as a fire that burns away all thoughts, desires, and veils from the heart. Yet when the lover is united with the beloved, "for whom is there longing, for whom is there love if not oneself?"[55] The language of love still implies duality. If love and longing reach unity, they will no longer exist.

In the thirteenth and final section on the perfection of love, Rūzbihān resumes his theme by equating God with love. Since passionate love *('ishq)* is a divine attribute, God loves himself; God is love, lover, and beloved. The perfection of *'ishq* is identical with divine *maḥabba.* This does not imply any distinction within the divine essence; God's multiple attributes are simply aspects of his beauty that he revealed to the spirits of humanity. Love remains an eternal quality. Rūzbihān calls it "the ivy of the ground of eternity, which has twined around the tree of the lover's soul. It is a sword that cuts off the head of temporality from the lover. It is the peak of the mountains of the attributes, where the soul of the lover who arrives there becomes the prisoner of love."[56] When lover and beloved become one, there is a complete transformation: "Then the lover becomes the ruler in the kingdom of the Real. When the Real overpowers him, his bodily form becomes heavenly, his soul becomes spiritual, his life becomes divine. He becomes the beloved of the beloved, the desired of the desired."[57] Many paradoxes follow. From one point

55. *Ibid.,* p. 136.
56. *Ibid.,* p. 139.
57. *Ibid.*

of view, love cannot be perfect, since the beloved has no limit. Yet the perfection of love is the essence of perfection. Love is also annihilation *(fanā');* when beauty is fully revealed, neither lover nor beloved remains. Lovers who find their life in the love of God cannot be said to die; they are like martyrs, always alive in God. Lovers become like angelic spirits, flying in the highest heaven with peacock angels, like Khiḍr, Ilyās, Idrīs, and Jesus. The world becomes subjugated by them, and they reveal themselves wherever they wish; this was the case with Abraham, Moses, Aaron, and Muḥammad. Some take earthly form, like the Sufi saints, or discard their bodies like veils. Ultimately, the limit of love is defined by the two stations of gnosis *(ma'rifat)* and unity *(tawḥīd).*[58] It is characterized by the final stages of annihilation and subsistence. But the perfection of love is the end of love; at its highest stage it no longer exists. It is at this point that it becomes appropriate to speak in terms of ecstatic expressions *(shaṭḥiyyāt)*, such as Abū Yazīd's "Glory be to me," or Ḥallāj's "I am the Real." The lover's experience of unity with God goes beyond all other modes of expression.[59]

In their meditations on the nature of love, Persian Sufis showed a remarkable consistency. The terms of the analysis multiplied over time, which is the natural tendency in the development of a tradition. Each generation refined on the insights it inherited, as individuals contributed their own nuances to the collective understanding. But the fundamental framework was the same. Love, together with its allied states, was conceived of as the ultimate form of the divine-human relationship. The principal factor that elevated this love above the mundane was recognized as early as Rābi'a: divinized

---

58. *Ibid.*, p. 145. It may be asked why Rūzbihān, in his treatise on 1001 stations, places the stations of love in a relatively low position; out of the twenty chapters of fifty stations each, the stations of the lovers *(muḥibbīn)*, those filled with longing *(mushtāqīn)*, and the passionate lovers *('āshiqīn)* occupy the sixth, seventh, and eighth chapters, while the later chapters are reserved for the higher ranks of the spiritual hierarchy. The apparent discrepancy between this arrangement and the thrust of the *'Abhar al-'āshiqīn* may be explained by the fact that the description of 1001 stations is intended for spiritual novices *(Mashrab al-arwāḥ,* pp. 3-4), while the *'Abhar al-'āshiqīn* (like other treatises dedicated to love) is reserved for the elite. The same difference of emphasis can be observed in the works of Anṣārī, mentioned above.

59. See my *Words of Ecstasy in Sufism* (Albany: SUNY Press 1984), esp. Part I.

love goes beyond the desires of the ego (it is precisely on the point that the Sufis differed most profoundly from the profane love theorists, who rejected any possibility of selfless or mystical love). The Sufis conveyed this understanding of love through the characteristic analysis of inner experience into spiritual states and stations, and the richness of their psychological analysis is what distinguishes their view of love. The number and sequence of these stations might differ from one author to another, or might show different emphases in separate works by the same author, according the requirements of the audience. Yet the comparison of the lists of the stations of love has shown significant consistencies throughout. The impulse to categorize and define love at times took on a rationalistic character, as in the semi-philosophical presentation of Daylamī. Sufis such as Rūzbihān, however, were able to reconnect their classifications to the mystical understanding of love and the annihilation of the ego. In the end, however, even the most ingenious explanations of the nuances of love were less than satisfactory. If writing on the stations of love was connected to a mystical teaching, its purpose seems to have been to indicate the sense of progression towards a goal of union with God. Yet as so many authors insisted, attainment of that goal makes the language of love an unacceptable dualism. It was the genius of these Sufi writers to express all the delicate shades of spiritual progress while at same time indicating the inadequacy of their explanations, thus pointing to what lay beyond. As Sumnūn 'the Lover' put it, "Nothing explains a thing except something that is subtler, and there is nothing subtler than love, so what can explain it?"[60]

60. Sumnūn al-Muḥibb, in Sulamī, *op. cit.,* p. 196.

Dervish Dancing. MS. Ouseley Add. 95, f. 49a. ca. 1019/1610. (Courtesy of the Bodleian Library).

"The Breath of Felicity:"
Adab, Aḥwāl, Maqāmāt and Abū Najīb al-Suhrawardī

Ian Richard Netton

Like the more famous Abū Ḥāmid al-Ghazālī (450/1058 – 505/1111), the Persian mystic 'Abd al-Qāhir Abū Najīb al-Suhrawardī (490/1097 - 563/1168) had a career which embraced both the academic and the mystical. Like Abū Ḥāmid, too, he later taught for some time at the Niẓāmiyya College in Baghdad. Earlier, Abū Najīb had studied *fiqh* at this college but he had left his academic work there "in order to associate with Shaykh Aḥmad al-Ghazālī [i.e. Abū Ḥāmid's brother] who wafted upon him *the breath of felicity*[1] *[nasīm al-sa'ādat]* and guided him along the Sufi Path. He cut himself off from ordinary society in order to lead a life of seclusion and retreat. *Murīd*s came to put themselves under him and the fame of his *baraka* spread widely."[2] But it is also clear that he did not totally turn his back on the life of academe. Indeed, again like Abū Ḥāmid al-Ghazālī, Abū Najīb al-Suhrawardī made a return to academic life when he assumed a Chair of *fiqh* in the Niẓāmiyya.[3] And these two aspects of his life, the academic and the mystical, merge most neatly

1. My italics.
2. Al-Subkī, *Ṭabaqāt* (Cairo: al-Maṭba'a al-Ḥusayniyya 1905-1906, repr. Beirut: Dār al-Ma'rifa, n.d.), vol. 4, p. 256, trans. by J. Spencer Trimingham, *The Sufi Orders in Islam* (Oxford: Clarendon Press 1971), p. 34. For a brief life of Abū Najīb al-Suhrawardī, see Menahem Milson, abridged trans. and introduction, *A Sufi Rule for Novices: Kitāb Ādāb al-murīdīn of Abū al-Najīb al-Suhrawardī* (Cambridge, Mass., and London: Harvard University Press 1975), pp. 10-16. [This work is hereafter referred to as Milson, *Sufi Rule].*
3. See Milson, *Sufi Rule,* p. 13, esp. n. 30.

in his famous manual of instruction, the *Kitāb Ādāb al-murīdīn.*[4] This title has loosely but accurately been rendered into English by Milson as *A Sufi Rule for Novices.*[5] However, other renditions of the Arabic could produce *The Book of the Manners of the Novices* or even *The Book of the Courtesies of the Novices;* and one of the themes of this paper will be that of Sufi correct behavior, manners or courtesy *(adab,* plural: *ādāb),*[6] as exemplified in Abū Najīb's famous text: two secondary themes will be his treatment here of *aḥwāl* and *maqāmāt.* The *Kitāb Ādāb al-murīdīn* will be the basic framework within which these three themes are explored.

However one chooses to translate *adab*, there is no doubt that the word has a special role throughout Abū Najīb's book. As Milson puts it: *"Kitāb Ādāb al-murīdīn* is unique among Sufi compositions

---

4. For the Arabic text see Abū Najīb al-Suhrawardī, *Kitāb Ādāb al-murīdīn,* edited by Menahem Milson, Max Schloessinger Memorial Series, Texts 2 (Jerusalem: Hebrew University of Jerusalem, Institute of Asian and African Studies 1977 [distributed by the Magnes Press]). [This work is hereafter referred to as *Ādāb al-murīdīn.]*

5. See above n. 2.

6. *Adab* is an Arabic and Persian word with a wide variety of meanings. For a survey, see F. Gabrieli, art. *"Adab"* EI[2], vol.1, pp 175-176. *In a technical Sufi sense* Trimingham defines it as "the conduct and discipline of the Sufi in relation to his Shaykh and associate Sufis." *(The Sufi Orders in Islam,* p. 300) Perhaps one of the best renditions is "proper behavior." This is the sense preferred by Jo-Ann Gross, "Interpretations of Improper Behaviour in the Hagiographies of Khwāja Aḥrār," paper presented at the conference on 'The Legacy of Mediæval Persian Sufism', SOAS, University of London 1990. (A revised version of this paper, entitled "Authority and Miraculous Behavior: Reflections on *Karāmāt* Stories of Khwāja 'Ubaydullāh Aḥrār" later appeared in L. Lewisohn [ed.], *The Legacy of Mediaeval Persian Sufism* [London: KNP 1992], pp. 159-71). As Ibn al-'Arabī shows, *adab* could be 'courtesy' extended towards the Deity Himself when it was a matter of allocating responsibility for good and evil deeds respectively. See William C. Chittick, *The Sufi Path of Knowledge: Ibn al-'Arabi's Metaphysics of Imagination* (Albany: SUNY Press 1989), pp. 209-210. By contrast, for an excellent review of *Adab as a literary genre,* see S.A. Bonebakker, *"Adab* and the concept of belles-lettres" in Julia Ashtiany *et al* (eds.), *The Cambridge History of Arabic Literature: Abbasid Belles-Lettres,* (Cambridge: Cambridge University Press 1990), pp. 16-30. (This chapter also contains a brief survey of pre-literary usages, see *ibid.,* pp. 17-19).

(The following valuable sources should also be consulted in any study of *adab:* Dj. Khaleghi-Motlagh and Ch. Pellat, s.v. *"Adab"* in *Encyclopedia Iranica,* vol. 1, pp. 431-44; J. Nurbakhsh, "The Rules and Manners of the Khānaqāh", *In the Tavern of Ruin* [New York: KNP 1975]; G. Makdisi, *The Rise of Humanism in Classical Islam and the Christian West* [Edinburgh 1989] –ED.)

known today in that Sufism in its entirety is viewed here from the standpoint of *ādāb* (rules of conduct)."[7] Milson contrasts the prominence of the theme of *adab* in the work with the relatively low profile of such typical Sufi themes as *aḥwāl* and *maqāmāt:*

> A full exposition of Sufi mystical theory is not included in it. One reason for this omission may lie in the fact that the system of stations and states *(maqāmāt* and *aḥwāl)* had already been explained by famous Sufi authors in the two centuries preceding Abū Najīb. A more important reason is that the mystical theory and, in particular, the matter of mystical states *(aḥwāl)* constituted the inner aspect of Sufism, whereas novices, for whom the book was primarily intended, were expected to become versed in the external aspect as a first step. This is presumably why, except for a brief summary on the stations and states, Abū al-Najīb deals with the stations *only insofar as the matter was required for novices.*[8]

In the light of this, it is intended here to (1) survey the *structure* of the *Kitāb Ādāb al-murīdīn,* (2) assess the major role played by *adab* with its real meaning and significance for Suhrawardī, together with the more minor roles within that *adab* taken by *aḥwāl* and *maqāmāt*, and finally (3) attempt an answer to two questions: how *successful* was Suhrawardī in incorporating, or 'institutionalizing', within the framework of a Rule (a code of Sufi *adab* or 'earthly manners'), such spiritual states as the *aḥwāl,* the *maqāmāt* and other aspects of Sufi spirituality? What is the true significance of his *Kitāb?*

Before examining the structure however, it is worth trying to identify the exact nature of the clientele for whom the Manual was intended. From its title, it is clear that they are novices *(murīdīn)* within a Sufi order. But what *kind* of novices? Were they permanent or temporary? Did they live all their lives within the kind of Sufi *ribāṭ* founded by Abū Najīb?[9] Or were the novices more akin to the tertiary (also called third order or secular) members of Roman Cath-

7. Milson, *Sufi Rule,* p. 16.
8. (My italics), *ibid.,* pp. 16-17.
9. See Milson, *Sufi Rule,* p. 13.

olic mendicant orders of Friars like the Carmelites[10] and Franciscans, or the oblate members of the Benedictine order of monks.[11] In other words, did they live their spirituality out in the world? What clues does the text provide?

Certainly, we know that the last proposition was a possibility. Suhrawardī did this himself and notes that some Sufis "when they had reached the state of stability, became commanders and administrators, and mixing with the people did not damage their religious position."[12] But here the author refers to *experienced* Sufis. We also know that those *inexperienced* in the Sufi life could nonetheless 'collect' affiliations to the great Sufi orders with little effort, spiritual or otherwise. The great fourteenth century traveller Ibn Baṭṭūṭa is an excellent example of one who did just that.[13] Certainly, he never troubled with the formality of a novitiate as such.[14]

What then, was the status of those for whom Suhrawardī wrote his famous text? Quite simply, a cursory glance at the text shows that it is directed at two types of Sufi; the amount of space devoted to each type however, is quite disproportionate and disparate. Overwhelmingly, Abū Najīb's text addresses the Sufi who is able to live in community and, thus, as a novice *(murīd)* to "choose only pure food, drink, and clothes,"[15] "render service to his brethren" and "not leave his Shaykh before the eye of his heart opens,"[16] "to associate with people of his kind and those from whom he can benefit" and

10. See, for example, *The Rule of Life of the Secular Order of Discalced Carmelites,* printed in Michael D. Griffin OCD, *Commentary on the Rule of Life,* The Growth in Carmel Series, (Washington: Teresian Charism Press 1981), pp. 156-67.
11. See "Lay Affiliation with English Benedictine Monasticism" in Dom Gordon Beattie (ed.), *The Benedictine and Cistercian Monastic Yearbook 1991* (York: Ampleforth Abbey 1991), pp. 24-25.
12. Milson, *Sufi Rule,* p. 36, p. 13, n.30; *Ādāb al-murīdīn,* p. 17.
13. Indeed, Ibn Baṭṭūṭa was invested with the robe of the Suhrawardī Sufi Order itself: see *Riḥlat Ibn Baṭṭūṭa,* (Beirut: Dār Ṣādir 1964), pp. 200-202; see also Ian Richard Netton, "Arabia and the Pilgrim Paradigm of Ibn Baṭṭūṭa: A Braudelian Approach," in Ian Richard Netton (ed.), *Arabia and the Gulf: From Traditional Society to Modern States,* (London: Croom Helm 1986), p. 38, and *idem.,* "Myth, Miracle and Magic in the *Riḥla* of Ibn Baṭṭūṭa," *Journal of Semitic Studies,* vol. 29:1, (Spring 1984), pp. 134-135.
14. Netton, "Myth, Miracle and Magic," p. 135.
15. Milson, *Sufi Rule,* p. 41; *Ādāb al-murīdīn,* p. 26.
16. Milson, *Sufi Rule,* p. 43; *Ādāb al-murīdīn,* p. 31.

"to undertake to serve his brethren and companions (*khidmat al-ikhwān)* and help them in obtaining their sustenance."[17] These are just a few examples of the manner in which the good Sufi, and aspirant or novice, should behave. It is clear that such actions are best, and most easily undertaken, within the context of a resident community.

Yet Suhrawardī does have a few words to spare in his text for those analogous to the tertiaries mentioned above.[18] These are the "associate" or "lay members" of the Sufi Order or Brotherhood.[19] Abū Najīb calls them in one place in his text *muḥibbūn* (lovers, i.e. of God),[20] and Menahem Milson comments:

> Although the affiliation of lay members to Sufism was a phenomenon both very common and of great consequence to the Sufi orders, this subject is hardly discussed in the Sufi manuals. Abū al-Najīb seems to have been the first Sufi author to deal explicitly with this form of association with Sufism and to propose a doctrine of Sufi ethics that would accommodate it. To this effect, Abū al-Najīb uses... the concept of *rukhṣa.*[21]

Any examination of the structure of the *Kitāb al-murīdīn* must, therefore, be undertaken in the light of the *dual* constituency at whom the text is directed (and an awareness that some dispensations *(rukhaṣ)*, originally designed just for the "lay members" were adopted by full members of the Brotherhood as well).[22] It is clear, then, that the concept of 'dispensation' *(rukhṣa)* from some of the severer Sufi practices is, in the view of Suhrawardī, a licit part of Sufi *adab.* Bearing this in mind, we will now survey briefly the general structure of Suhrawardī's work, emphasizing in conclusion those areas which were particularly designed for, or reflect, "lay member" practice. In what follows I have preferred not to adopt Milson's major fourfold division, nor his more extensive dissection of the text into

---

17. Milson, *Sufi Rule,* pp.45-46; *Ādāb al-murīdīn,* pp. 34-35.
18. See n. 10 above.
19. See Milson, *Sufi Rule,* pp. 9, 18-20.
20. *Ādāb al-murīdīn*, p. 68; Milson, *Sufi Rule,* p. 66, see also p. 19.
21. Milson, *Sufi Rule,* p. 19.
22. *Ibid.,* p. 20.

208 sections;[23] rather, as a *via media,* I have delineated a chronological sequence of *fifteen* discrete parts or sections which is intended to achieve a clearer presentation of the structure while at the same time incorporating sufficient detail for the purposes of this paper. Like Milson's, my divisions or sections are not contained within the text but are imposed by myself according to what I believe are the *fifteen* principal sections of Suhrawardī's work.

After a very brief *Foreword* (Section 1), which begins by invoking a blessing on Muḥammad and his family, Suhrawardī moves to an *Outline of Islamic Dogmatic Theology* (Section 2), which stresses God's Oneness using an almost Neoplatonic negative terminology. Reference is made to such fundamentals of Islamic dogma and debate as God's attributes, the uncreatedness of the Koran and various aspects of eschatology. Having set the scene in a traditionally orthodox fashion, the writer moves to an *Outline of Sufi Belief and Ritual* (Section 3), surveying such aspects of this as Sufi poverty, the love of God, the nature of miracles and the Sufi ritual of *samā'*. Suhrawardī then turns to deal with *Sufism within an Islamic Context* (Section 4), identifying three types of religious scholar: traditionists, jurists and Sufi religious scholars. A further threefold division occurs in the following section on the *Sufi Hierarchy and Character* (Section 5): there are three grades of Sufi, namely the Novice, the Initiate and the Gnostic Master.[24] Suhrawardī then pursues his evident liking for classification in threes by identifying three classes of people and different kinds of *ādāb* which they espouse.

What might be termed the first major section on *Sufi Spirituality* (Section 6) now appears. Here Suhrawardī deals with those classic aspects of the Sufi journey, the stations *(maqāmāt)* and the states *(aḥwāl)* before turning to an extended discussion of *Sufi Epistemology* (Section 7). It is after this that the real *Rule Book for Novices* (Section 8) *qua* Rule Book seems to begin with its frequent references to the proper and appropriate behavior of the novice,

23. See *ibid.*, pp. 25-26. I do not follow, either, the manuscript's division of the *Kitāb Ādāb al-murīdīn* into 26 unequal chapters *(fuṣūl).*
24. These are my renditions of the Arabic terms *murīd, mutawassiṭ,* and *'ārif* or *muntahin:* see Milson, *Sufi Rule,* p. 35; *Ādāb al-murīdīn,* p. 16.

whether that be from the point of view of food and drink, repentance, or service to his companions. The next section might conveniently be labelled *The Sufi and the World I* (Section 9). Here the author deals with such areas of life (and possible hazards!) as companionship, association, visiting, entertainment, and travel. It is succeeded by a section on *The Sufi and Himself* (Section 10) where such matters as dress, food and sleep are covered. Suhrawardī follows this by discoursing at some length on *The Sufi Office and Ritual* (Section 11) and provides an illuminating account of correct behavior during the *samāʻ*, with many apposite quotations. He then reverts to a previous theme of the Sufi's external relations with the outside world and discusses the topics of marriage and begging. This section might neatly be called *The Sufi and the World II* (Section 12), and it is followed by one dealing with *The Testing of the Sufi* (Section 13). Here our author covers such matters as illness, death and other trials. Stress is laid on the spiritually beneficial results of illness and the way it can purge sin. The last major section deals with *Dispensations* (Section 14) and the whole work concludes with a *Prayer* (Section 15).

This brief survey of the contents and structure of Suhrawardī's *Kitāb Ādāb al-murīdīn* shows that the regular Sufi, who belonged to and lived within the kind of Sufi brotherhood or convent envisaged by the author, was viewed as being very much a part of the classical Sufi tradition: for example, he was an ascetic, traversing a spiritual path, following a defined code of *adab*, with a detachment from worldly things yet a courtesy towards people of the world. Mystical experience, in terms of *aḥwāl*, may figure on the journey; and the Sufi who travels the spiritual path is characterized as a seeker *(ṭālib)*, a wanderer or voyager *(sā'ir)* or an arriver (*wāṣil)* according to whether he is respectively a novice, initiate or gnostic master.[25]

Thus far, in our survey of the structure and contents of the *Kitāb Ādāb al-murīdīn,* we have concentrated on the role of the regular full-time member of the Sufi brotherhood. Yet, as we noted above, it is clear that there was a genuine place and role for the "affiliate," the "lay member" or "adherent," who was not able to undertake the

25. See *Ādāb al-murīdīn,* p. 16.

full community life or rigors implicit in the full Rule, yet who wished, nonetheless, to share in the spirituality of the brotherhood.[26] It is to these lay members we now turn in our survey of Suhrawardī's work.

Before his final discussion of the dispensations, and their primary orientation towards the lay membership of the Brotherhood,[27] Suhrawardī, in his text, draws attention to the lay members both as *providers* of hospitality and as *recipients* of one of the charisms of the Brotherhood. The Sufi brother, on arrival at a town, should pay his respects to the local Sufi Shaykh or, failing that, in the absence of such a Shaykh, he should go to the place where the Sufis congregate. However, it may be that the town lacks both a formal Sufi brotherhood and place of meeting. If this be the case, the itinerant Sufi is advised to lodge with one of these townspeople who loves the Sufis.[28] This is a clear reference to the lay members.[29] That this whole procedure is regarded as a formally meritorious and correct aspect of Sufi *adab* and behavior, is signalled in the text by the words which open the section, *wa min ādābihim…*[30] and it stresses that the provision of hospitality for fellow Sufis who were itinerant must have been one of the major offices of the lay members.

Yet these *providers* of hospitality also shared in some of the *privileges* of their full-time brethren. When Sufi garments were torn up and distributed, and lay members *(muḥibbūn)* were present, they too were entitled to a share. However, the clothing of such lay members was not considered suitable for tearing and distribution, but was to be sold or given to the reciter instead.[31] There is clearly a division of Sufis here, from a hierarchical point of view, into the first and second class according to whether one is a regular or lay Sufi; and, in view of the statements that "they approve of tearing the 'patched mantles' *(muraqqa'āt)* only for the purpose of deriving *baraka* from them" and that "it is preferable to tear to pieces the *khiraq* of the

---

26. See Milson, *Sufi Rule,* p. 19.
27. See Milson, *Sufi Rule,* pp. 19-20.
28. *Ādāb al-murīdīn,* p. 50; Milson, *Sufi Rule,* p. 53.
29. See Milson, *Sufi Rule,* p. 19, n.53.
30. *Ādāb al-murīdīn,* p. 50; Milson, *Sufi Rule,* p. 53.
31. *Ādāb al-murīdīn,* p.68; Milson, *Sufi Rule,* p. 66.

regular Sufis, if they can be used for patching, so that each one can get his share," it is also clear that the degree of *baraka* judged to attach to the garb of the regular Sufi was rather more than that deriving from the lay member's clothing. The latter for Suhrawardī thus shared in some of the privileges or fruits of his Brotherhood; but he did not share in the rank of the regular member nor have parity of esteem with him.

By way of interesting contrast, we may briefly compare the position of such a Sufi lay member to that of the modern member of the (Roman Catholic) Secular Order of Discalced Carmelites, a group with sometimes striking similarities to those of the mediaeval lay Sufis. "The Secular Branches of every Mendicant Order," comments Griffin, "are truly part of the Order."[32] Article 1 of the *Rule of Life of the Secular Order of Discalced Carmelites* states: "The Secular Order forms an integral part of the Carmelite family; its members are therefore sons and daughters of the Order...[33] However, Griffin again comments that it is clear "that there is little similarity to the way the life is lived [by the Friars and Nuns]" and that "the participation of the Lay Carmelite in the life of the Order is different because of their members living a different lifestyle. ...Today in the Order one hears of the *one family of Carmel* and of the three branches living the *same Teresian charism.*"[34] The implications are clear: though the Carmelite Order as a whole may comprise First, Second and Third Orders or Sections (i.e. Friars, Nuns and Seculars), the principal difference between them is one of type and lifestyle rather than *rank.* There is a total lack of stress on hierarchization in both the Carmelite *Rule of Life of the Secular Order* which we have cited, and its principal *Commentary.*[35] But, by total contrast, hierarchy for Suhrawardī in his *Sufi Rule for Novices* is clearly part of Sufi *adab* and, as such, is 'enstructured' or encoded in the *Rule* in the manner outlined above.

32. Griffin, *Commentary of the Rule of Life,* p. 12.
33. See *The Rule of Life* in *ibid.,* p. 158. See also Marie Janinek OCDS, "Aspirants Knock, Seek, and Ask Questions," in *Welcome to Carmel: A Handbook for Aspirants to the Discalced Carmelite Secular Order,* The Growth in Carmel Series, (Washington: Teresian Charism Press 1982), p. 74.
34. Griffin, *Commentary on the Rule of Life,* p. 13.
35. See n. 10 above.

In view of this, it is perhaps somewhat ironical—though extremely human!—that some of the regular Sufis, proud as they must have been of their ascetic lifestyle and mortifications, clearly adopted, or availed themselves of, some of the dispensations *(rukhaṣ)* primarily designed for the lay membership.[36] Structurally, the section on "Dispensations" in the *Kitāb Ādāb al-murīdīn* occurs towards the end of the book. (In Milson's artificial division of 208 sections, it comprises Sections 166-207).[37] Suhrawardī lists here a total of forty dispensations and Milson reminds us that forty was a favorite number among Arab authors.[38] (A memorable example of this is al-Nawawī's famous collection known as *Forty Ḥadīth).* The forty dispensations listed by Suhrawardī in his text cover a wide variety of material ranging from permission to engage in business[39] to permission to joke[40] through permission to visit old women[41] and soothe poets with payment![42] The final *rukhṣa* listed is that which allows one "to show annoyance and exasperation upon encountering that which is absurd and which should not be tolerated."[43] At the end, however, Suhrawardī makes it very clear *who* is permitted such dispensations: it is the "lay members" of the brotherhood, called here, *non-pejoratively,* in Arabic *al-mutashabbihūn* ("the simulators," or "those who pretend to be Sufis"), but qualified by the adjective *al- Ṣādiqīn,* "the truthful."[44] As Suhrawardī puts it:[45]

> He who adheres to the dispensations and accepts the rules which govern them is one of *the truthful simulators,* about whom the Prophet said: 'Whoever makes the effort to resemble a group of people is one of them'... Whoever adopts the dispensations is one of the beginners, and he should strive to enhance his inner state and ascend to the heights of the *aḥwāl.* Whoever falls below the level of the 'dispensations' thereby renounces Sufism

36. See Milson, *Sufi Rule,* p. 20.
37. *Ibid.,* pp. 72-82; *Ādāb al-murīdīn,* pp. 80-99.
38. Milson, *Sufi Rule,* p. 20.
39. Milson, *Sufi Rule,* p. 73; *Ādāb al-murīdīn,* p. 82.
40. Milson, *Sufi Rule,* p. 75; *Ādāb al-murīdīn,* p. 85.
41. Milson, *Sufi Rule,* p. 79; *Ādāb al-murīdīn,* p. 92.
42. Milson, *Sufi Rule,* p. 80; *Ādāb al-murīdīn,* p. 95.
43. Milson, *Sufi Rule,* p. 81; *Ādāb al-murīdīn,* p. 97.
44. Milson, *Sufi Rule,* pp. 18, 82; *Ādāb al-murīdīn,* p. 98.
45. (my italics) trans. Milson, *Sufi Rule,* p. 82; *Ādāb al-murīdīn,* pp. 98-99.

> and is forbidden to enjoy the gifts and endowments which are made for the Sufis, and the Sufi congregation should excommunicate him.

The passage quoted clearly addresses two audiences: there are the "lay members," or "truthful simulators" according to Milson's translation, who are covered by the dispensations with no blame; and there are the regular members of low calibre who are classified as "beginners" and who may yet, it is hoped, aspire and ascend to greater heights. Suhrawardī's Sufi *adab* or courtesy here dictates that a measure of 'humanity' is built into the rigors of the *Rule*. While it is clear that such dispensations as the permission to engage in business were primarily and initially directed at the lay member[46] because of his family dependents, and equally clear that Suhrawardī believed the regular Sufi should avoid marriage,[47] it is also clear from the passage we cited above that dispensations from a variety of strictures *were* available to the lowest grade of regular Sufi who would not, however, advance very far in his spiritual journey until he had abjured such "comforts" as these *rukhaṣ.*[48]

We have referred several times already in the course of what has preceded to the concept of *adab.* This is perhaps a useful point at which to pause and try to assess the real meaning and significance of that term for Suhrawardī, before going on to evaluate the parts played within that *adab,* and within his text, by other terms like *maqāmāt* and *aḥwāl.* It is a truism that the term *adab* has a multitude of different meanings;[49] only those which pertain to the field of *taṣawwuf* will be mentioned here. We have already suggested translations such as "Sufi correct behavior" (modelled on Jo-Ann Gross's usage), "manners" and "courtesy." The latter is particularly felicitous with its connotations both of mediaeval chivalry and an attitude of loving gentleness towards one's God and one's fellow man. Trimingham, we have noted above, defined *adab* as "the *conduct and discipline* of the Sufi in relation to his Shaykh and associate

46. Milson, *Sufi Rule,* p. 73; *Ādāb al-murīdīn,* pp. 82.
47. See Milson, *Sufi Rule,* p. 67; *Ādāb al-murīdīn,* p. 69.
48. See Milson, *Sufi Rule,* pp. 81-82; *Ādāb al-murīdīn,* p. 98.
49. See above, n. 6.

Sufis;"[50] and Milson follows him, translating *ādāb* as "rules of conduct",[51] "ethical conduct"[52] and also just "ethics."[53] R.A. Nicholson's rendition of the term in his translation of Hujwīrī's Persian *Kashf al-maḥjūb* stresses the aspects both of "manners" and "discipline" implicit in the word:

> The Apostle said: "Good manners *(ḥusn al-adab)* are a part of faith." ...You must know that the seemliness and decorum of all religious and temporal affairs depends on rules of discipline *(ādāb)* ...[54]

In *Kitāb Ādāb al-murīdīn* Suhrawardī himself shows a considerable awareness of the nuances and the richness of the term *adab*. He says that from the point of view of *adab* people fall into three categories: there are the people of this world *(ahl al-dunyā),* the religious people *(ahl al-dīn)* and God's elite among the last group *(ahl al-khuṣūṣiyya min ahl al-dīn).* (Here we might note in passing that the usual contrast of *dīn* and *dunyā* is given a Sufi gloss with the addition of a third category.) In Suhrawardī's eyes, the *ādāb* of the people of this world comprise such things as eloquence, rhetoric, preserving or memorizing the (traditional) sciences, *(ḥifẓ al-'ulūm),* history, and poetry. The *ādāb* of the religious people include learning, discipline, refinement of character and eagerness to do good. But the *ādāb* of the final group, those whom I have translated as 'God's Elite', go far beyond such normative behavior as is prescribed for the second group. This third group is clearly that of the Sufis: their *ādāb* are (mysteriously) characterized as the preservation of hearts *(ḥifẓ al-qulūb)* —a direct contrast with the previously cited *ḥifẓ al-'ulūm* of the first group—as well as compliance with the secrets "and being the same both secretly and outwardly."[55]

Adab, then, as a term in the eyes of both modern translators and

---

50. See above, n. 6 (my italics).
51. Milson, *Sufi Rule,* p. 16.
52. *Ibid.,* p. 25.
53. *Ibid.,* p. 45.
54. Reynold A. Nicholson, *The Kashf al-Maḥjūb: the oldest Persian Treatise on Sufiism* by 'Alī B. Uthmān Al-Jullābī Al-Hujwīrī, trans. from the text of the Lahore edn., E.J.W. Gibb Memorial Series, vol. 17 (London: Luzac, repr. 1970), p. 334.
55. Milson, *Sufi Rule,* pp. 36-37; *Ādāb al-murīdīn,* p. 18.

such mediæval authors as Suhrawardī clearly has a variety of layers of meaning and carries a considerable weight of what might be termed "cultural baggage." However, I would like to suggest here that, apart from its obvious senses in *taṣawwuf*, already suggested, of "discipline" and "rules of conduct", there is another, perhaps more literary way of looking at the term. This is that *adab* is a useful *literary motif* which provides a convenient *structure* or *frame* within which may be articulated the whole of Sufi life. Parallels with frame stories such as occur in the *Panchatantra, Kalīla wa Dimna* and *The Thousand and One Nights* are not hard to find. But I suggest that one comes even closer, in literary terms, if one looks at the genre of *Riḥla* literature and observes how that genre served as a notable vehicle or *frame* for, *inter alia,* descriptions both of the pilgrimage to Mecca and Medina, and surveys of those holy cities themselves.[56] For Suhrawardī, we can say that *adab* is both the context or Frame of the internal literature of Sufism, as well as the context or frame of the external Sufi life as it is lived and which it directs and moulds to itself. It is therefore Structure, Frame and Rule all at once.

It is thus from the primary perspective of *ādāb* as frame that I now wish to evaluate, within that frame, Suhrawardī's treatment of the *maqāmāt* and in particular the *aḥwāl.* These "stations" *(maqāmāt)* and "spiritual states" (*aḥwāl)* —the first "to be effected by the individual's endeavor" and the second to be "regarded as divine gifts" for they "do not result from human action or volition but from God's favor"[57]—are specifically held by Suhrawardī in his text to be an integral part of Sufism.[58] Suhrawardī shows, however, that he considers them to be a very special part of Sufism, which possesses its own external and internal facets *(ẓāhiran wa bāṭinan).* The first consists in behaving ethically with regard to one's fellow man *(isti'māl al-adab ma'a al-khalq),* the second in engaging the *aḥwāl* and the *maqāmāt* with regard to God Himself,[59] called here

56. See Netton, "Myth, Miracle and Magic" and *idem.,* "Arabia and the Pilgrim Paradigm of Ibn Baṭṭūṭa."
57. Milson, *Sufi Rule*, p. 5. One of the best treatments of the *aḥwāl* in English is to be found in Javad Nurbakhsh, *Spiritual Poverty in Sufism,* trans. L. Lewisohn (London: KNP 1984), see esp. Chap. 4, pp. 63-80.
58. Milson, *Sufi Rule,* p. 81; *Ādāb al-murīdīn,* p. 98.
59. Milson, *Sufi Rule,* p. 36; *Ādāb al-murīdīn,* p. 17.

"The True" or "The Real," *al-Ḥaqq*. As always, the *bāṭin* is to be elevated above the *ẓāhir*, in this statement as elsewhere. We note also, here, the use of *adab* in the sense of "code or rule of ethics" but perhaps even more significantly, the triple, and surely deliberate, contrast between *ẓāhir* and *bāṭin*, *adab* and *aḥwāl* plus *maqāmāt,* and the corporeal (i.e. man) and the divine (i.e. God).

Here, then, earthly *adab* is contrasted with the two progressions in the spiritual life of *maqāmāt* and *aḥwāl.* This is a very significant contrast for it serves to root *adab* among matters terrestrial and corporeal while it elevates the *maqāmāt* and *aḥwāl* by associating them with the Divine. Here, in a nutshell—and we shall return to this point later—is a mirror of what Suhrawardī attempts in his *Kitāb Ādāb al-murīdīn:* the propagation of an earthly, or earth-bound and earth-designed Rule, which attempts to "ground" within it, or encapsulate, in some way, whether it be by contrast or stress, the stations and states which properly belong to the divine world. Here, there is a *contrast* of *adab* in the sense of "ethical rule" on the one hand, and *maqāmāt* and *aḥwāl* on the other. However, we may also present the latter two terms as *part* of *adab* if we adopt the suggestion which I formulated earlier of *adab* as 'literary' and 'life' *frame*. This idea finds some logical support within Suhrawardī's own text where he notes that "it is said that the whole of Sufism is *adab*; each moment (*waqt*), each state, and each station has its *adab.*"[60] We have stressed above that Suhrawardī specifically cites the *maqāmāt* and *aḥwāl* as part of Sufism.[61] It is because the structure constitutes a frame such as I have described, and that frame is *adab,* that I have spent a considerable amount of time surveying this structure and the contents it encapsulates.

The discussion of the spiritual stations and mystical states in the *Kitāb Ādāb al-murīdīn* is low-key and unsophisticated. The primary, *but not the only* constituency towards whom the work was directed was the Sufi novice.[62] Nonetheless, though the material be

60. *Ibid.*
61. Milson, *Sufi Rule,* p. 81; *Ādāb al-murīdīn,* p. 98.
62. Milson, *Sufi Rule,* pp. 16-17. See also pp. 20-21, however, where Milson remarks: "It should be noted that although *Kitāb Ādāb al-murīdīn* is intended primarily for novices, it presents, in fact, an ethical doctrine for Sufis in general."

lightweight, it is still of considerable interest. Definitions and lists of the stations and states are many. A useful and very early passage illustrating the distinction between a *maqām* and a *ḥāl* occurs in the *Kashf al-Maḥjūb* of Hujwīrī, who writes:

> 'Station' *(maqām)* denotes anyone's 'standing' in the Way of God, and his fulfillment of the obligations appertaining to that 'station' ...'State' *(ḥāl),* on the other hand, is something that descends from God into a man's heart, without his being able to repel it when it comes, or to attract it when it goes, by his own effort. ...*'Station' belongs to the category of acts, 'state' to the category of gifts.*[63]

Seyyed Hossein Nasr has drawn attention to one of the oldest Persian Sufi descriptions of the *maqāmāt,* the *Forty Stations (maqāmāt-i arba'īn)* ascribed to the fourth/eleventh century Persian Sufi master Abū Sa'īd ibn Abi'l-Khayr. (We note in passing the stress again on the number 'forty').[64] Abū Sa'īd begins with intention *(niyya)* as the first station, and concludes with a fortieth which is Sufism *(taṣawwuf)* itself.[65] Prof. Nasr adds that some of the *aḥwāl* described by other Sufis appear in Abū Sa'īd's list as *maqāmāt.*[66] Furthermore, for Abū Sa'īd, the station of 'subsistence-in-God' *(baqā'),* usually regarded by others as the highest "because it is the station of the Union with God"[67] ranks only as the twenty-second station.[68]

If we turn now to examine Suhrawardī's own text, the *Kitāb Ādāb al-murīdīn,* we find a similar lengthy list of mixed *maqāmāt* and *aḥwāl;* this particular list, however, lacks the descriptions attached to each item found on Abū Sa'īd's list of forty spiritual stations. However, Suhrawardī also has a slightly later, and shorter, list to which we will come, which does contain a brief definition of the mystical terms. We should note, firstly, that Suhrawardī makes

---

63. (my italics), Nicholson, *Kashf al-Maḥjūb*, pp. 180-181; see also Seyyed Hossein Nasr, *Les Etats Spirituels dans le Soufisme*, (Rome: Accademia Nazionale dei Lincei 1973), pp. 10-11.
64. Milson, *Sufi Rule,* p. 20.
65. See Nasr, *Les Etats Spirituels,* pp. 15-21.
66. *Ibid.,* p. 21.
67. *Ibid.*
68. See *ibid.,* pp. 18-19.

Table 1

SUHRAWARDĪ (ca. 490/1097–563/1168)

Maqāmāt *

Intibāh (awakening out of carelessness)
Tawba (repentance)
Ināba (returning)
Wara' (moral scrupulosity)
Muḥāsabat al-nafs (examination of the soul)
Irāda (aspiration)
Zuhd (renunciation)
Faqr (poverty)
Ṣidq (veracity)
Taṣabbur (forbearance [the final station of novices])
Ṣabr (patience)
Riḍā (satisfaction)
Ikhlāṣ (total sincerity)
Tawakkul (trust in God)

Aḥwāl **

Murāqaba (attentive observation)
Qurb (nearness)
Maḥabba (love)
Rajā' (hope)
Khawf (fear)
Ḥayā' (diffidence)
Shawq (yearning)
Uns (intimacy)
Ṭuma'nīna (serenity)
Yaqīn (certainty)
Mushāhada (experience of vision [the final *ḥāl*])

The *aḥwāl* are followed by such "indescribable things" as:***
Fawātiḥ (revealed signs)
Lawā'iḥ (appearances of light)
Manā'iḥ (graces)

*The translations here follow Milson, *Sufi Rule*, p. 38; *Ādāb al-murīdīn*, pp. 20-21.
**For translations, see *ibid.*
****Ibid.*

HUJWĪRĪ (d. between 465/1072–469/1077)

*Maqāmāt**	*Aḥwāl*
Tawba (repentance): *Maqām* of Adam	No formal lists but we may include *inter alia:*
Zuhd (renunciation): *Maqām* of Noah	*Maḥabba* (love)§
Taslīm (resignation): *Maqām* of Abraham	*Muḥādatha* (conversation)§§
Ināba (contrition): *Maqām* of Moses	*Musāmara* (nocturnal discourse)≠
Ḥuzn (sorrow): *Maqām* of David	Beyond the *aḥwāl* lies the grade of *tamkīn* (see the text for definition)
Rajā (hope): *Maqām* of Jesus	
Khawf (fear): *Maqām* of John	
Dhikr (praise): *Maqām* of Muḥammad	
Other *maqāmāt* cited in the text, not in the above list:	
Tawakkul (trust in God)**	
Faqr (poverty)¥	

Riḍā (satisfaction), "the end of the 'stations', and the beginning of the 'states'."¥¥

*Translations here and below by Nicholson, *Kashf al-Maḥjūb,* p. 371. Hujwīrī also provides a list of the "ten stations of spirits" (p. 265) and a shorter list of stations (p. 181).

***Ibid.,* p. 181.

¥*Ibid.,* p. 58.

¥¥*Ibid.,* p. 182; see also pp. 157, 176-77.

§*Ibid.,* p. 157; see also p. 309.

§§*Ibid.,* pp. 380-81.

≠*Ibid.*

it clear in his work that all questions about the spiritual stations and states are to be directed to "the masters of Sufism" *(a'immat al-Ṣūfiyya).*[69] For him, "*Maqām* signifies the position of man in worship before God... Junayd defined *ḥāl* as a form of inspiration which comes down to the heart but does not stay in it permanently."[70]

Milson, in his introduction to the *Sufi Rule* makes several comparisons between parts of Suhrawardī's work and' al-Kalābādhī's *Ta'arruf.*[71] By way of contrast, therefore, we will, instead, note Hujwīrī's *maqāmāt* and *aḥwāl* beside those listed in Suhrawardī's text (see Table 1). We have already noted that Suhrawardī has two basic lists: since the first mixed listing of *maqāmāt* and *aḥwāl* does not, however, provide a useful definition in the text after each *maqām* and *ḥāl,*[72] we will not cite it here, though it should be noted that it is in this stark but lengthy listing that the key words *fanā'* and *baqā'* appear, while they do not appear in the listings given in Table 1. For the latter, Suhrawardī provides brief textual definitions, stresses the last spiritual station designated for novices and emphasizes which is the last of the mystical states, all clearly in a didactic and pedagogical fashion.

It is proposed now to present a few comparisons between the works of Suhrawardī and Hujwīrī with regard to the *maqāmāt* and *aḥwāl,* before turning for a further comparison, by way of complete contrast, to one mediaeval and one modern Christian *Rule.*

Of the two works, the *Kashf al-maḥjūb* and the *Kitāb Ādāb al-murīdīn,* the *Kashf* is considerably the longer, and it is directed to a much wider Sufi audience. It embraces a wide body of material ranging from chapters on Poverty, important Imams and Sufis to a series of chapters characterized as the uncovering of various veils: there are eleven of the latter, and they constitute the primary formal frame within which discussion takes place in the latter part of the

69. Milson, *Sufi Rule,* p. 35; *Ādāb al-murīdīn,* p. 15.
70. Milson, *Sufi Rule,* p. 38; *Ādāb al-murīdīn,* pp. 20-21.
71. See Milson, *Sufi Rule,* pp. 21-22; for the work of al-Kalābādhī (d. 390/1000), see his *Kitāb al-ta'arruf li-madhhab ahl al-taṣawwuf,* 2nd edn. (Cairo: Maktabat al-Kulliyyāt al-Azhariyya 1980); and A.J. Arberry's English translation of the same as *The Doctrine of the Sufis* (Cambridge University Press 1977; repr. of 1935 edn.).
72. See Milson, *Sufi Rule,* p. 35 (which omits the translation of the list); *Ādāb al-murīdīn,* p. 15.

Kashf.[73] The section which perhaps best equates to the material of the *Kitāb Ādāb al-murīdīn* is that entitled "The Uncovering of the Ninth Veil: Concerning Companionship, Together with its Rules and Principles."[74] This includes discussion of the rules of companionship, rules of discipline for resident Sufis, rules for travel, eating, sleeping, speech, silence, begging, marriage and celibacy. If only because of its length, and the wider intended audience, Hujwīrī's is inevitably the profounder of the two works.

Hujwīrī declines "to enumerate every *ḥāl* and explain every *maqām*"[75] though it is clear that, as with Suhrawardī, both *aḥwāl* and *maqāmāt* have a major role to play in the Sufi path. But it is instructive that with neither master do these stations and states become an end in themselves. Both their texts indicate levels of progress and spirituality beyond the *maqāmāt* and *aḥwāl.* Hujwīrī, for example, stresses the evanescent quality of such stations and states—"the fleeting state *(ḥāl)* of the saint is the permanent station *(maqām)* of the prophet"[76]—and later notes:

> Now I, 'Alī b. Uthmān al-Jullābī, declare... that annihilation comes to a man through vision of the majesty of God and through the revelation of Divine omnipotence to his heart, so that in the overwhelming sense of His majesty this world and the next world are obliterated from his mind, *and 'states' and 'stations' appear contemptible in the sight of his aspiring thought.....*[77]

Even on a formal level, Hujwīrī divides the "Way to God" into the three kinds of *maqām, ḥāl* and *tamkīn* and, indicating that the latter is the highest of the three, defines it as "the residence of spiritual adepts in the abode of perfection and in the highest grade. . ."[78] Indeed,

73. See Nicholson, *Kashf al-Maḥjūb,* pp. 267 ff.
74. *Ibid.,* pp. 334-366.
75. *Ibid.,* p. 371.
76. *Ibid.,* p. 236, see also p. 157.
77. *Ibid.,* p. 246 (my italics); see also p. 243.
78. *Ibid.,* p. 371. Nicholson translates the word *tamkīn* as "steadfastness" *(Kashf al-Maḥjūb,* p. 371). It can also mean "dignity" and "authority" in Persian. Julian Baldick's preferred rendition is "fixity;" see his *Mystical Islam: An Introduction to Sufism,* (London: Tauris 1989), p. 63.

there is a type of *tamkīn* in which God's influence so predominates that even such key terms as *fanā'* and *baqā'* cease to have real meaning.[79]

Suhrawardī likewise, has a triple division of levels of spirituality: *maqāmāt, aḥwāl, fawātiḥ,* etc. He however, prefers to talk of the grade above the *aḥwāl* as comprising such indescribable things as *fawātiḥ* (revealed signs), *lawā'iḥ* (appearances of light), and *manā'iḥ* (graces).[80] These last three, while by no means the same as Hujwīrī's *tamkīn,* constitute nonetheless Suhrawardī's own parallel grade of highest spirituality. Significantly, while the terms *fanā'* and *baqā'* appear in Suhrawardī's long list of *maqāmāt* and *aḥwāl,*[81] Hujwīrī in his *Kashf* makes it clear that such terms are distinct from the *maqāmāt* and *aḥwāl* and, indeed, beyond them.[82] There is thus some comparability, and some divergence in the use of terminology; but perhaps the highest divergence of all between the texts of Suhrawardī and Hujwīrī is structural: Suhrawardī's teachings fall within a text whose constant frame is *adab.* This is clearly signalled in several places by such phrases as *min ādābihim* but a reading of the entire text shows, as I have stressed above, that the whole work is set within a frame of *adab.* Hujwīrī, too, saw a role for *adab*[83] but not as an all-embracing frame: his *adab* is part of a broader fabric; his *rules* of Sufi life figure as one aspect of that life.

Before moving to our conclusion, it is illuminating, briefly, to make one final comparison, between the Islamic *Rule* of Suhrawardī and two Christian *Rules* of spirituality: (i) the early mediaeval sixth-century monastic Rule of the Christian Saint Benedict, and (ii) the modern (1979 version) of the *Rule of Life of the Secular Order of the Discalced Carmelites.*

Of the former, Benedictine Rule, Henry Chadwick noted:

79. Nicholson, *Kashf al-Maḥjūb,* p. 373.
80. Milson, *Sufi Rule,* p. 38; *Ādāb al-murīdīn,* p. 21.
81. See *Ādāb al-murīdīn,* p. 15.
82. See Nicholson, *Kashf al-Maḥjūb,* pp. 242-246.
83. See *ibid.,* pp. 334, 341.

> [Benedict's] rule was one of simplicity and self-discipline, not of penitential austerity and self-inflicted mortification.[84]

The principle of restraint identified here and elsewhere[85] by Chadwick as a major facet of the Benedictine Rule is clear from any casual examination of the *Rule* itself.[86] It is full of sound common sense and ranges in its subject matter from "Restraint of Speech" *(De Taciturnitate)*[87] through "The Celebration of the Divine Office during the Day" (*Qualiter Divina Opera per Diem Agantur)*[88] to "Brothers working at a Distance or Travelling" *(De Fratribus qui Longe ab Oratorio Laborant Aut in Via Sunt)*[89] and "The Good Zeal of Monks" *(De Zelo Bono quod Debent Monachi Habere).*[90] From a structural point of view it seems that the shape of the *Benedictine Rule* is fairly clear "even though the connections between parts are sometimes loose or unclear."[91]

> The spiritual doctrine is given first... followed by the regulations... After the Prologue and the opening chapter on the kinds of monks, the ascetical program is laid down in three successive articulations: the abbot and his advisers... a catalogue of good works... and the three capital virtues of the monk: obedience, silence and humility... The Second part of the *RB* prescribes the necessary elements of institutional structure and discipline.[92]

Parallel examination of the two texts, the *Benedictine Rule* and the *Kitāb Ādāb al-murīdīn* of Suhrawardī, will clearly reveal that both manuals have points in common. We might loosely observe that

---

84. Henry Chadwick, *The Early Church.* The Pelican History of the Church, vol. I (Harmondsworth: Penguin 1967), p. 183.
85. See *ibid.,* p. 179.
86. See *Regula Sancti Benedicti* [hereafter referred to as *RB]* in Timothy Fry O.S.B. (ed.), *RB 1980: The Rule of St. Benedict,* in Latin and English with Notes, (Collegeville: Liturgical Press 1981), pp. 156-297. I am most grateful to Dom Benedict Couch O.S.B., Prior and Novice Master of Buckfast Abbey (in Buckfastleigh, Devon, England) for sending me a copy of the above edition of the *Rule* (which he uses with his own novices) together with a useful bibliography.
87. *RB,* pp. 190-191.
88. *RB,* pp.210-211.
89. *RB,* pp. 252-255.
90. *RB,* pp. 292-295.
91. *RB,* ("Introduction"), p. 91.
92. *RB*, ("Introduction"), pp. 91-92.

perhaps the *Benedictine Rule* concentrates rather more on the practical aspects of community life, though the author is always aware of the *spiritual* reasons for monastic observances.[93] Significantly, Chapter 73, the last of the *Benedictine Rule*, is entitled "This Rule [is] only a Beginning of Perfection" (*De Hoc quod non Omnis Justitiae Observatio in hac Sit Regula Constituta).*[94] And though Benedict characterizes his "little rule" as having been "written for beginners" *(hanc minimam inchoationis regulam descriptam),*[95] there is no doubt that he intends by this phrase "beginners in the monastic and spiritual life" (i.e. the majority of monks for, perhaps, most of their lives), rather than just the novices as with Suhrawardī's work. Indeed, St. Benedict has only one separate chapter in his *Rule* devoted to novices out of a total of 73.[96]

While aspects of what Suhrawardī would regard as *maqāmāt* are clearly present in the *Rule*—for example, the two spiritual stations of *zuhd* (renunciation) and *faqr* (poverty) mentioned by Suhrawardī have their parallels in the renunciation of possessions by the would-be Benedictine monk[97]—it is clear that there is no formal concentration on a Suhrawardīan-type order of *maqāmāt* or *aḥwāl as such,* although the pages of the *Rule* are imbued with the 'character' of some of what the Muslim author might have characterized himself as 'states'. For example, monks are to show "to God, loving fear" *(amore Deum timeant).*[98] (However, full discussion of such things as *baqā'* and *fanā'* is absent.) In other words, where with Suhrawardī the would-be-mystic is not to progress from one spiritual station to the next until the *ādāb* of the first have been mastered[99] (and these *maqāmāt* themselves form part of a formal and ordered structure of *maqāmāt, aḥwāl* and *fawātiḥ,* etc.), with Benedict, though the spirituality may sometimes be the same in essence,

93. *RB,* ("Introduction"), p. 94.
94. *RB,* pp. 294-297.
95. *See RB,* pp. 296-297.
96. See *RB,* pp. 266-271: Chapter 58: "The Procedure for Receiving Brothers" *(De Disciplina Suscipiendorum Fratrum).* See also pp. 442 ff.
97. See *RB,* pp. 268-269.
98. See *RB,* pp. 294-295.
99. See Milson, *Sufi Rule,* p. 43; Suhrawardī, *Ādāb al-murīdīn,* p. 29; Compare Hujwīrī, *Kashf al-Maḥjūb,* p. 181.

it is far less structured and much more practical. The Benedictine monk, it is true, does have some formal gradations or signposts on his spiritual journey but these are marked by the progression through simple and solemn vows and, for clerics, ordination, rather than a formal progression through *maqāmāt,* much less, *aḥwāl.*

The *Benedictine Rule* was a merciful and generous *Rule* which made due allowance for the frailties of the sick and the elderly.[100] Such relaxations or dispensations in the *Rule* as were allowed are obviously paralleled by the much more extensive passages on the *rukhaṣ* in Suhrawardī's text. And this brings us briefly, and neatly, to our final point of comparison, that between the *Rule* as enunciated by Suhrawardī and the *Rule of Life of the Secular Order of Discalced Carmelites.* I have chosen Carmelite tertiaries as the point of comparison here, rather than, say, Benedictine Oblates, to provide a comparison with a fresh perspective and spirituality. The primary point of interest is in the *rukhaṣ* permitted by Suhrawardī and the 'easier' or rather *different*, lifestyle of the secular Carmelites.[101] Secular Carmelites, as the name implies, live *in* the world and, for example, recite a reduced Office of Lauds and Vespers and, if possible, Compline.[102] Secular Carmelites thus share the same spirituality as that of the Friars and Nuns but their lifestyle is quite different. Furthermore, and this is significant, the Carmelite Friars and Nuns of the Order are not expected, or indeed permitted, to adopt the 'dispensations' of the Secular Order. However, as we have seen from our study of Suhrawardī, the regular Sufis adopted elements of the *Rule* originally designed for the Sufi tertiaries or lay members.[103]

How successful, then, was Suhrawardī in attempting to integrate earthly 'manners' and 'spiritual states' in a single document for novices? Certainly his frame of *adab* appears to work well at first sight. It is perhaps most successful on the practical level. But there is, inevitably perhaps, a tension between the written "frame" and the material it encapsulates. The various *maqāmāt* and *aḥwāl* are mainly

100. See *RB,* pp. 234-37, 252-53.
101. Griffin, *Commentary on the Rule of Life,* p. 13.
102. See *The Rule of Life* in Griffin, *Commentary on the Rule of Life,* p. 159.
103. See Milson, *Sufi Rule,* p. 20. See below, no. 109.

listed but hardly discussed in depth. There is little attempt to show the novice—or regular Sufi for that matter—how to progress from station to station, beyond enjoining a proper achievement of each before progression to the next. The listings of *maqāmāt* and *aḥwāl* give the impression of having been incorporated for the sake of completeness. They have little real *didactic* value in the text especially for the novice or regular Sufi who might aspire later to the higher reaches of the mystical path.

For Milson, apart from its *adab* orientation, the real significance of Suhrawardī's text lay in the fact that "Abū al-Najīb believed that the Sufi's sphere of activity is within society."[104] As we have already noted, the high-flying Sufi could indeed return to that society.[105] Both Suhrawardī and Abū Ḥāmid al-Ghazālī did just that in a literal way.[106] Milson thus suggests that "Abū al-Najīb presents an ethical doctrine that is applicable to social reality."[107] This is all true. We have, in other words, a *Rule* or guide which is not confined or applicable just to the fastness of the Sufi house but one with a much broader area of action. The key to this, of course, lies primarily in the existence of the 'lay members', rather than just those 'regulars' who returned to society.

But I would like to go beyond Milson here by way of conclusion and suggest that the very existence of these 'lay members', with the *rukhaṣ* built into the *Rule* for them, posed a real problem or even a threat: it incorporated an *element of instability* into what was supposed to be a stable frame of spirituality. It represented moreover, in a very real way, a *decline* from the 'high ground' of a Hujwīrī, whose *Kashf al-maḥjūb* had this to say on the subject of *rukhaṣ,* here translated as "indulgences" by Nicholson. Speaking of al-Shāfi'ī and Sufism, Hujwīrī notes: "It is related that he said: 'When you see a divine busying himself with indulgences (*rukhaṣ),* no good thing will come from him'."[108]

Finally, the *rukhaṣ* in Suhrawardī's *Rule* represented, in one

104. *Ibid.,* p. 17.
105. *Ibid.,* p. 13 n. 30.
106. *Ibid.*
107. *Ibid.,* p. 17.
108. Nicholson, *Kashf al-Maḥjūb,* p. 116.

sense, a *return to 'society'*, an arena fled by many other Sufis including Suhrawardī himself, at various times. (By 'society' I mean the 'material', 'secular' world as opposed to the 'spiritual' world, in addition to the usual connotations of the term).

The three concepts of *instability, decline* and *return to "society"*, which I have extrapolated from the *Kitāb Ādāb al-murīdīn,* herald—though it is not suggested here that they directly caused in any way—the later degeneration in some of the Orders and some areas of *taṣawwuf* which Arberry[109] and others have graphically

109. See A.J. Arberry, *Sufism: An Account of the Mystics of Islam* (London: Allen & Unwin 1950), pp. 119ff. Julian Baldick (*Mystical Islam,* p. 72) notes significantly: "It is interesting that, although the Suhrawardī brotherhood became noted for its emphasis on severity, some of its members were also conspicuous for their self-enrichment, collaboration with temporal rulers and enjoyment of worldly pleasures." However, this does not represent the whole picture and I am grateful to my colleague Dr. Leonard Lewisohn for drawing my attention to the way in which scholars have taken other, opposing views regarding *rukhaṣ*. Dr. Lewisohn (letter to the author, July 1992) adds the following important caveat to what I have written in this article:

"Religious tolerance (in the form of *rukhaṣ),* was a dynamic and original element in Sufism which actually prevented decay in the social fabric of mediaeval Islam. This viewpoint has been elaborated by many scholars; see, for instance, F. Meier ('Soufisme et Déclin Culturel' in *Classicisme et Déclin Culturel dans l'Histoire de l'Islam,* Actes du Symposium Internationale d'Histoire de la Civilisation Musulmane, organisé par R. Brunschvig and G.E. Von Grunebaum [Paris 1957], where he notes (p. 236, after translating *rukhaṣ* as 'tolérance'): "La disposition du Soufisme au compromis a donc servi ici à enrichir et à élargir la culture religieuse islamique." *Rukhaṣ* might be as well interpreted as 'tolerance', as much as 'laxity' and 'indulgence', and thus not viewed as a decline from the high ideals of Sufism: for although on the level of one's personal spiritual life, seeking after indulgences may be a decline in discipline, this seems to be less true when it comes to the particular social phenomenon of *rukhaṣ* described by Abū Najīb. And when Abū Najīb's nephew (and founder of the widespread Sufi Order which bears his surname) Abū'l-Ḥafṣ 'Umar Suhrawardī, instituted the Orders of *Futuwwah*—those fraternities of chivalry during the reign of the caliph al-Nāṣir (r. 577/1181–620/1223)—he carried on his uncle's tradition of humanistic tolerance, by declaring that "according to the code of chivalry—unlike the religious Law which does not pardon the sinner who begs forgiveness—if a man commits a sin seventy times over and begs forgiveness seventy times over, he should be excused." (from his *Treatise on Chivalry,* ed. M. Sarrāf, *Rasā'īl-i jawānmardān* [Tehran; French-Iran Institute 1973], p. 133). ...Western orientalists are at variance concerning the role of Sufism in the cultural decline of Islamdom. If we compare the views of M. Hodgson (see esp. *The Venture of Islam,* II 455-67) or F. Meier with those of A.J. Arberry on this so-called decline of Sufism, there appears a vast difference of opinion."

described. These are the textual or exegetical semiotic indicators of an *adab,* or frame of manners or conduct for Sufis, *which has weakened itself from within,* albeit with the best of intentions. The 'return to society' represents in some ways a 'flight from the desert' taking that word in both its spiritual and physical aspects. But a return to the eremitical tradition with its proverbial love of the 'desert' clearly characterized the mediaeval Christian Carthusian and Cistercian reformist Orders.[110] The relaxations by the Carmelites of the Ancient Observance, or Calced Carmelites, of their *Rule* were later followed by the reformist zeal of the discalced St. John of the Cross (1542-1591) and St. Teresa of Avila (1515-1582).[111] And for the Islamic mystical Orders, the degeneration in some areas of *taṣawwuf* down the centuries which was to follow the death of Abū Najīb Suhrawardī and other mystics, was halted by the rise of such Orders as the Sanūsiyya and the Tijāniyya.[112]

110. I am indebted to my good friend Professor C. Holdsworth, Emeritus Professor of History in the University of Exeter, for valuable advice on the significance of these Orders.

111. See "Saints of Carmel" in *Welcome to Carmel,* pp. 133-147.

112. See Jamil M. Abun-Nasr, *The Tijaniyya: A Sufi Order in the Modern World,* Middle Eastern Monographs: 7 (London: OUP 1965); Nicola A. Ziadeh, *Sanūsīya: A Study of a Revivalist Movement in Islam* (Leiden: E.J. Brill 1968).

The Concept of *Wilāya* in Early Sufism

Bernd Radtke

In order to introduce the historical background of the concept of saintship or 'friendship with God' *(wilāya)* in early Sufism, it may be useful to provide a chronological framework for our study. I understand the third/ninth century to be the period of Early Sufism and not, as it may be suggested, the second/eighth century. Although a reading of Abū Nu'aym's *Ornament of the Saints (Ḥilyat al-awliyā')* reveals that sayings on friendship with God *(wilāya)* and the friends of God *(awliyā')* were already being transmitted by mystics of the second/eighth century,[1] these dicta present, as so often happens in the intellectual history of Islam, only *disjecta membra* which can hardly, if at all, be put together to form a coherent picture.

This changed during the third/ninth century—more exactly during the second half of that century. Two treatises are preserved which deal with the subject of friendship with God, although they differ remarkably in size and contents. The smaller one, called *Kitāb al-Kashf wa'l-bayān,* was written by the Baghdadian Sufi Abū Sa'īd al-Kharrāz (d. probably 286/899).[2] The author of the second book, which is much larger than al-Kharrāz's small treatise, is al-Ḥakīm al-Tirmidhī. It may be in order here to present some short remarks on al-Tirmidhī's life and works.

Abū 'Abdallāh Muḥammad b. 'Alī al-Tirmidhī, called al-Ḥakīm (the Sage), was born between 820/1417 and 830/1427 in Tirmidh on

---

1. Abū Nu'aym al-Iṣfahānī, *Ḥilyat al-awliyā'*. 1-10. (Cairo: Maṭba'at al-Sa'āda 1352 ff.). Cf. e.g. *Ḥilya* II: p. 210, 215, 286; VI: p. 94, 165.
2. Paul Nwyia, *Exégèse coranique et langage mystique* (Beirut: Imprimerie Catholique 1970), p. 231 f.

the northern bank of the river Amū Daryā (Oxus) in Transoxiana. He came from a family of theologians and his father is mentioned as a transmitter of prophetic traditions *(muḥaddith)* of some renown. Al-Tirmidhī was educated in *fiqh* and *ḥadīth.* At the age of twenty-eight he made the pilgrimage to Mecca and following his return devoted himself to an ascetic and mystical life. He suffered some persecution by his former colleagues, the theologians, but finally he was able to surmount this. He died in about 298/910.[3]

Al-Tirmidhī was by far the most productive author of Classical Islamic mysticism, perhaps even more productive than al-Sulamī. All his writings were, of course, in Arabic, but he is the first mystic—at least as far as I know—who translated some Arabic concepts into Persian.[4] Traditionally the title of al-Ḥakīm al-Tirmidhī's main work is given as *Khatm al-awliyā'* or *Khatm al-wilāya.* Although this title is quoted in the available literature, beginning with al-Sulamī in the 10th century, it is not used by al-Tirmidhī himself. Without going into extraneous details here, this fact together with other arguments allow us to assume that the original title of the book was *Sīrat al-awliyā'*. This may be deduced from the fact that al-Tirmidhī himself repeatedly quotes from a book which he calls *Sīrat al-awliyā',* and these quotations correspond to the contents of *Khatm al-wilāya/al-awliyā'*.[5]

Al-Kharrāz's treatise on friendship with God *(Kitāb al-Kashf wa'l-bayān)* was edited and published in 1967 by Qāsim al-Sāmarrā'ī together with some other *Rasā'il.*[6] The *Sīrat al-awliyā'*

---

3. Bernd Radtke, Al-Ḥakīm al-Tirmiḏī. *Ein islamischer Theosoph des 3./9 Jahrhunderts* (Freiburg: Klaus Schwarz 1980), p. 16-38; hereafter quoted as *ḤT.* He did not die in the year 930, contrary to what can be read in Geneviève Gobillot, "Un penseur de l'Amour *(Ḥubb)*, le mystique khurāsānien al-Ḥakīm al-Tirmidhī (m. 318/930)," in *Studia Islamica* LXXIII [1991], p. 25) .
4. See the list in *ḤT,* p. 137 f., and Bernd Radtke, "Zweisprachigkeit im frühen persischen taṣawwuf," in *Orientalia Suecana* 38 - 39 (1991), p. 128 f.
5. The book was edited under the title *Kitāb Khatm al-awliyā'* by 'Uthmān Yaḥyā (Beyrouth: Imprimerie Catholique 1965). For the discussion concerning the title see Bernd Radtke, *Drei Schriften des Theosophen von Tirmid.* Bibliotheca Islamica 35 a (Beirut/Stuttgart: Franz Steiner 1992), Einleitung, p. 3-5; hereafter quoted as *Drei Schriften.*
6. Ed. Qāsim al-Sāmarrā'ī (Baghdad 1967).

by al-Tirmidhī, previously considered lost, was discovered in Istanbul, in two manuscripts, by 'Uthmān Yaḥyā, and in 1965 he published his famous edition. Unfortunately one must state that neither book was treated by its editor as it deserved. In the case of al-Kharrāz, this becomes particularly evident in the introduction to the edition, the impossibilities of which have been sufficiently dealt with by Paul Nwyia in his *Exégèse coranique et langage mystique.*[7]

Although Yaḥyā's edition was hailed enthusiastically by certain scholars, alas, from the standpoint of philology, it does not deserve the adjective 'careful'. His edition was based on only two manuscripts, one of which is extremely bad. A comparison of these two manuscripts with the text edited and published by Yaḥyā proves that his collation was not very exact.[8]

Since the focus of the present essay is mainly on al-Tirmidhī, only some short remarks on al-Kharrāz's treatise, which has already been treated by Nwyia in his *Exégèse coranique,* will here be offered. The book shows little coherence, and as Nwyia rightly remarked[9] a conceptual structure is missing. Some problems concerning *wilāya* and *awliyā'* are dealt with, and although these issues are met also in al-Ḥakīm al-Tirmidhī, the two works are independent of each other. Therefore, as may be inferred, the issues in question were the common property of Islamic mysticism during the third/ninth century. A detailed list of the questions al-Kharrāz deals with is as follows:

1. The relationship between the *walī* and prophet. Al-Kharrāz rejects the teaching of certain Sufis, whose names he does not provide, that the rank of the friend of God is above the rank of the prophet.[10]

---

7. *Exégèse,* pp. 239 ff.
8. It is my hope that my new edition of the text which just has been published will provide a more reliable text. My edition is based on two more manuscripts than Yaḥyā could utilize. I am preparing as a second volume an English translation with a commentary. The translation will be published as Bibliotheca Islamica 35 b.
9. *Exégèse,* p. 238.
10. *Rasā'il,* pp. 31 ff.

2. The question whether the friend of God can receive inspiration *(ilhām).*[11]
3. The difference between the miracles of the prophets *(āyāt)* and those of the friends of God *(karāmāt).* Al-Kharrāz accepts the possibility that miracles can be performed by the friends of God.[12]

In contrast with al-Kharrāz's book—and I cannot agree with Nwyia on this point[13]—al-Ḥakīm al-Tirmidhī's treatise shows a clear structure and a conceptual framework. One reason that this has not been appreciated until now is the unstructured and confused nature of Yaḥyā's edition. On the other hand, it would be going too far to make al-Tirmidhī's book a relative of al-Fārābī's *Perfect State* or to derive its structure from a source in late Antiquity.[14] As is characteristic of Classical Sufism in general, al-Ḥakīm al-Tirmidhī is still outside the tradition of Classical philosophy—as Louis Massignon already in 1922 demonstrated in his *Essai sur les origines du lexique technique de la mystique musulmane.*

Within the framework of al-Ḥakīm al-Tirmidhī's complete works, the *Sīrat al-awliyā',* to a certain degree, holds a special position partly because of its particular terminology, not found in his other works.[15] However, it does not directly contradict his usual terminology, as is the case with a number of other writings which are wrongly ascribed to him, namely *al-Farq bayna al-ṣadr wa-l-qalb wa-l-fu'ād wa-l-lubb,*[16] *Ghawr al-umūr;*[17] *al-Ḥajj wa-asrāruhū;*[18] *Ma'rifat al-asrār.*[19] The fact that this distinction between his

11. *Ibid.,* p. 35.
12. Ibid., p. 35 f.
13. Cf. *Exégèse,* p. 238.
14. *Drei Schriften,* Einleitung, p. 31.
15. E.g. *walī ḥaqq Allāh;* cf. footnote 37 below.
16. Ed. Nicholas Heer (Cairo 1958).
17. Still unedited; cf. Bernd Radtke, "Theologen und Mystiker in Khurāsān und Transoxanien," in *ZDMG* 136 (1986), p. 555; quoted hereafter as TM; Bernd Radtke, "Psychomachia in der Sufik" in *Studia Iranica* 11 (1992), p. 135.
18. Ed. Ḥusnī Naṣr Zaydān (Cairo 1969); cf. *ḤT,* p. 35 f.
19. Ed. Muḥammad Ibrāhīm al-Geyoushy (Cairo 1977); cf. Bernd Radtke, "Ibn al-'Arabī's Kommentar zu al-Ḥakīm al-Tirmiḏī's *Sīrat al-awliyā:* Einige filologische Bemerkungen," in *Tirmiḏiana Minora* (forthcoming in *Oriens* 34).

genuine and false works has not been sorted out properly has led to some severe errors in chronology as well as misinterpretations of his thinking.[20]

The *Sīrat al-awliyā'* has had a special fate—*habent sua fata libelli.* It is noteworthy that only four manuscripts have survived (in fact only three and a half) although the book was widely known and read. This is shown by quotations from it by al-Sulamī, 'Abd al-Qādir al-Jīlānī, 'Ammār al-Bidlīsī, the teacher of Najm al-Dīn al-Kubrā, Ibn Taymiyya,[21] as well as al-Qushayrī who probably also quotes from it in his *Risāla.*[22] Neither 'Abd al-Qādir al-Jīlānī, al-Bidlīsī nor al-Qushayrī give the name of the author of their source, nor indeed does 'Aṭṭār. In the latter's biography of al-Tirmidhī in the *Tadhkirat al-awliyā'* there are a number of literal translations and some paraphrases of parts of the *Sīrat al-awliyā'*.[23] Sulamī's quotations in his commentary on the Koran, the *Ḥaqā'iq al-tafsīr,* are in part very distorted.[24]

The main impact of the book on later authors, however, is due to the fact that Ibn al-'Arabī wrote a commentary on parts of it in his *Futūḥāt al-Makkiyya.* This commentary has been dealt with in recent studies by Michel Chodkiewicz[25] and William Chittick.[26] It must be emphasized in this context that Ibn al-'Arabī's commentary does not explain anything of al-Tirmidhī's text but only provides a tool for Ibn al-'Arabī to develop and explain his own system of thinking.[27]

But what about al-Ḥakīm al-Tirmidhī's text? How can one explain its structure? Another book by al-Tirmidhī may help us here. This is his autobiography, *Bad' sha'n Abī 'Abdallāh,* edited for the

---

20. E.g. the confusion concerning the date of his death; cf. footnote 3 above.
21. *Drei Schriften,* Einleitung, pp. 5-25.
22. Cf. Richard Gramlich, *Das Sendschreiben al-Qušayrīs über das Sufitum* (Wiesbaden: Franz Steiner 1989), e.g. p. 359, 38.4, seems to be inspired by *Sīrat al-awliyā'* , p. 1.
23. Bernd Radtke, "Die Autobiografie des Theosophen von Tirmiḏ. Edition, Übersetzung und Kommentar." in *Tirmiḏiana Minora* (forthcoming in *Oriens* 34).
24. *Drei Schriften,* Einleitung, p. 6.
25. *Un océan sans rivage* (Paris: Seuil 1992), cf. Index des noms.
26. *The Sufi Path of Knowledge: Ibn al-'Arabī's Metaphysics of Imagination* (Albany: SUNY 1989), Index of Names.
27. Cf. Radtke, "Ibn al-'Arabī's Kommentar."

first time by 'Uthmān Yaḥyā together with *Khatm al-awliyā'*.[28] Here al-Tirmidhī describes his personal mystical path, interestingly enough to a great degree by means of dreams. A comparison between structure and content makes it clear that *Sīrat al-awliyā'* corresponds to the autobiography.[29] This book represents, in other words, the theoretical presentation of al-Tirmidhī's personal mystical experience and thus it actually describes "the life of the friends of God" (*Sīrat al-awliyā'*).[30]

At the beginning of the work, al-Ḥakīm al-Tirmidhī prefaces his remarks by declaring that there are two groups of friends of God, one of whom he calls *awliyā' ḥaqq Allāh*, and the other 'the friends of God' *(awliyā' Allāh)*.[31] The translation of *walī/awliyā' Allāh* does not present any difficulties, in contrast to the other term which is nearly untranslatable. This difficulty is increased by the fact that the term *walī ḥaqq Allāh* is used by al-Tirmidhī only in this book.[32] The concept of the different groups of friends of God, however, is to be found in other works also, albeit using a different terminology.[33] The term *walī/awliyā' Allāh,* as is known, is Koranic, whereas *walī/awliyā' ḥaqq/ḥuqūq Allāh* seems to be al-Tirmidhī's own creation. I have not met the concept in any other author, mystical or non-mystical. Perhaps it is influenced by the terminology of Ḥanafite *fiqh,* but this, for the moment, remains an unproven assumption.

It is interesting to observe that al-Tirmidhī's main word for mystic is *walī.* He never uses the term *ṣūfī.*[34] *Walī* is derived from the root *waliya,* 'to be close or near.' Thus a *walī Allāh* is someone who is close to God, and therefore 'a friend of God'. But it is God who determines the nature of this relationship rather than man. By God's

28. *Khatm al-awliyā'*, pp. 14-32.
29. Radtke, "Die Autobiografie des Theosophen von Tirmiḏ."
30. *Sīrat al-awliyā'*, p. 110, 3; cf. Einleitung, p. 5.
31. *Sīrat al-awliyā'*, p. 2, 4-5.
32. Cf. footnote 15 above.
33. E.g. *Masā'il ahl Saraḫs,* (in *Drei Schriften),* pp. 137 f.
34. Therefore it is totally misleading when Yaḥyā introduces the word *ṣūfī* into the text of his edition. Space does not permit us to go into details here concerning the reasons for al-Tirmidhī's usage. See the considerations in *ḤT,* p. 94 f., also Fritz Meier, *Bahā'-i Walad: Grundzüge seines Lebens und seiner Mystik* (Leiden: Brill 1989), p. 85.

eternal decree a person is close to God and becomes his friend because God wishes it and chooses him. This is the *walī Allāh.*[35] For the other type of mystic, however, the *walī ḥaqq Allāh,* things are more difficult. He has to fight to get closer to God by trying to fulfill the demands of the Law, the *ḥaqq.* No matter how hard he struggles, his rank will always be below that of the *walī Allāh.*

The opening chapters of *Sīrat al-awliyā'*[36] describe the path of the *walī ḥaqq Allāh* as consisting of renouncing the world *(tawba),* education of the soul, and the initial mystical experiences. For this path the common denominator is *ṣidq,* this being the most intensive inner commitment the mystic is able to produce out of his own powers. However, since *ṣidq* is only a product of the self, the mystic is confined within himself, i.e. the lower soul, *nafs.*[37] It is very impressive how al-Tirmidhī describes the dilemma *(iḍṭirār)* the mystic is confronted with; whereas on the one hand he has to fulfill the demands of both *ḥaqq* and *ṣidq,* on the other, this is precisely the main hindrance in coming to God, because *ṣidq* automatically means the strengthening of the ego, while the contrary is necessary to come nearer to God.[38]

As in later Sufism, the concept of the journey to God for al-Tirmidhī has already two connotations: the journey into the interior and the ascent through the macrocosm to God. The cosmological model he uses is that of the so-called 'Islamic cosmology',[39] based on the Koran and *ḥadīth* and differing from models used by the philosophers and later scholastics.[40] Here it is important to note that the

---

35. *Sīrat al-awliyā',* p. 33 f.; p. 104 f.; p. 109 f.
36. *Sīrat al-awliyā',* pp. 2-20, chapter 4-39.
37. See especially *Sīrat al-awliyā',* pp. 14-20, chapter 26-39; *ḤT,* p. 84-86; pp. 104-109; pp. 110-117. Bernd Radtke, "A Forerunner of Ibn al-'Arabī: Ḥakīm Tirmidhī on Sainthood," in *Journal of the Ibn 'Arabī Society* 8 (1989), p. 47.
38. Especially *Sīrat al-awliyā',* p. 14-17, chapter 27-32. See also Bernd Radtke, "Der Mystiker al-Ḥakīm at-Tirmidī," in *Der Islam* 57 (1980), p. 242 f.
39. Studied by Anton Heinen in his book *Islamic Cosmology* (Beirut/Wiesbaden: Franz Steiner 1982) (BTS 27).
40. TM, pp. 558-562; Bernd Radtke, *Weltgeschichte und Weltbeschreibung im mittelalterlichen Islam.* BTS 51. (Beirut/Stuttgart: Franz Steiner 1992), especially Chapter III, p. 139 ff.; Bernd Radtke, "Theosophie *(Ḥikma)* und Philosophie *(Falsafa).* Ein Beitrag zur Frage der *ḥikmat al-mašriq|al-išrāq,"* in *Asiatische Studien* 42 (1988), pp. 156-174.

ascent of the *walī ḥaqq Allāh* comes to an end at the border of the created cosmos. This is the throne of God, which is also called by al-Tirmidhī space *(makān)* or nearness to God *(qurba)*.[41] Therefore, although the *walī ḥaqq Allāh* comes near to God, he does not reach God himself.[42]

The *walī Allāh,* however, attains to God himself—not through his own endeavor, but by divine grace. The ascent beyond the throne of God consists of passing through the kingdoms of the divine Names which the mystic comes to know. These kingdoms of light surround the inconceivable unknowable divine Essence. Here al-Tirmidhī undoubtedly is influenced by Gnostic ideas.[43]

After having traversed all the kingdoms of the divine Names so that he knows God in all his Names, the *walī Allāh* is annihilated in God's Essence. His ego or his soul *(nafs)* is extinguished. Now he is in God's hand *(fī qabḍatihī)*. If he acts, it is God who acts through him. However, this state of annihilation, of giving up the ego, is at the same time a state of the highest possible activity in the world.[44] To properly understand this we have to look at al-Tirmidhī's famous concept of *khatm al-wilāya,* the seal of the friendship with God, which has to be considered within the framework of his idea of prophethood.

Muḥammad was the last and perfect prophet. He did not deserve this rank solely because he was the last in time—that would not be to bestow a great honour on him, as al-Tirmidhī sarcastically remarks.[45] Rather he deserved it because through him prophethood was made perfect—it was sealed.[46] For al-Tirmidhī the term 'seal of prophethood' has nothing to do with time; this seal is rather the completion of prophethood. Therefore he prefers to read the active participle *khātim* instead of the usual *khātam al-nubuwwa.*[47]

---

41. Radtke, "Theosophie," p. 161; *Sīrat al-awliyā',* Fihris al-iṣṭilāḥāt, s.v. *makān al-qurba.*
42. *Sīrat al-awliyā',* pp. 65, 17 f.
43. ḤT, p. 60; Radtke, "Theosophie," pp. 163-67.
44. *Sīrat al-awliyā',* pp. 58, 13 ff.; Radtke, "Die Autobiografie des Theosophen von Tirmiḏ."
45. *Sīrat al-awliyā',* p. 42, 11 f.
46. *Sīrat al-awliyā',* pp. 39-43, chap. 58-62.
47. *Sīrat al-awliyā',* p. 42 f., chap. 62.

Furthermore Muḥammad was entitled to be the *khātim al-nubuwwa* because he was the first of creation.[48] In this al-Tirmidhī not only meets with Shi'ite ideas,[49] but also with the Iraqian Sufi, Sahl b. 'Abdullāh al-Tustarī.[50] Here we have undoubtedly the forerunner of the concept of the *ḥaqīqa muḥammadiyya.*

The seal of prophethood had still another effect on the prophet Muḥammad. It protected him from error and sin *(ma'ṣūm).* The lower nature, the soul and the ego, and the devil had no power over him.[51] In this regard it is interesting to note that al-Tirmidhī had a very special understanding of the Satanic verses, although space does not permit us to go into details here.[52]

Muḥammad was the leader of the *umma* through divine revelation *(waḥy).* He had knowledge of the unseen *('ilm al-ghayb)* and was able to perform miracles *(āyāt).* Because Muḥammad had completed—sealed—prophethood, it was impossible that another prophet could come after him.[53] But—to pose the fundamental question of Islamic theology and politics—who was to lead the *umma* following the death of the Prophet? As far as I know, three answers to the question were given during the first three centuries of Islamic history:

1. The Shi'ite explanation. The leadership of the Islamic community *(umma)* according to Shi'ite political theory is passed down to the descendants of the Prophet who by virtue of birth are qualified for it. Their inborn capacity endows them with a type of knowledge which ranks above that of ordinary Muslims. It is called *'ilm al-bāṭin,* to be translated as esoteric knowledge, and enables the Shi'ite Imām to understand and interpret the Koran and Sunna in the correct 'divine' way.[54]

2. The Sunnite solution. This answer was diametrically opposed

48. *Sīrat al-awliyā',* p. 39, chap. 57.
49. Radtke, *Weltgeschichte,* p. 230 f.
50. Julian Baldick, *Mystical Islam* (New York: New York University Press 1989), p. 38.
51. *Sīrat al-awliyā',* p. 41, 13 f.
52. *Sīrat al-awliyā',* p. 52 f.
53. *Sīrat al-awliyā',* p. 46, chap. 67.
54. Cf. *Encyclopaedia Iranica,* s.v. "*Bāṭen.*"

to the Shi'ite belief in a purely genealogical transmission of Prophetic authority. According to Sunni theory, the true heirs of the Prophet are the *'ulamā',* as espoused by the *ḥadīth,* 'The scholars are the heirs of the prophets' *(warathat al-anbiyā' al-'ulamā').* Their mastery of *fiqh* and *ḥadīth* qualifies them for leadership of the *umma* in collaboration with the Caliph.[55]

3. The mystics' interpretation. This solution was given, among others, by al-Ḥakīm al-Tirmidhī, and declared that neither relationship of blood nor the ordinary knowledge of the law are in themselves sufficient qualifications for the leadership of the *umma.* The leadership was to be bestowed upon the forty chosen men whom al-Tirmidhī calls either *ṣiddīqūn* or *awliyā' Allāh.* After the death of the Prophet these took over the leadership of the world.[56] Their rank is below that of the Prophet (—one may recall the first question dealt with by Abū Sa'īd al-Kharrāz.[57]) It is known that later authors, such as al-Dhahabī, maintained that al-Tirmidhī placed the friends of God in rank above the prophets—and this assertion was repeated, at least for some time, in Western literature.[58]

As the second of creation these forty men form the second spiritual hierarchy of the cosmos. Their characteristic is not *nubuwwa,* but *wilāya* 'friendship of God'. Like the prophets, but by virtue of *wilāya,* they are gifted with extraordinary capacities. The prophetic gift of revelation *(waḥy)* corresponds to their inspiration *(ilhām)*[59]. They can perform *karāmāt,* as the prophets performed *āyāt.*[60] Like the prophets they also possess knowledge of the unseen *('ilm al-ghayb).*[61] They do not bring a new *Sharī'a* to the people,[62] because the Law had been revealed in its totality by Muḥammad, but they

---

55. Bernd Radtke, "Der sunnitische Islam," p. 6, in Werner Ende/Udo Steinbach, *Der Islam in der Gegenwart* (München: Beck 1991).
56. *Sīrat al-awliyā',* p. 44 f.
57. See above, pp. 485-6.
58. *ḤT,* p. 92.
59. *Sīrat al-awliyā',* Fihris al-iṣṭilāḥāt, s.v. *"ilhām."*
60. *Sīrat al-awliyā',* p. 82 f.; cf. Einleitung, p. 4.
61. *Sīrat al-awliyā',* pp. 85-87, chaps. 110-111.
62. *Sīrat al-awliyā',* p. 50 f., chap. 73.

guarantee through their knowledge the perfect explanation and presentation of the revealed Law.

The knowledge of these friends of God, which al-Tirmidhī terms *'ilm al-bāṭin,* is at the highest level *al-'ilm billāh,* 'the knowledge of God.'[63] This is not—as in Shi'ite contexts—an esoteric knowledge, but rather a knowledge of the inner laws of creation and revelation which are hidden from normal consciousness, which the mystic attains by his own endeavor.[64]

In the hierarchy of the forty there is also a highest 'perfect one' who corresponds to the rank of the Prophet Muḥammad, who is the 'seal of friendship with God' *(khatm al-wilāya; khātam/khātim al-wilāya).* He is not a seal because he is the last of the friends of God—rather he deserves this rank because he has perfected his 'friendship with God', that is, he has 'sealed' it.[65] As with the Prophet Muḥammad, this 'seal' protects him against his enemies, the lower soul *(nafs)* and Satan. Thus he is protected like Muḥammad, but not sinless, because his sin was decreed by God *(maqdūr 'alayhi).*[66]

To briefly recapitulate the above discussion: the highest friend of God is a person chosen by God. After Muḥammad, he is the second person in creation. He is gifted with inspiration, knowledge of the unseen, can perform miracles—for example, is able to walk on water. His mystical ascent ends in annihilation in God. Furthermore, all his gifts are perfected by the the seal of the friendship of God. Therefore acting in the outer world cannot harm him. And as it becomes clear from his autobiography, al-Ḥakīm al-Tirmidhī perceived himself as this highest friend of God, as the *khatm al-wilāya.*[67]

As for the structure of *Sīrat al-awliyā',* after a very impressive description of the final failure of the *walī ḥaqq Allāh* who is unable to transcend creation because of self-entanglement, al-Tirmidhī turns to the *walī Allāh,* describing the latter's mystical ascent, his

63. *ḤT,* pp. 71-74.
64. *Bāṭen;* TM, pp. 557-61.
65. *Sīrat al-awliyā',* p. 44 f., chap. 64.
66. *Sīrat al-awliyā',* p. 90, 17.
67. Radtke, "Die Autobiografie des Theosophen von Tirmiḏ."

gifts, his relationship to the Prophet—by means of a fictitious dialogue between master and student.

CONCLUSION

The above considerations concerning al-Ḥakīm al-Tirmidhī will no doubt lead the historian to ask for the sources of such a system of thought. Here we must keep in mind that there are two aspects to the problem of sources in mysticism in general: on the one hand we have the individual mystical experience, which cannot be simply derived from sources, on the other, there is the theoretical understanding of this individual experience.

Al-Ḥakīm al-Tirmidhī reports some of his mystical experiences in his autobiography, but he does not tell us anything about the origin of his theories. He probably knew the writings of al-Muḥāsibī[68] and names his contemporary Yaḥyā b. Muʿādh al-Rāzī (d. 258/872) with whom he held discussions in the *Sīrat al-awliyāʾ*.[69] But the bulk of opinions which are discussed and partly very harshly rejected in the book, are quoted anonymously *(qāla nās, takallama nās)*.[70] From this at least one can infer that the problems dealt with in *Sīrat al-awliyāʾ* were generally discussed at the time and had not been 'invented' by al-Tirmidhī himself.

The *isnāds* of the *ḥadīths* quoted in *Sīrat al-awliyāʾ* always point towards the West, very often to Basra[71] where al-Tirmidhī stayed on his pilgrimage.[72] Much of the *ḥadīth*-material used by al-Tirmidhī in *Sīrat al-awliyāʾ* is also to be found in Ibn Abīʾl-Dunyā's *Kitāb al-awliyāʾ*, written at almost the same time. However, the *isnād*s differ and the latter book lacks seemingly any kind of conceptual structure.[73] Thus we can state that al-Ḥakīm al-Tirmidhī made use of subjects and materials on the theme 'friendship of God' which were known to the broader public during the second half of the third/ninth century and were discussed—not only in Sunnite circles, as it is

68. Radtke, "Die Autobiografie des Theosophen von Tirmiḏ."
69. *Sīrat al-awliyāʾ*, p. 78, 11 f.; p. 91, 8.
70. E.g. *Sīrat al-awliyāʾ*, p. 1, chapter 1 *(ṭāʾifa min al-nās)*.
71. E.g. *Sīrat al-awliyāʾ*, p. 99, 8-11; see also *ḤT*, pp. 29-32.
72. *ḤT*, p. 1; Radtke, "Die Autobiografie des Theosophen von Tirmiḏ."
73. *Drei Schriften*, Einleitung, pp. 29-31.

shown by Ibn Abī'l-Dunyā, but also in Shi'ite contexts, as for example in al-Kulaynī.[74]

The system, however, which al-Tirmidhī develops in *Sīrat al-awliyā'* seems to be his very personal creation. One may posit the question as to whether he perhaps made use of already existing systems, maybe deriving from a local East Iranian tradition. The *Sīrat al-awliyā'* would then have to be regarded as a representative of a special Eastern Persian mysticism. It would be easier to give an answer to this question if we knew more about his contemporary countrymen, and here I mean more than the later collections of their sayings contain.

Something should also be said concerning the nature of our sources for third/ninth century Sufism in general. On the one hand our information derives from texts written by the masters themselves, especially in the case of al-Ḥakīm al-Tirmidhī. On the other hand we depend on later collections and handbooks. And the picture these later books give of the life and teachings of earlier personalities are very often quite contradictory. This could be demonstrated in the case of al-Tirmidhī.[75]

Unfortunately, for example, all the writings of al-Ḥakīm al-Tirmidhī's compatriot Abū Bakr al-Warrāq al-Tirmidhī (died 906-7) are lost.[76] Later authors as Hujwīrī and Farīd al-Dīn 'Aṭṭār have wrongly made him a student of al-Ḥakīm al-Tirmidhī.[77] Abū Bakr al-Warrāq was close to the mystics of Balkh where he spent his life—and with all due caution one may assume that al-Ḥakīm al-Tirmidhī held opinions that were opposite to those of the mystics of Balkh. One of the most important statements in *Sīrat al-awliyā'*—that the *khātim al-wilāya* can go out to act in the world, seems to have been rejected in Balkh.[78] We have his correspondence with Muḥammad b. al-Faḍl al-Balkhī[79] and Abū 'Uthmān al-Ḥīrī of

74. *Drei Schriften,* Einleitung, p. 31 f.
75. *Drei Schriften,* Einleitung, p. 6; here footnote 24.
76. TM, p. 546.
77. *ḤT*, p. 38.
78. Radtke, "Die Autobiografie des Theosophen von Tirmiḏ."
79. *ḤT,* p. 86; a German translation *ibid.*, pp. 119-26. The first letter was edited by Muḥammad Ibrāhīm al-Geyoushī in *Al-Masā'il al-maknūna li'l-Ḥakīm al-Tirmidhī* (Cairo: Dār al-turāth al-'arabī 1980), pp. 71-6.

Naysābūr,[80] whose opinions he did not share. Furthermore it can be demonstrated that his language was different of that of contemporary Western, *i.e.* Iraqian mysticism.[81] Does he represent thus already an Eastern tradition or was he himself the creator of the special terminology partly used in his writings? But I must confess that I feel uncomfortable in using, especially for earlier times, concepts like 'Persian', 'school', etc., if more than a local characteristic is implied. We observe independent personalities—'schools' grew up later on—if at all.

Although the *Sīrat al-awliyā'* was read and copied—all the extant manuscripts are from the 'West'—its very sophisticated psychological and theosophical system did not have much influence on later Sufism—at least not until the advent of Ibn al-'Arabī. What was kept and used was the 'buzzword' *khatm al-wilāya*—but without any of the psychological implications described in *Sīrat al-awliyā'*. In modern times its most important influence was on the African orders of the Tijāniyya[82] and the Khatmiyya. This influence, however, was not exercised directly by the *Sīrat al-awliyā'*,[83] but through the writings of Ibn al-'Arabī who made use of it.

80. *ḤT*, p. 86; a German translation *ibid.*, p. 117-119. The text is now edited in *Drei Schriften*, pp. 190-192.
81. An easy comparison can be made between the terminology of a fourth/tenth century 'Western' handbook on Sufism (cf. Bernd Radtke, *Adab al-mulūk. Ein Handbuch zur islamischen Mystik aus dem 4./10. Jahrhundert.* BTS 37 [Beirut/Stuttgart: Franz Steiner 1991]) and al-Tirmidhī's terminology by studying the *Fihris al-iṣṭilāḥāt* of both books.
82. Bernd Radtke, "Gesetz und Pfad in der frühen islamischen Mystik. Einige Bemerkungen," (Rome 199-forthcoming); Radtke, "Die Autobiografie des Theosophen von Tirmiḏ."
83. Bernd Radtke, "Lehrer - Schüler - Enkel. Aḥmad b. Idrīs, Muḥammad 'Uṯmān al-Mīrġanī, Ismā'īl al-Walī," in *Oriens* 33 (1992); Radtke, "Ibn al-'Arabī's Kommentar zu al-Ḥakīm al-Tirmidī's *Sīrat al-awliyā'*."

Contemplative Disciplines in Early Persian Sufism

Muhammad Isa Waley

I. INTRODUCTION: CONTEMPLATION AND ACTION IN ISLAM

Islam is commonly thought of as a highly activist faith, but its teachings on the inner life are rich and varied. The present study aims to present an outline of two important inner aspects of the science of Sufism—the disciplines of invocation *(dhikr)* and of reflection or meditation *(fikr)*—according to the teachings of some of the Persian Sufis of the early period. Far from being a mark of inactivity or passivity, invocation and meditation are among the highest forms of activity. Many spiritual masters teach that they are also among the most necessary, and that the disastrous state of the world today is very much connected with our neglect of them. The anti-spirituality of modern civilization, and the almost total incompatibility between the mechanization of work and the use of working time for spiritual benefit, are cause and effect in the process that has made the remembrance of and meditation on God and His Creation appear to many people almost as alien to reality.

All religions are concerned with the meeting between the mortal and ephemeral on the one hand and the Eternal on the other. Those who would seek God must seek Him within the time-frame of this earthly life. Bereft of the impulsion to do so, those who confine their aspirations to this world can but seek to forget—for a short while—the end of this lifetime. The spiritual seeker looks to 'conquer time' through contact with the Eternal. According to an Arab proverb,

"Time is a sword, and if you do not cut through time it will cut through you."

In the traditional world of Islam, combining a highly active life in the temporal realm with one of devotion and contemplation was a possibility to some degree attainable by everyone. The Koranic doctrine[1] that Man is God's Caliph or representative on Earth, together with the absence of priesthood, makes it incumbent upon Muslims to seek within themselves a focus of spiritual purity, fervour, and contemplation whatever the hardships of worldly life. What, then, is the nature of this obligation to pursue an interior life of remembrance and contemplation, according to the doctrines of Islam? And what form did it take in Sufism, whose mystic lore and practices are so central to Muslim spirituality?

II. SUFI LITERATURE IN HISTORICAL CONTEXT

Although there is an abundance of source material concerning the spiritual disciplines of Sufism, most of the early works on *taṣawwuf* were written by Persians, several of them in the Arabic language. In the space available, one can only introduce a few ideas and illustrate some of them with excerpts from writings by Sufi masters of the period. All the texts cited, apart from passages from the Holy Koran and Traditions *(Aḥadīth)* of the Prophet Muḥammad, are from the works of Persian authors.

These works are of various types: some are prose treatises aiming at a comprehensive discussion of all aspects of the spiritual life, while others are devoted to a particular topic. Also of importance is the *tadhkira* literature, which deals with the sayings as well as the acts and virtues of the saints of the past. In addition, there is also Sufi poetry, one of the glories of Islamic culture replete with teachings concerning, and evocations of, the stages and states of the Path and its methodology. In this essay only a very small selection of material can be presented.

In the earliest Sufi manuals, such as Hujwīrī's *Kashf al-maḥjūb,*[2]

---

1. See e.g. Koran II: 30; VI: 165.
2. R. A. Nicholson (transl.), *The Kashf al-Maḥjūb: The oldest Persian treatise on Sufiism* (London: Luzac, repr. 1970).

much is said about the lives of Sufis and their descriptions and definitions of particular terms and states. On the other hand, very little if anything is said about the actual techniques of their invocation and meditation, a fact which at first may appear puzzling.[3]

Sufi treatises were never intended as substitutes for personal instruction. The earliest writers, like Abū'l-Qāsim Qushayrī and 'Alī Hujwīrī, were concerned to establish *taṣawwuf* as a licit and a vital field of learning and activity, and also to spell out their doctrine, methodology and views on issues over which there was controversy between Sufis. Like all writings, however elevated, they are a product of their time. Thus it is that in some passages of the *Kashf al-maḥjūb* one finds a mode of argumentation that seems to detract from the spiritual atmosphere normally associated with Sufism. The arguments are there, at least partially, to uphold viewpoints that the author considered it vital to defend at a crucial juncture in the historical unfolding and diffusion of Sufism.

Another consideration governing the tone and content of written works and the *dicta* of so many early Sufi saints makes their silence less difficult to fathom, and that was the need for strict secrecy regarding some of its esoteric methods and doctrines. To publish or be associated with statements offensive to the scholars of the Law could entail the loss of one's life, as is shown by the fate of Ḥallāj, 'Ayn al-Quḍāt Hamadhānī, and Shaykh al-Ishrāq Suhrawardī. Abū Hurayra, one of the great companions of the Prophet, allegedly remarked that he had been given two vessels by the Messenger of God and added, "I have divulged the contents of one; but were I to reveal what the other contained, this throat would be cut." Factors such as these may help to explain why it was only later, after the wider diffusion and acceptance of Sufism among the general Muslim community, due to the teachings of Ghazālī and others, that many actual details of contemplative practice and gnostic vision began to find their way into the technical literature.

The Sufi masters were also mindful of the acute dangers awaiting any person who wished to undertake certain spiritual practices

3. On this question see also the remarks of W.C. Chittick in his *Faith and Practice of Islam: three thirteenth-century Sufi texts* (Albany: SUNY 1992), pp. 20-21.

without undergoing the necessary initiation, training and supervision. The *'ulamā'* were required to study entire texts by reading them with a teacher before they could be authorized to teach. In the same way, and indeed *a fortiori, taṣawwuf* as one of the sciences of the Faith requires the strictest control and the closest guidance.

For this reason too, the earlier treatises are very largely silent as to the details of the techniques of *dhikr* and *fikr.* Yet it is wrong to infer that the Sufis of the time were not practising them, although there is little doubt that the practices of invocation became still more diverse from about the sixth/twelfth century as Sufism spread to many regions of the Muslim world.[4]

III. SOURCES OF *DHIKR* AND *FIKR*

Numerous writers, including some Muslims, have alleged that the spiritual practices associated with Sufism were introduced from sources outside Islam and have no legitimate place in it. In response, the basic orthodoxy of Sufism has been established by numerous authorities possessing expert knowledge of the *Sharī'a* and its canonical sources as well as practical and theoretical knowledge of the Path.[5] Almost every introductory or general work on Sufism written by a Muslim, down to the present day, contains a section wherein the author quotes passages from the Holy Koran and the Traditions of the Prophet and explains—if any explanation seems necessary—how the text validates certain Sufi doctrines and practices. The Holy Scripture of Islam accords great importance to the activities known in Arabic as *dhikr* and *fikr.* It may be useful to cite one or two of the canonical sources on this question.

One of many Koranic passages bearing on the subject is the following (III: 190-91), which extols both the practice of *dhikr* and its

4. Cf. J. S. Trimingham, *The Sufi Orders in Islam,* (London: Oxford University Press 1973), p. 199; L. Massignon, *Essai sur les origines du lexique technique de la mystique musulmane,* nouvelle édition (Paris: Vrin 1968), p. 106.
5. Among the numerous studies along these lines, see in particular, Victor Danner, *The Islamic Tradition: An Introduction* (New York: Amity House 1988); *idem.,* "The Necessity for the Rise of the Term Sufi," *Studies in Comparative Religion* (1972); Martin Lings, "The Origins of Sufism," *Islamic Quarterly* (1956); *idem., What is Sufism?* (London: Allen & Unwin 1983).

complement, *tafakkur* ('reflection', or 'contemplation'):

> *Surely in the creation of the heavens and earth*
> *and the alternation of night and day*
> *are signs for those possessed of insight*
> *who remember God standing and sitting*
> *and reclining and reflect upon*
> *the creation of the heavens and earth:*
> *Our Lord, Thou hast not created this for vanity.*
> *Glory be to Thee! Guard us against*
> *the chastisement of the Fire.*[6]

The performance of *dhikr* is also directly prescribed in a number of Koranic verses. These include XXXIII: 41: "O you who have faith, remember God with much remembrance" (or, "invoke God with much invocation"); and LXXII: 8, "Invoke the Name of your Lord, and devote yourself to Him wholeheartedly." Sufi authors cite a great many *Aḥadīth* on the subject of *dhikr,* of which the following *Ḥadīth* is particularly relevant, if, comparatively little known:

> It is related of the Prophet that he once assembled a group of the foremost companions in a room and ordered them to close the door. He then said aloud, three times, *Lā ilāha illā'llāh* ('No god but God') and ordered the Companions to do likewise. They did so, and he then lifted up his hands and said, "O God, have I conveyed what was to be conveyed?" He then said, "Glad tidings for you: God Almighty has forgiven your sins."[7]

The Koranic praise of meditation has already been instanced. Other verses bearing on the subject include the following, in which the word *dhikr* is generally interpreted as signifying the Holy Koran itself:

---

6. Translation by A.J. Arberry, *The Koran Interpreted* (Oxford University Press, reprinted 1983), with minor changes.
7. Quoted by Najm al-Dīn Rāzī, *Mirṣād al-'ibād min al-mabdā' ilā'l-ma'ād,* ed. Muḥammad Amīn Rīyāḥī, 2nd ed., (Tehran 1365 A.Hsh./1986), p. 280; cf. Hamid Algar (transl.) *The Path of God's Bondsmen* (New York: Caravan Books 1982), pp. 277-8. This *Ḥadīth* is found in the *Musnad* of Ibn Ḥanbal: see Algar's footnote on p. 278.

> ...and We have revealed unto you the Reminder *(al-Dhikr),* so that you may make clear to mankind what has been sent down [from Heaven] to them, and that they may reflect.[8]

Among the Traditions of the Prophet frequently cited by the Sufis is the following, which is intended not to be taken literally but rather to indicate rhetorically the immense importance of meditation: "An hour of contemplation is better than a year of worship."[9]

IV. *DHIKR:* THE KEY CONCEPTS

Having looked briefly at the sources of the disciplines of invocation and meditation in Islam, we now turn to the various meanings of the term *dhikr,* normally rendered in English as 'remembrance' or 'invocation', and the doctrines and practices associated with it in Sufism. Later on, we shall examine the complementary concept of *fikr,* usually translated as 'thought', 'reflection', or 'meditation', and also consider the relationship between *dhikr* and *fikr.*

Dhikr as an act of worship[10] can be said to possess four basic meanings. First of all, it can be understood as the act or state of striving to be constantly mindful of God in every waking moment of one's life. In other words, it is the opposite of *ghafla,* 'heedlessness' or 'negligence', being the essence of the struggle against Satan who is eager to make us forget God. This 'ethical' or 'moral' *dhikr,* so to speak, brings about in the soul at each moment a state acceptable to God: patience in adversity, thankfulness in receiving goodness; repentance at wrongdoing; hope of forgiveness. That in turn increases the soul's degree of faith *(īmān),* and heightens its consciousness.

A second meaning of *dhikr* is the methodical and repeated invocation of a formula, divine Name, or litany *(wird).* Some of the for-

8. Koran XVI: 44.

9. *Tafakkuru sā'atin khayrun min 'ibādati sanatin.* Cited by Abū Ḥāmid al-Ghazālī, in the *Kitāb al-Tafakkur,* vol. 4, pp. 410-35 of his *Ihyā' 'ulūm al-Dīn* (4 vols., reprinted Cairo 1289/1987). For more discussion of the place of *tafakkur* in devotional practice, see below, X.

10. Here I follow in part the work of K. Nakamura in his translation of the "Book of Invocations and Supplications" (*Kitab al-Adhkār wa'l-da'awāt*) from the *Iḥyā' 'ulūm al-dīn,* the monumental corpus of Islamic knowledge and wisdom by Abū Ḥāmid al-Ghazāli (d. 505/1111): *Invocations and Supplications: Kitāb al-Adhkār wa'l-da'awāt* (Cambridge: Islamic Texts Society 1990 [2nd ed.]).

mulae and techniques employed are discussed below. Masters of Sufism emphasize the importance of performing invocation correctly, which requires sincerity of intention *(ikhlāṣ)*, awareness and concentration *(ḥuḍūr)* and, not least, authorization *(idhn)* and instruction *(talqīn)*.

In the third place, the term *dhikr* can denote an inner state *(ḥāl)* in which fear and awareness of God *(taqwā)* and the act of remembrance and invocation overwhelm the traveller on the Path and he or she becomes truly divorced from concern for the world. The poetry of Persian Sufis is replete with beautiful expressions of this mystical state.

A fourth meaning of *dhikr* is the attainment of a stage or *maqām* in which invocation and mindfulness are spontaneously maintained through Divine help and the power and blessing of the *dhikr* itself, described in the renowned Sacred Tradition *(Ḥadīth Qudsī)* as follows:

> My servant continues to draw near to Me with supererogatory works until I love him. When I love him I am his hearing with which he hears, his seeing with which he sees, his hand with which he strikes, and his foot with which he walks. Were he to ask of Me, I would surely give to him, and were he to ask Me for refuge, I would surely grant him it.[11]

Here we have a canonical source for the doctrine that God becomes the Agent in every word and action of those whom He sanctifies. Sufi masters speak of this degree as *fanā'*, Annihilation.

Ghazālī uses the word *dhikr* to refer to the practice of calling to mind and assessing the nature and significance of one's states and actions in daily life, the fact that one will be brought to Judgement to answer for them; and the events and conditions of the Afterlife. A lengthy chapter of Ghazālī's *magnum opus* is devoted to this practice.[12] Here the object of *dhikr* is a contingent event or entity, rather than God Himself. It is clear that *dhikr* in this sense is akin to other

---

11. This *Ḥadīth* is related by Bukhārī: see *Al-Nawawī's Forty Ḥadīth*, trans. E. Ibrahim and D. Johnson-Davies, (Beirut and Damascus: The Holy Koran Publishing House 1976; 2nd edition), pp. 118-19.
12. *Kitāb Dhikr al-mawt wa mā ba'dah*, trans. T.J. Winter, as *The Remembrance of Death and the Afterlife* (Cambridge: Islamic Texts Society 1989).

contemplative disciplines of Sufism: *fikr,* meaning meditation or thought, and *muḥāsaba,* self-examination (see below, part IX).

Further significations for the word *dhikr* can be found in the Koran or in Sufi writings. In some passages of the Holy Koran, it signifies 'Scripture', or 'Message': "Truly it is We Who have revealed the Scripture *(al-dhikr),* and We are its Preservers."[13] Reading and studying the Koran is itself a potent form of *dhikr,* as will be seen later.

V. DOCTRINES OF *DHIKR*

From Sufi writings it is possible to extract some cardinal doctrines on *dhikr* and what its practice can actualize. *Dhikr,* as we have seen, is the quintessence of worship and the central means of spiritual actualization. But what is the philosophy and doctrine underlying the practice of *dhikr* as a spiritual discipline as depicted in the literature of Sufism?

i. One of the main doctrines is that *dhikr* as act or state is obligatory for all humankind.

The authors of treatises customarily begin their exposition of each subject or activity by citing the support for it in the Koran, Prophetic Tradition, and the deeds and words of pious Muslims of early times. It is also not uncommon to find views or acts ascribed to earlier Prophets. As mentioned above, the practice of *dhikr,* the various meanings of which have already been discussed, is prescribed repeatedly as an obligation in the Koran. A Persian treatise of the late fifth/eleventh or early sixth/twelfth century expresses this as follows:

> Know that God the Glorious and Mighty has singled out His remembrance *(yād)* from among other acts of obedience in four respects. For one thing, He did so by ordering that it be [performed] much: "O ye who have faith! Remember God with much remembrance!" (Koran XXXIII: 41) For another, by calling it "greater": "And verily the remembrance of God is greater." (XXIX: 45) Again, He ordered that it be constant *(paywastagī),* saying "So

13. Koran XV: 9. See also above, p. 502.

> remember God while standing and sitting." (IV: 103) Furthermore, He promises to remember [in turn], for He has declared: "So remember Me, and I shall remember you." (II: 152)[14]

Sufi authors also cite the many Prophetic Traditions commending the practice of *dhikr.* These include one *Ḥadīth* in which it is described as still more meritorious than fighting *jihād* in defence of the Faith until one's sword breaks and giving vast amounts in charity.[15] It is reported that the Prophet Muḥammad once declared that an 'invoker' (or 'rememberer': *dhākir)* of God, compared to those who neglect to do so, is like a fighter for a righteous cause compared with deserters.[16] According to 'Alī Hujwīrī, *dhikr* is a spiritual station *(maqām),* and the station of Muḥammad is that of *dhikr:*

> *Maqám* (station) denotes the perseverance of the seeker in fulfilling his obligations towards the object of his search with strenuous exertion and flawless intention. Everyone who desires God has a station *(maqám),* which, in the beginning of his search, is a means whereby he seeks God. Although the seeker derives some benefit from every station through which he passes, he finally rests in one, because a station and the quest thereof involves contrivance and design *(tarkīb wa ḥīla),* not conduct and practice *(rawish wa mu'āmalat).* God hath said: *"None of us but hath a certain station"* (Kor. xxxvii, 164). The station of Adam was repentance *(tawbat),* that of Noah was renunciation *(zuhd),* that of Abraham was resignation *(taslím),* that of Moses was contrition *(inábat),* that of David was sorrow *(huzn),* that of Jesus was hope *(rajá),* that of John (the Baptist) was fear *(khawf),* and that of our Apostle was praise [or remembrance] *(dhikr).*[17]

ii. No less significant than the doctrine of obligation—and evidently allied to it—is what might be termed the doctrine of reciprocity of *dhikr.* In accordance with the Koranic verse, "So remember Me, and

---

14. Abū Naṣr Ṭāhir Khānaqāhī, *Guzida dar taṣawwuf wa akhlāq,* ed. Īraj Afshār (Tehran 1347 A.Hsh./1968), p. 48.
15. al-Daylamī, *al-Firdaws bi-ma'thūr al-khiṭāb,* ed. al-Sa'īd Zaghlūl (Beirut 1405/1986), vol. 3, p. 454; see e.g. Ghazālī, *Iḥyā', Kitāb al-Adhkār wa'l-da'awāt;* trans. Nakamura, p. 7.
16. Abū Nu'aym al-Iṣfahānī, *Ḥilyat al-awliyā'* (Cairo 1351-7/1932-8), vol. 6, p. 181. This and the previous quotation are cited by Ghazālī, a Persian, from works compiled by Persians.
17. *Kashf al-Maḥjūb*, trans. R.A. Nicholson, p. 370-1.

I will remember you (II: 152)," God responds to man's remembrance of Him, "remembering" Him in turn. Divine Knowledge of all things being perfect and eternal, what this expression signifies is that the *dhikr* of God actuates a blessing upon the one who performs it. Such a blessing may be indescribably immense:

> The Envoy of God said, "When you come upon the pastures of Paradise, feed upon them." "What are the pastures of Paradise?" he was asked. "The circles of *dhikr,*" he replied.[18]

The Prophet's characterization of *dhikr* implies that to perform *dhikr Allāh* is in a certain sense to enjoy a taste of Paradise on Earth.

iii. Another primary doctrine concerning *dhikr* is that in essence the invocation, the invoker, and the Invoked One (in Arabic: *dhikr, dhākir,* and *Madhkūr)* are one. This is a mystery that can only be touched upon very briefly here. It has found expression, however, in many wonderful verse and prose texts, including the literature of *shaṭḥiyyāt:* the commentaries of Rūzbihān Baqlī[19] on the ecstatic utterances of Bāyazīd Bisṭāmī and others, contained in his "Commentary on the Paradoxes of the Sufis" *(Sharḥ-i shaṭḥiyyāt)* provide striking and profound examples. The 'content' of *dhikr Allāh* as practiced by Sufis consists of Divine Names and of formulae from the Koran which is the Divine Speech. At the unitive level of Reality which stands above all others, neither Names nor Speech are separable from the Divine Essence. It is in this context—explaining one of the paradoxical dicta of Ḥallāj —that Rūzbihān cites (or writes) this Arabic verse: "His remembrance is my remembrance, and my remembrance is His / How could two [mutual] rememberers possibly not be together?"[20] Again, since God is absolute and infinite, even the creatures who worship Him with their prayers and invocations—utterly dependent upon Him as they are—ultimately have no existence apart from Him. Thus, commenting on the ecstatic saying

---

18. Reported by Tirmidhī on the authority of Anas; see al-Khaṭīb al-Tabrīzī, *Mishkāt al-maṣābīḥ,* 32: 2 *(Dhikr Allāh),* 40; cf. translation by J. Robson, 2nd ed. (Lahore: Ashraf 1973), vol. 2, p. 479.
19. Rūzbihān Baqlī, *Sharḥ-i shaṭḥiyyāt (Commentaire sur les paradoxes des soufis),* ed. H. Corbin (Tehran: Dānishgāh-i Tihrān 1345 A.Hsh./1966).
20. *Ibid.,* p. 519.

(shaṭḥ) of Abū Bakr al-Wāsiṭī, "Whoever invoked Him uttered a calumny *(buhtān);* whoever was patient showed heroism; and whoever gave thanks acted presumptuously *(takalluf kard),"* Rūzbihān pronounced:

> This means that anyone who has remembered [God] and imagines that he has succeeded in remembering Him fittingly is guilty of fabrication. Even if he be the one remembering, remembrance is connected with the One Remembered, and the Remembered One is Infinite...When the temporal invokes the Eternal, it commits the ultimate fabrication...The All-embracing Name is 'Allah'. [Only] Allah is Allah. [Only] Allah says, 'Allah'. The reality of Allah, from Allah, is none other than Allah. When you say 'Allah', the instrument of [interposing] temporality is yours. When an invoker who is in thrall to the bondage of temporality says 'Allah, Allah', he is like a source of interference between the Name and the Named One. Since the Name is inseparable from the Named One, how can you describe the Eternal before you yourself have become Eternal? When the awesome Presence of His Majesty manifests Itself in the epithets of remembrance, [all Existence] from the [Divine] Throne to the Earth's surface is ground into atoms.[21]

iv. A fourth doctrine of *dhikr* is that it represents *anamnesis,* the 'unforgetting' of that which, in our deepest core, we already know. God created us for this purpose. The Sufis' reference to this doctrine is more Koranic than Platonic. As explained in the Koran (VII: 172), He has told us that He is our Lord; we have borne witness to it.

The Islamic doctrine of 'unforgetting' is highlighted in a particularly fascinating fashion in the writings of the founder of the Kubrawiyya Order, Najm al-Dīn Kubrā (ca. 1145-1220), upon whose work the teachings of Najm al-Dīn Rāzī are based to some extent (his own spiritual master, Majd al-Dīn Baghdādī, being a direct disciple of Kubrā). Kubrā's own major work, *Fawā'iḥ al-jamāl wa fawātiḥ al-jalāl,*[22] is an extraordinary combination of teachings on the practice of *dhikr* together with accounts of his own visionary experiences. He teaches that the heart possesses subtle organs of perception, which are progressively purified by the

21. *Ibid.,* pp. 280-1.
22. *Die Fawā'iḥ al-ǧamāl wa-fawātiḥ al-ǧalāl des Naǧm ad-dīn al-Kubrā,* edited with a study by F. Meier (Wiesbaden: Steiner 1957).

performance of *dhikr,* together with other spiritual disciplines and exercises:

> Our Path is the method of alchemy. It is essential that the subtle centre of light *(laṭīfa)* be released from beneath those mountains [i.e. the veils constituted by the four elements of corporeal existence]. ...Mystical tasting *(dhawq)* is brought about through existential and spiritual transformation ...this necessitates a transmutation of the faculties of sense-perception whereby the five senses are changed into senses of a different kind.[23]

The point of concern here, in relation to the doctrines of *dhikr,* is that the spiritual Path is an *inward* journey. We creatures already know what we are, but are veiled by the darkness of our individual existence. As Najm al-Dīn Kubrā expresses it:

> The lower soul, the Devil, and the Angels are not realities external to you. You *are* them. So, too, Heaven, Earth, and the Divine Throne are not outside you; nor are Paradise, Hell, Life, or Death. All exist within you, as you will realize once you have accomplished the initiatic journey and become pure.[24]

When illuminated by the power of the seeker's aspiration and by Divine Grace, each particle of the *dhākir*'s being finds its counterpart in the Unseen, and attains to the corresponding vision and knowledge, for like is attracted to like. According to Najm al-Dīn Kubrā again:

> You can only see or witness an object by means of some part of the same object. As we said, it is only the mine whence it came that a precious stone sees, desires and yearns for. So, when you have a vision of a sky, an earth, a sun, stars, or a moon, you must know that the particle in you which has its origin in that same mine has become pure.[25]

This takes us back to the doctrine, already touched upon above (iii), that from one point of view the invoker *(dhākir)* is inseparable from God, the Invoked One *(Madhkūr).*

---

23. *Ibid.,* sections 10-11.
24. *Ibid.,* p. 32.
25. *Ibid.,* p. 28.

VI. ASPECTS OF *DHIKR*

Dhikr, as already mentioned, can be performed in many different forms or modes. In addition to these, writers such as Abū Ḥāmid Ghazālī stress that every act of worship, and ideally every action, should be accompanied by an act of remembrance. Among the Prophetic Traditions on the subject of *dhikr* the following is very apposite to a situation today so very prevalent in which both time and knowledge seem in short supply:

> 'Abdullāh ibn Busr reported that a man said, "O Messenger of Allah, the Laws of Islam are too many for me, so tell me something that I may cling to." He replied, may God bless and him and give him peace, "Let your tongue never cease to be moist from invoking Allah."[26]

While important for the generality of Muslim worshippers, the performance of *dhikr* is *par excellence* the field of the Sufis. Here space permits consideration only of some of the most notable forms of *dhikr,* these being recitation of the Holy Koran, and invocation of Divine Names, sacred formulae, *awrād* (litanies), and poetry. Invocation may be audible or silent, individual or collective. Notable practices of *dhikr* include those of seclusion or *khalwa,* traditionally of forty days' duration; and the practice of audition to spiritual music *(samā').*

1. The Koran.

In his chapter of the *Iḥyā'* concerning the recitation and interpretation of the Koran, Ghazālī enumerates ten outward and ten inner duties to which the seeker must conform during this type of worship.

The outward requirements are ritual purity and correct comportment; maintaining a regular amount of recitation daily, weekly and monthly; dividing the text of the Koran according to that amount; writing the sacred text correctly and beautifully; reciting slowly and clearly *(tartīl);* to weep—or make oneself weep—while reciting; to

---

26. Related by al-Tirmidhī, Ibn Māja, and others; cf. Muḥammad Ṣāliḥ 'Ajjāj, *Jewels of Guidance: Advice from the Prophet Mohammad,* trans. M.I. Waley (London 1993), p. 31.

perform prostration at the required points in recitation; supplicatory prayer before and after reciting; to read silently or aloud as appropriate to the circumstances and to one's own state; and to recite as clearly and beautifully as possible.[27]

The inward actions required in recitation of the Koran are: understanding the divine origin of the Holy Book; magnifying its Author; paying full attention to the message and abandoning the chatter of the lower soul; pondering the meanings of the text; understanding each verse; ridding oneself of the psychological and doctrinal obstacles to such understanding; realizing the specific import of each verse to oneself; feeling the appropriate emotion or sensation whilst reciting; endeavouring to rise progressively to the state where it is as though the reader were hearing the sacred text from God Himself; and finally, to rid oneself of any sense of possessing the slightest power or ability of one's own—and to cease to regard oneself as being in the least satisfactory or pure.[28] Here consideration will be given to the third, fourth and fifth of these conditions, which are particularly germane to the matter of contemplation.

The third inward act is to concentrate on the meaning of the text and disregard the lower soul's attempts to distract one from it. Ghazālī cites the Koran (XIX: 12), in which the Divine Command was issued to the Prophet Yaḥyā (John the Baptist) to "Hold to the Book strongly," as signifying the imperative need for complete concentration. He adds that those who truly know the Koran realize that it contains everything that the higher part of the human soul can desire. It has been said that the Koran contains fields, gardens, closets, brides, brocades, meadows, and caravanserais. (Ghazālī defines each of these images: each letter *mīm* is a field, *rā*'s are gardens, Sūrahs beginning with the letters *Ḥā Mīm* are brocades, etc.) While reading and studying the sacred text in the prescribed manner, one enters these fields, enjoys their fruits, sees the brides, wears the brocades and so forth. Such delights absorb the reciter entirely and keep him from seeking any diversions. While emphasizing here the

---

27. Ghazālī, *Iḥyā'*, 8, *Kitāb Ādāb tilāwat al-Qur'ān,* vol. 1, pp. 261-5; translated by Muhammad Abul Quasem, *The Recitation and Interpretation of the Qur'an: al-Ghazali's Theory* (London 1979), pp. 34-55.
28. Ghazālī, *Iḥyā'*, Book 8, vol. 1, p. 265; transl. Quasem, *Recitation,* p. 56.

unique power and beauty of the Sacred Book, Ghazālī is perhaps suggesting also that real concentration ensures God's help in avoiding distraction and so guarantees the efficacy of the exercise.

The next inward act required is profound reflection on the message itself as it is recited. Ghazālī asserts that the entire purpose of reading the Koran is to ponder over it, whence the necessity of reading slowly and clearly, and quotes 'Alī ibn Abī Ṭālib as having said that there is no good in any act of worship which the one performing it does not understand, nor in any reading of the Koran unaccompanied by meditation. Reflection on a passage may be helped by multiple repetition in recitation, a practice recorded in the Prophetic Sunna (for instance, the repetition of the *Basmala* of each Sūrah of the Koran twenty times over). One pious man of yore spent six months reading and meditating on the Sūrah of Hūd (XI) again and again, states Ghazālī.

The fifth inner requirement is the intellectual duty to penetrate and grasp the meaning of each verse recited. The Koran encompasses the knowledge of God's Names, Attributes, and Actions, the *exempla* and life stories of the Prophets, the circumstances and final destruction of those who denied the previous Divine Revelations, the orders, threats and promises of God towards His creatures, and the descriptions of Paradise and Hell. When he encounters a verse relating to any one of these, the reciter must be eager to gain the knowledge inherent in them so as to deepen his knowledge and understanding.[29]

It is not feasible to go further here into the details of all the intellectual and mental disciplines of Koran reading andstudy. However, it is evident that Ghazālī's exposition opens up a whole range of possible meditational disciplines centered on the Holy Scripture.

2. *Litanies* (awrād)

The practice of reciting *awrād,* or litanies, can be traced to the teaching of the Prophet, who recommended the utterance of particular formulae on different occasions in daily life: these still vitally affect the life of many, if not most, Muslims today, who say every day as

29. Ghazālī, *Iḥyā',* 8, vol. 1, p. 267-70; trans. Quasem, *The Recitation,* pp. 2-69.

a matter of course, 'In the Name of God' *(Bi'smi'llāh),* 'God-willing' *(In shā' Allāh),* 'All praise belongs to God' *(al-Ḥamdu li-'llāh),* 'As God wishes' *(Mā shā' Allāh),* 'I ask God's forgiveness' *(Astaghfiru'llāh)*—all formulae including the comprehensive Divine Name 'Allāh'. For some of his Companions the Prophet prescribed a certain number of repetitions of certain verses or formulae at fixed times of the day, in most cases after the five ritual prayers. In one interesting instance, which is found in the *Ḥadīth* literature, the Prophet urged Abū Hurayra to earn complete forgiveness from God by glorifying, praising and magnifying God thirty-three times after each ritual prayer *(ṣalāt),* saying 'All glory to God' *(Subḥān Allāh),* 'All praise to God' *(al-Ḥamdu li-'llāh),* and 'God is Supreme' *(Allāh Akbar);* and then to repeat as a litany, up to one hundred times: 'There is no god but God. He is One, without partner. To Him belongs all Kingdom and Glorification, and He is omnipotent over all.' *(La ilāh illā'llāh, waḥdahu lā sharīka lah, lahu'l-mulk wa lahu'l-ḥamd wa huwa 'alā kulli shay'in qadīr).*[30]

An example of a *wird* used by an early Persian Sufi is found in Farīd al-Dīn 'Aṭṭār's account, in his biographical compilation *Tadhkirat al-awliyā',* of the life and states of Sahl ibn 'Abdullāh Tustarī (d. 282/896). The narrative also bears on the related topics of *murāqaba* and *khalwa,* self-observation and spiritual retreat, both to be discussed below.

> It is related that Sahl said, "I remember God Most High asking, 'Am I not your Lord?',[31] and myself replying 'Yes indeed', and Him answering me. I also remember being in the belly of my mother." He also said, "I was three years of age when I started rising at night to worship. My maternal uncle Muḥammad ibn Suwār would weep as he prayed, on account of my night worship, and tell me: 'Sahl, go to sleep. You are distracting my heart'. But I used to watch him, whether secretly or openly, until I reached the point when I told my uncle, 'I am in a difficult spiritual state: I see my head in prostration before the [Divine] Throne'. 'Little one', he told me, 'keep this state a secret. Tell nobody.' Then he said, 'Invoke in your heart. When you are in your nightclothes and turning over from side to side, and your tongue is moving, say

30. Muslim, *Saḥīḥ;* also 'Ajjāj, *Jewels of Guidance,* p. 29.
31. Koran VII: 171. See also above, p. 508.

> 'God is with me; God watches me; God witnesses me'. I began reciting this," recounted Sahl, "and informed my uncle. 'Say it seven times each night', said he. I did so, and again informed him. 'Say it fifteen times', said he, and I did so. After that, a sweetness manifested itself in my heart. After a year had passed, my uncle told me: 'Keep to what I have taught you, and practise it constantly until you enter the grave, so that you may enjoy its fruits in this world and the Hereafter'. Years went by, and I recited the same invocation until its sweetness appeared in the secret part of my heart *(sirr).* Then my uncle said, 'Sahl, How can anyone who has God with him, observing him, disobey God? May it be God's wish for you that you never disobey Him'. I then went into retreat *(khalwat).*"[32]

Abū Ḥāmid Ghazālī devotes a chapter of his *Iḥyā'* to the subject of *awrād,* in the broad sense of invocations, supplications and other acts of worship to be practiced at regular times of each day. Such regularity is regarded by Ghazālī as a prerequisite for a full spiritual life. He prescribes that a schedule be established whereby every period of twenty-four hours is divided into twelve parts, in each of which a fixed *wird* is recited.[33] Similar regimes were prescribed by Shaykh 'Umar Suhrawardī in his *'Awārif al-ma'ārif* (under the heading of *Tawzī' al-awqāt),* and by other masters of Sufism.

The importance of maintaining recitation of the *awrād* in Sufism is underlined in an anecdote concerning the great Junayd of Baghdad (d. 298/910). When it was suggested that in view of his advanced age and high station he should give up some of his recitation of *wird* he replied that since all that he had gained at the beginning of his discipleship had come about through the practice of *wird* it would be unthinkable to abandon it at the end.[34] *Awrād* in the sense of litanies to be chanted collectively do not seem to figure in Persian *taṣawwuf* during the period under discussion. In later times they assumed a central importance in many brotherhoods.

---

32. 'Aṭṭār, *Tadhkirat al-awliyā',* ed. Muḥammad Qazwīnī, 4th ed. (Tehran: Markazī, 1346 A.Hsh./1968), vol. 1, pp. 227-8; cf. *Muslim Saints and Mystics,* transl. A.J. Arberry (London: Routledge & Kegan Paul 1966), p. 154.
33. Ghazālī, *Iḥyā',* vol. 1, pp. 333-67: *Kitāb Tartīb al-awrād.*
34. Hujwīrī, *Kashf al-maḥjūb,* trans. Nicholson, p. 303.

3. Ritual Prayer (ṣalāt, namāz)

The five daily ritual prayers in themselves provide a framework within which the practising Muslim may organize his or her day. The need to keep track of the times for prayer inculcates consciousness of the importance of time and timekeeping: "Prayers are prescribed for believers at fixed times."[35] The Arabic word for 'ritual prayer' *(ṣalāt)* is derived from a verbal root which has the meaning of joining or linking. In this act of worship, the individual human links himself or herself to the Eternal and so in a sense conquers time. In microcosmic terms, this meeting takes place in the human heart. According to a saying often quoted by Sufis as a *Ḥadīth Qudsī* or Sacred Tradition, in which God Himself is the Speaker through the mouth of His Prophet Muḥammad: "Neither My Heaven nor My Earth can contain Me, yet the heart of My truly believing servant contains Me."

The ritual prayer as an act of *dhikr* is prescribed and discussed by 'Alī Hujwīrī who notes:

> Etymologically, prayer *(namáz)* means remembrance (of God) and submissiveness *(dhikr ú inqiyád),* but in the correct usage of lawyers the term is specially applied to the five prayers which God has ordered to be performed at five different times...

Hujwīrī elaborates further in the same section:

> Prayer is a term in which novices find the whole way to God, from beginning to end, and in which their stations *(maqámát)* are revealed. Thus, for novices, purification takes the place of repentance, and dependence on a spiritual director takes the place of ascertaining the *qibla,* and standing in prayer takes the place of self-mortification, and reciting the Koran takes the place of inward meditation *(dhikr),* and bowing the head takes the place of humility, and prostration takes the place of self-knowledge, and profession of faith takes the place of intimacy *(uns),* and salutation takes the place of detachment from the world and escape from the bondage of "stations."[36]

35. Koran IV: 103.
36. Hujwīrī, *Kashf al-maḥjūb,* trans. Nicholson, pp. 300-1.

For Hujwīrī, then, ritual prayer is *par excellence* the act of *dhikr*. Other authorities may not express it so, but stress in various ways that the remembrance of God is an essential part or concomitant of the prayer, and that while a prayer performed in a state of heedlessness may be acceptable from the narrow viewpoint of the Law, from the spiritual viewpoint it has no value in the sight of God or benefit to the heart of the worshipper. Mindfulness in prayer is best assured by means of the constant practice of *dhikr* throughout one's waking hours—and, one may add, by the constant maintenance of ritual purity.[37]

Perhaps the most eloquent expression of the essential need for recollection in the ritual prayer comes, once again from Abū Ḥāmid al-Ghazālī. He cites a number of Traditions, including this, related by Abū Dā'ūd and by al-Nasā'ī: "A man gains nothing from the prayer, except from those parts of which he is fully conscious." Next, Ghazālī compares the payment of alms tax *(zakāt)*, fasting, and performance of the Pilgrimage, three compulsory Muslim observances which are intrinsically difficult for the lower self *(nafs),* with the ritual prayer.

> In contrast to these other religious duties, ritual Prayer consists only in remembrance, recitation, bowing, prostration, standing erect and sitting down. As for remembrance, it is proximity to God, Great and Glorious is He, and communion with Him. If its purpose is not conversation and dialogue, it must be a verbal and vocal exercise, set to test the tongue in the same way as the belly and the genitals are tested by abstinence during the Fast, as the body is tested by the ordeals of Pilgrimage, or as one is tested by having to part with beloved money on paying the Alms. Without a doubt, the latter supposition must be wrong, for nothing comes more easily to the heedless than idle tongue-wagging. It cannot, therefore, be simply a physical exercise. The sounds produced are significant only when they form articulate speech. Articulate speech must be expressive of what is in the heart and mind, and this is not possible without conscious awareness. What is the point of praying: 'Show us the Straight Path', if one is in a state of absentmindedness? If it is not intended as a humble entreaty and supplication, why bother with the idle mouthing of the words,

37. See Ghazālī, *Iḥyā', Kitāb Asrār al-ṣalāh.*

> especially if it has become a habit?[38]

By the same token, adds Ghazālī, the recitation of the Holy Koran in the ritual prayer is intended as the worshipper's glorification and entreaty of God; and the purpose of the movements of bowing and prostration is to express veneration for Him. The author concludes that the reason why ritual prayer is the prime Pillar of Faith in Islam is that its external features are inseparably linked to the purpose of intimate communion between mankind and the Creator. "To sum up, attentiveness of the heart is the very spirit of ritual Prayer."[39]

Later on in the same Book of his *magnum opus,* Ghazālī enumerates and discusses the six inner realities *(al-ma'ānī al-baṭina)* required in order to "give life to" the prayer. They are attentiveness of the heart; understanding the significance of the words uttered; magnification of Almighty God; feeling awe at the fact of addressing Him; maintaining hope in God's Mercy and good will; and feeling shame on account of one's deficiencies. Remembrance of God is the key, as we are again reminded by this narrative:

> It is related that God said to Moses: "Moses, whenever you remember Me, let every part of your body tremble at your remembrance of Me. While remembering Me, be humble and be tranquil. When you remember Me, keep your tongue behind your heart. When you stand before Me, stand as a lowly slave stands. Commune with Me with quaking heart and sincere tongue."[40]

4. Supplicatory Prayer (du'ā)

That supplication *(du'ā)* is potentially a fruitful and inspiring form of *dhikr* is finely expounded by Ghazālī in his *Iḥyā 'ulūm al-dīn.* The value of *du'ā* is not negated by Predestination, since if God averts afflictions in response to human supplications this is itself predestined. Ghazālī goes on to observe that

---

38. *Iḥyā' 'ulūm al-dīn,* vol. 1, pp. 159-61: *Kitāb Asrār al-ṣalāh, al-Bāb al-thālith fī al-shurūṭ al-baṭīna min a'māl al-qalb* (The Mysteries of Ritual Prayer: Book 3, 'On the inward conditions for actions of the heart'). Translation by M. Holland, *Inner Dimensions of Islamic Worship* (Leicester: Islamic Foundation 1403/1983), pp. 34-9.
39. *Ibid.*
40. *Iḥyā',* vol. 1, pp. 161-3. Translation by M. Waley.

> Supplication has the same benefit as we mentioned with regard to invocation *(dhikr)*. For supplication requires the presence of the heart with God, and this is the apex of the acts of worship. Accordingly, the Emissary of God (may God bless him and grant him peace) said, "Supplication is the marrow of worship." The propensity of human beings is for their hearts not to turn to the remembrance of God (Great and Glorious is He!) save in cases of need *(ḥāja)* and suffering from a calamity. *Truly man, once ill luck befalls him, is full of endless supplication.*[41] Need requires supplication, and supplication brings back the heart to God with humility and submission, so that there results the remembrance [of God], which is the noblest of the acts of worship...[42]

Ghazālī lays down no fewer than ten principles to be applied when making supplication to God. Every opportunity must be taken to avail oneself of the most efficacious times for *du'ā*. One should take advantage of the best times (e.g. Ramaḍān, or any Friday) and occasions (e.g. while fasting or in prostration); one should face the *qibla* and raise one's hands. The voice must be kept neither loud nor silent; the words of prayer should be spontaneous and not affected, and hence rhymed prose is to be avoided. It is advisable to learn and to use the exact wording of prayers recorded as having been uttered by the Prophet, his Companions, or other pious Muslims of early times. When supplicating, the worshipper should be humble and submissive, and filled with longing and fear. Also essential is sincere trust and faith that one's prayers will be answered; and each request should be made earnestly and uttered three times. Above all is that the worshipper should call upon his or her Lord with complete humility, submission, and sincere contrition for past misdeeds.

The benefits of *du'ā* as an act of contemplation include the habitual reminder or realization that one's fate at every moment of life is in the hands of the Creator, upon whom one is utterly dependent. Because there are appropriate formulae of prayer and remembrance for every kind of event or occasion each instant of one's existence offers the opportunity to recall the underlying reality of the human situation and to petition for Divine Blessings and Mercy.[43]

---

41. Muslim, *Dhikr*, 12.
42. Ghazālī, *Iḥyā', Kitāb al-Adhkār wa'l-da'awāt;* trans. Nakamura, *op. cit.*, p. 90.
43. Ghazālī, *Iḥyā', (Kitāb al-Adhkār wa'l-da'awāt)*, vol. 1, pp. 303-9.

Mawlālā Jalāl al-Dīn Rūmī counsels the seeker to practice *du'ā* with *dhikr:*

> *Remember God the Truth so much that you forget about yourself and bend double in supplication, like the "r" in "prayer."*[44]

5. Poetry as Dhikr

The use of sung poetry as a support for *dhikr* is of course well-documented, especially in the context of *samā'*. A well-known example is the *Diwān-i Shams-i Tabrīzī* of Jalāl al-Dīn Rūmī, the poems of which were arranged by metre in some manuscripts, almost certainly in order to facilitate and systematize their use in *samā'*.[45] The use of a single verse as a formula for invocation in solitude is far more uncommon but is documented in the case of Abū Sa'īd ibn Abī'l-Khayr (d. 440/1049), the great Khurāsānian saint.[46] It was a Sufi named Abū'l-Qāsim Bishr-i Yāsīn who first counselled Abū Sa'īd to endeavour to remove all self-interest *(ṭama')* from his dealings with God. Bishr was also the author of many of the *ruba'iyyāt* quoted by Abū Sa'īd in his discourses. Again, it was Bishr who gave the young boy his first instructions in *dhikr:*

> "Do you wish", he asked him, "to talk with God?" "Yes, of course I do," said Abū Sa'īd. Bishr told him that whenever he was alone he must recite the following quatrain, no more and no less:
>
> *Without Thee, O Beloved, I cannot rest;*
> *Your goodness towards me I cannot reckon.*
> *Tho' every hair on my body becomes a tongue,*
> *A thousandth part of the thanks due to You I cannot tell.*

---

44. (*Mānanda-'i dāl-i du'ā*). Rūmī, *Kulliyyāt-i Shams ya Dīwān-i Kabīr,* ed. Badī' al-Zamān Furūzānfar, 2nd ed., vol. 7 (Tehran: Amīr Kabīr 1355 A.Hsh./1976), p. 137.
45. A. J. Arberry, in *Mystical Poems of Rūmī: first selection, poems 1-200* (Chicago 1968), pp. 2-3.
46. For further analysis of Abū Sa'īd's spiritual poetics, see above, pp. 94ff. –Ed.

Abū Sa'īd was constantly repeating these words. "By the blessing which they brought," he says, "the Way to God was opened to me in my childhood."[47]

6. Spiritual Retreat (khalwa)

The practice of *khalwa* involves the continuous and intensive practice of *dhikr* in solitude over a period of days or even weeks. Although the subject merits consideration in a separate study we mention it here insofar as it constitutes a particular aspect of *dhikr* with a special place in Sufi methodology. In such early Sufi treatises as the *Kitāb al-Luma'* of Abū Naṣr Sarrāj (d. 378/988), the *Ta'arruf* of Kalābādhī (d. 380/990) , or Hujwīrī's *Kashf al-maḥjūb,* the term *khalwa* is not mentioned. It may be wrong to read too much into this, though, for it is generally the case that a great deal that is implicit during the earlier historical phases of a given tradition has later to be made explicit in view of the decline in the overall level of spiritual aptitude. At all events, more information concerning the doctrine and method of *khalwa* is found in Sufi literature from Najm al-Dīn Kubrā (d. 618/1221) onwards.[48] The injunction to "keep solitude in society" *(khalwat dar anjumān)* accords with the prevalently anti-monastic spirit of Sufism; it was particularly characteristic of the Naqshbandī Order but widely accepted by other Sufis, formalizing a principle that was already implicit in earlier Sufi doctrine.

In his *Mirṣād al-'ibād,* a comprehensive guide to the spiritual life, Najm al-Dīn Rāzī furnishes an excellent account of the principles and procedures to be followed in undertaking the spiritual retreat. After citing Koranic passages and Traditions in support of the practice, which he considers to have been undertaken by every Prophet, Rāzī enumerates eight rules for *khalwa.*

---

47. Translated by R.A. Nicholson, in *Studies in Islamic Mysticism* (Cambridge University Press 1980 rprt.), p. 5; cf. Jamāl al-Dīn Luṭf Allāh ibn Abī Sa'īd Sa'd, *Ḥālāt wa sukhanān-i Shaykh Abū Sā'īd Abī'l-Khayr,* ed. V.A. Zhukovskii (St. Petersburg 1899); ed. Īraj Afshār (Tehran 1963), pp. 1-17.
48. See e.g. M. I. Waley, "'Azīz al-Dīn Nasafī on Spiritual Retreat *(Khalwa),*" *Sufi: A Journal of Sufism,* 17 (Spring 1993), pp. 5-9.

The first rule is to sit alone in an empty chamber, facing the *qibla,* crosslegged and with the hands resting upon the thighs. The disciple must first have made the major ablution *(ghusl),* his intention being that of washing a corpse, taking the chamber to be his grave, leaving it only for ablution, calls of nature, and the ritual prayers. The cell must be small and dark, and curtained off to prevent light and sound from entering, in order that the faculties of sight, hearing, speech and walking may cease to function and that the Spirit, unpreoccupied by sense-perceptions and sensory phenomena, commune with the Suprasensory World. With the outward senses no longer engaged, the veils and afflictions that entered the Spirit through the doorways of the five senses are eliminated by means of invocation and the negation of stray thoughts *(khawāṭir).* That [sensory] kind of veil falls away, the Spirit experiences intimacy with the Suprasensory World, and its familiar communion with mankind is negated.

The second condition is to maintain constantly a state of ritual purity, so that the disciple is armed and Satan cannot overcome him. "Purity is the armor of the believer" *[Ḥadīth].* The third is perpetual recitation of the formula *Lā ilāha illā 'llāh* ("No god but God"). God's saying, "They who remember God standing, sitting, and on their sides"[49] is an allusion to the practice of perpetual invocation. The fourth is to persist in rejecting stray thoughts *(khawāṭir).* Whatever thought may come to mind, be it good or ill, is to be negated by the words *Lā ilāha,* as if the initiate were telling himself, "I desire nothing but God." The Koranic verse, "Whether ye reveal what is within your souls or conceal it, God will call you to account for it,"[50] alludes to the negation of thoughts... Until the mirror of the heart is cleansed and purified of all marks it cannot accommodate the forms of the Suprasensory World or knowledge instilled directly by God, nor receive the lights of direct contemplation and spiritual revelations.

The fifth [condition] is continual fasting [in daytime]. ...This is enormously effective in severing human attachments and attenuating animal, bestial attributes. ...The sixth is constant silence. The disciple must speak to no one except the Shaykh, and then only the minimum when consulting him about a vision *(wāqi'a).* For the rest, let him say, "He is saved who is silent," and move his tongue only in invocation.

The seventh is to concentrate upon the Master's heart. The disciple must continually fix his heart upon that of the Shaykh,

49. Koran III: 191.
50. Koran II: 284.

seeking help from it. Revelations from the world beyond the senses, and the breeze of the exhalations of Divine Grace, at first reach the disciple through the heart of the Shaykh. Initially the disciple is held back by many veils, and being accustomed to the world of the senses *('ālam-i shahādat)* cannot turn towards the Almighty Presence as required. But if the bond of discipleship is firm he may readily concentrate upon the heart of the Shaykh. The Shaykh's heart is turned towards the Divine Presence and is nourished by the Suprasensory World, whence an effusion of Divine Grace reaches it at every moment. Insofar as the disciple's heart is directed towards that of the Shaykh, suprasensory help is transmitted from the Shaykh's heart to that of the initiate. Thus his heart first grows accustomed to receiving help through the intermediary of the Shaykh, then gradually advances to the point where it is capable of receiving Grace directly: "Their Lord shall give them drink of a pure wine."[51] In the first place they drink of the same wine, but it is given them in the goblet of the sainthood of the Shaykh: "Therein shall they be given to drink of a cup mixed with ginger."[52] Later, God's Cupbearer will give them the pure wine of direct vision, in the goblet of the Blessed Prophet Muḥammad, for "Their Lord shall give them drink of a pure wine" ...The disciple should always consider the directive power *(himmat)* of the Master as his guide and escort on the Way.

...The eighth condition is to abandon all contention either with God or with the Master. Abandoning contention with God signifies being content with whatever He sends from the Unseen, be it spiritual contraction or expansion, pain or comfort, sickness or health, oppression or opportunity; submitting to God, never turning away from Him, and being steadfast. ...The initiate must not object to any of the Master's words, deeds, states, or attributes that he may observe. He must submit to the Master's outward and inward work upon him. He must view the Shaykh's behavior and states with the eye of discipleship, and not apply the short-sighted eye of reason, for submission to the sainthood of the Master is the paramount condition of the Path. ...There are also many usages *(ādāb)* relating to the retreat; but the eight conditions of the retreat are as expounded above.[53]

---

51. Koran LXXVI: 21.
52. Koran LXXVI: 18.
53. *Mirṣād al-'ibād,* pp. 281-6. For a full translation, see Algar, *The Path of God's Bondsmen,* pp. 279-85.

The Chamber of Spiritual Retreat *(chilla-khāna)* Adjacent to the Mausoleum of Aḥmad Yasawī (d. 562/1166) in Turkestan. The Yasawiyya Order stressed the practice of *khalwa.* (Photo by Mehmet Yalcin).

7. Mystical Audition with Music and Poetry (Samāʿ)

Of the many aspects of Sufism which have given rise to controversy, probably no other question has been more strongly contested than that of the legitimacy of *samāʿ*. Listening to chanting and music, and performing sacred dance, gave rise to grave misgivings not only among non-Sufi Muslims but also among many Sufis. As with some other facets of *taṣawwuf,* such as visiting and praying at the tombs of the saints, it is the abuses of legitimate practices that have caused most trouble.

According to Hujwīrī, author of the earliest extant Sufi manual in Persian, *samāʿ* should not be practiced too often, lest familiarity diminish the reverence of the seeker for it. Essential conditions are the presence of a qualified Shaykh; the absence of any outsiders; the dispelling of all worldly thoughts; and seriousness of intention without artificial effort or formality *(takalluf).* The musicians involved, too, must be respectable persons. Hujwīrī enjoins dervishes to maintain a state of composed sobriety so far as possible. When the *samāʿ* begins to enrapture those present, they must take care to avoid any state or behavior which does not arise spontaneously:

> Until the *samāʿ* shows its power it is essential not to force it; but once it gains power one must not resist it. One must follow the 'moment' according to what it indicates. If it arouses you, be aroused; if it makes you calm, be calm. One taking part in *samāʿ* must possess enough discernment to be able to receive the divine influence and recognize its true value. When that influence shows itself in the heart he must not try to repel it, and when its power dies down he must not try to hold onto it. Whilst in a state he may neither expect assistance from anyone nor refuse anyone's help if offered. He must not disturb any other participant in *samāʿ* nor cogitate on the meaning of a verse [he hears].[54]

Although caution about *samāʿ*, and emphasis on proper observance of its proprieties, was voiced by other authorities—such

---

54. *Kashf al-maḥjūb,* ed. Zhukovskii, pp. 544-5; cf. Nicholson's translation, pp. 418-9; cf. J.-L. Michon, "Sacred Music and Dance in Islam," in (ed.) S.H. Nasr, *Islamic Spirituality II* (New York: Crossroad 1991), p. 476.

as Shihāb al-Dīn ʿUmar Suhrawardī[55] and Abū Ḥāmid Ghazālī—contrary to the opinion of many modernist Muslims, these masters perceived *samāʿ* as an activity of the greatest value in the devotional life. Their reservations arose from the need to ensure that those who participated were qualified and prepared for what could otherwise prove to be a spiritually dangerous experience. For them, the effect of *samāʿ* depends entirely upon whether the soul of the listener be inclined towards the desires of the lower self or of the Spirit—a viewpoint shared by most of those who deem such practices permissible.

The most comprehensive and informative text on *samāʿ* to have appeared in print is *Bawāriq al-ilmāʿ*, attributed to Aḥmad Ghazālī,[56] brother of Abū Ḥāmid Ghazālī. In the space available one can do little more than summarize the contents of this very important treatise. The author describes his work as a treatise on audition, its benefits, and conditions for performing it, with evidence from the Koran, the Sunna, and other traditions (of the Sufi saints).

> Know...that the audition of this party is a reference to the observation of strange secrets in the delicate poems which the *qawwāl* recites while joined to the ecstasy which arises in the heart of the gnostic *(ʿārif)* who works and the novice *(murīd)* who is perfect. It induces them to put off resistance, to be drawn to the Presence of the One, the Powerful, and to ponder delicate things and secrets.... So when a person hears the analogies which pertain to notes which include the realities *(maʿānī)* which pertain to taste [i.e. direct mystical experience] and the Truths which pertain to the Unity, the being inclines to all those, and every bodily member receives its portion separately. The hearing [receives] the things of the unrestrained analogies; the sight, the analogies of the movements; the heart, the delicate things of the realities; and the intellect, the inner consciousness of the unrestrained analogies. When the bodily members are united in affairs which are suitable, the law of contention is removed and the law of mutual agreement

55. For the arguments for and against *samāʿ* and the conditions to be met, see especially Shihāb al-Dīn Abū Ḥafṣ ʿUmar Suhrawardī, *ʿAwārif al-maʿārif* (Beirut: Dār al-Kitāb al-ʿArabī 1983), pp. 173-91.
56. Edited and translated by James Robson in *Tracts on listening to music* (London: Royal Asiatic Society 1938), pp. 63-184. Also valuable is the introduction, pp. 1-13, wherein Robson summarizes numerous statements regarding *samāʿ* from other early Sufi texts.

> appears. Contention pertains to darkness and mutual agreement to light, and when the darkness is removed and the light spread abroad, matters and verities are revealed which could not be reached by a thousand efforts.[57]

The author proceeds to explain that correct time, place and brethren are essential. Spiritual progress in *samā'* is facilitated by being in the company of congenial souls in a mosque or *Khānaqāh* (Sufi meeting-house). He is at pains to establish that singing or playing the *daf* (large tambourine), and listening to such music is both lawful and in accordance with the Sunna or usage of the Prophet, and furthermore that the same applies to dancing provided that the decencies are observed.[58] Jurists who claim otherwise stand in danger of rejecting the Sunna.[59]

After that rather polemical passage, the author of *Bawāriq al-ilmā'* explains the symbolism of the tambourine, singing voice, flute, breath, dancing, leaping, detachment, etc. in relation to the body and the Spirit. The unprejudiced intelligence can readily appreciate the nobility of *samā'*, for which six reasons are adduced. Firstly, in *samā'* the Spirit is drawn upwards and the body follows. Secondly, the spiritual nourishment gained though audition strengthens the practitioner's heart and inward faculties, as life and light from the Suprasensory World by Divine Grace enter the Spirit. Third, detachment from sensory phenomena and attraction towards the subtle realms of the Spirit lead to ecstasy, travel in those realms, and the attainment of the Station of Union *(wuṣūl)*. In the fourth place, when the Divine Name *Huwa* (He) is recited, it penetrates the seeker's being, releasing the Spirit and removing the veil over inner realities and truths. Fifthly, because *samā'* involves external motion and internal stillness, and the external and internal aspects of worship are interlinked, the inner nature of *samā'* in its various

---

57. *Bawāriq,* (trans. Robson), pp. 70-72.
58. It is interesting in this regard that the treatise concludes (pp. 111-18) with a mention of the musical "instruments of diversion" considered by the author to be prohibited—harp, viol, lute, and reedpipe; of the conditions governing audition (no beardless youths are to be present, and ecstasy must be spontaneous, never feigned); and of the qualities and qualifications required in a true jurist or judge of the old school, Abū Ḥanīfa being cited as an exemplar.
59. *Ibid.,* pp. 72-81.

ascending degrees includes the inner realities of the five exoteric Pillars of Islam (the Testimony of Faith, prayer, fasting, giving of alms, and *Ḥajj*). Finally, audition comprises the perfection of the stations of the mystical Path: "So he who engages in audition rises to high stations and divine favours which one could not attain to by a thousand efforts and the most perfect religious exercises."[60]

Having completed his exhaustive defence of the practice of *samā'*, the author of the *Bawāriq* describes the procedures of a session and the conditions governing it. Such gatherings normally take place by prior arrangement, after performance of prayers, a *wird,* or *dhikr.* Often proceedings begin with the recitation of appropriate passages from the Holy Koran, followed by a commentary from the spiritual director —whose presence is generally agreed to be essential—on their esoteric meaning (examples are given in the text). Next, a *qawwāl* or minstrel with appropriate gifts and qualifications recites poetry to inspire love and yearning for God (again, examples are provided). The description of physical attributes of the Beloved must be understood as applying to the spiritual personality of the Prophet Muḥammad. As the subtle attraction builds up, the participants are stirred to perform the sacred "dance." Once their state of rapture begins to subside, the Sufis one by one sit down; the chanting then gradually brings them back to a state of repose. Finally, the session over, they disperse and sit to await whatever spiritual revelations may be vouchsafed them as fruit of their *samā'*[61]

VII. *DHIKR:* DISCIPLINE AND PSYCHOLOGY

Both before and after Sufi circles developed into fully formalized Orders or *Ṭuruq* (singular *Ṭarīqa*), the Masters of the Way imposed conditions and disciplines on their novices. Inasmuch as the Sufi Path means war on the powers of evil within the soul, such a disciplinary framework is essential. One danger is that the seeker may unknowingly perform *dhikr* with the intention of gaining prestige, or visions, or other experiences. There is also a risk of misinterpreting one's experiences and imagining oneself to have attained to

60. *Ibid.,* pp. 101-4.
61. *Ibid.,* pp. 105-11.

some advanced degree of sanctity or gnosis. Najm al-Dīn Rāzī in the *Mirṣād al-'ibād* tells of a disciple who fancied that he had been blessed with some tremendous vision of light. When he told his spiritual instructor, the latter told him: "You immature man, that was the light of your ritual ablution *(wuḍū')!*"[62]

As is shown by the importance attached to the 'genealogies' of Orders or individual Sufis, authorization *(idhn)* is perceived as essential in guaranteeing the integrity of the seeker's guidance through a line of masters stretching back to the Prophet Muḥammad himself. Abū'l-Mafākhir Yaḥyā Bākharzī's treatise[63] includes three versions of his initiatic pedigree. The treatises stress the need for an authorized and fully qualified *murshīd* or spiritual director qualified to impart *talqīn* or instruction in invocation and to guide the seeker during its performance.

The kind of discipline imposed on disciples is exemplified by the 'Eight Rules' associated with the Persian Sufi Junayd of Baghdad. These were later adopted by Najm al-Dīn Kubrā, founder of the Kubrawī Order, who added two more rules which circulated widely in a short treatise by Kubrā entitled *al-Uṣūl al-'ashara* (the 'Ten Principles').[64] They prescribe constant observance of ritual purity, fasting, silence, seclusion, and invocation (using the formula *Lā ilāha illā 'llāh),* keeping the heart fixed forever upon the Shaykh, abandoning one's own will entirely, and referring to him for interpretation and guidance concerning his spiritual experiences. All thoughts and mental impulses *(khawāṭir)* are to be put aside the moment that they occur. Finally the disciple must surrender totally to the will of God. The rules added by Najm al-Dīn Kubrā are to eat and drink only the bare minimum and to observe moderation when breaking the fast.[65] Essentially the same rules are prescribed by Najm al-Dīn Dāya Rāzī, who belonged to the Kubrawī Order founded by Kubrā, in regard to the spiritual retreat (excerpts were cited

---

62. *The Path of God's Bondsmen,* p. 295.

63. *Awrād al-aḥbāb wa Fuṣūṣ al-ādāb.* The second part, *Fuṣūṣ al-ādāb,* has been edited by Īraj Afshār (Tehran 1345 A.Hsh./1966).

64. *Fawā'iḥ,* pp. 2-3. For further details see 'Abd al-Ghafūr Lārī's Persian translation of and commentary on Kubrā's *al-Uṣūl al-'ashara,* ed. Najīb Māyil Harawī (Tehran 1363 A.Hsh./1984).

65. *Fawā'iḥ,* ed. Meier, pp. 2-3.

above, pp. 519-21).

The diagnostic analysis of the origins and nature of stray thoughts *(khawāṭir)* is dealt with in detail by Sufis of various Orders, but was especially a subject of concern and literary exposition on the part of the Kubrawiyya. Learning to discriminate between these categories of 'inspiration' is of critical importance in spiritual development; this faculty grows stronger as the heart is progressively purified.[66]

It should be stressed here that the 'heart' *(qalb, dil)* spoken of here is conceived of as a subtle spiritual faculty rather than the physical organ to which it is in some respects analogous, and human spiritual health is inescapably linked to this faculty of subtle perception. Fundamental to the practice of *dhikr* is the teaching that it acts upon the subtle heart. In its state of primordial purity the heart sees clearly into the depths of the worlds of the Spirit; but in ordinary worldly people it is disordered and its vision curtailed by the desires and perceptions of the senses and the mind. The invocation of the heart must go beyond utterance by the tongue, although long and persistent practice is normally required before that can be attained. The subtle aspects of the heart are analyzed by Najm al-Dīn Rāzī in a chapter on *dhikr* in his *Mirṣād al-'ibād:*

> The heart has five senses, like those of the bodily frame. Just as the soundness of the bodily frame consists in the health of its five senses whereby it perceives all the manifest world, the same applies to the heart. When healthy, the heart perceives with its five senses the whole of the unseen world—essences and spiritual realities. The heart has an eye with which it enjoys visions of the Unseen; an ear with which it listens to the speech of the inhabitants of the Unseen, and the Speech of God; nostrils with which it smells the perfumes of the Unseen; and a palate whereon it perceives the taste of love, the sweetness of faith, and the savour of gnosis. Just as the sense of touch is distributed between all parts of the body, that through all of them it may gain benefit from tactile objects, so too the intelligence is present throughout the heart, that it may in its entirety derive benefit from all intelligibilia through the intelligence.[67]

66. *Fawā'iḥ,* ed. Meier, p. 11.
67. *Mirṣād,* p. 20; cf. *The Path of God's Bondsmen,* transl. Algar, pp. 205-6.

> After that, thanks to the light of *dhikr* and the negation of thought-impulses, the heart finds deliverance from the turbulence of the lower soul and of Satan. It must concern itself with its own states and gain for itself the taste of *dhikr.* [The heart] takes over the *dhikr* from the tongue, and busies itself with the invocation. The attribute of *dhikr* will begin removing from the heart all the obscurity and veils that had reached and taken root in it owing to the workings of the Devil and the lower soul. As the darkness and the veils lessen, the light of *dhikr* will shine on the jewel of the heart, and quaking and fear will appear in the heart: "The believers are they alone whose hearts quake when God is mentioned."[68] Later on, when the heart is watered with *dhikr,* the hardness all departs from it and softness and gentleness appear: "Then are their hearts and skins softened unto the remembrance of God."[69]

Najm al-Dīn Rāzī goes on to explain how further progression leads to the establishment of the *dhikr* in the *sirr* or innermost secret part of the heart. Once thoughts of and attachments to created things are eliminated, "the Sultan of Divine Love" descends to subdue any remaining unruly elements in the soul, to purify "the City of the Heart," and install the virtues therein definitively. The heart now finds true joy, and God's Command holds sway over every attribute of the seeker's personality and every action of his limbs, in accordance with the Sacred Tradition quoted above.[70]

Rāzī proceeds to describe the five aspects or senses of the subtle heart. These are the breast *(ṣadr),* which is the locus of submission or Islam, or of its opposite; the heart *(qalb),* which is the seat of true faith *(imān),* intellect, and vision; the pericardium *(shaghaf),* the source of love and mercy towards mankind; the *fu'ād,* or locus of gnosis and mystical witnessing; the grain of the heart *(ḥabbat al-qalb),* source of love for the Divine Presence; and finally the dark core *(suwaydā),* receptive to revelations of the Unseen and of God-given esoteric knowledge *('ilm-i ladunnī).*[71] Najm al-Dīn goes on to comment that

---

68. Koran VIII: 2.
69. Koran XXXIX: 23. *Mirṣād al-'ibād,* p. 204; cf. transl. Algar, pp. 215-6.
70. See p. 503. *Mirṣād al-'ibād,* pp. 205-9; cf. transl. Algar, pp. 216-9.
71. *Ibid.,* transl. Algar, pp. 207-10. For an exhaustive discussion of these aspects of the heart in Persian Sufism, see J. Nurbakhsh, *The Psychology of Sufism* (London: KNP 1992), pp. 71-112.

> The heart has a variety of features, and each of them holds many wonders and innumerable mysteries *(ma'ānī);* even a multitude of books expounding them could not do justice to them. Imām Muḥammad Ghazālī, may God sanctify his spirit, has composed a book on the wonders of the heart without encompassing even one-tenth of them."[72] .

VIII. TECHNIQUES AND FORMULAE OF *DHIKR*

A feature of great interest, not least to the outsider who may have heard or seen something of the Whirling Dervishes or the fire-eating fakirs or snake-teasing marabouts, is the question of the actual techniques involved in the practice of *dhikr.* Mir Valiyuddin's study of the *Contemplative Disciplines in Sufism*[73] contains much interesting detail concerning the techniques employed in a number of Sufi Orders. These include special kinds of breath control; directing the breath towards the heart or elsewhere; the visualization of letters of the Divine Name; and concentration on centres of perception. Another distinctive style of loud invocation is that of the 'saw' *('arra) dhikr,* associated mainly with the Yasawiyya *Ṭarīqa* of Central Asia but also practiced in other regions. It is so called because of the repeated guttural sounds produced by the dervishes practising it, reminiscent of a saw passing through wood. The revolving *samā'* of the Mevlevī dervishes, formalized after the period with which we are here concerned, has its origins in the practice of Jalāl al-Dīn Rūmī who often turned around and around as he composed his ecstatic yet finely controlled poetry. In the earlier literature little is said about such techniques. The facts that close supervision of *dhikr* was deemed essential and the disclosure of too much information to outsiders undesirable may help to explain this.

On one matter at least all main authorities are agreed. There are three degrees of proficiency in *dhikr.* First of all, it is uttered with the tongue; one must then establish at a deeper level, it in the heart;

---

72. Rāzī, *Mirṣād,* p. 194; *The Path of God's Bondsmen,* p. 207. Rāzī is alluding to Bk. 21 of Ghazālī's *Iḥyā',* entitled "The Wonders of the Heart *('Ajā'ib al-qalb).*"
73. Published, London: East-West Publications 1980. There is also much valuable material in A. Schimmel's superlative *Mystical Dimensions of Islam* (Chapel Hill: University of North Carolina Press 1975), pp. 167-78.

but the accomplishment to be desired is that the *dhikr* of the initiate become so firmly rooted that it continues spontaneously and constantly in the heart, on the tongue, and even—as described in *Tartīb al-sulūk,* a work attributed to Abū'l-Qāsim Qushayrī[74]—by the entire body. The idea of three ascending degrees of *dhikr* has been formulated in many variants. According to the "oldest surviving general account of Sufism,"[75] the *Kitāb al-Luma'* by Abū Naṣr al-Sarrāj:

> I heard Ibn Sālim say, when asked about *dhikr,* "*Dhikr* is of three kinds: *dhikr* with the tongue, which is a good deed rewarded tenfold; *dhikr* with the heart, which is a good deed rewarded sevenhundredfold; and *dhikr* of which the reward is beyond weighing or counting, consisting as it does of being filled with love and with modesty *(ḥayā')* because of nearness [to God]."[76]

Another early Persian Sufi and contemporary of Sarrāj, Abū Bakr al-Kalabadhī (d. ca. 385/995) from Bukhārā, in his "authoritative textbook on Sufi doctrine," the *Ta'arruf,*[77] provides another threefold doctrine of *dhikr:*

> The categories of *dhikr* are three in number. First is *dhikr* of the heart: the One Invoked *(Madhkūr)* is not forgotten, and so one practices remembrance. Second is *dhikr* of the Attributes of the One Invoked. Third comes actual contemplation *(shuhūd)* of the One Invoked, so that the invoker passes away from invoking: the Attributes of the One Invoked cause you to pass away from your own attributes, and so you pass away from invoking.[78]

A more purist view was adopted by Rashīd al-Dīn Maybudī (d. 520/1126) in his celebrated early Persian *tafsīr,* or Koran

74. F. Meier, "Qušayrī's *Tartīb as-sulūk,*" *Oriens* 16, (1963), pp. 1-39.
75. A.J. Arberry, *Sufism: An Account of the Mystics of Islam* (New York 1970), p. 67.
76. Abū Naṣr al-Sarrāj, *Kitāb al-Luma' f'l-taṣawwuf,* ed. R. A. Nicholson (London: Luzac 1914), p. 219 (Arabic text).
77. A.J. Arberry, in the introduction to his translation of this text *(The Doctrine of the Sufis,* Cambridge University Press, 1979 rpt., p. xiii), observed that "It may be said, after the *Risālah* of Qushayrī and the *Qūt al-qulūb* of Makkī, Kalābadhī's *Ta'arruf* was esteemed by the Arabs, especially the Sufis themselves, as the most valuable compendium of Ṣūfism written."
78. *Kitāb al-Ta'arruf li-madhhab ahl al-taṣawwuf,* ed. Maḥmūd Amīn al-Nawāwī (Cairo: Maktabat al-Kulliyyāt al-Azhariyya, 1388/1969), p. 126.

commentary, *Kashf al-asrār*. Commenting on Koran III: 190-1 (cited above, p. 501), Maybudī emphasizes the connection between profundity of *dhikr* and purity of intention and spiritual state—and like Sarrāj and Kalābādhī before him, also itemizes his views in a ternary form:

> There are three types of invokers. One invokes God with his tongue while his heart is heedless: such is the invocation of the 'wrongdoer' *(ẓālim)*, who knows nothing of the invocation *(dhikr)* or the One Invoked *(Madhkūr)*. Another invokes Him with his tongue while his heart is attentive *(ḥāḍir)*: such is the *dhikr* of the 'frugal' *(muqtaṣid)* and the state of the 'hireling', who seeks a reward but whose seeking is excusable. The third type invokes God with his heart; his heart is filled with God, and his tongue utters no invocation: "He who knows God, his tongue flags." Such is the *dhikr* of the "foremost."[79] His tongue has entered the mystery *(sirr)* of the *dhikr;* the *dhikr* is in the mystery of the One Invoked *(Madhkūr)*, his heart is in the mystery of Love; Love is in the mystery of Light: his Spirit *(jān)* is in the mystery of direct vision [of the Unseen] *('iyān);* and direct vision is far from being describable![80]

However, as in every other aspect of Islamic piety, observance of the propriety and correct etiquette *(adab)* is a necessary condition for the practice of the *dhikr,* as is illustrated by the more technical account of invocation given a century later by Najm al-Dīn Rāzī:

> Know that invocation performed without regard to its customs and traditions is of no great benefit: the arrangement, customs and conditions of *dhikr* must first be upheld... Before performing *dhikr,* one should if possible make a major ablution *(ghusl)*, and otherwise the minor *(wuḍū)*, and put on clean clothes in accordance with the Sunna. He should prepare an empty, clean, dark chamber *(khāna);* if he burns some fragrance that also is best. Then one should sit cross-legged, facing the *qibla* [direction of the Holy Ka'ba]...
>
> While performing *dhikr,* [the disciple] should put his hands on his thighs, concentrate his heart, close his eyes, and then, with total reverence, begin to utter the formula *Lā ilāha illā 'llāh* ['No

79. *Sābiq:* see Koran LVI: 10.
80. Maybudī, *Kashf al-asrār wa 'uddat al-abrār,* edited by 'Alī Aṣghar Ḥikmat, 10 vols. (Tehran: Intishārāt-i Dānishgāhī 1331-39 A.Hsh./1952-60), II, p. 396.

> god but God'] with all his might. He must bring the words *Lā ilāha* up from the navel and direct the words *illā 'llāh* down to the heart in such a way that the effect and power of the invocation reach all parts of his body. He is not to raise his voice, however, but must keep it as hidden and as low as he can. God has commanded [Koran VII: 204]: "Remember [or 'Invoke'] your Lord inwardly in humility and fear, without making your speech audible."
>
> [The initiate] is to invoke in this way, vigorously and without cease, meditating on the meaning of the *dhikr* in his heart. In accordance with the meaning of *Lā ilāha* he must negate any passing thought that may enter his heart. By doing so he says, in effect, "I desire nothing, seek nothing, and have no aim or love. 'but God *(illā 'llāh)*." Having negated all passing thoughts with *Lā ilāha,* he affirms the Mighty Presence to be his one and only goal, purpose and Beloved. Negating all stray thoughts with *Lā ilāha,* he affirms the Presence of Divine Majesty as his only goal, purpose and Beloved with *illā 'llāh.*[81]

As the above quotation demonstrates, formulae employed in invocation include the Divine Names, especially the Name 'Allah'; and the phrase *Lā ilāha illā 'llāh* (There is no god but God). Rūmī is reported to have said, "Our *dhikr* is 'Allāh! Allāh! Allāh!' We are Allāhīs."[82] A vivid account of the method and power of invoking this particular divine Name is found in the biography of Abū Sa'īd ibn Abī'l-Khayr. As a young student Abū Sa'īd lived at the town of Sarakhs, where he encountered a venerable Sufi named Abū'l-Faḍl. On their first meeting, he taught Abū Sa'īd about *dhikr* using the Divine Name:

> "Abū Sa'īd!" he said, "all the hundred and twenty-four thousand prophets were sent to preach one word. They bade the people say 'Allah' and devote themselves to Him. Those who heard this word with the ear alone, let it go out by the other ear; but those who heard it with their souls imprinted it on their souls and repeated it until it penetrated their hearts and souls, and their whole being became this word. They were made independent of the

81. Najm al-Dīn Rāzī, *Mirṣād al-'ibād,* ed. Riyāḥī, pp. 271-3; cf. Algar, *The Path of God's Bondsmen,* pp. 271-2.
82. Aḥmad Aflākī, *Manāqib al-'ārifīn,* ed. T. Yazıcı, 2 vols. (Ankara: Türk Tarih Kurumu 1957).

> pronunciation of the word, they were released from the sound and the letters. Having understood the spir-itual meaning of this word, they became so absorbed in it that they were no more conscious of their own nonexistence."[83]

The account continues with the young Abū Sa'īd finding himself wholly in the grip of what the Shaykh had said. In the morning he attended a lecture on scriptural exegesis *(tafsīr)* in which the text commented upon was Koran VI: 91: "Say 'Allah!' then leave them plunging in their idle talk." Hearing these words, Abū Sa'īd entered a mystical state. His teacher noticed this and asked the reason. Learning that Abū Sa'īd had been with Shaykh Abū'l-Faḍl, he told Abū Sa'īd: "It is not lawful for you to come back from that subject (meaning Sufism) to this discourse."

Completely bewildered, Abū Sa'īd returned to the *Khānaqāh* of Abū'l-Faḍl, who remarked in verse: *"Mastak shuda'ī hamī nadānī pas u pīsh,"* meaning, "Thou art drunk, poor youth! Thou know'st not head from tail." The Shaykh ordered Abū Sa'īd, "Come in and sit down. Devote yourself entirely to this Word, for this Word has much work to perform on you." He then initiated him into the *dhikr.* After some days Abū Sa'īd was sent away again. Returning to his home town of Mayhana, he forsook his studies and concentrated for seven years on the continuous *dhikr:* "Allah! Allah! Allah!" According to Abū Sa'īd's biography,

> Whenever drowsiness or inattention arising from the weakness of human nature came over me, a soldier with a fiery spear—the most terrible and alarming figure that can possibly be imagined—appeared in front of the niche *[miḥrāb]* and shouted at me, saying "O Abū Sa'īd, say Allah!" The dread of that apparition used to keep me burning and trembling for whole days and nights, so that I did not again fall asleep or become inattentive; and at last every atom of me began to cry aloud, "Allah! Allah! Allah!"[84]

***

83. Muḥammad ibn Munawwar Mayhanī, *Asrār al-tawḥīd fī maqāmāt al-Shaykh Abī Sa'īd,* ed. V.A. Zhukovskii (St. Petersburg 1899), pp. 23-4; translation here from R.A. Nicholson, *Studies in Islamic Mysticism,* p. 7.
84. Muḥammad ibn Munawwar, *op. cit.,* ed. V.A. Zhukovskii; translation by Nicholson, *Studies,* pp. 8-9.

Aside from the spiritual practices relating to *dhikr* which we have examined above, contemplative disciplines in Sufism may also be discussed under three other headings: *murāqaba* (vigilance, watchfulness), *muḥāsaba* (self-examination) and *fikr,* or *tafakkur* (meditation).

IX. CONTEMPLATIVE VIGILANCE: *MURĀQABA*

Constant vigilance, in outer life and while performing *dhikr* and other acts of worship, is known as *murāqaba* (contemplative watchfulness). Just as God watches over Man, one of His Names being 'The Watchful' *(al-Raqīb:* see Koran IV: 1; XXX: 52), so the seeker on the Path must not only remember that God sees him at every moment but also guard his own heart against distractions and evil thoughts. Only when free from distractions can the mind gain tranquillity and the heart be illumined. Concerning the effect of *murāqaba* upon the mind, Ibrāhīm ibn Adham (d. ca. 161/778), a great early Persian Sufi of Central Asia, commented, "Vigilance is the *ḥajj* of Reason *(al-murāqaba ḥajj al-'aql).*"[85] True *murāqaba* marks the highest level of self-mastery if it can be maintained.[86] As the *Sharī'a* defines it, *murāqaba* signifies control over external faculties *(jawāriḥ);* over the internal faculties: that is, one's state of the soul (dispelling evil thoughts and retaining concentration on the Divine Presence); and lastly, control over the innermost part of the heart, wherein "No god but God" is to be realized as an illumination untainted by the least concern for anything other than the Beloved One. It will be noticed that these three elements of *murāqaba* resemble the three levels of *dhikr* referred to earlier.

In his *Risāla,* one of the most influential of all early Sufi texts, Abū'l-Qāsim Qushayrī (d. 465/1072) defines *murāqaba* in terms of the *Ḥadīth* wherein Gabriel asked the Prophet the meaning of the terms 'Submission', 'Faith' and 'Excellence' *(Islām, Imān, Iḥsān).* The reply was that *Iḥsān* means that you worship God as though you

85. Abū Nu'aym al-Iṣfahānī, *Ḥilyat al-awliyā';* quoted by Louis Massignon, *Essai sur les origines du lexique de la mystique musumane* (Paris: Vrin 1968, 2nd ed.), p. 256.
86. Compare Hujwīrī on *dhikr* as a spiritual station: see p. 505 above.

see Him, and if you do not see Him yet He sees you.[87] Qushayrī comments as follows:

> This is an allusion to *al-murāqaba,* for *murāqaba* is the servant's knowledge of his Lord's (be He glorified) watchfulness of him. Such knowledge is extended through *murāqaba* (watchful contemplation) of his Lord. This is the very root of all good for [the seeker]. He can scarcely attain this degree until he has perfected *muḥāsaba* (calling himself to account). When he has called his soul to account for what is in the past and has rectified his state in the present time, and has held fast to the Way of Truth, and has made excellent the heart's vision between himself and his Lord, and maintained each breath [in contact] with God Most High, and has contemplated God in all his states—then [the seeker] knows that He, Most Glorious, is the Watcher over him. ...Whoever is heedless or unaware of all these matters is unable even to begin the journey [to Union with God], let alone witness the mysteries *(ḥaqā'iq)* through nearness to Him.[88]

In this passage Qushayrī explains *murāqaba* as a mutual 'keeping watch' between the Creator and the seeker on the Sufi Path. As mentioned above (cf. p. 535), one of the Divine Names mentioned in the Koran is *al-Raqīb,* the 'All-Vigilant', which means that one who seeks to realize this Name must in turn, keep watch over their heart, looking for the signs of God's will and wisdom in what transpires at every moment and how it affects the heart. To acquire and maintain such clarity of awareness requires the constant practice of *dhikr.* Such vigilance, according to the masters of Sufism, is a powerful method of achieving closeness *(qurb)* to God. A detailed section on principles of *murāqaba* is to be found in Quṭb al-Dīn 'Abbādī's (d. 547/1152) Persian treatise on Sufi methodology entitled *al-Taṣfiya fī aḥwāl al-mutaṣawwifa.*[89]

---

87. For this renowned Tradition, see e.g. Muslim, *Saḥīḥ, Īmān,* 1.
88. Qushayrī, *al-Risālat al-Qushayriyya,* ed. 'Abd al-Ḥalīm Maḥmūd and Maḥmūd ibn al-Sharīf (Cairo: Dār al-Kutūb al-Ḥadītha, n.d.), vol. 1, pp. 463-4. Cf. B.R. von Schlegell (trans.), *Principles of Sufism by al-Qushayri* (Berkeley: Mizan 1990), p. 158.
89. 'Abbādī, *al-Taṣfiya fī aḥwāl al-mutaṣawwifa (Ṣūfī-nāma),* ed. Ghulāmḥusayn Yūsifī (Tehran: Bunyād-i Farhang-i Īrān, 1347/1968), pp. 142 -4. This chapter on *murāqaba* is complemented by the next section of the work, the subject of which is modesty *(ḥayā).*

Vigilance in discriminating between thought-impulses *(khawāṭir)* is deemed by a number of authorities to be one of the most essential weapons in the armoury of the Sufi. *Khawāṭir* arising during the practice of invocation or meditation can provide important indications to the state of the disciple's spiritual being. Najm al-Dīn Kubrā, for example, describes them as being of four kinds, according to their origin: diabolic *(shayṭānī),* from the soul *(nafsānī),* angelic *(malakī)* and Divine *(raḥmānī).* The science of discernment between these different thought-impulses is a branch of the subtle knowledge which the Shaykhs seek to inculcate, but which by its nature can be taught only through general rules and indications.[90]

Shaykh 'Umar Suhrawardī in his *'Awārif al-ma'ārif*—perhaps the most celebrated manual of Sufi practice in the mediæval period—devotes an entire chapter to the question of thought-impulses, their origin and significance, and the subtle science of their diagnosis.[91] Suhrawardī explains that rigorous self-discipline is an indispensable condition for obtaining the power of discrimination between good and bad impulses. The desire of the untrained *nafs* for sensual and psychic gratification and for dignity among people deprives it of the ability to distinguish with certainty between angelic and satanic promptings.

> In Basra I heard Shaykh Abū Muḥammad ibn 'Abdullāh al-Baṣrī say, "There are four types of thought-impulse: the impulse from the lower soul, the impulse from God (or 'Truth' *Ḥaqq),* the impulse from Satan, and the impulse from an angel. Those emanating from the soul can be sensed within the heart itself *(fī arḍ al-qalb);* those from God, above the heart; those from an angel, to the right of the heart; and those from Satan, to the left of the heart."[92]
>
> However, what the Shaykh said only holds good for one who has dissolved his lower soul by means of immediate awareness of God *(al-taqwā)* and asceticism and purified his being, maintaining absolute correctness in his outward and inward comportment. His heart then will be like a finely polished mirror: Satan cannot approach it from any direction without being seen by it, whereas

90. Concerning the basic categories of *khāṭir,* see Kubrā, *Fawā'iḥ,* pp. 11-14. For more on this subject *per se,* see Quṭb al-Dīn 'Abbādī, *al-Taṣfiya,* pp. 143-4.
91. Chap. 57: *Fī ma'rifat al-khawāṭir wa tafṣīlihā.*
92. *'Awārif al-ma'ārif,* pp. 463-4.

when the human heart is black and tainted with rust then it cannot perceive Satan.[93]

X. *MUḤASABA* (SELF-EXAMINATION)

Muḥasaba, associated above all with the name of the ascetic master Ḥarith al-Muḥasibī of Baghdad (d. 243/857), is discussed in a number of classical treatises.[94] The concept of *muḥāsaba*—if not its use as a technical term—dates back to early Islamic times, and Sufis often quote a saying attributed to 'Alī: "Call yourselves to account before you are called to account *(Ḥāsibū anfusakum qabla an tuḥāsabū)."* Self-knowledge is both the condition and the goal of the mystical quest, as attested by the saying attributed to the Prophet—the Islamic version of the famous Delphic maxim—"One who knows himself knows his Lord *(man 'arafa nafsah fa-qad 'arafa Rabbah)."*

Already well before the time of al-Muḥāsibī, the great early Sufi ascetic Ḥasan Baṣrī reportedly said that "Reflection *(fikr)* is the mirror which shows what good and what bad there is in you."[95] Purgative aspects of inner knowledge involve rigorous and regular self-examination. Practices advocated by Sufi masters include admonishing oneself each morning and making a firm intention to spend each breath in a befitting way, for every breath will be accounted for on the Day of Resurrection. During daily life and acts of worship, one must exercise the strictest self-control.

The night time, especially the moments before retiring to sleep, is suited to the practice of *muḥāsaba;* recalling, and calling oneself to account for, each action. Perhaps the supreme example of self-accounting is the now-lost journal of the Kubrawī master Sayf al-Dīn Bākharzī, described by Yaḥyā Bākharzī in his above-mentioned treatise, *Awrād al-aḥbāb wa Fuṣūṣ al-ādāb.* In it Shaykh Sayf al-

93. *Ibid.,* pp. 462-3.
94. Concerning whom, see Margaret Smith, *An early mystic of Baghdad: a study of the life and teachings of Ḥārith b. Āsād al-Muḥāsibī, A.D. 781-857* (London: Sheldon Press 1977 reprt.).
95. Massignon, *Essai,* p. 192, quoting Ibn 'Iyāḍ as cited in Abū Nu'aym al-Iṣfahānī, *Ḥilyat al-awliyā'.* 'Abdullāh Anṣārī, in his *Manāzil al-sā'irīn,* describes true *muḥāsaba* as a spiritual station *(maqām),* closely connected with spiritual poverty *(faqr)* and annihilation of the self *(fanā').*

Dervish practising *Murāqaba.* From a sixteenth-century album; MS. Laud Or. 149, folio 6. (Courtesy of the Bodleian Library, Oxford).

Dīn recorded all the details of his life, the wrongs done him by others, the acts of worship performed by him with the intention of expiating those wrongs; and many other matters.[96]

In assessing his or her own record of intentions and deeds for the past day, the believer is also urged to call to mind at least once daily the certain and imminent prospect of death, the Resurrection, the Judgement, and the Afterlife. One should anticipate each stage of this journey to the Next World, feeling as though one were actually experiencing it in the present moment. This encourages softening of the heart, making it receptive to Divine Mercy, and lessens attachment to the vain hopes of the world. The classic treatment of this subject is found in the 'Chapter on the Remembrance of Death and the Afterlife' in the final book of Ghazālī's *Iḥyā'*, already mentioned above. The author begins with a chapter stressing the importance of remembering one's impending death regularly and frequently. This is followed by sections on the need to avoid cherishing long-term hopes *(ṭūl al-āmāl);* the pain of the pangs of death, and the emotions and states which accompany it; and the exemplary deaths of the Prophet, the Righteous Caliphs and other saintly men, together with their sayings of the subject on death and the Afterlife. The second part of the Book is devoted to Ghazālī's detailed and awe-inspiring description, based on the Koran and Prophetic Tradition, of the events which all must experience after death, from the questioning in the grave by the Angels to the Resurrection, the Gathering and Judgement, and the arrival in Paradise or Hell.

According to Ghazālī, there are two reasons for the tendency of humankind to procrastinate and to cherish long-term hopes of this world. The first is love of the world, which makes us reluctant ever to contemplate the idea that we must leave it. The second factor is ignorance—for practical purposes—of the fact that death does not come at a fixed age but may overtake us at any moment.[97]

> Upon thus having grasped that its cause is ignorance and the love of the world, one must cure oneself by destroying this cause. Ignorance is effaced by clear meditation with an aware heart, and

---

96. *Fuṣūṣ al-ādāb,* ed. Īraj Afshār, p. 8.
97. *Iḥyā',* book 40, vol. 4, p. 441.

> through hearing eloquent wisdom issuing from hearts that are pure.
>
> In case of love of the world, the cure by which it is driven from the heart is harsh, for this is a chronic illness the treatment of which sorely exercised the ancients and the moderns alike. Its treatment lies only in faith in the Last Day, and the great punishment and generous award which shall then be assigned... When one perceives the meanness of this world and the great preciousness of the next, one will despise any inclination towards worldly things; and this would be so even if one were to be given authority over the earth from East to West.[98]

Besides contemplating those of one's acquaintances who have passed away, and the circumstances of their passing, Ghazālī prescribes the contemplation of our own death, saying:

> Let man in every hour look to his limbs and his extremities. Let his thoughts dwell upon how the worms must needs devour them, and upon the fashion in which his bones shall rot away. Let him wonder whether the worms are to begin with the pupil of his right eye or his left; for there is no part of his body that shall not be food for the worm. He can do nothing for himself but to understand, and to act sincerely for the sake of God (Exalted is He!). And in like fashion, let him meditate upon that which we shall presently relate concerning the Punishment of the Grave, the Inquisition of Munkar and Nakīr, and the Congregation and Quickening, together with the terrors of the Resurrection, and the sounding of the Call on the Day of the Greatest Exposition. For it is thoughts such as these which prompt anew the remembrance of death in the heart, and summon one to make ready for it.[99]

X. *TAFAKKUR* (MEDITATION, CONTEMPLATION)

It would be wrong to suggest that among Muslims the practice of contemplation was confined to Sufis alone. To name but one example, the great exoteric scholar Fakhr al-Dīn Rāzī outlined in resounding terms the method and visionary goal of the contemplative:

> The heart's invocation of God is that a man meditates on the secrets of the things created by God Most High until each atom of

98. *Iḥyā'*, book 40, vol. 4, p. 442. Translation by T.J. Winter from *The Remembrance of Death*, p. 27.
99. *Ibid.* Translation by T.J. Winter.

> all their atoms become like a polished mirror set over against the unseen world, and when the servant of God looks with his mind's eye on created things the rays of his seeing pass from them to the world of majesty.[100]

Probably the most elaborate exposition of the doctrines of contemplative meditation *(fikr* or *tafakkur)* in Islam is found in Abū Ḥāmid Ghazālī's 'Chapter on Meditation' *(Bāb al-Tafakkur)* in the *Iḥyā'*, the main lines of which are worth summarizing here. Ghazālī begins by establishing the merit and importance of *tafakkur* by citing dicta of numerous great Muslims, including the Prophet himself and certain of his Companions. One example is related from Bishr al-Ḥāfī (d. 227/841-2), who said, "If people were to meditate on the Majesty of God (Great and Mighty is He), they would not be disobedient towards Him."

In the second part of his chapter, Ghazālī explains the true nature and the benefits of meditation. True contemplation is differentiated from ordinary thinking inasmuch as the latter always in making two observations and them drawing a conclusion from the relationship between them. Ghazālī proceeds to offer a painstaking analysis of the various modes of meditation and reflection, revealing the many rich varieties of this discipline. He distinguishes between *tafakkur* (reflection, meditation, contemplation), *i'tibār* (considering, learning lessons), *tadhakkur* (mindfulness, recalling), *naẓar* (speculation or mental examination), *ta'ammul* (reflection), and *tadabbur* (pondering).[101] The nature and benefits of each form of contemplation is analyzed with an exactitude characteristic of the author. *Tadabbur, ta'ammul,* and *tafakkur,* says Ghazālī, are almost synonymous terms. *Tadhakkur, i'tibār,* and *naẓar,* on the other hand, all connote a single process—that of passing on from two related observations to arrive at a third cognition—but with different nuances. This process of extending one's cognition and understanding through disciplined and regular meditation ought to be a continual one, limited only by the length of one's life-span.[102]

---

100. Fakhr al-Dīn Rāzī, *Lawāmi' al-bayyināt,* p. 29; translated by Constance Padwick in her *Muslim Devotions* (London: SPCK 1961), p. 245.
101. *Iḥyā', Bāb al-Tafakkur,* vol. 4, p. 412.
102. *Ibid.*

The third part of the *Kitāb al-tafakkur* discusses which subjects are appropriate and licit for mental reflection. These are divided by the author into two categories. The first comprises human qualities and their corresponding actions—that is, acts of obedience or of disobedience to the creator: on the one hand those which lead to perdition, and on the other, those which bring salvation and reward in the Afterlife. The second category refers to meditation upon God and His creation. Meditation upon the Essence *(Dhāt)* of God was forbidden by the Prophet, for the mind attempting to reach It can never succeed but can easily be led into madness or heresy. The Divine Names and Attributes, however, are fertile ground for the practice of contemplation, as are the manifestations of God's Wisdom and creative Power within the human soul and in the created world around us. In an eloquent passage the author describes the wisdom inherent in numerous facets of Nature and in the human form and soul, amply demonstrating that if Man fails to utilize his innate ability to learn from the signs that surround him this cannot be blamed upon any shortage of scope or material for contemplation.

> There exists no creature great or small which does not contain innumerable wonders! Do you think that the spider learned its art by itself? Or that it brought itself into existence; or that a human being did so, or taught it? Or that it could have had no guide or teacher? Can any person endowed with perception doubt that that creature is tiny, weak and powerless? But if the elephant, a great creature whose strength is manifest, is incapable of doing the same [as the spider does], how can that feeble creature do it? Is not that [spider], with its form and figure, its movements, its self-direction, and its marvelous handiwork, testimony to its own Omniscient Maker, the Almighty and All-Wise Creator? ...And so this chapter might continue without end, the creatures being innumerable in their forms, ways and character.[103]

Ghazālī also provides extensive analysis of the processes and benefits of *fikr* in its various modalities. He relates the various forms of meditation as effect and, especially, as cause of *dhikr* in the sense of mindful remembrance (his discussion of the four meanings of the

103. *Iḥyā'*, IV, p. 426.

term *dhikr* is especially significant in this respect). His central argument is that true *tafakkur* brings to the heart a knowledge which transforms it and heightens the consciousness and spiritualizes the action of the seeker. In this sense Ghazālī argues—at least for the rhetorical purposes of this section of the *Iḥyā'*—that meditation or reflection *(fikr)* is of still greater benefit than invocation *(dhikr)*.

> The fruits of meditation, then, consist of varieties of knowledge, states and actions. The fruit specific to each, however, is nothing other than a form of knowledge. When knowledge is acquired within the heart, the state of the heart is altered. When the heart's state changes, the actions of the bodily members change. Thus action follows spiritual state, states follow knowledge, and knowledge follows meditation. Meditation is therefore the beginning of and the key to all action.
>
> What we have said thus far will show you how excellent a thing is meditation *(tafakkur)* and how it surpasses invocation *(dhikr)* and remembrance *(tadhakkur)*. For reflection *(fikr)* is *dhikr* with something else added. *Dhikr,* for its part, is better than any physical action: if an action be good, it is so by virtue of the *dhikr* accompanying it. Consequently, meditation is better than any other deed.
>
> Should you wish to understand how meditation transforms one's state, then take for example what was stated earlier about the Afterlife. Given that meditation upon it brings us the knowledge that the Afterlife is preferable [to the life of this world], once such knowledge is firmly rooted in our hearts as a matter of certainty, our hearts change, turning in longing for the Life Beyond and renunciation of worldly things. That is exactly what we mean by the term 'state'...
>
> ...In this connection five separate stages can be distinguished. First: remembrance or invocation *(tadhakkur)*, which consists in bringing to mind two cognitions. Second: meditation or reflection *(tafakkur),* which is the search for the cognition which one seeks to obtain from the two concepts already in mind. Third: obtaining the desired cognition, and the heart's illumination by it. Fourth: a change in the heart from its former state, by virtue of the illumination attained. Fifth: service performed for the heart by the bodily members in conformity with the new state prevailing within it.[104]

One of the most eloquent authorities on meditation among the

---

104. *Iḥyā',* vol. 4, pp. 412-3.

early Persian Sufis, exposing its dangers and expousing its benefits, is the Khurāsānian Shaykh Aḥmad-i Jām (d. 535-6/1141-2). In one of his treatises entitled *Ḥadīqat al-ḥaqīqa* (which is not to be confused with Sanā'ī's great poem of the same name),a chapter *(Faṣl* 6: 'On Invocation *[dhikr]* and meditation *[tafakkur]'*) is dedicated to the relationship between *dhikr* and *fikr.* Some extracts serve to illustrate a distinctive standpoint on the cautious side as regards the relationship between invocation and meditation.[105]

> We now come to the question of *fikr, dhikr* and heart-discernment *(firāsat),* and their respective origins and the nature of imagination *(khiyāl).* For those in the material realm *('ālam-i arkān), dhikr* is preferable *(faḍiltar)* to *fikr.* 'Invocation is the provision of the lover in his search for the Beloved'. Whoever lives in the spiritual realm *('ālam-i bāṭin)* and has knowledge of the heart, *fikr* is better for him than *dhikr,* for 'Reflection is the heart's guard against drowning in the sea of forgetfulness'.
>
> In the material world, *dhikr* can assume forms—since *dhikr* is on the tongue and the tongue is a material entity. *Fikr,* on the other hand, does not coalesce in forms; *fikr* is in the heart, and he [the seeker still in the material world] has not attained to the heart. It is better for him to perform *dhikr.* It is not appropriate, at this stage, for him to perform *fikr* as a [regular] imposition *(ba-takalluf),* for the heart has yet to be illumined by the lights of contemplating the Spiritual World. He is not yet free from the bonds and prison of the lower self, the lower world, desire, and Satan; nor has love of rank and wealth removed itself from his vision *(dīda).* For the seeker to practice contemplation at this stage would be like a man setting out on a dark, cloudy night, on a route unknown and unfamiliar. However far he might go, it would be as though he had not gone at all *(na-rafta buwad).* It would be a rare event if he went aright, and since "there is no rule governing the exception," he may get lost in this manner. He will not be able to find the road unless he endures much suffering. Such a journey is better not made at all.
>
> Know also that his meditation will not serve to open his heart, it being neither the time nor the place for that. To be occupied with *dhikr* is more beneficial for him, since *dhikr* softens the heart,

105. A different reason sometimes given for preferring *dhikr* is that while *fikr* is a human attribute, *dhikr* is also attributable to God: see for example 'Abd al-Raḥmān Sulamī's reply to Abū 'Alī Daqqāq, as quoted in Maybudī's *Kashf al-asrār,* vol. 4, p. 396.

> illumines the eye of the heart, and unlocks the heart's contemplation *(fikr):* "Invocation lights the way to happiness and opens the way to mastery." And He knows best. As God Most High has said, "Enter houses by their doors." [Koran II: 189] Invocation with the tongue is the key that opens the door to heart's meditation; should one lose the key, the door will never be opened. And all success is from God."
>
> Invocation is to the heart what fruit is to the tree. To expect fruit from the tree before it has been watered, grown verdant and come into leaf is a mistake; [the fruit] will not come. That is not the season for fruit, but for tending *('imārat)* the tree and for digging out and keeping away weeds, thorns and brushwood from around it, and for awaiting the wind of auspicious fortune *(sa'ādat)* and the sun of Divine Grace *('ināyat).* Then the tree may grow sappy and fresh, and put forth leaves and blossom. Once the tree has become so, its natural production of fruit will function aright and in due season. Confirmation of this in the Book of God Almighty. As He says, "And those who strive for Us, We shall surely guide upon Our Ways." [XXIX: 69] "Striving" *(mujāhada)* is invocation with the tongue, and "guidance upon the Way" is the opening up of meditation to the heart.[106]

Practised under the proper conditions and guidance, contemplation brings an abundant spiritual harvest. Tranquillity is engendered in the heart, and the lights of gnosis may appear through Divine Grace. Shaykh Aḥmad-i Jām's description of this realization is eloquent. Having explained (see above, section IX) that *fikr* is for the adept rather than the novice, he goes on to say that one of the fruits of meditation is *firāsat,* 'intuition' or 'heart-discernment', which arises in the *fu'ād,* the core of the heart. This *firāsat,* he says, is one of God's emissaries *(rasūlān-i Ḥaqq).*

> This emissary never leaves empty the hands of any believing servant of God who practices meditation *(tafakkur),* but constantly brings gifts and presents: now he brings the Light of Certainty, now Thankfulness, now the Light of Endurance, now the Light of hearing the arcane Mysteries, now the Light of beholding Divine Effulgences, now the Unveiling of that which is shrouded in mystery...now the gift of Love, now Intimacy with the Holy Presence

---

106. Aḥmad-i Jām, *Ḥadīqat al-ḥaqīqa,* ed. Muḥammad 'Alī Muwaḥḥid (Tehran 1343 A.Hsh./1964), pp. 148-9.

> *(uns-i quds).* When he reaches this point, he is emancipated from bondage to himself and the world *(khalq)* and becomes absorbed *(mashghūl)* with the signs of God's Unicity."[107]

XII. CONCLUSION

Despite the modest amount of material cited in this essay it can be seen that the spiritual and literary heritage of the early Persian Sufis contains a rich treasury of wisdom and practical instruction with regard to the practices of invocation, remembrance, and contemplation. It has emerged also that invocation and meditation, correctly understood and performed, are not in conflict but rather complement and enhance one another.

> *It is the traveller's Contemplation that journeys on the Path—*
> *Contemplation that has benefited from his Invocation.*[108]

> *This much have we said; go and think out* (fikr) *the rest.*
> *If thought freezes up, then go and perform* dhikr.
> Dhikr *endows meditation with lively movement:*
> *when* fikr *is frozen make* dhikr *the sun to melt it.*[109]

Even a master like Mawlānā Rūmī, whose verse is full of exhortations to leave thought behind, clearly holds the same viewpoint. His strictures against reflection *(fikr)* and rumination *(andīsha)* are directed against excessive preoccupation with worldly matters and anxieties, and against rationalism, not against true and objective Reason, for, as Rūmī puts it, "The partial intellect has given [the Universal] Intellect a bad name"[110] Elsewhere in the *Mathnawī,* he presents his opinion about the complementariness of *dhikr* and *fikr,* saying of the Sufis that

> *They polish their breasts with invocation and meditation,*
> *That the mirror of the heart may receive images of virginal purity [from the Unseen World].*[111]

---

107. *Ḥadīqat al-ḥaqīqa,* pp. 150-1.
108. 'Aṭṭār, *Muṣībat-nāma.* Cited by H. Ritter, *Das Meer der Seele* (Leiden: Brill 1970), p. 21.
109. Rūmī, *Mathnawī-yi ma'nawī,* ed. R.A. Nicholson, 8 vols. (London: E.J.W. Gibb Memorial Series, n.s. 4, 1925-40), *Daftar* VI: 1475-6.
110. *'Aql-i juz'ī 'aql-rā badnām kard. Ibid., Daftar* V: 463.
111. *Mathnawī, Daftar* I: 3154.

The magisterial authority of the great Sufis is frequently combined with beauty of expression in a literature of which it is likely that important texts still await discovery and/or publication, let alone exploration. The few passages quoted in this essay serve to illustrate in some measure the range and profundity of the early Persian Sufis' teachings on the contemplative disciplines.

We have heard from Sufis who attained exalted degrees of realization. It would be a mistake, however, to think that it is a case of 'all or nothing'. Provided the conditions of *dhikr* are met, the sincere soul may hope to gain great benefit even if unable to follow the Path to its heights. And given that the practices of invocation and contemplation are by no means confined to the Sufis—or to the mystics of any one religion—the possibility of some benefit exists for all who seek inner peace. As Mawlānā Jalāl al-Dīn Rūmī says:

> Never be without the remembrance *(yād)* of Him, for His remembrance gives strength and wings to the bird of the Spirit. If that purpose *(maqṣūd)* of yours is fully realized, that is "Light upon Light" (Koran XXIV: 35). But at the very least, by practising God's remembrance your inner being *(bāṭin)* will be illumined little by little and you will achieve some measure of detachment *(inqiṭā'ī)* from the world.[112]

Rūmī's concept of mindfulness expressed above *(yād* being the Persian word for *dhikr),* can be understood as embracing all the contemplative disciplines discussed in this essay. Let us conclude with two verses of Farīd al-Dīn 'Aṭṭār, concerning the place that *dhikr* should occupy in the alchemy of spiritual life.

> *Your soul must have a love that's good and hot;*
> dhikr *with a tongue that's moistened, sleek and soft;*
> *you need dry piety, from fear and faith,*
> *and a chill sigh from stone-cold Certainty.*[113]

---

112. Rūmī, *Fīhi mā fīhi,* ed. Badī' al-Zamān Furūzānfar (Tehran 1348 A.Hsh./1969, 2nd ed.), p. 175.

113. Farīd al-Dīn 'Aṭṭār, *Muṣībat-nāma,* ed. Nūrānī Wiṣāl (Tehran 1338 A.Hsh./ 1959), p. 11. Cf. A. Schimmel, *Mystical Dimensions of Islam* (Chapel Hill, N.C. 1975), p. 168.

VII

Chivalry and Early Persian Sufism

Muhammad Ja'far Mahjub

The term 'chivalry' (in Persian *jawānmardī;* in Arabic *futuwwa)* has the overall connotation of being a pleasing trait of character, a positive quality of the human personality—such as honesty, candour and purity of mind. Indeed, chivalry can be categorized as one of the virtues, but with one important difference: which is that chivalry is not simply a single virtue, but constitutes a whole collection of praiseworthy moral qualities. Hence, while there is no difficulty in defining the meaning of such virtues as 'courage' or 'honesty', many people are immediately at a loss to define which of the virtues chivalry actually constitutes and are unable to give a comprehensive definition of chivalry. Even if we suggest that chivalry *(futuwwa)* is an assemblage of pleasing traits of human character, viewing it, for example, as an aggregate of virtues such as honesty, generosity, courage, modesty, and trustworthiness, we only touch on one of the meanings of this term: its outer, literal significance and not the deeper idiomatic sense of the word. By way of illustration consider the following example.

Literally, the word 'Sufism' *(taṣawwuf)* means the wearing of woolen garments. If we were to insist on applying the literal definition of the term, we can undoubtedly say that anyone who clothes himself or herself in woolen garments without any intervening underclothing is to be called a 'Sufi' (=wearer of wool). However, does this definition have any meaningful relation to what we consider to be the ideals and realities of the path of Sufism? Obviously not. The evident reason for and explanation of this phenomenon is the fact that each word *(lafẓ)* has one or several senses *(ma'ānī)* which are supposed to communicate its meaning. Thus, for example the term 'bread' is meant to signify a certain kind of food made of flour. However, with the passage of time and the expansion of the scientific and intellectual horizons of mankind, to the original meaning of certain words additional meanings were gradually added. Thus, the word 'living' came to signify 'making a living' and, by extension, 'income' – while the term 'bread' extended its significance to encompass the idea of one's 'daily bread' or sustenance. Such extended connotations of words came to be called their 'metaphorical' or 'figurative' meanings, and if this particular connotation was applied to a certain art or science then it was termed its 'technical' meaning. Now, the situation is the same today when we employ the words 'Sufism' or 'chivalry'. Today we do not use these words with their literal meaning in mind but rather with a special 'technical' sense which has been developed over the many centuries of the evolution of Persian culture—perhaps long before the appearance of Islam in that land—during which these two traditions had their own particular patrons and supporting organizations interested in fostering their development among the Persian people.

Sufism and chivalry have many characteristics in common, and have never been, in fact, totally separate from one another. Thus Ḥusayn Wā'iẓ Kāshifī, the author of the 'The Royal Book of Chivalry' *(Futuwwat-nāma-yi sulṭānī),* the largest text on chivalry in Islamdom, justly states that, "The science of chivalry is a branch of the science of Sufism."[1] Just as the principles and practices of Sufism have undergone many changes and transformations throughout its long history, and various masters have added, according to their own taste and understanding, new rules to its method and amplified the scope of its etiquette to meet the changing needs of their own disciples and times —by the same token, the tradition of chivalry has also experienced significant alteration over the course of centuries down to the present day, when, due to the social upheavals of the contemporary world, it has now totally disappeared as a living

1. *Futuwwat-nāma-yi sulṭānī,* edited by M.J. Maḥjūb (Tehran: Bunyād-i Farhang-i Īrān 1350 A.Hsh./1972), p. 7.

tradition!

In coining a comprehensive definition of chivalry we also encounter the same difficulty which we did in defining Sufism. Just as there are a multitude of definitions of Sufism in Islamic mystical texts, the same goes for chivalry. Authors of Sufi treatises, composers of tracts on *futuwwa,* romancers and storytellers all manage to furnish us with an amazing variety of definitions of chivalry, each of which significantly differs in its conception and interpretation of the subject. Shaykh Abū ʻAbdullāh Muḥammad ibn Abī'l-Makārim, otherwise known as Ibn Miʻmār Ḥanbalī Baghdādī, the author of the oldest text on chivalry: the 'Book of Chivalry' *(Kitāb al-futuwwa),* while essaying a definition of the subject, comments:

> In the Sunna of the Prophet there are certain traditions concerning *futuwwa* to be found. The most select definition of the subject is that given by Imam Jaʻfar Ṣādiq [d. 148/765] which he related on the authority of his father, and the latter from his ancestor. [According to this Tradition, it is said that] the Prophet declared that, "The chevaliers *(jawānmardān)* of my community have ten characteristics." "O Prophet of God," they asked, "what are these characteristics?" He pronounced, "Honesty *(rāst-gū'ī),* faithfulness to their word *(wafā ba- 'ahd),* trustworthiness *(idā-yi amānat),* abandoning lying *(tark-i durūgh-gū'ī),* being charitable to orphans *(bakhshūdan bar yatīm),* assisting the poor and needy *(dastgīrī-yi sā'il),* giving away one's income *(bakhshūdan ānchih rasīda-ast),* great benevolence *(bisyārī-yi iḥsān),* hospitality—but foremost of all these is modesty *(ḥayā).*[2]

This quotation is especially important insofar as it represents the testimony of a member of the Ḥanbalite school – thus authentic from the standpoint of Sunnite legality and acceptable to the majority of Muslims. Asked to give his view of chivalry, it is related that Ḥasan Baṣrī said:

> The entire meaning of chivalry *(futuwwa)* is summed up in the following verse of the Koran: "Surely God bids to justice and

2. Ibn Miʻmār Ḥanbalī Baghdādī, *Kitāb al-futuwwa* (Baghdad: Maktabat al-Muthannā 1985), pp. 132-33. (The above translation is from Prof. Mahjub's Persian text, not Ibn Miʻmār's Arabic original. –TRANS.)

> good-doing and giving to kinsmen; and He forbids indecency, dishonour, and insolence, admonishing you, so that haply you will remember." [XVI: 90][3]

Definitions such as these, however, are innumerable, and mention of all or even a portion of them is obviously beyond the scope of the present study. Such definitions, for instance, abound in Abū 'Abd al-Raḥmān Sulamī's (d. 412/1021) *Book of Sufi Chivalry (Kitāb al-futuwwat al-ṣūfiyya)*[4] as well as in his *Ṭabaqāt al-ṣūfiyya*, not to mention *al-Risāla al-Qushayriyya* of Abū'l-Qāsim al-Qushayrī (d. 465/1072). Examining these definitions as they occur in such manuals leads one to the conclusion that chivalry from the very beginning had developed as a kind of sub-group of mainstream Sufism. It would often be said, for example, in describing the manner or personality of some eminent Sufi, that "among the Sufis, he followed the most chivalrous discipline," or "he was endowed with perfect chivalry." Just as the Sufis traced their line of initiatic affiliation by way of their 'dervish cassock' *(khirqa)*, handed down from master to disciple in successive generations, this becoming their connecting 'chain' *(silsila)* of mystical affiliation, the members of the fraternities of chivalry also adduced documents to prove their adherence to lines of chivalric Orders, and wore special attire, with their own special breeches *(sarāwīl)*, drawers *(tunbān)* and robes *(kiswat)*, to distinguish themselves from others. All these rites and lines of affiliation were traced, without exception, back to the Prophet's son-in-law, 'Alī ibn Abī Ṭālib, establishing him as the supreme source of the virtues of *futuwwa*.

In some treatises, chivalry is considered as an integral part of Sufism. In one of these texts the 'breeches' of the chevaliers and the 'crown' *(tāj)* and 'cassock' and of the Sufi are compared and described:

---

3. Ibn Mi'mār Ḥanbalī Baghdādī, *Kitāb al-futuwwa*, introduction (by Muṣṭafā Jawād), p. 12, citing p. 14 of the text. Koran translation by A.J. Arberry, *The Koran Interpreted* (Oxford University Press, rprt. 1982).
4. Translated by Tosun Bayrak al-Jerrahi as *The Way of Sufi Chivalry* (Vermont: Inner Traditions International 1991).

> The 'uniform' *(khirqa)*[5] of chivalry consists of trousers *(izār)* whereas the uniform of Sufism is the hat *(kulāh)*. This is because the first step in chivalry is chastity *('ifāf)* which is connected with the lower realms of Being, whereas the beginning of Sufism is ascent to the realm of divine illumination connected with Being's higher realms. Hence, whereas it is the custom in Sufism [for novices] to shave their heads, in chivalry this custom does not exist. One who would realize chivalry must struggle to acquire certain virtues and praiseworthy moral traits, the chevalier being one who is known to be 'accomplished' in certain fields. Sufism, on the other hand, involves detachment from the world and abstraction from material things *(tajrīd wa tafrīd)* and, ultimately, dissolution of the self *(fanā')*, its first beginnings being the removal of all obstacles to spiritual progress. Therefore, it is evident that the terminus of chivalry is the beginning of the cycle of 'Friendship with God' *(walāyat)* and that chivalry is a part of Sufism—just as 'Friendship with God' is one part of Prophecy *(nubuwwa)*.[6]

Although the precise term *futuwwa* does not occur in the Koran, derivatives of the word (stemming from the same verbal root) appear repeatedly—such as *fatā* (youth),[7] *fityān* (young men),[8] etc. In Koranic exegesis *(tafsīr)* as well, reference to 'chivalry' *(jawānmardī)* and the use of the Arabic term 'young knight' or 'chevalier' *(fatā)* is quite infrequent; an exception to which is, of course, interpretation of the traditional references found in the Koran to Abraham, Joseph and the story of the Seven Sleepers. Of course, in certain types of Koranic exegesis written with a Sufi or mystical bent, lengthy explanations of chivalry sometimes are encountered. Rashīd al-Dīn Maybudī's *Kashf al-asrār wa 'uddat al-*

---

5. The term *khirqa* literally means mantle, cassock or cloak, but here it is apparent that it is being used generically to signify the 'uniform' or 'canonical robes' of the Muslim mystic. –ED.
6. Shams al-Dīn Muḥammad ibn Maḥmūd Āmulī, 'Risāla futuwwatiyya' from his Nafā'is al-funūn fī 'arā'is al-'uyūn, ed. M. Ṣarrāf in *Rasā'il-i jawāmardān* (Tehran/ Paris: Maisonneuve 1973), p. 74.
7. Cf. Koran XXI: 60.
8. Cf. Koran XVIII: 13.

abrār,[9] completed in 520/1126, immediately comes to mind in this regard. It is interesting to note what Maybudī has to say on this subject:

> The character and conduct of the chevaliers is summed up in the statement made by Muḥammad to 'Alī: "O 'Alī! *(yā 'Alī),* the chevalier *(jawānmard)* is truthful *(rāstgū'ī),* faithful, trustworthy, compassionate, a patron of the poor *(darwīsh-dār),* extremely charitable and hospitable, a doer of good works and of modest demeanor." It is also said that the chief of all followers of chivalry was Joseph the Sincere – peace be upon him – who, upon encountering his jealous brothers, forgave them for the torments which formerly they had inflicted upon him, by saying, "There is no blame upon you this day."[10]
>
> It is also related that once the Prophet – peace be upon him – was seated [in a gathering] and a beggar entered, and petitioned for assistance. Turning to the assembly, the Prophet addressed his companions, saying, "Be chivalrous towards him." At this point, 'Alī left the room. Shortly, thereafter he returned with his alms in hand consisting of one dinar, five dirhams, and a loaf of bread. "What is all this, 'Alī?" asked the Prophet.
>
> "O Prophet of God!" he replied, "When the beggar first petitioned us, the thought entered my heart that I should give him a loaf of bread. Then another thought passed through my heart to give him five dirhams in alms; lastly it occurred to me to give him one dinar. It seemed entirely inappropriate not to follow the promptings of my heart and the stirrings of my conscience."
>
> Thence it was that the Prophet commented, *"Lā Fatā illā 'Alī:* (There is no man of chivalry like unto 'Alī).[11]

In the earliest Persian poetry one encounters much general overall praise—albeit succinct and brief—of the ideals of chivalry. Thus in 'Unṣurī's (d. ca. 431-42/1040-50) *Dīwān* one finds the following encomium:

> *Chivalry excels all works and deeds.*
> *Chivalry is a trait of the Prophet.*

---

9. Edited by 'Alī Aṣghar Ḥikmat, 10 vols. (Tehran: Intishārāt-i Dānishgāhī 1952-60)

10. Koran XII: 92.

11. *Kashf al-asrār,* V, p. 669.

And Firdawsī incites the reader of the *Shāhnāma* to

> *Make a habit of being chivalrous and of telling the truth,*
> *Make a habit of good thoughts.*

Later Sufi authors, also, would express their admiration for chivalry in the same manner. Thus Sa'dī writes:

> *If you are a man of chivalry,*
> *both the worlds are yours: both the worlds*
> *heaven and earth, are the chevalier's wages.*
> *The true chevalier is a saint and friend of God;*
> *Benevolence was the path of 'Alī, 'King of Men'.*[12]

On occasion, Sufi poets also provided extended poetic commentary on the theme of chivalry. Abū Sa'īd ibn Abī'l-Khayr's renowned definition of chivalry—delivered extemporaneously to a bath attendant in Nīshāpūr occupied in scrubbing the Shaykh's back—was thus retold by 'Aṭṭār:

> Abū Sa'īd of Mayhana was once at the baths being served by an uncouth masseur. Scrubbing the Shaykh's arm, he cupped some dead skin in his palm, drawing forth, before the Master's face, the scourings for display. "So, good Shaykh," said the masseur, "tell us what is chivalry?'"
>
> "Chivalry is to hide a man's dead skin from him, to conceal such scum from men's eyes," pronounced the Shaykh at once.
>
> The attendant fell at his feet abased and ashamed by Abū Sa'īd's superlative reply, begging his pardon. The masseur having admitted his own ignorance, the Shaykh accepted his apology.[13]

12. In using the term 'King of Men' *(shāh-i mardān),* Sa'dī also implies, by extension, 'King of the Chevaliers' *(shāh-i jawānmardān).*
13. The foregoing citations from the poetry of 'Unṣūrī, Firdawsī, Sa'dī and 'Aṭṭār are to be found in 'Alī Akbar Dihkhudā's *Amthāl wa ḥikam,* (Tehran: Amīr Kabīr, 7th ed. 1370 A.Hsh./1991), II, pp. 590-91.

A large section of the Persian poetic rendition of *Kalīla wa Dimna*[14] composed during the Seljuk period in the reign of Bahrām-shāh of Ghazna (512/1118–544/1153) by Qāni'ī Ṭūsī treats the theme of *futuwwa* and its principles. The following quotation (which in view of the relative scarcity of its text, is here cited in full) illustrates the high degree accorded to chivalry during this period:[15]

> The crown jewel of the body is virtue *(muruwwat),* and virtue is a sign of chivalry *(futuwwa).* Chivalry causes no ill-feelings. Chivalry makes a man carry his head high. Chivalry is the labor of the liberated and free in spirit, the pearl of great price. Chivalry makes renowned the name of men. Consider nothing to be higher or nobler than chivalry. Chivalry is not apart from Justice. Chivalry makes glad the heart of wise men. Chivalry is the key to righteousness; it broadcasts one's good name abroad. The tongue of one whose eminence comes from chivalry is never occupied with lies and calumny. The man of chivalry wishes no man ill; he forgives whenever he can. Whatever he permits and wills for himself amongst his superiors, he wishes also for the entire world as his equals. The chevalier's way is abstention from blameworthy acts so that he never demeans himself by wrongdoing. His sole aim is a fair name and character; he never becomes involved in scandal and corruption. His benevolence puts all at ease for his heart is far from vanity. Chivalry makes a man known as trustworthy, wise and pious throughout the land. Chivalry comes to you as the legacy of 'Alī, who was a 'Friend of God' *(walī)* endowed with wisdom and chivalrous character. Whoever is guided well in the way of chivalry perceives divine Reality *(ḥaqīqat)* through the 'cycle of mystical initiation *(walāyat).*[16] 'Alī, in whose shadow the sun itself reposed, held chivalry to be his supreme fortune. According to the ethos of

---

14. The famed Fables of Bidpai, originally Indian in origin. These lines are to be found in an edition of Qāni'ī Ṭūsī's *Kalīla wa Dimna* edited by M. Todua: Kalīla wa dimna-yi manẓūm (Tehran: Bunyād-i Farhang-i Īrān 1358 A.Hsh./1979-80), originally sent to the present writer for editing and review. A copy of the book was not available during composition of this article. These verses I noted down some time ago. They occur in the introduction and are composed in praise of the reigning monarch mentioned in the *takhalluṣ*.
15. The text translated here into prose is in Persian rhyming couplets.–TRANS.
16. 'Alī is revered as the leader of the path of Chivalry. Without his mediation (i.e., through initiation into Orders of chivalry or Sufism), says the poet, one can make little progress in divine matters *(ḥaqīqa).*–TRANS.

> chivalry, it is wrong for you to possess two coats meant for one body. Chivalry [in its principles] is a model of divine Obedience. Chivalry is the foundation of Courage. Chivalry does not let you heedlessly enjoy your satiety—while others remain yet hungry. Chivalry does not let you be conceited, nor regard others with disdain. Chivalry is the essence of all goodness: [through its practice] you cease to be 'you'.[17] Among people of honour and rectitude chivalry does not permit that anyone in the world become annoyed by you. Chivalry never lets you incur a loss. Chivalry cannot be realized by dishonesty. Who possesses chivalry in the world? Who else, besides this eminent monarch, whose virtues are priceless?[18]

From the foregoing discussion and quotations, it has been conclusively demonstrated, I think, that chivalry constituted a whole collection of praiseworthy moral qualities and spiritually acceptable forms of etiquette *(ādāb)*. However, little consideration has been given in what has so far been said to the social forms and institutional organization which the fraternities of *futuwwa* assumed in early Islamic Persia.

One of the essential sources for the study and understanding of *futuwwa* is the *Qābūs-nāma* composed circa 475/1082-3 by 'Unṣur al-Ma'ālī Kaykā'ūs ibn Iskandar ibn Qābūs Washmgīr, then Prince of Ṭabaristān. In the last and longest chapter (XLIV) of his book, the prince devotes extensive discussion to the antecedents of the tradition of chivalry. Despite the relatively wide diffusion of this book (which renderw unnecessary analysis of it here), there are several quite original points in its approach to chivalry which deserve mention. Firstly, the book's definition of chivalry is noteworthy:

> It is said that chivalry consists of three things. First, that you practice what you preach, performing in act all that you promise by word. The second is you do not lie or speak contrary to the truth. The third is that you exercise patience in all your conduct and affairs. All other moral precepts in chivalry *(jawānmardī)*

---

17. I.e. the practice of Chivalry annuls vanity, erases the marks of selfhood and conceit from one's conduct, transforming one's passional attributes *(nafs)* into divine Qualities.–ED.

18. An allusion to the poet's royal patron who is the object of praise *(mamdūḥ)* of the poem.

can be subsumed under these three headings.

Another interesting facet of the *Qābūs-nāma* is that the author outlines different conditions for members of chivalry according to their social class. Thus, for example, knights errant or soldiers of fortune (*'ayyār)*[19] have one kind of chivalry and merchants another. The Sufis' chivalry in turn demands an entirely different set of conditions and requirements. The chivalry of the [Abrahamic] prophets constitutes the highest and most demanding degree, the prophets being a level above all the rest in their realization of the chivalric virtues since chivalry originates from them. The following passage illustrates the chivalrous qualities demanded of the soldier of fortune or mercenary:

> Know that the mercenary knight *(jawānmardī 'ayyārī)* is one who possesses various types of accomplishments. He is brave, manly and patient in all he does. He adheres faithfully to his oath, and is chaste, modest and pure in heart. He does not allow his own advantage to be the cause of another's ill or injury, yet accepts injury or offense coming from a friend with equanimity. He does not torture prisoners; rather he assists them. He is a patron of the poor, and prevents villains from oppressing the virtuous. Just as he speaks only good so he hears only good, demanding that his corporeal faculties follow the course of 'justice' in all things. He will never cause offence to anyone who has offered him bread and board, nor will he recompense with evil anyone who has done him good... Hardship and misfortune in his eyes appears as ease. Now if you examine the matter closely, you will see that the source of all these accomplishments lies in those three things which we have mentioned.[20]

Chivalry in this period *(circa* the fifth/eleventh century) as understood by the author of the *Qābūs-nāma,* was primarily

19. *'Ayyār,* here translated as 'knight-errant' or 'mercenary', roughly means an outlaw or soldier of fortune, somewhat like the Italian *condottiere.* For the meaning of the term *'ayyār* in Persian chivalry, see Cl. Cahen's article on "Futuwwa" and Fr. Taeschner on "'Ayyār" in EI² as well as the lengthy article in *Encyclopædia Iranica,* III (s.v. "'Ayyār", pp. 159-63) by Cl. Cahen and W.L. Hanway. For its significance in Persian Sufism, see J. Nurbakhsh, *Sufi Symbolism: The Nurbakhsh Encyclopedia of Sufi Terminology,* (London: KNP 1992), VI, p. 119. –ED.
20. *Qabūs-nāma,* p. 247.

interpreted as a sort of code of ethics to be followed by various classes of society. Members of each class all strove, in their respective ways, to live up to its ideals. For this reason, one finds, on the one hand, athletes, wrestling champions, mercenaries and soldiers all professing to follow the chivalric code of discipline, and on the other, tradesmen, merchants, and members of various crafts and guilds also observing their own particular rites and conditions based on chivalry.[21] Likewise, Sufis and residents of the *khānaqāh*s took care to base their conduct upon the ideals and principles of chivalry, attributing the highest spiritual rank to those who exerted themselves most to uphold its code of etiquette. This respect for the chivalric ideal transcended class distinctions, intersecting all strata of the social hierarchy despite the vast material and spiritual differences between its various members.

In the annals of Islamic history one finds that when the fortunes of one class rose above that of another, the ideals of chivalry pertaining to the ruling class usually come to the fore. Thus, when a group of mercenaries (*'ayyār)* came to power, the athletic and heroic ideal was glorified; tales of prowess and courage became the talk of the day, as was the case, for instance, in 'Awfī's *Jawāmi' al-ḥikāyāt.* Likewise, when a society began to enjoy the fruits of peace and political security, and the economy began to flourish so that the situation of the workers and merchants improved, tracts and treatises devoted to chivalry paid more attention to the merchant class of society. Construction of *langar*s,[22] the institutional center of the artisans and craftsmen following the principles of chivalry, would consequently become widespread, and much mention would be made of the rites and ceremonies pertaining to their particular assemblies. At the same time, throughout all such social upheavals

---

21. The various types of etiquette observed by craftsmen and members of the guilds is described in the *Futuwwat-nāma-yi sulṭānī;* there were also short treatises *(futuwwat-nāma)* written for each guild, many of which have been published.

22. The *langar* is the meeting house of the practitioners of *futuwwa.* Despite certain distinguishing characteristics, it is in many respects similar to the *khānaqāh* of the Sufis. Perhaps the main distinction between the two institutions is that there was a certain room reserved for gymnastic exercises in certain *langar*s (in many respects similar to the role of the 'House of Exercise', *Zūrkhāna,* in Iran), which is a feature never found in any *khānaqāh.*

and political changes, the practice of 'Sufi chivalry', based on the mystics' celebrated virtues of altruism *(ithār),* purity *('iffat)* as well as their admirable ethics, held fast to its own course and traditional discipline.

Another important source of reference for the study of chivalry are popular stories and romances. In such literature, especially in the oldest Persian sources, the mercenaries *('ayyār*s) are given a special place. As was mentioned above, this mercenary ethos was directly connected to the Persian tradition of chivalry, insofar as the *'ayyār* was himself a sort of professional knight-errant *(jawānmard),* who was considered to possess the highest degree of *futuwwa.* Among the famous books which discuss this aspect of 'professional chivalry', two works are of particular importance: *Samak-i 'Ayyār* by Faramarz ibn Khudādād Arrajānī[23] and the *Abū Muslim-nāma.* And with the publication of a third book, the 'Tale of Fīrūz Shāh' *(Dāstān-i Fīrūz Shāh)* by Muḥammad Bīghamī, otherwise known as the *Dārāb-nāma Bīghamī,* the other two romances were brought to completion.

Samak-i 'Ayyār is the oldest Persian popular romance of its genre and is devoted to the tale of a knight-errant. Here and there in this text one finds mention being made of the rites, traditions and ideals of chivalry. It goes without saying that the sensational highlighting of the main character and the consequent hyperbole and exaggeration devoted to the hero's feats of bravery and prowess in such romances—part and parcel of the literary genre from which they derive—does not pose any obstacle to the serious student intent on obtaining important chivalric axioms and morals from the text. In order to extract general moral conclusions about the meaning of chivalry from such tales, it would be necessary to cull all the *futuwwa/jawānmardī* references from the text, set them side by side and compare them. This is a task obviously beyond the scope of this brief study. Instead, by way of illustration of the extraordinary ethical richness of *Samak-i 'Ayyār,* we will content ourselves here with only a few examples of the concept of chivalry therein:

---

23. Edited by P.N. Khānlarī in 5 vols. (Tehran 1338-53A.Hsh./1959-74).

Two youths were standing (by the door of a house). A prince (Khūrshīd-shāh) arrived and said to them, "Go tell the master of the chevaliers *(sar-i jawānmardān)* that a stranger has come and wishes to enter, if permission is given."

"The door of a chevalier's house is always open." they replied.

"That's true, but still, it is unchivalrous behavior *(nā-jawānmardī)* to enter a chevalier's house without his permission."

Now the two youths, who were confused about how to respond to this, went to Shaghāl Pīlzūr,[24] and informed him of what had happened.

"Go and bring the prince to me," said Shaghāl.

So they went and brought the prince inside. Shaghāl paid his respects, sitting the prince down and inquiring after his health. They brought in food and drink and when he had satisfied himself and was enjoying their company, he turned towards Shaghāl and said, "O champions, tell me, how many rules does chivalry have?"

"Although the rules of chivalry are innumerable," said Shaghāl, "its major part is made up of seventy-two aspects, out of which two have been selected as being of particular importance. The first is giving food to the hungry and the second is preservation of people's secrets. Now, tell me if there is anything I can do for you?"

The prince said, "Since preservation of secrets is a quality of men such as yourselves, I beg you that you give me your word that you will not reveal the secret which I wish to confide in you."

Shaghāl Pīlzūr said, "By God Almighty and All-Just, I swear that I will not tell anyone your secret, and that I will sacrifice my life if necessary to preserve your secret."

Shaghāl's companions took the same oaths accordingly. Then, Khūrshīd-shāh said...[25]

Following the above story, Samak takes the prince to visit a female musician by the name of Rūḥ-afzā, so that she can arrange a meeting between the prince and his lover. An account of Samak's meeting with Rūḥ-afzā is as follows:

---

24. A wise chevalier, and their leader.
25. *Samak-i 'Ayyār,* I, pp 44-45.

Finding an appropriate moment to address the lady, Samak stood up and made obeisance. Then he said, "O mother, do you know what chivalry *(jawānmardī)* is and whose profession it truly is?"

Rūḥ-afzā remarked, "Chivalry is, of course, the accomplishment of 'men' of chivalry, but if a woman acts with chivalrously *(zanī jawānmardī kunad),* then she is a 'man' in its practice as well."[26]

So Samak asked, "Of the arts of chivalry which do you possess?"

Rūḥ-afzā replied, "In chivalry I possess complete trustworthiness. If anyone asks for my help in some affair, I will do all I can for him or her, putting my life at stake for their sake, considering the accomplishment of their work as my mortal obligation. And if someone comes to me earnestly seeking refuge, I will protect him or her to my last breath. I will never divulge the secret of anyone who confides in me. This is what *I* understand of 'manliness' and chivalry *(mardī u jawānmardī).* Now tell me, what is *your* purpose in asking these questions from me? If you have any business, or any secret which you would confide in me, speak up."

Samak-i 'Ayyār applauded her words and said, "Yes, I do have a secret to tell you and a trust which I would like to deposit with you. But first I would like you to swear on oath that all you said above was true."

Rūḥ-afzā replied, "I swear by the Justice of God Almighty that I will divulge your secret to none, that I will lay down my life for your sake, and be the devoted friend of your friends, and the earnest enemy of your enemies. I will never divulge your secret to anyone nor ever let my words bring harm unto you. Neither shall I engage in intrigue or deceit, nor harbor ill thoughts of anyone. If preserving the bond of friendship with you be the cause of my ruination, so be it! I feel no regret. If I cannot obtain what you desire, then I am not a woman who acts in a manly fashion *(az zanān-i mard-kirdar nabāsham)!*"[27]

---

26. Rūḥ-afzā here directly intends to state that chivalry is not based on gender distinctions nor is it the exclusive accomplishment of members of the male sex, demonstrating the latent misogyny of those scholars who have translated *jawānmardī* as 'youngmanliness'.–TRANS.
27. *Samak-i 'Ayyār,* I, pp. 47-48.

As the above passage demonstrates, complete honesty and courage are counted among the foremost conditions of chivalry. When Samak and Rūḥ-afzā finally succeed in arranging a rendezvous between Prince Khūrshīd-shāh and the princess with whom he was in love, unforeseen circumstances cause the King to hear of their affair. The King summons Shaghāl Pīlzūr, Commander-in-Chief of his army, to his court. Shaghāl brings Samak and a few other comrades along with him to the King who demands a full explanation:

> When Samak-i 'Ayyār—that dashing youth, that just man invested with complete equipoise—saw how Shaghāl Pīlzūr stood with his head downcast, speechless before the monarch, he arose and made obeisance, saying, "May your life forever prosper! Know that there is nothing in the world better than honesty. It is one's mortal duty to speak out and tell the truth wherever one may be, whether among commoners or noblity, whether with simple rustics or wise savants. Especially in the presence of the king, we must speak naught but the truth, or else risk having our name struck from the book of men of chivalry. Even if we be renowned as mercenaries *('ayyār-pīsha)* we are in fact chevaliers *(jawānmardān)*, for one cannot be a mercenary without being also a chevalier. Chevaliers make the most of their character, undergoing great hardships and laying down their lives for others. Now, my purpose in saying all this is to let you know that my teacher—no, rather, my father—Shaghāl, is too ashamed to speak up before the King of the world. However, let me just say that Fīrūzshāh, the son of Marzbānshāh, one day came to the house of the chevaliers *(sarā-yi jawānmardān)* and entreated us to promise him refuge. O King, we endorsed his chivalry, arranged his affairs, and strove with heart and soul to fulfil his wishes."[28]

***

So far we have limited our discussion to elucidation of the essential humane and ethical principles of chivalry, which are in fact universal values appreciated and accepted by almost all the religious teachers and faiths of the world. At least on the face of it, almost no

---

28. *Ibid.*, p. 65.

one willingly condemns such values. However, propagation of the principles of this 'way of chivalry' necessarily required an organization and institutional structure to facilitate the training of aspirants in its discipline.

It should also be kept in mind that every spiritual teaching which becomes institutionally formalized runs the risk of corruption, allowing its teaching to become 'watered-down' by those wishing to take advantage of the social benefits of 'belonging' to a respected social group for purely personal ends. *Futuwwa* was no exception to this rule. Many joined its ranks and assumed the chevalier's mantle without exerting themselves in its practice and discipline, a phenomenon which necessarily led to a certain decadence in its ethic.

The study of Islamic history reveals this clearly. One encounters a group of arrant and cruel characters whose aims are entirely worldly and material in nature—hedonistic at the best and savage at the worst—excusing their own violent natures under the auspices of practicing chivalry. The values of courage and bravery which were originally meant to be applied in the context of legitimate religious and national self-defence, were unscrupulously adopted to encourage a aggressive and strong-man disposition—the same temperament which in modern Iran is known today as *dāsh-mashdī*—effecting the transmutation of chivalry. Here we see the 'ugly side' of chivalry appearing, in which the word *futuwwa* came to imply a type of hedonism, consisting of hard-drinking, carousing, music, dance, singing, brawling and prizefighting! Notwithstanding this truncation of principles, some of the values of chivalry, such as generosity, faithfulness to one's oath and honesty, remained intact.

At the end of the Umayyad period, during the first half of the second Muslim century (circa the first half of the eighth Christian century), an organized society of 'young men' *(fityān)* came into being who devoted themselves to drinking wine, banqueting, singing and musical performances. An essential part of their festive occasions involved the singing of erotic poetry and playing of various musical instruments. For a certain time during this period, Khālid al-Qaṣrī in his capacity as governor of Iraq, totally prohibited these gatherings, making an exception for only one person by the name of Ḥunayn Ḥayrī, whom he allowed to hold assemblies on the condition that neither adolescents nor anti-governmental elements be admitted to them. During the same period the principles of *futuwwa* gradually merged with *'ayyārī* customs, creating its own particular tradition, etiquette and even dialect. The followers of chivalry wore special distinguishing attire, greased their hair and we even hear of a group of so-called 'knights' carousing at the gravestone of Abū'l-Hindī Ghālib ibn 'Abd al-Quddūs—the first poet in Islam to write poetry in praise of wine—singing bacchanal hymns, drinking to his memory and making an oblation of wine on the poet's tomb.[29]

By the beginning of the third/ninth century this particular type of *futuwwa* had become well established in Islamicate society, and had its own particular distinguishing rites and rituals. Some of the followers of *futuwwat* even held the post of *Qāḍī*—such as Abū'l-Fātak 'Abdullāh Daylamī who was nicknamed the 'Judge of the Knights' *(Qāḍī al-fityān),* and mentioned in the history of Baghdad during this era as holding assemblies of *fityān* in his house during which he would preach to them the principles of chivalry, which they would note down. In this same text one finds a listing of the noble qualities of character attributed to him which all chevaliers were required to pursue.[30] It would appear that Daylamī's list constitutes the first written evidence in Islam concerning the chivalric tradition.

From here on, the *futuwwa* tradition increasingly penetrated literary studies *(adab),* and especially poetry, so that poets embraced chivalry as a way of life and chevaliers also composed poetry. In the renowned *Kitāb al-Aghānī* of Abū'l-Faraj Iṣfahānī (d. 356/967) anecdotes of many of these poets are quoted. We read of 'Alī ibn Jahm (d. 249/863), for instance, a poet who frequented the company of the followers of chivalry in Baghdad, in whose honour a party was held in the house of some of the local knights to celebrate his being freed from prison and return from exile. During this celebration he com-

---

29. Some years ago in the Persian journal *Yādigār* the late 'Abbās Iqbāl Āshtiyān sent out a request to scholars to inform him of their research concerning the custom of making oblation of wine upon tombs. The response was quite informative and many important and interesting articles were published as a result. (See Year 1, nos. 6, 8, the articles by Muḥammad Qazwīnī, Muḥammad Mu'īn, Ghulām Ḥusayn Ṣadīqī. See also Dihkhudā's *Amthāl wa ḥikam,* IV, p. 1895, s.v. *Wa-li'l-ārḍ min ka's 'l-kirām naṣīb.)*

30. From an abridged version of *Mu'jam al-alqāb,* IV, p. 297, cited by Dr. Muṣṭafā Jawād in his introduction to the *Kitāb al-futuwwa.*

posed a famous poem in which he describes the chevaliers' rituals in detail, mentioning their 'Houses of Conviviality' *(ṭarab-khānahā),* their organizational hierarchy, as well as the beautiful women and handsome adolescent boys to be found in their assemblies.

The account given of these groups of so-called chevaliers in the third/ninth century by Abū Ḥayyān al-Ṭawḥīdī (d. after 400/1009) in his *al-Baṣā'ir wa 'l-dhakhā'ir*[31] reproves them for their complete immorality and decadence; no sin or perversion did they abstain from, even homosexuality, he relates. Once someone asked a judge who adhered to the *futuwwa* practice, Abū Ḥayyān notes, to give his legal opinion of homosexuality: should it be classed in the same category of offenses as adultery? The 'chivalric' judge then gave his opinion that homosexuality was far less sinful than adultery and he reproached his questioner for placing the two in the same category.

And it is during the same period that we hear of the vizier of the Abbasid Caliph al-Mutawakkil (reg. 232/847–247/861), Fatḥ ibn Khāqān's notorious homosexual affair with a slave-boy named Shāhak, in which the vizier's boon-companion, Abū 'Abdullāh ibn Ḥamdūn acted as a go-between between them. Despite their attempts at secrecy, news of this affair reached the ear of the Caliph, who told Ibn Ḥamdūn, "I selected you from the masses to be my close companion and servant, and not to act as pimp for my male slaves." Ibn Ḥamdūn protested his complete innocence of the incident and swore that all the allegations were false. When the truth, however, was eventually exposed, Ibn Ḥamdūn because of his false oath was obliged to divorce all of his wives and free all his slaves. He was also commanded to make the pilgrimage to Mecca thirty times; making this journey his annual legal obligation. Finally al-Mutawakkil exiled him to Tikrīt, ordering one of his slaves, called Zarrāfa, to cut off one of Ibn Ḥamdūn's ears. While executing the Caliph's orders, Zarrāfa told Ibn Ḥamdūn, "The Caliph told me to inform you that this is the punishment which the chevaliers inflict upon one another for this crime." A slightly different version of the

31. Edited Ibrahīm Keilanī, 3 vols. (Damascus: Librairie Atlas et Imprimerie Al-Incha 1964).

same story is given by Shābushtī (d. 390/1000) in his *al-Diyyārāt* and later retold by Yāqūt al-Rūmī (d. 626/1229), citing Amīn al-Dawla Afṭasī, in the *Mu'jam al-udabā'*:[32]

> It is said that [the Caliph] al-Mutawakkil tread the path of Abū Nuwās.[33] A handṣome slave boy came into the room. Ibn Ḥamdūn was enchanted by the slave, staring at him in a flirtatious manner. Al-Mutawakkil asked him at that time, "What punishment is exacted by the followers of chivalry upon a chevalier who flirts with another chevalier's slave?" Ibn Ḥamdūn answered, "Cutting off an ear." Thus al-Mutawakkil addressed him, "Likewise we order the same punishment for you." And the Caliph commanded that his ear be cut off.

The chivalric tradition became very widely diffused among the populace during this period: it was, one could say, the chosen *modus operandi* and ethos of the age. Of the many famous personages who embraced the *futuwwa* path was Isḥāq ibn Khalaf, otherwise known as Ibn Ṭayyib Ḥanafī Bahrānī, who frequented the company of the mercenaries *('ayyārān)* and 'hustlers' *(shaṭṭārān),*[34] hunted with hounds, and patronized lutanists *(ṭanbūr-nawāzān)* and minstrels. Once he was accused of a crime and thrown into prison where he began to compose and declaim poetry, arts at which, it is said, he demonstrated an exceptional talent. Until his death in 230/845, he was known for his chivalry, his love for music and playing the *ṭanbūr*. Many other such characters are frequently encountered in the annals of Arabic literature and *adab* during this age. One reads, for instance, of Abū 'Ataba Aḥmad ibn Faraj Kindī Ḥaṣmī (d. 219/834), a resident of Sūq al-Rastan, sitting with a group of chevaliers drinking wine, who in event of a shortage of drink, often used his beard

32. The story also appears in another version in the *Nathr al-durr* of Manṣūr Ābī.
33. That is to say: Mutawakkil had similar homosexual leanings as Abū Nuwās (d. 199/814), one of the greatest classical Arab poets (son of a Persian washerwoman), known for his sacrilegious erotic—often homosexual—allusions in his poetry. Abū Nuwās' homosexual tendencies are also the subject of certain tales in the *Thousand and One Nights*.
34. The word may mean 'swift-footed', 'fleet' as well as 'sly', 'adroit', 'villain', but here a special guild of Sunnite *futuwwa* is meant, rather than the Indian Sufi Order of the same name which traces its initiatic affiliation back to Bāyazid Bisṭāmī.–TRANS.

to strain the dregs of the wine![35]

Examined as a whole, these examples demonstrate that the adherants of chivalry during this era were usually closely connected with those social groups known as *shaṭṭār* and *'ayyār,* groups which also identified themselves as followers of *futuwwa,* so that by the fourth/tenth century the terms *fatā* and *futuwwa* had become completely synonymous with *shaṭṭār* and *'ayyār.* An interesting example of the association between the two groups during this century occurs in Abī'l-Ḥasan 'Alī ibn Ḥusayn Mas'ūdī's *Murūj al-dhahab.* Discussing the kings of China, Mas'ūdī mentions a certain rebel and outlaw

> called Yānshū who did not belong to any royal lineage. He had an evil and riotous disposition, and gathered about himself many infamous ruffians. Those in authority ignored him, however, thinking him not worthy of being worried about. Gradually, however, his affairs prospered and his notoriety increased, which boosted his arrogance and conceit. He was joined by many wicked men from across the realm, increasing the size of his army, and he set out on campaigns, plundering and pillaging the towns throughout the land...[36]

Mas'ūdī concludes his account of Yānshū with the comment, "He was an evil man who laid claim to *futuwwa.*"

From this time onwards, it became a common practice for brigands and highwaymen to ply their trade in the name of *futuwwa.* Historians recount how the famous philosopher Abū Naṣr Fārābī (d. 339/950) was once traveling from Damascus to 'Asqalān (Askelon) when he was waylaid by a band of thieves claiming to be *fityān.* Fārābī suggested that they help themselves to his clothes, horse and weapons and let him go free. The brigands rejected this offer, how-

---

35. See Khaṭīb Baghdādī, *Ta'rīkh Baghdād,* vol. 4, pp. 339-41, cited by Muṣṭafā Jawād in his introduction to *Kitāb al-futuwwa;* also cf.: Zayn al-Dīn Wāṣifī, *Badāyi' al-waqāyi',* written in Tashkent in 1538/9 (ed. A.N. Boldyrev, 2 vols., Moscow 1961), I, p. 579, who tells the tale of a certain orator who, during wine banquets, also used to strain the dregs of the wine with his beard.

36. Published in Cairo 1384/1964, translated into Persian by Abū'l-Qāsim Pāyanda: Mas'ūdī, *Murūj al-dhahab wa ma'ādin al-jawhar* (Tehran: B.T.N.K. 1344 A.Hsh/ 1965), I, p. 135.

ever, forcing him to fight them. Fārābī and all of his traveling companions were killed. News of this incident so deeply disturbed the rulers of the area that they pursued and arrested the entire gang of thieves, hanging them beside the philosopher's tomb.

A well-known facet of the biography of one of the earliest Persian Sufis, Fuḍayl ibn 'Iyāḍ (d. 187/778)[37]—known as the "Shaykh of the *fityān*"—is that he began his career as leader of a gang of brigands. While his followers ambushed caravans and took booty, he dressed as a pious ascetic, carried a rosary in hand, and regularly celebrated lauds. The stolen goods were brought to him to divide up among them as he saw fit. Despite his criminal activities, he did, however possess a small degree of chivalry, and it was this chivalry which, when one day he heard a verse of the Koran being recited, eventually effected his penitence, so that he forswore his past misdeeds and took to earning a honest living.

There are many other tales of 'pious brigands' which bear witness to their ready wit and refined sensitivity. They are to be found in works such as Qāḍī Tanūkhī's *al-Faraj ba'd al-shiddat* and, later, in Ibn Jawzī's *Kitāb al-adhkiyā'*. The following tale merits citation in this context:

> A certain brigand among the adherents of chivalry ambushed a fruit farmer and ordered him to strip. An exchange took place between them, the owner of the orchard telling the thief, "I swear to God that I will strip off all my clothes and give them to you when I reach my orchard."
>
> "That's unacceptable," said the thief, "because it is related by Imām Mālik ibn Anas that one needn't keep an oath given under duress to a thief."
>
> "But I solemnly swear by God Almighty that I will be glad to strip off all my clothes and give them to you if only you take me back to my orchard!" cried the fruit farmer.
>
> The thief lowered his head a moment. Coming out of his meditation, he remarked, "Do you know what I was thinking? I reviewed in my mind all the works wrought by brigands from the time of the Prophet (blessings be upon him!) down to the

37. In his entry on Fuḍayl in the *Ṭabaqāt al-ṣūfiyya,* Sulamī notes that he was born in Samarqand and lived in Khurāsān, and was "a famous Sufi and *'ayyār.*" Further biographical information on him may also be found in 'Aṭṭār's *Tadhkirat al-awliyā.*

> present day, and could not recall a single brigand who ever conducted any transaction solely on the basis of credit. Now, I have a great aversion to making an innovation *(bid'atī)* in the religion of Islam—for then the sin of this innovation would fall on my shoulders, and I would bear the burden of anyone who decided to imitate my practice until the Day of Judgement. So take off your clothes."
>
> The fruit farmer said, "But are you willing that I strip off my clothes and my private parts be exposed?"
>
> "Don't worry," the brigand retorted, "because it is related on the authority of Mālik ibn Anas, that a man whose nakedness becomes exposed in public may easily regain his religious purity by performing the correct ablutions."
>
> "But people will pass by me here and see my nudity!"
>
> The brigand rejoined, "If there was as much traffic of people on this highway as you say there is, I would never have been able to stop you."
>
> The farmer said, "I see that you are a man of subtle wit and insight. Let me just return to my garden—I will gladly strip there and give you my clothes."
>
> "Never!" replied the brigand. "You plan to return to your orchard, call four of your workers to catch me, who will then take me to the sheriff, who will throw me in jail, and flog my body and put my feet in the stocks. Now, strip off your clothes!"
>
> So the brigand made him strip, took his clothes and went on his way.

During the Shi'ite Būyid rule of Baghdad and domination of the caliphate in Iraq, groups of *jawānmardān* and *'ayyārān* whose religious fanaticism—whether in opposition to or cooperation with each other—usually surpassed their fraternal solidarity, gained increasing power and influence. It is interesting to read what Ibn 'Athīr, describing the political events of the year 361/972, says of this:

> In this year a great calamity came over Baghdad and people were divided into various opposing camps. The mercenary bandits *('ayyārān)* became powerful and well-organized, wreaking much evil and havoc... Among them, there were several groups such as the 'Nubuwiyya'[38] and the *fityān*. The Shi'ites, Sunnis and the mercenary bandits began fighting amongst themselves; many were killed, people's properties and estates were ransacked, many houses and businesses were burnt and looted, such

> as Karkh—the Shi'ite quarter and financial and trade center of Baghdad. It was then that the bitter enmity between the Shi'ite *naqīb* of the 'Alīds, Abū Aḥmad Mūsawī [d. 396/1006], father of the *sharīf* Raḍī, and Vizier Abū'l-Faḍl Shīrāzī deepened. In the resulting disturbance, certain groups of mercenary bandits (*'ayyārān*) divided up the rule and control of Baghdad between themselves. In the same century, the emperor of Byzantine attacked the city of Ruḥā [Edessa] and advancing to its outskirts, reached the town of Naṣībīn, destroying and burning Muslim towns and villages and taking many prisoners. He also wrecked havoc throughout Anatolia. Refugees from the cities destroyed by the Byzantine invasion poured into Baghdad, inciting its citizens to wage war on the Byzantine invaders. The refugees flocked to the mosques and made speeches, describing the horrors of the foreign invasion and warning the local Muslim population [of Iraq] of the real danger of further Byzantine incursions eastward. They also said that no obstacles lay in the path of the Byzantine armies, greedy to pillage the cities of Islamdom. As a consequence of their tales, a public outcry was raised; large demonstrations were held and people marched on the caliph's palace, accusing him of weakness, pusillanimity and shirking the duties which his religious and political office required him to uphold.[39]

In the same period, 'Izz al-Dawla Bakhtiyār (the son of the former Būyid chief at Baghdad Mu'izz al-Dawla Daylamī), who ruled Iraq and parts of Iran, pretended to go on a hunting expedition, intending in fact to battle with 'Umrān ibn Shāhīn, an outlaw who had taken control of the city of Wāsiṭ. A number of the citizens of Baghdad approached 'Izz al-Dawla and reproached him for having gone hunting or to battle with 'Umrān ibn Shāhīn—who, outlaw or

---

38. The Nubuwiyya were a group of Sunnite futuwwa strongly opposed to the Shi'ites, known to kill Shi'ites wherever they were found. Despite this, like most other *futuwwa* organizations, they expressed deep devotion to 'Alī.

39. Thus, in later Islamic history, the last Abbasid Caliph al-Mu'taṣim (d. 1258) attacked the powers of Byzantine Rome once, due to incursions by crusaders against Muslim cities and their taking a Hāshimite woman captive. His armies marched into Anatolia, wrecked Ankara, captured and burnt the city of Amorium, and brought back the city gate with them to Baghdad. Poets wrote odes celebrating this event as a great victory for Islam. It would seem that the populace of fourth/tenth century Baghdad expected similar military action of the caliphate and Būyid government at this time.

not, was at least a Muslim who observed the basic formalities of Islamic prayer—arguing that defending the country against the Byzantine invasion took precedence over petty domestic conflicts. Now, although 'Izz al-Dawla promised them that he would prepare himself for battle with the Christian 'infidels', he lacked the necessary military resources to do so, and the promised *jihād* never took place.

Due to such lack of initiative on the part of their leaders, the common people began to take the law into their own hands, arming themselves against the feared foreign intruder. Weapons—spears, bows, swords—were to be seen everywhere on the streets of Baghdad; riots became rife. A certain beggar by the name of Aswad al-Zabid, known for his destitution, seeing others once poorer than himself now in positions of power, also armed himself and soon became a very successful gangster, accomplished in the high arts of murder, arson, and robbery. Despite his demonic temperament and conduct, he was quite handsome in appearance, and was quite notorious for his love affairs, womanizing and a long train of admirers. As head of the mediæval Baghdad mob, he became a warlord in his own right, and acquired a vast following. He played the prince, dispensing largesse and granting boons to secure his leadership through the bribery of beneficence.

Despite his thoroughly ruthless nature, which refrained from no crime or sin, Aswad did have a certain quasi-chivalrous side to his character. Thus, one day he purchased a slave-girl in the town Mosul for a thousand dinars. When at night he tried to satisfy his lust with the girl, she rejected him. When he asked for her reasons, she rebuked him for his misconduct and public ill-fame, saying that he repelled her. "So what should I do with you?" said the warlord. "Resell me." she replied. "Would you rather that I free you and give you a thousand dinars as dowry?" asked Aswad. "So much the better," she said. So he took the girl to the local magistrate's court of Qāḍī Ibn al-Daqqāq near the Ibn Raqbān Mosque, manumitting her with a thousand dinars. According to the mores of that age, had Aswad murdered the girl, scarcely anyone would have noticed anything amiss—but giving her a writ of total emancipation caused popular astonishment. This magnanimous and 'chivalrous' conduct in face of the maid's cold disdain and shrewish temper became the talk of Baghdad, so that all marvelled at his *futuwwa.*

Although Ibn Athīr states that the beginning of the proliferation of religious sects and opposing groups of mercenary brigands (*'ayyārs)* and riots dates back to precisely the year 361/972, the truth of the matter is that long before this date such divisions and strife had been smoldering like coals under the hot ashes of that society. Socio-economic conditions, however, until this date had been inappropriate for any explosion of strife and manifestation of the differences between these groups. Furthermore, the branches or types of chivalric societies are not be strictly limited merely to those, such as the Nubuwiyya mentioned by Ibn Athīr, for other contemporary sources such as the *Kitāb al-futuwwa* of Ibn Mi'mār Ḥanbalī feature a number of other important *futuwwa* groups of the time, such as the Rahhāṣiyya, Shaḥīniyya, Khalīliyya, and Mawlidiyya.[40]

In the middle of the fourth/tenth century, the *'ayyārān* and *fityān* attempted to give the principles of their ritual and practices of *futuwwa* a religious foundation, whether or not there was any real historical or textual source or precedent to justify their action. Unfortunately, instead of uniting the forces of the various knightly orders and fraternities, this attempt to give the 'way of chivalry' some direct religious relevance and authority only deepened the sectarian divisiveness of their movement, and increased the possibility of greater religiously-motivated violence in Islamic society. Instead of unifying the movement and orienting it in word and deed towards one common goal to be shared by all the different chivalric groups, the chevaliers became divided into different opposing camps, and infighting flourished among these rival groups of contrary sectarian persuasion. Fighting merely to preserve their own party, they exhibited fanatical devotion to their own particular rites and interpretation of the chivalric tradition—ruthlessly murdering, robbing, mugging and crushing their opponents. Needless to say, such strife created a serious problem for the ruling authorities in Baghdad during this period—the Būyid dynasty and the Abbasid theocracy—who, to stem the stream of violence and crime filling the capital, decided to curb their powers and deal them a decisive blow.

---

40. *Kitāb al-futuwwat,* p. 146.

However, aside from a few lines of political protest, satirical allusions and stray words of disapprobation, little record remains in the history books of the struggle between these knights—now decked out in the intellectual armor of religious dogmatics—and the state authorities. One indication of the conflict, for instance, appears in one of the objections recorded about the comportment of Caliph al-Mustakfī (reg. 944-946)—that his Arabic diction carried a heavy *'ayyārī* drawl and that before his ascension to power he had been a bird-fancier with a special interest in archery spending his leisure hours carousing and amusing himself in gardens—all habits typical of the adherents of chivalry of the day.

Riots and disturbances caused by this conflict continued throughout the reign of the Būyid dynasty in Baghdad, especially during the decline of their power. Sometimes the government was virtually brought to a standstill by this struggle. The *'ayyārān* riots in Baghdad between the years 422/1031 and 426/1035 led by Abū 'Alī Burjumī—feared so much by the town's inhabitants that they hardly dared to refer to him by any other epithet but *qā'id* (=boss, chief)—were directly connected to the *futuwwa/jawānmardī* movement as well, one proof of which is Burjumī's own overt chivalry: he was known never to bother women or to seize their property. The political ascendancy of these bandit knights was often quite highly profiled as well. One hears, for example, of an incident where a huge mob of people gathered in a demonstration at the Ruṣāfa mosque in Baghdad, forcing the preacher, Abū'l-Ḥusayn ibn al-Gharīq to stop his sermon, threatening him that he should only use the name of Burjumī in the *khutba,* rather than that of caliph or king!

In the first few decades of the fifth/eleventh century groups of knights following the principles of *futuwwa,* known as *aḥdāth* (each of whom was addressed as *ḥadath),* appeared in certain areas of Asia Minor—the mediæval Shām, now encompassed by the countries of Jordan and Syria. This word soon entered the common parlance as a synonym for *fatā* (chivalrous youth). The most famous *aḥdāth* of Shām resided in Aleppo and Damascus, and were known for their unabashed pursuit of political power, in the course of which they often entered the field of battle supporting or opposing one local amir over another. Literature concerning the activities of these *aḥdāth* is quite abundant; anyone interested in this phase of Islamic chivalry need only examine the frequent references to them in the historical texts of the era.[41]

There was, however, some difference between the practices and conduct of the *aḥdāth,* the *'ayyārān* and the *jawānmardān.* The *aḥdāth* acted in normal circumstances as a local gendarmes in charge of preserving law and order in towns, and during crises, such as the outbreak of fires, they functioned as the fire brigade. They also acted as a standing army ready to be called up against external invaders in times of war. Although the *aḥdāth* corps were recruited by way of voluntary service from various social classes, they were under the command of two aristocratic families of the city. The member of each family in charge of the fraternities of *aḥdāth* was known as 'The Head' *(ra'īs al-balad);* he was in fact, the local mayor or Duke of the city as well. With responsibilities similar to modern-day town mayors, his influence and power usually surpassed that of the highest local religious judicial authorities. Sometimes these 'Heads' constituted dynasties of local nobility, reigning for generations from father to son, their names featured prominently in the histories of the region.

Needless to say, the significance and influence of the *aḥdāth* fraternities in maintaining law and order was greater in those cities which lacked an organized police force *(shurṭa).* The *aḥdāth* can thus be seen as a kind of homespun security unit designed for local needs to settle quarrels, adjudicate in disputes and maintain security in the absence of strong central political authority.

In the Seljuk period (reg. 429/1038–590/1194) the chivalric tradition as practiced by the *'ayyārān* and *shaṭṭārān* encountered fierce

41. The scope of the usage of the word *aḥdāth* also extended into Iran and Persian-speaking lands. During the Safavid era, the *Dārūgha*—a special night-watchman appointed to police the marketplaces of Persian towns and cities, and selected from among the chiefs of local *'ayyārs*—was also called *aḥdāth.* However, the Arabic plural of the word was employed as a singular noun (i.e. *aḥdāth* meant '*one* night-watchman') to designate the qualities of chivalry and *'ayyārī* which the officer was supposed to possess. Thus, one reads in the romance of *Ḥusayn-i Kurd* how the hero sets out every night to fight with the local town *dārūgha,* and, hurling a burning brickbat into the middle of the bazaar at the watchman, cries: "Good night to you, O *aḥdāth* of the night!" In the romance of *Amīr Arsalān* written in the Qajar period, the word again resurfaces, corrupted however, and spelled *A'ṭās;* and it is obvious that in this time the term had quite slipped out of use.

opposition. One reason for this was that their defiance and insubordination, their banditry and seditiousness had reached intolerable proportions; another is that the Seljuk rulers during the period of their greatest efflorescence and power were extremely powerful, with their own effective and strong police force, and were unwilling to tolerate any other powerful body with independent executive strength within their own kingdom.

Accounts of the encounter of the Seljuk state authorities with bands of *'ayyārs*[42] are so frequent in the historical sources of this

---

42. On these events, see especially Rāwandī's *Rāḥat al-ṣudūr*, ed. M. Iqbāl (Leiden 1921), p. 1070ff. It is interesting to note that Rāwandī's account attributes to Basāsīrī (see below, p. 577) the rank of *"Isfahsalār-i lashkar* (Army commander-in-chief)," which was a title used by the *'ayyārān* as well. The following tale from the romance *Samak-i 'Ayyār* details the duties, responsibilities, powers and the respect accorded to an *Isfahsalār* by the secular ruler during that period:

> "Suddenly a rider showed up from a distance with some men running swiftly and bravely alongside him. The gravity of his approach and the ripeness of his years inspired awe. Khūrshīd-shāh asked, "Who is this rider and who are his company?" Khwāja Sa'd said, "This man is called Shaghāl Pīlzūr. He is the leader of the chevaliers *(jawānmardān)* in this city. The other young man at his side dressed in rough feltcloth with daggers bound on either side of his waist is called Samak-i 'Ayyār. He is the head of the knight-errants *('ayyārān)* and Shaghāl's adopted son; the others are their friends. They have total executive authority by order of the Shāh and are the *Isfahsālār* of the city." *(Samak-i 'Ayyār*, I, p. 44)

Now long thereafter, a riot occurs in the city and the Shāh summons the *Isfahsālār* to his court for questioning. The vizier interogates him as follows:

> Shaghāl stood up. ...Samak-i 'Ayyār and a few other men were with him. When they reached the throne room, they stepped forward and made obeisance. Shaghāl was offered a chair beside the royal throne. Then Vizier Mihrān said, "O Isfahsālār Shaghāl, terrible events have recently occurred in the Shāh's kingdom. I do not doubt that you are fully cognizant of these circumstances, since such doings never take place without the Isfahsālār's prior permission. Last night, some bold vigilantes *(rindān)* broke into the prison and carried off all the detainees, killing some other people in the act. How could this have ever happened? I know that your bodyguards are not present and that this deed was the work of your men. This will not be forgiven or overlooked, for it demonstrates your contempt of his Royal Highness! It is not virtuous of you to act in this manner, and even if the Shāh has great respect for you, and does not take you to task for your deeds, such behavior is still completely inexcusable. You must explain yourself." *(ibid.,* I, p. 64).

It is highly probable that the romance of *Samak-i 'Ayyār* was written in the Seljukid period, because the above tale certainly reflects the shape of events taking place in the real political world of fifth/tenth century Persia.

period that we will have to limit our comments here to only few brief examples. The first of the Seljuk rulers, Rukn al-Dunyā wa al-Dīn Tughrïl (reg. 429/1038–455/1063) entered Baghdad in Ramaḍān 447/December 1055 and relieved the last of Būyid princes, Al-Malik al-Raḥīm (reg. 440/1048-447/1055) of his tenure of power. This caused the Būyid prince's powerful Turkish general Abū'l-Ḥārith Arslan Basāsīrī, who later stirred up so much trouble in the Abbasid's caliph's capital, to flee the city, and ultimately, effected his defeat and death at the hand of Seljuk forces in 451/1059. Through the clever manoeuvering of Tughrïl Beg's sagacious vizier 'Amīd al-Mulk Abū Naṣr Kundurī, the caliph, stripped now of most of his temporal powers, became a virtual puppet and appointee of the Seljuk warlord.

As a direct consequence of the Seljukid seizure of power and exercise of *force majeure,* the influence of the followers of martial chivalry was severely curbed; the *jawānmardān* were forced to go underground, conducting their activities in secret and assuming different names. Directly or indirectly, given their Shi'ite proclivities and admiration of 'Alī, the Baghdadī chevaliers in the fifth/tenth century were probably already ardent supporters of the Fāṭimid caliphate of Egypt, who considered themselves defenders of the 'Alīd cause.

Perhaps the two most famous leaders of the *jawānmardān* during the second half of the fifth/eleventh century were the poet, humanist *(adīb)* and calligrapher Abū Naṣr Muḥammad ibn 'Abd al-Bāqī Khabbāz—renowned as Ibn Rasūlī—and 'Abd al-Qādir Hāshimī Bazzāz. The latter was the chief proponent of the path of chivalry during this period and those who gained initiation into its rites generally referred to themselves as his students. Assuming for himself the title of 'Secretary of the Knights' *(Kātib al-fityān),* 'Abd al-Qādir issued his students with special diplomas *(manshūr),* sending matriculated knight-errants out to outlying provinces on missions as his special envoys. In addition to this, he codified the practices of chivalry, organizing a mission for propagation of its tenets and ideals, and defining the proper etiquette to be observed during the knights' assemblies. Furthermore, he is known to have written a letter to Rayḥān Iskandarānī, a highly-place slave of the Fāṭimid caliph who resided in Medina. After this, he soon became recognized as a leading authority on chivalry, and all incoming mail on chivalry-related questions would be sent directly to him and he would deliver his own opinion regarding its contents.[43]

Ibn Rasūlī also composed a treatise explaining the spiritual precedence and significance of the rules and manners of *futuwwa* in the context of Islamic piety. From the mid-fifth/eleventh century (the time of the composition of Ibn Rasūlī's treatise) onwards, we witness increasing literary efforts being made to demonstrate the antiquity of, and establish a historical lineage for, Islamic chivalry. In this vein, Ibn Rasūlī claimed in his treatise that *futuwwa* is the legacy of the Abrahamic prophets and Islamic Imams, that its origins go back to the time of Adam, who, he states, was the first to follow the code and uphold the ideals of chivalry. Following Adam's demise, the mantle of chivalry was handed down to his favourite son and spiritual heir *(waṣī)* the Prophet Seth. From Seth, the mantle of prophecy passed to Noah and then to his son Sām (Shem), and thenceforth to Abraham, whose chivalry is invoked in the Koran (XXI: 60). In Moses' time, writes Ibn Rasūlī, the path of chivalry, especially regarding its esoteric dimension, experienced a great revival, and Moses handed down the lore of chivalry to Aaron. *Futuwwa* resurfaced during the epoch of Jesus, and reached its culmination in the Prophet Muḥammad.

Ibn Rasūlī's treatise, which was later summarized by the Ḥanbalite preacher, Ibn al-Jawzī (d. 597/1200) in his world-history *al-Muntaẓam,* represents the first genuine attempt to provide documentary evidence of the historical lineage of the *futuwwa* tradition in Islam. Despite such efforts, the chevaliers of this period still lacked any real outer institutional structure such that one might label them an organized 'society', although historical texts do acknowledge their leanings towards the Fāṭimid caliphs in Egypt, an issue on which Ibn Rasūlī wrote verbosely.

Gradually his missionary activities on behalf of organized chivalry paid off and his followers and the quantity of his supporters increased vastly, to the point that a full roster of the members of his

43. Ibn Mi'mār, *Kitāb al-futuwwat,* introduction (by Muṣṭafā Jawād), pp. 38-9; Ibn Jawzī, *Al-Muntaẓam,* vol. 8, pp. 326-7.

organization, annotated with their full agnomens and their various party and kin affiliations, was published in two thick volumes! Amongst his members and sympathizers could be counted more than one hundred of the leading notables—aristocrats, merchants, political leaders and local politicians—of the day. His followers regularly congregated in the Barāthā Mosque in western Baghdad, the door of which had fallen into disrepair and which Ibn Rasūlī undertook to restore.

However, when Ibn Rasūlī reached the zenith of his popularity and fame, the true political motives underlying his activities—propaganda for the Fāṭimid caliph—were uncovered by disciples of the Shāfi'ite preacher Abū'l-Qāsim 'Abd al-Ṣamad, who accused him of being a Shi'ite extremist attempting to further Fāṭimid aims under the aegis of chivalry. These allegations were brought to the attention of 'Amīd al-Dawla Ibn Jahīr (reg. circa 472/1080–476/1084), vizier to the Abbasid Caliph al-Muqtadī, who ordered that both Ibn Rasūlī and 'Abd al-Qādir Hāshimī Bazzāz be arrested. In the month of Dhū'l-Ḥijja 773/May 1081 they were both seized and all their writings confiscated. Among the many documents found by the police was Ibn Rasūlī's letter to Rayḥān Iskandarānī. With this damning evidence in hand, Ibn Jahīr proceded to interrogate Ibn Rasūlī, asking him to supply the names of all those who had joined his *Fityān* organization. These Ibn Rasūlī revealed; a mass arrest of his followers was immediately made, some of whom, however, managed to flee. The clerical establishment now stepped into the act, with the jurists obliging the police by issuing fatwas anathematizing the followers of chivalry, obliging them to publicly recant their faith and its 'heretical' doctrines. The Seljuk Sultan's ambassador to the caliph in Baghdad, the *shaḥna,* who was also empowered as a kind of military governor to carry out juridical decisions pronounced by the clerics, used this fatwa as a pretext to ransack the residences of many Baghdadi citizens, pillaging their wealth and properties.

In conclusion, the essential factor underlying the decline of *futuwwa* during this period was the conscious affiliation and connection of these knights with the Egyptian Fāṭimids. Notwithstanding such persecution, the *'ayyārān* and the *shaṭṭārān* did not withdraw their support for the Fāṭimids. This close connection between the adherents of *futuwwa* and the Fāṭimids was also the main reason why, during the final years of the Abbasid caliphate, during the reign of the caliph al-Nāṣir li-Dīn Allāh (reg. 575/1180–622/1225), all the *futuwwa* organizations and centres were dissolved and forced to formally pledge their allegiance to the Abbasid caliph as the supreme leader of his new state-sponsored 'Order of knights'.[44]

Following the arrest of Ibn Rasūlī and the persecution of his followers, the historical texts of the period are full of accounts of persecution by and conflict with the state on the part of the *jawānmardān* and *'ayyārān.* Full discussion of this conflict, which is such a highly important and central issue in the domestic politics of the Seljuk period that it merits an entire monograph of its own, however, is beyond the scope of the present study.

Following the death in 547/1152 of the Seljuk Sultan Mas'ūd, under the rule of the Abbasid caliph al-Muqtafī ibn al-Mustaẓhir (reg. 530/1136–555/1160) caliphal authority in both the religious and temporal spheres was greatly strengthened; on several occasions, al-Muqtafī even successfully stood his ground against the Seljuk sultans. Al-Muqtafī also substantially relieved the pressure upon and persecution of the mercenary-brigands *('ayyārān)* and *jawānmardān,* incorporating many of them as mercenaries in his new private army (which was designed to preserve the independence of the Abbasid caliphate), and sending them out on combat missions against the caliph's enemies in the neighboring cities of Iraq.

By the end of the fourth/tenth century, the highly martially oriented *aḥdāth* of Shām increasingly gained the upper hand, to the point that their influence was felt in Iraq. The sporadic warfare and feuding between the *jawānmardān* of Iraq and the chevaliers of Shām added a new dimension to the age-old violence of these conflicts. Ibn Mi'mar thus comments:

> In this fashion, the tradition of chivalry was handed down from father to son, a tradition which is still being transmitted at the present day. Alas, however, so many different sects, schools, branches and confederations of chevaliers sprung up ...with so

---

44. For a fuller discussion of Nāṣirian chivalry, see the original Persian of the second part of the author's present article, in *Ṣūfī: faṣlnāma-yi Khānaqāh-i Ni'matullāhī* (No. 12, Fall 1370 A.Hsh./1991), pp. 6-18.

> much strife and disagreement between them, that each one held its own party to be God's own and the others astray and in error.

The bloody feuding between the various camps of the knights of Shām continued well into the sixth/twelfth century. Violent conflicts between the *'ayyarān* and *jawānmardān* of Iraq was also hardly less protracted. Especially during periods of weak central government, their disruptive activities served to fuel anarchism and disorder in society. On the other hand, the ancient tradition of Sufi *futuwwa* continued on its own course alongside that of martial chivalry, spreading its own spiritual teachings of devotion, austere piety, other-worldliness, pacifism, and compassion to all humanity throughout the lands of Islam.

Translated from Persian by L. Lewisohn and M. Bayat

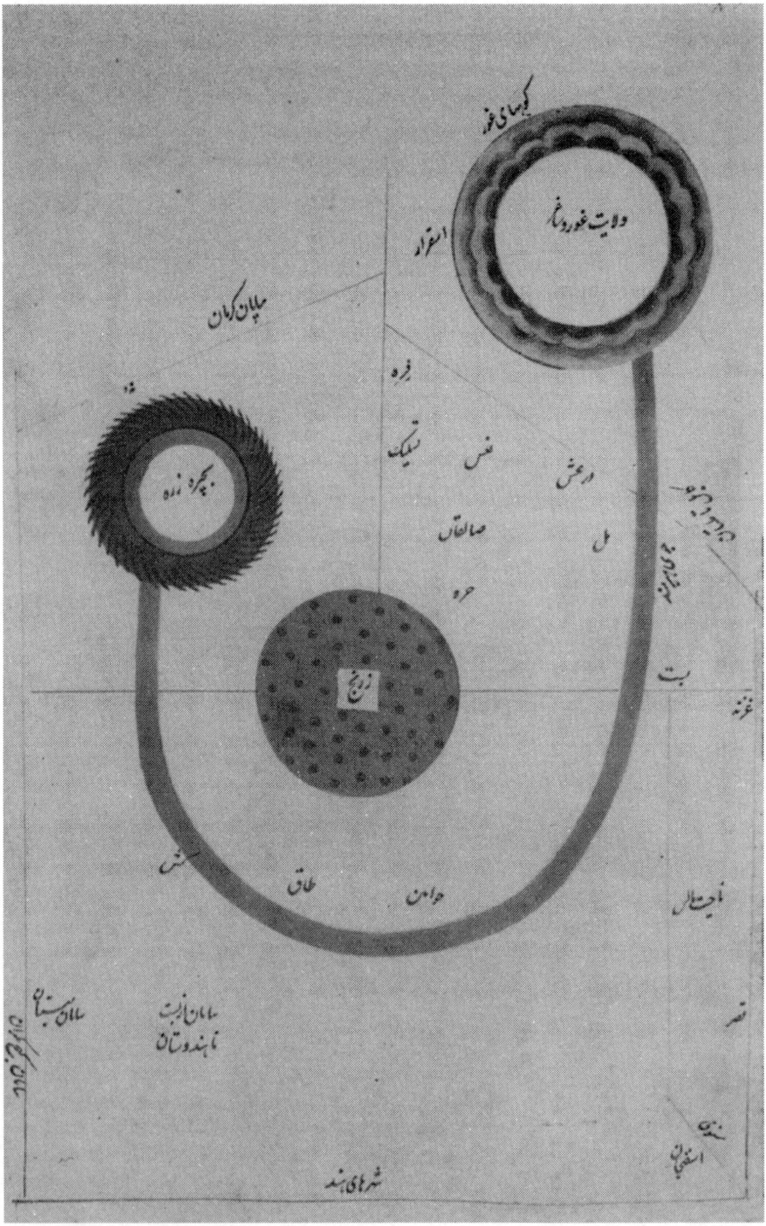

Mediæval Persian Map of Khurāsān. From Al-Iṣṭakhrī's *Ashkāl al-'ālam*. Copied 1835. Add. 23542, f. 76r. (Courtesy of the British Library).

Ḥakīm Tirmidhī and the *Malāmatī* Movement in Early Sufism

Sara Sviri

I. INTRODUCTION

The history of the formative years of Sufism has yet to be written. Much of our knowledge and understanding concerning the early spiritual centres, teachers and teaching, their interaction and the formation of their mystical vocabulary has been shaped by the compilations of later generations. These compilations have become a treasure trove not only of information, but also, and more importantly, of accumulative wisdom, insight and imagery of the mystical tradition of Islam. Yet the main object of the Sufi compilers from the end of the tenth century onwards, both explicitly and implicitly, has been to present a picture of a uniform spiritual tradition, based on the reconciliation of the normative extroverted religious aspect of Islam *(sharīʿa)* with the individualistic, experiential vision of its Reality *(ḥaqīqa)*. In this endeavour, the didactic and practical implications of which have become the bone and marrow of Sufism, the compilers have deliberately ironed out the dynamic multifaceted dialogue which had taken place between the various centres and teachers of the first few generations. Yet hints and allusions to this dialogue have been sown in abundance in the fertile soil of the Sufi compilations, and it is the purpose of this study to trace some of them in order to reconstruct, albeit in a preliminary manner, the outlines of a chapter in the history of the early mystical movements of Islam.

One of the most fascinating and illuminating chapters in the history of these formative years is that of the Nīshāpūrī 'Path of Blame', the *Malāmatiyya*. In any attempt to draft the early history of Islamic mysticism, the *Malāmatiyya* movement is indispensable.

Yet it is also, and to a no lesser degree, an invaluable phenomenon in the History of Religion at large, especially for its attentiveness, its insights and its formulations pertaining to the psychological obstacles which confront any sincere seeker on the path of the spiritual quest. In the *Malāmatī* teaching the dialectic between the *nafs* (the 'lower self' and the centre of ego-consciousness) and the *sirr* (the innermost recesses of one's being) – the paradigmatic dialectic referred to by all mystical traditions – is carried almost *ad absurdum*. The *Malāmatiyya* represent an extremely introverted reaction to extroverted and ascetic forms of spirituality *(zuhd)*. In the course of time this reaction took various shapes and forms, some of them utterly outstripping all religious and social norms (as, for instance, the *Qalandariyya)*. Yet in the ninth century, the formative period with which this essay is concerned, the *Malāmatī* teachers seem to have proposed a system in which sincere self-scrutiny and self-criticism were interwoven into a highly acclaimed social code based on chivalry and altruism (as exemplified by the *futuwwa* fraternities), and in which the call for abandoning any outward marks of distinction or any inward claim to spiritual superiority meant in practice a strict adherence to the Islamic *sharī'a*.

II. NĪSHĀPŪR

The activity of the early *malāmatiyya* takes place in the Khurāsānī town of Nīshāpūr in the third/ninth – fourth/tenth century against the background of varied religious activity, especially on the part of circles with a distinctly ascetic and mystical flavor.

During this period Nīshāpūr,[1] together with Merv, Herat and Balkh, was one of the four main cities of Khurāsān. It stood at an important crossroads from which several main routes spread out: the westward route to Rayy and hence Baghdad; southwest to Shiraz and the Persian Gulf; southeast and then northeast to Herat, Balkh, Tirmidh, Bukhārā and India; and northeast to Ṭūs, Mashhad, Merv,

1. For a detailed description of Nīshāpūr, its geographical position and its social structure, see R.W. Bulliet, *The Patricians of Nishapur*, (Cambridge: Harvard University Press 1972), chap. 1, pp. 4-27. See also G. Le Strange, *The Lands of the Eastern Caliphate*, (London 1966), p. 383ff.

Samarqand, Central Asia and China.

During the reign of the Ṭāhirid Dynasty (820–873) Nīshāpūr was the governmental centre and the capital of Khurāsān.[2] Following the fall of Baghdad to the Buwayhids in 945, Nīshāpūr became the *de facto* centre of Sunnite Islam through to at least the mid-fifth/ eleventh century. In its heyday it consisted of a large number of quarters *(maḥallāt)*, originally villages which became absorbed into the expanding town.[3] Its flourishing agriculture was based on a fine and sophisticated irrigation system, with mostly subterranean canals, which efficiently used the water of the melting snow from the mountains surrounding the city as well as the water of the river which flows through its north-eastern part. It also had a flourishing industry based on weaving and pottery. The north-western part of the city, the Mānishāk suburb, was inhabited mainly by the poor, especially weavers and water-carriers. This was most probably the only area of the city which was not irrigated by canals.[4] The north-eastern sections, sometimes referred to as villages *(qaria, qurā)* – Mulāqabādh, Khordabādh and Nasrabādh – and also the southern suburb of Ḥīra, were inhabited mainly by merchants, well-to-do craftsmen and artisans, as well as by scholars and other members of what might be regarded as a well-established middle class.[5] These 'burghers' lived generally in well-irrigated villas, or owned estates

2. The Ṭāhirids, who ruled from their capital Nīshāpūr, were generally known as loyal to the Abbasids and as sincere upholders of the Sunna in the face of 'suspicious' religious activity (e.g. Shi'ite propaganda, mystical teaching, extreme asceticism, etc.): see C.E. Bosworth, *The Islamic Dynasties,* (Edinburgh 1967), pp. 99-100, 103-06; *idem,* "The Ṭāhirids and Ṣaffārids" in *The Cambridge History of Iran,* IV, 1975, p. 98ff; A.H. Siddiqi, *Caliphate and Kingship in Medieval Persia,* (Philadelphia 1977) [= *Islamic Culture,* vols. 9-11, 1935-37].

3. On the expansion of Nīshāpūr after the Muslim conquest and on the possible identification of some quarters *(maḥallāt)* with earlier villages *(qurā),* see R.W. Bulliet, *op. cit.,* pp. 8-9.

4. See *ibid.,* pp. 11-13 and the sources cited there; on the irrigation system see Muḥammad ibn Aḥmad al-Muqaddasī, *Aḥsan al-taqāsīm fī ma'rifat al-aqālīm,* ed. M.J. De Goeje, (Leiden: E.J. Brill 1906), pp. 299, 329.

5. See Bulliet, *op. cit.,* p. 13 and the sources cited; on Mulāqabādh, Naṣrabādh and al-Ḥīra, see also pp. 92, 193 *et passim;* see also 'Abd al-Ghāfir al-Fārisī, *Al-ḥalqa al-'ūlā min ta'rīkh naysābūr al-muntakhab min al-Siyāq,* ed. Muḥammad Kāẓim al-Maḥmūdī, (Qum 1403/1982-3), no. 1, p. 7; no. 182, p. 97; no. 336, p. 196; on the number and size of the *maḥallāt,* see al-Muqaddasī, *op. cit.,* p. 315.

with large orchards. The most distinguished, and rich families of Nīshāpūr, those whom Richard Bulliet has termed "the Patricians of Nīshāpūr,"[6] lived mainly in the centre of town. These socio-historical observations have a bearing on the identification and characterization of the *Malāmatiyya* which will follow.[7]

Since the third/ninth century the well-being of Nīshāpūr and its inhabitants was impaired by violent religious struggles of a sectarian and fanatical nature. These struggles were known as *'aṣabiyyāt,* and they took place also in other parts of Khurāsān. It seems, however, that Nīshāpūr was the worst affected by them, and that it was they that brought about the eventual decline of the city in the sixth/twelfth century. These "wild sectarian struggles" – *al-'aṣabiyyāt al-waḥsha* – were carried out, according to the tenth-century geographer al-Muqaddasī, against the background of intense hostility between the different schools of religious law (the *madhāhib),* and first and foremost between Ḥanafites and Shāfi'ites.[8] (The Mālikites, Ẓāhirites and Ḥanbalites constituted only a small minority in Nīshāpūr.) There were also struggles between Shi'ite groups and the Karrāmiyya (for which see below), as well as between groups of 'vigilantes' *(mutaṭawwi'a)* and some extremists, such as remnants of the Khawārij. As a general rule, the *madhhab* segmentation correlated with the theological segmentation: most Ḥanafites belonged to the Mu'tazila, whereas most Shāfi'ites adhered to the *ahl al-Sunna wa'l-Ḥadīth,* namely Orthodox Islam, and subsequently to the Ash'arites.[9] It is against this factional and sectarian backdrop that the activities of the early *Malāmatī*s of Nīshāpūr take place.

---

6. See section III: 2 below, and Bulliet, *op. cit.,* Part II: Patrician Families, Introduction, pp. 85-88.
7. On the affiliation of Abū Ḥafṣ al-Ḥaddād, one of the main *Malāmatī* teachers, to Kurādabādh, a village on the north-eastern outskirts of Nīshāpūr, see Sulamī, *Ṭabaqāt al-ṣūfiyya,* ed. N. Sharība, (Cairo 1953), p. 115; the *nisba* of Abū 'Uthmān al-Ḥīrī, the teacher of the second generation of the Nīshāpūrī *Malāmatī*s, speaks for itself; for greater detail on these *Malāmatī* teachers, see below.
8. See al-Muqaddasī, *op. cit.,* p. 326; for the complex problem of determining the origin and typology of the *'aṣabiyyāt* struggles see Bulliet, *op. cit.,* pp. 30ff; see also W. Madelung, *Religious Schools and Sects in Medieval Islam,* (London: Variorium Reprints 1985), in particular "The Spread of Māturīdism and the Turks," II, pp. 109-68, and "The Early Murji'a in Khurasan and Transoxania," II, pp. 32-39.
9. See Page 587–>

III. SOURCES

1) The only source which deals specifically with the *Malāmatiyya* is Abū 'Abd al-Raḥmān al-Sulamī's work entitled *Risālat al-malāmatiyya.*[10] Sulamī (d. 412/1021), himself a native of Nīshāpūr and a member of one of the eminent families there,[11] was also—and this is significant—the disciple of Abū 'Amr Ismā'īl ibn Nujayd. The latter was Sulamī's maternal grandfather and one of the most distinguished disciples of Abū 'Uthmān al-Ḥīrī, one of the central Shaykhs of the *Malāmatī* circle at the end of the third/ninth century.[12] Sulamī's *Risāla* (Epistle) is in fact the only source upon which various scholars have based their historical and typological reconstruction of the *Malāmatiyya*. Some of the most important works are: R. Hartmann's "Al-Sulamī's *Risālat al-Malāmatiyya"*[13] as well as his "Futuwwa und Malāma;"[14] Abū'l-'Alā' al-'Afīfī's *Al-Malāmatiyya wa'l-ṣūfiyya wa ahl al-futuwwa*;[15] Kāmil Muṣṭafā al-

---

9. Madelung, *op. cit.*, pp. 109, 114. On the persecution of the Shāfi'ite-Ash'arites of Nīshāpūr by the Ḥanafite-Mu'tazilites in the eleventh century see H. Halm, "Der Wesir al-Kundurī und die Fitna von Nishapur" in *Die Welt des Orients,* vol. 6 (1971), pp. 205-33; see also *idem., Die Ausbreitung der safi'itischen Rechtsschule von den Anfängen bis zum 8/14 Jahrhundert* (Wiesbaden 1974), pp. 32-42.

10. = "The *Malāmatiyya* Epistle"; henceforth abbreviated as "M.E." There is a French translation of this work by Roger Deladrière: *Sulamī: La Lucidité Implacable (Épître des hommes du blâme),* (Paris: Arléa 1991).

11. Although Bulliet does not include the Sulamīs among the 'Patricians' of Nīshāpūr, several Sulamīs are enlisted among the "Qāḍīs of Nīshāpūr" (see Appendix II, pp. 256-9), starting with one Abū 'Amr Ḥafṣ al-Sulamī who died in 209/824. Abū 'Abd al-Raḥmān al-Sulamī is mentioned as the Sufi teacher of several sons of so-called 'Patrician' families, including Abū al-Qāsim 'Abd al-Karīm al-Qushayrī, the author of the famous *Risāla* or *Epistle on Sufism* (see *ibid.*, p. 152); see also E. Kohlberg's edition of Sulamī's *Jawāmi' ādāb al-ṣūfiyya* and *'Uyūb al-nafs wa mudāwātuhā,* (Jerusalem 1976), pp. 7-8; and Gerhard Böwering, "The Qur'ān Commentary of al-Sulamī" in (eds.) W.B. Hallaq & D. Little, *Islamic Studies Presented to Charles J. Adams* (Leiden: Brill 1991), pp. 43-45..

12. On Abū 'Amr Ismā'īl ibn Nujayd al-Sulamī (d. 366/977), see Abū 'Abd al-Raḥmān al-Sulamī, *Ṭabaqāt al-ṣūfiyya*, p. 454 and the sources cited. The only two teachers who are explicitly referred to by Sulamī in the *Ṭabaqāt* as "*malāmatīs*" are his grandfather Ismā'īl and Ḥamdūn al-Qaṣṣār (see also note 34 below).

13. *Der Islam* , Vol. 8, (1917-18).

14. *Z.D.M.G.* (1918), pp. 193-198.

15. Published: Cairo 1945, which includes a non-critical edition of al-Sulamī's *Risālat al-malāmatiyya.*

Shaybī's *Al-Ṣila bayna 'l-taṣawwuf wa'l-tashayyu';*[16] and J. Spencer Trimingham's *The Sufi Orders in Islam.*[17]

All these studies emphasize the paucity of source material and single out the *Malāmatiyya Epistle*'s value in this respect. In the last resort, in spite of the open scholarly debate by the writers mentioned above as to the relationship between *malāma* and *taṣawwuf, malāma* and *futuwwa, malāma* and *zuhd,* they all draw their scant information from one another, and ultimately, from Sulamī.

What is overlooked by all these scholars is the fact the Sulamī's text was never intended by its author as an historical document. It was written by a disciple and grandson of one of the apparently moderate members of the Nīshāpūrī school, known as the *Malāmatiyya,* with the triple purpose of: a) placing the *Malāmatiyya* in the arena of the mystical tradition within Islam (quite possibly with a view to counterbalancing the Baghdadi centre), of b) promoting the Nīshāpūrī teachers and evaluating their distinctive teaching as the purest in the mystical tradition, and c) vindicating them of the accusation of nonconformity and antinomianism (see below, III: 4).

Later sources, such as Hujwīrī's *Kashf al-maḥjūb,* Shihāb al-Dīn Suhrawardī's *'Awārif al-ma'ārif* or Ibn 'Arabī's *al-Futūḥāt al-Makiyya* are erroneously adduced in some of the aforementioned studies in the endeavor to trace the history of the *Malāmatiyya*—erroneously, since the writers in question are not at all interested in the historical set-up but rather, and solely, in the typological and psychological aspects of the Path of Blame.

2) In 1965 Richard Frye published three facsimiles of manuscripts which relate to a biographical work written probably at the end of the tenth century: *Ta'rīkh Naysābūr* by Abū 'Abdullāh Muḥammad ibn 'Abdullāh al-Ḥākim al-Naysābūrī al-Bayyi' (d. 404/1014).[18]

The original work by Ḥākim al-Naysābūrī has been lost, but large chunks of it were absorbed by al-Sam'ānī in his *Kitāb al-*

---

16. Published: Cairo 1969.
17. Published: Oxford 1971.
18. R.N. Frye, *The Histories of Nīshāpūr,* (Harvard Oriental Series No. 45, The Hague 1965). Al-Ḥākim al-Naysābūrī himself was a disciple of Abū 'Abd al-Raḥmān al-Sulamī: see E. Kohlberg, *op. cit.,* p. 8; *The Cambridge History of Iran,* IV, (1975), pp. 471-2.

Ansāb, by ʻAbd al-Qāhir al-Baghdādī (d. 529/1134) in his *Kitāb al-Farq bayna ʼl-firaq,* and especially by al-Subkī in his *Ṭabaqāt al-Shāfiʻiyya al-kubrā*. The first manuscript in Frye's collection is an abridged version of the *Taʼrīkh Naysābūr* in Persian, entitled *Aḥwāl-i Nishāpūr*. This abridged version covers the period which concerns us, the third/ninth and fourth/tenth centuries, and ends with contemporaries of Ḥakīm al-Naysābūrī.[19] The *Aḥwāl-i Nishāpūr* contains, as expected, biographical lists of the eminent scholars *(ʻulamāʼ)* and Shaykhs of Nīshāpūr in the third/ninth and fourth/tenth centuries. It mentions approximately fifty of the renowned mystics of the town. They are referred to neither as "Sufis" nor as "*Malāmatī*s" but rather as *zuhhād* (ascetics), *ʻubbād* (worshippers), *wuʻʻāẓ* or *mudhakkirūn* (preachers). The epithet "Sufi" comes up for the first time in this source as the attribute of Abū Bakr al-Wāsiṭī (d. 320/932). The latter indeed lived in Nīshāpūr for a number of years, but was not a native of it. He arrived there from Baghdad, where in his youth he had belonged to the circle of Junayd.[20] From the fourth/tenth century on, however, the epithet 'Sufi' appears with increasing frequency in front of the names of the local Shaykhs as well. The attribute *malāmatī* does not appear even once.[21]

---

19. The second text is a sequel to the *Taʼrīkh* composed by ʻAbd al-Ghāfir ibn Ismāʻīl al-Fārisī (d. 529/1134) entitled *Kitāb al-Siyāq li-taʼrīkh Naysābūr* and it covers the fifth/eleventh century. The third text is by Ibrāhīm ibn Muḥammad al-Sārifīnī (d. 641/1243) and is entitled *Muntakhab min K. al-Siyāq)* ("Selected excerpts from the *Siyāq").* For our purposes therefore only the first text is of relevance. The *Muntakhab* has since been edited and published by Muḥammad Kāẓim al-Maḥmūdī under the title of *Al-Ḥalqa al-ʼūlā min taʼrīkh Naysābūr al-muntakhab mina ʼl-Siyāq* (see note 5 above).

20. On Abū Bakr Muḥammad ibn Mūsā al-Wāsiṭī see Sulamī's *Ṭabaqāt,* p. 302; *idem,* M.E., pp. 98,105; al-Sarrāj, *Kitāb al-Lumaʻ,* see index; *Kitāb Aḥwāl-i Nishāpūr,* f. 27a, line 18: "Muḥammad ibn Mūsā al-Wāsiṭī Abū Bakr al-Ṣūfī, [known for] his mystical experiences *(ṣāḥib al-aḥwāl),* lived for a time in Naysābūr, then settled in Merv...and died there."

21. Note Bulliet's tables on pp. 41-2, especially the significant increase in the number of "Sufis" between the years of 314/926 and 335/946 (p. 41, n. 22). However, Bulliet's interpretation of the statistical data, that "from the ninth/third century to the twelfth/sixth, there was a late starting but extremely rapid growth in the specifically mystic Sufi current which absorbed to some degree the earlier ascetic and pietistic currents" (pp. 42-43) is based on the understanding that "Sufi" was the only epithet designating a Muslim 'mystic'. On the evidence from the Nīshāpūrī groups which calls for a modification of such an interpretation, see sections IV-VI below.

These manuscripts have been the basis for R.W. Bulliet's enlightening socio-historical study on the distinguished families of Nīshāpūr during the period between the third/ninth – sixth/twelfth centuries. Its title: *The Patricians of Nishapur, a Study in Medieval Islamic Social History,* speaks for itself.[22]

3) An important source for the history of Khurāsān in the fourth/tenth century are the first-hand descriptions of the famous traveller and geographer from Jerusalem, Abū 'Abdullāh Muḥammad ibn Aḥmad al-Muqaddasī (or Maqdisī, d. 380/990) in his book *Aḥsan al-taqāsīm.*[23] This source is particularly important for the history and characterization of the Karrāmiyya, which received its name from its founder Muḥammad ibn Karrām (d. 255/869). Ibn Karrām was an ascetic and preacher in Khurāsān who exerted an enormous influence, especially among the poor of Nīshāpūr (see below, section VI). Muqaddasī does not mention Khurāsānī 'Sufis' or '*Malāmatī*s' at all by either of these epithets in his book. He refers to the pietists, ascetics and mystics of this region as *'ubbād, zuhhād, wu''āẓ* and *Karrāmiyya,* in a similar way to al-Ḥākim al-Naysābūrī.

4) The earliest source known to me in which the *Malāmatiyya* are mentioned, and which to the best of my knowledge has not yet been adduced in scholarly discussions on the *Malāmatiyya,* are the chronicles of another author from Jerusalem, the historian Abū Naṣr Muṭahhar ibn Ṭāhir al-Muqaddasī, *Kitāb al-Bad' wa'l-ta'rīkh,* written circa 355/966. In the fifth volume of this book Abū Naṣr al-Muqaddasī writes:

22. The last two decades have seen a growing interest in the study of the religious groups in mediæval Khurāsān: Jaqueline Chabbi has used the above as well as other sources in her wide-ranging and profound analysis, written primarily from the point of view of social history: "Remarques sur le developpement historique des mouvements ascetiques et mystiques au Khurasan," in *Studia Islamica,* Vol. 46 (1977); Josef Van Ess has published the first three volumes of his encyclopedic work: *Theologie und Gesellschaft im 2. und 3. Jahrhundert Hidschra,* (Berlin/New York 1990-92), and Wilfred Madelung has published his *Religious Trends in Early Islamic Iran,* Columbia Lectures on Iranian Studies 4, (New York: SUNY Press 1988). On works concerning the Karrāmiyya, see below: note 47.
23. See above, note 4.

> The Sufi groups: among them are the Ḥasaniyya [after Ḥasan al-Baṣrī? or perhaps one should read "al-Ḥusayniyya" after Ḥusayn ibn Manṣūr al-Ḥallāj?], al-Malāmatiyya, al-Sūqiyya and al-Ma'dhūriyya. These are characterized by the lack of any consistent system or clear principles of faith. They make judgements according to their speculations and imagination, and they constantly change their opinions. Some of them believe in incarnationism *(ḥulūl),* as I have heard one of them claim that His habitation is in the cheeks of the beardless youth *(murd).* Some of them believe in promiscuity *(ibāḥa)* and neglect the religious law, and *they do not heed those who blame them...*"[24]

The significance of this mid-tenth-century text for clarifying historical and typological facts concerning the *Malāmatiyya* and other so-called Sufi groups related to them is obvious. There is no doubt that it relates to groups which had chosen to follow the peculiar Path of Blame *(malāma)* and it may thus allude to the unique characteristics of a mystical trend within Islam, practised by the masters of Nīshāpūr to whom Sulamī, barely a generation later, dedicated his *Malāmatiyya Epistle*. The historian Abū Naṣr al-Muqaddasī thus suggests that in the fourth/tenth century a group of "[people] who do not heed those who blame them," known as the *Malāmatiyya,* could have been classified as "Sufis." In itself it is an unfavourable and critical description. It suggests that the *Malāmatiyya,* and the other groups mentioned in association with it, were characterized by a strong antinomian trend with a clear nonconformist flavor. This information, which to the best of my knowledge is unique in the non-Sufi literature of the time, sheds light on the apologetics undoubtably underlying Sulamī's works, the *Malāmatiyya Epistle* as well as his great hagiographical *Ṭabaqāt al-ṣūfiyya:* to vindicate the spiritual teachers of his hometown,[25] in fact, his

24. Abū Naṣr Muṭahhar ibn Ṭāhir al-Muqaddasī, *Kitāb al-Bad' wa'l-ta'rīkh* (Beirut: n.d.), vol. 5, p. 148. According to F. Sezgin, *Geschichte des arabischen Schrifttums* (Leiden 1967), I, p. 337, the book was written in 355/966.

25. According to the Introduction of the *Ṭabaqāt,* Sulamī sets out to record the biographies of the *arbāb al-aḥwāl,* a very general term for Muslim mystics, namely: those who have mystical experiences. He starts off with the successors of the *tābi'ū al-tābi'īn* and finishes with his contemporaries. In his introduction to the M.E., on the other hand, he explicitly distinguishes between the "Sufis," to whom he refers as God's elect *(khāṣṣa),* and the "*Malāmatī*s," whom he refers to as the "elect of the elect" *(khāṣṣat al-khāṣṣa).*

own teachers, of the antinomian and nonconformist accusation, and to include them within the respectfully established "Generations of the Sufis."[26]

5) Additional material which is at our disposal are letters written by Ḥakīm al-Tirmidhī (d. ca. 295/908), a ninth-century mystic of great renown and authority from the Transoxanian town of Tirmidh, to two contemporary mystics associated with the early *Malāmatiyya:* Abū 'Uthmān al-Ḥīrī and Muḥammad ibn al-Faḍl al-Balkhī (see our discussion below of this correspondence, section X). Each of the three letters available to us, which Tirmidhī seems to have written in response to his correspondents' arguments or questions pertaining to the 'psychological' aspect of the mystical path (one to Abū 'Uthmān and two to Muḥammad ibn al-Faḍl), reads as a critique of a system which has been led astray by excessive concern with the negative, blameworthy aspects of the 'lower self' *(nafs)*. There is no doubt that these letters reflect a dynamic dialogue, which took place in ninth century Khurāsān, on the psychological issue, so intrinsic to the *Malāmatiyya,* of how to conquer the lower self. In fact, this issue touches upon a fundamental *malāmatī* problem: how far can one proceed on a spiritual path of uncompromising introverted purification, which entails elimination of any external traces of vanity *('ujb),* presumptuous pretension *(iddi'ā')* and delusion *(ghurūr),* to the point of incurring constant blame, without undermining the ethical and practical precepts of extroverted religion.

IV. MYSTICS NOT NECESSARILY SUFIS

One of the surprising deductions from the study of the various Sufi and non-Sufi sources is that from the third/ninth to fourth/tenth centuries not all Muslim mystics were known as Sufis. Addressing

26. According to the Introduction of the *Ṭabaqāt,* Sulamī sets out to record the biographies of the *arbāb al-aḥwāl,* a very general term for Muslim mystics, namely: those who have mystical experiences. He starts off with the successors of the *tābi'ū al-tābi'īn* and finishes with his contemporaries. In his introduction to the M.E., on the other hand, he explicitly distinguishes between the "Sufis," to whom he refers as God's elect *(khāṣṣa),* and the *"Malāmatī*s," whom he refers to as the "elect of the elect" *(khāṣṣat al-khāṣṣa).*

Muslim mystics with the comprehensive name *ṣūfī* and identifying Islamic mysticism with *taṣawwuf* seems to be the direct result of the compilatory literature of the late fourth/tenth century and later. With Kalābādhī's *Kitāb al-Ta'arruf,* Sarrāj's *Kitāb al-Luma',* Sulamī's *Ṭabaqāt al-ṣūfiyya* and, later on, Qushayrī's *Al-Risāla fī 'ilm al-taṣawwuf* and Hujwīrī's *Kashf al-maḥjūb,* one may trace a clear attempt to present an amalgamated picture of the different schools and centres, without losing sight – albeit subtly and tacitly – of the compiler's own affiliation and allegiance. One may thus argue that Sulamī's *Ṭabaqāt al-ṣūfiyya,* in which he includes mystics of different schools under one heading, complements the more locally particularistic *Malāmatiyya Epistle:* both works are the response of a Khurāsānī-Nīshāpūrī compiler to the emphatically Baghdadi slant of the earlier compilations of Kalābādhī and Sarrāj.

The last two authors, in spite of their Khurāsānī origin, represent in their compilations mainly the Baghdadi school of the third/ninth century. One of Sarrāj's main authorities is Ja'far al-Khuldī (d. 348/959), who appears to have been the main transmitter of sayings and traditions emanating from Junayd, the central Baghdadi teacher during most of the ninth century.[27] In the same vein it is significant to note that in Sarrāj's *Kitāb al-Luma'* the Khurāsānī Shaykhs are scarcely mentioned; some of them are totally glossed over (e.g. Ḥamdūn al-Qaṣṣār and Ḥakīm al-Tirmidhī). This reticence is not at all accidental. It reflects an early split between Baghdad and Khurāsān, a split which, notwithstanding the later amalgamation, has left its traces in the Sufi tradition.[28] This split is highlighted by a curious comment made by the same Ja'far al-Khuldī and recorded by Sulamī in his *Ṭabaqāt,* concerning Ḥakīm al-Tirmidhī:

---

27. On Abū Qāsim al-Junayd (d. 910), see Ali Hassan Abdel-Kader, *The Life, Personality and Writings of al-Junayd: A Study of a Third/Ninth Century Mystic with an Edition and Translation of his Writings*, (London: Luzac & Co., E.J.W. Gibb Memorial Series 1976); see also Sarrāj, *Kitāb al-Luma' fī al-taṣawwuf,* ed. R.A. Nicholson (Leiden 1914), Index. On Abū Muḥammad Ja'far ibn Muḥammad al-Khuldī see Sulamī, *Ṭabaqāt al-ṣūfiyya,* p. 434; Sarrāj, *op. cit.,* index. On his affiliation to Junayd, see also J.S. Trimingham, *The Sufi Orders in Islam,* (Oxford University Press 1973), Appendix A, p. 261.
28. On the 'archetypal' Baghdadi/Junaydi line vs. the Khurāsānī/Bisṭāmī line, see Trimingham, *op. cit.,* pp. 51ff.

> ... I heard Ja'far ibn Muḥammad al-Khuldī say: "I own a hundred and thirty odd works by Sufis." I asked him: "Do you own any of the works of al-Ḥakīm al-Tirmidhī? He said: "No, I do not count him among the Sufis."[29]

At first sight it would appear that in this comment Ḥakīm al-Tirmidhī is snubbed by Khuldī. It may well be understood though as reflecting, behind the fastidious tone, the pre-compilatory period in which the terms *ṣūfī*, *ṣūfiyya* and *taṣawwuf* designated exclusively the Baghdadī teachers. Indeed, in the vast corpus of Tirmidhī's works there does not seem to occur even one reference to 'Sufis', and yet his works are deeply mystical. This assumption is also corroborated by the fact, mentioned above, that in Ḥākim al-Naysabūrī's lists the first to be accorded the title *al-ṣūfī* is Abū Bakr al-Wāsiṭī, who had left the Baghdadi school before moving to Khurāsān. The statistics provided by Bulliet in his study of *Aḥwāl-i Nishāpūr* are also relevant: they show that the distribution of the attribute *ṣūfī* attached to the names of Nīshāpūrī Shaykhs becomes more frequent only from the fourth/tenth century onwards.[30] Sulamī himself seems to explicitly acknowledge this fact in his *Ṭabaqāt* when he remarks about Abū 'Uthmān al-Ḥīrī, the central Nīshāpūrī Shaykh at the end of the third/ninth century (on whom see below, sections V and X), that "...the Sufi system in Nīshāpūr spread from him..."[31] Does this necessarily mean that before Abū 'Uthmān there were no adepts of the mystical path, or only a small number of them, in Nīshāpūr? Or may it not rather suggest that Abū 'Uthmān, a moderate *malāmatī* as well as the spiritual teacher of Sulamī's grandfather, could have adequately represented for Sulamī himself an early attempt to amalgamate the Baghdadi and the Khurāsānī mystical schools under the comprehensive title "Sufi."

It is my contention that Sulamī, who is almost our only positive source of information for the early *Malāmatī* movement in Nīshāpūr, is also the author who is responsible—especially via his *Ṭabaqāt al-ṣūfiyya* in which he includes both Baghdadi and Khurāsānī teachers—for creating the deceptive impression that

29. *Ṭabaqāt al-sūfiyya*, edited by N. Sharība, (Cairo 1953), p. 434.
30. See above, note 21.
31. ... *minhu intashara [sic] ṭarīqat al-taṣawwuf bi-naysābūr, Ṭabaqāt*, p. 170.

taṣawwuf was a homogeneous movement in the formative years of Islamic mysticism. The *Ṭabaqāt* is in fact the main source which has shaped our knowledge and ideas on early Sufi history, so great has been the suggestive impact of his compilations and methods on modern as well as mediæval students.

And yet, having said all this, the bottom line of this brief historical discussion is that ultimately Sulami's *Ṭabaqāt*, as well as Qushayrī's *Risāla* and other compilations, *do* reflect the all-inclusive mystical tradition within Islam. Indeed, the various Shaykhs mentioned and referred to in these compilations are all mystics: seekers for whom a direct numinous experience and the psychological transformation which this experience entails is the end and meaning of their lives and teachings. These seekers and teachers were known in the first few centuries of Islamic history by various names: *ahl al-ma'rifa, ahl al-ḥaqīqa, al-'ārifūn, al-sālikūn, al-zuhhād, al-fuqarā'* etc. At times they were named after their particular teachers: *al-Ḥakīmiyya, al-Ḥallājiyya, al-Qaṣṣāriyya...*[32] They were distinguished by local qualifications related to etiquettes and occupation. It seems most probable that the mainstream of Islamic mysticism in the third/ninth century, that is, the Baghdadi school, adopted the name *ṣūfiyya*.[33] It is possible that this term had initially related to certain ascetical groups.[34] It was not until the

32. See Hujwīrī, *Kashf al-Maḥjūb,* trans. R.A. Nicholson, (London: Luzac & Co. 1936), chap. 14, pp. 176-266; cf. the passage quoted above from Abū Ṭāhir al-Muqaddasī's *Kitāb al-Bad' wa'l-tārīkh*.. Also see note 25 above.

33. Note the telling attempt of Abū Naṣr al-Sarrāj, in one of the introductory chapters of his *Kitāb al-Luma'*, to defend the use of the name *ṣūfiyya* against the accusation of innovation: "The argument that [the name *ṣūfī]* is an innovation invented by the Baghdadis is absurd, since the name was known at the time of Ḥasan al-Baṣrī..." (eds. 'Abd al-Ḥalīm Maḥmūd and 'Abd al-Bāqī Surūr, Cairo/Baghdad 1960, p. 42). Sarrāj's testimony, even if taken at face value, strongly suggests that the adjective *ṣūfī* originally, possibly since pre-Islamic times, had designated a [solitary] ascetic wearing wool; and that subsequently it was adopted by the Baghdadis [probably of Junayd's circle] as the collective denomination for Muslim mystics.

34. On the curious *ṣūfiyyat al-mu'tazila,* see J. van Ess (ed.), *Frühe Mu'tazilitische Häresiographie, Zwei Werke des Nāshi' al-Akbar (g. 293 H.),* (Beirut 1971), p. 50 (text) and pp. 43-44 of the introduction; see also *idem., Theologie und Gesellschaft,* Vol. 4 (forthcoming), 4.2.3: Später Verträter der *Ṣūfiyat al-Mu'tazila,* in section 4.2 entitled "Bagdader Mu'taziliten" (this reference accords with the contents given in Vol. 1 of the *op. cit.).*

second half of the fourth/tenth century – mainly as a result of the compilatory activity – that the terms *ṣūfiyya* and *taṣawwuf* became the comprehensive terms for Muslim mystics and Islamic mysticism at large, including all the various paths and schools within its scope.

V. TWO STREAMS WITHIN THE NĪSHĀPŪRI SCHOOL IN THE THIRD/NINTH CENTURY: ḤAMDŪN AL-QAṢṢĀR AL-MALĀMATĪ, AND THE FOLLOWERS OF ABŪ ḤAFṢ AL-ḤADDĀD AND ABŪ 'UTHMĀN AL-ḤĪRĪ

In the Sufi compilations from the fourth/tenth century onwards, including Sulamī's *Ṭabaqāt,* there is only one Nīshāpūrī Shaykh who is consistently referred to by the attribute *al-malāmatī:* Ḥamdūn al-Qaṣṣār (d. 271/884). According to Sulamī's *Ṭabaqāt* he was the founder of the *malāmatī* school in Nīshāpūr.[35] A close scrutiny of the hagiographical material concerning the third/ninth-century teachers of Nīshāpūr against the backdrop of Sulamī's *Malāmatiyya Epistle* shows that in fact there had been two distinct circles within the Nīshāpūrī Path of Blame: the circle of Ḥamdūn, which was extreme and non-compromising in its pursuit of *malāmat al-nafs,* or 'incurring blame on oneself'[36] and the more moderate circle of Abū

35. Of all the Nīshāpūrī teachers it is Ḥamdūn al-Qaṣṣār alone who is accorded the attribute *Malāmatī* by all of the following hagiographers: Sulamī *(Ṭabaqāt,* pp. 123, 129); Abū Nu'aym al-Iṣfahānī in the *Ḥilyat al-awliyā',* 10 vols., (Cairo 1932-38), vol. 10, p. 231; Qushayrī in the *Risāla* (p. 19) and Hujwīrī in the *Kashf al-maḥjūb.* The latter dedicates a whole chapter to the topic of "Blame" (chap. 6, pp. 62-9), where he says: "The doctrine of Blame was spread abroad in this sect by the Shaykh of his age Ḥamdūn Qaṣṣār (p. 66); likewise he dedicates a separate section to the "Qaṣṣārīs" or followers of Ḥamdūn Qaṣṣār (pp. 183ff.), in which he writes: "Hamdun's doctrine was the manifestation and divulgation of 'blame' *(malāmat).*" Ḥamdūn is also mentioned in the *Aḥwāl-i Nishāpūr,* f. 21b-22a and f. 70a, but with no reference to the epithet *Malāmatī.*

36. According to information culled from the *Ṭabaqāt,* the following list of Ḥamdūn Qaṣṣār's close circle may be drawn: (1) 'Abdullāh ibn Muḥammad ibn Munāzil (d. 331/943)–*Ṭabaqāt,* pp. 123, 366ff; and see also Qushayrī, *Risāla,* p. 26; (2) Abū 'Alī ibn 'Abd al-Wahhāb al-Thaqafī (d. 328/940) – most probably a direct disciple of Ibn Munāzil (–*Ṭabaqāt,* pp. 366, 369); and see also M.E., p. 118; Qushayrī, *Risāla,* p. 26; (3) Abū Bakr Muḥammad ibn Aḥmad al-Farrā' (d. 370/980) – probably the main disciple of Thaqafī and Ibn Munāzil – see *Ṭabaqāt,* pp. 507-8; Qushayrī names him as Muḥammad ibn Aḥmad "al-Malāmatī" *(Risāla,* p. 20); al-Farrā' was one of Sulamī's direct informants (see, e.g. M.E., p. 116).

Ḥafṣ and Abū 'Uthmān. It was the latter circle to which Sulamī's grandfather, as one of the closest disciples of Abū 'Uthmān, adhered.[37]

Ḥamdūn's insistence on the principle of hiding away all external signs of spirituality is exemplified by many stories in the Sufi tradition. The following is what seems to be a candid appraisal of Ḥamdūn by a co-patriot, Nūḥ al-'Ayyār, who probably belonged to one of the more extroverted spiritual circles in Nīshāpūr:

> I [Nūḥ]...wear a patched frock...in order that I may become a Sufi and refrain from sin because of the shame that I feel before God; but you put off the patched frock in order that you may not be deceived by men and that men may not be deceived by you..."[38]

An indication of Ḥamdūn's denunciation of overt spiritual practices we may read in the following passage from the *Malāmatiyya Epistle,* in which Ḥamdūn al-Qaṣṣār criticizes the audible *dhikr* (the practice of remembering God vocally[39]):

> When some of the teachers were in a gathering with Ḥamdūn al-Qaṣṣār a certain master was mentioned and it was said that he practiced *dhikr* profusely. Ḥamdūn remarked, "Still, he is constantly heedless." Someone who was present inquired, "But is he not obliged to be grateful that God bestows upon him the ability to commit himself to the audible *dhikr?*" Ḥamdūn said, "Is he not obliged to see his limitation when the heart becomes heedless by the [audible] *dhikr?*"[40]

---

37. The list of the immediate circle of Abū 'Uthmān, as culled from the *Ṭabaqāt,* is naturally more extensive; here are the names of a few disciples only: Maḥfūẓ ibn Maḥmūd (d. 304/916), who probably became the successor of Abū 'Uthmān (see *Ṭabaqāt,* pp. 273-4, 417, 501; also M.E., p. 102); Abū Muḥammad al-Murta'ish (d. 328/940) – see *Ṭabaqāt,* p. 349; Abū Muḥammad 'Abdullāh al-Rāzī (d. 353/964) – see *Ṭabaqāt,* p. 451, *Kitāb Aḥwāl-i Nishāpūr,* f. 70a; M.E., p. 119; Abū 'Amr Ismā'īl ibn Nujayd al-Sulamī, one of the closest disciples of Abū 'Uthmān – see *Ṭabaqāt,* p. 454. In the *Kitāb al-Luma'* the latter seems to feature as Sarrāj's direct transmitter of sayings ascribed to Abū 'Uthmān – see *K. al-Luma',* pp. 103, 208, 277.
38. *Kashf al-Maḥjūb,* p. 183.
39. On the distinction between vocal and non-vocal *dhikr,* see Muḥammad Isa Waley's essay in this volume. –Ed.
40. M.E., pp. 91-92.

As for Abū 'Uthmān al-Ḥīrī, one of the correspondents of Ḥakīm al-Tirmidhī mentioned above (see also below, section X), he was the central Shaykh of the Nīshāpūrī school from *circa* 270/883 to 298/910. He was born in Rayy, where he became the disciple of Shāh Shujā' Kirmānī. Hujwīrī tells us how on a visit with his teacher to Nīshāpūr, he became deeply impressed with their host Abū Ḥafṣ Ḥaddād, one of the leading spiritual teachers of his day. Abū Ḥafṣ "saw" intuitively the struggle in Abū 'Uthmān's heart—torn between loyalty to his teacher and the strong inclination towards Abū Ḥafṣ. The latter therefore asked Shāh Shujā' to leave his disciple behind. Thus Abū 'Uthmān became Abū Ḥafṣ' closest disciple, and eventually, his successor.[41] The *Malāmatiyya Epistle* tells us that Abū 'Uthmān trained his disciples in the middle path that ran between his teacher's method and that of Ḥamdūn. Thus, according to Abū Ḥafṣ' teaching the disciples were encouraged to carry out many spiritual practices, the merits of which were emphasized. According to Ḥamdūn, on the other hand, spiritual practices were criticized and denounced in order to eliminate conceit and inflation. Abū 'Uthmān taught the middle path. He said:

> Both ways are correct; each, however, in its right time. At the beginning of his novitiate we train the disciple in the path of practices and we encourage him to follow it and establish himself in it. However, when he is established and consistent in this path he becomes attached to it and dependent on it. Then we show him the shortcomings of this path of actions [or efforts] and our disregard for it, until he becomes aware of his helplessness, and sees how remote his efforts are from completion. Thus we make sure that first he becomes grounded in practices, yet does not (later on) fall into self-delusion. Otherwise, how can we show him the shortcomings of his practices if he has no practices?... Between the two this is the most balanced way.[42]

---

41. See Hujwīrī, *Kashf al-Maḥjūb,* pp. 132-4; on Abū 'Uthmān Sa'īd ibn Ismā'īl al-Ḥīrī see also Sulamī, *Ṭabaqāt,* p. 170ff. On Abū Ḥafṣ 'Amr ibn Salama al-Ḥaddād al-Naysābūrī (d. 260/874), see Sulamī, *Ṭabaqāt,* p. 115ff; both Abū Ḥafṣ and Abū 'Uthmān are mentioned in the *Aḥwāl-i Nishāpūr* (f. 70a) among the Nīshāpūrī sages *(mashāyikh)* without any reference to either 'Sufi' or *'Malāmatī'*. On the special relationship between Abū Ḥafṣ and Abū 'Uthmān see also Sarrāj, *Kitāb al-Luma',* p. 177.

42. M.E., p. 103.

In response to a letter from Muḥammad ibn al-Faḍl al-Balkhī, a close companion of Abū 'Uthmān and another of the correspondents of Ḥakīm al-Tirmidhī mentioned above (also see below, section X), who asked him how one can perfect one's actions and states, Abū 'Uthmān wrote:

> No action or state can become perfect unless God brings it about without any wish on the doer's part and without any awareness of the doing of the action, and without awareness of another's observation of the action.[43]

It is interesting to note that after Abū 'Uthmān's death the Nīshāpūrī centre seemed to lose its attraction and many of the disciples found their way to other centres, especially the one in Baghdad.[44]

VI. *MALĀMATIYYA* AND *KARRĀMIYYA*

The *Malāmatī* school of Nīshāpūr during the third/ninth century advocated the realization of a spiritual experience of rare psychological purity. The key terms in *malāmatī* psychology are: *riyā', iddi'ā'*, *'ujb* and *ikhlāṣ*. *Riyā'* (hypocrisy, acting ostentatiously) relates to the psychological dangers which arise when spiritual attainments become ostensible; *iddi'ā'* (pretense, presumption) relates to self-delusion; *'ujb* (conceit, vanity) to the pride and inflation which are bound up psychologically with the perception of one's own spiritual attainments; *ikhlāṣ* (sincerity) relates to a state in which one's actions and perceptions become free of the contamination of the ego or the lower self *(nafs)*. The main aim of the *Malāmatiyya* is to reach a stage in which all one's psychological and spiritual attainments become totally introverted. This aspiration is succinctly expressed in the following saying attributed to its central teacher Abū Ḥafṣ Ḥaddād (as well as by many similar sayings scattered throughout the relevant literature):

---

43. M.E., p. 106.
44. Thus, e.g. Abū Muḥammad al-Murta'ish, Abū 'Amr al-Zajjājī, 'Alī ibn Bundār – according to Sulamī's *Ṭabaqāt*.

> They [the *malāmatīs*] show off what is blameworthy and conceal what is praiseworthy. Thus people blame them for their outward [conduct] while they blame themselves for their inward [state]..."[45]

There is no doubt that as a mystical path the *malāmatiyya* represented a sharp, albeit subtle and well-codified, reaction against movements known for their extreme asceticism, movements which had a tremendous following in third/ninth-century Khurāsān. The *malāmatī* reaction is itself a continuation of the anti-*zuhdī* tendency of certain circles within Islam right from its very beginning.[46] Islamic mysticism – contrary to what one may expect – is steeped in this anti-*zuhdī* tendency.[47]

From the *Aḥsan al-taqāsīm* of al-Muqaddasī, as well as from the biographical lists of Ḥākim al-Naysābūrī, the *Ṭabaqāt al-Shāfi'iyya* and other heresiographical and hagiographical sources, we learn of

---

45. M.E., p. 89.

46. On this anti-*zuhdī* attitude in early Islam, see the author's "*Wa-rahbāniyyatan ibtada'ūhā* – An Analysis of Traditions Concerning the Origin and Evaluation of Christian Monasticism," in *Jerusalem Studies in Arabic and Islam,* vol. 13, (1990), pp. 195-208.

47. The intriguing dialectic between 'mysticism' and 'asceticism' in the Sufi tradition deserves a separate discussion. Suffice it to mention here the reluctance of Sufis to accept at face value the etymological derivation of *ṣūfī* from *ṣūf* (= wool, woolen garment), preferring the more linguistically awkward derivation from *ṣafā'* (= purity). See, for example the opinions voiced by Hujwīrī *(Kashf al-Maḥjūb,* pp. 30ff); Qushayrī *(Risāla, bāb fī'l-taṣawwuf,* p. 126). A warning that the ascetic custom of wearing rough wool or a patched garment might become "ostentatious" *(shuhra)* is voiced by Muḥāsibī (d. 243/857) in his *Al-Masā'il fī a'māl al-qulūb wa'l-jawāriḥ,* (Cairo 1969), pp. 103ff); see, e.g., p. 108: "I would beware of ostentation *(shuhra)* [in wearing ascetic-like clothes] lest it should corrupt the hearts so that they become contrived or conceited or arrogant or domineering..." In this vein it is related by Muḥāsibī that Sa'īd ibn al-Musayyib, one of the *tābi'ūn,* when asked about the type of clothing that should be worn by pious Muslims, said; "Purify your heart and wear whatever you like!" Ḥakīm Tirmidhī (d. ca. 295/908) attacks vehemently the so-called ascetics *(al-mutazahhidūn):* see, e.g. his *Nawādir al-uṣūl,* (Istanbul 1294/1877), p. 64, where he comments on "those who seemingly abstain from the things of this world for the sake of appearances and reputation... thinking that abstention *(zahāda)* means vilifying the world, eating from refuse, wearing wool [!], disparaging the rich and celebrating the poor..." Also cf. the dictum ascribed to Bayāzīd Bisṭāmī: "Three [types] of men are the most obscured from God: the scholar *(al-'ālim)* by his erudition, the pious worshipper *(al-'ābid)* by his piety, and the ascetic *(al-zāhid)* by his asceticism" (M.E., pp. 96-7). Many more references can be adduced from the wide range of Sufi works.

the popularity and the tremendous influence exerted by the Karrāmiyya – the followers of Muḥammad ibn Karrām – on the lower classes of Khurāsān and especially Nīshāpūr.[48] Edmund Bosworth in his studies describes an extremely militant and ascetic movement, which, on account of its popularity among the weavers and water-carriers who inhabited the north-western sections of Nīshāpūr (according to Bulliet's description, the poor district known as Mānishāk), became a threat to the Ṭāhirid rulers. The disciples of Ibn Karrām were apparently the first Muslims who established a quasi-monastic institution in Khurāsān, which they named *Khānqāh*. Indeed, al-Muqaddasī refers to them also as *Khānqāhiyyūn*.[49] Although the Karrāmiyya are attacked in the pro-Shāfi'ite heresiographies for their theological opinions, their extreme asceticism is nowhere disputed. In his *Ṭabaqāt al-Shāfi'iyya* al-Subkī, who cannot be accused of favoring them, gives the following description of their leader Ibn Karrām:

> ...He used to exhibit a great deal of piety *(tanassuk)*, Godfearing *(ta'alluh)*, devotional worship *(ta'abbud)* and asceticism *(taqashshuf)* ... Special assemblies were conducted for him, and when he was asked about his ideas he would say that they come from divine inspiration *(ilhām)*...

Quoting al-Ḥākim, al-Subkī continues:

> I was told that he was followed by a group of the poor *(fuqarā')*, that he used to wear dyed but unsewn sheep skin; on his head he used to wear a white *qalansuwwa*, and that he used to sit in a stall [at the market]...preaching... The governor of Sijistān had expelled him...but was afraid to execute him because of his ostensible piety and asceticism *(al-'ibāda wal-taqashshuf)* which attracted to him many followers *(iftatana bihi khalq kathīr;* lit.: 'by which many people were deluded ...')[50]

48. On the Karrāmiyya in Khurāsān, see C.E. Bosworth in EI^2: "Karrāmiyya," IV, pp. 667-9; *idem,* "The Rise of the Karāmiyya [sic] in Khurāsān," *Muslim World,* (1960), pp. 6-14; R.W. Bulliet, *The Patricians of Nishapur,* pp. 62-4; J. Van Ess, *Ungenutzte Texte zur Karramiya, Eine Materialsammlung,* (Heidelberg 1980); W. Madelung, "Sufism and the Karrāmiyya" in *Religious Trends,* pp. 39-53.
49. See also *K. al-Ansāb,* s.v. *Khānqāhī*.
50. *Ṭabaqāt al-Shāfi'iyya,* (Cairo 1964), Vol. 2, pp. 304-5. Cf. J. Van Ess, *Theologie un Gesellschaft,* Vol. 2, p. 609ff.

From al-Sam'ānī's *Kitāb al-Ansāb* we have an indirect piece of evidence for the critical attitude with which the *Malāmatiyya* regarded the Karrāmiyya's extroverted asceticism. He tells us about a confrontation between Sālim ibn Ḥasan al-Bārusī, one of the teachers of Ḥamdūn al-Qaṣṣār al-Malāmatī, and Muḥammad ibn Karrām:

> Sālim ibn al-Ḥasan al-Bārusī came to Muḥammad ibn Karrām. [Muḥammad] asked [al-Bārusī]: "What do you think of my followers?" He said: "If the longing of their interior were seen manifest in their exterior, and the asceticism of their exterior were concealed in their interior then they would have been 'men'.[51] And he added, "I see much prayer, fasting and humiliation; yet I cannot see the light of Islam upon them."[52]

Interestingly, in the early Sufi literature there is no mention of the Karrāmiyya. Hujwīrī in the fifth/eleventh century is the first Sufi author who mentions one of their teachers – Aḥmad ibn Ḥarb.[53] This reticence is very significant. In Sufi ethics polemics is counter-advocated. This, therefore, must have been the way in which the early Sufi tradition chose to alienate itself from these extreme ascetic circles: to simply ignore them. Bearing in mind the tendency of the later compilatory literature to standardize and amalgamate the different mystical schools, this silence has very loud reverberations. It reflects the on-going dialectical attitude of Islamic mysticism towards extroverted ascetical behaviour and practice.

VII. THE CHIVALRIC TRADITION *(FUTUWWA)*

The tradition of spiritual chivalry *(futuwwa* = chivalry, generosity; literally 'youth')[54] concerns us here because it was an important part of the socio-religious scene in Khurāsān, and because many of the Khurāsānī and Nīshāpūrī teachers refer to themselves as *fatan* (= youth; the Persian equivalent of which is *jawānmardī),* naming their disciples *fityān* (the plural form), and dedicating many sayings and

---

51. *Rijāl:* i.e., those who have attained the rank of 'spiritual manhood' *(rujūliyya);* see notes 56-57.
52. Sam'ānī, *Kitāb al-Ansāb,* p. 159 (quoted by 'Affifi, *Malāmatiyya,* p. 38); see also J. Van Ess, *Theologie und Gesellschaft,* Vol. 2, p. 610.
53. On Aḥmad ibn Ḥarb, see J. Van Ess, *op. cit.,* p. 609.
54. On chivalry and Sufism during this period, see above, pp. 549-81. –Ed.

even whole treatises to the topic of *futuwwa*. Sulamī composed an entire book on spiritual chivalry, the *Kitāb al-Futuwwa;* one finds, likewise, a special chapter devoted to this theme *(bāb fī 'l-futuwwa)* in Qushayrī's *Risāla*. The use of *futuwwa* terminology, similar to that of *zuhd* terminology, has caused great confusion in the study of the historical implications and the terminology of the early Sufi lexicon. Hartmann, Taeschner, Trimingham and others are all concerned with the differentiation between *futuwwa* and *malāma*.[55]

The *futuwwa* organization has a primarily socio-ethical connotation: it is the name given to the system of closed societies of crafts and professions in mediæval Persian towns. These societies were exclusive and esoteric. Members were not only required to belong to the relevant professions but were required to abide by the strictest ethical and professional standards. It seems that the most important of these ethical norms was *īthār* – extreme altruism or self-sacrifice, to the extent of always giving precedence to one's neighbour, especially to the fellow members of the fraternity. The etiquette of the *fityān* also concerned specific garments and items of clothes by which they were distinguished. It is evident from Sufi compilations as well as from the *Malāmatiyya Epistle* that the social-professional *futuwwa* and the mystical *futuwwa* were interrelated. Qushayrī's *Risāla* abounds with anecdotes about Sufi *fityān,* most of whom it appears are affiliated to Khurāsānī teachers.

Study of the relevant source material has led me to the conclusion that the interrelatedness (rather than identity) between *Futuwwa* and *Malāmatiyya* was based on the following principles:

1) The *Malāmatiyya* identified with the *fityān* in regard to their attitude to altruistic self-sacrifice or *īthār*.

2) The *Malāmatiyya* masked their mystical life under the guise of the social *futuwwa*. Many of the *malāmatī* teachers and disciples bore epithets indicating crafts and professions: *al-Ḥaddād* (=the

---

55. See, e.g. R. Hartmann, "Futuwwa und Malāma" in *Z.D.M.G.*, (1918), pp. 193-8; F. Taeschner, "Der Anteil des Sufismus an der Formung des Futuwwideals" in *Der Islam,* Vol. 24 (1937), pp. 43-74; *idem,* "Futuwwa" in E.I.^{2}, Vol. 2, pp. 961-969 and the sources cited there. See also J.S. Trimingham, *The Sufi Orders in Islam,* p. 24; M. Hodgson, *The Venture of Islam* (Chicago & London: University of Chicago 1974-77), II, pp. 126ff.

ironsmith), *al-Qaṣṣār* (=the bleacher), *al-Ḥajjām* (=the cupper), *al-Khayyāṭ* (=the tailor). Thus, in the *Malāmatiyya Epistle* Ḥamdūn al-Qaṣṣār says to ʻAbdullāh al-Ḥajjām:

> It is better for you to be known as ʻAbdullāh *al-Ḥajjām* (the bath-attendant, cupper) than as ʻAbdullāh the Mystic *(al-ʻĀrif)*, or as ʻAbdullāh the Ascetic *(al-Zāhid)*.[56]

3) The *Malāmatīyya* adopted the term *futuwwa* (youthful chivalry) as a code-name for one of the stages in the mystical hierarchy, perhaps the one preceeding manhood *rujūliyya*. Such terms as 'man' *(rajul)*, 'manliness' (*rujūliyya)*, 'men' *(rijāl)* as well as 'perfect manliness', 'complete maturity' *(kamāl al-rujūliyya)* appear quite often in Sulamī's writings. In the *Malāmatiyya Epistle*, for instance, we read:

> Abū Yazīd was asked: "When does a man reach the stage of manhood in this business *(matā yablughu al-rajul maqāma al-rijāl fī hādhā al-amr)?* He said: When he becomes aware of the blemishes of his lower self *(nafs)* and when his charge against it increases *(idhā ʻarafa ʻuyūb nafsihi wa qawiyat tuhmatuhu ʻalayhā)*.[57]

Most illuminating in this regard is a saying ascribed to Abū Ḥafṣ, in which he assesses the spiritual attainments of Abū ʻAbdullāh ibn Muḥammad al-Rāzī (d. ca. 310/922):

> It was told that Abū Ḥafṣ had said [concerning the above]: A 'youth' *(fatan)* grew up in Rayy; had he kept [faithfully] to his path and to the [behaviour appropriate to] this attribute, he would have become one of the 'men' (*rijāl)*."[58]

---

56. M.E., p. 94. Likewise Sulamī (M.E., p. 109) recounts how Bishr al-Ḥāfī (= the Barefoot) one day knocked at the door of one of the Shaykhs. "Who is it?" a voice asked. "It is I**...** Bishr al-Ḥāfī." he replied. The Shaykh's daughter replied: "If you had bought yourself a pair of sandals for two *dāniqs*, you would have gotten rid of this name *(lau ishtarayta naʻla bidāniqayn lasaqata ʻanka hādhā al-ism)*."
57. M.E., p. 95. Cf. also Sulamī's adage: "He who abides by the right rules of conduct during the occurrence of mystical states has reached the stage of 'men' *(man lazima ādāb al-awqāt balagha mablagh al-rijāl)*" (*Ṭabaqāt*, p. 119).
58. *nash'a bi-l-rayy fatan; in baqiya ʻalā ṭarīqatihi wa-simatihi ṣāra aḥada al-rijāl* –*Ibid*., p. 288.

VIII. *MALĀMATIYYA* AND *ṢŪFIYYA*

As explained above, *ṣūfiyya* and *malāmatiyya* are two terms pertaining to two different mystical schools in the third/ninth century: the Baghdadi and the Khurāsānī schools respectively. Between these two schools there were relationships and communications. From the *Ṭabaqāt al-ṣūfiyya* we know of disciples who moved from one centre to another: there were Baghdadis such as Abū Bakr al-Wāsiṭī who moved to Khurāsān, and Khurāsānīs who moved to Baghdad or stayed there for a while on their journey *fī ṭalab al-'ilm* (in search of knowledge). Analyzing the somewhat dry biographical material supplied by the *Ṭabaqāt* it seems that the Nīshāpūrī centre reached its zenith during the time of Abū Ḥafṣ al-Ḥaddād, Ḥamdūn al-Qaṣṣār and Abū 'Uthmān al-Ḥīrī in the second half of the third/ninth century, when it attracted disciples from far and wide. After Abū 'Uthmān's death, however, it appears that the Nīshāpūrī disciples started to wander off. Many found their way to the Baghdadi centre of Junayd (Junayd died between six to ten years after Abū 'Uthmān, and at least twenty years after Abū Ḥafṣ).

There exists at least one interesting record of a meeting between the teachers of the two schools—Abū Ḥafṣ and Junayd—with their disciples in Baghdad. From this anecdote, which is related by Sulamī in the *Ṭabaqāt* (pp. 117-18), in the interaction between these two Shaykhs, one can detect the subtle dialectics which operated between these two schools. This interaction illustrates the notion of proper manners and dignity conceived according to the strict code of *adab* (code of conduct, behaviour, proper manners or etiquette), especially *īthār,* and at the same time it contains also a hidden rebuke:

> When Abū Ḥafṣ came to Baghdad the Shaykhs of Baghdad gathered round him and asked him what the *futuwwa* was. He said: "You speak first, because you possess eloquence."
>
> Junayd said: "*Futuwwa* is that one obliterates the vision [of one's acts and merits] and stops taking notice of them *(isqāṭ al-ru'ya).*"
>
> Abū Ḥafṣ said: "How eloquently have you spoken! Yet for me *futuwwa* is that one should conduct oneself according to what is right and just *(inṣāf)* without expecting to be treated according to what is right and just."

> Junayd said: "Arise, my friends, for Abū Ḥafṣ has transcended Adam and his descendants!"

In the last words of Junayd one can discern a subtle irony, perhaps even a concealed criticism of Abū Ḥafṣ' over-submissiveness to the *īthār* code, while there is no doubt that Abū Ḥafṣ' praise of the Baghdadi eloquence is also double-edged. Indeed, just before departing, when he is again pressed by the Baghdadis to give his definition of *futuwwa* Abū Ḥafṣ says:

> *Futuwwa* is practiced by actions not by speech *(al-futuwwa tu'khadhu isti'mālan wa mu'āmalatan lā nuṭqan).*

It is also related that Abū Ḥafṣ could not speak Arabic at all, but by way of a certain charismatic power *(karāma)* vouchsafed to him he was enabled to understand the Baghdadi brethren and even answer them in their language.

IX. *MALĀMATĪ* PRINCIPLES

The main principle on which the *Malāmatī* Path is based requires that one always behold one's self as blameworthy. Rather than being an ethical postulate, this principle stems primarily from a psychological understanding of the nature of the self. The 'self', or more accurately the 'lower self' *(nafs),* is understood by the *Malāmatī* mystics as being the tempting element in the psyche, *al-nafs al-ammāra bi'l-sū':* 'the soul which prods one to evil' and in this capacity it functions as the *agent provocateur* of Satan, the lusts and all evil inclinations. Yet it is also understood as the centre of ego consciousness. Most mystical systems agree that the more one's energy is absorbed in satisfying and gratifying the requirements of the ego, the less energy can be put into the process of psychological and spiritual transformation. However, by ascetic practices alone the humiliation and surrender of the *nafs* cannot be achieved. On the contrary, the ascetic path often brings about an inflated hardening of the *nafs*. Inflation and conceit derive from both one's self-appraisal *(riyā', 'ujb)* as well as from external social feedback *(shuhra, ri'āsa)*. The Nīshāpūrī school known as the *Malāmatiyya* therefore taught that the only way to neutralize the *nafs* is to expose it to blame and humiliation in all circumstances and conditions. The blame and humiliation should be incurred from both external agents and from the *malāmatī* himself. Blame should be drawn upon one's self not only in accordance with what is considered *blameworthy* by social, religious and ethical standards, but also—and first and foremost—with disregard to what is accepted as *praiseworthy* by these standards. Evidently, this lends the *malāmatiyya* a clear nonconformist character.

Perhaps the most paradoxical and bewildering aspect of *malāmatī* teaching concerns blame in the arena of spiritual practice and mystical experience. Thus we read in Sulamī:

> Most of the *[malāmatī]* Shaykhs warn their disciples against relishing the taste of devotional worship. This is considered by them a grave offense [*min al-kabā'ir*). This is because when the human being finds anything to be sweet and desirable it becomes important in his eyes; and whoever regards any of his actions as good and desirable, or regards any of his actions with satisfaction, falls from the stage of the eminent ones.[59]

In psychological terms, the *malāmatī* teachers are warning their disciples against inflation of the ego which may accompany spiritual realization. However, the ultimate purpose of this path of contrariety is to reach a psychological stage of equanimity where no importance is attached to either praise or blame.[60]

Perhaps the best way to illustrate the complexity of the *malāmatī* masters' teaching, and to expose the principles of the mystical methods to be followed in order to combat the wiles of the ego, is to examine their own words. The following excerpts from Sulamī's *Malāmatiyya Epistle* reveal some of the depth of their psychological speculations in this regard:

> Ḥamdūn al-Qaṣṣār was asked, "What is the Path of Blame?" "It is to abandon in every situation the desire to smarten up in front of people," he said, "to renounce in all one's states and actions the need to please people, and to be at all times beyond blame in fulfilling one's duties to God."

---

59. M.E., p. 96.
60. In the chapter "On Blame" in the *Kashf al-Mahjūb* (pp. 68-9), Hujwīrī relates a personal anecdote as an illustration of the state of equanimity towards both praise and blame which he had realized through being subjected to abuse by fellow Sufis.

The *malāmatīs* outwardly have no special marks distinguishing them from other people, and inwardly make no claims with God, so that their innermost consciousness *(sirr),* which lies between them and God, can be perceived by neither their inner hearts *(af'ida)* nor outer hearts *(qulūb).*

No man can attain the rank of these people [the *malāmatīs*] unless he regards all his actions as hypocrisy *(riyā')* and all his spiritual states as presumptuous pretense *(da'āwā).*

One of the *[malāmatī]* teachers was asked, "What are the first steps in this affair?" He answered, "To humiliate and abase the lower self *(nafs)* and deprive it of what it relies upon, of that which it finds comfort with, and of what it inclines towards; to respect others, to regard others with favour, to justify the wrongdoings of others and to rebuke one's own self.[61]

The *malāmatīs* are those over whose innermost consciousness *(asrār)* God keeps watch, drawing over their innermost consciousness the curtain of formal appearances, so that outwardly they participate in all activities performed by their fellows, keeping company with them in the marketplaces and in earning a means of livelihood, while in their true essence and [spiritual] conduct they associate with God alone.[62]

Spiritual states are valuable assets deposited in the hearts of their trustees; whoever externalizes them forfeits the rank of a trustee.[63]

He who wishes to understand the waywardness of the lower self *(nafs)* and the corruption of the instinctual nature let him observe himself when praised. If he notices that his lower self is favourably affected, even minutely, by what he hears, he should realize that it has deviated from the Truth, for the lower self relies on praise which has no truth in it, and is disturbed by blame which has no truth in it.[64]

One of them was asked concerning the path of Blame. He replied, "It is to abandon being conspicuous *(shuhra)* in all matters which may distinguish one in the eyes of people, whether in one's manner of dressing, walking or sitting... He should rather adopt the

61. M.E., p. 90.
62. *Ibid.*, p. 91.
63. *Ibid.*, p. 92.
64. *Ibid.*, p. 96.

external behaviour of the people in whose company he is, while at the same time be isolated from them by way of contemplation, so that his exterior person conforms with society so as not to be distinguished in any way, while his interior reality is in utter distinction."

One of them was asked, "Why do you not participate in *samāʿ* gatherings [musical concerts conducive to ecstasy]?" "It is not," he replied, "out of objection to *samāʿ* that we abstain from attending its gatherings, but rather out of fear that we may not be able to conceal our inner spiritual states, and this is grave for us."[65]

One of their principles is that there are four grades of remembrance of God *(dhikr):* the *dhikr* of the tongue, the *dhikr* of the heart, the *dhikr* of the innermost consciousness *(sirr)* and the *dhikr* of the spirit *(rūḥ)*. If the *dhikr* of the spirit is sound the heart and the innermost consciousness are silenced: this is the *dhikr* of contemplation *(mushāhada)*. If the *dhikr* of the innermost consciousness is sound, the heart and the spirit are silenced: this is the *dhikr* of awe *(hayba)*. If the *dhikr* of the heart is sound the tongue is silenced: this is the *dhikr* of divine graces. If the heart is heedless of the *dhikr* then the tongue takes over, and this is the *dhikr* of habit. Each one of these grades has a fault. The fault of the *dhikr* of the spirit is to be perceived by the innermost consciousness. The fault of the *dhikr* of the heart is that the lower self *(nafs)* should take note of it and admire it, or that it should seek to gain by it the reward of attaining one of the spiritual ranks.[66]

X. ḤAKĪM AL-TIRMIDHĪ & THE NĪSHĀPŪRI MASTERS

Among the many treatises and epistles written by Abū ʿAbdullāh Muḥammad ibn ʿAlī al-Ḥakīm al-Tirmidhī (d. ca. 295/908) are a number of letters in which he responds to questions addressed to him by eminent correspondents. Among these, one letter is addressed to Abū ʿUthmān al-Ḥīrī, the Nīshāpūrī *Malāmatī* Shaykh. Two other letters are addressed to Muḥammad ibn al-Faḍl (d. 319/931) from Samarqand, a close companion of Abū ʿUthmān (more on whom below).

65. *Ibid.*, p. 103.
66. *Ibid.*, p. 104.

Ḥakīm al-Tirmidhī himself did not belong to the Nīshāpūrī school or any other mystical school.[67] He appears to have led his mystical and literary life away from the contemporary centres. Perhaps he did not even have a teacher in flesh, and thus belonged, as the Sufi tradition permits, to the *Uwaysiyyūn,* those whose teacher is the eternal prophet al-Khiḍr. Traditions in this vein are reported by Hujwīrī,[68] and 'Aṭṭār as well.[69] Ḥakīm al-Tirmidhī himself voices explicit reservations about the depending upon "a created being *(makhlūq)*" in the mystical quest rather than upon "the Creator *(al-khāliq).*"[70]

Yet, as we can see from his letters, he maintained direct links with some of his contemporaries among the mystics of Khurāsān. His letter to Abū 'Uthmān al-Ḥīrī, as well as the other two letters mentioned above revolve around the important issue of how best to deal with the ego *(nafs)* which undermines all spiritual attainments. Touching on this question, Ḥakīm al-Tirmidhī writes to Abū 'Uthmān:

> I have received your letter, my brother, one letter after another. You confirm repeatedly [how] the blemishes of the lower self *(nafs)* [are an obstacle] in the [attainment] of [spiritual] knowledge. My brother, if you can refrain from being occupied by this obstacle, since this is other than Allāh, do so. For Allāh has servants who indeed have knowledge of Him, and they ignore all things but Him. They are wary of being occupied with the lower self and instead they fear Him. Whenever anyone of them is afflicted by its memory, his stomach turns[71] as if he were about to vomit. How can one who strolls through gardens of roses, jasmine

67. On Tirmidhī's mystical affiliation, cf. B. Radtke's essay above, pp. 483-96.–ED.
68. *Kashf al-Maḥjūb,* p. 229.
69. See A.J. Arberry (tr.) *Muslim Saints and Mystics*: Episodes from the *Tadhkirat al-Auliya'* ("Memorial of the Saints") by Farid al-Din Attar (London: RKP 1979 rprt.), pp. 244ff.
70. See his "Answer to a letter from Rayy", in which he seems to respond to an anguished correspondent who feels he has regressed in his spiritual path after having met which a so-called teacher. Tirmidhī's response is: "This is what happens when one searches for the Creator by means of a created being." *(hākadhā yakūnu sha'nu man yaṭlub al-khāliq bi'l-makhlūq).* –B. Radtke, *Drei Schriften des Theosophen von Tirmid,* (Beirut 1992), pp. 171-2 (Arabic section).
71. I prefer to read here M'DTH *(ma'idatuhu* = his stomach) rather than M'RQH as in Radtke's edition.

> and wild lilies graze in valleys of thorns? How can one who is nourished by the remembrance of the Majestic be aware of anything but Him?[72]

Tirmidhī's objections to an exaggerated preoccupation with the *nafs* in the mystical quest is expressed here as well as in other letters and in many passages throughout his writings. In his letter to Abū 'Uthmān he presents the nucleus of his own understanding and approach in which the *nafs* is conceived as the centre of negative qualities: lust, desire, fear, anger, doubt, idolatry and forgetfulness. A transformation *(tabdīl)* of these negative qualities into positive ones is possible. This transformation is possible, however, only by means of the heart, that is, by the capacity of the heart to "see things in their essence" *(ḥaqā'iq al-umūr)*. The heart's vision is obscured by the negative qualities of the lower self which cause a veil *(ghiṭā')* to fall between it and the Truth. This vicious circle can be broken by faith *(īmān)* which resides in the heart. Faith is reinforced by the grace of God, and its light intensifies gradually. As the light of faith intensifies in the heart, the impact of the 'veil' becomes weaker. As it weakens, 'the essence of things' becomes clearer and more visible to the heart. When the heart 'sees' the 'essence of things', its faith is transformed and becomes 'certitude' *(yaqīn)*. At this stage, when the heart has attained 'certitude', the full transformation occurs: the desire of the *nafs* becomes desire for God, fear becomes fear of God, anger becomes anger for the sake of God, lust becomes longing for God, doubt becomes certitude, idolatry becomes pure unity and forgetfulness becomes determination.

Evidently Ḥakīm al-Tirmidhī's teaching, although revolving around the same psychological issues and obstacles which occupied the *malāmatiyya,* advocates an utterly different approach. Excessive concern with the *nafs,* regardless of its prominence in counteracting the sincere spiritual and devotional quest, will lead nowhere as long as the seeker's attention remains focused on it alone. Tirmidhī's method, as he reiterates in his letter, is based on "the science of God" *(al-'ilm bi'llāh),* whereas the method of Abū 'Uthmān and the Nīshāpūrī school—who are not mentioned by name but are

72. See B. Radtke, *op. cit.,* p. 191 (Arabic section).

undoubtedly implied—is based on "the science of the self" *(al-'ilm bi'l-nafs)*. If one focuses one's attention on the science of the self – says al-Tirmidhī – one will never be released from the self. "If one occupies oneself with the knowledge of the self's blemishes, one will spend all one's life in the attempt to be released from it *(fa-'in ishtaghala al-'abd bi ma'rifat al-'uyūb baqiya 'umrahu fīhā wa fī 'l-takhalluṣ minhā),"* he comments. On the other hand, if one focuses one's attention on the science of God, the heart becomes stronger and its vision of Divine revelations clearer. These revelations revive the heart, and its antithesis, the self, withers away. "When the self gives up because of the impact of the Divine revelations, the heart is revived by the Lord; what blemish remains then?"[73]

In the two letters addressed to Muḥammad ibn al-Faḍl al-Balkhī Tirmidhī expounds the same teaching. Muḥammad ibn al-Faḍl lived for many years in Samarqand, after having been expelled from his hometown of Balkh.[74] Although he cannot be said to have belonged to the Nīshāpūrī school, he was closely linked to Abū 'Uthmān al-Ḥīrī. In his *Ṭabaqāt* Sulamī quotes Abū 'Uthmān as saying, "If I were strong enough I would have travelled to my brother Muḥammad ibn al-Faḍl to find in his company solace for my inner-most heart *(sirrī)."*[75] Qushayrī too, in his *Risāla,* mentions the great esteem in which Abū 'Uthmān held Muḥammad ibn al-Faḍl.[76]

The two letters of Ḥakīm al-Tirmidhī to Ibn al-Faḍl are found in my unpublished critical edition – *Masā'il wa-rasā'il* - based on MS. Leipzig 212.[77] In one of these letters,[78] Tirmidhī seems to be answering Muḥammad's question as to how one attains the knowledge of the self. Here Tirmidhī reveals an uncompromisingly passionate sarcasm in his criticism of those who spend their entire life incurring blame on their selves. (Interestingly, al-Tirmidhī uses the terms *dhamm* and *lawm* rather than *malāma.)* To think that in this way

---

73. *Ibid.,* pp. 191-2 (Arabic).
74. See Sulamī, *Ṭabaqāt,* pp. 212-16, and the sources mentioned there.
75. *Ṭabaqāt* , pp. 212-3.
76. For letters of Abū 'Uthmān to Muḥammad ibn al-Faḍl see Sulamī, M.E., p. 106; Qushayrī, *Risāla,* p. 25.
77. See S. Sviri, "The Mystical Psychology of al-Ḥakīm al-Tirmidhī," Ph.D. Thesis, (Tel-Aviv 1979); in Hebrew and Arabic; Vol. 2, pp. 77-86 (Arabic section).
78. (MS. Leipzig, f. 66a-68b); *ibid.,* pp. 82ff. (Arabic).

they are going to eliminate the self is sheer delusion. The self is cunning and wily. It will turn the means whereby one attempts to destroy it to its own advantage. Its essence is pleasure and enjoyment. When one makes efforts to fight it, the self finds pleasure in these very efforts. If this is done publicly, the self will gain strength from the admiration and respect this will draw from the public. Thus all these efforts are to no avail. He who has eyes to see without deluding himself knows that the obstacle of the self will not be removed by the knowledge of the self or by blaming the self. Only the Creator of the self can eliminate it. He who knows this finds refuge with Him without Whom there is no refuge.

* * *

This correspondence, which has involved three Khurāsānī mystics of the third/ninth century, is a first-hand source that corroborates the contention expressed throughout this paper that towards the end of the third/ninth century there existed in Khurāsān (as well as in Baghdad) a number of mystical circles, centered around various important teachers. These circles were mutually related to each other by a complex and dynamic interaction revolving mainly around questions of mystical psychology. Perception of the many-faceted personal and communal relationships of these schools as well as the versatility of their opinions and methods is somewhat blurred and obscured in the later Sufi compilations, which were written with the purpose of solidifying and standardizing the Sufi tradition at large. The existence of such multifarious traditions, however, can be traced even within these very Sufi compilations, and when analysed alongside additional sources, both Sufi and non-Sufi, may present a fuller, richer and more accurate picture of the early development of Islamic mysticism.

Bibliography

Abū Ḥayyān ʻAlī b. Muḥammad Tawḥīdī. *Muqābasāt.* Edited by H. Sandūbī. Cairo: 1929.

ʻAbdū'l-Ḥaq, M. "ʻAyn al-Quḍāt Hamadānī's Concept of Time and Space in the Perspective of Sufism." *Isl. Qtly.* XXXI (1987).

Abun-Nasr. *The Tijaniyya: A Sufi Order in the Modern World.* Middle Eastern Monographs: 7. London: OUP, 1965.

Abū Sāʻīd Abī'l-Khayr. *Ḥālāt u sukhanān-i Shaykh Abū Sāʻīd Abī'l-Khayr.* s.v. "Sa'd, Jamāl al-Dīn Luṭfullāh ibn Abī Saʻīd."

______. *Asrār al-tawḥīd fī maqāmat al-Shaykh Abū Saʻīd.* s.v. "Ibn Munawwar."

______. *Abū Sāʻīd-nāma: Zindagī-nāma-yi Abū Sāʻīd Abī'l-Khayr.* s.v. "Damadī."

Āfāqī, Ṣābir. "Ṣūfiyān-i Kashmīr wa naqsh-i ānān dar nashr-i farhang wa adab-i fārsī." *Hunar va mardum.* Nos. 112-13, February-March (1972): 66-87.

Affīfī, Abū al-ʻAlā'. *The Mystical Philosophy of Muḥyid'Dīn Ibnul-ʻArabī.* Reprinted, Lahore: 1992.

Aflākī, Shams al-Dīn Aḥmad al-. *Manāqib al-ʻārifīn.* 2 vols. Ankara: Türk Tarih Kurumu, 1959-61.

Ahmad, A. *Change, Time and Causality, with Special Reference to Muslim Thought.* Lahore: 1974.

ʻAjjāj, Muḥammad Ṣāliḥ. *Jewels of Guidance: Advice from the Prophet Mohammad.* Translated by M.I. Waley. London: 1993.

Altınay, A.R. *Türkiye Tārīḫi.* İstanbul: Kütübḫāne-i Ḥilmī, 1923.

Aminrazavi, Mehdi. "Suhrawardī's Theory of Knowledge." Ph.D. Thesis, Temple University, 1989.

______. "Suhrawardī's Metaphysics of Illumination." *Hamdard Islamic-*

us XV/1 (1992).

Anawati, G.-C. and Louis Gardet. *Mystique musulmane, Aspects et tendances - Expériences et techniques.* Études Musulmanes VIII. 4th ed. Paris: Librairie Philosophique J. Vrin, 1986.

'Anṣārī, 'Abdullāh. *Manāzil al-sā'irīn.* Edited by A.G. Ravān Farhādī. Tehran: Intishārāt-i Mawlā, 1361 A.Hsh./1982.

______ . *Ṭabaqāt al-ṣūfiyya.* Edited by 'Abd al-Ḥayy Habībi. Kabul: 1961. Edited by Muḥammad Sarvar Mawlāyī. Tehran: Sahāmī 'ām, 1362 A.Hsh./1983.

______ . *Sukhanān-i Pīr-i Herāt.* Edited by Muḥammad Jawād Sharī'at. 3rd ed. Tehran: 1361 A.Hsh./1982.

______ . *Manāzil al-sā'irīn: matn-i 'arabī bā muqāyasa bā matn-i 'Ilal al-maqāmat wa Ṣad maydān, tarjama-yi darī-yi Manāzil al-sā'irīn wa 'Ilal al-maqāmat wa sharḥ-i kitāb az rūyi āthār-i Pīr-i Harāt.* Edited by A.G. Ravān Farhādī. Kabul: 1350 A.Hsh./1971; reprinted, Tehran: Mawlā 1361 A.Hsh./1982.

Arasteh, A.R. *Growth to Selfhood.* London: 1980.

Arberry, A.J. *The Doctrine of the Sufis.* Cambridge University Press, 1977. Translation of Kalābādhī's *Kitāb al-ta'arruf.*

______ . *Muslim Saints and Mystics.* London: RKP, 1966. Excerpts from the *Tadhkirat al-awliyā'* of 'Aṭṭār.

______ . *Mystical Poems of Rūmī: first selection, poems 1-200.* Chicago: 1968.

______ . *A Sufi Martyr: The Apologia of 'Ain al-Quḍāt al-Hamadhānī.* London: Allen & Unwin, 1969.

______ . *Sufism: An Account of the Mystics of Islam.* London: Allen & Unwin, 1950.

______ . "The Works of Shams al-Dīn al-Dailamī." *BSOAS* 29 (1966).

Arjomand, Said Amir. *The Shadow of God and the Hidden Imam: Religion, Political Order and Societal Change in Shi'ite Iran from the Beginnings to 1890.* Chicago and London: 1984.

Arnaldez, R. *Réflexions chrétiennes sur la mystique musulmane.* Paris: O.E.I.L., 1989.

Arrajān, Faramarz ibn Khudādād. *Samak-i 'ayyār.* 5 vols. Tehran: 1959-74.

Āshtiyānī, Mīrza Mihdī Mudarris. *Commentary on Sabzawārī's Sharḥ-i Manẓūma.* Edited by A. Falāṭūrī and M. Moheghegh. Tehran: 1973.

'Aṭṭār, Farīd al-Dīn. *Dīwān-i ghazaliyyāt wa qaṣā'id.* Edited by T. Tafaḍḍulī. Tehran: 1341 A.Hsh./1962.

______ . *Ilāhi-nāma.* Edited by H. Ritter. Tehran: 1980.

______ . *Le Livre de l'épreuve (Muṣībatnāma).* Translated into French by Isabelle de Gastines. Paris: 1981.

______. *Muṣībat-nāma.* Edited by Nūrānī Weṣāl. Tehran: 1977.

______. *Tadhkirāt al-awliyā'.* Edited by R.A. Nicholson. 2 vols. London/ Leiden: 1905-7.

Austin, R.J.W. "The Lady Niẓam: An Image of Love and Knowledge." *Journal of the Muhyiddin Ibn 'Arabi Society* VII (1988): 53-48.

Avicenna (Ibn Sīnā). *Al-Ishārāt wa'l-tanbīhāt.* With the commentaries of Naṣīr al-Dīn al-Ṭūsī and Quṭb al-Dīn al-Rāzī. 3 vols. Tehran: 1951.

Awn, Peter. *Satan's Tragedy and Redemption: Iblīs in Sufi Psychology.* Leiden: E.J. Brill, 1983.

'Aydarūs, 'Abd al-Qādir ibn Shaykh ibn 'Abdullāh Bā 'Alawī al-. *Ta'rīf al-Ahyā' bi-faḍā'il al-Iḥyā'.* Printed on the margin of *Iḥyā' 'ulūm al-dīn.* Cairo: 1352/1933.

Badawī, 'Abd al-Raḥmān. *Mu'allafat al-Ghazālī.* 2 vols. Cairo: 1961.

______. *Shahīdat al-'ishq al-ilāhī, Rābi'a al-'Adawiyya.* Cairo: al-Nahḍa, 1946.

Baffioni, C. *Atomismo e antiatomismo nel pensiero islamico.* Naples: 1982.

Baghawī, Abū Muḥammad al-Ḥusayn b. Mas'ūd. *Miṣbāḥ al-Sunna.* 4 vols. Beirut: 1987.

Baghdādī, Ismā'īl Bāshā al-. *Hadīyat al-'arifin asmā' al-mu'allifin wa-athār al-muṣannifin.* 2 vols. Istanbul: 1951-55.

Baghdādī, Ibn Mi'mār Ḥanbalī. *Kitāb al-futuwwat.* Baghdad: Maktaba al-Muthannā, 1985.

Bākharzī, Abū'l-Mafākhir. *Awrād al-aḥbāb wa Fuṣūṣ al-ādāb.* Vol. 2: *Fuṣūṣ al-ādāb.* Edited by Īrāj Afshār. Tehran: 1979.

Baldick, J. *Mystical Islam: An Introduction to Sufism.* London: I.B. Tauris, 1989.

Bamzai, Prithvi Nath Kaul. *A History of Kashmir.* 2nd ed. New Delhi: Metropolitan Book Company, 1973.

Bayhaqī, Abū'l-Faḍl Muḥammad ibn Ḥusayn. *Tā'rīkh-i Bayhaqī.* Mashhad: Firdawsī University Press, 1971.

Behler, E. *Die Ewigkeit der Welt.* München: 1965.

Bektaş, Hacī. *Velī Velāyetnāmesi.* Edited by B. Noyan. Ankara: Doğuş Matbaacılık, 1985.

Beldiceanu-Steinherr, I. "Le règne de Selim Ier: Tournant dans la vie politique et religieuse de l'Empire Ottoman." *Turcica* 6 (1975).

Bell, Joseph. *Love Theory in Later Ḥanbalite Islam.* Albany: SUNY Press, 1978.

Berge, M. *Pour un humanisme vécu: Abū Ḥayyān al-Tawḥīdī.* Damascus: 1979.

Bertel's, Y.E. *Taṣawwuf wa adabiyāt-i taṣawwuf.* Translated into Persian by Sīrūs Īzadī. Tehran: Amīr Kabīr, 1976.

Bībī, Ibn. *Die Seltschukengeschichte des Ibn Bībī.* Translated by H.W. Duda. Copenhagen: Munksgaard, 1959.

Birge, John K. *The Bektashi Order of Dervishes.* Connecticut: Hartford Seminary Press, 1937.

Blake, William. *Blake: Complete Writings.* Edited by G. Keynes. London: Oxford University Press, 1972.

Bloch, M. *The Historian's Craft.* Translated by Peter Putnam. New York: 1953.

Bodrogligeti, A. "Ahmad's *Baraq-Nāma:* A Central Asian Islamic Work in Eastern Middle Turkic." *Central Asiatic Journal* 18 (1974).

Bonebakker, S.A. "Adab and the concept of belles-lettres." *The Cambridge History of Arabic Literature: Abbasid Belles-Lettres.* Cambridge: University Press, 1990.

Bosworth, C.E. *The Islamic Dynasties.* Edinburgh: 1967.

______ . *Bahā' al-Dīn al-'Amilī and his literary anthologies.* Journal of Semitic Studies Monograph, no. 10. Manchester: 1989.

Bouyges, Maurice. *Essai de chrononlogie des oeuvres de al-Ghazali.* Beirut: 1959.

Böwering, Gerhard. "'Abū Sā'īd Fażlallāh b. Abi'l-Kayr." *Encyclopædia Iranica.* I: 377-80.

______ . "'Alī b. Šehab-al-Dīn b. Moḥammad Hamadānī." *Encyclopædia Iranica.* I: 862-64.

______ . *The Mystical Vision of Existence in Classical Islam.* Berlin: 1980.

______ ., ed. *The Islamic Case.* New York: 1981.

______ . "The Ādāb Literature of Classical Sufism: Anṣārī's Code of Conduct." *Moral Conduct and Authority: The Place of Adab in South Asian Islam.* Edited by Barabara Metcalf. Berkeley: 1984.

______ . "The Qur'ān Commentary of al-Sulamī." *Islamic Studies Presented to Charles J. Adams.* Edited by W.B. Hallaq & D. Little. Leiden: E.J. Brill, 1991.

______ . "Ibn 'Arabī's Concept of Time." *God is Beautiful and Loves Beauty: Festschrift for Annemarie Schimmel.* Edited by J.C. Bürgel and Alma Giese. Leiden: Peter Lang, 1994.

Brandon, S.G.F. *History, Time and Deity.* Manchester: 1965.

Brockelmann, Carl. *Geschichte der arabischen Litteratur.* 2 vols. plus 3 suppl. vols., Leiden: E.J. Brill 1943-49.

Bukhārī, 'Abd al-Ḥaqq Muḥaddith Dihlawī al-. *Akhbār al-akhyār fī asrār al-abrār.* Edited by Muḥammad 'Abd al-Aḥad. Delhi: Maṭba'-i Mujtabā'ī, 1913-14.

Bukhārī, Sharāf al-Dīn. *Nām-i ḥaqq.* Lucknow: 1889.

Bulliet, R.W. "'Abu'l-Qāsem 'Alī b. Moḥammad b. Ḥosayn b. 'Amr." *Encyclopædia Iranica*. I: 357.

______ . *The Patricians of Nishapur.* Cambridge: Harvard University Press, 1972.

Bürgel, J.C. "Musicotherapy in the Islamic Middle Ages." *History of Medicine.* New Delhi: 1980.

______ . *The Feather of Simurgh: The "Licit Magic" of the Arts in Medieval Islam.* New York University Press, 1988.

Bylebyle, M. "The Wisdom of Illumination: A Study of the Prose Stories of Suhrawardī." Ph.D. Thesis, University of Chicago, 1976.

Cahen, Claude. *Pre- Ottoman Turkey: A General Survey of the Material and Spiritual Culture and History, c. 1071-1330.* Translated by J. Jones-Williams. New York: Taplinger Publishing Company, 1968.

______ . "Baba Ishaq, Baba Ilyas, Hadjdji Beḳtash et quelques autres." *Turcica.*1 (1969).

______ . "A propos d'un article récent et des Babâ'is." *Journal Asiatique* 268 (1980).

______ . "Tribes, Cities and Social Organization." *The Cambridge History of Iran.* IV: *From The Arab Invasion to the Saljuqs.* Cambridge: University Press 1975, pp. 305-28.

Campbell, J., ed. *Man and Time: Papers from the Eranos Yearbooks.* Bollingen Series. Princeton: 1957.

Caskel, W. *Das Schicksal in der altarabischen Poesie.* Leipzig: 1926.

______ . "Aijām al-'Arab." *Islamica* 3. Suppl. (1930).

Chadwick, H. *The Early Church. The Pelican History of the Church.* Vol. 1. Harmondsworth: Penguin, 1967.

Chalabī, Ḥājjī Khalīfa Muṣṭafā ibn 'Abdullāh Kātib. *Kashf al-ẓunūn 'an asāmī al-kutub wa al-funūn.* 2 vols. Istanbul: 1310.

Chittick, William C. *The Sufi Path of Love: the Spiritual Teachings of Rumi.* Albany: SUNY, 1983.

______ . *The Sufi Path of Knowledge: Ibn al-'Arabī's Metaphysics of Imagination.* Albany: SUNY, 1989.

Christensen, A. *Recherches sur les Rubā'iyāt de 'Omar Ḫayyām.* Heidelberg: 1905.

______ . *L'Iran sous les Sassanides.* 2nd ed. Copenhagen: 1944.

Çiftçioğlu, N. A. ed. "Tevârîḫ-i Âl-i 'Osmān." *Osmanlı Tarihleri.* Istanbul: Türkiye Yayınevi 1949.

Coomaraswamy. *The Dance of Siva: Fourteen Indian Essays.* New York: 1924.

Corbin, H. *Les motifs zoroastriens dans la philosophie de Sohrawardī.* Teheran: Société d'Iranologie, 1946.

______ . *Terre céleste et corps de résurrection: de l'Iran mazdéen à l'Iran shî'ite.* Paris: 1978.

______ . "Le Temps Cyclique dans le Mazdéisme et dans l'Ismaélisme." *Eranos-Jahrbuch* XX (1951).

______ . *Creative Imagination in the Sufism of Ibn 'Arabi.* Translated by Ralph Mannheim. Bollingen Series 99. Princeton University Press, 1969.

______ . *En Islam iranien.* 4 vols. Paris: Éditions Gallimard, 1972.

______ and O.Yahya (eds). *"Jāmī' al-asrār:" La philosophie shi'ite.* Tehran-Paris: 1969.

______ . *Cyclical Time and Ismaili Gnosis.* Edited by H. Corbin. London: 1983.

Currie, P.M. *The Shrine and Cult of Mu'īn al-Dīn Chistī of Ajmer.* Delhi: Oxford University Press, 1989.

Dabashi, Hamid. "'Ayn al-Quḍāt Hamadhānī wa *Risāla-i Shakwā'l-gharīb*-i ū." *Iran Nameh.* XI/1 (1993): 57-73.

Dabbāgh, 'Abd al-Raḥmān. *Kitāb mashāriq anwār al-qulub wa mafātiḥ asrār al-ghuyub.* Beirut: Dār Ṣādir, Dār Bayrūt, 1959.

Daftary, Farhad. *The Ismā'īlīs: Their History and Doctrines.* Cambridge University Press, 1990.

Damadī, Sayyid Muḥammad. *Abū Sā'īd-nāma: Zindagī-nāma-yi Abū Sā'īd Abī'l-Khayr.* Tehran: 1973.

Danish-pazhūh, Muḥammad-Taqī, ed. *"Silsila al-awliyā'-yi* Nūrbakhsh"*Mélanges offerts à Henry Corbin.* Edited by S.H. Nasr. Tehran: Institute of Islamic Studies, McGill University, Tehran Branch, 1977.

Dankoff, R. "Baraq and Burāq." *Central Asiatic Journal.*15 (1971).

Danner, Victor. *The Islamic Tradition: An Introduction.* New York: Amity House, 1988.

Daylamī, Abū al-Ḥasan. *Sīrat-i shaykh-i kabīr Abū 'Abd Allāh ibn Khafīf al-Shīrāzī.* Translated into Persian by Rukn al-Dīn Yaḥyā ibn Junayd Shīrāzī. Edited by Annemarie Schimmel. Ankara: 1955. Repr. ed., Tehran: Intishārāt-i Bābak, 1984.

Daylamī, 'Alī ibn Aḥmad al-. *Kitāb 'aṭf al-alif al-mā'lūf ilā'l-lām al-ma'ṭūf.* Edited by Jean-Claude Vadet. Vol. 20 of *Textes et Traductions d'Auteurs Orientaux.* Cairo: Institut Français d'Archéologie Orientale, 1962.

______ . *al-Firdaws bi-ma'thūr al-khiṭāb.* Beirut: 1986.

De Bruijn, J.T.P. "Sanā'ī and the Rise of Persian Mystical Poetry." Actes du 8me Congrès de l'Union Européenne des Arabisants et Islamisants. Aix-en-Provence: 1978.

______ . *Of Piety and Poetry: the Interaction of Religion and Literature in the Life and Works of Ḥakīm Sanā'ī of Ghazna.* Leiden: E.J. Brill 1983.

______ . "The *Qalandariyyāt* in Persian Mystical Poetry, From Sanā'ī Onwards." *The Legacy of Mediæval Persian Sufism.* Edited by Leonard Lewisohn. London: KNP, 1992.

Deladrière, Roger., trans. *Sulamī: La Lucidité Implacable (Épître des hommes du blâme).* Paris: Arléa, 1991.

Dermenghem, Émile. *Vies des saints musulmans.* Algiers: 1942.

DeWeese, Devin. "The Eclipse of the Kubravīyah in Central Asia." *Iranian Studies* 21 (1988): 45-83.

Dhahabī, Muḥammad ibn Aḥmad. *Siyar a'lām al-nubalā'.* Beirut: 1981-85.

Dinānī, Ghulam-Ḥusayn. *Shu'a'i andīsha wa shuhūd dar falsafa-yi Suhrawardī.* Tehran: Ḥikmat, 1985.

During, Jean. *Musique et extase, L'audition mystique dans la tradition soufie.* Paris: Albin Michel, 1988.

Efendi, M. *Şaḳâyıḳ Tercümesi.* Istanbul: 1853.

Eickelmann, D. "Time in a Complex Society: A Moroccan Example." *Ethnology* 17 (1977)

Eklund, R. *Life Between Death and Resurrection According to Islam.* Uppsala: 1941.

Eliade, M. *Cosmos and History: The Myth of the Eternal Return.* New York: 1954.

Elwell-Sutton, L.P. "The 'Rubā'ī in Early Persian Literature." *The Cambridge History of Iran.* Vol. 4: *From The Arab Invasion to the Saljuqs.* Cambridge: 1975, pp. 633-57.

Encyclopædia of Islam. New Edition. Leiden: 1960-.

Ernst, Carl. *Words of Ecstasy in Sufism.* Albany: SUNY Press, 1984.

______ . "The Symbolism of Birds and Flight in the Writings of Rūzbihān Baqlī." *The Legacy of Mediaeval Persian Sufism.* Edited by Leonard Lewisohn. London: KNP, 1992.

______ . "Rūzbihān Baqlī on Love as 'Essential Desire'." *God is Beautiful and Loves Beauty: Festschrift for Annemarie Schimmel.* Edited by J.C. Bürgel and Alma Giese. Leiden: Peter Lang, 1994.

Faḍullāh, Rashīd al-Dīn. *Jāmi' al-tawārīkh.* 2 vols. Edited by Bahmān Karīmī. Tehran: Dunyā-yi kitāb, 1983.

Farac, Abu'l-. *Tarihi.* Translated by Ö.R. Doğrul. Ankara: Türk Tarih Kurumu Yayınları, 1950.

Farāhī, Abū Naṣr. *Niṣāb-i al-ṣibyān.* Edited by 'Alī ibn Naẓar 'Alī. Lithograph edition. Tabriz: 1308/1890.

Faris, Nabih Amin. *The Book of Knowledge.* Lahore: Sh. Muhammad Ashraf, 1962. Translation With Notes of the *Kitāb al-'ilm* of al-Ghazāli's *Ihyā' 'ulūm al-dīn.*

______ . *The Foundations of the Articles of Faith.* Lahore: Sh. Muhammad Ashraf, 1963. Translation With Notes of the *Kitāb Qawā'id al-'aqā'id* of Ghazālī's *Ihyā' 'ulūm al-dīn.*

Fārisī, 'Abd al-Ghāfir al-. *Al-ḥalqa al-'ūlā min ta'rīkh naysabūr al-muntakhab min al-Siyāq.* Edited by Muḥammad Kāẓim al-Maḥmūdī Qum: 1982-3.

Frank, R.M. *The Metaphysics of Created Being according to Abū'l-Hudhayl al-'Allāf.* Istanbul: 1966.

Fraser, J.T. "A Report on the Literature of Time 1900-1980." *The Study of Time* IV. Edited by J.T. Fraser. New York: 1981.

______ . *The Voices of Time.* Amherst: 1981.

______ . *Time: The Familiar Stranger.* Amherst: 1987.

Frye, R.N. "The Sāmānids." *The Cambridge History of Iran.* IV: *From The Arab Invasion to the Saljuqs.* Cambridge: 1975, pp. 136-61.

______ . *The Histories of Nīshāpūr.* Vol. 45 of Harvard Oriental Series. The Hague: 1965.

Furūzānfar, Badī' al-Zamān. *Sharḥ-i Mathnawī-yi sharīf.* Tehran: Dānishgāh-i Tihrān, 1967-69.

______ . *Sharḥ-i aḥwāl wa naqd wa taḥlīl-i āthār-i Shaykh Farīd al-Dīn Muḥammad 'Aṭṭār Nishābūrī.* Tehran: Diḥkhudā, 1974.

______ . *Ahadīth-i Mathnawī.* Tehran: Amīr Kabīr, 1361 A.Hsh./1982.

Gairdner, W.H.T. *Al-Ghazzali's Mishkat Al-Anwar ("The Niche for Lights").* Lahore: Sh. Muhammad Ashraf, 1952. Translation with Introduction. Reprint of the Royal Asiatic Society edition, London: 1924.

Gale, R.M., ed. *The Philosophy of Time.* Sussex: 1968.

Gardet, L. "Moslem Views of Time and History." *Cultures and Time.* Paris: 1976.

______ . "The Prophet." *Time and the Philosophies.* Paris: 1977.

Ghanī, Qāsim. *Baḥth dar āthār wa afkār wa aḥwāl-i Ḥāfiẓ.* 2 vols. 3rd edition. Tehran: Zawwār, 1977.

Ghazālī, Aḥmad. *Sawāniḥ: Aphorismen über die Liebe.* Edited by H. Ritter. Bibliotheca Islamica 15. Istanbul: Staatsdruckerei, 1942.

______ . *Sawāniḥ: Inspirations from the World of Pure Spirits, The Oldest Persian Sufi Treatise on Love.* Translated by Nasrollah Pourjavady. London: KPI, 1968.

Ghazālī, Abū Ḥāmid Muḥammad ibn Muḥammad al-. *Iljām al-'awāmm 'an 'ilm al-kalām.* Cairo: 1309.

______. *Fātiḥat al-'ulūm.* Cairo: 1322.

______. *Tahāfut al-falāsifa.* Edited by Maurice Bouyges. Beirut: 1927.

______. *Tahāfut al-falāsifa. Al-Ghazālī's Tahafut al-Falasifah (Incoherence of the Philosophers).* Translated by Sabih Ahmad Kamali. Lahore: 1958.

______. *Ihyā' 'ulūm al-dīn.* 4 vols. Cairo: 1352 A.Hsh./1933.

______. *Ihyā' 'ulūm al-dīn.* Vol. 1. Bk. 1. *The Book of Knowledge (Kitāb al-'Ilm).* Translated by Nabih Amin Faris. Lahore: Sh. Muhammad Ashraf, 1962.

______. *Ihyā' 'ulūm al-dīn.* Vol. 1. Bk. 2. *The Foundations of the Articles of Faith. (Kitāb al-'Qawā'id al-'aqā'id).* Translated by Nabih Amin Faris. Lahore: Sh. Muhammad Ashraf, 1963.

______. *Ihyā' 'ulūm al-dīn. Invocations and Supplications: Kitāb al-Adhkār wa'l-da'awāt.* Translated by K. Nakamura. 2nd ed. Cambridge: Islamic Texts Society, 1990.

______. *Ihyā' 'ulūm al-dīn. The Remembrance of Death and the Afterlife: Kitāb Dhikr al-mawt wa mā ba'dah.* Translated by T.J. Winter. Cambridge: Islamic Texts Society, 1989.

______. *Iḥyā' 'ulūm al-dīn.* Selected passages from the *Kitāb Asrār al-ṣalāh, al-Bāb al-thālith fī al-shurūṭ al-baṭīna min a'māl al-qalb* translated by M. Holland in *Inner Dimensions of Islamic Worship.* Leicester: Islamic Foundation, 1983.

______. *Ihyā' 'ulūm al-dīn. Imam Gazzali's Ihya Ulum-id-Din.* Abridged translation by Al-Haj Maulana Fazul-ul-Karim. 4 vols. Lahore: Sind Sagar Academy, 1971.

______. *Ihyā' 'ulūm al-dīn.* Vol. 1. Bk. 8. Translated by Muhammad Abul Quasem. *The Recitation and Interpretation of the Qur'ān: al-Ghazālī's Theory (Kitāb Ādāb tilāwat al-Qur'ān).* Kuala Lumpur: University of Malaya Press, 1979.

______. *Qānūn al-ta'wīl.* Edited by Muḥammad Zāhid al-Kawtharī. Cairo: 1359/1940.

______. *Mishkāt al-anwār.* Translated by W.H.T. Gairdner. Reprinted, Lahore: 1952.

______. *Mishkāt al-anwār.* Edited by Abū al-'Alā 'Afīfī. Cairo: 1383/1964.

______. *Mīzān al-'amal.* Edited by Sulaymān Dunyā. Cairo: 1964.

______. *Jawāhir al-Qur'ān.* Reprinted Beirut: 1981.

______. *Kitāb-i kīmīyā-yi sa'ādat.* Edited by Aḥmad Ārām. 2nd ed. Tehran: Kitābkhāna-i wa Chāpkhāna-i Markazī, 1955.

______. *Faḍa'ḥ al-bāṭiniyya.* Edited by 'Abd al-Raḥmān Badawī. Cairo: 1383/1964.

Ghurāb, Maḥmūd al-. *Sharḥ Fuṣūṣ al-ḥikam.* Damascus: 1985.

Giffen, L. A. *The Theory of Profane Love Among the Arabs: The Development of the Genre.* New York: 1971.

Gimaret, Daniel. *Les noms divins en Islam.* Paris: Cerf, 1988.

Gnoli, G. "L'évolution du dualisme iranien et le problème zurvanite." *RGR.* 201 (1984)

Gobillot, G. "Un penseur de l'Amour *(Ḥubb),* le mystique khurāsānien al-Ḥakīm al-Tirmidhī (m. 318/930)." *Studia Islamica* LXXIII (1991).

Goldman, S.L. "On the Beginnings and Endings of Time in Medieval Judaism and Islam." *The Study of Time.* Ed. J.T. Fraser. New York: 1981.

Goldziher, I. *Die Ẓāhiriten, ihre Lehrsystem und ihre Geschichte.* Leipzig: 1884.

Gramlich, Richard. "Vom islamischen Glauben an die 'gute, alte Zeit." *Islamwissenschaftliche Abhandlungen Fritz Meier zum sechzigsten Geburtstag.* Edited by R. Gramlich. Wiesbaden: 1974.

______ . *Die schiitischen Derwischorden Persiens. Zweiter Teil: Glaube und Lehre.* Wiesbaden: 1976.

______ . "Zur Ausdehnung der Zeit und Verwandtem." *Die islamische Welt zwischen Mittelalter und Neuzeit.* Edited by U. Haarmann and P. Bachmann. Beirut: 1979.

______ . "Der Urvertrag in der Koranauslegung (zu Sure 7, 172-3)." *Der Islam* 60 (1983).

______ . *Das Sendschreiben al-Qušayrīs über das Sufitum.* Wiesbaden: 1989.

______ . *Schlaglichter über das Sufitum.* Stuttgart: 1990.

______ . *Die Wunder der Freunde Gottes.* Wiesbaden: 1987.

Gross, Jo-Ann. "Authority and Miraculous Behavior: Reflections on Karāmāt Stories of Khwāja 'Ubaydullāh Aḥrār." *The Heritage of Sufism* Vol. II. Edited by L. Lewisohn. Oxford: Oneworld Publications, 1999.

Habshī, 'Abdullāh al-. *Al-ṣūfiyya wa l-fuqahā fi'l-Yaman.* Sana'a: 1976.

Ḥāfiẓ, Shams al-Dīn Muḥammad. *Dīwān-i Ḥāfiẓ.* Edited by Parwīz Nātil Khānlarī. Tehran 1359 A.Hsh./1980.

Ha'iri, M.H. *The Principles of Epistemology in Islamic Philosophy: Knowledge by Presence.* New York: SUNY Press, 1992.

Ḥājjī Khalīfa, Muṣṭafā ibn 'Abdullāh Kātib Chalabī. *Kashf al-zunūn 'an asāmī al-kutub wa al-funūn.* 2 vols. Istanbul: 1310.

Ḥākimī, Ismā'īl. *Samā' dar taṣawwuf-i Islām.* Tehran: 1989.

Ḥallāj, Manṣūr al-. *Diwān al-Ḥallāj.* Edited by L. Massignon. Paris: 1929; Edited by K.M. Shaybī. Baghdad 1974.

Halm, H. "Der Wesir al-Kundurī und die Fitna von Nishapur." *Die Welt des Orients* 6 (1971)

______. *Die Ausbreitung der safi'itischen Rechtsschule von den Anfängen bis zum 8/14 Jahrhundert.* Wiesbaden: 1974.

Hamadani, Agha Hussain Shah. *The life and works of Sayyid Ali Hamadani (A.D. 1314-1385).* Islamabad: National Institute of Historical and Cultural Research, 1984.

Hamadhānī, 'Ayn al-Quḍāt. *Tamhīdāt.* Edited by Afif Osseiran. Tehran: 1962.

______. *Nāmahā-yi 'Ayn al-Quḍat Hamadhānī.* 2 vols. Edited by Afif Osseiran. Tehran: Intishārāt-i bunyād-i farhang-i Īrān # 73, 1969.

Hawking, S. *A Brief History of Time.* London & New York: 1988.

Heiler, Friedrich. *Wesen und Erscheinungsformen der Religion.* Stuttgart: 1961.

Heinen, A. *Cosmology.* Beirut/Wiesbaden: Franz Steiner, 1982.

Hidāyat, Riḍā Qulī-Khān. *Majma' al-fuṣaḥā'.* Edited by 'Alī Aṣghar Ḥikmat. Tehran: 1957.

Hodgson, M. *The Venture of Islam.* 3 vols. Chicago & London: University of Chicago, 1974-77.

Horovitz, J. *Koranische Untersuchungen.* Berlin/Leipzig: 1926.

Hujwīrī, Alī b. Uthmān al-. *Kashf a-maḥjūb.* Islamabad: Markaz-i Taḥqīqāt-i Fārsī-i Īrān wa Pākistān, 1978.

______. *The "Kashf al-maḥjūb:" The Oldest Persian Treatise on Sufism.* Translated by R.A. Nicholson. Gibb Memorial Series, no. 17. 1911. Reprinted London: 1976.

______. *Kashf al-maḥjūb.* Edited by V.A. Zhukovskii. St. Petersburg 1899. Reprinted, Leningrad 1926.

Humā'ī, Jalāl al-Dīn. *Ghazālī-nāma.* Tehran: Furūghī, 1938.

Ibn al-'Arabī. *Kitāb al-Futūḥāt al-Makkiyya.* Cairo: 1329.

______. *Mawāqī' al-nujūm wa-maṭāli' ahillat al-asrār wa'l-'ulūm.* Cairo: 1325/1907.

______. *Ta'wīlāt.* Beirut: 1968.

______. *Sufis of Andalusia: The Rūḥ al-quds and Al-Durrat al-fākhirah..* Translated by R.W.J. Austin. London: 1971.

______. *The "Tarjumān Al-Ashwāq": A Collection of Mystical Odes by Muḥyīu'ddīn ibn al-'Arabī.* Edited and translated by R.A. Nicholson. London 1911. Reprinted, 1978.

______. *Bezels of Wisdom.* Translated by R.J.W. Austin. New York: Paulist Press, 1980.

______. *Traité de l'amour.* Translated by Maurice Gloton. Paris: Albin Michel, 1986.

Ibn Baṭṭūṭa. *Riḥlat Ibn Baṭṭūṭa*. Beirut: Dār Ṣādir, 1964.

______. *The Travels of Ibn Baṭṭūṭa (A.D. 1325-1354)*. Translated by H.A.R. Gibb. 4 vols. Cambridge: University Press, 1958.

Ibn Fāris, Abū'l-Ḥusayn Aḥmad. *al-Ṣāhibī fī fiqh al-lughah wa sunan al-'arab fī kalāmihā*. Edited by Muṣṭafā al-Shuwaymī. Beirut: 1963.

Ibn al-Jawzī, 'Abd al-Raḥmān. *Naqd al-'ilm wa'l-'ulamā' aw talbīs Iblīs*. Cairo: 1928.

Ibn Khallikān, Aḥmad. *Wafayāt al-a'yān wa anbā' abnā' al-zamān*. Beirut: 1965.

Ibn Munawwar, Muḥammad. *Asrār at-tawḥīd fī maqāmāt Shaykh Abū Sa'īd*. Edited by V.A. Zhukovskii. St. Petersburg 1899. Re-edited A. Bahmanyār, Tehran: 1978. Edited by Dhabīḥullāh Ṣafā. Tehran: 1953. Reprinted, Tehran 1969 & 1975. New edition by M.R. Shafī'ī-Kadkanī. 2 vols., incl. study and notes. Tehran: 1987. Arabic trans. E. A. Qandil. Cairo: 1966. French trans. M. Achena, *Les étapes mystiques du shaikh Abu Sa'īd*. Paris: 1974.

Ikhwān al-Ṣafā. *Rasā'il fī qawl al-ḥukamā' annā'l-insān 'ālam ṣaghīr*. vol. 2. Beirut: Dār Ṣādir/Dār Bayrūt, 1957.

Iṣfahānī, Abū Nu'aym al-. *Ḥilyat al-awliyā'*. 10 vols. Cairo: Maṭba'at al-sa'āda, 1932.

Izutsu, T. "Mysticism and the Linguistic Problem of Equivocation in the Thought of 'Ayn al- Quḍāt Hamadānī." *Studia Islamica* XXXI (1970).

Jām, Aḥmad-i (Muḥammad ibn Muṭahhar, farzand-i Zhanda-pīl). *Ḥadīqat al-ḥaqīqa*. Edited by Manūchihr Sitūdih. Tehran: B.T.N.K., 1343 A.Hsh./1964.

Jāmī, Nūr al-Dīn 'Abd al-Raḥmān ibn Ahmad al-. *Nafaḥāt al-uns*. Edited by Mihdī Tawḥīdīpūr. Tehran: 1336 A.Hsh./1957.

Jandī, Mu'ayyid al-Dīn. *Sharḥ Fuṣūṣ al-ḥikam*. Edited by S.J. Āashtiyānī. Mashhad: Dānishgāh, 1361 A.Hsh./1982.

Junayd, al-. *The Life, Personality and Writings of al-Junayd: A Study of a Third/Ninth Century Mystic with an Edition and Translation of his Writings*. Edited and translated by Ali Hassan Abdel-Kader. Gibb Memorial Series. London: Luzac & Co., 1976.

Jurjānī, 'Alī b. Muḥammad. *Kitāb al-Ta'rīfāt*. Beirut: 1969.

Kalābādhī, Abū Bakr Muḥammad. *Kitāb at-Ta'arruf li-madhhab ahl al-taṣawwuf.* Edited by A.J. Arberry. Cairo: 1934.

______. *Kitāb al-Ta'arruf li-madhhab ahl al-taṣawwuf.* 2nd. ed. Cairo: Maktabat al-Kulliyyāt al-Azhariyya, 1980.

Kāshifī, Fakhr al-Dīn 'Alī ibn Ḥusayn Wā'iz al-. *Rashaḥāt-i 'ayn al-ḥayāt*. 2 vols. Edited by 'Alī Aṣghar Mu'miyān. Tehran: 1970.

______. *Futuwwat-nāma sulṭānī.* Edited by M.J. Maḥjūb. Tehran: Bunyād-i farhang-i Īrān, 1972.

Khān, Muḥammad Riyāż. "'Khadamāt-i Amīr-i Kabīr Mīr Sayyid 'Alī Hamadānī dar shabh-i qāra-i Pākistān wa Hind (qarn-i hashtum)'." *Ma'ārif-i islāmī.*6 (1968): 95-96.

______. *"Futuwwatnāma* az Mīr Sayyid 'Alī Hamadānī." *Ma'ārif-i islāmī* 10 &11 (1970): 32-39.

Khānaqāhī, Abū Naṣr Ṭāhir. *Guzida dar taṣawwuf wa akhlāq.* Tehran: 1347 A.Hsh./1968.

Khawlānī, 'Abd al-Jabbār. *Ta'rīkh Darāyā.* Damascus: 1984.

Kiyānī, Muḥsin. *Tārīkh-i khānaqāh dar Īrān.* Tehran: Ṭahūrī, 1369A.Hsh./ 1991.

Köprülü, M.F. *Türk Edebiyatında İlk Mutasavvıflar.* 2nd ed. Ankara: Diyanet İşleri Başkanlığı Yayınları, 1966.

______. "Anadolu'da Islāmīyet: Türk istilāsından soñra Anadolu tārīḫ-i Dīnīsine bir naẓar ve bu tārīḫiñ menba'ları," *Dārü'l-fünūn Edebiyāt Fakültesi Mecmū'asī* 2 (1922-23).

Koran. *The Meaning of the Glorious Koran.* Translated by Mohammed Marmaduke Pickthall. Many editions and printings exist.

______. *al-Qur'an al-Karim.* 2nd ed. Cairo: Dar al-Kutub al-Misriyah, 1952.

______. *The Koran Interpreted.* Translated by A.J. Arberry. Reprinted, Oxford University Press, 1983.

Kraemer, Joel L. *Philosophy in the Renaissance of Islam: Abū Sulaymān al-Sijistānī and his Circle.* Leiden: E J. Brill, 1986.

Krupp, A. *Studien zum Menāqybnāme des Abu'l- Wafā' Tāğ al-'Ārifīn: Das historische Leben des Abu l-Wafā' Tāğ al-'Ārifīn.* Munich: Rudolf Trofenik, 1976.

Kubrā, Najm al-Dīn al-. *al-Uṣūl al-'ashara.* Translated into Persian by 'Abd al-Ghafūr Lārī. Edited by Najīb Māyil Harawī. Tehran 1363 A.Hsh./1984.

______. *Die Fawā'iḥ al-ğamāl wa-fawātiḥ al-ğalāl des Nağm ad-dīn al-Kubrā.* Edited with a study by F. Meier. Wiesbaden: Steiner, 1957.

La Capra. *Rethinking Intellectual History: Texts, Contexts, Language.* Ithaca: 1983.

Lāhawrī, 'Abd al-Karīm. *Sharḥ-i Sawāniḥ.* Persian MS. 218. New Delhi: Jamia Millia Islamia.

Lambton, Ann K. *Continuity and Change in Medieval Persia: Aspects of Administrative, Economic and Social History, 11th-14th Century.* London: I.B. Tauris, 1988.

Landolt, Hermann. "Two Types of Mystical Thought in Muslim Iran: An

Essay on Suhrawardī Shaykh al-Ishrāq and 'Aynulquẓāt-i Hamadānī." *Muslim World* 68 (1978).

Lane, E.W. *An Arabic-English Lexicon.* London: 1863-93.

______ ., trans. *The Arabian Nights Enertainments.* New York: 1927.

Laugier de Beaurecueil, Serge de. *Anṣārī: Chemin de Dieu, trois traités spirituels: Les Cent Terrains* (Sad Maydān), *Les Étapes des Itinérants vers Dieu* (Manāzil al- sā'irīn), traduits du Persan et de l'Arabe, presentés et annotés. Paris: Sindbad, 1985.

______ , ed. *Kitāb 'ilal al-maqāmāt.* Mélanges Massignon. Damacus: 1956.

______ . *Khawādja 'Abdullāh Anṣārī (396-481 H./ 1006-1089), mystique hanbalite.* Vol. XXVI of Beirut: Recherches d'Institut de lettres orientales de Beyrouth, 1965.

______ ., trans. *Anṣārī: Cris du coeur.* Paris: Sindbad, 1988.

Lawrence, Bruce B. "The Chishtiya of Sultanate India: A Case Study of Biographical Complexities in South Asian Islam." *Charisma and Sacred Biography.* Edited by Michael A. Williams. Chico: 1982.

Lazard, G. "Pahlavi, Pârsi, Dari: Les Langues de l'Iran d'après Ibn al-Muqaffa'." *Iran and Islam.* Edited by C.E. Bosworth. Edinburgh: University Press, 1971.

______ . "The Rise of the New Persian Language." *The Cambridge History of Iran.* IV: *From the Arab Invasion to the Saljuqs.* Edited by Richard N. Frye. Cambridge: University Press, 1975.

Le Strange, G. *The Lands of the Eastern Caliphate.* Cambridge: 1905.

Lewisohn, Leonard. "Shabistarī's Garden of Mysteries: The Aesthetics and Hermeneutics of Sufi Poetry." *Temenos: A Review Devoted to the Arts of the Imagination.* No. 10 (1989): 177-207.

______ . "The Life and Poetry of Mashriqī Tabrīzī (d. 1454)." *Iranian Studies.* vol. 22. nos. 2-3. (1989): 99-127.

______ . "Muḥammad Shīrīn Tabrīzī." *Sufi: A Journal of Sufism.* Issue 1, (1988-89) 30-35.

______ ., ed., *The Heritage of Sufism.* Vol. II. Oxford: Oneworld Publications, 1999.

______ ., ed., *Divān-i Muḥammad Shīrīn Maghribī.* Persian text edited with notes, introduction, and indices. Wisdom of Persia Series. (Tehran: McGill Institute of Islamic Studies, Tehran Branch; London: SOAS 1994).

______ ., "Zindigī va dawrān-i Kamāl Khujandī." *Iran Nameh* (in Persian) 10/4 (1992).

Lings, Martin. "The Origins of Sufism." *Islamic Quarterly* (1956).

Little, D.P. "Religion under the Mamlūks." *The Muslim World* 73 (1986).

López-Baralt, L. *San Juan de la Cruz y el Islam.* Puerto Rico: 1985.
______ . "De Nūrī de Bagdad a Santa Teresa de Jesús: el símbolo de los siete castillos o moradas concéntricas del alma." *Vuelta* 80. July (1983).
______ . *Huellas de Islam en la literatura española.* Madrid: 1985.
Lukes, S. "Relativism in Its Place." *Rationality and Relativism.* Edited by Martin Hollis and Steven Lukes. Cambridge: MIT Press, 1982.
Lyall, C.J. *Translation of Ancient Arabian Poetry, Chiefly Pre-Islamic, with an Introduction and Notes.* London: 1885.
Madelung, W. *Religious Schools and Sects in Medieval Islam.* London: Variorium Reprints, 1985.
______ . *Religious Trends in Early Islamic Iran.* Columbia Lectures on Iranian Studies 4. Bibliotheca Persica. Albany: SUNY, 1988.
Maghribī, Muḥammad Shīrīn. *Divān-i Muḥammad Shīrīn Maghribī.* Edited by Leonard Lewisohn. Tehran: 'Wisdom of Persia' Series, McGill Institute of Islamic Studies, and London: SOAS 1993.
Mahdi, M. "The Book and the Master as Poles of Cultural Change in Islam." *Islam and Cultural Change in the Middle Ages.* Edited by S. Vyronis Jr. Wiesbaden: Otto Harrassowitz, 1975.
Makdisi. *The Rise of Colleges: Institutions of Learning in Islam and the West.* Edinburgh: University Press, 1981.
______ . *The Rise of Humanism in Classical Islam and the Christian West.* Edinburgh: University Press, 1989.
Malamud, M. "Sufism in the Twelfth-century Baghdad: The *Ādāb al-murīdīn* of Abū Najīb al-Suhrawardī." Paper presented at the 1991 MESA conference.
Manheim, R. "Time in Islamic Thought." *Man and Time, Papers from the Eranos Yearbooks.* Edited by J. Campbell. Bollingen Series XXX.3. Princeton: 1957.
Marrou, H.I. *Théologie de l'histoire.* Paris: 1968.
Massignon, ed. *Akhbār al-Hallāj, texte ancien relatif à la prédication et au supplice du mystique musulman al-Ḥosayn b. Manṣour al-Ḥallāj.* 3 ed. Paris: 1957.
______ . *Essai sur les origenes du lexique technique de la mystique musulmane.* Études Musulmanes. 2 ed. Paris: Librairie Philosophique J. Vrin, 1968.
______ . *La Passion de Husayn Ibn Mansûr Hallâj, martyr mystique de l'Islam exécuté à Baghdad le 26 mars 922.* Vol. 4 of Paris: Gallimard, 1975.
______ . *The Passion of al-Ḥallāj: Mystic and Martyr of Islam.* Trans. H. Mason. Princeton University Press, 1982.

______ . *Receuil des textes inédits concernant l'histoire de la mystique en pays d'Islam.* Paris: 1929.

______ . "Le Temps dans la pensée islamique." *Eranos-Jahrbuch.* Zurich: 1951-2.

______ . *Opera Minora I.* Beirut: 1963.

Mason, Herbert. *The Death of al-Ḥallāj.* Notre Dame: University Press 1979.

Mas'ūdī, Abī'l-Ḥasan 'Alī ibn Ḥusayn. *Murawwij al-dhahab wa ma'ādin al-jawhar.* Persian translation by Abū'l-Qāsim Pāyanda. Tehran: B.T.N.K, 1965.

Maybudī, Rashīd al-Dīn. *Kashf al-asrār wa 'uddat al-abrār.* 10 vols. Edited by 'Alī Aṣghar Ḥikmat. Tehran: Intishārāt-i Dānishgāhī, 1952-60.

Maysarī, Ḥakīm. *Dānish-nāma.* Tehran: 1987.

Meier, F. "Soufisme et déclin Culturel." *Classicisme et déclin culturel dans l'histoire de l'Islam.* Actes du Symposium Internationale d'Histoire de la Civilisation Musulmane. Edited by R. Brunschvig and G.E. Von Grunebaum. Paris: 1957, pp. 217-45.

______ . "The Ultimate Origin and the Hereafter in Islam." *Islam and its Cultural Divergence.* Edited by C.L. Tikku. Urbana: 1971.

______ . *Abū Sa'īd b. Abī'l-Ḫayr (357-440/967-1049): Wirklichkeit und Legende.* Leiden, Tehran, Paris: 1976.

______ . *Bahā'-i Walad. Grundzüge seines Lebens und seiner Mystik.* Acta Iranica 27, troisième série textes et mémoires, vol. 14. Leiden: E.J Brill, 1989.

Milson, M. *A Sufi Rule for Novices: Kitāb Ādāb al-murīdīn of Abū Najīb al-Suhrawardī.* Cambridge, Mass. and London: Harvard University Press, 1973.

Mīnuvī, Mujtabā, ed., *Aḥwāl wa aqwāl-i Shaykh Abū'l-Ḥasan Kharaqānī wa muntakhab-i Nūr al-'ulū.* Tehran: Ṭahūrī 1359 A.Hsh./1980.

Molé, M. "Professions de foi de deux Kubrawīs: 'Alī-i Hamadānī et Muḥammad Nūrbakhsh." *Bulletin d'étude orientales [Institute français de Damas].*17 (1961-62): 133-204

______ . *Les Mystiques Musulmans.* Paris: Les Deux Océans, 1982.

______ . "La version persane du Traité de dix principes de Najm al-Dîn Kobrâ par 'Alî ibn Shihâb al-Din Hamadânî." *Farhang-i Īrān zamīn.* 6 (1958): 38-66.

______ . "Le problème zurvanite." *Journal asiatique.* (1959).

______ . "Les Kubrawiya entre sunnisme et shiisme aux huitième et neuvième siècles de l'hégire." *Revue des études islamiques.* 29 (1961).

Monnot, G. *Penseurs musulmans et religions iraniennes.* Paris: 1974.

Morris, James W. *The Wisdom of the Throne, translation of Al-ḥikma al-arshiyya.* Princeton: 1981.

Mughal, Munir Ahmad., trans. *The Hundred Fields Between Man and God.* Lahore: Islamic Book Foundation, 1983.

Muḥasibī, al-Ḥarīth al-. *Al-Masā'il fī a'māl al-qulūb wa'l-jawāriḥ.* Cairo: 1969.

Mulaqqin, Ibn. *Ṭabaqāt al-awliyā'.* Edited by Nūr al-Dīn Sharība. Egypt: 1973.

Muqaddasī, Abū Naṣr Muṭahhar ibn Ṭāhir al-. *Kitāb al-bad' wa'l-ta'rīkh.* Beirut: n.d.

Muqaddasī, Muḥammad ibn Aḥmad al-. *Aḥsan al-taqāsīm fī ma'rifat al-aqālīm.* Edited by M.J. De Goeje. Leiden: E.J. Brill, 1906.

Murata, Sachiko. *The Tao of Islam: A Sourcebook on Gender Relationships in Islamic Thought.* Albany: SUNY Press, 1992.

Mustawfī, Hamdullāh. *Ta'rīkh-i guzīda.* Reprinted, Tehran: Amīr Kabīr, 1985.

Nafīsī, Sa'īd, ed. *Sukhanān-i manẓūm-i Abū Sa'īd Abī'l-Khayr.* Tehran: Sanā'ī, n.d.

Nasr, S.H. "The School of Isfahan." *A History of Muslim Philosophy.* Edited by H.M. Sharif. 2 vols. Wiesbaden: O. Harrassowitz, 1966.

______ . *Ṣadr al-Dīn Shīrāzī and His Transcendent Philosophy.* Tehran: Iranian Academy of Philosophy, 1978.

______ . *Three Muslim Sages.* New York: Caravan Books, 1966.

______ . *Les Etats Spirituels dans le Soufisme.* Rome: Accademia Nazionale dei Lincei, 1973.

______ . "The Relationship between Sufism and Philosophy in Persian Culture." *Hamdard Islamicus* 6.4 (1983):

______ . "Why Was Fārābī Called the Second Teacher." *Islamic Culture* 59 (1985).

______ . *Islamic Art and Spirituality.* Suffolk, U.K: Golgonooza Press, 1987.

______ . "Spiritual Chivalry." *Islamic Spirituality: Manifestations II.* Edited by S.H. Nasr. New York: Crossroads 1991.

Nawawī, Al-. *An-Nawawī's Forty Ḥadīth.* Translated E. Ibrahim and D. Johnson-Davies. 2nd ed. Beirut and Damascus: The Holy Koran Publishing House, 1976.

Netton. "Myth, Miracle and Magic in the Riḥla of Ibn Baṭṭūṭa." *Journal of Semitic Studies* 29:1. Spring (1984)

______ . "Arabia and the Pilgrim Paradigm of Ibn Baṭṭūṭa: A Braudelian Approach." *Arabia and the Gulf: From Traditional Society to Mod-*

ern States. Edited by Ian Richard Netton. London: Croom Helm, 1986.

Neuwirth, A. "Symmetrie und Paarbildung in der koranischen Eschatologie, Philologisch-Stilistisches u Sūrat ar-Raḥman." *Melanges de l'Université Saint-Joseph.*

Newman, Andrew. "Towards a Reconsideration of the 'Iṣfahān School of Philosophy': Shaykh Bahā'ī and the Role of the Safawid *'Ulamā',*" *Studia Iranica.* XV/ii (1986): 165-99.

Ni'matullāh Walī, Shāh. *Rasā'il Ḥaḍrat-i Sayyid Nūr al-Dīn Shāh Ni'matu'llāh Valī.* 4 vols. Edited by Javad Nurbakhsh. Tehran: Intishārāt-i Khāniqāh-i Nimatu'llāhī, 1979.

Nicholson, R.A. *Studies in Islamic Poetry.* Cambridge: Cambridge University Press 1921.

______ . *A Persian Forerunner of Dante.* Towyn-on-Sea, N. Wales: 1944.

______ . *Studies in Islamic Mysticism.* Reprinted, Cambridge: 1980.

Niffarī, Ibn Abdī 'l-Jabbār al-. *The Mawāqif and Mukhātabat of Muḥammad Ibn Abdī 'l-Jabbār al-Niffarī with other fragments.* Edited with translation by A.J. Arberry. E.J.W. Gibb Memorial Trust. London: Luzac & Co., 1978.

Niẓām al-Mulk. *Sīyāsatnāma.* Edited by H. Darke. Tehran: B.T.N.K., 1340 A.Hsh./1961.

Nöldeke, T. "Vorstellungen der Araber vom Schicksal." *Zeitschrift für Völkerpsychologie und Sprachwissenschaft* 3 (1885).

Nurbakhsh, Javad. *Sufism: Meaning, Knowledge and Unity.* New York: KNP, 1981.

______ . *In the Tavern of Ruin.* New York: KNP, 1975.

______ . *Traditions of the Prophet.* 2 vols. Vol. 1: translated by L. Lewisohn; vol. 2: translated by T. Graham and L. Lewisohn. New York: KNP, 1981.

______ . *Spiritual Poverty in Sufism.* Translated by L. Lewisohn. London: 1984.

______ . *Dogs From a Sufi Point of View.* London: KNP, 1989.

______ . *Sufi Women.* Translated by L. Lewisohn. 2nd ed. London: KNP, 1990.

______ . "Two Approaches to the Principle of the Unity of Being." *The Heritage of Sufism.* Vol. II. Edited by L. Lewisohn. Oxford, Oneworld Publications, 1999.

Nwyia, Paul. "Le Tafsīr Mystique attribué à Ǧa'far Ṣādiq: Édition critique," *Mélanges de l'Université Saint-Joseph,* XLIII/4 (1968).

______ . *Exégèse coranique et langage mystique, Nouvel essai sur le lexique technique des mystiques musulmanes.* Recherches publiées sous la direction de l'Institut de Lettres Orientales de Beyrouth, Série I: Pensée arabe et musulmane, vol. XLIX. Beirut: Dar el-Machreq Éditeurs 1970.

______., ed. *Trois œuvres inédites de mystiques musulmans: Šaqīq al-Balkhī, Ibn 'Aṭā, Niffarī.* Recherches, Collection publiée sous la direction de la Faculté des Lettres et des Sciences Humaines de l'Université Saint-Joseph, Beyrouth, Série I: Pensée arabe et musulmane, vol. 7. 2nd ed. Beirut: Dar el-Machreq Éditeurs SARL 1982.

Ocak, A.Y. "Emirci Sultan ve zāviyesi. XIII. yüzyılın ilk yarısında Anadolu (Bozok)'da bir Babâi şeyhi: Şeref'üd-Din İsmail b. Muḥammed." *Tarih Enstitüsü Dergisi.* 9 (1978).

______. *Babaīler İsyanı.* Istanbul: Dergāh Yayınları, 1980.

______. *La Révolte de Baba Resul ou la Formation de l'Hétérodoxie Musulmane en Anatolie au XIIIe Siècle.* Ankara: Türk Tarih Kurumu, 1989.

______. "Les *Menakib'ul-Ḳudsıya fī Menāsib'il-Unsīya:* une source importante pour l'histoire religieuse de l'Anatolie au XIIIe siècle." *Journal Asiatique.* 267 (1979).

______ and İ. Erünsal, eds. *Menâḳıbu'l-ḳudsiyye fı menâsıbi'l-ünsiyye: Baba İlyas- ı Horasānī ve Sülālesinin Menkabevi Tarihi.* Istanbul: İstanbul Üniversitesi Edebiyat Fakültesi Yayınları, 1984.

Önder, M. "Eine neuentdeckte Quelle zur Geschichte der Seltschuken in Anatolien." *Wiener Zeitschrift für die Kunde des Morgenlandes* 55 (1959).

Osseiran, Afif., ed. *Muṣannafat-i 'Ayn al-Quḍāt Hamadhānī.* Tehran: Dānishgāh, 1962.

Paret, R. *Mohammed und der Koran.* Stuttgart 1957.

Parmaksızoğlu, İ. Olgun and İ., ed. *Ḳuṭbnāme.* Ankara: Türk Tarih Kurumu Yayınları, 1980.

Parmu, R.K. *A History of Muslim Rule in Kashmir, 1320-1819.* Delhi: People's Publishing house, 1969.

Pedersen, J. "The Islamic Preacher: wā'iẓ, mudhakkir, qāṣṣ." *Goldziher Mem.* Budapest: 1948.

Pines, S. *Beiträge zur islamischen Atomenlehre.* Gräfenhainichen: 1936.

______. *Nouvelles études sur Awḥad al-zamān Abu-l-Barakāt al-Baghdādī.* Paris: 1955.

______. and S. Sambursky. *The Concept of Time in Late Neoplatonism.* Jerusalem: 1971.

Pourjavady, N. *Mukātibāt-i Khwāja Aḥmad Ghazzālī bā 'Ayn al-Quḍāt Hamadānī.* Tehran: Intishārāt-i Khānaqāh-i Ni'matullāhī, 1977.

______. *Zindagī wa āthār-i Shaykh Abū'l-Ḥasan Bustī.* Tehran: 1985.

______ . "Selfhood and Time in the Sufism of Aḥmad Ghazzālī." *Sophia Perennis* IV (1981).

______ trans., ed. Aḥmad Ghazālī, *Sawāniḥ: Inspirations from the World of Pure Spirits.* London: KPI, 1986.

Qāsimī, M. "Sharḥ-i āwāz-i par-i Jibrā'īl." *Ma'ārif* 1. March-May (1984).

Qazwīnī, Zakariyya. *Athār al-bilād wa akhbār al-'ibād.* Beirut: 1960.

Quasem, Muhammad Abul. *The Recitation and Interpretation of the Qur'ān: al-Ghazzālī's Theory.* Kuala Lumpur: University of Malaysia Press, 1979.

Qushayrī, 'Abū'l-Qāsim al-. *The Principles of Sufism by al-Qushayri.* Translated by B.R. Von Schlegell. Berkley: Mizan Press, 1990.

______ . *Al-risāla fī 'ilm al-taṣawwuf.* Cairo: 1912.

______ . *Tarjama-yi Risāla-yi Qushayrī.* Edited by Badī' al-Zamān Furūzānfār. Tehran: 1345 A.Hsh./1982. Persian translation of the *Risāla* by Abū 'Alī Ḥasan ibn Aḥmad al-'Uthmānī.

______ . *al-Risāla al-Qushayriyya.* 2 vols. Cairo: 1966.

Radtke, B. "Ibn al-'Arabī's Kommentar zu al-Ḥakīm al-Tirmiḏī's *Sīrat al-awliyā:* Einige filologische Bemerkungen." *Tirmiḏiana Minora. Oriens* 34 (forthcoming).

______ . *Al-Ḥakīm al-Tirmiḏī. Ein islamischer Theosoph des 3./9 Jahrhunderts.* Freiburg: Klaus Schwarz, 1980.

______ . "Der Mystiker al-Ḥakīm at-Tirmidī." *Der Islam* 57 (1980).

______ . "Die älteste islamische Kosmographies. Muḥammad-i Ṭūsīs 'Ağā'ib ul-mahlūqāt." *Der Islam* 64 (1987).

______ . "A Forerunner of Ibn al-'Arabī: Ḥakīm Tirmidhī on Sainthood." *Journal of the Ibn 'Arabī Society* 8 (1989).

______ . "Theosophie *(Ḥikma)* und Philosophie *(Falsafa).* Ein Beitrag zur Frage der *ḥikmat al-mašriq|al-išrāq." Asiatische Studien* 42 (1988).

______ . *Adab al-mulūk. Ein Handbuch zur islamischen Mystik aus dem 4./10. Jahrhundert.* Beirut/Stuttgart: Franz Steiner, 1991.

______ . "Der sunnitische Islam." *Der Islam in der Gegenwart.* Edited by Werner Ende and Udo Steinbach. München: Beck, 1991.

______ . "Zweisprachigkeit im frühen persischen taṣawwuf." *Orientalia Suecana* 38-39 (1991).

______ . *Drei Schriften des Theosophen von Tirmid.* Bibliotheca Islamica 35a. Beirut/Stuttgart: Franz Steiner, 1992

______ . "Psychomachia in der Sufik." *Studia Iranica* 11 (1992).

______ . "Die Autobiografie des Theosophen von Tirmid. Edition, Übersetzung und Kommentar." *Tirmiḏiana Minora. Oriens* 34 (forthcoming).

______ . *Weltgeschichte und Weltbeschreibung im mittelalterlichen Islam.*

Beirut/Stuttgart: Franz Steiner, 1992.

______ . "Theologen und Mystiker in Khurāsān und Transoxanien." *ZDMG.* 136 (1986).

Rafiqi, Abdul Qaiyum. *Sufism in Kashmir from the Fourteenth to the Sixteenth Century.* Varanasi: Bharatiya Publishing House, 1972.

Rahman, F. "The Eternity of the World and the Heavenly Bodies in Post-Avicennan Philosophy." *Essays on Islamic Philosophy and Science.* Edited by G.F. Hourani. Albany: 1975.

______ . "The God-World Relationship in Mullā Ṣadrā." *Essays on Islamic Philosophy and Science.* Edited by G.F. Hourani. Albany: 1975.

______ . *The Philosophy of Mullā Ṣadrā.* Albany: 1975.

Rāwandī, Muḥammad ibn 'Alī ibn Sulaymān al-. *Rāhat al-ṣudūr wa 'āyat al-surūr dar tārīkh-i Āl-i Siljūq.* Tehran: Amīr Kabīr, 1985.

Rāzī, Najm al-Dīn. *Mirṣād al-'ibād min al-mabdā' ilā'l-ma'ād.* Edited by Muḥammad Amīn Riyāhī. 2nd ed. Tehran: 1986.

______ . *The Path of God's Bondsmen.* Translation of *Mirṣād al-'ibād* by Hamid Algar. New York: Caravan Books 1982.

Rāzī, Shams al-Dīn Muḥammad ibn Qays Rāzī. *Al-Mu'ajjam fī mu'āyīri ash'ār al-'ajam.* Edited by M. Qazwīnī and Mudarris Raḍawī. Tehran: n.d.

Reinert, B. *Die Lehre tawakkul in der klassischen Sufik.* Berlin: 1968.

Ricoeur, P. *Time and Narrative*. Chicago: 1984.

Ringgren, H. *Fatalism in Persian Epics.* Uppsala: 1952.

______ . *Studies in Arabian Fatalism.* Uppsala: 1955.

______ . "Islamic Fatalism." *Fatalistic Beliefs.* Edited by H. Ringgren. Stockholm: 1967.

Ritter, H. "Philologika VII: Arabische und persische Schriften über die profane und die mystische Liebe." *Der Islam* 21 (1933).

______ . "Die Aussprüche des Bāyezīd Bisṭāmī."*Westöstliche Abhandlungen.* Edited by F. Meier. Wiesbaden: 1954.

______ . *Das Meer der Seele: Mensch, Welt und Gott in den Geschichten des Farīduddīn 'Aṭṭār.* Leiden: 1978.

Rizvi, S.A.A. *A History of Sufism in India.* 2 vols. New Delhi: Mundshiram Manoharlal, 1978-83.

Rosenthal, F. *A History of Muslim Historiography.* 2nd revised ed. Leiden: 1968.

______ . *Sweeter than Hope.* Leiden: 1983.

Rūmī, Jalāl al-Dīn Muḥammad. *Fīhi mā fīhi.* Tehran: 1969.

______ . *Mathnawī.* Edited by M. Este'lami. 6 vols. Tehran: Intishārāt-i Zawwar, 1991. A critical edition with introduction, notes and indices.

______ .*The Mathnawí of Jalálu'ddín Rúmí.* Edited and translated by R.A. Nicholson with a commentary. 8 vols. London & Leiden: 1925-40. Reprinted, London: 1982.

______ . *Kulliyyāt-i Shams yā Dīwān-i kabīr.* Edited by Badī' al-Zamān Furūzānfār. 10 vols. Tehran: University Press 1957-67.

Rūmī, Ebū'l-Ḫayr. *Ṣaltuḳnāme.* Sources of Oriental Languages and Literatures, Turkish Sources 4. 7 vols. Cambridge, Mass: Harvard University, Office of the University Publisher, 1974-84.

Rūzbihān al-Baqlī al-Shīrāzī. *Tafsīr 'arā'is al-bayān.* Lucknow: Nawal Kishōr, 1983-4.

______ . *Kitāb mashrab al-arwāḥ.* Edited by N.M. Hoca. Istanbul: Maṭba'at Kulliyyāt al-Ādāb, 1973.

______ . *Sharḥ-i shaṭḥīyyāt.* Edited by H. Corbin. Bibliothéque Iranienne 12. Tehran: Departement d'iranologie de l'Institut Franco-iranien, 1966.

______ . *Le Jasmin des fidèles d'amour ('Abhar al-'āshiqīn).* Edited by H. Corbin and M. Mu'īn. Bibliothéque Iranienne, 8. Tehran: Institut Français d'Iranologie de Téhéran, 1958; reprinted, 1981.

Rypka. *History of Iranian Literature.* Dordrecht, Holland: D. Reidel Publishing Co, 1968.

Sabzawārī, H. *Asrār al-ḥikam fi'l-muftataḥ wa'l-mukhtatam.* Edited by Ḥ.M. Farzād (Tehran 1361 A.Hsh./1982-3.

Sa'd, Jamāl al-Dīn Luṭfullāh ibn Abī Sa'īd. *Ḥālāt u sukhanān-i Shaykh Abū Sā'īd Abī'l-Khayr.* Edited by V. Zhukovskii. St. Petersburg: 1899. Edited by Īraj Afshār. Tehran: 1963.

Ṣadrā, Mullā. *Sih aṣl.* Edited by S.H. Nasr. (Tehran: 1340 A.Hsh./1961.

Ṣafā, Dh. *Tā'rīkh-i adabiyyāt dar Irān.* 5 vols. Tehran: Amīr Kabīr, 1952-85.

Sahlajī, Abū'l-Faḍl Muḥammad b. 'Alī. *Kitāb al-nūr min kalimāt Abī Ṭayfūr.* Edited by A. Badawī in his *Shaṭaḥāt al-ṣūfiyya.* Cairo: 1949.

Saint-Quentin, Simon de. *Histoire des Tartares (Historia Tartarum).* Paris: Paul Geuthner, 1965.

Sakkakini, Widad el-. *First Among Sufis, The Life and Thought of Rabia al-Adawiyya, the Woman Saint of Basra.* Translated by Nabil Safwat. London: Octagon Press, 1982.

Ṣalībā', Jamīl. *Ta'rīkh al-falsafa al-'arabiyya.* Beirut: Dār al-kitāb al-kubnānī, 1986.

Sam'āni, Aḥmad. *Rawḥ al-arwāḥ fī sharḥ asmā' al-malīk al-fattāḥ.* Edited by M. Harawī. Tehran: Shirkat-i intishārāt-i 'ilmī wa farhangī, 1368 A.Hsh./1989.

Samarqandī, Dawlatshāh. *Tadhkirat al-shu'arā*. Edited by E.G. Browne. Leiden/ London: 1901.

Samartha, S.J. *The Hindu View of History*. Bangalore: 1959.

Sanā'ī, Abū'l-Majd Majdūd b. Ādam. *Ḥadīqat al-ḥaqīqat wa sharī'a al-ṭarīqat*. Edited by M. Raḍawī. Tehran: 1950.

______ . *Sayr al-'ibād ilā'l-ma'ād*. MS. Bağdatli Vehbi (Istanbul). No. 1672.

______ . *Fakhrī-nāma*. MS. Bağdatli Vehbi (Istanbul). No. 1672.

______ . *Makātīb Sanā'ī*. Edited by Nadhīr Aḥmad. Tehran 1362 A.Hsh./ 1983.

Sarfeh, L. Morris & R. *Munajat: The Intimate Prayers of Khwajih 'Abd Al-lah Ansari*. New York: Khaneghah Maleknia Naseralishah, 1975.

Sarrāj, Abū Naṣr al-. *Kitāb al-luma' fī'l-taṣawwuf*. Edited. by R.A. Nicholson. London/Leiden: 1914.

Schacht, J. *An Introduction to Islamic Law*. Oxford: 1964.

Scheftelowitz, I. *Die Zeit als Schickalsgottheit in der indischen und iranischen Religion (Kāla und Zurvān)*. Stuttgart: 1929.

Schimmel, A. "The Ornament of the Saints." *Iranian Studies* 7 (1974).

______ . *Mystical Dimensions of Islam*. Chapel Hill: University of North Carolina, 1975.

______ . *And Muhammad is His Messeenger*. Chapel Hill: University of North Carolina, 1985.

______ . *I am Wind, You are Fire: The Life and Work of Rumi*. Boston & London: 1992.

______ . *The Triumphal Sun :a Study of the Works of Jalāloddin Rūmī*. London/The Hague: 1978.

Schmitt, E. *Lexikalische Untersuchungen zur arabischen Übersetzung von Artemidors Traumbuch*. Wiesbaden: 1970.

Schrameyer. *Über den Fatalismus der vorislamischen Araber*. Bonn: 1981.

Şerafeddin, M. "Gazalî, nin Te'vil Hakkinda Basilmamiş bir Eseri." *Darülfünun İlahiyat Fakültesi Mecmuası*. IV/16 (Teşrinievvel: 1930): 46-58.

Sezgin, F. *Gescichte des arabischen Schrifttums*. Leiden: 1967.

Shabistarī, Maḥmūd. *Gulshan-i rāz*. Edited by Ṣamad Muwaḥḥid. *Majmū'a-yi āthār-i Shaykh Maḥmūd Shabistarī*. 2nd printing. Tehran: 1371 A.Hsh./1982.

Shaqīq al-Balkhī. "Ādāb al-'ibādāt." *Trois œuvres inédites de mystiques musulmans: Šaqīq al-Balkhī, Ibn 'Aṭā, Niffarī*. Edited by Paul Nwyia. Recherches, Collection publiée sous la direction de la Faculté des Lettres et des Sciences Humaines de l'Université Saint-Joseph, Beyrouth, Série I: Pensée arabe et musulmane, vol. 7. 2nd ed.

Beirut: Dar el-Machreq Éditeurs SARL 1982.
Shahrazūrī, Shams al-Dīn. *Nūzhat al-arwāḥ wa rawḍāt al-afrāḥ fī tārīkh al-ḥukamā wa'l-falāsifa.* Hayderabad: 1976.
Siddiqi, A.H. *Caliphate and Kingship in Medieval Persia.* Philadelphia: 1977.
Singh, Sir Jogendra. *The Invocations of Shaikh Abdullah Ansari.* London: John Murray, 1939.
Sirhindī, Aḥmad. *Maktūbāt-i Imām-i Rabbānī.* Lucknow: 1989.
Sīstānī, Amīr Iqbāl. *Chihil majlis* of 'Alā' al-Dawla Simnānī. Edited by 'Abd al- Rafī' Ḥaqīqat. Tehran 1979.
Smith, Margaret. *Rābi'ah the Mystic and Her Fellow-Saints in Islam.* Cambridge: Cambridge University Press, 1928.
______ . *An Early Mystic of Baghdad: a Study of the Life and Teachings of Ḥārith b. Āsād al-Muḥāsibī, A.D. 781-857.* London: Sheldon Press, 1977.
Soykut, R. *Ahi Evran.* Ankara: San Matbaası,1976.
Stewart, Devin J. "A Biographical Notice on Bahā' al-Dīn al-'Āmilī (d. 1030/1621)." *Journal of the American Oriental Society.* CXI/iii. July-Sept. 1991.
St. John of the Cross. Kavanaugh, K. & O. Rodriguez, trans., eds. *The Collected Works of St. John of the Cross.* Washington: ICS, 1979.
Storey, C.A. *Persian Literature: A Bio-Bibliographical Survey.* 2 vols. London: 1953-72.
Subkī, Tāj al-Dīn Abū Naṣr 'Abd al-Wahhāb b. 'Alī. *Ṭabaqāt al-Shāfi'iyya al-kubrā.* Reprinted, Beirut: Dār al-Ma'rifa, n.d.; Cairo: al-Maṭba'a al-Ḥusayniyya, 1905-6. Reprinted, Cairo: 1964.
Suhrawardī (Shaykh al-Ishrāq). *Opera Metaphysica et Mystica.* Edited by Henry Corbin. 3 vols. Tehran and Paris 1952-70.
Suhrawardī, Abū Najīb al-. *Kitāb Ādāb al-murīdīn.* Edited by Menahem Milson. Vol. 2 of Max Schloessinger Memorial Series, Texts 2. Jerusalem: Hebrew University of Jerusalem, Institute of Asian and African Studies, 1977 [distributed by the Magnes Press].
______ . *Adāb al-murīdīn.* Edited by 'Umar ibn Muḥammad ibn Aḥmad Shirakān. Tehran: 1984.
______ . *A Sufi Rule for Novices: Kitāb Ādāb al-murīdīn of Abū al-Najīb al-Suhrawardī .* Abridged trans. and introduction by Menahem Milson. Cambridge, Mass., and London: Harvard University Press: 1975.
Suhrawardī, Shihāb al-Dīn Abū Ḥafṣ 'Umar. *'Awārif al-ma'ārif.* Beirut: Dār al-Kitāb al-'Arabī, 1983.
Sulamī, 'Abd al-Raḥmān. *Jawāmi' ādāb al-ṣūfiyya* and *'Uyūb al-nafs wa*

mudāwātuhā. Edited by E. Kohlberg. Jerusalem: 1976.

______. *Ṭabaqāt al-ṣūfiyya.* Edited by N. Sharība. Cairo: 1953.

______. *Sulamī: La Lucidité Implacable (Épître des hommes du blâme).* Translated into French by Roger Deladrière. Paris: Arléa 1991.

______. R. Hartmann, "Al-Sulamī's *Risālat al-Malāmatiyya." Der Islam.* VIII (1917-18).

______. *Risālat al-malāmatiyya.* Edited by Abū'l-'Alā' al-'Afīfī in *Al-malāmatiyya wa'l-ṣūfiyya wa ahl al-futuwwa.* Cairo: 1945.

______. *The Way of Sufi Chivalry.* Translated by Tosun Bayrak al-Jerrahi. Vermont: Inner Traditions International, 1991. Translation of Sulamī's *Risāla al-futuwwa.*

Sulṭān Walad. *Dīwān-i Sulṭān Walad.* Edited by S. Nafīsī. Tehran: 1338 A.Hsh./1959.

Suyuti, Jalāl al-Dīn 'Abd al-Raḥmān ibn Abī Bakr al-. *al-Itqān fī 'ulūm al-Qur'ān.* 2 vols. Reprinted, Lahore: 1400/1980.

______. *al-Muzhir fī 'ulūm al-lughah.* Edited by Muḥammad Aḥmad Jād al-Mawlā, Muḥammad Abū al-Faḍl Ibrāhīm and 'Alī Muḥammad al-Bukhārī. 2 vols. Cairo: nd.

Sviri, Sara. "The Mystical Psychology of al-Ḥakīm al-Tirmidhī." Ph.D Thesis. Tel-Aviv, 1978.

______. *"Wa-rahbāniyyatan ibtada'ūhā* – An Analysis of Traditions Concerning the Origin and Evaluation of Christian Monasticism." *Jerusalem Studies in Arabic and Islam* 13 (1990).

Taeschner, F. *Gülschehrī's Mesnevī auf Achi Evran, den Heiligen von Kirschehir und Patron der türkischen Zünfte.* Wiesbaden: Deutsche Morgenländische Gesellschaft, Kommissionsverlag Franz Steiner 1955.

______. "Der Anteil des Sufismus an der Formung des Futuwwideals." *Der Islam* 24 (1937): 43-74.

Tahānawī, Muḥammad 'Alī ibn 'Alī ibn Muḥammad Ḥāmid al-. *Kashshāf Iṣṭilāḥāt al-funūn.* Edited by A. Sprenger. Calcutta: 1278/1861.

Takeshita, Masataka. "Continuity and Change in the Tradition of Shirazi Love Mysticism: A Comparison between Daylamī's *'Aṭf al-Alif* and Rūzbihān Baqlī's *'Abhar al-'āshiqīn." Orient* XXIII (1987): 113-31.

Taşköprīzāde, A. al-Shaqā'iq. *al-Numāniyya fī 'ulamā' al-dawlat al-'uthmāniyya.* Beirut: Dār al-Kitāb al-'Arabī, 1970.

Tavard, G. *Poetry and Contemplation in St. John of the Cross.* Ohio University Press, 1988.

Tawḥīdī, Abū Ḥayyān al-. *al-Baṣā'ir wa'l- dhakhā'ir.* Beirut: 1988; 3 vols. Damascus: Librairie Atlas et Imprimerie Al-Incha, 1964.

Tehrani, K. "Mystical Symbolism in Four Treatises of Suhrawardī." Ph.D. Thesis Columbia University, 1974.

Teufel, J.K. *Eine Lebenbeschreibung des Scheichs Alī-i Hamadānī (gestorben 1385): Die Xulāṣat ul-manāqib des Maulānā Nūr ud-Dīn Ca'far-i Badaxšī.* Leiden: E. J. Brill, 1962.

Thackston, Wheeler M. *Kwaja Abdullah Ansari: Intimate Conversations.* New York: Paulist Press, 1978.

Trimingham, J.S. *The Sufi Orders in Islam.* Oxford: Clarendon Press, 1971.

Ṭūsī, Ḥakīm Abū Naṣr 'Alī b. Aḥmad Asadī.*Garshāsp-nāma.* Edited by by Ḥabīb Yaghmā'ī. 2nd ed. Tehran: 1354 A.Hsh./1975.

Ülken, H.Z. "Anadolu tārīḫiñde Dīnī rūhīyāt müşāhedeleri," Medḫal: I. Burak Baba. II. Geyikli Baba. III. Ḥācī Bektāş Velī," *Mihrāb* 1 (1923).

Upton, Charles. *Doorkeeper of the Heart, Versions of Rābi'a.* Putney, VT: Threshold Books, 1988.

Van Ess, J. *Zwischen Ḥadīṯ und Theologie.* Berlin: 1975.

______ . *Ungenutzte Texte zur Karramiya, Eine Materialsammlung.* Heidelberg: 1980.

______ . *Theologie und Gesellschaft im 2. und 3. Jahrhundert Hidschra.* Berlin-New York: 1990-2.

Vryonis Jr., S. *The Decline of Medieval Hellenism in Asia Minor and the Process of Islamization from the Eleventh through the Fifteenth Century.* Berkeley: University of California Press, 1971.

Waley, M.I. "A Kubrāwī Manual of Sufism: The *Fuṣūṣ al-ādāb* of Yaḥyā Bākharzī." *The Heritage of Sufism.* Vol. II. Edited by L. Lewisohn. Oxford: Oneworld Publications, 1999.

______ . "Azīz al-Dīn Nasafī on Spiritual Retreat *(Khalwa)." Sufi: A Journal of Sufism* 17. Spring (1993).

Wāṣitī, Abū'l-Faraj al-. *Tiryāq al-muḥibbīn fī ṭabaqāt khirqat al-mashāyīkh al-'ārifīn.* Cairo: Maṭba'at al-Miṣr, 1887.

Watt, Montgomery. *Muslim Intellectual: A Study of al-Ghazali.* Edinburgh: 1963.

______ . *Free Will and Predestination in Early Islam.* London: 1948.

Webb, Gisella. "Suhrawardī's Angelology." Ph.D. Thesis, Temple University, 1989.

Weil, G. *Maimonides über die Lebensdauer.* Basel: 1953.

Weil, Simone. *Gravity and Grace.* Translated by E. Craufurd. London: ARK, 1987.

Wellhausen, J. *Reste arabischen Heidentums.* Berlin: 1897.

Wensinck, A. J. "On the Relation Between Ghazālī's Cosmology and His Mysticism." *Mededeelingen der Koninklijke Akademie van Weten-*

schappen. Afdeeling Letterkunde, Deel 75, Serie A, no. 6 (1933): 183-209.

______. *Concordance et indices de la tradition musulmane.* 8 vols. Leiden: 1936-88.

Wickens, G.M. *Morals Pointed and Tales Adorned: The Būstān of Sa'dī.* Leiden: E.J. Brill, 1974.

Wittek, P. "Yazijioughlu 'Alī on the Christian Turks of the Dobruja." *Bulletin of the School of Oriental Studies* 14 (1952): 639-668.

______. *Das Fürstentum Mentesche: Studie zur Geschichte Westkleinasiens im 13.-15. Jh.* Istanbul: Istanbuler Mitteilungen herausgegeben von der Abteilung Istanbul des Archäologischen Institutes des Deutschen Reiches, 1934.

Yaşar, H.H. *Amasya Tarihi.* 4 vols. İstanbul: Aydınlık Basımevi 1912-1935.

Yörükan. "Bir Fetva Münasebetiyle: Fetva Müessesesi, Ebussuud Efendi ve Sarı Saltuk." *Ankara Üniversitesi İlahiyat Fakültesi Dergisi* 1/ 2-3 (1952):

Yüce, K. *Saltukname'de Tarihī, Dinī ve Efsanevī Unsurlar.* Vol. 832 of *Kültür ve Turizm Bakanlığı Yayınları.* Ankara: Kültür ve Turizm Bakanlığı, 1987.

Yūsufī, G.Ḥ. s.v. "Andarz-Nāma." *Encyclopædia Iranica* II.

Zabīdī, Murtada, Muḥammad ibn Muḥammad al-Ḥusaynī al-. *Itḥāf al-sādah al-muttaqīn bi-sharḥ asrār Iḥyā' 'ulūm al-dīn.* 10 vols. Reprinted, Beirut: Dār Ihyā' al-Turāth al-'Arabī, n.d.; Cairo: 1311.

Zaehner, R. C. *Zurvan: A Zoroastrian Dilemma.* Oxford: 1955.

______. *Hindu and Muslim Mysticism.* New York: 1969.

Zarrīnkūb, 'Abd al-Ḥusayn. *Farār az madrasa: dar bāra-yi zindigī wa andīsha-yi Abū Ḥāmid Ghazālī.* Tehran: Amīr Kabīr, 1985.

______ *Justijū-yi dar taṣawwuf-i Īrān.* Tehran: Amīr Kabīr, 1978.

Ziadeh, N.A. *Sanūsīya: A Study of a Revivalist Movement in Islam.* Leiden: E.J. Brill, 1968.

Ziai, H. "Suhrawardī's Philosophy of Illumination." Ph.D. Thesis, Harvard University, 1976.

Zubayr, Abū Bakr 'Abdullāh b. al-. *al-Musnad.* Beirut: 1988.

Index of Places, Names, Terms and Koranic References